D0548105

HISTORY OF EARLY RUSSIAN LITERATURE

WORKS TRANSLATED UNDER THE RUSSIAN
TRANSLATION PROJECT OF THE AMERICAN
COUNCIL OF LEARNED SOCIETIES, AND PUB-
LISHED BY THE MACMILLAN COMPANY

W. CHAPIN HUNTINGTON, EDITOR

TOLSTOY AS I KNEW HIM
My Life at Home and at Yasnaya Polyana
By T. A. Kuzminskaya, sister-in-law
of Leo Tolstoy

THE LAW OF THE SOVIET STATE
By Andrei Y. Vyshinsky, Deputy Minister
for Foreign Affairs of the U.S.S.R.

HISTORY OF EARLY RUSSIAN LITERATURE
By N. K. Gudzy, member, Academy of
Sciences of the U.S.S.R.

HISTORY OF THE NATIONAL ECONOMY
OF RUSSIA
By P. I. Lyashchenko, member, Academy of
Sciences of the U.S.S.R.

ECONOMIC GEOGRAPHY OF THE U.S.S.R.
Edited by S. S. Balzak, V. F. Vasyutin,
and Y. G. Feigin

THE NATURAL REGIONS OF THE U.S.S.R.
By L. S. Berg

and numerous others

ПРОФ. Н. К. ГУДЗИЙ

История древней русской литературы

УЧЕБНИК ДЛЯ ВЫСШИХ УЧЕБНЫХ ЗАВЕДЕНИЙ

издание второе, переработанное

ГОСУДАРСТВЕННОЕ УЧЕБНО-ПЕДАГОГИЧЕСКОЕ ИЗДАТЕЛЬСТВО
НАРКОМПРОСА Р.С.Ф.С.Р.

МОСКВА
1941

History of
EARLY RUSSIAN
LITERATURE

by N. K. Gudzy

nikolai kallinikovich ii

TRANSLATED FROM THE SECOND RUSSIAN EDITION BY

SUSAN WILBUR JONES

INTRODUCTION BY

GLEB STRUVE

PROFESSOR OF RUSSIAN, UNIVERSITY OF CALIFORNIA,

BERKELEY

THE MACMILLAN COMPANY
New York: 1949

Foreword

THE Russian Translation Project of the American Council of Learned Societies was organized in 1944 with the aid of a subsidy from the Humanities Division of the Rockefeller Foundation. The aim of the Project is the translation into English of significant Russian works in the fields of the humanities and the social sciences which provide an insight into Russian life and thought.

In the difficult problem of the selection of books for translation, the Administrative Committee has had the counsel and cooperation of Slavic scholars throughout the United States and Great Britain. It is thought that the books chosen will be useful to general readers interested in world affairs, and will also serve as collateral reading material for the large number of courses on Russia in our colleges and universities.

Since Russian history is a continuum, the volumes translated are of various dates and have been drawn from both the prerevolutionary and postrevolutionary periods, from writings published inside and out of Russia, the choice depending solely on their value to the fundamental aim of the Project. Translations are presented in authentic and unabridged English versions of the original text. Only in this way, it is believed, can American readers be made aware of the traditions, concepts, and ideologies by which the thinking and attitudes of the people of Russia are molded.

It should, of course, be clearly understood that the views expressed in the works translated are not to be identified in any way with those of the Administrative Committee or of the Council.

THE ADMINISTRATIVE COMMITTEE
JOHN A. MORRISON, *Chairman*
HAROLD SPIVACKE
SERGIUS YAKOBSON
MORTIMER GRAVES
W. CHAPIN HUNTINGTON

491008

Translator's Acknowledgment

G RATEFUL acknowledgment is hereby made to the late Dr. Samuel Hazzard Cross, Professor of Slavic Languages and Literatures at Harvard University, for permission to use excerpts from *The Russian Primary Chronicle* (Harvard University Press, 1930) and from his then unpublished translations of *The Tale of Igor's Expedition* and *Zadonshchina,* and for the privilege of consultation.

The following works containing translations of Early Russian monuments or of selected passages were also helpful:

Anthology of Russian Literature from the Earliest Period to the Present Time, by Leo Wiener. Part I. G. P. Putnam's Sons, New York, 1902.

Der Briefwechsel Iwans des Schrecklichen mit dem Fürsten Kurbskii (1564– 1579), tr. Karl Stählin, Leipzig, 1921.

History of Russian Literature, A, by Prince D. S. Mirsky. New York, Alfred A. Knopf, 1927.

India in the Fifteenth Century. Being a Collection of Narratives of Voyages to India, in the Century preceding the discovery of the Cape of Good Hope; from Latin, Persian, Russian and Italian sources, now first translated into English. Edited, with an Introduction by R. H. Major, Esq., F.S.A. London: the Hakluyt Society, 1857.

Life of the Archpriest Avvakum by Himself. Translated from the Seventeenth Century Russian by Jane Harrison and Hope Mirrlees, with a Preface by Prince D. S. Mirsky. Hogarth Press, 1924.

Medieval Russian Laws, tr. George Vernadsky. New York, Columbia University Press, 1947.

Russian Religious Mind, The, by George P. Fedotov. Kievan Christianity. Cambridge, Harvard University Press, 1946.

Treasury of Russian Literature, A, ed. Bernard Guilbert Guerney. New York, Vanguard Press, 1943.

Introduction

IN Professor Gudzy's book the English-speaking students of Russia are offered, for the first time, a detailed and authoritative account of early Russian literature. Though he has also written on other literary problems and periods (for instance, on Tolstoy), Professor Gudzy is, above all, an authority on early Russian literature, one of the leading present-day scholars in this field, known also as the author of several specialized monographs, and the compiler of a standard anthology of early Russian literature which serves as a companion volume to the present work in the study of that literature in Soviet universities.

The study of early Russian literature offers many difficulties and problems, some of them common to the study of the early period in all European literatures, though in Russian literature they appear in a higher degree. There is, first of all, the problem of the actual content of that literature, of what is to be included in it and what is to be left out. It is obvious that we cannot approach early works of literature with the same literary criteria which we apply to modern literature. In Russia this is particularly the case, for, at least until the seventeenth century, purely literary works in it are extremely rare. In the earliest period literature is dominated by the Church, its contents are almost exclusively religious and ecclesiastical. Secular works are almost completely absent. Still rarer are the examples of what can be regarded as imaginative literature. The sole notable exception is the *Slovo o polku Igoreve* (Tale of Igor's Expedition), and it is not an accident that this unique, remarkable work still arouses some doubts with regard to its authenticity, at least outside Russia. In the sixteenth century there springs up an important political literature, of polemical, controversial character: the correspondence between Ivan the Terrible and Prince Kurbsky, the writings of Ivan Peresvetov, and some of the works of Maximus the Greek. Next to it we also find some monumental attempts at "codifying" the ideology and philosophy of life of the new Muscovite state. These two novel trends are the hallmark of sixteenth century literature. But we have to wait until the seventeenth century for the appearance on a more or less large scale of a literature—both translated and original—the primary object of which is to entertain.

Unlike some earlier, postrevolutionary Russian historians of literature, Professor Gudzy has solved this problem of the contents of early Russian literature in a liberal spirit. He says that his choice of material was determined—provided that material contained "specifically literary elements"—by the extent to which it reflected essential aspects of the historical reality. Accordingly we find him treating as literature such works as Vladimir Monomakh's *Testament* and as *Domostroy*, which were sometimes omitted by earlier historians of literature, though his treatment of *Domostroy* is too brief and cursory and does not do full justice either to its literary and linguistic or to its ideological importance. On the other hand he excludes such a work as *Russian Law*,* interesting though it unquestionably is from the point of view of language.

The second and even more difficult problem facing the historian of early Russian literature is the problem of chronology. This is especially true of the earliest, Kievan, period—whether we take translations or original works—with regard to which there is still a great deal of confusion and lack of agreement. Whether some of that confusion will ever be cleared away may be doubted. Even with regard to the early Russian chronicles there is still no complete agreement between Russian scholars, despite the enormous amount of clarifying work done by the late Shakhmatov: Professor Gudzy refers to the differences between Shakhmatov and Istrin with regard to some of the essential points bearing on the origin and chronology of the chronicles. With regard to some other works there is an even greater scope for varying conjectures. It is characteristic that new hypotheses as regards the dating of certain works are being constantly offered by Russian scholars. One of the reasons is, of course, that very few early transcripts have come down to us, and that in the existing versions we have to make allowances for possible alterations and interpolations by later scribes. As Professor G. Fedotov points out in his recent stimulating study of the Russian religious mind: "The puzzling element in the Kievan period is the richness of content, the variety of literary styles and spiritual trends requiring not one but several evolutionary series. This complexity in the cultural life, together with the scarcity of existing materials, defies all attempts to arrange the material in an evolutionary sequence." †

There is finally the problem of certain puzzling, enigmatic works. There is, for instance, that curious, presumably thirteenth century work known as the *Supplication of Daniel the Prisoner* which, apart from the puzzle of its author's personality and social status, poses before the student some problems

---

* *Russkaya Pravda.*

† George P. Fedotov, *The Russian Religious Mind: Kievan Christianity* (Cambridge, Mass., Harvard University Press, 1946).

of a literary nature, for in some respects it has no parallel in early Russian literature. The same, of course, is even more true of the *Tale of Igor's Expedition* which has been variously described in the context of contemporary literature as "an oasis in a desert" or "a mountain in the midst of a plain." Modern historians of literature tend to minimize somewhat this uniqueness of the *Slovo* by pointing out certain similarities of style, imagery, and so forth, in other contemporary or near-contemporary works, such as the homilies and orations of Bishop Cyril of Turov, or by stressing the stylistic indebtedness of the author of the *Slovo* to the Slavonic version of Josephus' *History of the Judaic War*. But these comparisons and juxtapositions do not essentially detract from the uniqueness of the *Slovo* as a poetic work. Some plausible explanations of this uniqueness have been offered by Russian scholars. It is nevertheless true that it was largely this unique character of the *Slovo* which started the original controversy about its authenticity. Professor Gudzy recounts this controversy in some detail. For him, as for all other scholars in Russia, it is a thing of the past. No doubt is left in their minds about the authenticity of the *Slovo* as a work of the twelfth century, and in 1938 its seven hundred and fiftieth anniversary was celebrated in the Soviet Union with great pomp and circumstance.

It must, however, be placed on record for the English-speaking reader that about the time when the first edition of Professor Gudzy's work was published, and before the publication of the second edition from which the present translation was made, the controversy was revived by Professor André Mazon, of the Collège de France, one of the foremost Slavic scholars outside Russia. In a course of lectures at the Collège de France he propounded anew the theory—later embodied by him in a book * the sequel to which is still to appear—that the *Slovo* was a spurious work. Starting from the premise that the fifteenth century *Zadonshchina,* instead of being a poor imitation of the *Slovo,* actually lay at the basis of it, he proceeded to the sweeping conclusion that the *Slovo* was an eighteenth century forgery, and even made an attempt to lay his finger on its author. His theory was indignantly rejected by all Russian scholars in the USSR, including Professor Gudzy, who discusses Mazon's views in the new (1945) edition of his *History of Early Russian Literature.* It is also rejected by such outstanding authorities outside Russia as Professor Roman Jakobson,† formerly of Brno and now of Columbia University.

Professor Mazon, it is true, mentions in his book a few names of those (including the Polish scholar Krzyzanowski) who were inclined to agree with

* *Le Slovo d'Igor* (Paris, Institut d'études slaves), 1940.
† Annuaire de l'Institut de Philologie et d'Histoire Orientales et Slaves. Vol. VIII, New York, 1945-1947, Includes Prof. S. H. Cross' Engl. trans. of the *Slovo.*

his views. In a private conversation with the present author he said that some of the young Russian scholars in Paris who assisted him in his research were prepared to go even further than himself. (This applied apparently in the first place to the talented young scholar Mikhail Gorlin, who perished during the war in a Nazi concentration camp.) In all fairness it must be said that Professor Mazon's attempt to prove that the *Slovo* is an eighteenth century fake lacks the last convincing touch, tempting though some of his arguments against its authenticity may appear to be. The very fact, however, that a scholar like Mazon finds it possible to raise the whole problem afresh and succeeds in enlisting some support is symptomatic and significant. Even if we fail to accept his conclusions (and his surmise about the actual eighteenth century author of the *Slovo* sounds quite fantastic) cautiousness compels us to admit that as things are at present there must still remain some room for doubting the twelfth century origin of the *Slovo*. Theoretically speaking, there are possibilities midway between the accepted Russian view and the forgery theory of Mazon, and such intermediate views have been voiced. When Professor Gudzy, Professor Orlov, and other eminent Soviet scholars indignantly reject all such doubts, there is no reason to question the sincerity of their conviction.

Another problem involved in the study of early Russian literature is the problem where to end this early period. Professor Guzdy adheres to the traditional view that the new period begins with the seventeenth century. He mentions, however, the opinion of Istrin, who was inclined to date the modern period from the middle of the seventeenth century, and admits that there is much to be said for regarding a great deal of seventeenth century literature as a totally new departure. The autobiography of Archpriest Avvakum with its entirely novel spirit, the appearance of such new literary forms as social satire, syllabic poetry, and the drama as well as the adaptations of medieval romances and the appearances of an original narrative literature devoid of any religious and moral bias (as exemplified in the picaresque *Story of Frol Skobeyev*), all this imparts to seventeenth century literature a new character, divides it sharply from the preceding period. In trying to define this difference we are inevitably struck by the growing *secularization* of literature. This entitles us to regard the seventeenth century in literature as a transition period, but we are hardly justified in looking upon it as the actual beginnings of the modern period. (In history it was also a critical period characterized by the same secularizing trend—Peter the Great's reforms were the finishing touch in this process.) Though foreshadowing the developments of the eighteenth century, it is not yet organically connected with eighteenth century literature. Therefore Professor Gudzy seems to us right in sticking to the traditional periodization.

The English-speaking reader of the book will be most of all struck, perhaps, by a fact which the author does not stress (nor has he any need to)— the fact of Russia's belated literary development, the fact that when Dante and Chaucer were active in western Europe, and even when the neighboring Poland had her Kochanowski, Russia had no poetry; that there was no theater and drama in Russia at the time of the Elizabethans; that when Cervantes had already written his immortal novel the Russians did not possess even the naïve and artless story of Frol Skobeyev's adventures. These facts are rooted in Russia's historical development, but to bear them in mind is important in approaching early Russian literature. But the more the reader is struck by these facts the more surprised he will be to realize how rapidly, literally in no time, beginning with Pushkin, Russian literature rose in the nineteenth century to occupy one of the foremost places in Europe and to exercise by our time such a significant influence.

On the other hand, without producing any works of world significance, early Russian literature, and especially during the earliest, Kievan, period, offers us works which afford pleasure to a modern reader, even leaving aside the *Tale of Igor's Expedition*. The early chronicles, with their quaint mixture of fact and fancy and their fresh, straightforward, vigorous, graphic style, make delightful reading. The twelfth century *Kievan Chronicle* * is widely held to be at least equal, as a literary and historical document, to the best European medieval annals. The early lives of the saints have many charming touches, and it is not surprising that modern Russian writers were attracted by them. Pushkin praised the Kiev *Paterikon* for "the charm of its simplicity and invention," while of later writers, Leskov, Remizov, and others drew inspiration from the old *Prologue* for their own work. The early Russian ecclesiastics, and especially Hilarion, the first Russian Metropolitan of Kiev, for all their imitation of Byzantine models, show a great oratorical mastery. Of later works the *Life of Archpriest Avvakum,* written by himself, though not meant as a work of literature, has outstanding literary qualities and has also influenced some modern writers, while it may also be pointed out (a fact not recorded by Professor Gudzy) that the German poet Chamisse took the subject of one of his poems from the Russian story of Shemyaka's judgment.

At the same time, from the overdetailed, analytical picture given by Professor Gudzy—a picture intended primarily for the Russian student—it may be difficult for the average foreign reader to grasp the essential features of the Russian mind as reflected in literature. Yet, to understand those features is also important for understanding the appreciation of modern Russian literature, for the latter in some of its aspects was the product no less of the

* Engl. trans. published by Harvard University Press, 1930.—Ed.

Russian mind and tradition than of Western influences. Some of those features are not brought out with sufficient clearness by Gudzy who, for reasons that can be easily understood, is chary of discussing at length the spiritual contents of early religious literature with its duality of Byzantine and native Russian elements. To supplement Gudzy's analysis of that literature and to place it in the context of the Russian religious mind, the American student interested in obtaining a more complete picture of Russian culture of the Kiev period would be advised to go to Professor Fedotov's above-mentioned volume on Kievan Christianity, for in it he will get something of the synthesis which Professor Gudzy fails to provide.

In Professor Gudzy's book there are relatively few conventional curtsies to the teaching of Marx and Lenin; this may be because, as Professor Gudzy points out, the Marxist-Leninist interpretation of early Russian literature is still in an embryonic state.

GLEB STRUVE

University of California
Berkeley
October, 1947

Contents

Author's Note

THE text here offered surveys in chronological sequence the basic aspects of the history of early Russian literature from the beginning of the eleventh century to the end of the seventeenth. The selection of the material subjected to study is determined—although there are specifically literary elements present in it—chiefly by the degree in which it reflects essential features of historical reality.

In dealing with the monuments of early Russian literature, as in dealing with those of the early literature of western Europe, the standard of "literary quality" commonly set for modern literary works is by no means always applicable, nor can the concept of "literature" itself be considered absolute or as possessing any earmarks so unmistakable that they can be arbitrarily established without regard to the epoch under discussion. Hence some difference of opinion is unavoidable as to whether this monument or that ought or ought not to be put under the heading of literature, though the author of the present book has endeavored, so far as in him lay, to keep the grounds for debate at a minimum.

The exposition is supplemented by bibliographical references to the most important literature on the question. An exhaustive bibliography did not enter into the author's calculations in writing a book the aim of which was first and foremost educational. The reader will find fuller bibliographical notes in Mezier's noted reference work, in the bibliographical apparatus to Pypin's *History of Russian Literature,* and so on, and also in the more recent studies on various questions which are mentioned in the book and which contain in the majority of cases a survey of previous literature on the topic.

HISTORY OF EARLY RUSSIAN LITERATURE

Author's Introduction

IN the study of our literary heritage as part of our cultural heritage in
general, early Russian literature holds a position of note. This place belongs to it in view of the important eyewitness role that it has played in
helping us to understand our historic past. Early Russian literature was
fundamentally journalistic in character, concerned with the burning questions of the day, its purpose being more or less openly pragmatic. The concept of literary art as a province of culture in its own right, set off from other
such provinces, did not exist for us in olden times—at least if we take only
written literature into account and exclude the oral tradition. This circumstance at times permits us to discover, more easily than in subsequent literature, what historical and social interrelations existed between a given epoch
and one literary monument or another of that date.

Along with this, powerful as was the monopoly that the church exercised
over our culture in olden times, limiting in large measure the artistic possibilities open to early Russian literature, our ancient literature has also yielded
a good deal of valuable artistic material, particularly in the field of narrative.
One need only point to the *Tale of Igor's Expedition,* certain specimens of
chronicle narrative, and of the later war narrative, and such a genre tale as
the story of *Gore-Zlochastie.* Even the traditional church categories, for instance the lives of saints, afford examples of remarkable artistic force, particularly where they have absorbed the elements of oral poetry or taken on the
lineaments of real life. Cases in point are the *Story of Peter and Fevronia*
or the *Life of Archpriest Avvakum,* written by himself.

Then, too, a number of the monuments of early Russian literature owe
their existence to an extensive international literary exchange, thanks to

which our ancient literature merges with world literature, making a specific contribution and showing itself capable of absorbing the literary material of the world at large. Certain monuments, of legendary and apocryphal literature, for example, borrowed by us from outside and here revised in accordance with the social background of their adoption, have not as yet come to light at their point of origin; the existence of the Russian text of such a monument helps fill in the picture of the development of foreign literatures which influenced ours. On the other hand early Russian literature, as affected by the literatures of neighboring peoples, itself became in turn an influential factor in the Slavic literatures related to it—the Bulgarian and the Serbian. All this constrains us to regard it not as an isolated phenomenon in the realm of culture but as something closely interconnected with the literary process of medieval Europe as a whole.

There can be no doubt that before the rise of a written literature in our country a body of oral creation existed. This is demonstrated both by direct analogy with the history of the development of oral and written creation among other peoples and by unmistakable instances of the reflection of oral poetry in early monuments of learned literature. But what this oral tradition was in Old Rus we do not precisely know, owing to the fact that with us the recording of oral poetry began very late—not before the seventeenth century. Nor can we set any exact date for the first appearance of written literature here. There is, however, every reason to postulate its existence in Rus well before the middle of the eleventh century—date of the first extant monuments of Russian writing. Such a postulation is based on the fact that at this time we already get examples that show a considerable degree of literary proficiency and hence it is difficult to believe that we had hitherto possessed no written works whatever; probably they have simply not come down to us.

As a provisional date for the end of early Russian literature and the beginning of modern literature we shall perhaps do well to take the end of the seventeenth century and the beginning of the eighteenth. By that time the Europeanization of our patrician ruling class was pretty clearly defined and along with it the Europeanization of its literature, of the leading literature, since "the ideas of the ruling class are for each epoch the ruling ideas; that is, the class which controls the *material* power of a society will at the same time be in control of its *spiritual* power." [1] Certain historians are inclined, however, to date the end of early Russian literature and the beginning of modern from the middle of the seventeenth century. This position was very circumstantially argued by V. M. Istrin, who regarded the second half of the seventeenth century as the starting point for the modern period of Rus-

[1] O. L. Feuerbach, K. *Marx and F. Engels,* "Arkhiv Marksa i Engelsa" (Moscow, State Publishing House, 1930), Bk. I, p. 230.

sian literature in view of the following symptoms of an increased Western influence upon Russian literature: (1) the Great Schism; (2) the contest of Great Russian scholars with those of the Ukraine as to what set Russian life was to assume—the old Byzantine, or the new Roman-Catholic-Polish; (3) the appearance of new literary forms: drama, miracle play, syllabic verse, and (4) the influx of a new narrative literature derived from works in German, Polish, and Latin.[2]

The facts pointed out by Istrin are indeed of the very essence of that new quality which chiefly differentiates Russian literature in the second half of the seventeenth century from that which had gone before. We might even add to the peculiarities of the literature of the second half of the seventeenth century listed by Istrin the increased penetration into it of folklore elements, though these had been in evidence since the beginning of the century. None the less, inasmuch as the victory of secular elements over religio-ecclesiastical does not profess to be complete in Russian literature until the eighteenth century, and inasmuch as the literature of the eighteenth century is the *immediate* and organic preliminary of nineteenth century Russian literature, it is historically more correct to accept the traditional point of view and bring early Russian literature down to the beginning of the eighteenth century; that is, down to the break in Russia's cultural fortunes associated with the reforms of Peter the Great.

Thus early Russian literature covers a period of approximately six and a half centuries.

However, just as the historical situation underlying the development of Russian literature was all this while unintegrated, so our early literature lacked integration from one end of its existence to the other.

The earliest period of Russian literature, down to the beginning of the thirteenth century, is associated with Kievan Rus, and is therefore commonly called the *Kiev period* or, less happily, by association with the subsequent Tartar domination over Rus, the pre-Mongol period.

Kievan Rus was a state with far-flung territories including not only Kiev and adjoining areas, but the districts of Novgorod, Suzdal, and Rostov as well. "As the empire of Charlemagne," writes Marx, "was antecedent to the formation of present-day France, Germany, and Italy, so the empire of the dynasty of Rurik was antecedent to the formation of Poland, Lithuania, the Baltic States, and Turkey, as well as of the Muscovite state itself."[3] Toward

---

[2] See V. M. Istrin, *Vvedeniye v istoriyu russkoy literatury vtoroy poloviny XVII v.* (Introduction to the History of Russian Literature in the Second Half of the Seventeenth Century) (Odessa, 1903), pp. 1–2, 22–24. A. I. Sobelevsky answered Istrin in *Izv. otd. russk. yaz. i slov.* (Journal of the Department of Russian Language and Literature, 1903), Bk. II, pp. 138–146.

[3] Marx, *Sekretnaya diplomatiya XVIII v.* (Secret Diplomacy in the Eighteenth Century).

the end of the eleventh century, a gradual falling apart of Kievan Rus took place—of the "rag-bag empire of the dynasty of Rurik," as Marx terms it—into the separate and independent feudal principalities of Kiev, Chernigov, Smolensk, Galicia, Volynia, Rostov-Suzdal, Novgorod, and others. And within these new organisms the same process of feudal disintegration was carried over into the future. Later the economic impoverishment of the Kiev district, which had started back in the middle of the twelfth century, began to make itself felt; it had been occasioned by the separatist trends in other Russian areas, aggravated (in consequence of the Crusaders' conquest of Constantinople) by the loss in importance of the great water route "from the Varangians to the Greeks," and finally consummated by the devastation of the south (and of Kiev in particular) by the Tartars. From that time on, the political existence and the cultural life of the individual districts of Old Rus went their separate ways, centering about rising regional political organisms each of which had a distinct historic destiny of its own. In the north the first state to emerge as a political and cultural center for the federate groups of Great Russians was Rostov-Suzdal; South Russia—the future Ukraine and the future White Russia—became part of Lithuania and, in the fifteenth century, of the Polish-Lithuanian state.

The social structure of Kievan Rus during the eleventh, twelfth, and thirteenth centuries was characterized by the development of feudal relationships which determined the whole social structure as early as the beginning of the eleventh century and took final form during the thirteenth century. The system was based on the enserfing of the rural population of Old Rus, the conversion of the peasant, formerly free, into a bondman. (Lenin writes that "landowners enslaved peasants even at the time of the Russkaya Pravda.") [4] The former tribal retinue was transformed into a feudal landowning nobility thriving on its exploitation of the peasants. At the same time the creation of a feudal class society brought about primary differentiation, the separating out of the early feudal town. In its political development this young feudal society in process of assembly is at the first stage of feudal disintegration. The presence in Kievan Rus of two basically antagonistic classes —the landowners and the serf-peasants—with the existence of slave labor, defines the class struggle, the reflection of which is chiefly to be found in chronicle literature.

The principal focus of literary production during this period was South Russia, with its chief political and cultural center Kiev, which, in the eleventh century, according to Marx and Engels, "aped Constantinople in all things and was called the *second Constantinople*." [5] Marx and Engels evi-

---

[4] Lenin, *Sochineniya* (Works), Vol. III, p. 150.
[5] Marx and Engels, *Sochineniya* (Works), Vol. IX, p. 439. Italics by Marx and Engels.

dently had in mind the words of the famous eleventh century historian Adam of Bremen, who called Kiev the rival of Constantinople and the "lustrous jewel of Greece"; that is, of the Christian East. Somewhat earlier even than this, the German chronicler Thietmar of Merseburg had written that at the end of the tenth century and the beginning of the eleventh, Kiev was a very large city, having approximately four hundred churches, eight markets, and an enormous number of inhabitants. In the *Laurentian Chronicle* under the year 1124 there is an entry about a two-day fire in Kiev at which time about six hundred churches were burned down. Even if these statements and figures are exaggerated there can be no doubt that in many respects Kiev rivaled in importance the great cultural centers of medieval Europe. But besides Kiev, even though on a considerably smaller scale, there were other towns both in the south (Chernigov, Turov, Galich) and in the north (Novgorod, Smolensk, Rostov) where written monuments and works of literature were independently produced. Works originating in the south enjoyed a wide circulation in the north and have for the most part come down to us in North Russian copies; the language, apart from certain specific phonetic variants, was the same in northern and southern manuscripts—the old literary language, basically very similar to old Bulgarian. From this point of view the literature of the Kiev period must be viewed as a literature common to Great Russians, Ukrainians, and White Russians alike. It is the first stage in the development of Old Russian literature and coincides with the period of the breaking up of feudalism.

Next, in connection with the continuing condition of break-up, when "the state fell apart into separate districts, partly even into principalities preserving lively traces of former autonomy," [6] there set in an epoch of *provincial* development in Russian literature which lasted down to its unification during the sixteenth century under the Muscovite state. But from the fourteenth century to the beginning of the sixteenth, there appears within this breaking up a process of feudal concentration which gradually becomes more pronounced and constitutes a sort of "order in disorder" (Engels). The organization of the nationalistic and centralized Muscovite state in the early decades of the sixteenth century was the summing up of this process. With us the organization of a centralized state was accelerated "by requirements of self-defense (invasion by Turks, Mongols, and so on)" and "occurred earlier than the liquidation of feudalism, consequently earlier than the formation of the nation." [7] Political preeminence in the struggle between the boyars and the court nobility was finally secured to the court nobles by the support

[6] Lenin, *Sochineniya* (Works), Vol. I, p. 73.
[7] Stalin, *Marksizm i natsionalno kolonialnyi vopros* (Marxism and the National-Colonial Question), 1939, p. 87.

of the merchant class. From the very beginning of the sixteenth century we must speak of a *common Russian literature* in this state. In the second half of the sixteenth century and in the seventeenth century, the literature of the nobility is firmly established as dominant. But along with it, in the seventeenth century, especially in the second half, a literature of the tradespeople and also, in part, of the peasantry is already developing.

The social determinants for the literature of this whole period from the eleventh to the eighteenth century were, first, the formulation of the ideology of the ruling class of feudal lords, in its successive modifications; secondly, the coming to a head of the fundamental social conflict of the era of feudalism, the class struggle between feudal lords and peasants; and thirdly, the rise of a town merchant opposition and its subsequent formulation of a bourgeois ideology as early as the eighteenth century. In written literature the peasant as antagonist of the ruling class could, for perfectly comprehensible reasons, make almost no showing. The literary process can therefore be reconstructed in its entirety only if we take into account the existence of an oral poetry among the peasantry.

A discussion of the history of early Russian literature must necessarily be preceded by some decision as to its *scope;* that is, as to what monuments of early Russian literature, generally speaking, we propose to regard as specifically literary. The fact is that early Russian literature over a considerable period cannot in most cases be isolated from that syncretic whole in which literary and nonliterary elements are found fused in an undifferentiated mass. In view of this fact, it is only proper in selecting monuments for inclusion in a history of early Russian literature to limit that inclusion to material that shows in some measure an attempt on the part of the author at picturesque expression, stylistic, or genre effect, as distinguished from the effect sought by routine cultural monuments of a purely journalistic, historical, ecclesiastico-theological, juridical, or technical nature.

Literature in Rus catered at first to the interests of the Christianized ruling class, and for this reason the literature of Old Rus, like the literature of medieval Europe as a whole, was in the earliest times both in form and in content chiefly ecclesiastical, a medium of religious instruction. Of the predominant role of ecclesiastical ideology throughout medieval Europe, Engels wrote in *The Peasant War in Germany:* "This sovereign domination of theology in all provinces of intellectual activity was at the same time a necessary consequence of the fact that the Church was the highest generalization of and sanction for the existing feudal order." [8] Ecclesiastico-religious tendencies characterize even the handful of early translated works on secular themes. Even in the very earliest times, however, historical literature called

[8] Marx and Engels, *Sochineniya* (Works), Vol. VIII, p. 128.

forth by interests purely secular and governmental was appearing here. These interests find still more effectual expression in the *Tale of Igor's Expedition.* But inasmuch as the Church was closely linked to the state, being in a way its political agent, even literature which was ecclesiastical in form served not only the interests of the Church as such but those of the state as well. Again, in his article "On the Extent of Popular Participation in the Development of Russian Literature," Dobrolyubov wrote: "Almost from its inception, literature refused to confine itself to exclusively religious interests: it served as a tool of secular power as well, even though it did not leave the sphere of spiritual subjects." [9]

Governmental patronage of the Church and of ecclesiastical literature was perfectly natural since it was the struggle to consolidate the political structure of formative Russian feudalism that had defined the role of the Church as the great political and ideological factor in this process. The Church took an active part in the political life of society, looking out for the interests, chiefly, of the feudal heads. The "worldly" tastes of the layman either at the top or—still more so—at the bottom of the social ladder were principally gratified by an oral poetry which, down to the middle of the seventeenth century, only in rare individual cases found its way into a book and exercised only a sporadic influence on written literature. The "worldly" interests of the Old Russian reader were also met by historical literature (the chronicle) and by story literature, translated and original.

The bias of the corpus of early Russian literature was further conditioned by the fact that an ecclesiastical center was in olden times not only in large part the creator but also the monopolistic guardian of the literary tradition, preserving and multiplying in manuscript only the material that accorded with its interests, and treating with indifference or hostility material which was unsatisfactory for its purposes or antagonistic to them. A substantial obstacle to the development of secular literature in the earliest times was the circumstance that down to the fourteenth century the writing material in use was parchment, the costliness and scarcity of which precluded the possibility of any extensive outlay of it on manuscripts which did not prosecute immediate aims of a religious and edifying character. But even religious and edifying literature found free circulation only in so far as it was approved by the ecclesiastical censorship. There existed a considerable class of so-called "apocryphal" literature, of "spurious" or "proscribed" books, having the disapproval of the official Church and by it prohibited for reading, although in some cases the Church authorities, through their own faulty discrimination among apocrypha, inadvertently permitted these to circulate.

[9] N. A. Dobrolyubov, *Polnoye Sobraniye Sochinenii* (Complete Collected Works), ed. P. I. Lebedev-Polyanskii (Goslitizdat, 1934), Vol. I, p. 222.

If we also take into account the destruction of individual literary monuments—especially those circulating in a small number of copies—resulting
from various natural calamities (fires, the plundering of libraries in time of
war, and so on), it becomes quite evident that we are not in possession of all
the material of early Russian literature that once existed, and therefore the
very building up of its history can of necessity be only more or less approximate. If it had not been for the chance discovery, in 1795, in a provincial
monastery, of the unique copy of the *Tale of Igor's Expedition,* our idea of
early Russian literature would be considerably poorer than it now is. But
we have no assurance that there did not exist in ancient times monuments
of the same type as the *Igor* which met a less fortunate fate.

Academician [10] N. K. Nikolsky justly observed in his time:

> The *Tale of Igor's Expedition,* the *Supplication of Daniel the Exile,* fragments
> of historical legends in the chronicles, the *Discourse of the Ruin of the Land of
> Rus,* and like productions show that in the first centuries of Russian life there
> existed and developed, in addition to ecclesiastical and didactic literature, a secular
> literature which attained a notable flowering in southern Rus. For the *Tale of
> Igor's Expedition* to have been the only thing of the kind in its epoch would,
> naturally, amount to a historical absurdity.[11]

Academician A. I. Sobolevsky, though taking issue with Nikolsky's assertion
as to the notable flowering of secular literature in ancient Rus, none the less
agreed that there were many works of the same type as the *Igor* in early Rus,
and explained their disappearance as due to loss of interest in their content
on the part of generations immediately following.[12]

The circulating medium for the products of early Russian literature was
almost exclusively the *manuscript.* Book printing, which made its appearance
in Rus only in the second half of the sixteenth century, though in a general
way a fact of enormous cultural importance, was chiefly utilized for service
books not only in the sixteenth century but practically throughout the seventeenth century as well. The manuscript tradition in early Russian literature
contributed to the mutability of literary monuments, which frequently went
through an evolutionary process in thought development, composition, and
style, conditional upon the historical setting and the social milieu into which
a given monument chanced to find its way. The concept of literary property
and the monopoly of an individual author over a literary product did not
exist in Old Rus. The copyist of a work was often at the same time its editor
and had no scruples about adapting the text to the needs and tastes of his own

[10] Member of the Academy of Sciences of the USSR.—Ed.
[11] N. K. Nikolskii, *Blizhaishie zadachi izucheniya drevnerusskoy knizhnosti* (Immediate
Problems in the Study of Early Russian Learned Literature) (St. Petersburg, 1902), p. 10.
[12] A. I. Sobolevskii, *Neskolko mysley o drevney russkoy literature* (Some Reflections on
Early Russian Literature), *Izv. otd. russk. yaz. i slov.* (1903), Bk. II, p. 152.

time and surroundings. Hence a history of early Russian literature must keep in view not only the history of its monuments but also the history of the redactions of those monuments.

That the editor should have felt free to do as he liked with an author's text was all the more natural since in most cases the author did not consider it necessary to indicate his name, while in some instances Russian writers, to give greater authority to what they had written, signed their productions with the names of popular Byzantine writers. As a result anonymity and pseudonymity are so common in the monuments of early Russian literature as to complicate considerably the problem of building up its history.

Sometimes indirect historical indications here come to the aid of the investigator if they are consistent and if they carry sufficient weight. An analysis of the thought and style of a monument which leads to more or less positive results has substantial significance, however, only when we apply it not only to the work of which the authorship is in doubt but also to works which unquestionably belong to the given author.

The peculiar difficulty attending the study of the history of early Russian literature has as its further condition the fact that even in cases where a work may be associated unquestionably with the name of a definite author, we for the most part know nothing about the author except his name. Thus in building up a history of old Russian literature one substantially important aid which is at our disposal in dealing with modern literature practically drops out; namely, acquaintance with a writer's biography and the circumstances under which he did his work.

At times it is a very complicated matter even to establish a chronology for works of ancient Russian literature, especially in the very earliest period. The oldest works of Russian literature are extant not in original drafts but in copies, and very late copies at that in the vast majority of cases. Thus a more or less approximate dating of our ancient literary works is effected on the basis of indirect historical data derived from the works themselves, and by no means always exhaustive or reliable, in addition to a linguistic analysis of the copy, if it has preserved the archaic traits of the original. What has been said of the difficulty of dating our old original literature is even more applicable to translated literature, in the Russian dating of which historical references can, of course, play almost no part.

The absence of original drafts of the works of ancient Russian writers hampers extremely the establishment of authoritative texts. This difficulty becomes more considerable in proportion as the number of extant copies of a text becomes less, or the copies less accurate, and the more remote they are chronologically from the original. Upon the number of copies, their relative state of preservation, their relative distance in time from the original, depends the degree of authority with which the original text may be established, the text itself remaining hypothetical, however, whatever the degree of authority.

The evolution of early Russian literature paralleled, in general, the evolution of the literary language. The latter was based on the language of the service books brought into Rus at the time of the adoption of Christianity; that is, on Old Bulgarian, also known as Old Slavonic or Church Slavonic. In the earliest period it took over the phonetic and morphological peculiarities of spoken Russian, and in works of a secular character (for example, the *Tale of Igor's Expedition*) or semisecular (for example, the chronicle), its lexical elements as well. In the initial stage of the history of early Russian literature, the adoption of Old Bulgarian as the literary language was facilitated by the relative similarity of the Slavic languages to each other. Later on, especially in the Muscovite period of the history of early Russian literature, the current spoken language gradually began to prevail, particularly in literary works not specifically ecclesiastical, becoming predominant by the second half of the seventeenth century.

The literary process in Old Rus was closely associated with a change in the material and technique of writing. Until the fourteenth century manuscripts had been executed on parchment (also known as "charter," "calfskin," and "leather") prepared from calf's hide, and had been written in a hand which was termed *uncial* and whose peculiarity was the painstaking formation of letters by tracing straight lines, square corners, and ovals; each letter during the given period retained in general a uniform shape. It is quite evident that both the nature of the material and the character of the handwriting in very early times were unfavorable to the growth of a manuscript profession: manuscripts were costly and took time to produce. In the second half of the fourteenth century, paper is introduced and uncial gradually gives place to *semiuncial,* a more fluent hand in which straight lines are replaced by broken and slanting lines, and the regularity of corners and ovals and the uniformity of letters disappear. At about the same time *cursive writing* also came in. Thus the cost of a manuscript was reduced and the work on it took less time; the book became more accessible, it was democratized, and literary production itself showed a tendency toward expansion.

For a clarification of perspectives in the study of early Russian literature, it is necessary to dwell at some length on the basic stages of that study.

The scientific study of early Russian literature was preceded by an extended period of collecting, registering, describing and, finally, of publishing the monuments appertaining to it. This work began back in the earliest period of Russian letters, at the time when the monastery libraries started to be centers of manuscript scholarship, and to do the sorting that went with it. From the end of the fifteenth century, several inventories of monastery libraries are extant, among them an inventory of manuscripts in the monastery of St. Cyril at Byelozersk [White Lake], listing 957 books and anticipating in its cataloguing methods the latest scientific bibliographical works.[13] From the end of the seventeenth century comes a bibliographical undertaking closely resembling in execution the inventory of manuscripts in the St. Cyril Monastery: "Index of books, who composed them,"[14] formerly attributed to Sylvester Medvedev, but as a matter of fact probably the work either of Epiphanius Slavinetsky or of his disciple the monk Euphemius of the Miracle Monastery.

In the eighteenth century, with the commencement of historical studies, the collection of manuscript material broadened its scope considerably, and further attempts were made at scientific cataloguing and investigation; many monuments important to literary history were printed in special publications. Much was done in this connection by Tatischev and Damaskin-Rudnev, and also by Kol, Paus, Bauze, Bakmeister, Miller and Schlözer. In 1768 there appeared in a German periodical, in German, the anonymous "Information About Russian Writers."[15] This gave character sketches of forty-two eighteenth century writers. A sequel was announced but never saw the light. The year 1772 brought the printing of N. I. Novikov's *Attempt at a Historical Dictionary of Russian Writers*,[16] which embraced more than three hundred names and went back to the very beginning of Russian letters. Novikov's dictionary, while attempting to appraise the importance of various authors from the viewpoint of literary history and giving a brief, though sometimes quite successful, sketch of each author's work, did little more than itemize purely external data on the lives and literary careers of authors, at times defining their importance in general terms, and praising almost all of them to excess. However, as reference material this *Dictionary* has not lost its value even now. In 1773–1774 Novikov brought out the *Old Russian Library* (ten parts), reissued in 1788–1791 (in twenty parts). Here, along with a great

[13] Published by N. K. Nikolskii in *Izd. Obshchestva Lyubiteley Drevney Pismennosti* (Journal of the Society of Friends of Early Literature) (St. Petersburg, 1897), CXIII.

[14] Published in *Chteniya Obshchestva istorii i drevnostey rossiiskikh* (Papers of the Society of Russian History and Antiquities) (1846).

[15] Reprinted in Russian translation in N. A. Efremov's *Materialy dlya istorii russkoy literatury* (Materials for the History of Russian Literature) (St. Petersburg, 1867), pp. 129–144. It is commonly attributed to the actor I. A. Dmitrevsky, but apparently without sufficient grounds. A more probable authorship would appear to be that of P. Ya. Shtelin, son of the celebrated Academician, or that of the playwright V. I. Lukin. See V. N. Vsevolodsky-Gerngross, "I. A. Dmitrevsky," *Ocherki po istorii russkogo teatra* (Historical Outline of the Russian Theater) (Berlin, Petropolis, 1923), pp. 223–234. (All undesignated footnotes are those of the Author.—Ed.)

[16] Reprinted in N. A. Efremov, *op. cit.*, pp. 1–128.

deal of historical material, he printed a few monuments belonging specifically to early Russian literature. Ancient literary monuments were also
printed separately in eighteenth century periodicals both general and special, and in the scholarly publications of the Academy of Sciences.

Such were the first steps in the accumulation of literary-historical material, as yet undifferentiated, however, from historical material in general;
and such were the first attempts to make a roster of the authors of literature
produced in Russia down to the eighteenth century.

To this time belong the first attempts to collect song material, those of
M. Chulkov: *Sobranie Raznykh Pesen,* first edition, in four parts, 1770–
1774; here, out of a total of eight hundred songs, more than three hundred
and thirty are folk songs. In 1780–1781 this work, with additions by N. I.
Novikov, came out in six parts. Twenty years after the first publication of
Chulkov's songs (in 1790), there appeared *A Collection of Russian Folk
Songs in Part Form, Set to Music.* The compiler of the collection was a
kinsman of Derzhavin, N. A. Lvov; the text of the songs was set to music by
I. Prach. Here again, art songs were mixed with folk songs, but for all that,
Lvov's collection was a step forward from Chulkov's. In 1795 an ama-
teur of archaeology, Count A. I. Musin-Pushkin, acquired the collection
containing the *Tale of Igor's Expedition,* which immediately sent the interest in early Russian literature rocketing.

In the nineteenth century the activity of a wealthy Maecenas, Count N.
P. Rumyantsev, was of very great importance not only to the collection of
literary-historical material, but to its publication and study. Being a man of
unlimited financial resources, Rumyantsev acquired old manuscripts in
great numbers and organized at his own expense expeditions to monastery
libraries, in the course of which his assistants inventoried the stocks of manuscripts in these libraries and uncovered priceless monuments of early Russian literature. Rumyantsev's acquisitions went to make up the rich
manuscript collection which became the nucleus of the Rumyantsev Museum, now the Lenin Library of the USSR. In 1842 appeared the celebrated
*Catalogue of the Rumyantsev Museum's Russian and Slovenian Manu-
scripts* (473 in all), compiled by the outstanding philologist, A. Vostokov.
Rumyantsev did not confine his activity, however, to the collecting of manuscripts, but made arrangements for their scientific publication and study as
well. Rumyantsev's staff included, in addition to Vostokov, the noted scholars
K. Kalaidovich, P. Stroyev and the metropolitan, Eugene Bolkhovitinov.
Kalaidovich produced such works as *Old Russian Poems of Kirsh Danilov*
(1818), first scientific edition of genuine works of folk creation discovered
in eighteenth century records; *Monuments of Twelfth Century Russian*

Literature (1821), and *John, Exarch of Bulgaria* (1824), a study devoted to an outstanding Bulgarian writer of the tenth century (Bulgaria's literary golden age), who was also popular in early Russian literature. Stroyev's most important publication is his edition of the *St. Sofia Annals* (1820). From 1829 to 1835, Stroyev headed an archaeographical expedition which covered almost the whole north of Russia and collected an enormous amount of priceless manuscript material, for the scientific ordering of which a special Archaeographical Commission was set up in 1837. The most important of Eugene Bolkhovitinov's works are the *Historical Dictionary of Old Russian Writers Belonging to the Clergy of the Russian Greek Church* (two two-volume editions, 1818 and 1827), and the posthumous *Dictionary of Native Russian Secular Writers and of Lay Foreigners Writing in Russia* (two volumes, 1838 and 1845). Both dictionaries were the result of very painstaking study of manuscript material, chiefly unpublished, and constituted a manifestation of remarkable scientific value which retains its importance as a bibliographical reference work even to this day.

The year 1822 saw the first attempt at a *historical* survey of the fortunes of Russian literature from the earliest times to the 1820's. It was made in a book entitled *Attempt at a Short History of Russian Literature* and came from the pen of N. I. Grech, later a notorious reactionary and the associate of Bulgarin. Being at that time a teacher in the middle schools and not specifically engaged in the scientific study of Russian literary history, Grech availed himself of the works of his predecessors, among them Eugene Bolkhovitinov's *Dictionary of Writers Belonging to the Clergy,* and plotted a historical perspective of the development of Russian literature, which was, however, far from being free from chronological errors. Grech's modest volume was none the less interesting, if only for the fact that it first gave an outline of the development of literature in Russia which, however imperfect, was drawn up with a certain amount of system.

After Grech's survey, similar brief surveys of the history of Russian literature were brought out by Timayev (1832), Plaxin (1833), Glagolev (1834), Georgievsky (1836). In 1838 M. A. Maximovich's *History of Early Russian Literature* was published in Kiev. Originally a botanical specialist, Maximovich, in his enthusiasm over the romanticist theories concerning nationality, next turned to the study of oral poetry (in 1827 he published a collection of Ukrainian folk songs). He later turned to archaeology, ethnography, linguistics, history, and the history of early Russian literature. As professor in the University of Kiev, Maximovich was the first to hold a university chair in the history of Russian literature. He was particularly interested in the literary past of the Ukraine and in the *Tale of Igor's Ex-*

pedition, concerning which he advanced a number of valuable opinions.[17] Maximovich prefaces his *History of Early Russian Literature* by the establishment of periods in the development of Russian literature generally, taking the seventeenth century as the end of the early period and making the period division itself conform to facts in the general history of Russia. Next comes a historiographical survey of materials and of works bearing on the history of Russian literature, and after that a special historical introduction to the early period of Russian literature, Maximovich's account of which extends only to the thirteenth century and, as had been the case with his predecessors, amounts to little more than a bibliographical survey of the corpus of early Russian writing and an enumeration of its producers. The remaining, and major, part of the book is devoted to the fortunes of the Russian, Ukrainian, White Russian and Old Slavonic languages.

Maximovich's book, the work of a specialist, represents a notable advance over previous attempts to frame a history of literature, chiefly by reason of the very breadth with which it states its theme and the endeavor made to relate the historico-literary process to the general course of history.

During the 1830's and 1840's, I. P. Sakharov's publications played an important part in the study of the fortunes of Russian literature, particularly his *Legends of the Russian People,* which began appearing in 1836. Here many monuments of oral composition and of early Russian literature found a place. Later on it was discovered that Sakharov's approach to his material had been uncritical, that he had deliberately altered songs, and so forth, but for all that, the great interest in ancient times and in folk creation aroused by Sakharov's efforts bore abundant fruit in subsequent, much more strictly scientific, historico-literary studies.

A stage in the study of Russian literature important for its own day was the course of lectures by a Moscow University professor, S. P. Shevyrov, which began appearing in 1846 under the title, *A History of Russian Literature with Special Reference to the Early Period.* In 1858–1860 a second edition of the course came out in four parts, bringing the fortunes of Russian literature down to the end of the fifteenth century and also including an analysis of works of oral poetry. By the 1870's and 1880's Shevyrov's book had already lost scientific importance, although it was reissued by the Academy of Sciences in 1887, a patent anachronism. The book was keyed to a set of reactionary, romantic notions concerning the moral and religious elevation of Old Russian spiritual practice. Sentimental idealization of the past pervades the work throughout. Shevyrov failed to draw any line of demar-

---

[17] Most of Maximovich's studies are printed in his *Collected Works* (Kiev 1876–1880), Vols. I–III. His studies in early Russian literature, among them the *History of Early Russian Literature,* are reprinted in the third volume.

cation between the history of literature and the history of the Church. A literary monument interested him primarily in proportion as its study might aid him to reconstitute the spirit of Old Rus and the predominantly ecclesiastico-religious mode of existence. In speaking, for example, of the lives of saints, he approaches them not as a specific literary genre, but as material capable of giving an idea of the ecclesiastical personages of Old Rus, who were his prime interest. A high-flown style and sentimental journalistic moralizings in a spirit of jingoistic patriotism are the distinguishing mark of Shevyrov's method of interpreting his monuments.

In spite of all these glaring defects, however, Shevyrov's course, what with its wealth of material and the serious erudition of its author, who was well informed as to all the results of previous research, represented an extraordinary accomplishment at the time when it appeared and served as a profound inspiration to subsequent investigators. Of these, so great a scholar as Academician Tikhonravov, who had been Shevyrov's pupil, valued his teacher's book highly as the first serious attempt to build up a history course on the basis of factual material at that time already extensive.

The section of the book that retained its value longer than others was the introduction, where Shevyrov gave a general inventory and a detailed analysis of sources and of aids to the study of early Russian literature, introduced the reader to state and privately owned manuscript collections, and inculcated some very important points from the field of sciences ancillary to the history of literature—paleography and bibliography.

By the 1850's the study of early Russian literature was getting on firm ground and thenceforward was prosecuted by a succession of scholar-specialists, of whom Buslayev, Pypin, Tikhonravov, and Alexander Veselovsky may be designated as the ones who did most toward giving definition to the earliest stages of prerevolutionary research.

The advances made in historico-literary studies in Russia at this time were associated with influences exercised on our literary scholarship by western Europe, Germany in particular.

Between 1810 and 1820 there had arisen in Germany, chiefly through the efforts of Bopp and the brothers Grimm, the so-called "historical school," an outgrowth of the post-Napoleonic nationalistic movement centering in a study of the history of German language and literature, especially the folk epos, on the principles of comparative history. From the viewpoint of this school, both language and folk poetry have their roots in remote antiquity and retain an imprint of phases in the development of thought, custom, and mythology that go back to the farthest depths of the past. Similarity as to the elements of linguistic culture and community of motifs and plots in the poetic material of the separate peoples belonging to the so-called "Indo-

European" language family are evidence, according to the teaching of this school, that these peoples had a common ancestry. In the oral poetry of "Indo-European" peoples, this school saw the reflection of a complete mythological system assembled in that common cradle from which these people went their different ways, carrying over into our own time the fundamentals of their primordial mythology. The theoretical formulations of this school paralleled the idealistic philosophies of Fichte and Schelling and the romantic movement in literature. The basic positions of the Grimm school were developed here by such scholars as Afanasyev, Or. Miller, Potebnya, and Konstantin Aksakov.

The labors of Bopp and the brothers Grimm set the pattern for the scientific activity of one of our greatest literary historians, F. I. Buslayev, professor in Moscow University, and afterwards Academician. Buslayev began his scholarly career in the mid-1840's with studies in Russian linguistics written in the spirit of the comparative-history school. In connection with these studies, he printed, in 1861, his *Historical Anthology of Works in the Church Slavonic and Old Russian Languages*, which included a great number of Old Russian literary monuments, largely appearing for the first time. This work of Buslayev's has retained its scientific importance down to the present. In his early studies in the history of literature and the oral tradition— collected in the two-volume *Essays in the History of Russian Folk Literature and Art* (1861)—Buslayev kept in a general way to the mythological theory, but avoided going to any such extremes in applying it as Afanasyev or Or. Miller had done. Along with the mythological factor, Buslayev took into account those elements in oral works which are determined by cultural-historical, geographical, or literary influences. Thus, in a number of his articles, he noted the interaction between oral poetry and monuments of recorded literature. Later, under the influence of Benfey's *Panchatantra* (1859), which gave predominance to the theory of borrowing, whereby the similarity of motifs and plots among various peoples is explained not on grounds of common ancestry but as due to widespread international exchange, Buslayev abandoned the mythological theory and became an adherent of the theory of borrowing. In the process of the development of capitalistic relations, attended by the subjugation of colonies, it had become clear that a community of literary elements may be found not only among peoples of the same linguistic stock but also where there can be no question of kinship. Buslayev, forced to recognize the justice of this observation, himself developed the new school's positions in "The Migration of Tale and Story," an article first published in 1874 and afterwards reprinted in the two-volume collection, *My Leisure Hours* (1886).

Possessing wide knowledge in the field of Old Russian and western European art, and having written a number of valuable studies about both, Buslayev embarked upon the very fruitful parallel study of style in literature and style in graphic art. Deserving of mention is the notable mastery of exposition that characterizes his writings. A fine artistic sense, a picturesque and extremely elegant use of language are the distinguishing marks of everything that Buslayev wrote, and won for him the reputation of being not only a first-rate scholar but a brilliant educator and man of letters as well.

A. N. Pypin made his first published appearance, as a youth of twenty, with a number of serious historico-literary studies, and in 1857, at the age of twenty-four, presented the brilliant master's dissertation, *An Essay in the Literary History of Ancient Russian Tales and Stories*, which was immediately issued under the imprint of the Academy of Sciences. In this book, remarkable for its time, Pypin established and studied a body of material, chiefly old translated stories in circulation here previous to the eighteenth century, and determined, in so far as the state of knowledge permitted, the Byzantine and western European sources. The author's great erudition, his fine command of western European literature on the question, and his practical exhaustion of the Russian manuscript material at his disposal immediately placed his study on a footing with outstanding Western historico-literary studies, and the book itself not only became a point of departure for all subsequent workers in the province of Russia's ancient narrative literature, but remains to this day a *sine qua non* for those interested in this field.

Pypin was also interested in apocryphal literature, and devoted several monographs to its study. He thus became the first to occupy himself specifically with a voluminous and very curious section of our early translated literature previously almost unnoticed by scholars. Shortly afterwards, in 1862, he published in the third number of Count Kushelev-Bezborodko's *Monuments of Ancient Russian Literature* a large collection of apocryphas under the title, "Spurious and Prohibited Books of Russian Antiquity"—a very valuable issue notwithstanding numerous shortcomings pointed out, for the most part, in Tikhonravov's review.

Accused of free thought and of communications with Chernyshevsky, Pypin was forced in the early 1860's to cut short his professorial career, then just begun (he was not elected Academician until the late 1890's), and to confine his efforts almost exclusively to periodicals—chiefly to the liberal *Vestnik Yevropy* [Messenger of Europe]. There he published a large number of studies concerning various stages in the history of nineteenth century Russian literature having a connection with social movements, and in the history of trends in Russian thought, likewise with reference to the nineteenth century. These studies subsequently formed separate books on social movements in Russia under Alexander I, and on Belinsky, Saltykov-

Shchedrin, Nekrasov, and others. In 1890–1892 Pypin published a four-volume *History of Russian Ethnography* in which a good deal of space was given to the history of literary studies, and 1898–1899 brought the first edition of his *History of Russian Literature*, likewise in four volumes, the first two of which are devoted to early literature. (The fourth volume ends with Gogol.) Although not a systematic presentation of the historical fortunes of Russian literature, this work of Pypin's is a compendium of special studies covering many years, a summing up of his own and other scholars' researches. Pypin was an adherent of the cultural-history school, which drew no line between literature, as a specific form of ideology, and general culture. At the same time he leaned toward a publicistic interpretation of literary facts consonant with liberal-bourgeois doctrine and Occidental ideology. On this account his studies, though still of value for the abundance of facts they bring together, have in large measure lost their significance when it comes to giving an inner explanation and interpretation of those facts.

With the name of N. S. Tikhonravov, who became adjunct in the late 1850's, afterward professor in the University of Moscow, and finally Academician, is linked that whole fruitful period in Russian literary scholarship which was principally characterized by an intensified development of the vast manuscript resources of Russian literature through critical editions and analytic study. Tikhonravov saw clearly that a comprehensive picture of the literary process could only be built up through the more or less adequate acquisition of a critically verified, scientifically edited corpus of literary monuments, and to this task he devoted much strength and energy. From 1859 to 1863, Tikhonravov published *Annals of Russian Literature and Antiquity* (eight numbers were issued), in which he and other scholars printed much valuable material relating to pre-eighteenth-century Russian literature and oral poetry as well as a number of articles of the research type. In 1863, in connection with his studies in apocryphal literature, Tikhonravov published, from authoritative copies, two volumes of *Monuments of Repudiated Russian Literature*—an issue notably superior scientifically to the analogous work that Pypin had produced a year earlier. In 1894 the start Tikhonravov had made on a third volume of apocryphas was posthumously published by the Academy of Sciences. Paralleling his studies in the history of the old Russian theater, Tikhonravov published in 1874 the texts of Russian dramatic works from 1672 to 1725 (two volumes) and thereby laid a solid foundation for the study of old-time dramaturgy and the old Russian theater. The wide experience that he had acquired in his work on early Russian texts enabled Tikhonravov to edit in a manner exemplary for his time the first critical (the so-called "tenth") edition of the works of Gogol, brought to completion after Tikhonravov's death by Shenrok.

Though he did not abandon the positions of the comparative-history method, Tikhonravov none the less gave most of his attention to the fortunes on Russian soil of individual monuments, tracing their literary history as shown in successive redactions. This method of study appeared to him the only rational one, inasmuch as any genuine study of the history of Russian literature is inconceivable without a knowledge of the evolution of the manuscript tradition, primarily within the bounds of individual literary monuments. Basic methods for the scientific working up of a history of literature, ancient literature included, were very clearly indicated by Tikhonravov in 1878 in his extended critique of Galakhov's *History of Russian Literature*. Against Galakhov's aesthetic method of work, Tikhonravov set the strictly historical method—in his opinion the only one capable of giving scientific illumination to the process of literary history. For wealth of facts and breadth in stating problems, this critique was in itself not only a genuinely scientific conspectus of the history of Russian literature, chiefly early literature, but a very full program for future studies by Tikhonravov's pupils and disciples, who afterwards formed a complete school of literary scholarship (M. I. Sokolov, V. M. Istrin, M. N. Speransky, and others). Individual members of this school, however, in many cases carried the basic principles of its founder to extremes and encumbered their studies with scrupulous textualistic researches, making these an end, as it were, in themselves, and not carrying through to those general conclusions which their teacher himself had always made the essential thing.

Tikhonravov did not confine himself to early Russian literature but wrote a number of studies in eighteenth and nineteenth century literature, the most valuable of which are those on Zhukovsky. But owing to his profound instinct for scientific precision, he would delay publishing his studies, meaning to deepen and expand them later on; thus several valuable papers by Tikhonravov remained for decades in manuscript and were only published after the author's death, in the three-volume (four-part) collected works issued in 1898.

A major figure not only in Russian but in world-wide literary scholarship was the Petersburg University professor and Academician, Alexander Veselovsky, who began his scholarly career in the late 1850's with studies in western European (chiefly Italian) literature, and afterwards turned his attention to studies in early Russian literature primarily, both written and oral, and in Byzantine and modern Russian literature (a book about Zhukovsky). From the early 1880's to the end of his life (he died in 1906), Veselovsky was hard at work on the formulation of a historical theory of poetry.

Commanding an impressive range of material, and distinguished by extraordinary erudition in the literatures of the most widely varying peoples,

Veselovsky left a notable legacy to science in all these fields, one almost unparalleled in European literary scholarship. Reared in the traditions of the 1860's, an assiduous reader of Feuerbach and Bokl, a positivist and empiricist in his habits of mind, Veselovsky showed from the very beginning of his scholarly career a leaning toward those scientific systems which avoided metaphysical concepts unverified by experience and relied on deductions as obtained by the natural and historical sciences. Such an intellectual bias predetermined his attitude of suspicion toward the mythological school, the basic principles of which he did not discard entirely but drastically restricted, advancing the theory of borrowing to first place in his own studies, broadening its scope and deepening the foundations laid by Denlop-Librecht, Pypin, and Benfey. In the course of time, however, Veselovsky adopted the views of the so-called "anthropological school," which maintained the "spontaneous generation" of motifs and plots and explained their common possession by various peoples as due not to mutual intercourse but to an identity in the psychic attributes of human beings at fixed stages of cultural development. It is noteworthy that the basic positions of this school had been anticipated by Veselovsky himself in his early studies, where they were treated as organic to the theory of international literary exchange.

From the very first stages of his scholarly activity, Veselovsky revealed himself a partisan of the evolutionary-sociological method of studying the literary process. His acquaintance with the works of Darwin and Spencer and, later, of Taylor and Lang, helped him, as much by the wealth of material they contained as by their basic theoretical principles, to verify his own work in this direction. The most profound and many-sided application of the evolutionary-sociological method was made by Veselovsky in his studies in historical poetics.

The first major work by Veselovsky to have a direct bearing on the history of early Russian literature, and in its own way to constitute an epoch in the history of Russian literary scholarship, was his doctor's dissertation, *From the History of Literary Intercourse Between East and West: the Slavic Legends of Solomon and Kitovras and the Western Legends of Morolf and Merlin* (1872). It largely determined the veering to Veselovsky's positions of his teacher Buslayev, who was very much in sympathy with this book of his pupil. Veselovsky followed it up by a number of other works relating to the study of early Russian literature. Chief among these were *Essays in the History of the Development of Christian Legends* (1875–1877), *Researches in the Field of Russian Spiritual Verse* (1879–1891), *From the History of the Romance and the Tale* (two volumes, 1886–1888), and many others.

Such were the fundamental stages in the study of early Russian literature in the nineteenth century in connection with the general development of literary scholarship in Russia. Here the most important place belongs to the works of Veselovsky, who laid the foundations for the sociological study of literature. The subsequent efforts of Russian scholars specializing in the study of early Russian literature carry on in a general way the traditions that Tikhonravov and Veselovsky were chiefly instrumental in establishing.[18] The Marxist-Leninist study of early Russian literature is as yet in the embryonic stage. To build up a genuinely Marxist course in the history of early Russian literature is a problem of first importance to the general system of Soviet literary scholarship. A fully successful solution of this problem is, however, inconceivable without special investigations of separate sections of the broad period from the viewpoint of Marxist methodology, investigations which are now under way.

At the present time this work is being conducted chiefly by fellows of the Institute of Literature of the Academy of Sciences of the USSR (Leningrad), a number of whose investigations have been published in *Trudy Kommissii po drevnerusskoy literature*[19] (Vol. I, 1932) and in *Trudy otdela drevnerusskoy literatury* [20] of the Institute (Vols. I–III, 1934–1936) and by fellows of the A. M. Gorky Institute of World Literature of the Academy of Sciences of the USSR (Moscow). Work in the Leningrad institute has been focused on the volumes on early Russian literature which will form part of the multivolume *History of Russian Literature* projected by the USSR Academy of Sciences for the purpose of elucidating the development of Russian literature in accordance with the principles of Marxism-Leninism.

[18] On the history of the study of Russian literature, with particular reference to early literature, see A. N. Pypin, *Istoriya russkoy etnografii* (History of Russian Ethnography), Vols. I–II (St. Petersburg, 1890–1891); V. Ikonnikov, *Opyt russkoy istoriografii* (Experiment in Russian Historiography) (Kiev, 1891–1892, 1908), Vols. I–II; I. Yagich, *Istoriya slavyanskoy philologii* (History of Slavic Philology) (St. Petersburg, 1910); A. Archangelskii, *Vvedenie v istoriyu russkoy literatury* (Introduction to the History of Russian Literature) (St. Petersburg, 1916), Vol. I; M. N. Speransky, *Istoriya drevney russkoy literatury* (History of Early Russian Literature): Introduction, Kiev Period, 3rd ed. (Moscow, 1920), pp. 1–112; V. N. Peretts, *Kratkii ocherk metodologii istorii russkoy literatury* (Brief Sketch of the Methodology of the History of Russian Literature) (Petrograd, 1922). In connection with the centenary of the birth of Aleksandr Veselovsky, the *Izv. akad. nauk USSR* (Journal of the Academy of Sciences USSR), *Otd. obshchestv. nauk* (Division of Social sciences) (1938), No. 4, published a number of valuable studies of his legacy to science (articles by V. F. Shishmarev, V. N. Zhirmunsky, V. A. Desnitsky, M. K. Azadovsky, and M. P. Alexeyev).

[19] The Works of the Commission on Early Russian Literature.

[20] The Works of the Department of Early Russian Literature.

Translated Literature
of the Kiev Period

IN the earliest period of the development of Russian letters, while original Russian literature was still only in the formative stage, the important role had, naturally, to be assumed by translated literature stemming from Christian culture. Nor could the translated material fail to influence our own literary creation.

What the Christianization of Rus meant in terms of progress may be precisely defined as participation, with the aid of translated literature, in a culture considerably higher than that of pre-Christian Rus. At first this translated literature not only broadened the intellectual horizon of the Old Russian writer and reader, but also introduced new moral and juridical concepts, and contributed to the adoption of more advanced forms of community life. At the same time it supplemented largely the stock of artistic means of expression already existent in oral folk poetry. Later on, however, and down to the end of the sixteenth century, the translated literature chiefly in circulation here was of a specifically ecclesiastical nature, often couched in rhetorically bombastic, set phrases, and then, both in itself and through its influence on original literature, it came to have a retarding effect on the artistic and conceptual development of Russian letters.

The principal fund available to original Old Russian literature was Byzantine literature, the monuments of which were known to Rus largely through South Slavic translations, though to some extent in Russian versions as well.

Our chief purveyor of Byzantine literature was Bulgaria, which in the tenth century, the epoch of Tsar Simeon, was passing through its golden age of letters. But some works of Byzantine literature were translated directly from the Greek in Rus itself during the period of awakened activity in translation under Yaroslav the Wise. In the *Primary Chronicle*, under the year 1037, the chronicler, speaking of Yaroslav's love of books, of which he "wrote many and deposited them in the Church of St. Sophia," writes:

Yaroslav loved religious establishments and was devoted to priests, especially to monks. He applied himself to books, and read them continually day and night. He assembled many scribes, and translated from Greek into Slavic. He wrote and collected many books through which true believers are instructed and enjoy religious education.

However, to determine just which works were translated in this country at that time is, in many cases, difficult.[1]

Byzantine literature played the leading role here down to the middle of the seventeenth century. The existence, even in very early times and particularly in the fifteenth and sixteenth centuries, of a number of translated works—monuments not so much of literature, however, as of letters western European in origin and derived from Latin, or, more often, from German originals—does not alter the general character of early Russian translated literature. This Western translated material for the most part offered nothing essentially new, nothing different from the traditional Byzantine stock, in themes and general trend.

What Old Rus appropriated in translation from the Byzantine storehouse was determined on the one hand by her degree of cultural development, and on the other by the fact that Russians engaged in literary pursuits belonged chiefly to ecclesiastical circles: specifically secular literature, free from ethical or religious taint, of which Byzantium had an abundance, was not known in Rus at all. Besides devotional literature, the books that came in from Byzantium were biographical, apocryphal, and patristic writings, works of church history and, finally, narratives secular in plot but having some degree of religious coloration, and legendary literature, similarly tinged, dealing with Creation and with the animal and vegetable kingdoms.

On the whole, as we see, our translated literature was very considerable in quantity. It embraced almost all provinces of medieval European culture. That so large an influx of translated material was required to meet the demands of the Russian reader, itself testifies to the extraordinary cultural level of Old Rus, which, though it had no more than just become a participant in the European enlightenment, was already showing an ability to appropriate the varied output of medieval letters. It is well to point out in

---

[1] An attempt to ascertain what monuments were translated from the Greek in Rus during the earliest period was made by Academician A. I. Sobolevsky in the article entitled "Distinguishing Marks of Russian Translations of the Pre-Mongol Period." See *Materialy i issledovaniya v oblasti slavyanskoy philologii i arkheologii* (Materials and Investigations in the Field of Slavic Philology and Archaeology) (St. Petersburg, 1910), pp. 152–177.

this connection that the widespread infiltration into early Rus of Byzantine literary works did not prevent early Russian literature's showing from the very beginning of its existence significant traits of independence. Even in cases where native Russian literature borrowed from translated works, it by no means lost the marks of originality in so doing. Alexander Veselovsky expressed himself very well on this subject in his report on studies made in 1863. He wrote:

We have subsisted by large and frequent borrowings. Needless to say, the borrowings themselves lived anew; while introducing fresh material into the moral and intellectual life of the people, they were themselves modified by the joint influence of both. . . . In this impact between the native and the foreign, or invading, influence, it is hard to determine which outweighed the other. We think that the former did. The influence of the foreign element is always conditioned by its inner accord with the level of the milieu upon which it happens to be at work. Anything which departs too much from this level remains uncomprehended or is comprehended in its own way, is brought into equilibrium with the environment. Thus the independent development of a people subjected to the documentary influence of foreign literatures remains inviolate in its principal features: the influence operates more in breadth than in depth; it contributes material rather than introduces new concepts. The people itself creates such concepts as are possible to its given state of development.[2]

Like original literature, translated literature was usually subjected on Russian soil to a process of editorial revision lasting as long as it continued to circulate, and at the same time it became an inseparable part of the literary stream as a whole, where any dividing line between native and foreign was obliterated. In this sense it became as much a fact of Russian literature as, for example, Zhukovsky's translations were to become at a later time.

Simultaneously with the adoption of Christianity by Rus, service books, for the most part in Old Bulgarian, were imported, these including—besides material to guide in the organization of church ritual—church prayers and chants, the poetic formulae of which influenced both learned and oral literature. The prayers and chants were found in the so-called monthly "Service Minyei," in the triodia, service books, and missals. Extant in a late eleventh century copy are Novgorod Service Minyei of 1095–1097 (for September, October, and November) and from the same century several undated Service Minyei besides.

At approximately the same time there also appeared in Rus books of "Holy Scripture" from both the New Testament and the Old. Among the former belonged gospels of two types: the so-called "Aprakos" (that is, those in which readings were arranged by days of the week to fit the Church service)

2 *Zhurnal min. nar. provs.* (Journal of the Ministry of Public Instruction) (1864), No. 3, p. 132.

and the Four Gospels (with the material arranged by Evangelists). Gospels of the second type appeared later than the Aprakos. The earliest extant copy of an Aprakos gospel (abridged, containing readings only for Sundays and certain holidays) is the *Ostromir Gospel*, copied in 1056–1057 by Deacon Gregory for Ostromir, Mayor of Novgorod. The oldest known copy of a Four Gospels (1144) is the *Galician Gospel*. There is reason to believe that an Aprakos version of the apostolic books was also known in Rus during the earliest period. Among the Old Testament books known in eleventh century copies is the Psalter both in its usual form and also in variants: a divinatory and an explanatory psalter. Certain other Old Testament books were also known in the earliest period but until the end of the fifteenth century a full codex of the biblical books did not exist in Rus: what had circulated instead from of old was the so-called *Pariminik,* containing passages selected from the Old Testament to meet the requirements of the Church service.

The influence of biblical texts on early Russian literature was very marked. Not to mention the lavish use of biblical quotations and sayings, there was considerable employment of the biblical style as well.

SAINTS' LIVES

Of literature intended for reading, that which enjoyed the largest circulation was biography, or hagiography (from the Greek *hagios,* sacred) by means of which the Church sought to give its flock examples of the practical application of abstract Christian principles. The conventional, idealized picture of a Christian ascetic whose life and work ran their course in a setting of legend and miracle seemed the most suitable guide to that ideology which it was the mission of the Church to propagate. The problem before the hagiographer, the author of the life of a saint, was primarily to give a picture of the saint that would conform to the established concept of an ideal ecclesiastical hero. From his life only such facts were taken as fitted this conception, and whatever diverged from it went unmentioned. Nay more, in many cases incidents were invented which had not occurred in the saint's life but which furthered his apotheosis; it even happened that facts from the life of some popular saint were attributed to another ascetic of whose life very little was known. Thus, for example, in the practice of Russian hagiography there were cases where, in writing the life of a native saint, the author borrowed what had been said about a Byzantine saint of the same name.

Such freedom in dealing with factual material resulted from the hagiographer's aiming not so much at a truthful presentation of events as at the teaching of a lesson. The saint must, by the example of his life, confirm the truth of the basic principles of Christian doctrine. Hence the elements of rhetoric and panegyric inherent in the majority of saints' lives; hence, too, the set thematic and stylistic pattern which defined the genre.

Usually a life of a saint began with brief mention of his parents, who for the most part proved to be pious folk and at the same time persons of quality. The saint is born to "orthodox and pious parents," "noble and pious," "great and illustrious," "rich." But sometimes the saint is the son of impious parents, and it is then emphasized that in spite of the unfavorable conditions of his upbringing he none the less became an ascetic. Next came an account of the future saint's behavior in childhood. He is distinguished by modesty, obedience, studiousness, shuns games with boys his own age, and is wholly imbued with piety. Next, frequently as a youth, his ascetic life begins, for the most part in a monastery or in a hermitage. It is attended by ascetic mortification of the flesh and struggle with all manner of passions, among them physical desire. In order, for example, to rid himself of the temptation of women, the saint inflicts physical pain upon himself: he cuts off a finger, thereby diverting his attention from the lusts of the flesh (compare the analogous episode in Leo Tolstoy's *Father Sergius*), and so on. Often the saint is persecuted by demons which are incarnations of the same temptations to sin, but through prayers, fasting, and abstinence he gets the better of the devil's evil suggestions. He possesses the power to perform miracles and enters into communication with the heavenly powers. The saint's death is, in most cases, peaceful and calm: he departs painlessly for the other world, and posthumously his body gives forth fragrance; miracles of healing are performed at his coffin and on his tomb: the blind receive their sight, the deaf their hearing, the sick are made well. The biography usually ends with a eulogy of the saint.

The inner structure of the life shows the same general features found in secular narrative literature. The saint's life often contains psychological characterizations, particularly of the chief character, whose own reflections are largely used for this purpose; of common occurrence are monologues revealing the spiritual state of the characters and now and again taking the form of a threnody, a lament. Common, too, is the dialogue form, which serves to enliven the narrative and give it dramatic quality. In a number of instances, the hagiographer turns aside from the consecutive exposition of the saint's destiny to indulge in reflections himself, often of a sentimental cast, and reinforced by quotations from "Holy Writ." Finally, some lives give a physical portrait of the saint, drawn schematically, a mere enumeration of his principal distinguishing marks.

The canonical form for saints' lives was worked out on Byzantine soil in the fourth century. By this time we already have the most typical example, the *Life of Antonius the Great,* by Athanasius of Alexandria. The basic theme of this *Life*—which underwent artistic metamorphosis during the nineteenth century in Flaubert's *Temptation of St. Anthony*—is the saint's strenuous conflict with devils. The finishing touch was given to Byzantine lives of saints by a compiler from the second half of the tenth century, Simeon Metaphrastes, whose work served to fix the hagiographical tradition in a groove.

Translated lives had circulated here from of old either in long form or in short. In the long form they existed separately or became part of collections known as *Chetyi Minyei;* that is, books intended for reading and having the material arranged by days of the month; the second, or short, formulary of the saint found a place in the prologues or (in Greek) synaxars, and in menologies. (The Russian designation "prologue" resulted from a Russian editor's mistaking *prologos,* denoting the introduction of a synaxar, for the title of the collection.) *Chetyi Minyei* apparently existed in Rus as early as the eleventh century. (The earliest extant copy made in Rus, the Uspensky *Chetyi Minyei* for the month of May, dates from the beginning of the twelfth century,[3] the earliest *Prologue* from the twelfth century.) On Russian soil the latter included, in addition to saints' lives, edifying legend-novellas borrowed from the paterikons (see below), and articles of an instructive character. It was presumably produced by collaboration between South Slavic and Russian ecclesiastics at some joint meeting place, most probably Constantinople. The early edition already includes, along with biographies of Greek and South Slavic saints, "memorials" of Russian saints: Boris and Gleb, Princess Olga, Prince Mstislav, Theodosius of the Crypt Monastery. Later the *Prologue* was very much augmented on Russian soil and became an extremely popular book with the religious reader; its plots were used in art literature of the nineteenth and early twentieth centuries, in works by Herzen, Leskov, Tolstoy, Remizov, and other writers.[4]

Among the translated lives known in Rus in separate copies during the

[3] The first part of this was published by A. A. Shakhmatov and P. A. Lavrov. See "A Twelfth Century Collection from the Uspensky Cathedral of Moscow" (Moscow, 1899), Pt. 1, in *Chtenii obshchestva istorii i drevnostey rossiikikh pri Moskovskom universitete* (Papers of the Society of Russian History and Antiquities at the University of Moscow).

[4] See N. I. Petrov, *O proiskhozhdenii i sostave slavyano-russkogo "Prologa"* (On the Origin and Composition of the Slavo-Russian Prologue) (Kiev, 1875). Separate items from the *Prologue* (for Sept.-April) are printed in *Pamyatniki drevnerusskoy tserkovno-uchitelnoy literatury* (Monuments of Early Russian Ecclesiastico-Instructional Literature), ed. A. Ponomarev (St. Petersburg, 1896–1898), Pts. 2 and 4. In 1916, part of the second edition of the *Prologue,* as found in a Bulgarian fourteenth century MS., was brought out as Publication CXXXV of the Obshchestvo lyubiteley drevney pismennosti (Society of Friends of Early Literature).

eleventh and twelfth centuries were those of Nicholas the Wonder-Worker, Antonius the Great, John Chrysostom, Savva the Consecrated, Basil the New, Andrew the Simple, Alexis, Man of God, and Wenceslas of Bohemia (a West Slavic production).

To illustrate the saint's life as a genre, let us make a study of the biography of Alexis, Man of God, from the text of a fourteenth-fifteenth century manuscript.[5]

To the pious Roman citizens Euphimian and Aglaida, in response to their urgent prayers, a son was born, whom they named Alexis. When the boy reached the age of seven, he was sent to school, where in no time he made his mark. Upon his attaining maturity, the parents married Alexis to a girl of royal blood. But on the wedding night Alexis returned his spouse her ring and, after disclosing some secret to her, left Rome unobserved, took ship and departed for Syria. Upon reaching shore, Alexis disembarked and, having prayed to God, came in the company of some donkey drivers to the city of Edessa, there sold all his belongings and distributed the money to the poor, and himself sat in beggar's raiment at the church porch and spent his life in vigil and fasting, distributing to the poor all the alms that were given him. Meanwhile the grief-stricken father sent three hundred servants out to look for his son. Upon arriving at Edessa they found him at the church porch and gave him alms, not knowing that it was he. Alexis thanked God that he had been deemed worthy to receive alms of his servants. After Alexis had spent seventeen years at the porch of the temple of the Virgin, in a manner wholly pleasing to God, the Virgin appeared to the sexton in a dream and said: "Bring the man of God into my church, for he is worthy of the kingdom of heaven. . . . As the sun shines upon the world, so has his life shone forth to all the world in the sight of God and in the sight of His angels." And the sexton went out to seek this man and could not find him. At last, in accordance with the Virgin's instructions, Alexis was found and brought into the church. His fame spread throughout the city, and to escape from it, Alexis proposed to depart into Catalonia. "By the will of God," the ship on which he had taken passage was borne out of its course by the wind and driven to Rome. Upon landing, Alexis, in order not to be a burden upon strangers, decided to take up his abode in his father's house, trusting that he might escape recognition. He appealed for asylum to his father, who, thinking that it was a stranger who asked him, bade his servants lodge Alexis in an attic cupboard, wait upon him, and give him food and drink from the master's table.

[5] Published as a supplement to V. P. Adrianov's *Zhitie Alekseya-cheloveka bozhiya v drevney russkoy literature i narodnoy slovesnosti* (Life of Alexis, Man of God, in Early Russian Literature and Folk Literature) (St. Petersburg, 1917), pp. 476–483.

Alexis' mother had, after his disappearance, shut herself up in the house, curtained the windows, strewn ashes upon her head, and stopped going out anywhere. His wife, like a "faithful turtledove bereft of its mate," had also decided not to leave the house until she should receive news of her husband. Meanwhile the servants constantly mocked at Alexis, beat him, poured slops on him. Alexis accepted this treatment gladly and bore it with rejoicing. So he passed seventeen years in his father's house unrecognized of any. However, when his end drew near, he bade that a "parchment" be brought him, and in it he wrote all the secrets that he had with his mother and father and what he had said to his bride as he gave her the ring, and he described his whole life—doing all this that his own might know him.

At this time there issued from the altar of the church a voice prophesying that on Friday, at dawn, a man of God now in the house of Euphimian would die. The two reigning emperors of Rome, Honorius and Arcadius, sent to upbraid Euphimian that "having such grace in his house," he had neglected to inform them of it. Euphimian swore that he knew nothing of the matter. The emperors, the archbishops, and the "emperors' men" came to call upon Euphimian. Alexis' mother and his wife wondered what all the noise and excitement going on outside could mean. Alexis' servants, to whose care Euphimian had formerly entrusted the beggar who came to him, hazarded the guess that this beggar who had spent all his time in fasting and nightly vigil and had submitted to persecution by the servants, was the man of God miraculously mentioned in the temple. Euphimian went to the man, but he was already dead and lay with the parchment in his hand. The father attempted to take the parchment in order to find out what was written there, but Alexis would not let go of it, and only at the request of the emperors, the archbishops, and the nobles did he render the parchment up to the emperors and an archbishop. After hearing its contents, the father rent his garments, began to tear his gray hair, and to kiss the dead body of Alexis and mourn over it. Then Alexis' mother uttered a lengthy lamentation: "Like a lioness from the hunt she clambered through the door, and rent her garments and tore her hair, looking wildly toward heaven," and, lastly, Alexis' wife did likewise, "swathed in black robes" and wailing: "Woe is me, a turtledove bereft; how many years have I longed to hear your voice or your conversation or news of whither you had gone, yet you did not come to me. How many years was my heart empty for your sake. Today I am made a widow, with no one to look to, no one to wait for. I no longer have strength to bear up but shall henceforth weep out my pierced heart and my wounded soul."

By command of the emperors and the archbishop, the cot with Alexis' body upon it was set up in the midst of the city. To his body thronged the deaf, the blind, lepers, and those possessed of devils, and all were miraculously healed. When the body of Alexis was carried to the church for burial, such a multitude of people gathered that the emperors and archbishops who were carrying the coffin could not force their way through. In order to clear a way, they commanded that much gold and silver be scattered, but even this failed to distract the people, who continued to crowd about the coffin. The body of Alexis was laid in a golden shrine set with precious stones. In the shrine, "by the grace of God," a fragrant font of consecrated oil bubbled up wherewith the sick anointed themselves and obtained of God all that they asked.

As may readily be seen, the *Life of Alexis* gives us the above noted series of moments essential to the biographical pattern: here we have the saint's descent from pious parents of noble birth, his early inclination for study, disdain for the blandishments of earthly life, strict asceticism, blissful end, and, finally, the performance of posthumous miracles at his tomb. In this life we get both dialogue and lyrical monologue-laments. The exposition itself contains elements of the embellished rhetorical style in connection with the author's lyric flights. Traditional, too, in this life are the indicated childlessness of the saint's parents previous to his birth, his departure from the parental roof, distribution of his goods to the poor, avoidance of popular renown, and so forth.[6] The *Life of Alexis,* like other monuments of early Russian literature, saints' lives in particular, underwent editorial revision down to the seventeenth century, exercised an influence on a number of subsequent original Russian literary works, and, finally, became a basis for popular spiritual verse.

Our great interest of old in the *Life of Alexis* is explained by the fact that it deals with the life of a man whose disdain of all that the rich landowning gentry lived for awakened sympathy in those who did not belong to the upper ranks of society. Another attractive feature was its general lyric tone.

Also known in Rus during the earliest period were translated collections of short novellas dealing with sundry edifying episodes from the lives of Christian ascetics and called "paterikons" or "otechnikons." Each was a congeries of tales about ascetics or hermits living in a given locality or a given monastery or about events and various vital happenings of which these recluses had been observers or eyewitnesses. Elements of the entertaining, the anecdotal, the naïvely superstitious, here curiously intertwined with everyday episodes of a purely secular character, helped to promote the wide circulation of these story collections, which made extensive levies upon the stock in trade of migratory international plots going back to pagan mythology.

[6] For further details see Adrianov, *op. cit.,* Chap. 3, pp. 127–144.

The popular *Prologue* included a good many paterikon legends, and was largely dependent upon them for its interest.

Two paterikons were especially popular in olden times, the *Holy Land* or *Sinaitic Paterikon* of John Moschus (seventh century), giving incidents from the lives of the Syrian monks, and the *Egyptian Paterikon,* which, as a rule, bore the title, *Legend of the Egyptian Monks,* and utilized as its principal source of material the *Cloister Roll* of Bishop Palladius of Elenopolis, compiled in 420. Both paterikons were already known in Rus in the eleventh century. Somewhat later, though still during the Kiev Period, the *Roman Paterikon,* compiled in the West, became known in this country.[7]

Let us cite one story from the *Egyptian Paterikon,* that about Mark. Palladius says:

This Mark, while still a youth, knew the Old and New Testaments by heart; he was very mild and peaceful, more so than almost any other. Once I went to see him and, sitting by the door of his cell, began listening to what he said and did. Completely alone in the cell, a man almost a hundred years old, without a tooth, he was still fighting with himself and with the devil, and saying: "What more do you want, old man? You have drunk wine and anointed yourself with oil—what else do you require of me? You gray-haired glutton, you belly-worshipper, shame on you!" Then, turning to the devil, he said: "Leave me, devil, avaunt! Through my sloth you have grown old with me. On the pretext of bodily infirmity you have had me ask for wine and oil and have made a voluptuary of me. Is there anything I still owe you? You shall get nothing more out of me, so leave me, enemy of man." Then he said to himself in a joking way: "Now then, chatterbox, gray-haired glutton, esurient old man, how much longer shall you and I be together?"

Let us next study a tale from the *Sinaitic Paterikon,* the one about Herasimus and the lion of which Leskov made an artistic adaptation.

It is told of the ancient Herasimus that once on the bank of Jordan he met a lion roaring with pain from a splinter that had become lodged in its foot. Herasimus, seeing the lion's plight, sat down, pulled out the splinter,

---

7 The text of the *Sinaitic Paterikon* from an eleventh-twelfth century Russian MS. was published by I. Sreznevskii in *Svedeniya i zametki o maloizvestnykh i neizvestnykh pamyatnikakh* (Information and Notes on Little Known and Unknown Monuments) (St. Petersburg, 1879), LXXI–XV, pp. 49–110. A study of it was made by I. Smirnov, *Sinaiskii paterik v drevneslavyanskom perevode* (Sinaitic Paterikon in Early Russian Translation) (Sergiev Posad, 1917), Pts. 1 and 2. On the *Egyptian Paterikon* see I. P. Eremin's article, "K istorii drevnerusskoy perevodnoy povesti" (Toward a History of the Early Russian Translated Narrative) in *Trudy otdela drevnerusskoy literatury* (Works of the Division of Early Russian Literature) (1936), III, pp. 37–57. On the *Roman Paterikon* see F. I. Buslayev's *Istoriya russkoy literatury* (Moscow, 1905), Pt. 3, pp. 26–41. See also V. Preobrazhenskii's *Slavyano-Russkii skitskii paterik* (Slavo-Russian Hermitage Paterikon) (Kiev, 1909), and I. P. Eremin, *Svodnyi paterik v pivdenno-slovyanskikh, ukrainskomy ta moskovskomy pismenstvakh* (Composite Paterikon from Church Slavonic, Ukrainian, and Muscovite Manuscripts) (Kiev, 1927), reprinted from *Zapiski istorichno-philologichnogo viddilu* (Notes of the Historico-Philological Division), Academy of Science of the USSR, Bks. XII, XV.

and cleansed the foot of pus. Thereafter, the lion he had healed followed the ancient and would not leave him. The ancient began to feed him and soon the lion was entrusted with pasturing the donkey that hauled water to the monastery from the Jordan. Once the donkey wandered off by itself and a certain merchant coming with camels from Arabia took the donkey with him; but the lion, having lost the donkey, went to the monastery "very sad and despondent." When the ancient asked him where the donkey was, the lion "stood silent with downcast eyes, like a person." Thinking that the lion had eaten the donkey, Herasimus bade the lion now bring water to the monastery himself. Just then a soldier came to the ancient about a prayer and, seeing the lion carrying water, took pity on him and gave the ancient three pieces of gold that he might buy a donkey and release the lion from such work. Some time afterwards, the merchant who had made off with the donkey came again along the Jordan with camels and the stolen donkey, and, catching sight of the lion, took to flight; then the lion seized the donkey's rope in his mouth and joyously led him to the ancient, together with three camels. Herasimus then understood that the lion had been unjustly accused, and gave him the name Jordan.

After that, the lion passed more than five years at the monastery, never leaving the old man's side. But Herasimus died and was buried, and at this time "God saw to it" that the lion was not in the monastery. When the lion returned and, not finding the ancient, began searching for him, one of the monks told him that the ancient was dead, and started to offer him food, but the lion refused the food and kept looking for Herasimus, "roaring greatly," as though his despair were too much for him. Neither the monks' caresses nor their condolences could assuage the lion's grief or check his sobs: with voice and face and eyes he expressed his sorrow at not seeing the ancient. Then a monk took the lion to the tomb of Herasimus and himself knelt beside it. Seeing this, the lion knelt too, and weeping and beating his head upon the ground, forthwith gave up the ghost. All this (concludes the narrator) was not because the animal had "understanding" but because it had pleased God to glorify one who had glorified Him not only in life but also in death, and to indicate to us what manner of obedience the animals had shown Adam before his fall.

The *Roman Paterikon* of Pope Gregory Deuterologos was Western in its cultural associations and therefore largely free from the traits of somber Byzantine asceticism which characterize most of the stories in the *Egyptian* and *Sinaitic* paterikons. Let us cite as a sample of the *Roman Paterikon* one of its most poetic tales—that of the pious Scholastica.

Scholastica had been dedicated to God from childhood. Once a year it was her custom to pay a visit to her brother, the monk Benedict; they would meet near the monastery gates. Upon one occasion the brother and sister passed the whole day in uplifting conversation and toward evening supped together. And when the brother was about to part from his sister, she besought him not to depart from her but pass the night in converse about the joys of the heavenly life. But Benedict answered: "What are you saying, Sister? The rule forbids my remaining longer outside the monastery." And the sky was at that time very clear (observes the narrator), not a single cloud to be seen in it. Upon hearing her brother's refusal, Scholastica bowed her head and started to pray earnestly to God. The moment she raised her head there was a flash of lightning, a crash of thunder, and such a great rain fell that Benedict and the monks who were with him could not move from the spot. So a pious woman (explains Gregory Deuterologos), with head bent in prayer, shed floods of tears, whence came abundant rain out of a clear sky. Seeing that by reason of the thunder storm he could not return to the monastery, Benedict said reproachfully to Scholastica: "May almighty God have mercy upon you, Sister! What is this that you have done?" Scholastica answered: "Lo, I besought you and you would not hearken unto me; but when I besought my God he heard me." And Benedict must perforce remain until morning in pious converse with his sister. The story ends with the following words by the compiler of the paterikon:

A woman's soul performed a great miracle by the will of almighty God. Nor is it to be wondered at that a woman who had long desired to see her brother should at that moment have been more capable of accomplishment, since, in the words of the Evangelist John, "God is love," wherefore she who had the more love was the more capable of accomplishment.

By inclusion in the *Prologue,* the paterikon stories became accessible to the widest range of readers and exercised a great influence on original book literature and on the oral tradition.

APOCRYPHA

Among the translated works already circulating in Rus during the earliest period belong the monuments of so-called apocryphal literature, associated chiefly with biblical themes. Literally translated, the word "apocryphal" means "secret," "hidden," accessible only to persons with special knowledge, to experts, not to the public at large. The word had this meaning back in the pre-Christian era and retained it during the first centuries of Christianity. In this sense an apocrypha was not regarded even on Christian soil as anything harmful or contradictory to canonical literature but, on the contrary, being a sort of literature for the chosen few, was held in special respect and esteem. Such respect was enjoyed, particularly among the early Christians, by the Apocalypse of St. John the Divine, likewise numbered among apocryphal books. But later on, in connection with the growth of "heresies" in opposition to the official Church, apocryphas were extensively used by various "heretical" offshots of Christianity, and at that time the official Church began suppressing and prohibiting them. On the other hand, during the struggle of various "heretical" teachings against orthodox Christian doctrine, a struggle which often had deep underlying social causes, the apocryphas were an indirect reflection of the critical attitude of the "heretics" toward the basic principles of canonical Christian literature as maintained by the orthodox Church.

This state of affairs in the long run demanded the establishment of a fixed body of religious and ecclesiastical literature held by the official Church to be true and to merit full confidence, and therefore termed "canonical." In the fourth century a listing was projected of the books of "Holy Writ" recognized as canonical, side by side with which there existed writings of two other sorts: those that lacked plenary sanctity, "divine inspiration," but were consistent enough with the canon to be considered harmless and at times even helpful for persons ill prepared to perceive the complicated Christian dogma, and which were consequently permitted to circulate (the so-called *homologoumena*), and those positively harmful, spurious, false (*nopha*) and hence reprobated by the church, forbidden (*aporreta*). Complete agreement as to the qualifications of individual writings did not exist between the two Churches. It sometimes happened that a writing recognized as canonical in the Eastern Church was regarded by the Western as a prohibited or "repudiated" work and vice versa. Even within the two Churches opinion differed on the matter. Next, the middle category of writings—those permitted to circulate—lost its independent status and was divided between the two others, and *nopha* and *aporreta* became synonymous with *apokrypha;* a "repudiated" book became an apocryphal one. With the apocryphal writings were lumped the so-called "forgeries" (*pseudepigrapha*); that is, writings which, for the sake of added authority, were improperly attributed to the pen of some prominent Church dignitary. Such writings fell into the prohibited, or apocryphal, category even when they contained nothing contradictory to canonical literature, a case in point being the *Gospel of Jacob.*

Thus in the final acceptation of the term on Christian soil, apocryphas were a sort of religious-legend literature which, though closely connected in theme with the canonical writings of the Old or of the New Testament, included in their subject matter itself or in their treatment of it, "heretical" elements reprobated by orthodox Church teaching. To the apocrypha class were also relegated works falsely attributed to genuine Church dignitaries.

It is obvious that the canonical books of the Bible, the gospels not excepted, also belong in the category of religious legend, but the biblical legend, being the one employed by the official Church for its purposes, was sanctioned by it, while the apocryphal legend, being in disagreement with the canonical legend, did not receive the official sanction of the Church.

Also classified as apocryphal works were individual lives of saints, literature of an apocalyptic and eschatological tenor; that is, professing to settle questions relating to the end of the world; likewise catechistic monuments, written in the form of questions and answers, on the highly varied subjects that interested the old-time reader, and finally so-called "false" prayers, exorcisms, astrological and divinatory books, and so forth. Of the Old Testament personages, those accorded most attention in apocryphal literature were Adam and Eve, Enoch, Abraham, David, Solomon, and the twelve patriarchs, particularly Joseph. Works associated with New Testament events were the apocryphal gospels of Jacob, Nicodemus, and Thomas, Aphroditian's legend of the miracle in the land of "Persia" (the Magi adoring the newborn Christ), several legends about Christ (how he was "made pope," how he "plowed," and so forth), legends about the "tree of the cross," "acts" and "tours" (journeys) of the apostles. The apocryphal lives of the saints include the "martyrdoms" of Theodore of Tyre, Georgius the Victor, Nikita, and so forth. Among the apocalyptic and eschatological apocryphas belong such works as *The Virgin's Visit to Hell, The Apostle Paul's Revelation, The Revelation to St. John the Divine on Mount Tabor, The Revelation of St. Methodius of Patara*. With them are associated apocryphal legends about paradise (concerning Agapius, Macarius, Zosima). The most notable of the apocryphas written in question-and-answer form is the *Colloquy of the Three Prelates*. Add to all this the divinatory and astrological books, the "false" prayers and exorcisms, for the most part in circulation here as early as the fifteenth and sixteenth centuries, and we get a rough picture of the vast store of apocryphal material present in our ancient literature and constituting an important part of the poetical reserve drawn on by the chronicle tale, the sermon, the pious pilgrimage narrative, folk lore, and icon-painting.

The sources of the apocryphas, both Old Testament and New, were primarily the early Hebrew oral and written traditions and legends not included in the so-called "canon of Esdras," particularly the numerous "books of Wisdom"; in part these legends and traditions showed the influence of philosophers of the Hellenistic epoch—of the Neoplatonists and the Gnostics.

Another source of apocryphal literature is found in the dualistic religious teachings of the ancient, and of the early Christian, East. On the basis of these, as mediated by the Manichean, Paulician, the Messalian "heresies," there arose in Bulgaria in the tenth and eleventh centuries a movement known as "Bogomilism," associated with the name of Bogomil—in all probability to be identified with Pope Jeremiah, accredited with the compilation of a collection of apocryphas—and preaching an explicit religious dualism. According to the Bogomil teaching, the world is ruled by two powers enjoying equal rights—God and the Devil. God's domain is the spiritual principle in the world, identifiable with good, the Devil's the material principle, embodying what is evil upon earth. The Devil created man's body, and God breathed the soul into it. An echo of this belief is found in our *Primary Chronicle*, where, under the year 1071, we read:

How was man made? . . . God washed himself in the bath, and after perspiring dried himself with straw and threw it out of heaven upon the earth. Then Satan quarreled with God as to which of them should create man out of it. But the Devil made man, and God set a soul in him. As a result, whenever a man dies, his body goes to the earth and his soul to God.

The history of mankind from the moment of man's creation is, according to this teaching, the history of a persistent struggle between these two principles, with man simultaneously the object and the subject of the struggle. Having had its rise during the clash between the enslaved Bulgarian peasantry and the feudal gentry, Bogomilism reflected the protest of the lower social stratum against its enslavers and against the latter's ally, the official Church, with its ritualistic cult—in Bogomil opinion, neither more nor less than an embodiment of the satanic, material, evil element in the world.[8] Victory over the material forces of life was obtained, so the Bogomils taught,

[8] As early as the beginning of the 1870's, A. N. Veselovsky gave a very successful characterization of the social situation which fostered Bogomilism and the legend born of it: "The people offered the most favorable soil possible for the spreading of a heresy. . . . The reasons are clear: the people were the ones who suffered most from the disorders and from the arbitrary government of the feudal lords, from the mass of ills which had descended from no one knew where in the way of famine, bad crops, and massacre by the enemy. They were accustomed to this element of accident, of fatality, and deduced from it the existence of some sort of specific principle of evil, independent, having sovereign power in the world. The dualistic doctrine explained the origin of evil in the world in images that their fancy could grasp, whereas the Church theologians put the question too abstractly for them, since it required some mental exertion to reconcile with the concept of one God, source of all good, the concept of evil as something subject to him. It was to the imagination of a people which had not yet broken away from the mythological habit of mind as expressed in rites and superstitions that the dualists keyed their fantastic cosmogony, fabulous tales concerning the beginning of the world, their eschatology. Hence their teachings were immediately taken up by the people and passed over into their songs and stories." *Slavyanskie Skazania o Solomone i Kitovrase i zapadnye legendy o Morolfe i Merline* (Slavonic Legends of Solomon and Kitovras and Western Legends of Morolfus and Merlin) (St. Petersburg, 1872), pp. 147–148.

through inner self-perfection and ascetic practice, whereby man's spiritual nature was set free. Hence, the heavily underlined moral didacticism of apocryphas emanating from the Bogomil background. That these apocryphas were also read in democratic circles is due to the embodiment in them of elements of legend and fantasy as well as realistic themes, a trait characteristic of apocryphal literature as a whole but particularly marked in the Bogomil writings. These possess to a superlative degree all the marks of what may be termed "folk religion."

Bulgaria had already transmitted to us during the early period of Russian letters the Bogomil apocrypha produced there, the "fables" and "blasphemies" of Pope Jeremiah, and these had found a perfect soil in the ambiguous religious state of the old Russian reader, who was little more than a formal adherent of Christianity, inexperienced in the subtleties of orthodox dogma. Also chiefly through the medium of Bulgaria, apocryphas were imported which had been given a literary going over in Byzantium, though it occasionally happens that some apocrypha in circulation here, known to derive ultimately from a Byzantine text, has never turned up on Byzantine soil.

Most of the Russian texts of apocryphas are to be found in late copies— in sixteenth and, some of them, in fifteenth or fourteenth century manuscripts—but, to judge from the language, a large part of them were known here during the first centuries of Russian letters, and some are even preserved in eleventh and twelfth century copies; for example, the eleventh century copy of the *Acts of the Apostle Paul and Thekla* and the twelfth century copies of the *Ascension of Isaiah,* the *Virgin's Visit to Hell,* and the *Martyrdoms of the Three Children and Daniel.* Later on, Old Testament apocryphal material reached the Russian reader in abundance through the *Explanatory Paleya* and the *Historical Paleya,* which did duty with the Russian reader as a biblical codex, something that did not appear in this country until the end of the fifteenth century and even then did not supersede the *Paleya* with the general reader until the end of the seventeenth century.[9]

[9] Most important published texts of Russian apocryphal literature:
Pamyatniki otrechennoy russkoy literatury (Monuments of Proscribed Russian Literature) (Moscow and St. Petersburg, 1863), Vols. I–II, collected and published by Tikhonravov, the fullest, most accurate and best critical edition. Tikhonravov also prepared for publication a third volume of the *Pamyatniki* but delayed publication and it was printed only in part (6 folios): *Apokrificheskie skazaniya* (Apocryphal Legends) (St. Petersburg, 1894), *Sbornik otd. russk. yaz. i slov.* (Collection of the Division of Russian Language and Literature) Academy of Sciences of the USSR, Vol. LVIII, No. 4.
Lozhnye i otrechennye knigi russkoy stariny (False and Proscribed Books of Russian Antiquity) collected by A. N. Pypin, *Pamyatniki starinnoy russkoy literatury* (Monuments of Ancient Russian Literature) (St. Petersburg, G. Kushelev-Bezborodko, 1862), Pt. 3; I. Ya. Porfiryev: *Apokrificheskie skazaniya o vetkhozavetnykh litsakh i sobytiakh po rukopisyam Solovetskoy biblioteki* (Apocryphal Legends About Old Testament Personages and Events

However, apocryphal legend drifted into Rus not only through the medium of writing but also by oral transmission, after the manner of migratory international tales and legends in general, and thus found its way into the earliest monuments of Russian literature, beginning with the eleventh century. In this connection commercial and political relations played an important part, as did the military clashes with Byzantium, Bulgaria, and the Orient, and last but not least the pilgrimages of Russians to Palestine, an abounding storehouse of apocryphal legend. Whole throngs of pilgrims, "sandal walkers," would set out for the "Holy Land," purposing

> In the holy of holies their prayers to say,
> On the tomb of the Lord their lips to lay,
> In Jordan wash their sins away,
> And dry on the vestment immune to decay,

and they brought back to their own country a good many apocryphas, both Old Testament and New.

Whether a work formally belonged in the apocrypha class was a matter of its being entered in the Index, in the list of "spurious" or "forbidden" books. Sometimes a monument clearly apocryphal in character escaped suppression simply because it had not found its way into the Index or because the compilation of which it formed a part had not been indexed. Thus, several apocryphas not listed in the Index were included at the middle of the sixteenth century in such a strictly official Church collection as the *Chetyi Minyei*, edited by the metropolitan Macarius; on the other hand indexed apocryphas found a hospitable welcome in the *Paleya*, not accounted a forbidden book.

Indexes were imported into Rus from Byzantium as early as the eleventh century. In *Svyatoslav's Miscellany*, 1073, there is a translated Greek article by "Theologue of the Word," which enumerates along with "true" books and those that do not rank as true, "secret"; that is, apocryphal books. The total number of forbidden books here indexed is twenty-five. Just which of the books listed in this index were known in Rus even in later translations we do not know. Later on, we encounter similar indexes, again translated from the Greek, in the *Taktikon* of Nikon of Montenegro, and in the so-called *Pilots*, collections of statutes and regulations pertaining to ecclesiastical law. Extant in a fourteenth century manuscript, is the Pogodin *Nomokanon*, which contains an index of forbidden books compiled during

---

from Manuscripts in the Solovetsky Library) (St. Petersburg, 1877); *Apokrificheskie ska-zaniya o novozavetnykh, etc.* (St. Petersburg, 1890).

See also A. I. Yatsimirskii, *Bibliograficheskii obzor apokrifov v yuzhno-slavyanskoy i russkoy pismennosti: spiski pamyatnikov* (Bibliographical Survey of Apocryphas in South Slavic and Russian Literature: Lists of Monuments), No. 1, Pt. 1, *Old Testament Apocryphas* (St. Petersburg, 1921).

the eleventh century but already originating in Bulgaria. This index, entitled "Canon of the Laodicean Council," enumerates not only the apocryphas known to the Greek indexes but also those circulating in Bulgaria, particularly—and in considerable numbers—the Bogomil apocryphas, here attributed to Pope Jeremiah.

A specifically Russian index makes its appearance in the fourteenth century. We find the first such index in the *Prayer Book* of St. Cyprian; it is known to us through an extract made in the fifteenth century by the Metropolitan Zosima. This draws upon the Greek indexes and the Bulgarian one given in the Pogodin *Nomokanon* but, in addition, enumerates superstitious and divinatory books, "anathema and detestable to God," then circulating in Rus. During the fifteenth and sixteenth centuries the Index underwent further development here, was enlarged by new proscriptions; specific additions found in sixteenth century indexes were the astrological and divinatory books, already coming to us not from Byzantium and not from the South Slavs, but from the West. The Index took final form toward the end of the sixteenth century and as then constituted is included in the so-called *Book of St. Cyril,* 1644, a work which enjoyed special popularity among the Old Believers.[10]

Let us study the content of a few apocryphas, beginning with one which preserves echoes of the Bogomil heresy, an apocrypha on the creation of Adam and Eve.

God created man in the land of Midian "from the eight elements": his body from earth, his bones from stone, his blood from the sea, his eyes from the sun, his thoughts from the clouds, his glance from light, his breath from the wind, his warmth from fire. And when God went to get eyes from the sun, he left Adam by himself, lying there on the ground. During His absence, "accursed Satan" came and smeared Adam with mire and mucus. And when the Lord came back He wanted to put the eyes in Adam, but, seeing man so besmeared, was wroth with Satan and cursed him. And, like lightning, the Devil vanished into the earth from before the face of the Lord. But the Lord, having removed from Adam the "filths of Satan" and mixed them with his tears, created of them a dog, bade it keep Adam clean as a mirror while he himself went to high Jerusalem for Adam's breath. And Satan came a second time and wanted to drop evil filth upon Adam, but, scared off by the dog, which ran at him barking, he took a tree and pierced man full of holes and created in him seventy diseases. And the Lord came from high Jerusalem and, seeing Adam pierced by the tree, took pity on him

[10] On the history of the Slavo-Russian Index, see A. N. Pypin, "Dlya obyasneniya stati o lozhnykh knigakh" (In Explanation of Articles Concerning False Books), *Letopis zanyatii arkheograficheskoy komissii* (Chronicle of the Studies of the Archaeographical Commission) (St. Petersburg, 1861–1862), Pt. 1, pp. 1–55.

and said to Satan: "Accursed devil, what have you done to this man? Why have you inoculated him with these ills?" The Devil explained that if man were not afflicted he would never remember God; but that if afflicted he would call upon Him. And the Lord chased the Devil off, and the Devil disappeared as darkness disappears before light, and the Lord put the ailments of man inside of his body. Then the Lord dispatched his angel to take the letters of Adam's name (*A, D,* and *M*), to the east, to the west, to the north and to the south. Adam became tsar over all lands and over the birds of the sky and the beasts of the field and the fish of the sea, and God gave him "absolute power," making the heavenly bodies subject to him and every earthly creature. And God planted Paradise on the east and commanded Adam to dwell there. On the sixth day God caused sleep to come upon Adam, took a rib from his left side, and from the rib "produced arms and legs and a head" and so made a wife for him. Then the Lord showed him His death, crucifixion, resurrection, and ascension five and a half millenniums later.[11] And Adam saw the Lord crucified, Peter going to Rome, and Paul teaching in Damascus and preaching the resurrection of Christ.

Adam awoke in great consternation. He told the Lord of his dream and the Lord said unto him: "It is meet that I should come down to earth for your sake, be crucified, and on the third day rise again; but tell no man of your dream until you shall see me sitting at the right hand of my Father, and then grieve thereat."

And Adam dwelt in Paradise seven days, whereby the Lord symbolized the life of man: "At ten years is his infancy fulfilled; at twenty, his youth; at thirty, his prime; at forty, middle age; at fifty, senescence; at sixty, old age; at seventy, death." Seven days symbolized also the seven thousand years that the world is to exist, and the eighth thousand will have no end, for it is eternal.

As we see, this apocrypha does not fully reflect the Bogomil doctrine, whereby the body of the first man was created by the Devil and only his spirit by God: here God is equally creator of the material and the spiritual nature of man, but none the less the Devil appears as a sufficiently imposing power to enter into competition with God. In contrast to the style usual in canonical writings, we here have a vividly expressive realistic manner, permitting an extremely concrete presentation of biblical events. Here we also see a limitation of divine omnipotence, and the attribution of human traits both to God and to the Devil. Naturally such a narrative could not elicit the approval of the official Church.

Solomon was the biblical personage to whom apocryphal literature paid

[11] The period from the creation of the world to the birth of Christ was 5508 years according to ancient calculation.

the most attention. No Russian manuscripts of apocryphas about Solomon are earlier than the second half of the fifteenth century, but, to judge from the language of extant texts, the translation itself dates from a considerably earlier time. The *Explanatory Paleya,* 1477, and subsequent paleyas, contain an apocrypha about Solomon and Kitovras. In substance it is as follows:

When Solomon was building the temple at Jerusalem, he tried to find a way to hew stones without the use of iron. Upon learning that such a method was known to Kitovras (a supernatural being, the Greek centaur, the ancient Hindu gandarv), Solomon sent his best boyar to Kitovras' place of abode and with him servants bearing an iron chain and a hoop, whereon was inscribed an incantation in the name of God, and also wine, mead, and sheep's wool. Kitovras was away when the delegation arrived, and, seeing three wells, they bailed out the water, stopped up the pits with wool, poured wine into two of the wells and mead into the third, then went and hid. Kitovras came home thirsty, and when he did not find water in the wells, drank up the wine and mead that had been poured in, became intoxicated, and fell fast asleep. Then the boyar put the chain about his neck and, when he awoke and wanted to get it off, told him that it had the name of God on it and a spell. Upon learning this, Kitovras submitted and meekly followed the boyar.

It was his habit always to take the straight road, and when he came to Jerusalem they cleared the way before him, razing any houses that stood in his path. But when he passed a widow's house that blocked his course, the widow implored him not to destroy her dwelling. Kitovras bent himself about the corner of the house without turning aside from the straight road, broke a rib and said: "A soft word breaks a bone, but a harsh word arouses anger." Passing through the market place and hearing a man ask for shoes that would last seven years, he burst out laughing. Seeing another man telling fortunes, he likewise laughed; seeing a wedding, he wept; seeing a drunken man who had lost his way, Kitovras put him on the right road.

And they took Kitovras to Solomon's palace, but upon the first day Solomon did not summon him into his presence. When Kitovras asked why the king had not summoned him, they answered that the king had drunk to excess the evening before. Kitovras, hearing this, put stone upon stone, and when they told Solomon of it, he interpreted this as meaning that Kitovras bade him go on drinking. When they did not summon Kitovras into the king's presence the next day either, explaining that he was ill from having overeaten the day before, Kitovras took stone from stone. On the third day Solomon finally summoned Kitovras. And Kitovras said to the king: "God gave the universe unto you to possess it, and you were not content, but took me also." To which reproach Solomon replied: "Not for any need of mine did I bring you hither, but at the Lord's command, to inquire of you how I may build a temple without using iron to square the stones."

Kitovras instructed Solomon how to obtain a shamir,[12] with the aid of which the stones of the temple might be squared. Upon the advice of Kitovras, Solomon's boyar and servants were dispatched to a distant place, to the nest of a bird which, in Russian copies of the apocrypha, is sometimes called a "nogotch," sometimes a "kogot." [13] Kitovras had given them a glass. This they fitted over the kogot's nest when he flew off after food for his young. Unable then to get into the nest, the kogot flew for a shamir, but when he was about to cut the glass with it, Solomon's servants scared the kogot off and the bird dropped the shamir, which was then conveyed to Solomon.

When Solomon afterwards asked Kitovras why he had laughed at the man who was looking for shoes that would last seven years, Kitovras answered that it was because the man would not live seven days longer. When Solomon asked why he had laughed when he saw the fortuneteller, Kitovras said that this fortuneteller, who was revealing secrets to others, did not himself know that a gold treasure was buried under his feet. Solomon gave orders to find out if this were true, and they found that it was. His tears at sight of the wedding Kitovras explained as being because he knew that the bridegroom would not live another thirty days. This too, when investigated, turned out to have been correct. He helped the drunken man find his way, so he said, because he had learned through a voice from the sky that this was a righteous man, and consequently he had been obliged to do him the service.

Kitovras remained at Solomon's palace until the temple was finished. Once Solomon said to Kitovras: "I perceive that your strength is as the strength of a man, and not more than ours, since I was able to seize you." And Kitovras said: "If you would know my strength, take this chain from me and give me the ring from your hand." Solomon complied with this request, and Kitovras, after swallowing the ring, smote Solomon with his wing and knocked him to the edge of the Promised Land, where his sages and wise men found him. From that time Solomon began to fear Kitovras by night and gave orders that sixty soldiers should guard his bed, armed with swords.

No Greek text of the apocrypha is known to us, but on the other hand we have a Hebrew Talmudic apocrypha about Solomon and Asmodeus, very much like ours, which goes back to Iranian legend and even beyond— to Indian legend—and which is closely related to Jewish legends of the

---

[12] A Hebrew word, meaning "diamond."

[13] The meaning of this word is obscure. A. Veselovsky (*Slavic Legends about Solomon and Kitovras*, pp. 213–215), by associating "nogotch" with "noga" (leg), interprets it as "vulture," "kite," "hawk," and even "ostrich." But this interpretation does not accord with the indication in the text that the "nogotch" or "kogot" was a small bird.

building of Solomon's temple. (Compare I Kings 6:7: "And the house when it was in building, was built of stone made ready before it was brought thither: so that there was neither hammer nor ax nor any tool of iron heard in the house while it was in building.") South Slavic texts of the apocrypha of Solomon and Kitovras are also lacking, though there is every reason to suppose that such texts existed, to judge from the Pogodin fourteenth century Bulgarian *Nomokanon,* which prohibits "fables and blasphemies concerning King Solomon and concerning Kitovras." One is led to believe, with Veselovsky, that there also existed inextant Byzantine texts of the apocrypha from which were derived, among other things, the Western legends of Solomon and Morolphus and also the legends about Merlin which figure in the romances of the Round Table. The name Kitovras itself, a very close distortion of the Greek "centaur," argues for a Byzantine original to which, through a South Slavic medium, the Russian text of the apocrypha must be traced. In this connection we need not be disturbed by the presence in our text of the Hebrew word "shamir," which most probably did not make its appearance until the *Explanatory Paleya* in the fifteenth century, as a result perhaps of some connection between the *Paleya* text and the heresy of the "Judaizers." On South Slavic soil, whence the apocrypha evidently passed direct to our country, it probably came out under the influence of the Bogomil heresy, inasmuch as A. N. Veselovsky shows that "the contest of Solomon with the demon, which constitutes the substance of the legend, gives fully appropriate expression to the dualist concept of the feud between the principles of good and evil." [14]

In addition to the apocrypha about Solomon and Kitovras, the *Explanatory Paleya* also includes judgments of Solomon, which characterize him as an eminent wise man and justify the following reference to him in the Bible: "And God gave Solomon wisdom and understanding exceeding much, and largeness of heart, even as the sand that is on the sea shore. And Solomon's wisdom excelled the wisdom of all the children of the east country, and all the wisdom of Egypt" (I Kings 4:29–30). First Kings tells of the judgment of Solomon upon two women who were quarreling about a child. Each of them maintained that the child belonged to her. Solomon proposed that the women cut the child in two and share the parts between them. One of the contestants agreed to this, but the other preferred to give up all claim to the child if only it were not killed. After that it was not hard for Solomon to decide which of the rival women was the real mother.

Older texts of the *Explanatory Paleya* carry eight of the judgments of Solomon. Let us study a few of them. In the first judgment the argument was over three vessels which had been bequeathed by a father to his three

14 *Slavonic Legends of Solomon and Kitovras,* p. 156.

sons. The first vessel was found to contain gold, the second, bones, the third, earth. When the sons disagreed about the division of the vessels and referred the matter to Solomon, he interpreted the father's will thus: that the eldest son should possess the gold, the middle son the cattle and slaves, the youngest, the fields and vineyards. A father having a daughter and six sons died, leaving a thousand pieces of gold to his daughter and all his property to his eldest son. After the father's death the sons against whom discrimination had been made demanded of their elder brother that he share the estate with them. When he refused, all six referred the matter to Solomon. Solomon told them that he could not settle their dispute until he had seen the right arm of their father, whom they were to exhume. The sons betook themselves to their father's tomb, and when five of them were about to break into it, the sixth, the eldest, cried out and restrained them, agreeing to share the estate, if only they would leave his father's remains undisturbed. The servants of Solomon, who had been sent after the brothers, observed the behavior of all six and reported to Solomon concerning it. Solomon recognized the father's arrangement as just, saying to the brothers who would have amputated their father's arm that they had been begotten upon their mother by "adulterous men." That he might verify his conclusion, Solomon bade that the mother be called, and she confirmed what he had said.

In other instances Solomon distinguishes himself by his ability to guess hard riddles. Sometimes subject devils help him to get the answer. Thus, in the *Explanatory Paleya*, we find the following riddle propounded to Solomon by the Persian king Darius, the purport of it, however, being explained to Solomon by devils. There was a shield, and on the shield was a hare, and a falcon flew down and took the hare, and an owl perched on the shield. As a prize for guessing this riddle, Darius promises Solomon three barrels of silver. Solomon invokes the devils in his service and proposes that they guess the riddle, promising them a third of the silver which he is to receive from Darius. In the twinkling of an eye, one of the devils said: "The shield is the earth, and the hare on the shield is truth, but the falcon's taking the hare means that an angel took the truth that was on earth; and the owl perched on the shield is falsehood: truth went to heaven, and what remained on earth was falsehood." Upon receiving the answer to his riddle, Darius sent Solomon the three barrels of silver, which Solomon bade the devils divide between themselves and him. The devils assigned two barrels to Solomon, and the third, as agreed, they kept for themselves. Then Solomon ordered that this third barrel be turned upside down and the contents poured over the devil's head. The devil asked Solomon: "Why do you deal falsely instead of upholding the truth?" And the king said: "False devil, you have been your own judge: truth was taken up into heaven, and falsehood remained here."

This riddle about right and wrong, to which Solomon's judgment upon the devils is the sequel, clearly reflected the basic dualistic concept of the Bogomil heresy concerning the struggle in life between two principles—good and evil.

The Bible tells how "when the queen of Sheba heard of the fame of Solomon concerning the name of the Lord, she came to prove him with hard questions. . . . And Solomon told her all her questions: there was not any thing hid from the king, which he told her not." (I Kings 10:1–3.) The *Explanatory Paleya* cites a number of riddles correctly guessed by Solomon. When the queen of Sheba, or of the South, brought fair boys and girls before Solomon all dressed alike, Solomon twice distinguished the boys from the girls. The first time, he had all of them wash; the boys washed "hard and fast," the girls "gently and delicately." The second time he bade them pick up vegetables that had been strewn about; the boys started to gather them in their skirts, the girls, in their sleeves.

The queen's wise men said to Solomon's wise men: "We have a well that is far from the city; in your wisdom, move it to our city."

Solomon's wise men answered: "Braid ropes of bran and we will move your well into the city."

"And the queen's wise men asked them: "When knives spring up in the field, with what do you reap them?"

"The horn of an ass," answered Solomon's wise men.

"But when have asses horns?" asked the former.

"When do knives spring up in the field?" answered the latter, and so on. The last two riddles go back to Talmudic story.[15]

New Testament apocryphas of great popularity in Old Rus were the apocryphal gospels, of which three were known here: Jacob, Nicodemus, and Thomas. In them the personality of Christ stands out in much more realistic outlines than in the canonical gospels. This is particularly true of the *Gospel of Thomas*, which tells of Christ's childhood, and pictures him as a self-willed and at times a cruel boy. The neighbors complain to Joseph, his foster father, about Christ's pranks; falling into a passion with some refractory playmates, he had cursed one and the boy pined away; at his word another fell down dead; those who persecuted Jesus went blind. In school he was distinguished for his intellectual abilities and intelligence; he was endowed with miraculous power: he modeled out of mud birds that came to

15 See A. N. Veselovskii, *Zametki po literature i narodnoy slovesnosti* (Notes on Literature and Folk Literature), *Sbornik otdeleniya russkogo yazyka i slovesnosti akademii nauk* (Collection of the Division of Russian Language and Literature of the Academy of Sciences) (St. Petersburg, 1883), Vol. XXXII, No. 7, pp. 1–8.

life and could fly; with a word he could destroy buildings and raise them up, cure the bite of a viper, raise the dead—for example, the comrade who fell off a roof and was crushed to death.

In conclusion let us make a study of the *Virgin's Visit to Hell,* an apocrypha which was very popular in Rus for several centuries. Like other apocryphas, it reached us through a South Slavic medium, and in content is very closely related to an extant Byzantine text of the monument. The oldest Russian copy of it dates from the twelfth century. The contents of the apocrypha in this earliest Russian copy are as follows:

The Virgin wished to see how human souls are tortured, and requested the archangel Michael to show her the tortures of sinners. And the archangel bade the angels of the south to appear, and hell was opened and the Virgin saw those that were in torment. She saw there a multitude of men and women and heard a great wailing. When the Virgin asked who these people were, the archangel answered: "These are they that did not believe in the Father and the Son and the Holy Ghost, forgot God and put their faith in 'creatures' that God had made for the service of man; they deified sun, moon, earth, and water, beasts and reptiles; they accounted Troyan, Khors, Veles, and Perun to be gods. Therefore they are here and in torment."

Seeing in another place a great darkness, the Virgin bade the angels dispel it that she might see the damned that were there. But the angels in charge of the torture answered that they had been enjoined against letting the sinners see light until the Son of the Virgin should appear, "brighter than seven suns." The Virgin grew sorrowful and herself bade the darkness disappear that she might see this torment. And the darkness lifted and the seven heavens were revealed and the Virgin saw there a multitude of men and women crying and shrieking. "What have ye done, ye wretched and accursed that you should be here?" the Virgin asked them, weeping. But not a voice was raised.

"Why do you not answer?" the angels asked them. And those in torment said:

"O gracious one, for centuries we have not seen the light and we cannot lift our eyes." And looking upon them, the Virgin wept anew; but they said to her: "How is it that you have visited us? Your gracious Son came upon earth and did not ask after us, nor did Abraham the patriarch, nor Moses the prophet, nor John the Baptist, nor the apostle Paul, "beloved of God"—no one asked, yet you, most holy Virgin, intercessor, protector of the Christian race, you are praying to God concerning us."

The tortured, according to Michael, were being punished for not believing in God, not believing even in the Virgin, and not preaching her name or the fact that Christ was born of her. And again the Virgin wept, saying to the sinners: "Why did you fall into temptation? Do you not know that all creation honors my name?" And again darkness enfolded them.

Next, the cherubim and seraphim and four hundred angels took the Virgin to the south where flows the river of fire, and there likewise she saw a multitude of men and women; some were submerged in the river waist-high, others breast-high, a third group to the neck, and a fourth to the top of their heads. And seeing this, the Virgin cried out in a loud voice and asked the archangel for what sin the people here were being tortured. Archangel Michael explained that those submerged in the river to the waist were those who had brought upon themselves the curse of their parents; those submerged breast-high, godparents who had quarreled with each other or committed adultery; those submerged to the neck had eaten human flesh; and, finally, those who were completely submerged had broken an oath sworn upon the cross. And then the Virgin saw a man hanging head down and being consumed by worms. He proved to be a money-lender who had taken interest on gold and silver. The Virgin also saw a woman suspended by the teeth; snakes were proceeding from her mouth and devouring her. She proved to be a gossip who had gone from house to house, eavesdropping on conversations, gossiping about them, and sowing mischief between neighbors. Of her the Virgin said: "It would be well for such a person never to have been born into the world at all."

Wishing to see all the tortures, the Virgin bade Michael take her to the north. There she saw a cloud spread out flat, and in the midst of it flaming beds on which lay a multitude of men and women. These were people who had not got up for matins during Holy Week but had lain lazily abed like corpses. On an iron tree with iron boughs and branches, a multitude of people were hanging suspended by their tongues. To the Virgin, weeping at the sight of the sinners in torment, Michael explained that the ones hanging there were slanderers and babblers who had parted brother from brother and husband from wife. There, too, hung women tied by the feet; flame was proceeding from their mouths and burning them and from the flame came forth serpents and clung to them. The transgressors wailed and prayed for mercy, since they were undergoing the most grievous tortures. The Virgin, again weeping, asked for what sin such torment had been visited upon these women, and learned from Michael that the sufferers were priests' wives who had not respected their husbands but had made second marriages after their death. Next them, nuns who had committed adultery lay in the fire, and serpents devoured them. Into the river of fire that flowed like blood there were thrown fornicators, adulterers, thieves, gossips, slanderers, drunkards, cruel princes, bishops and patriarchs, kings who had not done God's will, avaricious usurers, lawbreakers. There, too, the Virgin wept and said: "Grievous is the lot of sinners; it would be better for them if they had never been born into the world."

After this, all the angel host escorted the Virgin to the west. Here she saw the river of pitch, shrouded in darkness; waves of fire boiled in the river as in a sea, and broke over the sinners that were in it; the insatiable worm gnawed at them and the gnashing of its teeth was heard. This time the very angels in charge of torturing the sinners prayed to the Virgin and to the archangel Michael concerning them; and the sinners themselves prayed for mercy. At the end of the prayer, the storm on the river abated, the waves were still, and the sinners emerged in numbers like unto mustard seed. The Virgin, weeping, asked Michael who was being tortured here, but upon learning that it was the Hebrews, at whose hands her son had suffered, and those who, being Christians by baptism, had fallen away from God and put their trust in demons; likewise those who had committed adultery with godmothers, mothers, and daughters, and also poisoners and murderers, she said: "As their deeds were, so be it." And again the stormy river and the waves of fire covered the sinners, and darkness enshrouded them.

The spectacle of the countless tortures of hell finally moved the Virgin to beseech Michael to permit her to be tortured along with the Christians, since they are called the children of her Son. But Michael's answer was: "Abide in paradise." Then the Virgin requested Michael to assemble the army of the seven heavens and all the angel host that they might pray God for mercy upon the sinners, and bade him take her up to the peak of heaven and set her in the presence of the invisible Father. And at the command of the archangel, cherubim and seraphim appeared and bore her up to heaven and set her before the throne of the invisible Father. With hands uplifted, the Virgin prayed him to have mercy on the sinners, for, upon learning their tortures, she had herself wished to suffer along with the Christians. God refused to pardon the sinners: how could he pardon them, seeing the nails in the hands of his Son? But the Virgin persisted, saying that she was praying not for the Jews but for the Christians, and she went on to mention the fact that all men in all situations turned to her for help. But the Lord was inexorable. Then the Virgin called upon the prophet Moses to help her and upon all the prophets and the apostle Paul and upon "Sunday, the pride of Christianity," and the power of the "holy cross," which had delivered Adam and Eve from the curse. In response to this appeal, the archangel Michael and all the angels, and Moses, and John the Evangelist and the apostle Paul prayed God to have mercy upon the sinners. But this prayer also proved fruitless. Again the Virgin addressed herself to all the heavenly powers, besought them to intercede for the sinners, and reproached them for their indifference to the fate of those in torment. Once more the heavenly powers prayed for pardon for the sinners, and this time God was moved to pity "for the sake of his only-begotten son" and bade Christ descend from the invisible throne to hear the prayer of the saints and show his face to the sinners.

And Christ descended from the throne, and the sinners, seeing him, cried out with one voice for forgiveness. Christ reminded them of the breaking of the commandment given to the first man and woman in paradise, of his own coming down to earth to free mankind from original sin, of the impenitence of sinners and, in conclusion, of his Father's compassion and his Mother's prayers and tears, and then, for the sake of the archangel Michael and the host of His holy martyrs, he accorded them rest by day and by night from Holy Thursday to Pentecost (about two months). And they all replied: "Glory be to thy mercy."

We have in our text one very characteristic insert not found in the Greek text: among the sinners being tortured in hell are included worshippers of the Slavic pagan gods—Troyan, Khors, Veles, Perun. It is possible that this interpolation did not get into the apocrypha on South Slavic but on Russian soil.

How are we to explain the fact that a monument so vividly descriptive of the tortures of hell and, one would suppose, so capable of frightening sinners and bringing home to them some idea of the necessity of righteous living, should have been prosecuted by the Church and relegated to the category of "spurious" and "forbidden" books? First of all, apparently, because in its basic trend it involved a critical revaluation, a revision, as it were, of the traditional tenets concerning divine justice that canonical literature upheld. The lively sympathy for tormented sinners which is always moving the Virgin to tears is here set over against the stern and impassive justice of God. Only after the Virgin's persistent prayers, supported by those of the saints and angels, whom, incidentally, the Virgin upbraids for their indifference to human sufferings, do the sinners obtain temporary respite from their tortures. The whole apocrypha is permeated by a liberal, free-thought attitude toward the established norms and concepts about deity: He is unsparing not only of ordinary sinners, but even of those who, by reason of their hierarchic position, were under the protection of the official Church: bishops, patriarchs, nuns, cruel princes, and kings who did not do the will of God. The *Virgin's Visit to Hell* reflected the opposition attitude of a certain group of believers toward the teaching of the Orthodox

Church and at the same time presented a moral reconsideration of strait-laced and spiritless official Christian doctrine.

Furthermore, quite apart from its thought content and artistic force, this apocrypha must have attracted the reader by its lively realistic coloring, at once decorative and extremely graphic. Not to mention the fact that the sinners are frequently persons guilty of the common sins of everyday life (gossips who wash dirty linen in public, babblers, sluggards who oversleep matins, and so on), even the central figure of the apocrypha—the Virgin—possesses, notwithstanding her epic quality, all the characteristics of a real human personality. She is sketched as a being actively in sympathy with human distress, but at the same time as an ordinary woman and mother, to whom a feeling of indignation in matters touching the fate of her son is natural. Only in passing does she rebuke sinners for disrespect to herself (apparently a reference to the Nestorian heretics who repudiated the worship of the Virgin), but she speaks with anger of those whom she regards as responsible for the sufferings of Christ: "As their deeds were, so be it." Finally, the very picture of the tortures of hell, in all its detail, produces a twofold effect. The terrors of that picture cannot have failed to act on the old-time reader's imagination, while at the same time the apocrypha as a whole, thanks to its central figure, the Virgin, served to awaken that lyric mood which secured for it a wide circulation in manuscript down to the nineteenth century and occasioned its infiltration into oral poetry.[16]

[16] To the history of this apocrypha in Russian written and oral literature, N. K. Boka-dorov devoted a special study entitled, "The Legend of the Virgin's Visit to Hell," *Izbornik Kievsky* (Kiev Miscellany) (Kiev, 1904), pp. 39–94. In Dostoevsky's *Brothers Karamazov*, Ivan Karamazov, in a conversation with Alyosha, gives a résumé of the *Visit* and says: "There is, for example, one little monastic poem (from the Greek, of course), the *Virgin's Visit to Hell*, which has descriptive passages, and an audacity, not inferior to Dante's."

The most important general works on apocryphas are: N. S. Tikhonravov, "Forbidden Books of Ancient Russia," *Works* (Moscow, 1898), Vol. I, pp. 127–255; A. N. Pypin, "Forbidden Books," *History of Russian Literature*, 3rd ed. (St. Petersburg, 1907), Vol. I, Chap. 10; I. Porfiryev, *Apocryphal Legends Concerning Old Testament Persons and Events* (Kazan, 1872–1873); A. Veselovsky, *Slavic Legends of Solomon and Kitovras and the Western Legends About Morolfus and Merlin* (St. Petersburg, 1872), reprinted with additions in his *Collected Works, Izd. otd. russk. yaz. i slov.* (Publications of the Division of Russian Language and Literature of the Academy of Sciences) (Petrograd, 1921), Vol. VIII, Pt. 1; M. I. Sokolov, *Materials and Notes on Old-Time Slavic Literature* (Moscow, 1888); N. Speransky, *Slavic Apocryphal Gospels* (General Survey) (Moscow, 1895); I. Franko, *Apocryphas and Legends from Ukrainian Manuscripts* (Lvov, 1896, 1899), Vols. I–II; *Pamyatki ukrainsko-russkoy movi i literaturi* (Monuments of Ukraino-Russian Ballad and Literature) (Introductory articles to the volumes give a detailed account of the history of the apocrypha in written and oral literature and also a history of the study of apocryphas); P. V. Vladimirov, "The Scientific Study of Apocryphas—Forbidden Books of Russian Literature—in the Second Half of the Nineteenth Century, *Universitetskie izvestiya* (University News) (Kiev, 1900).

HISTORICAL, "NATURAL-HISTORICAL,"
AND PATRISTIC WORKS

Ecclesiastico-historical literature, containing a good deal of story material, was represented in Rus in the earliest times by translations of the Byzantine chronicles, which started from the creation of the world and concerned themselves with all history, though principally with the Hebrew and the Byzantine, and chiefly from the ecclesiastico-religious point of view. It is very indicative that not one secular historical work of the many current in Byzantium was known in Rus. As early as the eleventh century, translations existed here of the chronicle of John Malalas of Antioch (sixth century), Georgius Sincellus (eighth-ninth centuries) and Georgius Hamartolas—"the sinner"—(ninth century). The first, consisting of eighteen books, was translated in Bulgaria in the tenth century, in Tsar Simeon's time, but no trace of it has been preserved in Bulgarian literature. When imported into Rus, it enjoyed no great popularity here either, is not extant in a single complete copy, and can only be partially restored on the basis of later Russian compilations.[17] The reasons for this chronicle's scant popularity in Rus were its inclusion of a large amount of pagan, fantastic-legendary, secular material, reflecting ancient and Oriental mythology, and its relative poverty in items of Church history. The narrative is brought down to the time of Emperor Justinian; that is, to the middle of the sixth century. The *Chronicle of Georgius Sincellus* was also little known here; it was translated (apparently in Rus) from a much abridged Greek version and, furthermore, only carried events down to the Emperor Diocletian; that is, only to the third century.[18]

The chronicle which enjoyed the greatest popularity in Rus was that of Georgius Hamartolas, which came down to 864, and included supplementary material for the following century from the *Chronicle of Simeon Logothetes*, which terminated with 948, the reign of the Byzantine Emperor Román. In this amplified form it too appeared here at the middle of the eleventh century, possibly in Russian translation.[19] The oldest Russian copy dates

[17] This was done by V. M. Istrin: see "Khronika Ioanna Malaly v slavyanskom perevode" (Chronicles of John Malalas in Slavic Translation), Bks. 15–18 and appendices, *Sbornik otd. russk. yaz. i slov.* (Collection of the Division of Russian Language and Literature of the Academy of Sciences, USSR) (St. Petersburg, 1914), Vol. XCI, No. 2, which indicate publications where the preceding books of the *Chronicles* have been printed. See also D. Abramovich, "Fragment of the Chronicle of John Malalas in the Twelfth Century Zlatostrui" (Leningrad, 1928), Vol. CI, No. 3, pp. 19–24.

[18] See V. M. Istrin, *Investigations in the Field of Early Russian Literature* (St. Petersburg, 1906), I–IV, pp. 2–34.

[19] See V. M. Istrin, *Annalistic and Descriptive Books of Georgius the Monk, the Chronicle of Georgius Hamartolas in Early Slavo-Russian Translation*, text, study, and glossary (Academy of Sciences, 1920–1930), Vols. I–III. Istrin also made the assertion that the

from the thirteenth-fourteenth century; later on, it was copied several times more. The chronicle of Hamartolas included a large body of facts relating to Byzantine ecclesiastical life and to monastic history; it gave information about heretical movements, about miraculous "signs," and caught up a good many instructive anecdotal tales. Academician Istrin conjectures that the material of the *Chronicle of Georgius Hamartolas* was also presented in abridged form in the eleventh century on Russian soil in the so-called "chronograph according to the long text," which is not extant in manuscript but which may be reconstructed from surviving monuments. This also includes some rudimentary items from Russian history. On the basis principally of the chronicles of Malalas and Hamartolas, there appeared in Rus in the eleventh-twelfth centuries a first edition and in the thirteenth a second, considerably revised and enlarged, of the so-called "Greek and Roman Chronicler." Later, apparently not before the fifteenth century, the works of the twelfth century chroniclers, John Zonara and Constantine Manassius, became known in this country.

Russian literature, particularly the narrative, utilizes all the above-mentioned chronicles not only for their content but also for their stylistic formulae.

A good deal of historico-literary importance also attaches to such medieval "natural science" encyclopaedias as the *Hexaemeron* and the *Physiologus*.

The *Explanatory Paleya* opens with a hexaemeron; that is, a book expounding the history of the six days of creation on the basis of information drawn by the Middle Ages from Greek and Oriental sources. The hexaemerons were composed in Byzantium and were there immediately subjected to theological elaboration, chiefly in the form of running commentary on the items included. The hexaemeron most popular in Byzantium was that of Basil the Great, and this was the principal source of the *Hexaemeron* of John, Exarch of Bulgaria, already known in Rus during the early period.[20]

Chronicle of Hamartolas was translated directly from Greek into Russian in the time of Yaroslav the Wise. Istrin was answered by Academician P. Lavrov (*Slavia* [1925], No. 3, pp. 461–464, and [1926] No. 4, pp. 657–683), who declared in favor of a South Slavic translation of the *Chronicle*.

N.B. One of the most compendious philological studies of the *Chronicle of Georgius Hamartolas* was the investigation made by N. A. Dobrolyubov, as an undergraduate, at the advice of his teacher, Academician I. I. Sreznevsky, for his bachelor's thesis upon graduation from the Teachers' Institute. This study, entitled "On the Old Slavonic Translation of the Chronicle of Georgius Hamartolas," was written in 1857 but was never published in full until 1934 in Vol. I of Dobrolyubov's *Complete Collected Works*, ed. P. I. Lebedev-Polyansky, pp. 566–591. Dobrolyubov's study was used in part by I. I. Sreznevsky in his note, "Russian Version of the Chronicle of Georgius Hamartolas"; *Svedeniya i zametki o maloizvestnykh i neizvestnykh pamyatnikakh* (Information and Notes on Little Known and Unknown Monuments) (St. Petersburg, 1867), IV, pp. 20–26.

[20] In a Serbian copy of 1263, prepared for the press by O. M. Bodyanskii and published in *Chtenia Obshchestva istorii i drevnostey rossiiskikh* (Papers of the Society of Russian History and Antiquities) (1879), Bk. 3.

The legendary history of the creation given in the hexaemerons largely determined the ancient bookman's outlook upon nature, especially the world of plants and animals, to which it abundantly imparted elements of poetic fantasy. This quality of fantasy was present in still greater degree in a collection known by the name of *Physiologus*,[21] which dealt chiefly with animals, real and imaginary, and their peculiarities, but also had something to say about fantastic stones and trees. Items were accompanied by symbolic interpretations in the spirit of Christian beliefs. The *Physiologus* first appeared in the second or third century of our era. Its birthplace was, most probably, Alexandria, and its material was drawn from the ancient writers represented in monuments of Egyptian and biblical antiquity and in Talmudic legends. Slavic translations of the Greek *Physiologus* are known only in Russian copies, but to judge from the language of the earliest such copy (fifteenth century), they go back to a Bulgarian translation made in any event earlier than the thirteenth century. There are grounds for maintaining that the *Physiologus* was known here during the earliest period, at about the same time that the *Hexaemeron* became known, this, in turn, including a good deal of material from the *Physiologus* in sections dealing with the creation of the animal kingdom. Let us consider a few of the most representative *Physiologus* tales as given in I. N. Tsarsky's copy.

First, the lion is discussed. The lion has three peculiarities. Here is the first: when a lioness gives birth to a cub, she bears it dead and blind and tends it until the third day; then the lion approaches and breathes into its nostrils and it comes to life. "Such is also the case with pagan believers"; until baptism they are dead, but thereafter they are enlightened by "the Holy Ghost." Second peculiarity of the lion: he sleeps with his eyes open; even so did our Lord say to the Jews: "When I sleep, my eyes divine and my heart keep watch." Third peculiarity of the lion: when he flees, he sweeps away his footprints with his tail to conceal himself from the hunter; so too must you, O man, when you give alms, let not your left hand know what your right hand doeth, lest the devil confound you.

Of the eagle: the eagle lives a hundred years, and the end of his beak grows out and his sight is dimmed so that he cannot see and cannot hunt. Then he flies aloft and throws himself on a rock and breaks off the end of his beak. Then he bathes in the golden lake and sits directly facing the sun, and, as he warms, the scale falls from him and he becomes a fledgling again.

---

21 Texts and a study of the *Physiologus* are to be found in A. Karneyev's book, *Materialy i zametki po literaturnoy istorii Phiziologa* (Materials and Notes on the Literary History of the Physiologus), *Izd. obshchestva lyubiteley drevney pismennosti* (Society of Friends of Early Literature) (1890), XCII.

So too must you, O man, when you sin much, go aloft; that is, be filled with faith, and lament over the outgrowth of sin, and wash in your tears, warm yourself in the Church and cast your sins from you.

Of the phoenix: the phoenix is fairer than all other birds, fairer even than the peacock. The peacock may be likened unto gold and silver, and the phoenix unto jacinth and precious stones; it wears a crown on its head and shoes on its feet, like a king; it dwells in India, near the city of the sun. It lies for five hundred years on the cedars of Lebanon without food, but is fed of the Holy Ghost, and for five hundred years it fills its wings with fragrance. Then the priest of the city of the sun rings a bell and the bird comes to the priest and enters the church. The priest and the bird sit on the steps of the altar and the bird turns to ashes. The next morning, when the priest again enters the church, he finds there a young fledgling, but in two days' time the fledgling has become as "complete" a bird as before. And the priest salutes her and departs. How unreasoning then were the Jews not to believe in the resurrection of our Lord Jesus Christ on the third day! If he brings this bird to life, how then can he not raise himself up? Wherefore the prophet David says: "The just man shall flourish like the phoenix, like the cedar of Lebanon shall his seed be multiplied in the house of the Lord."

The other stories in the *Physiologus*, about fifty all told, are of the same sort. The *Physiologus* saga did not receive any particular literary elaboration in Rus. Only three complete copies of the *Physiologus* are extant; it was never transformed into anything like those widely circulated bestiaries of the West, which considerably expanded its scope and greatly reduced its allegorico-symbolical element. It was not until later, in the fifteenth-seventeenth centuries, that the *Physiologus* saga received some developments in our country. That the *Physiologus* should have fared thus on Russian soil is apparently explained on the one hand by the fact that its subject matter was for the most part alien to Russian nature, and on the other, by the fact that the collection's allegorical cast as such proved difficult of comprehension for the ordinary reader. None the less, with respect to its individual elements, its symbols and allegories, it was reflected, either directly or through the medium of the *Explanatory Paleya*, the *Hexaemeron*, and other collections, in a few works of early Russian literature and more particularly in the icon painter's art.

A translated Greek monument, which contained legendary-apocryphal elements in abundance in its explanation of the organization of the universe, is the *Christian Topography* of Cosmas Indicopleustes, extant in copies themselves not earlier than the fifteenth century but representing, to judge by the language, a very early translation.[22] Cosmas Indicopleustes—that is, sailor to India, lived in Alexandria in the sixth century after Christ and, while a merchant, made several journeys to the Orient (though not to India, which he described from other travelers' accounts). Later, having embraced monasticism, he decided to write a work in which he would refute, from the viewpoint of Christian doctrine, the Ptolemaic teaching as to the sphericity of the earth and demonstrate the necessity of trusting exclusively to "Holy Writ" on questions pertaining to the ordering of the universe. In passing, he gives items about certain plants and animals of India and Ceylon. Cosmas Indicopleustes held that the earth is not a sphere but an elevated plane, oblong, four sided, roofed by the vault of heaven, and similar in form to Noah's ark and the Tabernacle of the Covenant. It rests on a firm foundation and is surrounded on all sides by the ocean, at the edge of which rises a wall attached to the sky at the four corners. The sun, moon, and stars set behind a high mountain to the north. The motions of the heavenly bodies are regulated by angels appointed to each of them severally, entrusted with this task on the fourth day of creation, when the heavenly bodies were made, and destined to perform it until the end of the world when the stars shall fall from the sky and the heavenly forces advance. Russian manuscripts of the *Topography* are, like the Greek, provided with a large number of illustrations.

The works of the "Church Fathers" (patristic literature) also enjoyed a wide circulation here from the very beginning of letters, especially the "discourses" of John Chrysostom, Ephrem Syrus, Basil the Great, Gregory the Theologian, John Climacus, John Damascene, Athanasius of Alexandria, Gennadius of Constantinople.[23] Some of them (for example, Ephrem Syrus, author of the *Parenesis* collection) gave evidence of extraordinary poetic endowment. The poetry of Ephrem Syrus is very gloomy, permeated throughout with the ascetic spirit. Works by all these authors found place, to a certain extent, in collections, the best known of which are the two *Svyato-*

---

[22] For the text see *Izd. obshch. lyub. drev. pism.* (Publications of the Society of Friends of Early Literature) (1886), LXXXVI. For a study of Greek and Russian copies of the monument, as well as rich illustrated material, see E. K. Redin, *Khristianskaya topografiya Kosmy Indikoplova po grecheskim i russkim spiskam* (Christian Topography of Cosmas Indicopleustes from Greek and Russian copies), ed. D. V. Ainalov (Moscow, 1916), Pt. 1. See also I. I. Sreznevskii, *Sved. i zamet. o maloizv. i neizv. pam.* (Information and Notes on Little Known and Unknown Monuments) (St. Petersburg, 1867), XI, pp. 1–19.

[23] See A. Arkhangelskii, *K izucheniyu drevnerusskoy literatury: tvoreniya ottsov tserkvi v drevnerusskoy pismennosti* (Toward a Study of Early Russian Literature: Works of the Church Fathers in Russian Literature) (St. Petersburg, 1888); *Tvoreniya ottsov tserkvi v drevnerusskoy pismennosti; Izvlecheniya iz rukopisey i opyty istoriko-literaturnykh izuchenii* (Works of the Church Fathers in Early Russian Literature: Extracts from MSS. and Experiments in Historico-Literary Studies) (Kazan, 1889–1890), I–IV.

slav's Miscellanies—1073[24] and 1076[25]—and the *Zlatostrui*,[26] containing
the discourses of John Chrysostom and extant in a twelfth century copy.
The Miscellany of 1073 is interesting, all else apart, for the included article
by George Kherobosk, "On Images," which treats of tropes and figures of
speech (allegory, metaphor, personification, and so forth).

Short didactic adages and aphorisms culled from "Holy Writ," patristic
literature, and even from ancient secular writers formed a special collection,
the so-called *Bee,* which came out in Rus at the end of the twelfth century,
apparently, and represented the translation of two collections, that of John
Stobaeus (fifth century) and that of Maxim the Confessor (seventh century), as combined by the monk Antonius (eleventh century).[27] The
subject matter of the *Bee* is divided into discourses: "On Virtue and Vice,"
"On Wisdom," "On Chastity and Celibacy," "On Courage and Fortitude,"
and so forth. The adages are presented in the order of their authoritative-
ness, from the Gospels, the Apostles, the Old Testament (Solomon, Sirach,
and so on), from the "Church Fathers," from the works of ancient writers
and philosophers (Plutarch, Diogenes, Socrates, Pythagoras, Menander,
Aristotle, Epicurus, and so on). Sometimes, too, little stories and fables are
interspersed, for example: "The wolf, seeing the shepherd secretly eating
another's sheep in his hut, said: 'Why did you raise such a hue and cry
when I did it?'"

Early Russian authors made generous use in their works of material from
the *Bee,* citing aphorisms and adages found there, and referring them to
sources to which they had not in fact had access. Later on, the *Bee* was upon
a number of occasions augmented by adages and proverbs borrowed from
works of early Russian literature (for example, from the *Supplication of
Daniel the Exile*—see below) and also by oral proverbs, while certain of its
own adages passed over into proverbs.

[24] Pub. Obshch. lyub. etc. (Society of Friends of Early Literature) (1880).
[25] Published by V. Shinanovski (Warsaw, 1887). The most recent study is N. P. Popov's,
"L'izbornik de 1076, dit de Svjatoslav, comme monument littéraire," *Revue des études slaves*
(1934), Vol. XIV, Nos. 1–2, pp. 5–25. N. P. Popov holds that *Svyatoslav's Selection,* 1076,
originated in Rus.
[26] See V. Malinin, *Issledovanie Zlatostruya po rukopisi* (Study of the Zlatostrui from a
Twelfth Century MS. (Kiev, 1878), in the Imperial Public Library.
[27] See V. Semenov. *Drevnyaya russkaya Pchela po pergamennomu spisku* (Early Russian
Bee from Parchment Copy) (St. Petersburg, 1893); M. N. Speranskii, *Perevodnye sborniki
izrechenii v slavyano-russkoy pismennosti* (Translated Collections of Aphorisms in Slavo-
Russian Literature) (Moscow, 1904).

THE SECULAR NARRATIVE

Like most other works of translated literature, narratives in the earliest period came to us from Byzantium direct and were translated, at the middle of the eleventh century, in the time of Yaroslav the Wise, immediately into Russian; or they came by way of Bulgaria and, later, of Serbia. The generally ecclesiastical character of early Russian letters on the one hand and the cultural level of the old-time Russian reader on the other are shown in the selection of narrative material made on Russian soil. The material selected was chiefly moralistic, didactic, and informed to a greater or less degree with religious tendency even in cases where the subject under discussion was the life of a secular hero, his warlike exploits and adventures. Due to this fact, the translated narrative as it existed in Rus in antiquity was not so very different in general trend from the literature of Christian instruction, lives of the saints in particular. It is very indicative that not a single purely secular, let alone amorous, Byzantine romance (for example, Heliodorus, Achilles Tatius, Longus) was known in Old Rus.

The number of translated narratives that circulated here in antiquity is relatively small: the Church, which largely controlled written literature, was not interested in the popularization of material which did not immediately answer its problems, while the monastery libraries, acting as custodians of the manuscript tradition, naturally did not bother much about preserving and restoring monuments not directly in line with the general tendency of ecclesiastico-instructional literature.

More marked than in the case of any other translated genre was the evolution undergone by ancient narrative during its several centuries of existence as a part of Russian literature, an evolution exemplified in the modification and adaptation of subject matter, ideological content, and style to meet the demands of the milieu and the epoch being served.

A translated narrative of Kievan Rus which borders on the historical chronicle was the celebrated work of the Jewish writer and statesman Josephus Flavius, *History of the Judaic War*, known here under the title, *Narrative of the Destruction* (or *Capture*) *of Jerusalem*.[28] It deals with the conquest of Judea by the Romans. The narrative consists of seven books, giv-

[28] An edition of the Old Russian text of the *Judaic War* was brought out by the Institute of Slavic Studies in Paris; see *La prise de Jerusalem de Joseph le Juif*, "texte vieux-russe publié intégralement par V. Istrin" (Paris, 1934, 1938), Vols. I–II. For a description of the sixteenth century MSS. from the Volokolam Monastery containing the texts of the *Judaic War*, see I. I. Sreznevskii, *Svedeniya i zametki o maloizvestnykh i neizvestnykh pamyatnikakh* (Information and Notes on Little Known and Unknown Monuments) (St. Petersburg, 1879), LXXXV, pp. 140–144.

ing an account of events from the taking of Jerusalem by the Syrian Emperor Antiochus Epiphanes in 167 B.C. to the complete devastation of Judea in A.D. 72. Consequently Josephus' work embraces an epoch of almost two and a half centuries, beginning where the Bible leaves off, and thus offers almost a single source for the history of the Jewish people over a long period. For the Christian reader and, as such, for the Russian reader, it had paramount significance as material throwing light upon that period of Jewish history which immediately preceded the inception and consolidation of Christianity. Josephus states in his introduction to the *Judaic War* that he originally wrote it in his "native tongue," that is, in Aramaic, and afterward, in order to make it accessible to Roman citizens, translated it into Greek. This translation Josephus made in collaboration with Greeks of good literary training.

As literature, the *Judaic War* is an outstanding work. Josephus inherited his art of narrative from the best Greek and Roman historians. His exposition is distinguished by great elegance and verve; the speeches he puts into the mouths of his characters, his own speeches among them (Josephus here speaks of himself in the third person), are imbued with lofty sentiment and written with great oratorical skill.

The most moving events of the war are described with a genuine dramatic quality and very vividly. This is especially true of the pages that deal with the war in Galilee and with the siege and destruction of Jerusalem. The introduction of dreams and portents into the narrative does much to enhance this dramatic quality.

At the third book, where Josephus makes his transition to contemporary facts and persons, and in which he speaks of having seen this thing himself or heard about that from an eyewitness, he launches out into very detailed descriptions of places taken in battle and of all the chances and changes of war, giving minute descriptions of military episodes, implements of war, methods of attack and defense, and so forth.

The data derived from a linguistic analysis of the earliest extant Russian copy of the *Judaic War* bear indubitable witness to its having been translated directly from Greek into Russian. The Russian text of our monument, aside from separate copies of a later date, exists in a chronographic compilation known as the *Jewish*, or *Archival*, *Chronograph*. The extant copy of this chronograph dates from the fifteenth century, but goes back to a copy of 1262. Inasmuch as unmistakable traces of the influence of the style of the *Judaic War* are already observable in the *Tale of Igor's Expedition*, however, it follows that a translation of it existed by about the last quarter of the twelfth century. But there is reason to suppose that the *Judaic War* may even have been translated here under Yaroslav the Wise; that is, about the middle of the eleventh century, when a number of works were translated in Rus from the Greek, among them the *Chronicle of Georgius Hamartolas*.

A comparison of the Russian text of the *Judaic War* with the extant Greek text convinces us, however, that we are here dealing not so much with a translation in the literal sense of the word as with a free paraphrase of the foreign original into a language resembling that of Russian eleventh and twelfth century monuments, and most resembling that of the *Primary Chronicle*. In most cases the Greek original was appreciably abbreviated, but at some points the Russian translation amplifies the Greek text. Sometimes the indirect discourse of the original is replaced by direct discourse, and vice versa. Abbreviations most often consist not in the omission of sections of the Greek original but in a compressed paraphrase of them. As to additions found in the Russian text, the most substantial are those which contain references to John the Baptist and to Christ. Apart from these additions to the Russian text, there are two sharp thrusts at the Romans not found in the Greek text and also a caustic characterization of Herod the Great, likewise lacking in the corresponding passage of the Greek text, but implicit in a general way in the Greek original, though differently expressed.

In the first place the question naturally arises as to who was the author of all the indicated additions in the Russian text for which no counterparts exist in the Greek, and especially of the rather numerous references to John the Baptist and Christ.

In 1906 the German scholar Berendts, who had made a study of Russian copies of the *Judaic War*, hit upon the idea that the author of all the additions preserved in Russian copies was Josephus Flavius himself.[29] According to Berendts' hypothesis, Josephus translated his work from Aramaic into Greek and afterwards revised his Greek translation, omitting all passages which might displease the Jews; that is, first and foremost, the references to John the Baptist and Christ. The Christians did not preserve the original edition, presumably because these references were too scanty in comparison with the corresponding testimony of the Gospels, and because they revealed a certain scepticism. But how this vanished Greek edition got into the hands of the Russian translator, Berendts declines to explain. In 1922 Berendts' hypothesis gained an adherent in Academician Istrin,[30] who likewise hypothesized the existence of two Greek versions of the *Judaic War* from the pen of Josephus Flavius himself. Istrin thinks that, in going over his Greek

[29] A. Berendts, *Die Zeugnisse vom Christentum im Slavischen, De Bello Judaico des Josephus* (Leipzig, 1906).

[30] See his article, " 'Indeyskaya voina' Iosefa Flaviya v drevnerusskom perevode" (Judaic War of Josephus Flavius in Early Russian Translation), *Uchenye zapiski vysshey shkoly g. Odessy* (Scholarly Notes of the College of Odessa) (1922), Vol. II, pp. 27–40.

text for a second time, during the period when he was on intimate terms with the Emperor Titus and enjoyed a position of respect in Rome, Josephus on the one hand toned down those passages in his work which contained sallies at the Romans and, on the other, removed anything that might evoke the displeasure of the Jews. Touching Berendts' quandary as to how the Russian translator got hold of the discarded Greek version of the *Judaic War*, Istrin mentions the generally known fact that in old Slavo-Russian literature we frequently have to do with translations of Byzantine works in redactions which have not been preserved in the original.

However, the conjecture of Berendts and Istrin as to a secondary revision by Josephus of his Greek translation of the *Judaic War* from the motives they indicated, gives rise to definite objections. Along with everything else, it is very doubtful whether Josephus, as a member of the Pharisee sect, could have spoken with such sympathy of John the Baptist and Christ as is shown in the supposed first edition of the Greek translation of the *Judaic War*, which served, in the opinion of Berendts and Istrin, as the original of the Russian translation, and it is quite improbable that a Pharisee, or any Jew, could interpret the calamity of his people as retribution for the shedding of Christ's blood.

Nor are the Russian additions involving the sharp thrusts at the Romans and the caustic characterization of Herod, however problematical their origin, sufficient to justify Berendts and Istrin in postulating the existence of two author's revisions of the Greek translation of the *Judaic War*, from the second of which, made during the period of his intimacy with Titus, Josephus omitted the sharp thrusts at the Romans.

To begin with, Josephus was already intimate with Titus at the time of the siege and capture of Jerusalem; that is, before he set to work on his book at all. Furthermore, we encounter censorious references to the Romans here and there in the Greek text too, just as we find positive and even flattering opinions of them in the Russian text.

One last question remains to be settled: the source of those abridgments and paraphrases of the Greek text which we find in the Russian translation. There are three possible explanations for both. First, they may already have been in the Greek original from which the Russian translation was made; secondly, they may have been made on Russian soil, as Istrin admits, by some learned Greek who helped the Russian translator by compressing the original and simplifying its syntax; finally, it is possible to explain all the peculiarities of the Russian translation as originating with the translator. This last supposition, it seems to me, is the most probable in view of the presence in the translation of stylistic peculiarities which cannot be explained by the Greek context and are comprehensible only if we admit a

considerable amount of creative initiative on the part of the Russian translator.

There is no possibility of defining with exactitude the degree of this
initiative since we have no way of knowing exactly the peculiarities of the
Greek text that the Russian translator had at his disposal. There can be no
doubt, however, that the initiative of the translator is primarily revealed
where there occurs an intrusion of ideas, terminology, and phraseology
characteristic of thought processes and manner of living in prince-and-
retainer Rus and finding a counterpart in original Russian works contemporary with the translation, notably the chronicles. Such are the concepts of
honor and glory replacing different concepts found in the Greek text: exultation, lavish entertainment, reward. The Greek terms associated with martial life and the paraphernalia of war acquire in translation a specifically
Russian sound (quivers, spears, battering rams, banners, breastplates, ramparts, inner fortress, and so forth). The same is true of expressions typical of
Russian daily life in prince-and-retainer times: "father's throne," "council,"
"councilor," "and sitting on his golden throne," "and said things worthy of
his ancestral throne," "Ananus took counsel with his men," and so forth.

The translator's style asserts itself also in his rendering of the operations
and the mental states associated with the practice of war: "The Romans,
moreover, were likewise sweating," "the Romans with great sweat and toil
set the affairs up," "and they were filled with warlike spirit," "the troops were
full of fighting spirit," "whet your soul for revenge," "give heed to your
defense and stand firm, having gained it," and so forth. Most of these
expressions have parallels in our old chronicle texts.

The stylistic originality of the Russian translation is particularly evident
in the battle scenes. The terror and the grandiose proportions of the conflict
are usually pointed up by the din and crash of weapons breaking, the rain
of arrows darkening the sky, the streams of blood flooding large areas, the
enormous number of corpses, on which it is possible to walk as up a staircase or over a bridge: "And you could see the breaking of spears, and the
clashing of swords, and shields being cleft, and men being borne, and the
earth given blood to drink . . . and spears rustled as they were hurled from
saddle bows and arrows darkened the sun." Then: "The watercourses of
the city ran blood. . . . Blood flowed like a river and the bloody current
swept corpses along with it . . . and the Jordan was bridged with corpses
and the whole river was so filled with the drowned that they walked across
them as across a bridge." The flight of arrows is compared to rain: "And
the arrows pelted them like rain." In the heat of battle, the combatants,
having broken their swords, go on fighting hand to hand: "And there was
terrible slaughter about the machines that one side was striving to set on

fire while the other strove to prevent them, and a confused outcry went up from both sides, and sparks flew from their swords and they seized one another by the arm and hacked, and many of those in the forefront fell. . . . Then, having broken their swords also, they started to fight hand to hand, and any weapon found was his who found it." In the fury of battle, it sometimes became impossible to distinguish friend from foe: "And then, casting aside darts and spears, they drew swords and clashed, and in this clash no man could distinguish or judge against whom he was fighting, and with the men mixed and massed in the street, and the noise falling indistinct on the ear for its loudness, blood flowed on both sides like a river." The dust rising from the battle was also a hindrance: "And the battle being joined, the dust would not let them see with their eyes nor the noise let them hear with their ears, nor was it possible to recognize friend or foe . . . and for the thickness of the dust one did not recognize another and they wheeled like blind men and slashed at each other." The destructiveness and cruelty of war are thus described: "And there was slaughter of an uncounted number in the city and temple and palace, no pity being shown for young or old or for helpless women . . . and they had not the shame to spare either young or old, and there were killed on that day fifty thousand."

The majority of these and similar stylistic formulae have no counterparts in the extant Greek text of the *Judaic War,* but we encounter very close parallels in original Russian monuments contemporary or nearly so, with the Russian translation of Josephus, notably the chronicle and in the *Tale of Igor's Expedition.* Presumably, in these cases, the Russian translator, while to some extent utilizing the imagery of his original, none the less availed himself for the most part of the supply of poetic images already existing in Russian literature at the time he made his translation. There is, of course, also the possibility that he may have created them himself. Thus, in the Barsov copy we find this lovely image: "They go to death head on." The corresponding reading in the Greek text is: "They scorned death," and in the Volokolam copy: "They recked not of death."

Typical of the style of the translation are the similes which quite frequently figure in the Russian text: "This word struck both youths like a tempest," "the towns were close together and the villages thick as stars," "they howled like wolves," "and butted them like wild beasts," "like a beast angered at its own flesh and turning its teeth upon it, so they turned their hand against their kinsfolk," "they toppled down from their place four rocks as great as mountains," "youths who raced for the wood like wild animals," "some hankering for wealth as ravens for a corpse," and so forth. The majority of these similes have no counterpart in the Greek text.

Occasionally a rhythmic pattern is encountered in the Russian translation:

Consider too that they will be unarmed,
and we well armed;
they on foot,
and we on horseback;
they ungeneraled,
and we with generals.

So their ranks are firmly held,
and moreover quick at maneuver;
their ears are pricked for commands,
and their eyes on the standards fixed,
their hands for slaughter ready.
Thus they quickly can strike
wherever they like,
and wounds give
instead of receive.

When bowmen set arrows winging
and spearmen spears were flinging
and catapults stones were slinging,
the Jews no longer dared to stand on the ramparts.
The watercourse, being dry, prevented their skirting the bank,
and by sea no refuge existed,
and the rivers were raging torrents.

He who wreaks widespread destruction
unleashes widespread transgression.

The style of the *Judaic War,* and its individual poetic images, particularly those relating to war themes, influenced Russian narrative literature of the martial type down to the seventeenth century. In the Kiev period, Josephus' influence was particularly manifest in the *Tale of Igor's Expedition,* while the chronicle narrative showed it to some extent.[31]

One very popular narrative, in the East as well as in the West, was the story of Alexander of Macedon, the so-called *Alexandria,* a fabulous biography of the noted hero of antiquity (died 323 B.C.). This told of his extraordinary birth, of his exploits, his prowess in war, the lands he conquered, teeming with all manner of marvels, and of his early death, and sketched Alexander as a hero endowed with great intelligence, wisdom, a thirst for knowledge, and uncommon physical and psychical qualities. Legends about him which had apparently sprung up shortly after his death took form in the second-third centuries after Christ, probably in Alexandria, in a literary work attributed to Callisthenes, nephew of Aristotle, but clearly not from his pen since Callisthenes predeceased Alexander. In about the fifth century,

[31] See E. Barsov, *Slovo o polku Igoreve* (Tale of Igor's Expedition) (Moscow, 1887), Vol. I, pp. 213–273; V. N. Peretts, *K izucheniyu Slovo o polku Igoreve* (Toward a Study of the Tale of Igor's Expedition) (Leningrad, 1926), pp. 75–87.

the pseudo-Callisthenes *Alexandria,* in Hellenized form, began to circulate in Byzantium, having appeared in western Europe even earlier in the Latin version of Julius Valerius. On the basis of the latter, and of the Greek *Alexandria,* a new Latin version of the narrative was prepared in the tenth century by the Neapolitan Archpresbyter Leo, and from this were derived the numerous medieval European adaptations of the tale. The pseudo-Callisthenes *Alexandria* afterward penetrated to the Moslem east and the Slavic south.

It is difficult to determine exactly when the *Alexandria* appeared on Russian soil. There is reason to believe, however, that it already existed in Rus in the eleventh and twelfth centuries, and, very probably, the translation was itself made in Rus and went back to the second Greek edition of the pseudo-Callisthenes, none of the known copies of which can, however, be considered the original of the Russian translation. In translation it already carried the interpolation from Georgius Hamartolas, "On the Entry of Alexander into Jerusalem." With this interpolation it was included in the *Chronicle of John Malalas,* which we know as a component part of the *Greek and Roman Chronicle,* in two editions, and as part of the so-called *Jewish Chronograph.*[32]

The content of the oldest first Russian edition of the *Alexandria* is as follows.

Many have erroneously asserted that Alexander was the son of King Philip, but this is not so: he was the son of Nektanebus and Philip's wife Olympiada. Nektanebus, King of Egypt, possessed magic power with the aid of which he had been victorious over all his enemies. But when the Persians made war on him, he knew by divination that this time he could not vanquish the enemy and fled from Egypt to Macedonia; however, the god Serapis told the Egyptians that Nektanebus would return with his youth renewed and vanquish the Persians. The promise of Serapis was inscribed by the Egyptians on the statue of Nektanebus. At the time of Nektanebus' arrival in the capital of Macedonia, Philip was away. His beautiful wife Olympiada, who was childless and feared that Philip had left her to marry someone else, as he had threatened, turned for help to Nektanebus, who was celebrated for his magic powers even in Macedonia. Nektanebus promised her that she would bear a son if she had union with the Libyan god Ammon, whom she was to see that same night in a dream. Ammon did in fact appear to Olympiada in a dream and afterward she asked Nektanebus to have the god visit her in person. However, that night, in the form of

[32] See V. Istrin, *Aleksandriya russkikh khronografov* (the *Alexandria* of the Russian Chronographs) (Moscow, 1893), study and text. In the appendix, texts of four editions of the chronograph *Alexandria* are given.

Ammon, Nektanebus himself appeared to Olympiada, and she conceived by him. Philip, learning through a dream sent him by Nektanebus that his wife had had intercourse with Ammon and had conceived by him, reconciled himself to it as to the inevitable.

The appearance of Alexander at birth was unusual; his aspect was human, but he had a mane like a lion and sharp teeth like a serpent; one of his eyes looked down, the other sidewise. Teachers were appointed to instruct him in various arts and sciences, including music, geometry, and astronomy; philosophy was taught him by Aristotle. From childhood he showed strength and daring; in his twelfth year he accompanied his father on a campaign. Once, when he had gone outside the city with Nektanebus to observe the starry sky, Alexander brought Nektanebus to a pit and cast him into it. When the bruised and broken Nektanebus asked him why he had done this, Alexander replied: "You are making a fool of yourself, teacher: not knowing what is happening on earth, you study what is going on in the sky." With his dying breath, Nektanebus revealed to Alexander the secret of his birth. The son felt sorry for his father, threw the dead Nektanebus over his shoulders, unwilling that the beasts should rend his body, and took him to Olympiada, telling her all that he had heard from Nektanebus. She then realized that she had been "seduced by him through magic wiles," but buried him affectionately as the father of Alexander.

When he was fourteen, Alexander tamed an ox-headed horse that had been devouring the people, and thereby made Philip very happy, for the Delphic oracle had prophesied to him that whoever mastered the ox-headed horse would be ruler of the world. Shortly afterward, in the chariot races at Nyssa, he defeated King Nicholas of Acarnania, who had been plotting against him, and was crowned with the victor's wreath. And a proverb was made about the dead Nicholas: "He who plans to trick another shall himself be tricked." After his return to Macedonia, Alexander brought about a reconciliation between his mother and Philip, who, thinking to marry another woman, had left her. Presently Philip died of a wound dealt him by Pausanias, ruler of Thessalonica, and Alexander ascended the throne.

Next we are told about Alexander's numerous campaigns, particularly against the Persian king Darius, and about his founding of cities. Upon arriving in Egypt, he saw in the city of Memphis the statue of Nektanebus with the inscription announcing that Nektanebus would return to Egypt young again. Alexander explained that the rejuvenated king was himself, and proposed to the Egyptians that they should pay him the tribute that they had previously paid the Persians—he needed it to build the new city of Alexandria. The Egyptians willingly accepted Alexander's proposal. Then comes the interpolation from the *Chronicle of Georgius Hamartolas*, "On the Entry of Alexander into Jerusalem," portraying Alexander as a worshiper of the one invisible God. Having captured Tyre in Sidon, Alexander asks the Jews for help against the Persians. The Jews refuse to help him and Alexander advances against them. Accompanied by the clergy, the high priest Addus comes out to meet him, dressed in ceremonial robes on which the name of God is inscribed. At sight of this marvelous spectacle, Alexander leaps from his chariot, bows to the name of God, and embraces the high priest. In reply to the remonstrances of certain captains in his army, Alexander says: "I bowed not to the high priest but to his god, whose help he has given me against the enemy." It seems that Alexander had seen a vision in which, through the high priest, God had promised him victory over the Persians. Then, after offering a sacrifice to God in the temple at Jerusalem and honoring the high priest and the clergy with gifts, Alexander and the Jews advanced against the Persians.

On the way he meets emissaries of Darius, who hand him a letter, a whip, a ball, and a casket of gold. The letter said:

I, Darius, king of kings and kin of gods and myself a god, shining like the sun, do command you, Alexander, my slave, to return to your parents, to the lap of your mother Olympiada, since it is meet that you should still be in school and drawing your nourishment from the maternal breast, and therefore I am sending you a ball, a whip, and a casket of gold. Chose which you will. The ball means that you should still be playing with boys your own age, the whip that you ought to go back to school, and I send you a casket of gold whereby you may feed brigands like yourself when they return to their native land. But if you do not submit to me, I shall order my soldiers to seize and crucify you.

When his soldiers showed alarm, Alexander calmed them by comparing Darius to dogs that, "being large but not strong, bark much that thereby they may appear to be strong." After first deciding to crucify the messengers, Alexander in the end pardons them: "It is not my intention to destroy you," he says, "but to show you what a Greek king is like. . . . A king does not slay a messenger," and then he seats them at his own table. Alexander rejects the advice of the emissaries that he seize Darius by craft.

Following an exchange of mutually accusatory letters, a bloody battle takes place between Alexander and Darius:

The soldiers fell, one on another, in great numbers and nothing was to be seen but horses lying dead on the ground and slain men. There was no way to recognize Persian or Macedonian, or noble or foot soldier or cavalryman, for the great dust; neither was heaven visible, nor earth, for the much blood. And, moreover, the sun itself, taking pity on those that were no more and unable to look upon such disaster, clouded over.

The Persians, and Darius after them, turned and fled; his mother, wife, and children, being with the Persian Army, were taken captive by Alexander.

The latter received them with honor, commanded that the slain Persians be buried, and spoke words of comfort to the captives.

The vanquished Darius was in the meantime gathering his forces to attack Alexander again. Alexander advanced to meet him. Coming to the river Scamander, where Achilles had once paused to rest, Alexander himself felt inclined to repose there. Recalling the heroes of the Trojan War whom Homer had celebrated in song, he observed ironically that the present-day Trojans were unworthy of their ancestors. In response a poet there present said: "King Alexander, we shall outdo Homer in writing of your deeds."

Upon reaching the land of Persia, Alexander began debating which of his generals to send to Darius with the declaration that he was ready for battle. But in a dream the god Ammon bade him, instead of depending on a messenger who might betray him, to assume the form of Ammon and go to Darius himself. Alexander did so: he betook himself to Darius in the guise of an emissary, urging him to join battle at once, but, when recognized by one of the Persians, rose precipitately, slipped away from his pursuers and, "like a star shining down from the sky, walked alone and ran and the Persians had no idea what had become of him." After encouraging his army by the assurance that "any one of you can vanquish a thousand of the enemy barehanded," Alexander on his ox-headed horse advanced to the dread and ominous battle. "On both sides the war cry went up; some hurled stones, and great—like as clouds gathering in the sky until they obscure the light of day—was the commingling of attackers and attacked, and many were wounded by arrows and died, while others lay scarce alive. The sky was murky and bloody." Darius fled from the field of battle, and as he fled "many Persians were mowed down as if they had been sheaves in the field."

After this, Darius again made ready to do battle with Alexander, but in the midst of these preparations two satraps, desiring to win favor with Alexander, mortally wounded their king. Coming upon his dying enemy, Alexander took pity on him, wept over him, covered the body with his own cloak, laid the hands upon the breast and said: "Rise, King Darius, and rule in your land and be sovereign over your people; take your crown, be king over the Persian multitude and maintain your majesty." Bidding Alexander farewell and advising him not to be deluded by good fortune as he himself had once been deluded, Darius requested that Alexander perform his burial rites in person and that Macedonians and Persians walk behind his coffin; he entrusted his mother and his wife to Alexander's care and gave him his daughter Roxana to wife. After mourning for Darius and burying him with honor, Alexander ascended the Persian throne; he left the citizens their liberties but executed the murderers of Darius. By letter he informed the mother and the wife of Darius, and Roxana, of the death of Darius, and in a letter to Olympiada and Aristotle described the marvels that he had come across in the course of his campaigns: giants living in the forest, with long necks and arms; giants inhabiting the steppes, round, shaggy, red, with the faces of lions; anthropophagi coming out of the swamps and barking like dogs; men who were headless but capable of speech; many-eyed beasts roaming a land on which the sun did not shine but which was lighted by a sunless, moonless, starless glow, and where flew birds with human faces, speaking Greek.

Alexander's final exploit was his campaign against the Indian king Por, whom he vanquished in single combat, piercing him with a spear at the instant when some commotion among his troops made him turn his head. After burying Por, Alexander set out to visit the "naked wise men," the Rakhmans (Brahmans), who lived in tents and caves. The Rakhmans, hearing of Alexander's approach, sent a very old sage to him with a letter in which they said that if Alexander were coming to fight them, he would have no success since he would get nothing from them; but if he wanted to get what they had, there was no need to make war on them since a prayer would suffice, a prayer addressed, however, not to them, but to "supreme providence." Alexander came in peace to the land of the Rakhmans, which teemed with all manner of fruits, and carried on with its inhabitants—"lovers of wisdom"—a philosophical conversation, during which the Rakhmans treated him not as a king but as an equal. In reply to Alexander's offer: "Ask of me what you will and I will give it you," they all shouted: "Give us immortality!" Alexander answered that this he was unable to do, being himself mortal. "Then why do you, being mortal," the Rakhmans said to him, "fight so hard to get everything for yourself? Where will you put it all? Won't other people get it in the end?" In answer to this, Alexander explained that everyone's lot is apportioned him and that man is powerless to order his own fate. He would be glad to renounce warfare, but his nature drove him to it. If everyone had the same nature, the world would come to a standstill: no one would sail the sea or till the soil; no children would be born. In parting from the Rakhmans, Alexander presented their "prior" Dandamius with gold, bread, wine, and oil, asking that he accept it as a remembrance. Dandamius smiled and said that they had no use for any of it, but, in order not to appear proud, took the oil and poured it on the fire in Alexander's presence.

Next, Alexander went to India, to the "town of Prasiach." In it were two trees which had the gift of human speech. From them Alexander learned that he and his mother and his wife would perish in Babylon at the hand of Hindus. From India, Alexander set out for Persia and went to the palace of Semiramis to visit Queen Candacia, into whose presence he penetrated under an assumed name. But Candacia recognized him from a portrait which had been secretly painted by an artist of hers, and brought a blush to his cheek by saying that he was now "at the mercy of one woman." From Candacia, Alexander went to the country of the Amazons, took tribute from them and then started for the Black Sea, where he saw dog-headed men with eyes and mouth on their chests, and others with six arms. Thence he went to the "City of the Sun" on a certain large island, and after that to the "Sanctuary of Lusa" where, on a very high mountain, stood rich temples adorned with gold and silver. In one of these temples, Alexander saw a bird like a dove, which, with a human voice, and in Greek, bade him cease setting his face against God, go back where he belonged, and not presume to climb the road to heaven.

Upon his arrival in Babylon, Alexander received the sign indicating that he was to die. Shortly afterward one of his enemies sent into Babylon a strong poison destined for Alexander. This poison was administered at a banquet in the house of a Mede. Aware of the approach of death, Alexander left the banquet. On the following day he gave orders that his deathbed be set up in a high place and that his whole army file past him. And there was not one who did not weep when he looked upon Alexander dying. He decreed that if Roxana bore a son he should be made king of Macedonia; if a daughter, then let the Macedonians choose whom they would for their king. Afterward the air was filled with mist, in the sky appeared a new star moving toward the sea, and beside the star an eagle, and the idol of Babylon was shaken. When the star again ascended the sky, Alexander died. His body was buried at Alexandria in a shrine called "Alexander's Body." Alexander lived thirty-two years, having begun his reign at the age of twenty. He conquered twenty-two barbarian peoples and fourteen Greek peoples and founded twelve cities which he named Alexandria, after himself.

In the thirteenth century a second edition of the *Greek and Roman Chronicle* appeared, containing a second edition of the pseudo-Callisthenes *Alexandria,* which represented a considerable working over of the early text on the part of the Russian editor. This revision is chiefly a matter of numerous interpolations into the old text of the monument, borrowings by the editor from the chronicles of Georgius Hamartolas and Malalas, from the apocryphal *Revelation* of Methodius of Patara, the *Visit of the Three Monks to Macarius, Zosima's Visit to the Rakhmans,* from the *Legend of the Kingdom of India,* from the *Bee,* the *Physiologus,* and so on. Additions were particularly numerous in parts dealing with the wonders seen by Alexander in the course of his campaigns. The second edition is also distinguished from the first by its greater amount of moralizing. Its prevalent mood is one of submissiveness to fate and a sense of the limitations of human power, present in Darius and Alexander alike. This gives a pessimistic tinge to the reflections of both of them, emphasized by appropriate editorial explanations. In the new edition the style, too, has been somewhat altered in the direction of greater rhetorical flourish. Here similes are more frequently encountered, as, for example, the comparison of Alexander's impetuosity to the spring of the panther, the lion, and the leopard, or of battles to harvesting. ("They were cut down, and dropped like sheaves in the field.")

During the fifteenth century, in connection with the increased South Slavic influence at that time, a new edition of the *Alexandria* reached Rus from Serbia, the so-called "Serbian" edition, which was the translation of a special Greek edition, showing Romance influence in language as well as in subject matter.[33] It was distinguished from the pseudo-Callisthenes redaction by a greater interest, enlivening dialogue, and lyric embellishment. In it Alexander stands out as a Christianized hero, on friendly terms with the prophet Jeremiah, and professing monotheism. Arriving in Jerusalem and learning that the Jews acknowledge a single God, he exclaims: "Verily I too believe in him and profess him . . . and your God shall be my God, and may His peace be with me," and he did not take tribute from the Jews. Next, Jeremiah appears on the scene as the faithful guide and mentor of Alexander. The Jewish prophet predicts that he will die in his fortieth year and reminds Alexander of this prophecy when he is about to leave for Babylon.

Alexander's wife Roxana and the romantic relations of the pair are much more vividly described in the Serbian *Alexandria* than in the pseudo-Callisthenes. In the new edition of the narrative, Roxana's lament over the body of Alexander is very artistically rendered: "Moreover, Roxana, the queen, rent her royal purple robe to the ground and let down the hair of her head, and with grief and lamentation spoke to Alexander from her aching heart as if he had been alive: 'O Alexander, king of the whole world and my valiant lord, wisest among men, will you not look upon me whom you have left alone in a foreign land, while you yourself, like the sun, have gone down with the sun beneath the earth? O sky, sun, moon, and all you stars, sob me a woeful lament! O earth and ye foundations of eternal strength, mountains and hills, lament with me this day and tap your founts of tears until the lakes are filled and the mountains are drunk with their torrents, for the bitterest of all sorrows has befallen me this day!'" Then she stabbed herself upon

---

[33] The text of the Serbian *Alexandria*, from a seventeenth century copy, was printed in *Pubs. obshchestva lyubiteley drevney pismennosti* (Society of Friends of Early Literature) (1880–1887), LXVI and LXXXVII. See A. N. Veselovskii, "K voprosu ob istochnikakh serbskoy Alexandrii" (On the Question of the Sources of the Serbian Alexandria), *Zhurnal min. nar. prosy* (Journal of the Ministry of Public Instruction) (1884), Nos. 4, 9; (1885), No. 10; *K istorii romana i povesti* (On the History of Romance and Tale) (St. Petersburg, 1886), Pt. 1; V. Istrin, "History of the Serbian Alexandria," *Letopis istoriko-filologicheskovo obshchestva pri novorossiiskom universitete* (Chronicle of the Historico-Philological Society at the University of Novorossiisk) (1910), Pt. 16.

Alexander's body, and was buried with him in a golden shrine which is standing, even "to this day," on a pedestal in Alexandria.

The Serbian version, which from the fifteenth to the seventeenth century circulated in a hundred separate copies, quickly supplanted the second pseudo-Callisthenes redaction, and in turn influenced subsequent editions of the pseudo-Callisthenes, a work which ran to a total of five editions all told, including the earlier ones.

The complicated history of the monument on Russian soil, where certain of its episodes were reflected in the old learned literature, in the later chapbooks, and in oral literature, attests to its great popularity here over a period of several centuries. The fate of the idealized hero, endowed with qualities transcending the bounds of human capability, and at the same time subject to a norm that is higher than human existence, worked upon the imagination and upon the moral sense of the old-time reader, while the narrative itself entertained him by its abundance of all manner of unusual adventures and fantastic pictures. The narrative gratified the aesthetic tastes of such a reader and at the same time accorded with his religious bent. The force of cultural and literary tradition prevented any such artistic metamorphosis here of the romance of Alexander of Macedon as took place in the West, so overlaying the romance with the pigmentation of the everyday life of the time as to obliterate the dividing line between history and contemporaneity. But even on Russian soil the *Alexandria* did not remain stationary, was not passively recopied from century to century: here, too, its literary history shows it answering the new intellectual demands that arose as one epoch succeeded another.

The legends of Troy popular in medieval Europe also circulated to a considerable extent in Rus, the earliest example being a text included in the *Chronicle of Malalas* and entitled, "Concerning Trojan Times." [34] In the fifteenth century this legend, under the title of the "Parable of the Beauties," became known here as part of the translated Byzantine *Chronicle of Manassius,* and in conjunction with the chronicle at once found its way into the *Russian Chronograph* compiled by the Serbian immigrant Pakhomius Logothetes. The text of the "Parable of Beauties" goes back to a South Slavic translation made from a Romance original on the Dalmatian coast in the thirteenth-fourteenth centuries. The legends of Troy had as their source not the poems of Homer but later legends erroneously attributed to the Greek Dictys and the Phrygian Daretes. Apparently during the second half of the fifteenth century, a translation from the Latin came out here of a tale of Troy

[34] See A. N. Veselovskii, "The South Slavic Tale of Troy," *Iz istorii romana i povesti* (From the History of Romance and Tale) (St. Petersburg, 1888), Pt. 2, pp. 25–121. An appendix gives two texts of the tale from sixteenth century MSS.

by the thirteenth century Italian author, Guido da Colonna, whose style
had peculiarities similar to those of the Serbian *Alexandria*. This was afterwards included, in abbreviated form, in the later chronograph, replacing the
"Parable of the Beauties," and in Peter the Great's time became one of the
first printed books.

Another translated tale in circulation here during the earliest period was
the *Adventures of Digenis*.[35] The Russian text of this tale goes back to an
inextant text of a tenth century Byzantine romance based on the Byzantine
epos of the struggle between Greeks and Saracens and telling of the abduction by the Saracen king Amir of a noble Greek maiden, whom, having embraced Christianity, he marries, and of the exploits and amorous adventures
of their son Digenis Akritas. Later Byzantine versifications of this romance
(fifteenth-seventeenth century) have been preserved, but these were not the
source of the Russian text. The hyphenated name Digenis- (Greek: "of two
races") Akritas (Greek: "mingled") was adopted by the hero in view of his
mixed origin as son of a Saracen and a Grecian. On Russian soil the Greek
name Digenis was transformed into Devgeny.

The translation of the Byzantine romance directly into Russian, without
the mediation of a South Slavic text (no such text has at any rate come to
light), was made, to judge by certain peculiarities of language and style in
extant copies, not later than the twelfth-thirteenth centuries, the days of
Kievan Rus. The oldest Russian copy of the *Adventures of Digenis* (early
sixteenth century) was in the same collection with the *Tale of Igor's Expedition*. Of the text of this copy, only a few excerpts were preserved, made, for
the most part, by Karamzin. We now have at our disposal only two copies
of the tale, and late ones at that (mid-eighteenth century), both of which go
back to the same translation. Of these, the one formerly belonging to N. S.
Tikhonravov, and now preserved in the Lenin All-Union Library in Moscow, is, to judge by the fact that corresponding passages coincide with the
excerpts made by Karamzin from the sixteenth century copy, of the same
edition, while the other, discovered by A. N. Pypin, and preserved in the
Pogodin collection at the Saltykov-Shchedrin Public Library RSFSR in
Leningrad, represents a later Russianized edition of the old translation,
which reflected elements of the oral poetic tradition. Both copies are defective; in both the end is lacking. In the first the beginning has also been
lost and there is a large gap in the central section. We have no assurance that

---

[35] See M. N. Speranskii, *Devgeniyevo deyaniye: K istorii yevo texta v starinnoy russkoy
pismennosti* (Deeds of Digenis: On the History of Its Texts in Ancient Russian Literature),
study and texts, *Sbornik otd. russk. yaz. i slov.* (Collection of the Division of Russian Language and Literature of the Academy of Sciences) (Petrograd, 1922), Vol. XCIX, No. 7
(the appendix gives Karamzin's excerpts from the *Adventures of Digenis* in the Musim-
Pushkin MS., as well as the Tikhonravov and Pypin texts); N. S. Tikhonravov, "Adventures
of Digenis," *Works*, Vol. I, pp. 256–274.

the tale was translated into Russian in its entirety, however. The beginning of what is left of the text in the Tikhonravov copy is entitled, *Life of Digenis;* the Pypin copy is entitled, *Deeds of Former Times and of Brave Men, Concerning the Boldness and Courage and Prowess of Fair Digenis.* In presenting the content of the tale, we shall proceed from the Pypin copy, using the Tikhonravov to supply missing episodes.

In Byzantium there lived a certain pious widow of the imperial family who had three sons, "very handsome and celebrated," and one daughter, "very fair, and celebrated for the beauty of her person." Amir, King of Arabia, learning of the maiden's beauty, gathered a multitude of troops and set out to "make a raid into Greek territory for the sake of that maiden's beauty." He came to the widow's house when the brothers were out hunting and the mother at church and abducted the girl. When the mother returned from church and learned of her beautiful daughter's abduction she began to tear the hair of her head and rend her face and weep for her daughter. Presently the sons returned and asked their mother the cause of her grief. The mother informed them that their sister had been abducted by Amir. "And he has torn my heart up by the roots, and cast me away like a dead stick," she inveighed against Amir, then conjured her sons to set out in pursuit of the abductor and get their sister away from him or lay down their lives, in which case she will, as a childless woman, mourn her children.

The sons complied with their mother's wish, received her blessing, put on their armor, mounted their horses and rode off "like golden-winged hawks, and the horses under them fairly flew." They came to the border of the Saracen land over which Amir ruled and there met a Saracen of whom they inquired where King Amir was to be found. But the Saracen drew his sword and arrogantly advanced against them. The youngest brother hurled himself upon the Saracen and would have killed him, but the older brother restrained him, saying: "Why should we stain our sword on a Saracen subject? Let us stain it with the blood of King Amir, for it is he who has wronged us." After tying the Saracen to a tree, the brothers rode on, met Amir's large bodyguard of three thousand men, and advanced against it. The oldest brother rode "to the right hand," the second in the center, "against the bulk of the company," and the youngest "to the left hand." [36] They galloped at the Saracens and began to kill them, "as good haymakers cut grass"; some they cut down, others they bound and took to a high hill, driving them along

---

[36] Cf. the description of the march of the bogatyrs in the *byliny:*
        They cast lots among themselves
        Which of them should ride to the right hand,
        Which of them should ride to the left hand,
        Which be put in the middle to bear the brunt.
                —Kireyevsky, *Songs,* IV, 44.

before "like a good shepherd his sheep," and then they killed these as well, sparing only three men to conduct them to Amir. The Saracens who remained alive described Amir's costly tent, his brother, and his warriors strong and brave: "One can engage a hundred." Through these Saracens the brothers sent Amir word that they were advancing upon him, so that Amir could not say they had come upon him like thieves. Hearing of the approach of the brothers, Amir was alarmed and, summoning his retinue, said to them: "My brothers, powerful knights, I dreamed last night that three hawks beat at me with their wings and very nearly inflicted wounds on my body; now these brothers are approaching and starting to make trouble."

Upon arriving at Amir's tent the brothers asked where their sister was. Amir suggested that they go to a high hill where lay many women and fair maidens slain by Amir, among them their sister, because she had refused to do his will. Hurling threats at Amir, the brothers betook themselves to the designated mountain, but, not finding their sister there, returned to the king with the "angels'" song on their lips, firmly resolved to carry out their mother's instructions and lay down their lives for their sister. Amir proposed that they settle the dispute by single combat. The brothers agreed and cast lots. Three times the lot fell to the youngest brother, because he and his sister were twins. Amir was defeated and begged for mercy; he promised to be baptized "for love of the maiden" and proposed that the brothers take him as their brother-in-law. He informed them that their sister was alive and well and directed them to her dwelling. The brothers found her in a tent, sitting on a golden chair; her face was covered with a "costly magnesian veil." When her brothers asked how Amir had been treating her, she replied that the king had surrounded her with all manner of attentions, and only rode over once a month to look at her from a distance, without even coming into the tent. And if Amir should accept baptism, then her brothers could not find a better brother-in-law, for he was "famous with fame, strong in strength, and wise with wisdom, and rich in riches." The brothers gave their consent to the marriage and said: "Our mother's prayer shall unite you to King Amir." By craft Amir got out of Saracen territory, informing his mother and brother that he was going "on a foray into Greek territory," and took with him great riches—camels, gold, and silver. In Greek territory he was baptized by the patriarch and there married "the girl he loved." The wedding feast lasted three months. In the meantime Amir's mother, having grasped the fact that her son had deceived her, sent three Saracens in pursuit of him, providing them with much gold and with three horses, one named Gust of Wind, a second, Thunder, and the third, Lightning, upon which they were to convey Amir and his beloved to the Saracen country unobserved. The Saracens reached the land of Greece and stayed in hiding outside the city. On the night of their arrival, Amir's wife, the "beautiful girl queen," had a terrifying dream: a golden-winged falcon flew into her chamber, took her by the hand, and led her forth from the chamber, and then three ravens flew up and set upon the falcon, and the falcon let go of her. Her brothers, to whom she told her dream, gathered "scholars and Pharisees," who interpreted the dream as meaning that Amir (the falcon) intended, with the help of three Saracens (the three ravens), to take his wife and flee to the Saracen country. Amir, however, denied on oath what the interpreters of the dream had said about him, and in company with them and the brothers started for the outskirts of the city, where he found the Saracens, who, after disclosing the whole secret, received baptism and remained in the land of Greece.

After this "pre-story," the principal hero's story begins. To Amir and the Grecian was born a son whom they named Digenis the Fair. He was baptized by the patriarch himself, and the empress acted as godmother. At the age of ten, Digenis began spear practice, at twelve he began riding mettled steeds and was clever at performing feats on his bogatyr's mount while the charger curvetted under him. Moreover, the youth himself was very fair, his face white as snow and red as poppy flowers, his hair like gold, his eyes as large as chalices; he was "terrific" to look upon. His father chose for him a horse as white as a dove, with many little bells on its mane, and the "tinkling" of those bells was "beyond human imagining."

When he was thirteen, Digenis began to hunt all sorts of wild beasts, performing marvels of daring and strength. A fleeing elk he seized by its hind legs and tore in two; he caught a bear and tore that apart by the jaws; with his sword he sliced many another fierce beast in two and killed a four-headed serpent.

Presently Digenis began to contemplate various exploits. At this juncture Philippapa and his daughter Maximiana, who had the boldness and courage of a man, having heard about the strength and courage of Digenis, began plotting how they might "catch him like a hare in a trap." With a large army they went into Greek territory, halted at the river "Ephrantes" and sent him a deceitful letter in which they said: "O light, O radiant sun, illustrious Digenis, you are king over all of us who are brave and strong as the month of May is king over all the months: as in the month of May all earthly beauty is at its height and deciduous trees put on their leafy garments and heavenly beauty is also at its peak, just so are you the flower of such as we, illustrious Digenis; and now we beseech you, illustrious one, to take the trouble to come and visit us, with just a few men, by the Ephrantes River, that we may behold your beauty and strength, and we have no evil intentions against you."

Upon receiving the letter, Digenis laughed and began to make plans for meeting Philippapa and Maximiana. His father tried to dissuade him by warning him of the strength and courage of Philippapa and Maximiana and the strength and size of their army. But Digenis insisted on having his own way and, after receiving his parents' blessing, set out for the river Ephrantes with a small army. He hurled himself on the enemy force "like a stout falcon released from the hand of the hunter," and drove into it "as a good haymaker mows grass." At the first onslaught he killed a thousand of Philippapa's soldiers, at the second, another thousand, and at the third, struck Philippapa with the blunt end of his spear and unhorsed him. Seeing this, Maximiana set her spear and would have pierced Digenis with it, but Digenis smote her in the face with the palm of his hand, forced her to the ground, and bound father and daughter, while of the army he captured some alive and others he drove before him "as a good shepherd drives sheep or goats" and chased them to the other side of the river.

Philippapa afterward told Digenis of the existence of a king Stratig who was braver and stronger than Digenis himself, and that he had a beautiful daughter Stratigovna whom no one had as yet vanquished in single combat; perhaps Digenis would succeed in doing this. As a reward for this information, Philippapa begged that he release him. Digenis promised to do so if what he had said proved true. Maximiana, who had never up to this time been defeated by anyone and who had refused all the strong and courageous emperors and kings who had asked her in marriage, now proposed that Digenis should take her to wife and then no power need awe him. But saying that he had no need of human help, "with the grace of God and his mother's prayers," the wise Digenis opened a book and in it read that if he married Maximiana, he would live another sixteen years, but if he married Stratigovna, he would live another thirty-six, and he refused Maximiana's proposal and then commanded that father and daughter be taken to his parents.

After this Digenis began to plan how to win Stratigovna.

Once more against his father's advice, he set out for Stratig's kingdom, wearing costly raiment, and riding to the sound of dulcimers. Leaving his army five versts from the city, he set out alone for Stratig's court. Stratig and his sons were hunting at the time, but Stratigovna, sitting by her window and seeing Digenis, made up her mind that he was handsome but not strong. Digenis strove to attract Stratigovna's attention by having his army play various instruments and by himself riding up and down Stratig's courtyard on a horse with such bells on its mane as could "ravish" a person's wits. Stratigovna sent her nurse to tell Digenis to leave the town, and to threaten him with the speedy return of her father and brothers.

At this point the Pypin text of the tale breaks off. The Tikhonravov text tells how Digenis, after chivalrously warning Stratig and his sons that he was about to abduct Stratigovna, did abduct her, without any opposition on the part of her father and brothers. Afterward, however, Stratig, his sons, and a large army set out in pursuit of Digenis, who beats Stratig's army, and takes him and his sons captive, but later, at the request of Stratigovna, releases them; Digenis marries Stratigovna. From Stratig, his wife, and sons, he receives rich presents.

After this the Tikhonravov manuscript has a chapter entitled, the "Legend of How Digenis Vanquished the Emperor Basil," which resembles in content the episode of Digenis' fight with Philippapa and Maximiana.

The style of this tale is very much like that of the war stories, translated and original, of the Kiev period: Josephus' account of the destruction of Jerusalem, the chronicle war story, the *Tale of Igor's Expedition*. Take, for example, the similes still encountered in the older edition: "like a stout falcon," "like a young falcon," "his face was white as snow," "as a shepherd drives the sheep before him," "as a good haymaker mows grass," and so on, and the epithets in this same edition: a wild beast is "fierce," a horse "swift," a falcon "stout," "young," "fleet," a helmet "golden," strings "golden," and so forth. The same is also true of the lexical constituents of our monument which likewise find parallels in the very early narrative works mentioned.[37]

As indicated above, both the Tikhonravov and the Pypin texts of the tale go back to a single early translation, from which, in view of the fact that both date from the eighteenth century, they have naturally more or less departed stylistically. This is especially true of the Pypin text, which reflects to a marked degree the tastes of its editor, who imported into the text elements of the oral-poetry and to some extent of the popular-book tradition. The former is observable in the rather frequent use of folk-poetry epithets and similes, and also in the employment of tautology: "swift steed," "sounding" dulcimers, "face red as poppy flowers," "with fame famous, in strength strong, in wisdom wise, with riches rich," "emperors and sons of emperors, kings and sons of kings." To the mode of oral poetry is probably traceable the triple casting of lots among the brothers to decide which of them is to enter into single combat with Amir. The episode of the three miraculous horses on which Amir's mother sent the Saracens in pursuit of her son evidently has its source in fairy tale.[38]

The figure of Digenis, like the figure of Alexander of Macedon, is an embodiment of the concept of the ideal hero as worked out by feudal culture, but with this distinction, that the piety of Digenis is given considerably

[37] For details see M. N. Speranskii, *Devgeniyevo deyaniye* (Deeds of Digenis), pp. 59–77, 100–103.

[38] For more details see *op. cit.*, pp. 124–127.

greater emphasis than the piety of Alexander. He is not only a marvelous warrior, endowed with superior physical qualities, but also a God-fearing Christian, relying upon God in all matters and never undertaking anything without prayer and his mother's blessing.

At the outset, to judge from the later versified renderings, the Byzantine original of our tale described Digenis-Akritas as a guardian of the frontiers of Christian Byzantium against the attacks of "unbelievers"—Mahometans.

One of the first Byzantine tales to make its appearance here, evidently translated in Rus without intermediary, was the *Tale of Barlaam and Josaphat*, some elements in which relate it rather closely to the lives of saints.[39] Basically, it is a Christianized biography of Buddha. The Greek text of the narrative came from the Indian original of this biography by way of a Christianized Georgian version. In it the Oriental names Balavkhar and Budasaph were replaced by the Christian names Barlaam and Josaphat. The tale, rewritten on Byzantine soil, probably by the monk John of St. Savva Monastery, was traditionally attributed on insufficient grounds to St. John Damascene (eighth century). In the eleventh century, through the medium of a Latin translation, the *Tale of Barlaam and Josaphat* circulated widely in western Europe. At the same time, apparently, it also penetrated from Byzantium into Rus. Some of the parable-apologues it contained were known in this country, it would seem, even before a complete translation of the tale appeared. In particular, such parables found a place in the *Prologue*. The earliest Russian copy of the tale dates from the thirteenth-fourteenth centuries. Its content is as follows.

The Indian king Avenir, being a pagan, vigorously combated Christianity, which was infiltrating into his country. Avenir's hostility to the new religion intensified after one of his nobles embraced Christianity and became a hermit. When a son of uncommon beauty was born to Avenir—Josaphat they named him—fifty-five astrologers foretold wealth and power for him, but one said that the kingdom of Josaphat would not be of this world, that he was destined to become an adherent of Christianity. In order to prevent this, Avenir commanded that Josaphat be domiciled in a luxurious palace that had been built for him and that he be protected in every way from painful impressions which might lead to his thinking about the transitoriness of life. Isolation from the outside world, however, began to depress Josaphat

---

[39] Printed in *Pub. obshchestva lyubiteley drevney pismennosti* (Publications of the Society of the Friends of Early Literature) (St. Petersburg, 1885), LXXXIII. For comment see A. Kirpichnikov, *Grecheskie romany v noveishey literature* (Greek Romances in Modern Literature), *Povest o Varlaame i Iosafe* (Tale of Barlaam and Josaphat), *Zhurnal min. nar. prosv.* (Journal of the Ministry of Public Instruction) (1887), No. 7; I Franko, *Iosaf i Varlaam, staro-khristianskii dukhovnyi roman* (Josaphat and Barlaam, Old Christian Spiritual Romance) (Lvov, 1897).

and at his persistent request Avenir authorized that he be allowed to go out-side the palace precincts, ordering that watch be kept the while so that noth-ing should cross his son's path that could cause him sorrow. But once, un-beknown to the servants, Josaphat met two men, one leprous, the other blind, and learned that maladies exist in the world. Another time, he saw a decrepit person and learned that old age exists and that death lies in wait for men. Josaphat was deeply afflicted, began to reflect upon the vanity of life and to muse as to the existence of some other life and another world and to look for someone who would answer the questions that were tormenting him. By a revelation from on high, Barlaam, a hermit of the wilderness of Shinar, learned of Josaphat's spiritual state, came to India in the guise of a merchant, and informed Josaphat's tutor that he wanted to sell the prince a precious stone which possessed the power to illumine the hearts of men with the light of truth, cure the sick, make the blind to see, open the ears of the deaf, give the dumb a voice, make wise the foolish, drive out demons; but that only he could see this stone who had clear vision and a chaste body.

Josaphat desired to see this stone, but Barlaam said that he must first test his powers of reasoning, and to this end he delivered a number of apologues and parables, partly from evangelical but mostly from Oriental sources, with a Christian interpretation, however. One of these apologues—about a man pursued by a unicorn—was particularly popular here in antiquity, even circulating independently.

A man, fleeing from a unicorn and coming to a chasm, seizes the branch of a tree growing at the edge of the chasm and hangs in mid-air. Looking down, he sees that two mice, a white one and a black one, are gnawing at the roots of the tree, that at the bottom of the chasm lies a terrible snake with open jaws, and that from the sides four asps' heads are thrust forth. But noticing honey dripping from the branches of the tree, the man, disre-garding the dangers that beset him, greedily drinks it. Then comes an in-terpretation of the apologue in the spirit of Christian doctrine: the unicorn is death, lying in wait for man, the tree is man's journey of life, the honey dripping from the tree, the pleasures to which man abandons himself when overcome by temptations (the asps' heads), doing so in spite of the fact that day and night (the white mouse and the black) are undermining the roots of his life and that after death hell threatens him (the serpent at the bot-tom of the chasm).

After Josaphat has perceived the Christian doctrine, Barlaam baptizes him (this is the promised precious stone) and, preventing the prince from fol-lowing him, returns to the desert. Avenir, learning of Barlaam's visit to his son, gives orders that he be pursued, but Barlaam is not found. Then the king resorts to a pagan wise man and a magician with command over demons in the hope that they can disprove, to the prince, Barlaam's teaching, but both the wise man and the magician shortly become Christians themselves. Equally fruitless are his attempts to distract Josaphat from Christianity by women's charms and cares of state. (Avenir entrusts half his dominion to his son to govern.) Sensual temptations Josaphat escapes through prayer and fasting, and his subjects he converts to Christianity. In the end Avenir himself becomes a Christian and turns his whole kingdom over to Josaphat. After his father's death, having turned the kingdom over to one of his nobles, Josaphat, in spite of the people's entreaty, puts on the hair shirt left him by Barlaam, and departs for the wilderness of Shinar in search of the latter.

There he wanders for two years, overcoming all manner of hardships and temptations sent him by the devil; he is burned by the sun, tortured by thirst, pursued by wild beasts. Finally, he finds Barlaam, takes up his abode in the latter's cave and devotes himself to asceticism, surpassing even his teacher in its practice. Presently Barlaam dies; Josaphat buries him and, after spending another thirty-five years in the desert, comes to a peaceful end. In his hour of death, the hermit who had earlier showed him the way to Barlaam comes and buries him by Barlaam's side. This same hermit, by a command from on high, starts out for India and there reports the death of Josaphat. The noble to whom Josaphat had entrusted the kingdom, and a throng of people with him, set out for the desert of Shinar and find there the incorruptible and sweet-smelling bodies of the recluses, which they ceremoniously convey to the capital of India. The "relics" of Barlaam and Josaphat perform miracles and heal the sick, and many pagan peoples round about hear of this and are converted to Christianity.

Later, the *Tale of Barlaam and Josaphat* had a history on Russian soil. The second half of the fifteenth century brought a so-called "Athanasian travesty" of the tale, reflecting the Catholic tendency to give religious power precedence over secular that eventuated in one of the most influential ecclesiastical factions of that time, the "Josephites." [40] In the seventeenth century the *Tale* was printed first in White Russia, then in Moscow. Both editions in the last analysis derive, however, not from a Greek but from a Latin original. Both are provided with verses reminiscent of the oral spiritual verses about Prince Josaphat and the beautiful mother-desert.

In the lost manuscript which contained the *Tale of Igor's Expedition*, and immediately preceding it, was a tale entitled, *Sinagrip, King of the Adars and of the Alluvial Country*, commonly called, from the name of the

[40] See N. P. Popov, "Afanas'evskii izvod 'Povesti o Varlaame i Iosafe'" (Athanasian Travesty of the Tale of Barlaam and Josaphat), *Izvestiya otd. russk. yaz. i slov.* (News of the Division of Russian Language and Literature of the Academy of Sciences USSR) (1926), XXXI, pp. 189–230.

main character, the *Tale of Akir the Wise*.[41] It is one of the earliest monuments of narrative literature, having originated in the seventh century B.C.
in Assyro-Babylonia and afterwards spread to the Orient and then to Byzantium, where it apparently underwent some revision in line with Christian
principles, and so on. No Greek texts of the tale have been preserved but
their existence is confirmed, among other things, by the fact that the tale
influenced the Greek biography of Aesop.

The *Tale of Akir* is apparently made up of two tales which originally
existed independently. One of them narrates the fortunes of a royal adviser
who was slandered to the king by his nephew, condemned to execution, but
saved from death by a friend, and who afterwards, through his wisdom,
relieved the king of having to pay tribute to a foreign country; the other consists of the precepts and moral admonitions of uncle to nephew before the
betrayal and his reproaches after it. On Byzantine soil the two tales were
already known as a unit. The content of the tale may be summarized as
follows.

Akir, childless adviser to King Sinagrip, takes his nephew Anadan to
bring up, teaches him wisdom and inculcates all manner of edifying precepts to prepare him to become adviser to the king after his own death. But
by his profligacy Anadan roused the anger of Akir, who took a younger
brother into his service instead. Then Anadan in revenge defamed Akir
before Sinagrip as guilty of treason, informing the king that Akir was about
to betray the land of the Adars into the power of the Persian king and the
Egyptian pharaoh, and presented his libel in such a way that Sinagrip believed him and condemned Akir to death. His execution was entrusted to
a friend whose life he had himself once saved, and the friend executed a
slave in his place and hid Akir in a deep pit. When the Egyptian pharaoh
heard of the death of Akir, he rejoiced, and proposed that Sinagrip send
him a wise man who should build a house between earth and sky and guess
such riddles as the pharaoh should propound to him. If Sinagrip failed to
meet this demand, he was to pay tribute to Pharaoh for three years, and in
the opposite event, it should be the other way round. Sinagrip's wise men
advised him to send Anadan to Pharaoh, but Anadan begged off.

After the king had bewailed the fact that Akir was no longer alive to send
to Pharaoh, Akir's friend made known that his adviser still lived. Sinagrip
rejoiced at this news, went in person to take Akir from the pit, and then
sent him to Pharaoh. The demand of the Egyptian pharaoh that he should

[41] The oldest Russian text of the tale, from the fifteenth and early sixteenth century copy,
was published by A. D. Grigoryev as a supplement to his extensive study of it, *Povest ob
Akire Premudrom* (Tale of Akir The Wise) (Moscow, 1913). See also his "Tale of Akir
The Wise As a Work of Art," *Varshavskie universitetskie izvestiya* (Warsaw University
News) (1913), No. 4.

build a house between heaven and earth Akir decided to meet in the following manner. He ordered that two female eagles be trained to fly up into the air carrying two boys in a basket, and he ordered the boys to be trained to say, as they rose: "Bring lime and stone. The workmen have arrived." In Pharaoh's presence the eagles flew up into the air and the boys demanded material for building, but as their demand could not be met, Akir came off victor in the contest of wits with Pharaoh. He was also successful at guessing several riddles propounded by Pharaoh, and returned with tribute to the land of the Adars. As a reward he asked only Anadan, whom, having put in chains and subjected to a thousand stripes, he upbraided in parables, whereafter Anadan sulked and broke down. The tale closes with an aphorism that expresses its basic idea: "He who digs a pit for his friend shall himself fall into it."

This tale, of which no extant Russian copies are earlier than the fifteenth or early sixteenth century, was apparently rendered directly from the Greek, possibly in the earliest period of Russian letters, the eleventh century, as one of the Byzantine monuments translated under Yaroslav the Wise. The Old Russian reader was particularly attracted by its moralistic element, originally given the center of the stage, and reflected in such works as the *Supplication of Daniel the Exile* and the *Bee,* but later editions gradually cut down the didactic part, giving precedence to the interesting features of the plot itself. In the Novgorod redaction of the monument (a seventeenth century copy) we get a graphic example of the Russianization of a tale: town elders figure in it; Pharaoh calls a meeting of the Vetche; Akir detects in Anadan vices that were attacked in the *Domostroy* and the *Stoglav*—Russian sixteenth century works; Russian proverbs find their way into the tale, and so on. In the eighteenth century, under the pen of an editor well read in the secular narrative literature of that time, the *Tale of Akir* took on all the typical stylistic peculiarities of a story of Peter the Great's time.[42]

As is clear from what has been said of the character of our translated narrative literature in the Kiev period, this literature does not differ fundamentally in general tendency from other translated literature in Rus at that time. The surface interest of the translated tale was kept in harmony with the religio-instructional tendency that informed it in some degree even when the plot itself and the life histories of the characters did not warrant it. In some instances, for example in the *Tale of Akir* and the *Alexandria*, this produced an emphasis on edification in the spirit of Christian ethics which was peculiar to Russia, transforming a work secular in form and origin into an indirect

[42] See V. N. Peretts, "K istorii teksta 'Povesti ob Akire Premudrom' " (Toward a History of the Text of the Tale of Akir the Wise), *Izv. otd. russk. yaz. i slov.* (News of the Division of Russian Language and Literature of the Academy of Sciences) (1916), Bk. I, pp. 262–278.

instrument of ecclesiastical propaganda. At the same time the themes and style of the earliest translated tales exercised an influence on the original Russian tale and on the products of oral epic poetry.[43]

[43] Most important general works on the ancient translated tale: A. N. Pypin, *Ocherk literaturnoy istorii starinnykh povestey i skazok russkikh* (Sketch of the Literary History of Ancient Russian Tales and Folk Tales) (St. Petersburg, 1857); *Istoriya russkoy literatury* (History of Russian Literature), 3rd or 4th ed. (St. Petersburg, 1907, 1911), Vol. I, Chap. 11, "The Early Tale"; A. N. Veselovskii, "Monuments of Narrative Literature"; in A. Galakhov's *Istoriya russkoy slovesnosti, drevney i novoy* (History of Russian Literature, Ancient and Modern) (Moscow, 1880, 1894), 2nd, 3rd eds., Vol. I, Sec. 1; N. K. Piksanov, *Starorusskaya povest* (The Old Russian Tale) (Moscow, 1923); A. S. Orlov, *Perevodnye povesti feodal'noy Rusi i Moskovskovo gosudarstva XII–XVII vv.* (Translated Tales of Feudal Russia and the Moscovite State in the Twelfth to the Seventeenth Centuries) (Leningrad, 1934).

Original Literature
of the Kiev Period

THE ORATORICAL SERMON

THE development of a homiletic and didactic literature to propagate the basic dogma and ethics of the new religion was from the first a natural and necessary concomitant to the establishment of Christianity in Rus. A sermon addressed to the wider circle of listeners and readers dealt with the rudimentary principles of the Christian religion and employed simple and intelligible language. It contained no abstract philosophical elements, no picturesque expressions, no stylistic embellishment of any sort—in a word, nothing that could make it hard for the uninitiate to understand. Consisting only of a generally accessible statement and explanation of the simplest conceptions in religious dogma and ethics, the type of sermon exemplified by the discourses of Luka Zhidyata, Theodosius of the Crypt Monastery, and other, often nameless, preachers, did not contain a trace of poetic language or imagery, and for that reason stood outside the literary process. The pretentious sermon, with rhetorical embellishments modeled on the examples of the oratorical art offered by outstanding works of Byzantine ecclesiastical eloquence, is another matter. Such a sermon was in antiquity at once both a fact and a factor in our literary development.

The most noted exponent of this type of homiletic literature in Rus during the earliest period was Hilarion. Information about his life and his literary activity is extremely scanty. The only reference to him occurs in the *Primary Chronicle* under the year 1051, where we are told that Yaroslav in that year appointed Hilarion, previously presbyter in the Kiev suburb of Berestovoye, Metropolitan of Rus. This appointment was an act of major importance to the history of church and state in Rus, since it was a conscious step toward liberating the Russian Church from the administrative interference of the

84

Byzantine Church, which had been sending Rus its metropolitans. The occasion for Yaroslav's taking this step was the war with Byzantium in 1043 and subsequent strained relations between the Russian Church and the Byzantine. But in 1055 the *Novgorod Chronicle* already mentions the Greek Ephrem as Metropolitan of Rus, and nothing is anywhere said as to the fate of Hilarion. Whether he was dead at that time, or still alive, is unknown. M. D. Prisyolkov thinks that in 1053, upon the cessation of hostilities between the Greek Church and the Russian, Hilarion must have resigned in favor of the Greek, assumed the monastic habit under the name of Nikon, and taken up his abode in the Crypt Monastery at Kiev. In the opinion of M. D. Prisyolkov, he was that Nikon to whom A. A. Shakhmatov ascribes the composition of the so-called "Kiev Crypt chronicle compilation." Nikon died in 1088.[1] For all its astuteness, M. D. Prisyolkov's conjecture remains no more than a somewhat likely hypothesis.

Equally obscure is the problem of the extent of Hilarion's literary activity. The works that may with certainty be ascribed to Hilarion are the "Confession of Faith," an excerpt of only a few lines from a manual for presbyters, and the celebrated *Discourse of Law and Grace,* his principal work and the only one which can claim the attention of the literary historian. Hilarion's name is not indicated in any extant copy of the *Discourse,* but an argument for its ascription to Hilarion, in addition to a number of purely historical considerations, is the circumstance that in one manuscript, after the *Discourse,* and written in the same hand, occurs the "Confession of Faith," with the comment that it is the work of the "monk and presbyter" Hilarion. Besides this, a similarity of expression is observable in the two works: in particular, both call the great prince * "kagan."[2] Quite recently, on the basis, chiefly, of a stylistic analysis of the 1076 *Svyatoslav Miscellany,* N. P. Popov has advanced the idea of Hilarion's active participation in the composition and redaction of this collection, which thus becomes, from his point of view, a literary enterprise originating not in Bulgaria, as had been assumed, but on Russian soil. With Hilarion's authorship, N. P. Popov associates the "Instruction of Father to Son," the "Hundred Maxims," signed with the name Gennadius, and several other articles.[3] But quite apart from the

* Or Grand Prince.—Ed.

[1] See M. D. Prisyolkov (Prisyelkov), *Ocherki po tserkovno-politicheskoy istorii Kievskoy Rusi X–XII vv.* (Outlines of the Ecclesiastico-Political History of Kievan Rus in the Tenth-Twelfth Centuries) (St. Petersburg, 1913), pp. 109–111, 181–237.

[2] For a list of Hilarion's works and of all works ascribed to him on insufficient grounds, see N. K. Nikolsky's *Materialy dlya povremennovo spiska russkikh pisateley i ikh sochinenii X–XI vv.* (Materials for a Provisional List of Russian Writers and their Works, Tenth-Eleventh Centuries) (St. Petersburg, 1906), pp. 75–122. This catalogues the MSS. relating to him, and their editions, and lists the literature on Hilarion.

[3] See N. P. Popov, "Les auteurs de l'Isbornik de Svjatoslav de 1076," *Revue des études slaves* (1935), Vol. XV, Nos. 3–4, pp. 210–223.

fact that any definite conclusion as to Hilarion's participation in the composition of the 1076 *Miscellany* must be preceded by the establishment of at least an approximate date for Hilarion's death, something which N. P. Popov does not even attempt, the presence of the same tricks of style in the *Discourse of Law and Grace* and in the articles of the 1076 *Miscellany* may itself be explained as due to Hilarion and the authors of the articles having been of the same literary school, and having utilized the same examples of translated patristic literature.

However that may be, and regardless of the extent of Hilarion's literary activity, the work of primary importance for us is the *Discourse of Law and Grace,* which ranks infinitely above anything else attributable to him. It is preserved in a large number of copies, from the fifteenth century on, these copies being classifiable into four redactions. The *Discourse* dates from between 1037 and 1050: it mentions the Church of the Annunciation by the Golden Gates, which Yaroslav built in 1037, and speaks of Yaroslav's wife, Princess Irene, who died in 1050, as still living. Thus the *Discourse* was composed before Hilarion's promotion to the rank of metropolitan, and in all probability proved a substantial factor in Yaroslav's decision to make Hilarion head of the Russian metropolitanate.

In its long form the *Discourse* falls into three sections, as may be seen from the full title: "[1] Concerning the law given to Moses, and concerning grace and truth that came through Jesus Christ, and how the law departed and mercy and truth filled the whole world and the faith spread to all languages even to our Russian language, [2] and praise to our Kagan [4] Vladimir by whom we were baptized, [3] and a prayer to God from our whole land." The fundamental thesis developed in the first part of the *Discourse* is the superiority of the New Testament to the Old, of Christianity to Judaism. Hilarion's idea is that the relations between God and man in the Judaic epoch were founded on "law," on a principle unfree, coercive, so to speak, formal, but in the epoch of Christianity on "grace," signifying the free communion of man with God. Grace for Hilarion was synonymous with truth, while law was only the shadow and image of truth. Law is the servant and forerunner of grace, while grace is the servant of the age to come, of the life incorruptible. First law, then grace, first the image of truth, then truth itself. The relation of grace to law is then illustrated in detail by means of parallels from Old Testament history.

The image for law and grace is Hagar and Sarah, the slave woman Hagar and the free woman Sarah, first the former, the slave woman, then the latter, the free woman. Just as Abraham from his youth had to wife Sarah, the free woman, and not a slave, so had God even before the creation of the

---

[4] A Hebrew word, meaning "prince," transmitted to us by the Khazars.

world planned to send his Son into the world and thereby initiate grace. Sarah bore no child because she was barren; no, she was not barren, but destined to bear a child in old age. Obscure for a time and hidden, the wisdom of God was kept secret from angels and men, not as having failed to manifest itself, but as being temporarily concealed, and destined to be revealed at the end of the epoch of law. Sarah said to Abraham: "God has seen fit for me not to bear children; have union with my slave girl Hagar and beget a son by her"; and grace said to God: "If the time has not yet come for me to descend to earth and save the world, do thou go down to Mount Sinai and give men law." Abraham harkened to Sarah and had union with Hagar; God also harkened to grace and descended to Sinai. Hagar bore Abraham a slave, the son of a slave, and Abraham named him Ishmael; and Moses brought the law down from Mount Sinai, but not grace; the shadow of truth, but not truth itself. Then follow a number of other parallels worked out in the same way.

Hilarion next illustrates the concept of the universal role of Christianity by a whole series of references to the Old Testament and to the Gospels. After this he addresses himself to the glorification of Christ as planter of Grace.

The religion of grace has spread throughout all the earth and has reached even unto us the people of Rus, and the lake of the law ran dry while the fount of the Gospel welled up, covered all the earth, and overflowed upon us. . . . And for us, who were pagans, what the Scriptures say came to pass.

A number of quotations follow, after which comes the second section of the *Discourse,* a eulogy on Vladimir, through whose efforts Russia was brought to the Christian fold, beginning:

Rome sings the praises of Peter and Paul, through whom it came to believe in Jesus Christ, the Son of God; Asia, Ephesus, and Patmos praise John the Divine; India, Thomas; Egypt, Mark. All countries, towns, and peoples honor and glorify their teacher who taught them the Orthodox faith. Let us also, according to our power, praise with humble praises our teacher and instructor, who has done great and wondrous things, the great kagan of our land, Vladimir, grandson of old Igor, son of glorious Svyatoslav, who, ruling in their day, became famous for courage and valor in many lands, and are remembered even now and praised. For they did not rule in a poor and unknown country, but in Rus, which is known and celebrated to all the ends of the earth.

After praising Vladimir for his conversion to Christianity, his propagation of the Christian faith in the land of Rus and his generosity to the poor, and in all this likening the Russian prince to Constantine the Great, Hilarion passes to an apotheosis of Yaroslav as the man who continued Vladimir's work, after which comes an impassioned summons to the dead Vladimir to rise and see how the land of Rus and the Russian Church have prospered:

Rise, honored head, from your grave; rise, cast off sleep, for you are not dead but sleep to the day of the common resurrection. Rise, you are not dead, for it is not meet that you should die who have believed in Christ, the life of the whole world. Cast off sleep, raise your eyes and you will see that while deeming you worthy of such honors there on high, the Lord has also kept you in remembrance here on earth through your son. Rise, see your son George,[5] see your progeny, see your dearly beloved, see him whom the Lord produced from your loins; see him adorning the throne of your land, and rejoice; be glad. Likewise look upon her, your pious daughter-in-law Irene, see your grandsons and great-grandsons, how they live, how the Lord has preserved them, how they profess the faith with a devotion like your own, frequent the holy churches, praise Christ, bow before his name. See, too, the town shining in grandeur, see the churches flourishing, see Christianity growing, see the city gleaming with the light from holy icons and fragrant with thyme and vocal with praise and sacred chants raised to God. And, seeing all this, rejoice and be glad and praise the good God, architect of it all.

In conclusion Hilarion beseeches Vladimir to pray for the land of Rus, for its people, and for his son Yaroslav. The *Discourse* ends with a prayer to God made by the whole land of Rus.

The tenor of the *Discourse* was suggested to Hilarion in the first place by the living present, by the political situation that had developed in Yaroslav's time between the young state of Kiev and its cultural agent, the Church. The central moment of the *Discourse,* embodied in the eulogy of Vladimir, is an apology for the Russian prince as planter of the Christian faith in his country, in that same land of Rus which is "known and celebrated all over the world," and as founder of the Russian Church. The *Discourse* was undoubtedly evoked by a desire to defend the idea of the Russian Church's independence of Byzantium: the Church's right to independent existence was borne out by the whole course of historical events in Rus. Hilarion could not have been unaware of a basic tendency, spread here through the agency of the Byzantine Church, to regard Rus as indebted to Byzantium for the establishment of Christianity here. This tendency was very clearly reflected even in the chronicle accounts of the adoption of the Christian faith by Rus. And as a sort of tacit refutation, Hilarion emphasizes the point that Vladimir embraced Christianity on his own initiative and by immediate inspiration from on high. He merely heard of the "pious land of Greece, Christ-loving and strong in the faith," and at once his heart longed and his soul burned to become a Christian and give baptism to his country, nor would it appear from anything in the *Discourse* that Byzantium had taken any active part in Vladimir's conversion to Christianity. On the contrary Hilarion indicates that Vladimir had no examples and no influences from without which could have led him to think that Christianity was superior to paganism. Vladimir saw no apostle come to his land and in poverty,

[5] Yaroslav's Christian name.

nakedness, hunger and thirst seek to dispose him to humility, saw no devils banished in the name of Christ, no sick miraculously healed, no dead raised —and none the less believed and became a pious Christian, friend of the poor, consoler of the weak and infirm, intercessor for the oppressed and the enslaved. (Later, the chronicle asserted that the apostle Andrew made a journey through the land of Rus.) He fostered the spread of the Christian religion in all manner of ways, built churches and adorned them, protected the clergy, like Constantine the Great humbly took counsel with bishops about the establishment of law in the newly converted nation. Such an idealization of Vladimir in the spirit of Christian principles gives a picture that is rather in contrast to the idea that folk tradition built up of him as an "affable" prince, noted for his lavish feasts and his martial exploits. It seems possible that the aim of this championship of Vladimir as a Christian hero was to expedite his ecclesiastical canonization, something which had been opposed by Byzantium on account of political considerations. Hilarion praises Vladimir not only for his piety, however, but also for his courage and his services to the state, for the fact that he had subdued the surrounding countries, some peacefully, others—the refractory ones—with the sword. With Hilarion nationalistic interests are on a par with purely ecclesiastical interests. Not without reason does he mention, in the style of the later *Tale of Igor's Expedition,* that Vladimir was "grandson of old Igor, son of renowned Svyatoslav." He put a high valuation upon the best pages of his country's history and was undisturbed by the fact that both Igor and Svyatoslav had been pagans: as Russian princes distinguished for their bravery and courage, Hilarion mentions them with the same feeling of patriotic pride that he shows in speaking of his country.

But though referring to the past, Hilarion's *Discourse,* as above stated, had the living present in view. Praise of Vladimir's achievement was, on the lips of Hilarion, at the same time a program which the preacher was, as it were, prescribing for the illustrious prince's son Yaroslav—in Hilarion's opinion a worthy successor to his father. In addressing Vladimir, Hilarion says:

A very fine witness to your piety is your son George, whom the Lord has made heir to your dominion; he does not violate your statutes but maintains them, does not diminish what your piety decreed but increases it, does not confound but puts in order, finishes what you left unfinished, as Solomon finished what David began.

"The Eulogy attaches relatively less importance to Yaroslav's achievements than the chronicle does," says the foremost student of Hilarion's work, I. N. Zhdanov:

But if we remember the general motives underlying all such attempts to compare the accomplishment of contemporaries to that of personages who have already acquired a certain historical significance and are generally acknowledged to have attained a certain eminence, then we are forced to arrive at exactly the opposite conclusion. A desire to praise the present through the past is the essential purpose of any such endeavor as the "Eulogy of Kagan Vladimir." [6]

In corroboration of Zhdanov's words, examples might be adduced from later, or at least from eighteenth century, literature: Feofan Prokopovich, in his tragicomedy *Vladimir,* praises Vladimir as a religious reformer, at the same time indirectly praising Peter I as a political reformer; Lomonosov in his ode, "On the Day of Empress Elizabeth Petrovna's Accession to the Throne," extols not only Elizabeth but, still more highly, Peter I, whom he sets for her as a model; Kheraskov in the *Rossiad,* apotheosizes Ivan the Terrible as conqueror of Kazan and leaves his contemporaries to draw for themselves the analogy between Ivan the Terrible and Catherine II.

If the eulogy of Vladimir be taken as the thematic focus of the *Discourse,* then the preceding dissertation upon law as symbol of the Jewish religion, and grace as expression of Christian doctrine, becomes the logical introduction to the eulogy, showing the meaning and significance of the new religious principle that Vladimir had established in Rus, while the prayer by the land of Rus brings the whole *Discourse* to a triumphal conclusion. The idea that the supplanting of Judaism by Christianity constituted the chief moment in universal history is a common historico-ecclesiastical conception of the Middle Ages, and consequently there are no grounds whatever for discerning in the first part of Hilarion's *Discourse* indications of a polemic against hypothetical Jewish propaganda in Old Rus, as some scholars have supposed. There is still less reason to accept M. D. Prisyolkov's unconvincing conjecture that the main purpose of the first part of the *Discourse* is to contrast the period when the Russian Church was under the Bulgarian Ochrida patriarchate, as a time of law, of oppression, with the present era, inaugurated by the conquest of Bulgaria, as the epoch of grace and of freedom.[7] Quite apart from the fact that the very dependence of the Russian Church on the Ochrida patriarchate is only Prisyolkov's hypothesis, and not a very acceptable one at that, Hilarion could scarcely have resorted to such a very obscure allusion without risk of proving incomprehensible even to those select readers of his. Nor was there any point in settling accounts with the Ochrida Church, even if such had ever existed, once the dependence on Ochrida had become a thing of the past, whereas the dependence on Byzantium was not in the past but in the present.

[6] "Slovo o zakone i blagodati i pokhvala kaganu Vladimiru" (Discourse of Law and Grace and Eulogy of Kagan Vladimir), *Works of I. N. Zhdanov* (St. Petersburg, 1904), Vol. I, p. 46.

[7] See *Ocherki po tserkovno-politicheskoy istorii Kievskoy Rusi X–XII vv.* (Outlines of the Ecclesiastico-Political History of Kievan Rus in the Tenth-Eleventh Centuries), pp. 97–111.

In Hilarion's work we are dealing with an example of lofty oratorical art worthy to stand alongside the best products of Byzantine ecclesiastical eloquence. The *Discourse* reveals an author of outstanding literary culture, remarkable taste, and a real sense of proportion. It is informed throughout with fervent patriotic zeal, written with real inspiration and marked by a faultless harmony of outward form. Nor is it any exaggeration to say that early Russian literature has left us nothing else in the field of oratory as noteworthy as Hilarion's *Discourse*. It is a striking index to the high degree of literary proficiency that Rus attained during the early flowering of its culture under Yaroslav the Wise. Hilarion was presumably one of the foremost among those scholars whom Yaroslav gathered about him and with whose help, in the words of the chronicle, he "sowed the hearts of the faithful with the written word."

Hilarion's *Discourse* was addressed, as he himself states, not to ordinary listeners, for whose understanding it would have been too difficult both in content and in form, "not to the unlearned," but to "those who have banqueted their fill on the sweetness of books." Hence all its peculiarities of oratorical style: symbolical parallelism and simile, personification of abstract concepts, metaphors, antitheses, repetitions, rhetorical exhortations and questions, and so forth. We get examples of symbolical parallelism and simile when the law is compared to shadow, to moonlight, to night chill, and to the biblical personages Hagar and Ishmael; and grace with sunlight, with warmth, with Sarah and Isaac, when Jacob's blessing of Manasseh and Ephraim is set up as the prototype of the fate of the Hebrew and the Christian peoples, or when the two natures of Christ are discussed, and when Vladimir's achievement is compared to that of Constantine the Great.

A curious example of the type of parallelism in which a statement is made and then denied, with a view to expressing the idea with greater accuracy, is: "Sarah bore no child because she was barren; no, she was not barren, but destined to bear a child in old age." This example may be compared to the well known passage in the *Tale of Igor's Expedition*: "Then he loosed ten falcons upon a flock of swans . . . no, brothers, Boyan did not loose ten falcons upon a flock of swans." Metaphorical expressions are found throughout the *Discourse*. A few examples should suffice: "Then the gloom of idolatry began to depart from us, and the dawn of grace appeared; then the darkness of devil worship was dispelled and the sun of the gospel shone upon our land," or: "May the dayspring of your faith not be withered by the heat of infidelity but may it by rain of God's timely sending be made fruitful," or, finally, the following metaphor built up through a series of gradations and ending in a simile: "For you are clothed with justice, girded with strength, shod with truth, crowned with understanding and adorned with charity as with a gold collar and ornaments of gold." As an example of the personification of abstract concepts, the request may be cited that Grace makes when she asks God to descend to Sinai and impart the law.

As examples of antithesis, the following symmetrically constructed phrases will at least be indicative: "First law, then grace, first its shadow, then truth," or: "And thus we call those who are strangers to God his people, and call the enemies of God his sons; let us not censure the Jews, but let us bless the Christians; let us not take counsel how we may crucify him, but let us bow before him crucified; let us not crucify the Saviour but lift up our hands to him; let us not pierce his side, but let us drink of the imperishable fount that gushes from it," and so forth.

Examples of repetition are very strikingly assembled in the apostrophe to Vladimir quoted above. To these may be added the following: "New teaching, new bottles, new tongues, newness must be maintained. . . . Christ has conquered, Christ has won, Christ is king, and Christ is glorified. . . . We thy people seek thee, fall before thee, fondly beseech thee. . . . For we are thine, thy creation, the work of thy hand. . . . And our souls are in thy hand and our breath is subject to thy will." Rhetorical exclamations also occur in the apostrophe to Vladimir. A rhetorical question is encountered at the beginning of the Discourse: "And what did law avail, what grace?" And again: "How shall we praise thee, honored father, famed among earthly sovereigns, most valiant Basil;[8] how shall we show our wonder at thy kindness, thy fortitude and strength; how shall we render thanks to thee for making God known to us and delivering us from the worship of idols?" and so forth.

Finally, the Discourse in a number of instances yields examples of rhythmic pattern, consisting for the most part in a series of short phrases ending with assonant verbs: "The naked clothing, the hungry and thirsty supplying, to invalids comfort sending, for debtors a ransom providing, bondmen setting free . . . Armies you scattered, peace you established, countries subdued, hunger assuaged, boyars you schooled, towns you planted, your church you increased, your property tended, men and women and children you saved. . . . The few that you wounded you graciously cured; the few you offended you instantly cheered," and so forth.

Hilarion's whole Discourse is written in biblical language. The author not only uses this language himself but also introduces into his work a large number of biblical quotations. In certain passages the influence of Church chants, tropes, and acathists is also perceptible.[9] In the first, dogmatic

---

[8] Vladimir's Christian name.

[9] See F. G. Kalugin, "Ilarion, mitropolit Kievskii, i yevo tserkovno-uchitel'nye proizvedeniya" (Hilarion, Metropolitan of Kiev, and his Ecclesiastico-Instructional Works), in *Pam. Drev. tserkovno-uchitel'noy-literatury* (Monuments of Early Russian Ecclesiastical-Instructional Literature), ed. A. I. Ponomarev (St. Petersburg, 1894), Pt. 1, pp. 55–56.

part of the *Discourse,* Hilarion was considerably influenced by the *Discourse* of Ephrem Syrus on the Transfiguration and somewhat influenced by one of the colloquies of Cyril of Jerusalem, as was further pointed out by Shevyrov.[10] In the *Discourse* one also catches echoes from apocryphal literature, saints' lives,[11] and other sources.

In turn Hilarion's *Discourse,* especially the part constituting the eulogy of Vladimir, exercised an influence first of all on a whole series of Russian literary monuments. This influence is manifest in the *Prologue* eulogy of Vladimir (twelfth- thirteenth centuries), in the Volynian chronicler's eulogy of Vladimir, son of Vasilko, and his brother Mstislav (thirteenth century), in the life of Leontius of Rostov (fourteenth-fifteenth centuries), in the life of Stephen of Permia written by Epiphanius the Wise, and in several other monuments.[12] In the thirteenth century the Serbian monk Domentian utilized Hilarion's *Discourse* in two of his lives, those of the Serbian saints Symeon and Savva. Finally, curiously enough, we find echoes of the Vladimir eulogy from Hilarion's *Discourse* in the verses of the seventeenth century Ukrainian writer, Kassian Sakovich.

There were some very striking examples of the flowery rhetorical sermon here in the twelfth century as well. One of the prominent mid-century preacher-orators was a second Russian metropolitan, Clement of Smolensk, whom the chronicle signalizes as a bookman and philosopher without equal in the land of Rus. A typical peculiarity of Clement's writings as shown in his only extant, and textually complicated, work, the *Epistle to the Presbyter Thomas,* was an allegorico-symbolical manner of interpreting biblical texts and the world of nature. To judge from the epistle, which was "interpreted," that is, amplified and adapted, by some monk named Athanasius, Thomas had rebuked Clement for relying in his works not on the "Church Fathers" but on Homer, Aristotle, and Plato. This rebuke, of itself, regardless of its justification, argues for the work of Clement of Smolensk having been on the same high level as that of the prominent orators of the Byzantine middle ages.[13]

But the most talented and prolific exponent of the pompous, stylistically

[10] *Istoriya russkoy slovesnosti* (History of Russian Literature) (Moscow, 1860), 2nd ed., Pt. 2, p. 26. For further details see M. P. Petrovskii's article, *Ilarion, Mitropolit Kievskii, i Domentian, ieromonakh Khilandarskii* (Ilarion, Metropolitan of Kiev, and Domentian, Monk-Priest of Khilandar), *Izvestiya otd. russk. yaz. i slov.* (News of the Division of Russian Language and Literature) (1908), Bk. IV, pp. 89–94.

[11] See I. N. Zhdanov, *op. cit.,* pp. 13–16.

[12] Cf. in the life of Leontius of Rostov: "Rome praises Peter and Paul, Greece, the Emperor Constantine; the land and country of Rus, Prince Volodimer; the Rostov district blesses thee, great Bishop Leontius."

[13] On Clement of Smolensk, see N. K. Nikolskii, *O literaturnykh trudakh Klimenta Smolyaticha, pisatelya XII v.* (On the Literary Works of Clement of Smolensk, Twelfth Century Writer) (St. Petersburg, 1902).

elaborate sermon among us in the latter half of the twelfth century was Cyril, Bishop of Turov, who also revealed himself as a very unusual poet in the prayers he composed. Such extremely scant information as we have about his life comes only from such a none-too-trustworthy source as a note about him found in a fifteenth century copy of the old *Prologue*. To judge from this note, Cyril was the son of wealthy parents, was born in Turov, capital city of the principality of Turov, near Kiev. He early became a monk-ascetic and was much given to book reading and to "the interpretation of godly writings." His fame spread throughout the Turov district, and upon the urgent request of prince and people he was appointed Bishop of Turov. In enumerating Cyril's works, the *Prologue* account mentions his polemic against the heretic Bishop Theodorets, a series of epistles to Prince Andrew Bogolyubsky, based on the Gospels and the prophetic books, discourses on "the Lord's" holidays, and "many other edifying discourses," prayers, eulogies of saints, a great penitential canon, and "very many other works" besides.

Works which may unquestionably be assigned to Cyril of Turov are eight discourses on various Church holidays, two collects, about twenty-two prayers, and one canon.[14] Cyril's discourses are principally known as part of the so-called "festival manuals," collections of sermons and collects arranged for use on particularly solemn feast days and chiefly penned by the Byzantine "Church Fathers," John Chrysostom, Gregory the Theologian, Theodore of Studion, Cyril of Alexandria, and others. That the works of our author should be found in what the old-time Russian bookman regarded as such august company indicates the great esteem in which he was held.

Cyril of Turov, in such sermons of his as are extant, made almost no comment on the burning questions of his own day and showed no such pronounced publicistic proclivities as Hilarion. An exception is his "Parable of the Human Soul and Body and of the Transgression of God's Commandments," based on the Talmudic fable of the blind man and the lame man and identifiable as the polemic against Bishop Theodore ("Theodorets") of Rostov mentioned in the *Prologue* life of Cyril. Theodore was maneuvering to obtain for Rostov an autonomous episcopal chair, independent of the Kiev metropolitanate. Cyril felt that his presuming to do so was an imposition and came out against it in his "Parable."[15]

[14] Principal editions of the works of Cyril of Turov: K. Kalaidovich, *Pamyatniki rossiiskoy slovesnosti XII v.* (Monuments of Russian Twelfth Century Literature) (Moscow, 1821), and M. I. Sukhomlinov, *Rukopisi grafa A. S. Uvarova* (Manuscripts of Count A. S. Uvarov), Vol. II, *Pamyatniki slovesnosti* (Monuments of Literature) (St. Petersburg, 1858), Pt. 1. In 1880 the works of Cyril of Turov were published in Kiev by Bishop Eugene. See also *Pam. drev. tserk.-uchit. lit.* (Monuments of Early Russian Ecclesiastico-Instructional Literature), Pt. 1, pp. 126–177.

[15] See I. P. Yeremin, "Parable of the Blind Man and the Lame Man in Early Russian Literature," *Izv. otd. russk. yaz. i slov.* (News of the Division of Russian Language and Literature of the Academy of Sciences) (1925), Vol. XXX, pp. 323–352.

All his sermons are holiday eulogies with a lyric and often a dramatic tinge, designed to interpret by means of allegory and symbolical parallels and comparisons the significance of the holiday. Although powerfully influenced by the Byzantine "Church Fathers" and orators, Cyril of Turov was none the less no mere compiler mechanically taking over foreign models; he shows genuine creative talent and unquestionable poetic inspiration. He falls short of Hilarion's harmony and logical precision in the arrangement of material; his language is often marked by excessive exuberance and a sort of rhetorical self-sufficiency, but all his sermons none the less reveal him as a poet and orator of no mean ability. Cyril of Turov openly set preachers the task of surpassing secular writers in elegance and beauty of language. In one of his discourses, he said:

If historians and poets, that is, chroniclers and song writers, incline their ear to tales of bygone wars and conflicts between tsars that they may give verbal adornment to what they have heard and glorify with their crown of praise those who fought stoutly for their tsar and did not flee from before the enemy, then how much more ought we to add praise to praise for those courageous and mighty generals of God who have fought stoutly for God's Son, their tsar, our Lord Jesus Christ.

To get an idea of Cyril's homiletic style, let us study his *Discourse on the First Sunday After Easter.*

Here, having spoken of the significance of the Sunday after Easter and contrasted it with the feast of Easter, Cyril draws a picture of the renewal of nature in spring, relating it symbolically to the spiritual renewal of man in the Christian religion:

Today the heavens are bright again, freed from dark clouds as from a coarse garment, and by the clearness of the air they declare the glory of God; I speak not of the visible heavens but of the spiritual; that is, of the apostles who, ascending unto Zion, perceived the Lord and, having forgotten the sorrow and affliction wrought by the Jews, and having overcome the fear that was in their hearts, 'neath the sheltering presence of the Holy Ghost, preach plainly the resurrection of Christ. Today the sun in glory ascends the sky and rejoicing warms the earth; so Christ, the sun of righteousness, rose from the grave and saves all those that believe on him. Today the moon descending from its height does honor to a larger luminary; so the Old Testament, according to Scripture, ceased work on Saturday, while the Church does honor to Christ's Testament with Sunday. Today the winter of sin is dispelled by repentance and the ice of unbelief has melted away before knowledge: the winter of idolatry has been banished by apostolic teaching and by the Christian religion, as the ice of Thomas' unbelief melted at the sight of Christ's wounded side. Today spring is in its glory, bringing the world of nature to life, and the stormy winds, now blowing gently, bring increase of fruits, and the seed-nurturing earth puts forth green grass. Thus the lovely spring is faith in Christ, whereby, through baptism, human nature is reborn; and the stormy winds are sinful desires transformed by repentance into virtue and giving increase to the fruits of edification. . . . Today the newborn lambs and calves frisk and leap and presently, returning to their mothers, regale themselves, and shepherds playing on their pipes cheerfully praise Christ; the lambs are gentle pagans, but the calves are the idolaters of infidel lands, who . . . having accepted the law . . . are sucking the milk of instruction. . . . Today the trees put forth shoots and fragrant flowers burst into bloom and gardens give forth sweet perfume, while the farmers, laboring in hope, call upon Christ the giver of increase. Today the plowman of the Word, putting the bull calves of the Word, to the spiritual yoke, and sinking the plow of baptism into the furrows of thought, and drawing a furrow of repentance, and planting the spiritual seed, rejoices in hopes of blessings to come.

The second part of the discourse deals with the appearance of the risen Christ to the Apostle Thomas and gives the speeches of Christ and Thomas at great length. The discourse ends with a summons to believe in Christ and an invitation to praise him.

The sermons of Cyril of Turov are characterized by symbolism and allegory and also by their saturation with tropes and figures of speech: metaphor, personification, antithesis, rhetorical questions, and exhortations. In his sermons Cyril will now and again pass directly from a lyrical eulogy of the feast to a narrative of the event associated with the feast, dramatizing this narrative by the introduction of monologues, dialogues, and poetical lamentations, and describing the events themselves as though they were actually happening at the time. A particularly effective narrative dramatization of this type is found in the *Discourse on the Man with the Palsy,* which cites the dialogue between Christ and the man whom he has healed of the palsy. Cyril also made use in his sermons of the allegory-parable method ("Parable of the Human Soul and Body," parallels to which are found in the *Talmud* and in the *Arabian Nights'* tales, and "Parable of the Man in White Robes," which goes back to the *Tale of Barlaam and Josaphat).* Finally, Cyril's use of rhythmic pattern also deserves mention: this occurs particularly in his prayers, where the style in the main resembles that of the discourses.

In theme and style Cyril of Turov, as has been said, was not original. He was a great borrower, particularly from Byzantine authors, ranging all the way from the "Church Fathers"—Gregory the Theologian, John Chrysostom, Ephrem Syrus, and many others—to the Greek orators and grammarians of his own time. Thus the *Discourse on the First Sunday After Easter* is much influenced by the analogous discourse of Gregory the Theologian and by one of John Chrysostom's; the *Discourse on the Myrrh-bearing Women* was similarly influenced by discourses of Gregory of Nicomedea and Epiphanius of Cyprus and also by a canon of Simeon Metaphrastes.

It seems probable that Cyril of Turov read Greek himself, and he may even have gone through a rigorous schooling in the writer's art under the direct tutelage of one of those itinerant Greek scholars who undoubtedly appeared in Rus from time to time at that period.[16]

In order to give a concrete idea of Cyril's manner of borrowing from his sources, I shall quote a parallel to his *Discourse on the First Sunday After Easter* from Gregory the Divine's discourse on the same holiday, where he, too, speaks of the joyous renewal of nature:

Today the sky is pellucid; today the sun is higher and more golden; today the disk of the moon is brighter and the host of stars clearer. Today the waves are at peace with the shore, the clouds with the sun, the winds with the air, the earth with the plants, and the plants with our glances. Today the springs gush more limpid, today the rivers flow more abundantly, freed from winter's bonds. The meadow is fragrant, the plants blossom, the grass is clipped, and lambs leap in the golden fields. . . . Already the farmer is setting his plow to the earth, lifting his gaze on high and calling upon the giver of increase to aid him; already he is putting the ox under the yoke, cutting a splendid furrow, and rejoicing in his hopes. Already the shepherds and oxherds are tuning their pipes and playing a pastoral lay and welcoming in the spring under the trees and on the rocks. Already the industrious bee . . . shows its wisdom by flitting over the meadows.

The symbolical application of this picture, expressed in few words, does not come, with Gregory the Theologian, until the end of the description: "The queen of the seasons comes forth to meet the queen of days and brings as a gift" . . . whereas with Cyril of Turov, influenced as he was by the latest Byzantine orators, this application becomes an allegorized description of spring and is given piecemeal in various places—and at some length.

In summing up his observations on the relation of Cyril of Turov's sermons to their sources, V. P. Vinogradov, the most recent student of them, concludes:

The work of the celebrated early Russian orator is wholly of a compilatory character. But even compilation varies in kind and in value. There is compilation that is crudely mechanical and there can be compilation showing talent and artistry. The work of Cyril is an artistic mosaic. Here the minute individual elements are taken, like precious stones, ready-made from various sources. From these sources the plan itself is likewise taken, the design in accordance with which these literary pearls are to be set. . . . But the choice of them, their fitting to-

16 On the influence of Byzantine literature on Cyril of Turov, see: M. I. Sukhomlinov, "On the Works of Cyril of Turov," in *Rukopisi grafa A. S. Uvarova* (Manuscripts of Count A. S. Uvarov) Vol. II, pp. vii–lxxii, reprinted in *Issledovaniya po drevney russkoy literature* (Studies in Early Russian Literature) (St. Petersburg, 1908), pp. 273–349; A. I. Ponomarev, "Cyril, Bishop of Turov, and his Sermons," *Pamyatniki drevnerusskoy tserkovno-uchitel'noy literatury* (Monuments of Early Russian Ecclesiastico-Instructional Literature), Pt. 1, pp. 87–125, 184–198; V. P. Vinogradov, "O kharaktere propovednicheskovo tvorchestva Kirilla, episkopa Turovskovo" (On the Character of the Homiletic Genius of Cyril, Bishop of Turov) in the collection of articles, *V pamyat' stoletiya Moskovskoy dukhovnoy akademii* (In Commemoration of the Centenary of the Moscow Ecclesiastical Academy) (Sergiev Posad, 1915), pp. 313–392.

gether, in short, their blending into a new scheme of effects—all this is carried out independently and in a highly artistic manner.[17]

Let us conclude with some examples of rhythmically articulated language as used by Cyril of Turov. The most common method of articulation is through a series of hanging clauses, each ending with a verb:

> A model youth—celibacy ever preferring,
> the monkish order considering
> as ceaselessly extolling
> Christ, and miracles by God's grace performing . . .
> but in him living
> and for him dying
> and to him vows and prayers rendering . . .
>   —From the Sermon on Palm Sunday

Sometimes the final verbs make a rhymed couplet, as they do in Hilarion:

> Then the copper gate was rent,
> and the iron doorpost bent.
>   —From the Sermon on Easter

The extant discourses of Cyril of Turov, as was said above, show almost no reaction to contemporary life. But we cannot claim to possess all that Cyril wrote. If the *Prologue* account is to be trusted, he wrote not only an arraignment of Bishop Theodore but many epistles of Andrew Bogolyubsky as well. In these epistles in particular, granted their existence, Bishop Cyril can hardly have failed to mention some of the facts of contemporary life and would undoubtedly have expressed some reaction to them.

SAINTS' LIVES

With translated lives as a basis, saints' lives of our own also appeared here as early as the eleventh century. From the very beginning this literature was closely associated with the political interests of the time. Relatively few lives are extant from the earliest period as compared with later times. It is typical, however, that more lives of lay members of the ruling class were written than lives in which members of the clergy figure. This circumstance admirably points up the subordinate political role that the Church played here from the very first.

The most popular of our oldest biographical works were those associated with the names of Princes Boris and Gleb, sons of Vladimir. Works devoted to them include the chronicle account of their murder by Svyatopolk, and

[17] *Op. cit.*, pp. 392–393.

the *Prologue* legend and saints' calendar narrative, the *Legend and Passion and Eulogy of the Holy Martyrs Boris and Gleb*, ascribed, though on insufficient grounds, to the monk James, and Nestor's *Narrative of the Life and Death of the Blessed Martyrs Boris and Gleb*. The question of the interrelationship of these monuments and of their chronology still remains in dispute. The only point that may be regarded as more or less established is that the chronicle account of the death of Boris and Gleb preceded the anonymous *Legend* and Nestor's *Narrative* and influenced them in some degree.[18] Touching the question of the relationship existing between the *Legend* and the *Narrative*, the majority of older scholars (Makarius, Golubinsky, Khrushchov) considered that the *Legend* was written earlier than the *Narrative* and influenced it. This view was developed and further probed by S. A. Bugoslavsky.[19] The contrary opinion was advanced by A. A. Shakhmatov in his *Investigations into the Earliest Chronicle Compilations*, and received the support of N. I. Serebryansky (in his monograph, *Early Russian Princes' Lives*) and of D. I. Abramovich (in the preface to his edition of the lives of Boris and Gleb). Afterwards, however, Shakhmatov was led by S. A. Bugoslavsky's arguments to retract his earlier pronouncement as to the dependence of the *Legend* on the *Narrative*, while continuing to hold that there was no dependence in the other direction.[20] Both monuments date from the end of the eleventh or the beginning of the twelfth century. The oldest copy of the first dates from the twelfth century, of the second, from the fourteenth century.

Let us first consider the anonymous *Legend*.

After a brief eulogy the author enumerates the sons of Vladimir, mentioning that Svyatopolk was born "of two fathers who were brothers" since Vladimir, while yet a pagan, had taken the wife of his brother Yaropolk—whom he had murdered—when she was already "with child." Then without wasting any words, the author hastens to pass to his exposition of events. Twenty-eight years after being baptized, Vladimir fell grievously ill. At this moment Boris arrived from Rostov and his father dispatched him with an

[18] However, A. A. Shakhmatov assumes that the chronicle account, the *Legend*, and the *Narrative* all go back to a specific inextant life of Boris and Gleb, *Povest vremennykh let* ('Tale of Bygone Years) ('St. Petersburg, 1916), Vol. I, p. lxxv.

[19] "K voprosy o kharaktere i ob'yome literaturnoy deyatel'nosti prep. Nestora" (On the Question of the Character and Extent of the Literary Activity of the Reverend Nestor), *Izv. otd. russk. yaz. i slov.* (News of the Division of Russian Language and Literature of the Academy of Sciences) (1914), Bk. I, pp. 135–143.

[20] See *Povest vremennykh let*, Vol. I, pp. lxviii–lxxvii. Latest editions of the *Legend* and the *Narrative* are D. I. Abramovich's "Zhitiya sv. Borisa i Gleba i sluzhby im" (Lives of Saints Boris and Gleb and Services to Them), Pt. 2, *Pam. Drev. Lit.*, Pt. 2, *Pub. otd. russk. yaz. i slov.* (Publications of the Division of Russian Language and Literature of the Academy of Sciences) (St. Petersburg, 1916), and S. A. Bugoslavskii's *Pam'yatki xi–xvii vv. pro knyaziv Borisa i Gleba* (Monuments of the Eleventh-Seventeenth Centuries of the Princes Boris and Gleb) (Kiev, 1928).

army against the Pechenegs, who were on their way to attack Rus. Boris, "blessed" and "quick to obey," gladly set out against the enemy: "Here I stand before your eyes, ready to do whatever it is the will of your heart to command," he said to his father. Failing to make contact with the Pechenegs, however, Boris turned back, and at this point a messenger informed him of Vladimir's death and of the fact that Svyatopolk was keeping his father's death a secret. Upon hearing the news, Boris collapsed and, weeping so copiously as to be incapable of speech, said in his heart: "Woe is me, the light of my eyes, the dayspring and dawn of my countenance, my bridle has been taken from me, the admonition of my unwisdom! Woe is me, my father and my lord! To whom shall I turn, to whom shall I now look up? Where shall I satisfy my hunger for benign instruction such as yours and for your wise counsel? Woe is me! Woe is me! My sun has set; I can not go on living. . . . My heart is sad, my feelings confound my sense, and I know not to whom to turn, before whom to lay this bitter grief." He has an older brother (Svyatopolk) who lives for earthly vanity and who is planning his murder; but if he is killed—thinks Boris to himself—he will be a martyr in the sight of his Lord, because it is written: The Lord sets his face against the proud but is gracious to the humble; and again, in the Acts of the Apostles, it is written: Any man who says that he loves God but hates his brother speaks falsehood; and again it is written: In love there is no fear; perfect love banishes fear. And he reflected: What shall I say or what shall I do? I shall go to my brother and I shall say: "Be to me a father; you are my brother, my elder brother. What do you require of me, my lord?"

What if I go to my father's house? Boris next thought. There they may incite me to drive out my brother, as my father once did for the sake of worldly glory, before he became a Christian. But what would I gain thereby in the future life? What did my father's brothers gain by it, or my father? Where is their glory and all their wealth: silver, gold, sumptuous feasts and swift horses, fine large houses, tribute past reckoning? Already all this is as though it had not been: it all vanished with them, and none of it profits them, neither estates, nor multitude of servants, nor fame in this world. Wherefore even Solomon said, after he had studied all, seen and investigated all, and got all: All is vanity of vanities and everything is but vanity. Nothing profits a man but good deeds, true faith and unfeigned love.

And as he went his way he thought of the beauty and strength of his body; the tears welled up and he tried to hold them back but could not. And all who saw him sobbing lamented for his noble body and his upright mind and each man groaned in his spirit with heartfelt sorrow and all were beside themselves with grief. "And indeed," the author adds in his own person, "who could help lamenting when he pictured with the eyes of his heart how death should destroy this?"

But presently Boris' sorrow was replaced by joy at thought of the reward that awaited him in heaven.

In the meantime Svyatopolk, settling in Kiev after his father's death, suborned the citizens with rich gifts, then sent men to Boris with the flattering offer of his love and promises of lavish endowment, while he himself set out secretly by night for Vyshegorod, near Kiev, where he obtained the support of Governor Putsha and the men of Vyshegorod. The Devil, enemy of the good man since time immemorial, aware that Boris put all his trust in God, caught in his snares, as he had once caught Cain, Svyatopolk, this second Cain, and prompted him to destroy all his father's heirs so that he might get the whole power for himself.

Boris halted at the river Alta and pitched camp there. The retainers advised him to go to Kiev and with their support seize his father's throne. When Boris refused to take the field against his elder brother, the retainers forsook him; only his servants remained.

In tears and prayer, recalling to memory the death of other martyrs like himself, Boris awaited his fate. Those sent by Svyatopolk arrived while Boris was saying his morning prayers. They pierced the prince's body with a lance and murdered his beloved Hungarian servant, George, when he attempted to intervene in his lord's behalf. Grievously wounded, but not to the death, Boris besought them to give him a little time to pray; then, having ended his prayer, he touchingly addressed the soldiers, weeping and proposing that they finish the task they had been charged with. Hearing him, they could not speak for their tears, but in his heart every man praised him for his greatness of soul and for his meekness.

With Boris were killed many of his servants. His body was conveyed on a cart, but on the way, Boris started to raise his head and Svyatopolk ordered two Varangians to put a sword through his heart. He was buried in Vyshegorod in the Church of St. Basil.

It was now the turn of Gleb, who ruled in Murom. He was still in ignorance of Vladimir's death. Svyatopolk summoned him as if at the instance of their seriously indisposed father. Gleb set out at once, but at Smolensk, through messengers sent by his brother Yaroslav to warn him not to go to Svyatopolk, he learned of Vladimir's death and of the murder of Boris. Upon hearing these tidings, Gleb cried out in bitter lamentation and heartfelt grief, saying:

O woe is me, my lord! Two sorrows make me to lament and groan; with a double mourning am I bereaved and afflicted. Woe is me! Woe is me! I weep for my father; I also lament, with exceeding despair, for you, O brother and lord, Boris.

. . . Why did you meet destruction not at the hand of an enemy but at your brother's? Woe is me! It were better for me to die with you than to live on in this world solitary and bereft of you. . . . O my dear brother and lord! Pray for me who am beyond hope that I may be deemed worthy to endure the same passion and be where you are rather than go on living in this deceitful world.

Suddenly the wicked servants of Svyatopolk arrive with drawn swords, pitiless slaughterers, fierce brother-haters, endowed with the hearts of savage beasts. With an imploring look, brokenhearted and his eyes brimming with tears, Gleb beseeches Svyatopolk's warriors not to slay him, promising to be servant to his brother. "Do not reap me, my life is not yet ripe," he prays. "Do not reap the ear that is not yet full but still moist with the milk of innocence! Do not cut the twig not yet full-grown but capable of fruit!" But the murderers are inflexible. Gleb bids farewell to his father, his mother, Boris, Yaroslav, to his retainers, and even to Svyatopolk; then he addresses his father and his brother Boris again, as if seeking their protection, then says a last prayer, after which, at the command of Svyatopolk's soldier Goresyar, Gleb's cook Torchin slays him with a knife, like an innocent lamb, on the fifth day of the month, on Monday. Gleb's body was cast in a desert place. Passing merchants and shepherds and huntsmen saw above it now a pillar of fire, now burning candles, or heard the song of angels. So Gleb's body lay neglected until Yaroslav vanquished the accursed Svyatopolk. The victory took place on that same river Alta where Boris had been murdered and whither Svyatopolk came with a great number of Pechenegs. The battle is described in the style that had become traditional for tales of war: "And the plain beside the river Alta was covered with the multitude of soldiers, and at sunrise they clashed and the carnage on both sides was terrible. And they clashed three times and fought the whole day through." Toward evening Yaroslav was victorious and the accursed Svyatopolk fled, and he was beset by a demon and his bones were loosened so that he could not sit his horse but was carried in a litter. When he recovered, he fled, driven by the wrath of God, to the waste land between the Czechs and the Lyakhs and there gave up the ghost, having experienced the vengeance of the Lord, deprived in this world not only of his principality but of his life and doomed in the other to torment everlasting. And his tomb exists to this day and from it issues an evil odor "as a testimony to men."

From that time dissensions ceased in the land of Rus and Yaroslav assumed full sovereignty. He found the body of Gleb, uncorrupted and fragrant, and laid it in Vyshegorod beside the body of Boris.

The *Legend* ends with a eulogy of Boris and Gleb and a prayer addressed to them and to God. Later on, a brief descriptive sketch of Boris' outward appearance and inner nature and items about the brothers' posthumous miracles were incorporated in the *Legend*. The sketch of Boris, typical example of early Russian literary portraiture, reads thus:

> Now this pious Boris, being a good son, hearkened to his father, and was obedient to his father in everything. In body he was handsome, tall, round-faced, broad-shouldered, narrow-hipped, with kindly eyes, a cheerful face, scarcely any beard or mustache, for he was still young, and with a kingly air about him, strong of body, fair in all ways as a flower in the bloom of his youth, brave in battle, wise in counsel, and intelligent withal, and the grace of God flowered in him.

The *Legend* of Boris and Gleb departs considerably from the canonical form of the Byzantine saint's life. It lacks any consecutive exposition of the life of the saints as a whole or even of its basic moments, such as saints' lives usually had, and gives only one episode, their murder. The *Legend* is more like a history, striving to give an exact description of events and facts, complete with names of historic places and persons, and is at the same time a work made lyric by laments, monologues, prayers, and meditations put into the mouths of Boris and Gleb. The author himself does not view with detachment the events he narrates but shows a lyrical heightening of emotion when the narrative reaches its dramatic climax, and particularly at the end, in the eulogy of Boris and Gleb. But, though striving to be documentary as to purely outward circumstances and as to names and localities, in all other respects the author follows the typical pattern for lives of saints. All that Boris and Gleb think and say, how they act and how they are treated before their murder, is strictly the fruit of the author's invention, or, more exactly, the result of his adapting the ready-made diagrams and stereotypes of hagiography to the fate of given concrete personages. Rhetoric and lyric pathos, in many instances showing a good deal of talent, dominate the *Legend* throughout and are used as a substitute for any attempt to individualize the fate of the main characters. The author proposes to depict the psychological state of two young brothers confronted by the threat of death (he is particularly successful with the younger, Gleb), the struggle that takes place in them between their fear and despair and their faith in a heavenly reward; but this description is generalized, so to speak, from what he has heard, or thinks, pious persons in general experience under such circumstances. Just as general and unindividualized is the portrait given of Boris, a synthesis of the idealized inner and outer qualities of the Christian hero.

Although observing a superficial exactitude, the author is not only unable to give an honest, realistic description of the characters of Boris and Gleb, but does not even aspire to do so. (They were murdered in 1015, while the *Legend* was written at least sixty years later, consequently not by a contemporary.) Like all saints' lives, the *Legend* is, first and foremost, a tendentious work which sets itself a definite publicistic problem—in the given instance the preservation and maintenance of the political situation which, in the person of Yaroslav, had come out victorious in the settling of private accounts between the princes. The literary apotheosis of Boris and Gleb and their ecclesiastical canonization sixty years after their death—incidentally the first introduction of Russian saints into the Christian pantheon—was primarily a matter of obvious political calculation.

The literary and ecclesiastical championship of Boris and Gleb and the denunciation leveled at Svyatopolk performed two tasks simultaneously: on the one hand fratricidal quarrels between the princes were condemned, and on the other, through the whole conduct of the murdered brothers in not wishing to lift their hand against an elder brother, the idea of seniority in the system of princely succession was pointed up and reinforced with a view to strengthening the new feudal system. All this suited Yaroslav very well, and that is why he pressed the canonization of Boris and Gleb, while the Church, supporting princely political interests, seconded his initiative in word and deed.

It is curious that the unselfish act of Boris' retainer George, who perished only for love of his prince and who, according to Christian ideas, thereby exhibited the height of Christian virtue, is mentioned in the *Legend* only in passing. From the standpoint of political effect, a common soldier and his deed did not much matter, and neither the literary nor the ecclesiastical apotheosis of such a nameless hero came within the hagiographer-publicist's purview.

The saints-calendar narrative about Boris and Gleb contains an assemblage of the battle formulae typical of martial episodes:

It was on Friday at sunrise that Svyatopolk rushed up with his Pechenegs, and the two armies met, and there was terrible carnage, the like of which had never occurred in Rus. And they seized each other by the arm and hacked, and blood flowed down the valley; three times they clashed, and darkness enveloped them as they fought. And there was loud echoing thunder and heavy rain and lightning. Whenever the lightning flashed, their weapons flashed in their hands, and many of the faithful saw angels helping Yaroslav. As for Svyatopolk, he turned and fled.

The anonymous *Legend* enjoyed a very great popularity and is extant in more than one hundred and seventy copies; it became the basis for a religious poem about Boris and Gleb, but, as we have said, it was not a canonical life. This gap was filled in by Nestor, who wrote, in addition to the *Narrative of the Life and Death of Boris and Gleb,* a life of Theodosius, prior of the Crypt Monastery. His *Narrative* reflected the characteristic traits of Byzantine hagiography. After beginning with a prayer to God for help in writing the life, and a confession of the "coarseness and ignorance" of his heart, Nestor goes on to tell of the creation of the world and of man's fall. Next he deals with Christ's atonement for human sin and with Christianity's penetration to the land of Rus, which had at first lived "in the delusion of idolatry." God made the land of Rus his personal care, for no man told here about Christ nor did any apostles journey through here or preach the word of God. At that time the whole land of Rus was ruled by Prince Vladimir, a righteous man, kind to the poor and to widows and orphans, but in religion a pagan. And God enjoined him to become a Christian as he had once enjoined Placidus. To the pagan Placidus, a kindly and righteous man, Christ, whom he had honored without knowing him, appeared and bade him be baptized. Placidus was baptized, and his wife and children with him, and received the name Eustaphius. And so it was with Vladimir. He too was sent a revelation from God, was baptized, and received the name of Basil. Yesterday he was still ordering everyone to bring sacrifices to the idols; today he is commanding his nobles and all his people to be baptized. In this, Nestor, like Hilarion, emphasizes Vladimir's independence of Byzantium in the matter of baptism. But where Hilarion says that after Vladimir all were baptized, some of their own free will, but some, too, under compulsion, for fear of the prince, since in him piety was joined to power, Nestor asserts that all accepted baptism with joy.

Then comes the story of Boris and Gleb, who shone like "two stars shining in the darkness." From childhood Boris read godly books and passed his time in prayer, while day and night Gleb listened to his reading, never leaving his brother's side. The two brothers bestowed alms on all who were in need. The fact that Boris' baptismal name was Roman and Gleb's David prompts the author to a somewhat prolix comparison between the two Russian princes and the Byzantine saints Roman and David. As also happens in the Life of Alexis, Man of God, young Boris marries merely to comply with his father's wishes: "This the blessed one did not for lust of the flesh, not for that," Nestor explains, "but because of the kingly law and out of obedience to his father." The anonymous Legend speaks of Boris having been sent by his father to Rostov, and Gleb to Murom, but in the Narrative Boris turns up at Vladimir, while Gleb, being still a child, lives with his father. In his province Boris is such a model of kindness and gentleness that all the people marvel at him. Svyatopolk plots to destroy Boris so that after his father's death he may seize all the land of Rus for himself. Learning of this, Vladimir summons Boris to Kiev to prevent Svyatopolk's making an attempt upon his life. Svyatopolk, however, thinking that Boris means to seize the throne after their father's death, becomes still more incensed against him. So was it also with the patriarch Jacob. He loved his sons Joseph and Benjamin and for that reason Joseph was hated by his brethren, who assumed that he wanted to rule over them.

From this point on, facts are given in the *Narrative* approximately as they are in the *Legend,* except that here specific names and localities are almost never indicated. Thus, Boris sets out against "warriors" (not, concretely, against the Pechenegs as it says in the *Legend*), Boris' and Gleb's places of death are not mentioned, and so forth. Nor is anything said in the *Narrative* about Yaroslav's battle with Svyatopolk. The inhabitants of the "province" drive Svyatopolk out, he flees to foreign lands, and there "his life came to an end." After this, Yaroslav takes the power into his own hands. The *Narrative* ends with a detailed description of the miracles performed at the tombs of Boris and Gleb (analogous miracles in the *Legend* are a later addition), reproaches directed against young princes who show disobedience to older princes, a eulogy of Boris and Gleb, of their tomb, and of Vyshegorod where the brothers were buried, and with a request to readers to pray "to the blessed martyrs" for him, "Nestor the sinful."

Written in accordance with the set pattern of Byzantine hagiography, Nestor's *Narrative* is a fairly typical example of a hagiographical work. Rhetoric and edification are its predominant traits. As a literary manifestation it is less significant than the anonymous *Legend:* it lacks the relative lyric freshness perceptible in the *Legend;* its rhetoric is too cold and pompous, and the style highly artificial. This circumstance is apparently why it was less popular than the *Legend,* having survived in only twenty and some odd copies. In it we find approximately the same publicistic tendency as in the *Legend.*

In connection with the apotheosis of Boris and Gleb, in 1175, on May 2, the day upon which the feast to their memory was celebrated, an ecclesiastical personage to us unknown delivered in the cathedral at Chernigov a eulogistic sermon in honor of the brothers which is known as the *Discourse on the Princes.* It was composed in the interests of the future great prince of Kiev, Svyatoslav, who figures in the *Tale of Igor's Expedition,* at that time a competitor with Oleg Svyatoslavich, a junior prince, for the throne of Chernigov. The idea of the obedience of younger princes to older and the condemnation of quarrels between princes are even more energetically voiced in this discourse than in the *Legend of Boris and Gleb.* We read here:

Hearken, you princes who are opposing your elder brothers, raising armies against them and bringing in infidels! Will not God convict us at the last judgment through these two saints? See how they endured at their brother's hand the loss not only of dominion but of life as well! Whereas you cannot stand even a word from a brother, and for a trifling offense you raise mortal enmity . . . ! You ought to be ashamed to be at odds with your brothers, with others of the same religion as yourselves, and come before God with fear and lamentation! You are proposing to forfeit fame and honor for the sake of rancor and enmity.

An important part in the development of biographical literature was played by the Kiev-Crypt Monastery, which came into being toward the middle of the eleventh century and became the religious center of Rus and guiding spirit of the national ideology. An intramural chronicle was kept, embodying a series of life legends, on the basis of which there appeared, in part during the first quarter of the thirteenth century, a monument later called the *Kiev-Crypt Paterikon*. The point of departure was an exchange of letters between Simon, Bishop of Vladimir (died 1226), formerly a monk in the Kiev-Crypt Monastery, and Polycarp, a monk in that monastery. Dissatisfied with the humble role of an ordinary monk in the monastery, Polycarp, a man of unusual literary gifts and wide reading, complained to his friend Simon about having been passed over. In reply to Polycarp, who had shown a lack of the basic monastic virtue, humility, Simon wrote a reproachful letter, incorporating in it for his edification a few brief stories from the lives of Crypt monks and an account of the building of the Crypt church. All this material was supposed to impress Polycarp with a sense of the sanctity of the cloister where his modest position hung heavy on him. Evidently Simon's exhortation had its effect on Polycarp, and he in turn, in the form of an appeal to the Crypt prior Akindinus, added to Simon's work a number of new tales from the lives of the Kiev-Crypt monks.

Later on, just when is not known, the letters of Simon and Polycarp were brought together. The oldest manuscript including such a joint text of the two writers—with the addition of the legend of the earliest Crypt monks, Nestor's *Life of Theodosius,* prior of the Crypt Monastery, and certain other materials—dates from the beginning of the fifteenth century (1406). It was produced at Tver through the enterprise of Arsenius, Bishop of Tver, after whom it is called the "Arsenius" redaction of the *Kiev-Crypt Paterikon.* Also during the fifteenth century, in 1462, a new edition of the monument was brought out at the Crypt Monastery through the initiative of the monk Cassianus, the so-called "Cassian" edition, where it is for the first time given the name, *Crypt Paterikon.*[21] This in turn underwent further revisions down to the seventeenth century, when, in 1661, the *Kiev-Crypt Paterikon,* in an arrangement by Archimandrite Innocentius Gizel, was printed at Kiev.

[21] Both these editions were published by D. I. Abramovich in the Archaeographical Commission's series, *Pamyatniki slavyano-russkoy pismennosti:* "Paterik Kievo-Pecherskovo monastyrya" (Monuments of Slavo-Russian Literature: Paterikon of the Kiev-Crypt Monastery) (St. Petersburg, 1911). A very fine translation of the *Kiev-Crypt Paterikon* into modern Russian, showing a true artistic sense, was made by a woman pupil of Buslayev, M. Viktorova: *Kievo-Pecherskii paterik po drevnim rukopisyam v perelozhenii na sovremennyi russkii yazyk* (The Kiev-Crypt Paterikon of the Early Manuscripts Paraphrased into Modern Russian) (Kiev, 1870).

The principal sources for the writings of Simon and Polycarp were the inextant *Life of Antonius,* prior of the Crypt, Nestor's *Life of Theodosius,* the Crypt chronicle, and oral traditions. Both writers did some of their writing from memory. A marked influence was exerted on their writings by translated Byzantine paterikons, the *Sinaitic* and the *Jerusalem,* and also by the works of certain "Church Fathers" (Ephrem Syrus, John Climacus, and others). Quite possibly it was chancing upon the Grecophil life of Antonius that moved Simon to undertake a work devoted to the glorification of the Kiev-Crypt Monastery and its prominent worthies.[22] In Simon and Polycarp's work the Greek tendencies of this life were considerably toned down and the nationalistic aspect was advanced to first place.

The basic problem that Simon and Polycarp set themselves was the glorification of the Kiev-Crypt Monastery as religious center of Rus. This automatically exalted and reinforced the authority of the Church as a serious political factor in feudal society. At the same time it constituted a championship of the Kievan state, which had at that period lost its erstwhile political importance. The idea of glorifying the stronghold of Christianity in Rus, the Crypt Monastery, itself testified to the Russian clergy's growing consciousness of being a substantial force, a corporation exerting an influence on the historical life of Rus.

In all probability Simon began his work with an account of the building of the Crypt Church of the Virgin. The essentials of the account are as follows. In Varangia there lived a prince named Afrikanus who had two sons, Friand and Shimon. After the death of Afrikanus, his brother Yakun turned both nephews out. Shimon betook himself to the prince of Kiev, Yaroslav the Wise, and served with his son Vsevolod. When the Polovcians attacked Rus, Yaroslav's sons Izyaslav, Svyatoslav, and Vsevolod, and Shimon with them, set out against the invader. Antonius—prior of the Crypt Monastery —predicted the defeat of the Russian Army and the victory of the Polovcians; however, Antonius told Shimon that his life would be spared and that later, when his time came to die, he would be laid to rest in a church which he himself should build. The Russians did actually suffer a serious defeat on the river Alta. Shimon was wounded and, as he lay surrounded by

    [22] For further details see M. D. Prisyolkov, *Ocherki po tserkovno-politicheskoy istorii Kievskoy Rusi X–XII vv.* (Outlines of the Ecclesiastico-Political History of Kievan Rus in the Tenth-Twelfth Centuries) pp. 238–264. On the general subject of the *Kiev-Crypt Paterikon,* see: V. Yakovlev, *Drevne-kievskie religioznye skazaniya* (Early Kievan Religious Legends) (Warsaw, 1875); A. A. Shakhmatov, "Kievo-Pecherskii paterik i Pecherskaya letopis'" (Kiev-Crypt Paterikon and the Crypt Chronicle), *Izv. otd. russk. yaz. i slov.* (News of the Section of Russian Language and Literature of the Academy of Sciences) (1897), Bk. II; D. I. Abramovich, "Issledovanie o Kievo-Pecherskom paterike kak literaturnom pamyatnike" (Study of the Kiev-Crypt Paterikon as a Literary Monument) (1901), Bks. 3–4 (1902), Bks. 1–4.

corpses, saw in the sky the similitude of a church. He prayed to God and, as the result of this prayer, was healed of his wounds, whereafter he went to Antonius and Theodosius and told them about his coming to Rus. On leaving Varangia, he had taken from a cross that Afrikanus had erected, the gold belt, weighing fifty grivna, and the gold crown which had adorned the image of Christ on that cross. While he was on his way to Rus, a storm came up at sea, and it was then that Shimon first saw the church in the sky, while a voice from on high told him that he must build just such a church in Kiev. The dimensions were specified, length, breadth, and height, and it was predicted that Shimon should be buried in this church. Shimon delivered the belt and the crown to Antonius and Theodosius, and then with his whole household, including the clergy and the servants, transferred his allegiance from the Latin to the Orthodox faith. Upon his death he was buried in the Crypt Monastery as it had been foretold to him.

The story of how the Crypt Church came to be built is followed by the story of the arrival from Byzantium of four architects bringing a large amount of gold. They had been sent, it seems, by the Virgin herself, whose image in the Church of the Blachernae in Tsargrad had bidden them go to Rus to the monastery of Antonius and Theodosius and build a church there. On this occasion she had given them, as her contribution, some martyrs' relics and an icon for the church. For three days Antonius prayed God to send a sign telling him where the church should be built: let there be dew over the whole land, but let the place where the church was to be built remain dry. And so it came to pass. Then—as specified in a second prayer—the process was reversed: all around it was dry, but on the site where the church must be built there was dew. Thus was the site for the church determined. With Shimon's belt Antonius measured off the length and the breadth of the church, and Antonius prayed, and fire came down out of heaven, reducing the brushwood and blackthorn round about to ashes, drying up the dew, and leaving a hollow at the site blocked off for the church.

Ten years after the arrival of the architects, icon painters came from Tsargrad to adorn the church with icons. Approaching Kiev and seeing a church of greater size than the one they had contracted to decorate, the icon painters decided to turn back. They started to sail down the Dnieper, but twice a storm turned them upstream to Kiev, to the locality of the church. Then the painters understood that it was their obligation, laid upon them from on high, to decorate the church, and they set to work. Their efforts were attended by a miraculous appearance of the image of the Virgin, dazzling in its brilliance. From the Virgin's lips doves flew forth and fluttered about the church but would not let the icon painters catch them. And thereby all who were in the church knew it to be the dwelling place of the Holy Ghost.

The legend is curious in that it links the building of the Crypt church first with Scandinavia and secondly with Byzantium. This was due to the fact that on the one hand the Kiev-Crypt Monastery was on friendly terms with the princely house of Vsevolod, to which the house of Shimon and Varangian was bound by close family ties, while on the other we perceive the influence of a popular tendency which had been introduced by the Byzantine Church and which amounted to affirming the dependence of Russian Christendom on Byzantium; this tendency had informed the *Life of Antonius*, which was, as stated, a principal source of the *Kiev-Crypt Paterikon*. In the paterikon, however, it was considerably less pronounced than in the *Life of Antonius*: Theodosius almost always appears side by side with Antonius.

The *Kiev-Crypt Paterikon* is of interest to us, among other things, for the striking way its literary material reflects the struggle which was in progress between the monastery and the princes as the result both of their rivalry in respect to material interests and of the friction brought about by the monastery's interference in interprincely relations. At first the Kiev-Crypt Monastery attempted to maintain its independence and regarded the princes with favor only in so far as they were friendly to its growth. In the contrary event it was antagonistic to them. If Vsevolod and his son Vladimir Monomakh, patrons of the monastery, are depicted by the paterikon in a positive light, a different attitude is expressed, for example, toward Izyaslav Yaroslavich, his son Svyatopolk Izyaslavich, and his grandson Mstislav, son of Svyatopolk. Thus the story of wonder-worker Prokhor is very typical of the attitude of the paterikon toward Svyatopolk Izyaslavich.

Svyatopolk, son of Izyaslav, was a cruel and merciless prince. The distressful state of the Kievans during his reign was aggravated by Polovcian attacks, civil strife, robberies, and famine. At the same time no merchants could get through to Kiev from Galich and Przemysl with salt, and the whole land of Rus was left without salt; moreover, the merchants of Kiev took advantage of this condition to raise the price of it exorbitantly. Prokhor, a monk of the Crypt Monastery, came to the aid of the populace through his possession of the miraculous art of making bread (*khleb*) out of pigweed (*lebeda*) and turning ashes (*zola*) into salt (*sol*). The merchants complained to Svyatopolk that Prokhor by distributing salt to the Kievans was depriving them of their profits. Svyatopolk ordered that the salt be taken from Prokhor and carted to the prince's yard, calculating to enrich himself by likewise selling it at a high price. But as soon as the salt was removed from the monastery it turned back into ashes. After keeping it for three days, Svyatopolk ordered it thrown out, whereupon the ashes changed back into salt. The story ends with an account of Svyatopolk's shame upon learning

of Prokhor's miracles and how he betook himself to the Crypt Monastery
and made his peace with Prior John, under whose authority Prokhor was.
Previously—the narrator adds—Svyatopolk had been at odds with John, who
had reproached him for covetousness and cruelty, and he had even exiled
the prior to Turov, but afterwards, fearing "a revolt against himself by the
Christ-loving Vladimir Monomakh," had quickly returned him with honor
to the Crypt Monastery. Thus the story, while expressing dislike for Svyatopolk, manages at the same time to accentuate sympathy for Vladimir
Monomakh.

Or here is the story of Theodore and Basil. Theodore had at one time
been a rich man. But, reflecting that he was destined to die and that riches
offered no security in the future life, he decided to receive the tonsure in
the Kiev-Crypt Monastery and distribute his goods to the poor. He took up
his abode in a cave where Varangian treasure had once been buried, wherefore it was called the Varangian cave. But afterwards Theodore began to
repent of having forfeited wealth and the joys of secular life. Next to him
lived the pious monk Basil, who instructed him in the way of monastic
virtue and discipline, striving to divert his mind from worldly thoughts. For
a while Basil had a beneficial influence on Theodore. But once, when Basil
was away from the monastery for three months, the Devil came into his
own. He appeared to Theodore first in the form of Basil and then in the
form of an angel, showed him the location of the Varangian treasure and
incited him to dig it up and go with it to another monastery. When Theodore, having found the treasure, was preparing to leave the Kiev-Crypt
Monastery, Basil returned and kept him from taking any such step. Theodore reburied the treasure that he had dug up and prayed God to grant him
forgetfulness of the place where the gold was hidden so that he would not
again be tempted to dig it up. And Theodore's prayer was answered. Thus
put to shame, the Devil turned into a little hobgoblin which Theodore
tamed very cleverly. Once, for example, he made it grind five loads of grain;
another time he bade the Devil carry lumber to the top of a high hill for a
building. The Devil became Theodore's obedient implement. But later in
Theodore's life the following event took place: the Devil appeared to a
counselor of Prince Mstislav's in the form of Theodore's friend Basil and,
desiring to have vengeance on Theodore, said that Theodore was conceal-
ing a treasure in his cave. Mstislav, wishing to get possession of the treasure
himself, forced Theodore to come before him and demanded that he tell
where the gold was. Theodore said with a clear conscience that he did not
remember, since God had granted his request for oblivion as to the place.
And Mstislav commanded that the monk be put in chains, kept for three
days without food or water, and then put to the torture. He likewise tor-

tured Basil, who had been summoned as a witness. Both monks bore up stoically under torture and accused the prince. Mstislav shot an arrow at Basil. Basil drew the arrow from his body and predicted that Mstislav would himself be wounded by that arrow. Theodore and Basil died during the night, but not long afterwards Mstislav died, having been wounded in a skirmish with Prince Igor Davidovich.

The *Tale of Igor's Expedition* narrates touchingly how the young Prince Rostislav, son of Vsevolod, was drowned while attempting to cross the river Stugna. The author of the *Igor* shows a distinct liking for this prince. He feels sorry for him and for his grief-stricken mother, whose lament for her son elicits the sympathy of trees and flowers.

This same Prince Rostislav appears in a quite different light in the *Kiev-Crypt Paterikon* in the story of the Wonder-worker Gregory.

Once, it says, Gregory had gone to the bank of the Dnieper to cleanse a chalice that some unclean animal had got into. Just then Rostislav rode past with his brother Vladimir Monomakh, intending to pray at the Crypt Monastery before setting out against the Polovcians. Rostislav's retinue insulted Gregory and started to make sport of him. Then Gregory said in anger: "For calling me names you shall all drown along with your prince."

Rostislav shouted indignantly: "Why should I drown, who am such a good swimmer?" and gave orders to tie a stone around Gregory's neck and drown him in the Dnieper. Gregory was drowned. The infuriated Rostislav did not go to the Crypt Monastery to pray, whereas his brother Vladimir Monomakh fulfilled his Christian duty, prayed in the monastery and received a blessing there. And what happened? An event that the *Tale of Igor's Expedition* narrates with sympathy, and the *Kiev-Crypt Paterikon* with an evident malicious satisfaction. Rostislav, retreating from before the Polovcians, was drowned in the Stugna along with his retainers, while Vladimir Monomakh was spared on account of his respect for the Crypt Monastery.

As we see, grievous retribution falls on the head of a prince, even one belonging to the family of Vsevolod, which the Crypt monks esteemed, when he dishonors the monastery and its monks.

The sympathetic attitude toward Vladimir Monomakh comes out in other paterikon stories as well, for example, in those about the icon-painter Olimpius and the disinterested physician Agipit. The first of these stories, moreover, sketches the negative aspects of monastic life along with the positive—chiefly as evidenced in the covetousness of certain monks.

Speaking of the *Kiev-Crypt Paterikon* (in a letter to P. A. Pletnev in April, 1831), Pushkin went into raptures over its "charm of simplicity and invention." Pushkin's comment on the paterikon is perhaps illustrated by such a story as the legend of Mark the Sexton, who dug burial niches for dead monks.

Once when Mark was digging a niche he got tired and stopped without finishing, and when the deceased was brought, the coffin could not be squeezed in. Grumbling arose among the monks since, as the story says, they could not "lay out" the corpse; that is, arrange it and anoint it with oil, "because the space was narrow." Mark apologized to the brothers: "Forgive me, dear fathers, for my wickedness that I did not finish." But the monks began to scold him all the more. Then Mark appealed to the dead man himself: "It's a tight fit, brother, so just rouse up and take the oil and pour it on yourself." And a miracle took place: the dead man stretched out his hand and poured the oil, and his coffin squeezed itself into the narrow cave.

Another time, after the death of a monk, his friend came to the spot where there was to have been a niche prepared, and asked Mark when it would be ready. Mark replied: "Brother, go to the departed and tell him to wait until morning while I dig out his tomb." The monk said that there was no use asking his friend to postpone dying, since he was already dead. However, Mark persisted: "You can see the place is not finished; go and say: 'Stay one more day; die in the morning, and there will be a place ready.'" His visitor could only obey. He went to the deceased and transmitted Mark's request. To the amazement of all, the dead man opened his eyes, breath returned to him, and he remained alive for a day and a night, though he did not say anything. In the morning, after making sure that the place for his friend's burial was ready, the monk returned to the dead man and said: "Leave your temporal life and pass on to the life everlasting, for a place is prepared to receive your body." The resuscitated dead man immediately died again and was laid in the crypt that Mark had dug out for him.

Curious, too, is the following story based on the literal understanding of a word in its precise etymological sense, and related to fairy-tale motifs. It tells how the monk Theophilus, wishing to keep an accurate record of his virtues, obtained a special pitcher in which he collected all the tears that he shed at any time while praying. And behold, when his last hour came, an angel appeared to him bearing a fragrant pitcher, in which, it seems, were collected not those tears which the monk himself had gathered but those which he had in the literal sense shed (spilled outside the pitcher). It was only the tears not counted by Theophilus that had proved pleasing in God's sight.

Thus the *Kiev-Crypt Paterikon* combines politically tendentious tales with churchly legends which in some cases go back to oral-poetry motifs.

PILGRIMAGE LITERATURE

Quite early, probably soon after Russia's acceptance of Christianity, Russians began making pilgrimages to the "Holy Land"—to Palestine, to Mount Athos, and to Constantinople, as centers where objects sacred to Christians were concentrated. The fundamental incentive for such pilgrimages was the aspiration of the young Russian ecclesiastical corporation to recruit its strength by means of direct intercourse with the Christian East. Such intercourse undoubtedly increased the prestige of the Russian Church by bringing it within the sphere of inter-Christian relationships and thereby extricating it from a position of domestic isolation. Private motives for making pilgrimages were religious emotion and plain curiosity.

There is a tradition that Antonius, future founder of the Kiev-Crypt Monastery, made a pilgrimage to Mount Athos; it is known that Barlaam, prior of the same monastery, made a pilgrimage to Palestine in 1062. At the beginning of the twelfth century, Prior Daniel was in Palestine, while at the end of the same century, Dobrynya Yadreikovich of Novgorod went to Tsargrad, afterwards took the tonsure under the name of Antonius, and later became Archbishop of Novgorod. The two latter pilgrims left descriptions of their journeys.

As we see, those who betook themselves to the "Holy Land" were chiefly ecclesiastical personages, and not ordinary ones at that, but in most cases incumbents of some major hierarchical position. Of the names listed, only Dobrynya Yadreikovich was a layman at the time of his pilgrimage, but even he, upon his return to Russia, embraced monasticism. At first it was the materially well-off who made pilgrimages, those having the means to support not only themselves but their retainers, the servants who traveled with them. Later on, however, we find among the pilgrims to the "Holy Land" people belonging to the lower, the needy social classes; to them pilgrimages were a source of profit since on the way they were supported by alms, while on their return they fell into the category of ecclesiastically privileged persons. Toward the middle of the twelfth century, this category of pilgrims became so numerous that the Church even began to take prohibitory measures against them: mass absences from places of domicile disorganized the economic life of the country, and in its prohibitions the Church was evidently acting under governmental instructions.

Persons who had been to the "Holy Land" were termed palmers, pilgrims, or sandal-walkers. The first title was applied to them because they usually brought back a palm branch as souvenir of the "holy places"; the word "pilgrim" is derived from the Latin *peregrinus,* meaning "traveler"; finally, they were called "sandal-walkers" because during a pilgrimage special footgear was worn, the Latin term for which was *caliga* or sandal.

Of greatest interest from the literary point of view is the *Pilgrimage* to Palestine of Prior Daniel, who made the journey between 1106 and 1108. [23] Daniel remained sixteen months in Palestine. He lived chiefly in Jerusalem, at the monastery of St. Savva, whence he made trips all over the country, having as his guide a "good leader," one of the very well informed ancients of the monastery where he was stopping.

Daniel made his journey at the time when Palestine was in the hands of the Crusaders. King Baldwin of Jerusalem, who headed the Crusaders, gave Daniel assistance in his travels about the "Holy Land."

On the basis of the fact that Daniel mentions the river Snov, comparing it to the Jordan, it was at first supposed that Daniel was of Chernigov extraction, since a river of that name flows through the Chernigov district. It was later pointed out, however, that rivers of this name are also found in other localities, one, in particular, within the precincts of Voronezh. In any case the fact that the southern princes are specifically mentioned in the *Pilgrimage* suggests that Daniel was of southern origin.

Daniel's *Pilgrimage* is interesting in that it combines an accurate topographical description of Palestine with an abundance of legendary and apocryphal material, which the traveler drew partly from oral accounts and partly from pertinent literary sources with which he was, apparently, already well acquainted before undertaking his pilgrimage. In fact it is the presence of a considerable amount of this legendary and apocryphal material, together with the occasional lyric embellishment of the work as a whole, that determines its literary significance. The *Pilgrimage* enjoyed very great popularity here and in large measure predetermined the characteristics of the pious pilgrimage genre on Russian soil. Its wide circulation is also explained by the fact that it was written in language resembling the current spoken Russian. It is extant in approximately a hundred copies, dating from the fifteenth-nineteenth centuries.

Prior Daniel begins the story of his pilgrimage with his motives for going. He went to Jerusalem first of all in order to see with his "sinful eyes" the places which Christ with his feet had trod. Next he gives notice, as early

[23] The best edition of the text of Prior Daniel's *Pilgrimage* is found in Pts. 3 and 9 of Vol. I of the *Pravoslavnyi Palestinskii sbornik* (Orthodox Palestine Collection) (St. Petersburg, 1885). On Daniel, see: M. A. Venevitinov, "Pilgrimage of Prior Daniel to the Holy Land at the Beginning of the Twelfth Century," *Letop. zanyatii Arkheographicheskoy komissii* (Chronicle of the Studies of the Archaeographical Commission, 1876–1877) (St. Petersburg, 1884), Pt. 7, pp. 1–138; P. Zabolotskii, "The Legendary and Apocryphal Element in the Pilgrimage of Prior Daniel," *Russkii phil. Vestnik* (Russian Philological Herald) (1899), Nos. 1–2, 3–4.

Russian writers often did, that he is incapable of telling what he has seen and heard as it ought to be told, and asks that he be not condemned for his poverty of wit and his uncouthness; whoso visits these holy places in humility and the fear of God will, by God's grace, not sin in future; but Daniel had visited the holy places in an unseemly manner, in all manner of sloth, weakness, and drunkenness, doing all manner of unseemly things.

Needless to say, we are here dealing not with the real facts of Daniel's conduct, but with the routine self-abasement of the sinner typical of the old-time religiously minded writer.

Daniel was impelled to his pilgrimage by yet another circumstance. He wanted to describe for those interested in the holy places and in Palestine what they could not see for themselves, since not only is he saved who has himself looked upon the sacred relics, has himself touched them, but he too who has learned of them from others, if at the same time he does good deeds at home.

Daniel started to make notes while still on the way to Jerusalem, beginning at Tsargrad. In the town of Ephesus, he saw the crypt where lay the bodies of seven youths who had slept for three hundred and sixty years, and the bodies of three hundred holy fathers. There Daniel worshiped at the tomb of John the Divine.

Approaching Jerusalem, Daniel first saw the Pillar of David, then the Mount of Olives and the Church of the Resurrection, in which is the tomb of the Lord, and next he saw the whole city. "And at that moment," he writes, "great joy is wont to come upon any Christian, as he beholds the holy city of Jerusalem, and tears are wont to stream from the eyes of true believers. For no one can fail to drop a tear when he glimpses that longed-for land and looks upon the holy places where Christ our God suffered for us sinners." Next he describes in detail the Church of the Resurrection and the tomb of the Lord within it. Back of the altar of the church is the "navel" of the earth. At twelve sazhens * distance from it is Golgotha.

Daniel also saw, so he tells us, the altar of Abraham, where Abraham sacrificed a ram to God in place of his son Isaac; he saw the tomb of the Virgin, the cave in which Christ was betrayed, and another cave in which Christ began the instruction of his disciples, and the caves of John the Baptist and the prophet Elias, and the cave in which Christ was born.

He pays a good deal of attention to the river Jordan. Its water is very turbid and sweet and from this water no ill nor any sort of harm ever comes to any. At the feast of the baptism, when a multitude of people was gathered on the bank of the Jordan, Daniel saw the "grace of God": at that time the

* One sazhen equals seven feet.—Ed.

Holy Ghost came upon the waters of Jordan, and the deserving saw it, though the rest did not, yet joy and gladness visited the heart of every Christian. The Jordan looks just like the river Snov.

It is curious that in telling of the "light from heaven," which descended to the tomb of Christ on Holy Saturday, Daniel emphasizes the fact that the lamps of the Greeks were kindled by this light, as was the lamp that Daniel had placed there for the land of Rus, but the Frankish lamps, that is, those of the Latins, were not kindled; "divine grace" passed them by.

In conclusion Daniel says that he prayed zealously for his princes and for the whole Russian people. This prayer was one of the objects of his pilgrimage. He speaks of himself as the representative of the whole land of Rus, calling himself "Prior of Rus." At the feast of Easter, he places a "candle on the Holy Sepulchre from the whole land of Rus."

In describing his pilgrimage, Daniel concentrates chiefly on such moments as are connected with his religious interests. But along with these he mentions the natural peculiarities of Palestine, its fertility, and certain aspects of trade that attracted his attention.

In the *Pilgrimage*, Daniel's social physiognomy is very clearly shown. He is prior of a rich monastery, has the means to perform a long and difficult pilgrimage, enters into direct communication with Baldwin, King of Jerusalem. Baldwin shows a very great liking for Daniel. The figure of Daniel stands out in the *Pilgrimage* as that of a man of good birth and eminent position with sufficient material resources to pay for any services done him by those who show him Palestine's varied relics.

THE PRIMARY CHRONICLE: *Povest vremennykh let*

THE TALE OF BYGONE YEARS

One of our most ancient and widely developed literary genres was the chronicle. The method of chronicle composition consisted, first, in separate persons, for the most part from princely boyar or monastic circles, making records of various events which they had witnessed or of which they had been told. These records, along with legends, tales, or narratives about various persons or events, were next brought together into separate digests, which were thereafter amplified and modified down to the compilation of the first extant digest, which bears the title: "These are the narratives of bygone years regarding the origin of the land of Rus, who first began to rule in Kiev, and from what source the land of Rus had its beginning." This digest is extant in later collections of annals with subsequent digests subjoined. The oldest copies of annalistic collections of this type are the Laurentian, 1377, where the *Povest* is followed by a North Russian chronicle compilation dealing chiefly with events in the Suzdal area to the year 1305, and the Hypatian, written in the 1420's and including, along with the *Povest*, a South Russian digest dealing principally with events in the districts of Kiev and Galicia-Volynia and carrying the account down to 1292. The Novgorod chronicle, setting forth the destinies of northwestern Rus, is extant in a copy from the 1330's. Neither the original entries nor the tales, legends, and narratives in their pre-chronicle form, nor yet the earliest compilations that preceded the *Povest* are extant.

The question of the genesis of early chronicle compilations even now cannot be regarded as finally settled, notwithstanding the existence of an extensive literature devoted to the investigation of the chronicles. The most valuable studies of this question are those of Academician A. A. Shakh-matov [24] and Academician V. M. Istrin.[25] The results of his investigations led Shakhmatov to the following conclusions. Under the influence of a Bulgarian chronicle compilation, "the most ancient Kiev compilation" was assembled at Kiev in 1039 in connection with the establishment of the metro-politanate there; it was brought down to 1037, which year carried an entry concerning Yaroslav's patronage of book production and of translation. On the basis of this compilation and of the *Novgorod Chronicle* of 1036, there appeared in 1050 the "old Novgorod compilation." In 1073 at the Kiev-Crypt Monastery, through the efforts of Prior Nikon, the "first compilation of the Kiev-Crypt Monastery" was assembled; this took over the "most ancient Kiev compilation," introduced certain interpolations and extended it to include items on events from the death of Yaroslav the Wise (1054). In 1095 or thereabouts, the "first Kiev-Crypt compilation," supplemented by the "old Novgorod compilation" and its continuation, by material from the inextant *Life of Antonius* of the Crypt Monastery, and from the *Greek Chronograph* and the *Pariminik*, became the "second Kiev-Crypt compila-tion," in other words, the "primary compilation" that underlies the *Povest*, of which there were three editions.

The basic, or first, redaction of the *Povest* was made at the Kiev-Crypt

---

[24] Especially *Razyskaniya o drevneyshikh russkikh letopisnykh svodakh* (Researches Concerning Early Russian Annalistic Compilations) (St. Petersburg, 1908), and *Povest vremmennykh let* (Tale of Bygone Years) (St. Petersburg, 1916), Vol. I, introductory section, text, notes.

[25] "Zamechaniya o nachale russkovo letopisaniya" (Observations on the Beginning of Russian Chronicle Writing), *Izv. otd. russk. yaz. i slov.* (News of the Division of Russian Language and Literature of the Academy of Sciences) (1921), Vol. XXVI, and (1922), Vol. XXVII.

Monastery by Nestor,[26] in 1112, in a spirit of benevolence toward Kiev's unpopular Prince Svyatopolk Izyaslavich, for which reason it never got into circulation but was rewritten in 1116, after the death of Svyatopolk (1113), by Sylvester, prior of the Vydobichy Monastery. In this rewriting the person of Svyatopolk is relegated to the background, while that of Vladimir Monomakh is brought to the fore. Thus the second edition of the *Povest* came into being. The third edition dates from 1118 and was executed by Prince Mstislav Vladimirovich's confessor, a monk of the Kiev-Crypt Monastery, in an effort to rival the Vydobichy Monastery. The compiler of this edition, in view of the loss of the original Nestorian edition, availed himself of the second (Sylvester's) edition, amplifying it chiefly with items relating to Vladimir Monomakh, bringing it down to 1117, and at the end of the compilation copying in the instruction of Monomakh to his children.

When Istrin reexamined the edifice erected by Shakhmatov, he arrived at a series of conclusions that were at variance with those of Shakhmatov. First of all he disagreed with the asserted existence of the so-called "most ancient Kiev compilation" of 1039 and, consequently, of the "primary compilation" of 1095. Istrin did not agree with Shakhmatov about the redactions of the *Povest* either, or about the parts played by Nestor and by Sylvester in the writing of the chronicle. Shakhmatov's hypothesis as to the existence of a compilation of 1039 depended upon the relegation of a number of items in the *Povest* to the category of later interpolations. By analyzing these interpolations, and defining the relationship of the Hamartolas interpolations to the chronicle text, Istrin arrives at the following conclusions, which in some measure represent a return to old points of view.

---

[26] In his article, "Nestor letopisets" (Nestor the Chronicler), in *Zapiski Naukovogo t-va im. Shevchenka* (Notes of the Shevchenka Scientific Association) (1914), Vols. 117, 118, Shakhmatov adduces a number of reasons for recognizing Nestor as author of the *Povest*, despite established opinion that Nestor had nothing to do with the oldest Kiev chronicle. According to Shakhmatov, in 1110 Nestor, who would then have been about fifty-five years old, undertook to compile a new chronicle digest, which he called the *Povest vremennykh let*. This was based on the previous digest, supplemented, however, and rewritten on the basis of numerous written and oral sources. M. D. Prisyolkov arrives at very nearly the same opinion as Shakhmatov, as to Nestor's role in the writing of the chronicle, in his book, *Nestor letopisets* (Petrograd, 1923).

Another view on this question is maintained by S. A. Bugoslavsky in his article, "K voprosu o kharaktere i obeme literaturnoy deyatel'nosti prep. Nestora" (On the Question of the Character and Extent of the Literary Activity of Reverend Nestor), *Izv. otd. russk. yaz. i slov.* (News of the Division of Russian Language and Literature) (1914), Bk. I, pp. 131–136; Bk. III, pp. 153–191. In this very thorough study the author assumes that Nestor wrote the lives of Boris and Gleb, and of Theodosius, prior of the Crypt Monastery, during the first few years of the twelfth century, on grounds of the factual content of these lives, their style, and method of writing, and from this proceeds to the conclusion that this Nestor could be neither the author nor the editor of the following works which have been attributed to him: 1) legend as to how the Crypt Monastery got its name, 2) legend about the first Crypt monks, 3) tale of the transfer of the relics of Theodosius, and, finally, 4) the chronicle, *Povest vremennykh let*, or part of it.

The "chronograph according to the long text," an abbreviation and simplification of the chronicle of Hamartolas, was speedily, or perhaps even at the time of its appearance, continued to include an exposition of events from Russian history. This history was there narrated partly in accordance with tradition, partly from written sources, partly from a mixture of the two.

The "chronograph according to the long text" apparently ended with the legend of Vladimir's baptism. In the later 1050's, after the death of Yaroslav, Russian history was divorced from Greek history and received independent treatment. Istrin's *Povest* was formed through the mechanical separation of Russian from Greek events, the addition of a few new items, and a continuation covering the reigns of Vladimir and Yaroslav down to the death of the latter (1054). This was the first edition of the *Povest* and already bore the title: "These are the narratives of bygone years," and so forth. Its form was identical with that preserved in the Laurentian and Hypatian copies except that it lacked the extensive introduction and the legend of the beginning of the Crypt Monastery, entered under the year 1050. The history of the *Povest* for the rest of the eleventh century consisted simply in its continuation to include subsequent events. One such continuation may have been made by Nikon in the 1070's. It is possible that the next was made in the 1090's. But the continuators did not introduce anything beyond insignificant additions into the previous text.

Early in the second decade of the twelfth century, immediately after the death of Svyatopolk Izyaslavich, the prototype of the *Povest,* with all its continuations, was again continued through the death of Svyatopolk. The author of this continuation was Nestor, who added to the *Povest* a long introduction in which he again utilized the full text of the *Chronicle* of *Georgius Hamartolas* and a number of other sources. Such was the make-up of the second edition of the *Povest,* preserved in full (except for the accidental loss of the end) in the Laurentian copy. Nestor's work was copied verbatim in 1116, without editorial alterations, by Sylvester, who appended his name as copyist. After Sylvester had taken his copy, Nestor's original was returned to the Crypt Monastery, where it was continued as usual and became what is known as the *Kiev Chronicle,* represented by the Hypatian copy. From the copy made by Sylvester, or perhaps from a copy made from that copy, the last pages were, in the course of time, lost, without the disappearance, however, of Sylvester's signature, which had been written either on a special page or on the binding. The loss of these pages resulted in the Laurentian copy's breaking off at the year 1110, in the middle of a sentence. Such are Academician Istrin's basic conclusions as to the early history of Russian chronicle writing.

Another attempt to revise Shakhmatov's concept of the evolution of the chronicle in Rus is to be found in the most recent study of the *Povest,* by Academician N. K. Nikolsky.[27] N. K. Nikolsky fully shares A. A. Shakhmatov's basic position as to the political tendentiousness of the editor of the *Povest* as shown in the way he describes the rise of civil government in the land of Rus and the spread of Christian culture there. This editor was Normanist and Grecophil in his sympathies. His Normanism asserted itself in his affirmation of a Varangian origin for the Russian state, which was formed—in the chronicler's view—as the result of the Russian Slavs inviting in the Varangian princes headed by Rurik, while his Grecophilism is manifest in his tendency to attribute the spread of Christianity in Rus directly to the influence of Byzantium and the Byzantine Church, one illustration of which tendency is the so-called *Kherson Legend,* which asserts that Vladimir's baptism took place in the Greek town of Kherson, and first makes its appearance in the primary compilation, where it replaces the tradition of Vladimir's baptism at Kiev, found in the "most ancient compilation."

But the *Povest* editor's tendentiousness, in N. K. Nikolsky's opinion, is apparent not only in what he says but in what he wittingly leaves unsaid or purposely omits. One such silence in the *Povest* is the absence from it of any information as to the beginning of Russian letters. A special item on the translation of books into Slavic, inserted in the *Povest* as of the year 898, and regarded by Shakhmatov as a later interpolation, tells of the introduction of writing among the western and southern Slavs, but says nothing as to when writing appeared in Rus, nor is the subject mentioned elsewhere in the *Povest.* Such an omission, Nikolsky conjectures, was fully premeditated: the inextant West-Slavic (Moravo-Pannonian) source, which served as a basis not only for the legend about the translation of books but also for part of the extracts that precede the first chronicle year, 852, as well as for certain subsequent pages of the compilation, dealt with the primordial cultural and religious ties between Russian Slavdom, identified by the chronicler with the Polyanian tribe exclusively, and western Slavdom. The Normanist-Byzantine tendency of the *Povest* editor forced him to omit any indication on the part of his source as to the penetration of writing to the Russian Slavs from Pannonia and Moravia earlier than its penetration to them from Bulgaria, and also as to the penetration of Christianity previous to the arrival of the Greeks in Rus. But in the meantime such an earlier

27 "Povest vremennykh let kak istochnik dlya istorii nachal'-nogo perioda russkoy pismennosti i kul'tury" (Tale of Bygone Years as Source for the History of the Initial Period of Russian Literature and Culture), Pt. 1, *Sbornik po russkomu yaz. i slov. akad. nauk USSR* (Collection on Russian Language and Literature of the Academy of Sciences, USSR) (Leningrad, 1930), Vol II, Pt. 1.

penetration to this country of both writing and Christianity is attested to on the one hand by the lexical data of our ancient monuments, and on the other by the chronicle's characterization of the Polyanians as Christians who had been converted along with the western Slavs by the apostle Paul; that is, long before the baptism of Rus under Vladimir.

If, however, the legend about the translation of books into Slavic is not some chance interpolation but an organic part of the narrative concerning the historic destinies of the Polyanian tribe, then, so Nikolsky asserts, there are no grounds for supposing, with Shakhmatov, that the item about the translation of books among the Slavs made its first appearance in an all-Russian compilation such as the *Povest,* but there is every reason to suppose that it had already found inclusion in some historical work dealing chiefly with the destinies of Polyania-Rus.

With Solovyev, Kostomarov, Bestuzhev-Ryumin, Filevich, and Grushevsky, Nikolsky is inclined to think that the title itself, "These are the tales of bygone years," and so forth, refers not to the whole early twelfth century chronicle compilation but only to the first pages of it, to the introductory section; Nikolsky, however, admits the possibility that this title may embrace events down to the final years of the Vladimirian epoch. N. K. Nikolsky doubts whether the "most ancient Kiev compilation" of 1039, as reconstructed by Shakhmatov, owed its origin to the alien Greek clergy: if this had been the case, then, in Nikolsky's opinion, it would not have retained items that were scandalous from the viewpoint of the medieval moralist-clergymen (for example, Vladimir's reply to the Mahometans, and so forth), would have set aside more space for ecclesiastical happenings, about which it says almost nothing, and would have adhered more closely to Greek models.

In summing up his investigations, Academician Nikolsky arrives at the conclusion that

there are insufficient grounds for looking upon the legendary section of the *Povest* as the outcome of previous "compilatory" effort. This part, even in its present state, after having passed through the hands of several editors, still bears the obvious marks of an attempt at the tendentious adaptation, reorganization, and abridgment of a previous, better proportioned survey of very early Russian history (Tales of the Land of Rus) that has lost its original form through Sylvester's redaction, having kept only excerpts from "Tales of the Land of Rus," supplemented them in part by extracts from other sources, and adapted them to a new historiographical scheme; that is, to the Greco-Varangian theory.[28]

[28] *Op. cit.,* p. 166. Objections to the basic theses of Prof. Nikolsky were advanced by Acad. V. M. Istrin in a critical article, "The Moravian History of the Slavs and the History of Polyania-Rus as Conjectural Sources of the Russian *Primary Chronicle,*" *Byzantinoslavica* (1931), Vol III/II, pp. 308–332, and (1932), Vol. VI/I, pp. 36–57.

Thus the Russian chronicle, like the great majority of other monuments of early Russian literature, is, in the opinion of Shakhmatov and Nikolsky, shot through with definite publicistic tendencies. A. A. Shakhmatov writes:

The hand of the chronicler was guided in most instances not by the high ideal of a pious recluse remote from life and worldly vanity, capable of giving an unbiased appraisal of the events unfolding around him and of the persons who directed these events—the appraisal of a religious thinker hoping for the establishment of the kingdom of God in this earthly vale of tears—but by political passions and world interests; if the chronicler was a monk, then he gave even freer rein to his prejudiced appraisal where it coincided with the interests of his own cloister and the monastic flock who dwelt there.[29]

Shakhmatov further points out that many monasteries were bound to some prince from their very founding and accordingly became the "patrimonial archives and political chancelleries of the prince." In this respect even the relatively most independent of them, the Kiev-Crypt Monastery, was no exception: from time to time it registered protests against the policies of individual princes, but in the last analysis submitted to princely authority and gave moral sanction to it. On their side the princes, looking out for their own political interests, exercised a definite influence on the general trend of chronicle writing, and on the exegesis of separate historical facts, which they naturally desired to see presented in a light favorable to themselves.

The cardinal political tendency that informs the chronicle consists in the enunciation of the principle of Russian unity as practiced by the princes of the house of Rurik. The publicistic position of the chronicler, in the opinion of Shakhmatov, of Prisyolkov, and of Nikolsky, is also characterized by an inclination to emphasize the culturo-historical dependence of Rus upon Byzantium.

Our ancient chronicle has been justly esteemed not only by Russian but by western European scholars, who have asserted that for quality it not only holds its own among medieval European chronicles but in some respects even surpasses them. Notwithstanding the obvious bias of the chronicler's judgments as pointed out by Shakhmatov, the idea of Slavic unity on the one hand, and on the other the idea of a community of aims and interests in the land of Rus as a whole, permeate the exposition of events throughout. "It seems remarkable," says Klyuchevsky, "that in a society where, not much more than a hundred years before, human sacrifices were still being offered to idols, thought should already have schooled itself to a sense of the interconnection of world phenomena. At the beginning of the twelfth century, the idea of Slavic unity required an intellectual effort all the greater for

[29] A. A. Shakhmatov, *Povest vremennykh let*, Vol. I, p. xvi.

being in no wise borne out by contemporary conditions." And Klyuchevsky further emphasizes that the eleventh and twelfth centuries were characterized by an "awakening throughout society of that feeling that the land of Rus was something integral, the common national cause the obvious and compulsory concern of each and all, which both princes and chronicle writers so often mention." [30]

The literary importance of the chronicle is determined by the large number of stories, tales, and legends inserted at intervals among short paragraphs and references of a purely factual character. In Rus, as was also true of western Europe during the Middle Ages, the editors of chronicle compilations were ecclesiastical personages closely connected wth monasteries. But if the pious tales, legends, and sermons included in the chronicle are to be ascribed to a clerical milieu, then the tales dealing with martial incidents or with the private life of princes and their suites must have emanated from some secular milieu, in all probability the retinue. A great part of these tales were based on the traditions of oral poetry, in many cases compounded of motifs and plots drawn from the stock of international migratory tales. Most of the narrative material in the chronicle bears in some degree all the distinguishing marks of poetical treatment. At times the artistic merits of this material are outstanding. In substance it originated independently of the chronicle and was used there ready-made after being subjected to special revision by the chronicle editor; but it is inextant apart from the chronicle compilations and we know it only through them. It is this fact that makes the chronicles so valuable from a specifically historico-literary point of view. As K. N. Bestuzhev-Ryumin well describes it, the *Primary Chronicle*, the *Povest vremennykh let*, is an "archive which preserves the vestiges of works from our primordial literature now lost to us." [31]

As distinguished from the Byzantine chronicles, which begin with the creation of the world and then pass to the history of the Jewish people, the *Povest* begins with the partition of the earth among the sons of Noah and the confusion of tongues after the building of the tower of Babel. It next treats of the gemmation of the Slavic people from the tribe of Japhet, one branch, the Polyanian tribe, being the principal subject of attention for the first few pages of the *Povest*. As a sort of introduction to the history of the land of Rus—or, more exactly, to that of the Polyanian tribe—we get the legend of the visit of the apostle Andrew to Kiev and Novgorod. When he was teaching in Sinope and came to Kherson, Andrew, upon learning that the mouth of the Dnieper was nearby, conceived a desire to go by the

[30] V. Klyuchevskii, *Kurs russkoy istorii* (Course in Russian History) (Moscow, 1911), 4th ed., Vol. I, pp. 107, 248.
[31] *O sostave russkikh letopisey do kontsa XIV v.* (On the Corpus of Russian Chronicles to the End of the Fourteenth Century) (St. Petersburg, 1868), p. 59.

Dnieper to Rome. While ascending the river, he halted beneath the hills at the place where Kiev was subsequently built, and said to his disciples that the grace of God would shine upon these hills, that a great city with many churches would arise there. Having blessed the hills and set up a cross on them, Andrew continued his journey up the Dnieper and reached "the Slavs" at the point where Novgorod is now situated. There he was struck by the custom the inhabitants had of bathing in bathhouses warmed to an extreme heat and then lashing themselves with young reeds almost to the point of insensibility; he could not understand why people should voluntarily inflict such torture upon themselves. He told of this in Rome and his hearers marveled at the tale.

The oldest Russian monuments, among them Hilarion's *Discourse of Law and Grace* and, apparently, the previous *Povest* compilations, not only said nothing about the visit of apostles to Rus but on the contrary gave Vladimir credit for having adopted the Christian faith in spite of the fact that apostles had never come to Rus and consequently had in no way prepared the Russian people for baptism. Moreover the *Povest* itself in the story of the first martyrs—Varangians offered in Kiev as sacrifices to heathen gods—contradicts the legend of the visit of the apostle Andrew to Rus by saying: "Though the Apostles have not been here in person, their teachings resound like trumpets in the churches throughout the world." Furthermore, in the story of the baptism of the Kievans, we are told of the complaints made by the Devil, whom the baptism of the Russians had driven out of the dwelling place where he had expected to go on living indefinitely "since the apostolic teachings do not abide in this land, nor did this people know God."

It would appear that the legend about Andrew was a later interpolation, which, as we see, the editor of the *Povest* failed to reconcile with the subsequent narrative. There are hardly grounds for interpreting this legend with M. D. Prisyolkov [32] and V. M. Istrin [33] as an expression of Grecophil tendencies on the part of the Russian chronicler, however, the more so since the destination for which the apostle Andrew had set out was Rome, the center of Catholicism at the time the chronicle was compiled. On the contrary it would be more correct to link it up with the tendency of the Russian Church to emancipate itself from Byzantine tutelage. The point made is, clearly, that Rus, even before being officially united by Byzantium to Christendom, had been unofficially brought into touch with it through an immediate disciple of Christ, his apostle, whose authority, needless to

[32] *Ocherki po tserkovno-politicheskoy istorii kievskoy Rusi X–XII vv.* (Outlines of the Ecclesiastico-Political History of Kievan Rus in the Tenth-Twelfth Centuries), pp. 160–162.

[33] *Ocherki po istorii drevney russkoy literatury domoskovskogo perioda* (Outlines of the History of Early Russian Literature in the Pre-Mongol Period) (Petrograd, 1922), p. 130.

say, was, in the eyes of the chronicler, no whit inferior to the authority of the Byzantine Church. This is exactly how the legend of Andrew was taken in the sixteenth century by Ivan the Terrible in his dispute with the papal emissary, Antonius Possevinus, who was trying to win him over to the Catholic Church: the Terrible pointed out that the Russians had received Christianity not from the Greeks but from the apostle Andrew himself. The same thing was pointed out to the Greeks a century later by the priest-monk Arsenius Sukhanov, who had been sent to Greece by Tsar Alexis Mikhailovich on ecclesiastical business.[34]

The purpose of the legend in arranging such a roundabout and artificial route from Kherson to Rome for the apostle Andrew, was precisely to en-courage the belief that Rus had received, back in apostolic times, the seed of Christianity which was only later to germinate under Greek auspices.

At the same time the legend, having originated in the Kiev district, is informed with a manifestly ironical and derisive attitude toward the people of Novgorod: Andrew's sojourn in the south of Rus was signalized by the flattering prediction that the grace of God would shine on the future Kiev, while the visit of the apostle to the Novgorod area evoked nothing but a memory of the, in his opinion, absurd custom of self-torture in the baths. It is a curious fact that later on, in the precincts of Novgorod, another legend was built up to confute the compromising legend, a legend which was silent on the subject of baths and which told of Andrew's preaching in Novgorod and setting up his staff there. The literary source of the legend about the visit of the apostle Andrew to Kiev and Novgorod may have been the so-called *Tours of the Apostles,* which told of the preaching expeditions of the apostles to various countries. Evidently our legend was later reflected in the story by the sixteenth and seventeenth century Livonian historian, Fabricius, about how the monks of a Dominican monastery, being in need, asked the pope for a subsidy. The pope, before granting the monks' request, sent his legate to them to observe how they performed their offices. The monks gave the papal legate some beer to drink, then took him to the bath, where his unaccustomed southern eyes beheld approximately the same zealous steam-ing that the apostle Andrew had seen in Novgorod. The emissary concluded that the monks were mortifying their flesh, and informed the pope of the fact, whereupon the Dominican monks received the requested subsidy.[35]

Immediately after the legend about the apostle Andrew comes the story of the three brothers, rulers of their kin among the Polyanians, Kii, Shchek, and Khoriv, and their sister Lybed. The brothers built a town which they

[34] Cf. E. Golubinskii, *Istoriya russkoy tserkvi* (History of the Russian Church) (Moscow, 1901), 2nd ed., Vol. I, first half, pp. 27–28.

[35] See A. Sedelnikov, "Drevnyaya kievskaya legenda ob apostole Andreye (Early Kievan Legend About the Apostle Andrew), *Slavia* (1924), III, pp. 332–335.

named Kiev, after the oldest brother. Here, at the start, the rumor is refuted that Kii was a ferryman. If he had been a ferryman, he would not have gone to Tsargrad and would not have been received with honor by the emperor; no, Kii was no ferryman, he was chief of his kin. In this legend we catch the echo of a pre-Varangian theory concerning the origin of princely rule in Rus: this rule was linked not with the dynasty of Rurik, which had originally settled in Novgorod, but with a princely family which had established itself in southern Rus, among the Polyanian tribes. At the same time the legend reflects the widespread migratory motif of three brothers as founders of towns which underlies, for example, the Serbian ballad about three brothers founding the town of Skadr. The attempt to explain geographical names by matching them to hypothetical human beings is a common phenomenon in the field of ancient tradition. Thus the chronicler tells how the Radimichians and the Vyatichians were descended from two brothers, Radim and Vyatko, and later associates the founding of Kharkov with the name of a mythical Khark.

Speaking next of the peoples who made war on the Slavs, the chronicler mentions the Avars, who attacked the Greek emperor Heraclius, and all but conquered him. Avar oppression fell with special weight upon the Slavic tribe of the Dulebians: if an Avar had to go anywhere, he did not harness a horse or a steer to his cart, but three or four or five Dulebian women; thus did the Avars harass the Dulebians. The Avars were large of stature and proud of spirit, the chronicler concludes, and God destroyed them, and they all perished, and not one Avar survived; to this day there is a proverb in Rus: "They perished like the Avars; neither race nor descendants of them remain." The Avars or Obors were a warlike tribe who oppressed the Slavs and were finally crushed by Charlemagne. In the Slavic languages *obr* means "giant" (Czechish, *obr,* Polish, *olbrzym*). Traditions about giants doomed to destruction are generally current. Also widespread in folklore are legends about the harnessing of enslaved women. An echo of these legends occurs in an item from the chronicle of Velichka (seventeenth-eighteenth centuries) about the Poles harnessing women to the plow, their mothers, sisters, and wives. Of the Hungarian King Stephen there existed a tradition that after his victory over the Poles he plowed the field of victory with them and then planted a beechwood on it (hence the place name Bukovina); of Prince Román of Galicia the story was told that he harnessed Lithuanian women, and this gave rise to the proverb: "Román, you live ill, with Lithuania you till."

Having used for the opening pages of the *Povest* a source written in a spirit of sympathy toward the Polyanians, the chronicler characterizes the Polyanians as a mild and peaceful tribe, who showed respect for their daughters-in-law, sisters, mothers, and fathers, and had marriage customs. To judge from what is said of the Polyanians, they were Christians. In contrast to them, the Derevlians, Radimichians, Vyatichians, Severians, and Krivichians are represented as pagans, living "in beastly fashion, like cattle," killing one another, eating every unclean thing, and speaking obscenely before their fathers and their daughters-in-law. There were no marriages among them, but, by previous agreement, they abducted girls at the time of their games, which were accompanied by dances and devilish songs, and they had two or three wives apiece. For the dead they made a feast and then burned them on a pyre.

The model for such an ethnographical excursus in the chronicle was, apart from oral traditions, the description of the manners and customs of various peoples given in the *Chronicle of Georgius Hamartolas*, and cited by the chronicler immediately after his account of customs among Slavic tribes.

Resuming his narrative about the Polyanians, the chronicler states that after the death of Kii, Shchek, and Khoriv, the Khazars attacked the Polyanians and demanded tribute from them. The Polyanians paid tribute of a sword from each hearth; that is, from each house. When the Khazars bore this tribute to their prince and elders, the Khazar elders said: "Evil is this tribute, prince: we conquered them with a one-edged weapon called a saber, but their weapon is sharp on both edges and is called a sword; these men shall impose tribute upon us and upon other lands." And in his own person the chronicler adds that so it has come to pass; the Khazars spoke not of their own will but by God's commandment: as the Egyptians perished at the hand of Moses, though the Jews had previously been subject to the Egyptians, so the Khazars were first rulers themselves and then came to be ruled over; so do the Russian princes rule over the Khazars even to this day. This tradition, from the turn given it, is undoubtedly an echo of some ballad, composed, however, after the Rus had already been emancipated from Khazar domination. At least so one may conjecture from the fact that, a little farther on, the *Povest* speaks of the Polyanians paying tribute to the Khazars without a murmur, at the rate of a squirrel skin per hearth.

Up to this point the *Povest* account has not been dated. Now we find the first date (852) in connection with the accession of the Byzantine emperor Michael, when "the land of Rus was first named." In the reign of this emperor, the chronicle writer states, the Rus attacked Tsargrad, as is written in the Greek chronicle. Next the *Povest* notes the principal chronological landmarks from Adam to the death of Svyatopolk II; that is, down to 1113. Future items are given as of a definite year, and in several instances we have empty years; that is, years that are designated but not filled in with facts of any sort. The remainder of the *Povest* tells of the invitation of the North Russian Slavs to the Varangian princes headed by Rurik, of the occupation of Kiev by Rurik's generals Askold and Dir, of the reigns of Oleg, Igor, Olga, Svyatoslav, Yaropolk, Vladimir, Yaroslav, and other princes down to Svyatopolk II. Even here, material derived from folk-poetry traditions and migratory literary-fable motifs is largely used. A migratory motif is present first of all in the tradition about the inviting of the princes. Even so, in Irish tradition, did the inhabitants of Ireland invite three brothers from the Ostman tribe, Amelov, Sitarakh, and Ivor, who brought order to Ireland. In Wiedekind, tenth century German chronicler, when the Britons invited brothers to become their princes, they described their land in almost the same words that the Russians in the chronicle used to describe theirs to the Varangian brothers: *"Terra lata et spatiosa et omnium rerum copia referta"*; that is: "The land is wide and spacious and abounding in all manner of riches." Very similar traditions are preserved about the invitation to the Saxon princes, about the discovery of the island of Gotland and so on. The legend of the three brothers, Kii, Shchek, and Khoriv, family heads in the Polyanian tribe we encountered above; Slavic tradition also mentioned Lekh, Rus, and Chekh as heads of three Slavic tribes.

The poetical tradition about Oleg is chiefly associated with his attack on Tsargrad and his death through his horse. Oleg set out for Tsargrad by horse and by ship at the head of a multitude of various tribesmen; his ships numbered two thousand. Arriving before Tsargrad, he killed many Greeks and caused much woe. Then he commanded his warriors to mount the ships on wheels and, when the wind was favorable, bore down upon the city. The Greeks were afraid and begged for mercy, promising to pay Oleg such tribute as he should desire. They brought food and wine out to him, but Oleg refused their entertainment, for it was poisoned. The Greeks were afraid and said: "This is not Oleg, but St. Demetrius, whom God has sent against us." And the Greeks made an agreement whereby they paid Oleg tribute for his two thousand ships at the rate of twelve grivni per man and forty men to a ship, and in addition a tribute to the Russian towns, to Kiev, Chernigov, Pereyaslavl, Polotzk, Rostov, Lyubech, and the other towns; the agreement was ratified by oath; the Greeks kissed the cross, while the Russians swore in accordance with the Russian law by their weapons and by their gods, Perun and Volos, god of cattle. Following the text of the agreement between Oleg and the Greeks, there is an account of how Oleg gave orders that silk sails should be made for Rus—that is, for the Kievans—and linen ones for the Slavs—that is, for the men of Novgorod—and, hanging a shield upon the gates of Tsargrad in sign of victory, they started back. On the way the sails of the Novgorodians were torn by the wind, and, deciding that linen sails were not for them, they went back to their old canvas ones. So Oleg came to Kiev, bringing with him gold, silk, fruits, wine, and all manner of costly stuffs. And the people called Oleg a sage, for they were pagans and ignorant.

As Kostomarov pointed out in his day, the details of this story show very strong traces of poetic invention. Here is the usual heroic ballad's enumeration of the tribes who set out with Oleg for Byzantium, including some who were not even subject to him, and the enormous number of Oleg's ships, each of them carrying forty men, a figure also common in oral poetry legends; and the mounting of boats on wheels, which likewise finds parallels in folklore; and the poisoned food and drink, which figure in many migratory legends; and copious tribute from the conquered and the symbol of victory, a shield on the gates of Tsargrad. Finally, in the episode of the sails, where the unlucky Novgorodians come off short, we have an echo of the same ironical and derisive attitude of the people of Kiev toward those of Novgorod that we met in the legend of the visit of the apostle Andrew to the land of Rus: in both instances it is a reflection of motifs from historic folklore.

The widely known chronicle story of how Oleg's horse caused his death, basis of Pushkin's *Ballad of Oleg the Wise,* finds a very close parallel in the Scandinavian legend of the death, through his horse, of the Norwegian knight-errant, Orvar-Odd, who passed the greater part of his life in Rus. While he was still a child, a wise woman predicted that he would live a very long time, win renown in many lands, but that in the end he would die of his steed Faxi. In order to cheat the prophecy of its fulfillment, Odd killed Faxi, and throwing the carcass into a pit, heaped huge stones upon it. This marks the beginning of Odd's wanderings and exploits in various lands, Rus among them. Here he is entrusted with guarding the borders of the realm; he becomes the intimate of King Kvilanus, and his relations with the king are reminiscent of the relations of Oleg to Rurik. In Kiev, Odd marries the daughter of King Geraud, and after the death of Geraud becomes king himself. In extreme old age, notwithstanding his wife's attempts to dissuade him, he starts out upon a time for Norway and gets to the spot where he had once buried his horse. During his absence, fierce storms have cast down the stones with which he covered the pit where he had thrown Faxi. Odd now feels perfectly sure that the prediction of the wretched prophetess will not be fulfilled. Seeing the bleached skull of a horse, he conjectures that it is the head of Faxi and hits it a mighty blow, but as he does so, out crawls a serpent, and Odd dies of its sting.

The most recent student of the chronicle legend of Oleg's death, A. I. Lyashchenko, very plausibly identifies the Russian Oleg with the Scandinavian Odd. All the data, in A. I. Lyashchenko's opinion, favor the supposition that our chronicle legend is borrowed from the Scandinavian legend, and not the other way round. Back in the 1880's A. A. Kunik inclined to the opinion that Oleg and Odd were identical. Arguments against such an identification might appear to reside in the name Oleg and also in the Russian chronicle references to the death of Oleg in Rus and to his tomb, located, according to some accounts, at Kiev, according to others, at Ladoga. But etymologically Oleg is derived from the word Hegli; and this was an adjective which fairly early began to be used as a proper name, with the meaning of "saintly," "wise," "sage." Such a nickname might have been given by his retinue to a prince of Rus whose real name may perfectly well have been Odd. As to the references to Oleg's tombs in Kiev and Ladoga, *mogila* in early Russian meant hill or mound rather than place of burial. When news of Oleg's death reached the cities mentioned, a burial feast would have been held in his honor, and for this it would have been necessary to pile up a *mogila,* that is, a hill. Thus the inconsistency in the information about Oleg's death is removed. He died in Norway, where he had passed his childhood and youth, while his "tomb" in different cities of Rus were monuments reared in his honor.[36]

Aware, apparently, of the fascination of a story about the power of a soothsayer's prophecy over man, the chronicler follows this story by an item from the *Chronicle of Georgius Hamartolas* on the power of sorcery as revealed under the Roman emperor Domitian by the soothsayer Apollonius of Tyana.

The years 945 and 946 carry an account of the death of Igor and how his wife Olga took vengeance on those responsible for it, the Derevlians. The first story, which is an echo from retinue legend, depicts, first of all, the mutual relationships existing between prince and retinue. Igor's retinue began complaining to him that the retainers of Sveinald, one of his generals, were provided with weapons and fine raiment while they were naked, and they proposed to the prince that he should go forth with them after tribute: "You will profit and so shall we." Igor hearkened to his retinue, attacked the Derevlians, and, after collecting tribute from them, dismissed the greater part of his soldiers and with a small retinue turned back against the Derevlians to collect further tribute. Hearing that Igor was once more ap-

[36] See A. I. Lyashchenko, "Letopisnye skazaniya o smerti Olega Veshchego" (Chronicle Legends of the Death of Oleg the Wise), *Izv. otd. russk. yaz. i slov.* (News of the Division of Russian Language and Literature of the Academy of Sciences) (1924), Vol. XXIX, pp. 254–288. A Serbian tradition, similar to our chronicle legend, concerning the death of a Turkish sultan through his favorite horse, first brought forward by M. I. Sukhomlinov in his study, *O drevney russkoy letopisi kak pamyatnike literaturnom* (On the Early Russian Chronicle as a Literary Monument), A. I. Lyashchenko is, not without reason, inclined to regard as a variant on the Russian chronicle account of the death of Oleg.

proaching, the Derevlians consulted with Mal, their prince, saying: "If a wolf is wont to come among the sheep, he will take away the whole flock unless he be killed; even so with this man: if we do not kill him, he will destroy us all." Igor did not heed a warning given by the Derevlians and they slew him and his company. After the death of Igor, the Derevlians proposed to Olga through emissaries that she should marry their prince Mal. Olga pretended to agree to the Derevlians' proposal, but was actually plotting vengeance against them. First she put Derevlian emissaries to death, some by dropping them in a ditch and heaping earth on them, others by setting a bathhouse on fire, a third lot by getting them drunk and then killing them. The fourth vengeance of Olga consisted in demanding of the Derevlians, whom she had besieged in Izkorosten, three pigeons and three sparrows apiece (promising that after receiving these she would raise the siege), and bidding men tie brimstone to each of the birds and then release them. When the birds returned to their nests, they set fire to all Izkorosten, and of the Derevlians who fled from the city, Olga commanded her warriors to kill part and take part as slaves, while on the rest she imposed a heavy tribute. All four stories of Olga's vengeance are written as lively epic narrative and are lavishly garnished with dialogue.

As Sukhomlinov noted, the details of Olga's revenge in all three cases are reminiscent of what one reads in the Scandinavian sagas about Nyal and Stir. A very close parallel to Olga's fourth vengeance is presented by a story about the Scandinavian knight-errant Harald, son-in-law of Yaroslav the Wise, who likewise took a town in Sicily by means of birds to which incendiary materials had been tied. Kostomarov recalls as parallel to this fourth vengeance of Olga's the Bible story about Samson fastening firebrands to the tails of foxes, which he then turned loose in the fields of the Philistines.

Other parallels, both Western and Eastern, also exist on this theme, showing that we are here dealing with a migratory tale of some popularity.

The characterization of Svyatoslav, Olga's son, contains distinct echoes of an epic legend, composed no doubt within the retinue:

For he was brave himself, and stepping light as a leopard, undertook many campaigns. Upon his expeditions he carried with him neither wagons nor kettles, and boiled no meat, but cut off small strips of horseflesh, game or beef, and ate it after roasting it on the coals. Nor did he have a tent, but he spread out a garment under him and set his saddle under his head; and all his retinue did likewise. He sent messengers to other lands, saying: "I am coming to attack you."

In the chronicle Svyatoslav stands out as, practically speaking, the most warlike of the Russian princes. War is his natural element. His name alone strikes fear into his enemies; the Pechenegs flee in all directions when they imagine that Svyatoslav is coming against them. He conquers the Khazars, the Vyatichians, the Danubian Bulgars, the Greeks; against a hundred thousand Greek troops he advances with only ten thousand warriors. When the Rus were terrified at the multitude of the enemy forces, Svyatoslav made the following speech to them:

Now we have no place whither we may flee. Whether we will or no, we must give battle. Let us not disgrace Rus, but rather lay down our lives, dead we shall not be disgraced; if we flee we shall be; we must not take to flight, but will resist boldly, and I shall march before you. If my head falls, then look to yourselves.

In reply to this his warriors said: "Wherever your head falls, there we will lay down our own." And the carnage was great, and Svyatoslav was victorious and the Greeks fled, but Svyatoslav advanced toward Tsargrad, fighting and destroying towns that stand deserted to this day. The very death of Svyatoslav came about, according to chronicle tradition, as the result of his headstrong warlike fervor; he perished in a skirmish with the Pechenegs, and the Pecheneg prince made a cup from his skull and drank out of it.[37]

Traces of a retinue epos are numerous in the chronicle stories about Vladimir, particularly those having to do with the period before his baptism. When Yaropolk, brother of Vladimir, vanquished his other brother, Oleg, Prince of Derevla, and became sole ruler of all Rus, Vladimir seized Novgorod and said to the elders: "Go to my brother and say to him: 'Vladimir is advancing against you, prepare to fight with him'" (Yaropolk was in Kiev). Then he sent word to Rogvold of Polotzk: "I desire to take your daughter to wife." When Rogvold asked his daughter Rogneda whether she wished to marry Vladimir, she replied:

"I will not draw off the boots of a slave's son, but I want Yaropolk instead." Vladimir was considered the son of a slave, and the proud princess of Polotsk therefore refused to become his wife and go through the ceremony of drawing off his boots in sign of obedience. She preferred to marry Vladimir's brother Yaropolk, who was born of a free woman. When Vladimir's servants returned and reported to him what Rogneda had said, he collected a large army of Varangians, Novgorodians, Chuds, and Krivichians and marched against Rogvold, arriving at Polotzk just as they were on the point of conveying Rogneda to Yaropolk. Vladimir killed Rogvold and his two sons, and forced Rogneda to become his wife.

This story, interrupting the narrative sequence of Vladimir's campaign against Yaropolk, is undoubtedly a later interpolation. Like the account of Vladimir's campaign against Yaropolk, it is inserted under the year 980. In the *Suzdal Chronicle*, under the year 1128, where the sons of Vseslav are

---

[37] We get an analogous story in the *Chronicle of Georgius Hamartolas*. There the Bulgarian prince, having killed the Greek emperor Nikiphorus, makes a cup of his skull (see Istrin, *Khronika Georgia Amartola*, I, 187).

mentioned, we get a later variant of this story. Here Vladimir's uncle Dobrynya is introduced as his matchmaker to Rogvold. When the forcibly
wedded Rogneda, thereafter called Gorislava, had borne him a son, Izyaslav,
Vladimir lost interest in her and took to himself many other wives. Once
when, on a visit to Rogneda, Vladimir fell asleep, she tried to stab him, but
he awoke and stayed her hand. Rogneda explained her desire to kill him as
due to resentment that, after killing her father and seizing his lands, all
because of her, he now loved neither her nor their son. Vladimir, after ordering Rogneda to put on full royal attire as. for her wedding day and sit
on the bed, made ready to run her through with his sword. Rogneda did as
the prince had commanded her, then putting a naked sword into the hand
of her son Izyaslav, said to him: "When your father enters, you must step
forward and say: 'Do you think, father, that you are the only man here?'"
Upon hearing these words from his son, Vladimir cast his sword aside and,
on the advice of his boyars, who entreated him not to kill Rogneda for the
child's sake, restored Rogneda's inheritance and built for her and her son a
town which he called Izyaslavl. The story ends with the following words by
the chronicler: "And ever since then the grandsons of Rogvold have raised
their swords against the grandsons of Yaroslav." Judging from the fact that
this version of the story of Vladimir and Rogneda is found only in the all-
Russian compilation, it did not originate before the fourteenth century.
Both variants of this very poetical tale are undoubtedly based on retinue
epic tradition. Parallels exist in northern sagas and in Russian and Ukrainian
folk tales, which in turn are closely related to the epic traditions of the Germanic peoples as reflected in the *Song of the Nibelungs* and the *Tidrek
Saga*.[38]

Vladimir's new marriage, made in connection with his conversion to
Christianity, is discussed in the *Povest* under the year 988, after the story
of his examination of the religions. Vladimir attacked the Greek city of
Kherson and halted at the harbor, a bowshot from the town. The people of
Kherson put up a stiff resistance in the besieged town, though exhausted
from privation. Vladimir threatened to remain three years before the city
if the inhabitants did not surrender, yet they did not surrender; he constructed an earthwork just outside the city, but the people of Kherson undermined and gradually reduced it, carrying the earth into the town. Then a

[38] See B. M. Sokolov, *Epicheskie skazaniya o zhenit'be knazya Vladimira* (Epic Legends
About the Marriage of Prince Vladimir), German-Russian Relationships in the Field of the
Epic, reprinted from *Uchenye zapiski Gosud. Saratovskovo universiteta* (Scholarly Notes of
the State University of Saratov) (1923), Vol. I, Pt. 3, pp. 1–34. Also A. M. Lobodá's *Russkie
byliny o svatovstve* (Russian *Byliny* About Matchmaking) (Kiev, 1904), pp. 238–250.
Literary adaptations of this chronicle story were made by several writers of the end of the
eighteenth century and the first decades of the nineteenth. The best verse paraphrase is
Ryleyev's ballad, "*Rogneda*."

certain man of Kherson, Anastasius by name, shot an arrow into Vladimir's camp with a message advising him to divert the flow of a spring which was behind the Russian lines and from which water was piped into Kherson. Raising his eyes to heaven, Vladimir vowed that he would be baptized if he succeeded in doing as Anastasius had advised him. The pipes were severed, and the people of Kherson, overcome by thirst, surrendered. Vladimir entered the town with his *druzhina*** and then sent to Tsargrad to the emperors Basil and Constantine to demand that they give him their sister Anna in marriage, threatening that in the contrary event he would deal with Tsargrad as he had dealt with Kherson. The emperors consented to give Vladimir their sister in marriage only on condition that he be baptized. Vladimir agreed, saying that he had previously given some study to the Greek religion and that it was "pleasing" to him. With difficulty the brother emperors persuaded their sister to become Vladimir's wife, pleading that in so doing she would bring the land of Rus into the Christian fold and save Greece from destruction. Anna set out for Kherson. At that time Vladimir was suffering from a disease of the eyes so that he could see nothing. Anna advised him to be baptized with all speed in order to be cured of his malady. Vladimir took her advice, and no sooner had the bishop of Kherson laid his hand upon him than straightway he recovered his sight and glorified "the true God." Accompanied by the princess, Anastasius, and priests of Kherson, and taking the relics of St. Clement and of Phoebus, his disciple, sacred vessels, two bronze statues, and four bronze horses, Vladimir returned to Kiev, having first restored Kherson to the Greeks as a "marriage gift" to his bride. We are next told how the idols were overthrown in Kiev, how the priests of Kherson baptized the Russians, and how Vladimir built churches where the idols had previously been set.

In this version of the baptism of Vladimir, substituted, in Shakhmatov's opinion, for the primary version of the most ancient compilation of 1039 about the Russian prince's christening at Kiev, we are dealing with a learned work which originated independently of the chronicle and which utilized the folk-poetry tradition about a bold young man winning a bride by subjugating a city. This learned work, the text of which was established by Shakhmatov,[39] is known as the *Kherson Legend*. First it mentions Vladimir's worship of idols, then his insatiable lust, in which he is likened to Solomon: besides his lawful wives he had eight hundred concubines. (These data about Vladimir are also included in the *Povest*.) Then, judging from later

---

* *Druzhina*: a company or retinue serving as aids to the prince both as an armed force and as advisers and servitors. In general a *druzhina* did not exceed several hundred men.—ED.

[39] See the "Kherson Legend of the Baptism of Vladimir," *Sbornik statey v chest' V. I. Lamanskovo* (Collection of Articles in Honor of V. I. Lamanskii) (St. Petersburg, 1906), Pt. 2, pp. 1029–1153, and also *Razyskaniya* (Researches), pp. 133–161.

collections, the *Kherson Legend* told how Vladimir sent to the prince of Kherson to ask for his daughter's hand. When the prince of Kherson refuses this request, pleading the "paganism" of the suitor, Vladimir makes war on Kherson and takes it with the aid of the Varangian Zhidbern, who advises him by arrow to take the town through depriving it of water. Vladimir ravishes the prince's daughter in the presence of her parents, whom he then kills, and marries her to Zhidbern, whom he makes deputy of Kherson, while he himself, through Zhidbern and Oleg, who here appears as the general not of Igor but of Vladimir, seeks the sister of the Byzantine emperors in marriage. The rest of the story is approximately the same as in the *Povest*.

The *Kherson Legend*, as has been said, is a learned adaptation of folk-poetry motifs about a youth obtaining a bride, which are present, as Kostomarov further pointed out, in Christmas carols and other ballads, Ukrainian chiefly. Vladimir's threat that he would remain three years before Kherson if the town did not surrender, is, to judge by the use of the epic number three, likewise an echo from oral-poetry tradition. This is also true of the episode of the shooting of an arrow bearing an inscription, which is common in folk poetry: in Solun, for example, there is a similar story about a monk shooting an arrow from the town to the Turkish sultan with an inscription about diverting the water supply. To the ballad tradition must also apparently be referred the sending of the matchmakers Oleg and Zhidbern to Tsargrad, and so forth. The *Kherson Legend*, evidently from the pen of a Greek of Kherson, is based on the historical facts, corroborated by both Byzantine and Arabic sources, of Vladimir's attack upon Kherson, his taking of the city, and his marriage to a Greek princess. But all this was transformed into a literary legend which "fused into one, events that had occurred at different times, giving unity to what actually had no such unity. And though the legend is historical in its essential features, the treatment deflects it in the direction of legend and *bylina*." [40]

The *byliny* devoted to Vladimir assign a position of importance to his lavish feasts. Mention of these feasts—vestiges of *druzhina* epos—are also found in the *Povest*. Vladimir gave them every week, and provided much meat, both beef and game, an abundance of everything. Once, however, when the banqueters were drunk, they began to grumble about eating with wooden instead of with silver spoons. When he heard this, Vladimir ordered that silver spoons be molded, saying: "With silver and gold I could not secure a retinue, but with a retinue I can secure both silver and gold, as my grandfather and my father obtained gold and silver with their followers," for Vladimir loved his retinue and consulted with them concerning matters of administration, wars, and government.

[40] A. A. Shakhmatov, *Razyskaniya* (Researches), p. 135.

Assigned to the reign of Vladimir are the two following legends, one of which narrates the victory of a Russian youth over a Pecheneg and the other the incident of the Byelgorod porridge. The first legend tells how, during an encounter between Vladimir and the Pechenegs, it was decided, at the suggestion of the Pecheneg prince, that they have recourse to single combat between a Rus and a Pecheneg; if the Rus was victorious, then there was to be no war for three years, but if the Pecheneg won, there was to be war for three years in succession. For a long time no volunteer could be found on the Russian side, but finally an old man came to Vladimir and said that he had a son who once, when rebuked, had torn a tough hide to shreds in his hands. The youth was put to the test: a powerful bull that had been angered with hot irons was let loose upon him and, as it ran past, the youth seized the bull's flank in his hand and pulled off skin along with flesh. Then Vladimir decided that a suitable opponent had been found for the Pecheneg, and on the following day the contest took place. The Pecheneg was gigantic and fearsome and started to laugh at his adversary because he was of but moderate size. But the Russian seized the Pecheneg, crushed him to death in his arms and cast him upon the ground. The Pechenegs screamed and fled and the Russians pursued, cutting them down. On the spot where the combat had taken place, Vladimir founded a city and called it Pereyaslavl, "because this youth had won glory there," or, as Sobolevsky prefers to read it, "because the youth was named Pereyaslav." After rewarding the champion and his father, Vladimir returned to Kiev with victory and great renown. This tradition reflects, first of all, the very widely diffused migratory motif of victory over a giant, present even in the Bible (David and Goliath). Another parallel that may be cited is the folk tale of the battle between Nikita or Cyril Kozhemyak and the serpent. A single-combat motif, analogous to that just summarized and recurring in the *Tale of Igor's Expedition,* is also encountered in the chronicle story about Mstislav cutting down the Kassogian prince Rededya.

The story about the Byelgorod porridge emphasizes the stupidity of the Pechenegs, previously brought out in the chronicle account of the Pecheneg siege of Kiev in the reign of Svyatoslav. The Pechenegs attacked Byelgorod. Vladimir could not come to its assistance because he was in Novgorod and had too few troops. The harassed people of Byelgorod were ready to surrender to the Pechenegs, but one old man decided to fool the enemy. He directed the citizens to bring in a measure of oats, wheat, or beans, if no more, make a porridge of the product, dig a well, and sink the tub of porridge into it. In a second well he bade them put a tub of honey diluted with water, and then he invited the Pechenegs to see what was happening in the

besieged town. The inhabitants assured the Pecheneg envoys who entered
the town that however long the siege continued they would sustain it, for
the earth itself fed them. The amazed envoys tasted the porridge and honey
themselves and then took a pot of each to their princes, and the Pechenegs,
convinced that the inhabitants of Byelgorod had an inexhaustible supply of
comestibles, left for home. We find a similar legend in Herodotus' story of
the siege of Miletus by the Lydians; in Russian folklore popular anecdotes
are very widespread about simpletons who are easily duped by sharp swin-
dlers and crooks.

The examples cited are far from exhausting the cases in which the chronicle uses the traditions of folk poetry, existent chiefly in the form of epic
legends or lyric ballads composed by singer-poets like that Boyan whom the
Tale of Igor's Expedition mentions, and akin to the northern skalds. In the
monk-editor's literary adaptation, the poetic style of these traditions was
largely depersonalized, though not so much so as to wipe out all connection
with the oral-poetry tradition on which they were based. From this point
on, the *Povest* uses folk-poetry traditions less frequently, for subsequent
events narrated in the chronicle were, so to speak, a matter of yesterday, or
of today, for the editor.[41]

Side by side with oral traditions, the *Povest* used written sources both
Russian and foreign. An attempt to give a more or less exhaustive list of
these sources was first made by M. I. Sukhomlinov in 1856 in his book,
On the Old Russian Chronicle as a Literary Monument. As time went on,
Sukhomlinov's listings were repeatedly revised, made more exact, supplemented.[42] I shall not go into detail concerning the redactions of foreign
sources used in the *Povest*, but shall note only the sources themselves and,

[41] Concerning the connection of the chronicle with oral tradition and with folk poetry,
see M. I. Sukhomlinov: "O predaniakh v drevney russkoy letopisi" (On Traditions in the
Early Russian Chronicle), *Issledovaniya po drevney russkoy literature* (Studies in Early Russian Literature) (St. Petersburg, 1908), pp. 248–272; N. I. Kostomarov, "Predaniya pervonach-
al'noy russkoy letopisi v soobrazheniyakh s russkimi narodnymi predaniami v pesnyakh, skaz-
kakh i obychayakh" (Traditions in the Russian Primary Chronicle Considered in Relation
to Russian Folk Traditions in Songs, Folk Tales and Customs), *Collected Works,* Bk. V,
Vol. XIII, pp. 289–392.

[42] In addition to Shakhmatov's *Razyskaniya* (Researches) and his study, "Povest vremennykh let i yevo istochniki" (Tale of Bygone Years and Its Sources) in *Trudy otd. drevnerusskoy literatury* (Works of the Division of Early Russian Literature) (1940), IV, on this
problem see also P. Zabolotskii's "K voprosy ob inozemnykh pis'mennykh istochnikakh
nachalnoy letopisi" (On the Question of the Foreign Written Sources of the Primary Chronicle), *Russkii philologicheskii vestnik* (Russian Philological Herald) (1902), No. 1; P.
Potapov, "K voprosy o literaturnom sostave letopisi" (On the Question of the Literary Composition of the Chronicle) (1910), No. 1, and (1911), No. 1; V. Istrin, "Otkrovenie Mefodia
Patarskovo i letopis," (Revelation of Methodius of Patara and the Chronicle) *Izv. ORYAS
akad. nauk* (News of the Division of Russian Language and Literature of the Academy of
Sciences) (1924), Vol. XXIX.

at that, only such as may be regarded as beyond debate. To this category belongs, first, the *Chronicle of Georgius Hamartolas,* whence the *Povest* drew the items set forth in the first pages of the chronicle about the division of the earth among the sons of Noah, about the manners and customs of various peoples (this account carries on the face of it the reference: "Georgius says in his chronicle"), about the philosopher-soothsayer, Apollonius of Tyana, about various facts of Byzantine history, and so forth. From a non-extant Moravo-Pannonian source are derived the items about Polyanian Rus and about the translation of books into Slavic. From the *Life of Basil Neos* are borrowed the items about Igor's attacks on Tsargrad in 941 and 944. As indicated, the story of the baptism of Vladimir in Kherson goes back to a Greek source. The Greek philosopher's admonition to Vladimir before baptism and the philosopher's speech are, in Shakhmatov's opinion, derived from an account inextant but reflected in the Byzantine chronicle's account of the baptism of the Bulgarian king Boris. Vladimir's confession of faith is drawn from the "Confession of Faith" of Michael Syncellus. With the *Revelation of Methodius of Patara* is associated the account, under the date 1096, of the attack of the Polovcians, whom the chronicler considers descendants of Ishmael, who shall, at the end of the world, come forth with the other "unclean peoples" from the mountain where Alexander of Macedon inclosed them.

As to the Russian sources of the *Povest,* if we take into account the fact that the chronicle is a compilation consisting of a large number of separate narratives and tales, both oral and written, which had previously existed independently of it, the number of such sources becomes very considerable. They include both martial tales and monastic legends such as the legend of the beginning of the Crypt Monastery, biographical narratives, for example, the account of the murder of Boris and Gleb, legendary tales such as the legend about the magicians in Yaroslav's time, testaments such as those of Theodosius and Vladimir Monomakh, and narratives dealing with inter-princely relations, for example, the priest Basil's highly artistic and dramatic account of the blinding of Vasilko, Prince of Terebovl, and so forth.[43] As an example of a martial tale used in the chronicle, we may cite the poetical description, under the year 1024, of the battle of Listven between Yaroslav and Mstislav. This is how the battle is there described:

When night fell, there was darkness with lightning, thunder, and rain. And Mstislav said to his followers: "Let us attack them." And Mstislav and Yaroslav then attacked each other, and the Severians in the center met the Varangians,

---

[43] An attempt to sort out this material in the chronicle is made in I. P. Khrushchov's book, *O drevnerusskikh istoricheskikh povestyakh i skazaniyakh* (On the Early Russian Historical Tales and Legends) (Kiev, 1878).

who exhausted themselves in opposing them. Then Mstislav came up with his retainers to attack the Varangians, and the combat was violent. As the lightnings flashed, the weapons gleamed and the thunder roared, and the fight was violent and fearsome.

Under the year 1071 there is a story about magicians confounding the people in time of famine. In argument with Yan, son of Vyshata, they retail the Bogomil apocryphal legend of the creation of man by the Devil and God as set forth above in the section on apocryphas. Some incidents are told from the impressions of eyewitnesses, and stories of these events are accordingly written by the editor from memory. In addition to the long dramatic account, under 1097, of the blinding of Vasilko, attributable to the priest Basil and written in such realistic detail that it can only have been done from the words of an eyewitness, the *Povest* mentions, under 1065, in a piece about portents, the fact that some fishermen at that time pulled up in their net, from the river Setoml, a malformed child, and adds: "We gazed upon it till evening, when they cast it back into the water." Under 1096 is quoted an account of the attack of the Polovcians on the Crypt Monastery under the leadership of the Polovcian khan Bonyak, to which is appended: "They came to the Crypt Monastery while we were resting in our cells after matins, and they howled about the monastery. They planted two standards before the monastery gates, and we fled, some of us behind the building of the monastery, and others to its various rooms."

In proceeding to the establishment of the commonest characteristics of the chronicle style, it must be borne in mind that, owing to the variety of the material that goes to make up the chronicle, there can be no question of unity of style. The style is in large measure determined by the genre to which separate items in the chronicle belong. In the majority of cases the chronicle style is distinguished by its compression, its laconic quality, the best example of which is perhaps the account of Oleg's death through his horse:

Thus Oleg ruled in Kiev, and dwelt at peace with all nations. Now autumn came, and Oleg bethought him of his horse that he had caused to be well fed, yet had never mounted. For on one occasion he had made inquiry of the wonder-working magicians as to the ultimate cause of his death. One magician replied, "O Prince, it is from the steed which you love and on which you ride that you shall meet your death."

This laconic quality is particularly noticeable in short, purely factual paragraphs of only a line or so. In the long stories dialogue occupies an important place, bringing elements of drama into the account. Those passages of the chronicle which tell of battles give prominence to the stylistic formulae traditional for martial tales, expressions such as: "They clashed . . . and the carnage was terrible. . . . They seized each other by the arm and hacked so that blood flowed down the valley," and so forth.[44]

As an example I shall quote the description of the battle between Yaroslav and Svyatopolk:

It was then Friday. As the sun rose, the two met in battle, and the carnage was terrible, such as had never before occurred in Rus. The soldiers fought hand to hand and slaughtered each other, and three times they clashed so that blood flowed down the valley.

Another example of the style of the chronicle war story was cited above in the quotation from the description of the battle of Listven. Chronicle tales of the biographical type, such as the legend of the murder of Boris and Gleb by Svyatopolk, are comparatively verbose and rhetorical. This is partly due to the numerous biblical quotations, most frequently encountered, generally speaking, in parts of the chronicle having wholly to do with ecclesiastical tradition. In some cases, however, chronicle rhetoric offers examples of genuine poetic inspiration. Such, for instance, is the praise of books inserted by the chronicler under the year 1037, in connection with the account of the organization by Yaroslav the Wise of a translation project:

For great is the profit from book-learning. Through the medium of books, we are shown and taught the way of repentance, for we gain wisdom and continence from the written word. Books are like rivers that water the whole earth; they are the springs of wisdom. For books have an immeasurable depth; by them we are consoled in sorrow. They are the bridle of self-restraint.

Or the obituary eulogy to Princess Olga:

She was the precursor of the Christian land, even as the dayspring precedes the sun and as the dawn precedes the day. For she shone like the moon by night, and she was radiant among the infidels like a pearl in the mire, since the people were soiled and not yet purified of their sin by holy baptism. . . . She was the first from Rus to enter the Kingdom of God, and the sons of Rus thus praise her as their leader, for since her death she has interceded with God in their behalf.

A eulogy frequently accompanies the chronicle notice of the death of outstanding historical figures, princes chiefly, and along with the description of the inner qualities of the subject a description of his personal appearance is frequently given as well, a schematic portrait: "Rostislav was a man bold in war, fair of stature, and handsome of feature, and he was generous to the poor"; "For Gleb was generous to the poor and kind to strangers, reverent in church, warm in faith and gentle, beautiful to look upon"; "For Izyaslav

[44] A detailed analysis of the poetical formulae used in martial tales is made in A. S. Orlov's study, "Ob osobennostyakh formy russkikh voinskikh povestey, konchaya XVII v." (On Stylistic Idiosyncracies in Russian War Narratives, Ending with the Seventeenth Century) (Fuserti, Moscow, 1902), from Chtenii v Obshchestve istorii i drevnostey rossiiskikh (Papers Read Before the Society of Russian History and Antiquities).

was a man fair of appearance and imposing in stature, not malicious in temper, but a hater of injustice and a lover of rectitude. In him there was no guile, for he was a simple man who did not render evil for evil." In all these sketches, especially in the second and third, one senses the hand of the ecclesiastic for whom the moral-religious aspect of the dead prince is the most important thing. This tendency of the pious scholar is reflected, for example, in the sketch of Yaropolk, who died in 1086:

This blessed prince was calm, mild, moderate, and loving toward his brethren. He gave each year a tithe of his property to the Holy Virgin, and often addressed this prayer to God, saying: "O Lord, my God! receive my prayer, and grant me a death by an unknown hand like that of my kinsmen Boris and Gleb, so that I may wash away my sin with my blood, and thus escape this vain world and its confusion, as well as the snares of the devil."

And entirely different qualities are noted in the character sketch of Mstislav (died 1036): "Mstislav was corpulent and red-faced, with large eyes, bold in battle, merciful, and a great lover of his retainers, begrudging them neither treasure nor food nor drink." It is quite evident that such a characterization could issue only from the ranks of Mstislav's devoted retinue.

Accounts of the death of pagan princes commonly make mention of the fact that their tomb is standing even to "this day." Of Oleg's tomb it is said: "His tomb stands there to this day, and it is called the Tomb of Oleg." Of the Tomb of Igor: "His tomb is near the town of Izkorosten in Dereva even to this day." To the Tomb of Oleg, son of Svyatoslav, we find the following reference: "So they buried Oleg in the city of Vruchi and his tomb is there to this day." (Later on, in connection with Christian princes, it is customary to refer to their burial in such and such a church, sometimes with the addition, "which he himself had built.")

Mention of the attack on the Polovcians and the death of Prince Román Svyatoslavich is accompanied by a rhythmic refrain in the style of a Boyan ballad:

And his bones exist and lie there to this day—
son of Svyatoslav, grandson of Yaroslav.

In the description of the burial of princes, it is customary to mention the lamentation of relatives and of the populace. At the burial of Oleg: "All the people mourned for him in great grief"; at the burial of Olga: "Her son wept for her with great mourning, as did likewise her grandsons and all the people." When the populace found out about the death of Vladimir, "the boyars mourned him as the defender of their country, the poor as their protector and benefactor"; after the death of Yaroslav, "the people mourned for him. When they had transported the body, they laid it in a marble sarcophagus in the Church of St. Sophia and Vsevolod and all his subjects mourned him." When Izyaslav was killed at the plain of Nezhatina, "the chanting could not be heard for the lamentation and great mourning, since the whole city of Kiev bewailed him." Finally, when the young prince Rostislav, son of Vsevolod, was drowned in the Stugna, "his mother wept over him, and the people pitied him greatly because of his youth."

This traditional formula of lamentation obviously derives from the hagiographical style.

The language of the chronicle, while retaining in churchly narratives and in quotations from the Bible the vocabulary and form of Church Slavonic, reveals upon other occasions its vital connection with the spoken Russian of the eleventh and twelfth centuries. This is particularly shown in the use of proverbs and adages. The chronicler mentions current sayings: "They perished like the Avars"; "Famine as in Rodnya." The Derevlians, upon hearing that Igor was coming back for further tribute, said: "If a wolf is wont to come among the sheep, he will take away the whole flock unless he be killed." Vladimir's warriors ridicule the Radimichians, saying: "Those who live by the river Pyeshchan flee from a wolf's tail" (play upon words: Wolf's Tail was the nickname of the Kievan general who defeated the Radimichians). When Vladimir conquered the Bulgars, Dobrynya said: "I have seen the prisoners, and they all wear boots. They will not pay us tribute. Let us rather look for foes with bast shoes." When the Bulgars made peace with Vladimir, they confirmed it by oath: "May peace prevail between us till stone floats and straw sinks." The people of Novgorod, when refusing to accept Svyatopolk and his son as their princes, say to Svyatopolk: "If your son has two heads, you might send him," and so forth.

In its general character and tricks of exposition, our chronicle has much in common with the medieval chronicles of western Europe written in Latin by Gregory of Tours (fifth century), Lambert of Hersfeld (eleventh century), Martin Hall (twelfth century), Cosima of Prague (twelfth century), and others. The likeness between them is shown first of all in the fact that both the Russian chronicle and the Western ones as a rule adhere to the chronological principle. In cases where our chronicler has introduced some episode into his account in violation of the chronological sequence, his resumption of the interrupted narrative is prefaced by the words: "But let us return to the topic we were discussing," or, "We shall now return to the subject," "We shall now proceed to discuss," "We should also mention," corresponding to the formulae of western European chroniclers: *"Sed ad coeptum, unde digressi sumus, redeamus," "Ad coeptum potius revertamur,"* and so forth.

Both with the Russian and with the western European chronicler, the material included consists partly of short paragraphs, partly of detailed narratives. In short paragraphs and in more circumstantial accounts alike, what both of them talk about is, for the most part, enemy invasions, internecine wars, marriages of rulers, the birth of children to them, heavenly portents, and so forth. As with the Russian chronicler, so with his colleagues in western Europe, preference is given to the description of outward events and historical facts rather than to a discussion of the inner life, though ecclesiastical and monastic events are among those set forth. These events are sketched, as in the *Povest*, partly from traditional accounts, partly on the basis of written sources, and partly from the testimony of contemporaries and eyewitnesses.

Sketches of the moral and physical characteristics of the historical personages who figure in the Western chronicles are as short, schematic, and, in many cases, hackneyed as those that we have met in the *Povest*.

The medieval chronicler in western Europe was just as credulous about all manner of unusual anecdotal facts and occurrences as the Russian chronicler. As a parallel to the Russian chronicler's item about the malformed child which was taken out of the river Setoml, an item may be cited from a German chronicler of the beginning of the eleventh century, Thietmar of Merseburg, about a monster birth which brought on a pestilence. Another German chronicler, Wiedekind (tenth century), records: "In this year (942) occurred many heavenly portents. . . . A report was circulated that the mount where the Almighty Lord was buried had shot forth flame at many points. Also, a man's left hand, which had been cut off with a sword, grew again as he slept. . . . Upon these comets followed a terrible flood and upon the flood a cattle plague." Both the Russian and the western European chronicler regard heavenly portents as the presage of all manner of troubles and misfortunes. Both sometimes take exception to pronouncements, particularly those made by superstitious people. Thus in the *Povest* under 1073, following the account of the malformed child that had been taken out of the Setoml, we find the record: "Somewhat before this moment the sun also suffered alteration and, instead of being bright, became rather like the moon, and the ignorant said it had been consumed."

Thietmar of Merseburg writes: "In 989, on October 21, at five o'clock, there was a darkening of the sun. I exhorted the Christians not to believe that this had been brought about by the sorcery of evil women or by someone's swallowing the sun." Incidentally the *Povest*, as of 1071, carries an account of magicians falsely accusing women of being responsible for the crop failure that had occurred in the Rostov district. Finally, the Russian and the Western medieval chronicler both consider the will of God the source of all good; from it proceeds also the punishment of sin; while the source of enmity, treachery, and all manner of evil things is regarded by both as residing in the machinations of the Devil, and both express sorrow in connection with dishonorable and wicked acts which sow misfortune in their native land. Common expressions in the *Povest* are: "God implanted a good impulse in the Russian princes"; "God put it in the prince's heart"; "God sent the pagans upon us, not because he held them dear, but to chastise us"; "The Devil stirred up strife between the brothers," and so forth. Just so do the Western chroniclers explain good fortune and bad as the interference of God and of the Devil in human affairs. Thus Cosima of Prague writes: "The ancient serpent, enemy of mankind, who never slumbers nor ever ceases to disturb the repose of others, could not bear to see the brothers, King Vratislav and Bishop Gebhard living in peace, and sowed enmity between them." The pursuit of egoistic personal interests by those in power, to the detriment of public welfare and of the interests of the country, and to the profit of its enemies, are a common subject for censure on the part of the Western chronicler. We find the same thing in our own chronicler. Through the lips of the Russian princes at the Lyubech Conference he says: "Why do we ruin the land of Rus by our continued strife against one another? The Polovcians tear our country to pieces and rejoice that war is waged among us. Let us rather hereafter be united in spirit and watch over the land of Rus."

Thus, as we see, the Russian and the Western medieval chronicler coincide in the main as to methods of exposition, world outlook, and ways of expressing it.[45] This does not signify, of course, that our chronicler was acquainted with the Western chronicles; his resembling them is due to similarity in the literary manifestations of medieval culture exhibited by various peoples living under its influence. Specifically, the Russian chronicle resembles in the above-mentioned particulars not only the chronicles of western Europe but those of Byzantium as well, especially the *Chronicle of Georgius Hamartolas*, and again because the Byzantine chronicles were basically characterized by the same traits of medieval literary culture that are present in the Western chronicles.

At the same time the Russian chronicle clearly reflected national interests. The above-quoted opinion of certain scholars as to the presence in the chronicle of a marked Grecophil tendency is grave exaggeration. Virtually the only solid basis for discerning such a tendency is the *Kherson Legend*, but, in the first place, a Grecophil tendency could be quite as successfully demonstrated if the *Povest* asserted that he was baptized in Kiev instead of in Kherson, the more so as Vladimir had come to Kherson not as a humble pil-

[45] For more details on this, see M. Sukhomlinov, *ibid.*, pp. 139–196; V. S. Ikonnikov, *Opyt russkoy istoriografii* (Experiment in Russian Historiography) (Kiev, 1908), Vol. II, Bk. I, pp. 308–319.

grim desirous of joining the Christian faith, but as the stern conqueror of the city, of his bride, and, in effect, of the Church. On the other hand the chronicle so often, and sometimes even in contradiction of historical fact, tells of the triumph of Russian arms over Greek, that this alone would be enough to throw doubt on any consciously and systematically developed pro-Greek tendency on the part of the chronicler. Moreover, it is only necessary to note such a slip as "for the Greeks are deceivers even to this day," made in speaking of Svyatoslav's war with the Greeks, in order to arrive at a correct estimate of his Grecophilism.[46] However that may be, the Russian *Primary Chronicle,* taken along with other monuments of Russian literature from the eleventh and twelfth centuries, constitutes a very significant index to the growth of national consciousness in a people which had but recently become united to medieval European culture.

The *Povest* served as a point of departure for a whole series of annalistic compilations, which made use of it in more or less complete form for the exposition of Russian history as a whole down to the beginning of the twelfth century, and then continued it, chiefly with local items. Thus, during the twelfth and early thirteenth centuries, chronicles sprang up in southern Pereyaslavl, Chernigov, Volynia, Kiev, Vladimir (three compilations), Rostov, and Pereyaslavl in the Suzdal district which in turn became the basis for later annalistic compilations.[47] All the provincial chronicle compilations begin with the *Povest,* which, in the eyes of the chroniclers, constituted a synthesis of all the Russian history of the preceding age, and thereby clarified their connection with the interests not of one given province alone, but of the land of Rus as a whole.

THE TESTAMENT OF VLADIMIR MONOMAKH

Under the year 1096 the Laurentian copy of the *Povest* carries the *Testament* of Vladimir Monomakh, together with his letter to Prince Oleg of

[46] Incidentally, one ought not to overemphasize, as M. D. Prisyolkov does, the tendentiousness of the inextant *Life of Antonius,* Prior of the Crypt, as reflected in those pages of the chronicle which deal with the Kiev-Crypt Monastery. Cf. S. P. Rozanov, "K voprosu o zhitii Antonia Pecherskogo" (On the Question of the Life of Antonius of the Crypt), *Izv. otd. russk, yaz. i slov.* (News of the Division of Russian Language and Literature of the Academy of Sciences) (1914), Bk. I, pp. 34–46; V. Parkhomenko, "B kakoy mere bylo tendentsiozno nesokhranivsheesya do nas drevneyshee 'Zhitie Antoniya Pecherskogo?' (In What Measure Was the Inextant Oldest Life of Antonius of the Crypt Tendentious?) *ibid.,* pp. 237–241.

[47] On the scientific editions of chronicle texts and on the numerous works devoted to the chronicle, see *Opyt russkoy istoriografii* (Experiment in Russian Historiography), V. S. Ikonnikov, Vol. II, Bk. I.

Chernigov. The *Testament* is addressed by Monomakh to his children and continues with this outstanding historical figure's autobiography. It dates from between the end of the eleventh century and 1125—the year of Monomakh's death—and is a striking indication of the high cultural level which had been reached by Kievan Rus in the person of its greatest secular representatives. Monomakh shows a thorough knowledge of the translated reading matter in circulation in Rus at that time and of the service books, the Psalter in particular. He is acquainted with the genre, so popular in Byzantine medieval literature, of testaments of fathers to sons, beginning with those of Xenophon and Marius, which were included in *Svyatoslav's Miscellany* of 1076.[48] In his *Testament* Vladimir Monomakh stands revealed as a man wise through a large experience of life, noble, humanely disposed, always looking out for the good of his realm, and invoking protection for the weak against the strong and against those in power. At the same time he is an energetic prince, enterprising, endowed with warlike virtues, who spends his whole life in unceasing toil and in perilous military campaigns. When emissaries from his brothers come to him with the proposal that he join forces with them to expel the sons of Rostislav from their appanage and seize their domain, he refuses to do so because he does not wish to violate his oath on the cross. He counsels against taking an oath unless it can be abided by, but once an oath has been taken, the promise must be kept, lest one destroy one's own soul. He does not advise his children to save their souls in a hermitage or a monastery or by fasting, but only by repentance, tears, and almsgiving. Monomakh particularly urges them to protect all unfortunates and to invoke lenience even for criminals: "Above all things, forget not the poor," he says, "but support them to the extent of your means. Give to the orphan, protect the widow, and permit the mighty to destroy no man. Take not the life of the just or the unjust, nor permit him to be killed, even though he be guilty of murder. Destroy no Christian soul." Of himself he writes: "I did not allow the mighty to distress the common peasant or the poverty-stricken widow." They must honor old men as their fathers, young men as their brothers. In visiting their domains, they must not permit servants to injure either peasants belonging to them or those of another. They must give the beggar to eat and to drink, and must honor the traveler, be he simple or noble, and the emissary, and give them gifts, because these and others who travel through various lands give you a reputation as gener-

48 On the *Testament* see N. Shlyakov, *O pouchenii Vladimira Monomakha* (On the Testament of Vladimir Monomakh) (St. Petersburg, 1900), and I. M. Ivakin, *Knyaz' Vladimir Monomakh i yevo pouchenie* (Prince Vladimir Monomakh and His Testament) (Moscow, 1901), Pt. 1; M. P. Alexeyev, "Anglo-Saksonska Parallel k poucheniya Vladimira Monomakha" (An Anglo-Saxon Parallel to the Testament of Vladimir Monomakh), *Trudy otd. drevnerussk. lit.* (Works of the Division of Early Russian Literature) (1935), II, pp. 39–80.

ous or niggardly. "Visit the sick," Monomakh goes on to advise, "and accompany the dead, for we are all but mortal; pass no man without a greeting; give him a kindly word. Love your wives, but grant them no power over you."

Monomakh summons his children to an active life, to constant effort, and exhorts them never to live in idleness nor give themselves over to debauchery. They must not rely upon servants nor upon stewards, but go into everything themselves and supervise everything, lest some harm should befall. They must shun drunkenness and vice, for therein perish soul and body. Forget not what useful knowledge you possess, and acquire that with which you are not acquainted, even as Monomakh's father (Vsevolod), though he remained at home in his own country, learned five languages, whereby honor is acquired in other lands. (Vsevolod probably knew the following languages: Greek, Latin, German, Hungarian, and Polovcian.) In enumerating his many "journeys" and "hunts," Monomakh has it in mind to instruct by personal example his children and all who shall read his "manual," which, needless to say, was not written for the prince's children alone. Monomakh mounted, in all, eighty-three major campaigns, and does not even recall the minor ones. On hunting expeditions he many times underwent mortal dangers, of which he himself says:

Two bisons tossed me and my horse on their horns; a stag once gored me; one elk stamped upon me, while another gored me; a boar once tore my sword from my thigh; a bear on one occasion bit my knee and another wild beast jumped on my flank and threw my horse with me. But God preserved me unharmed. I often fell from my horse, fractured my skull twice, and in my youth injured my arms and legs when I did not reck of my body or spare my head.

In the *Testament* Monomakh expresses a poetical delight in the beauties of nature. Following the Psalter and the *Hexaemeron* of John the Exarch, he speaks with emotion of how marvelously the world was constructed "through God's devices—how the heaven was formed, the sun, the moon, the stars, the darkness of night and the light of day, and how the earth was set upon the waters." He is amazed at "the appearance of birds in the springtime in our own land first of all. Yet they remain not in one region, for both weak and strong, by divine commandment, fly over the whole earth, to populate the forests and fields." And all this "God has bestowed for the delight, sustenance, and pleasure of mankind."

However grim and war-hardened Vladimir Monomakh may have been, lyrical feelings were natural to him, and what sort of poetical expression he gave them is to be seen in his letter to Oleg, Prince of Chernigov. Izyaslav, the youthful son of Monomakh, had seized Murom, which belonged to Oleg, and he was killed. The father was deeply grieved over the death of his son, but in the end decided to make his peace with Oleg for the good of Rus, and wrote him a letter on the subject, asking him to send Izyaslav's widow to him so that they may mourn together for his slain son:

You might have returned to me my daughter-in-law (for in her there is neither harm nor profit) that I might embrace her and mourn her husband and her marriage, instead of uttering joyous songs. For, because of my sins, I did not behold their joy of other days nor their betrothal. But now, for God's sake, send her to me quickly with your first answer, so that I may mourn with her unceasingly and set her in the station that befits her: so may she sit languishing like a dove on a dry tree, and I shall be consoled in God!

The touching image of a dove mourning for its mate we find alike in the Psalter, in the *Hexaemeron*, in the *Physiologus*, in the "Church Fathers," and in folk poetry. Wherever Monomakh may have borrowed it, he did so with great artistic good taste.

THE TALE OF IGOR'S EXPEDITION: *Slovo O Polku Igoreve*

The most precious monument of ancient Russian literature, *The Tale of Igor's Expedition,* was written in connection with a disastrous foray made against the Polovcians by the Severian prince Igor, son of Svyatoslav, in conjunction with his brother Vsevolod from Trubchevsk, his son Vladimir from Putivl, and his nephew Svyatoslav, son of Oleg from Rylsk. The foray took place at the end of April and the beginning of May, 1185. Besides being the subject of the *Tale of Igor's Expedition,* it is described under this year in the Laurentian (comparatively short) and Hypatian (more detailed) chronicles, and also in subsequent chronicles based on these. As we shall see later, the *Tale* was written shortly after the campaign. It was discovered in 1795 by a collector and amateur of antiquities, Count A. I. Musin-Pushkin, as part of a collection acquired from the Yaroslav St. Saviour's Monastery and containing, besides the *Igor,* the *Chronograph, The Annals Which Are Called the Chronicle of the Russian Princes and the Land of Rus,* the *Legend of the Kingdom of India,* the *Tale of Akir,* and the *Adventures of Digenis.* In this collection the *Igor* was the next to the last item. The first announcement of its discovery was made by Karamzin, in 1797, in the *Spectateur du Nord.*

The text, with a translation into modern Russian, an introductory essay and notes, was first published in 1800 in Moscow by Musin-Pushkin in collaboration with the scholar specialists A. F. Malinovsky and N. N. Bantysh-Kamensky. The publication was entitled, *The Heroic Ballad of the Campaign Against the Polovcians of the Appanaged Prince of Severian Novgorod, Igor, Son of Svyatoslav, Written in the Ancient Russian Language at the End of the Twelfth Century, with a Paraphrase into the Idiom Now in Use.* This title, given the *Tale* by its first publishers, was in full accord with their opinion that in it "was to be seen the spirit of Ossian." Apparently, soon after the discovery of the monument, a copy was made for Catherine II. This was first published in 1864 by P. P. Pekarsky, as a supplement to the fifth volume of the *Records of the Academy of Sciences.* It was published a second time, with greater regard for accuracy, by P. K. Simon in 1890 in the Moscow Archaeological Society's *Antiquities,* Volume XIII. In 1812 Musin-Pushkin's Moscow house was burned down, and the manuscript containing the *Igor* perished along with other manuscripts kept there. Thus the one old copy of the *Igor* was lost, and we now possess only the copy made for Catherine at the end of the eighteenth century and the first printed text, most of the copies of which, stored in Musin-Pushkin's house, were likewise destroyed, so that this first printed text became a bibliographical rarity.[49]

At the time when Musin-Pushkin and his collaborators were working on the *Igor* manuscript, the science of paleography was still in the embryonic stage and therefore Catherine's copy and the first printed text of the *Tale* contain a number of readings that are beyond doubt erroneous. It is significant that in a number of cases the readings in the two texts differ in matters of detail: the Musin-Pushkin edition emended some readings which had earlier been established in the copy made for Catherine. There can be no doubt, however, that incorrect readings already existed in the *Igor* manuscript itself. Philological and paleographical criticism of Catherine's copy and of the first printed edition would appear to indicate that the lost manuscript dated from the sixteenth century, the beginning, perhaps, and consequently was more than three hundred years removed from the original monument.

Needless to say, this copy derived not directly from the original, but from some copy that had in turn been transcribed from an earlier copy. How many such intermediate copies separate the only known manuscript of the *Tale* from the original we do not know, but however many there may have been (more likely few than many), the interval of three hundred years is too long a period for a monument so unusual in style and so rich in factual

[49] Later it was several times accurately reproduced, first by D. Dubenskii, in his book on the *Tale* (1844), next as a supplement to Prof. P. V. Vladimirov's *Drevnyaya russkaya literatura Kievskogo perioda XI–XIII vv.* (Early Russian Literature of the Kiev Period, Eleventh-Thirteenth Centuries) (Kiev, 1900), then in phototype in editions by A. S. Suvorin (1904) and M. and S. Sabashnikov (1920).

content to have escaped corruption and mutilation. To the sixteenth century copyist much even of what had come over correctly would have been in large measure strange and incomprehensible. Hence the many obscure passages in the *Tale* which numerous learned commentators, both Russian and foreign, have already been one hundred and forty years trying to figure out.

The copy of the *Tale* lost in the burning of Moscow was made in the Pskov area and therefore reflected the phonetic peculiarities of the North Russian dialects, chief among which is the alternation of lingual and dental sibilants (*shizyi, rusitsi, Slovutitsyu, synov'chya, chepy*, and so on). The orthography of the manuscript is artificial: on the one hand it retains the traditional hard and soft signs, which in the spoken language had at that time already ceased to be pronounced or had gone over into *o* and *ye*, and confuses them at that (*p'rvykh', rzhut', byezhat'*, but *zovut', breshut'*, while on the other hand it uses the Bulgarian orthography which came into fashion in the fifteenth century, whereby the hard and soft signs are placed after the liquid consonants (*pl'k', vl'k', khr'sovy, pr'vyy*), frequently with the same confusion of the two (*pr'vye, pr'sty, chr'nyi*), and an un-iotized vowel is allowed to stand after another vowel (*vyeshchia, kopia, sia*).

At the very first, even before the loss of the manuscript of the *Tale*, several translations were made into modern Russian, including some in verse. The few attempts made to study the *Tale* amounted to little more than commentary upon individual obscure passages. Shortly after the publication of the monument, however, sceptics began raising their voices in denial of its antiquity. Thus the metropolitan Eugene Bolkhovitinov asserted that the *Tale* was not written until the sixteenth century, while Rumyantsov assigned it to the eighteenth century, regarding it as a manifest forgery. There were even some who went so far as to look upon the *Tale* as a forgery either by Musin-Pushkin himself or by Karamzin. The incredulity of certain stubborn sceptics as to the *Tale* being a genuine monument remained unshaken even after the publication, in 1838, of *The Communication and Legend of the Rout of Great Prince Dmitry Ivanovich*, which beyond doubt showed the reflected influence of the *Igor*.

Two of these sceptics in particular, Kachenovsky and Senkovsky, went on demonstrating against the genuineness of the *Slovo* down to the middle 1850's. The sceptical attitude toward it in the 1830's and 1840's was merely a specific manifestation of the general attitude of disparagement assumed by a group of historians and critics toward Russia's past, to them an epoch culturally very poor, almost barbarous. In relation to the *Slovo* in particular, the sceptics chiefly called attention, on the one hand, to the absence in Old Russian literature of monuments in any way approaching it as a work of art, and on the other hand pointed out that its linguistic peculiarities had no parallels in the language of the earliest Russian monuments. This stubborn disinclination on the part of certain students of the *Slovo* to recognize its genuineness only spurred their opponents to set to work the more painstakingly and more persistently on a study of early Russian literature precedent to or contemporary with the *Slovo*, and of the Old Russian language, in order to prove the affirmative point of view. As a result of these studies, the position of the sceptics had by the 1840's already become quite obviously untenable.[50] After the loss of the manuscript of the *Slovo*, the defenders of its authenticity concentrated chiefly on an analysis of linguistic peculiarities, on the interpretation of separate passages, and on historical commentaries. In line with their work, emended texts of the *Slovo* were printed, and modern Russian translations both in prose and verse. Researches were conducted by Y. A. Pozharsky (1819), P. Butkov (1821), N. Grammatin (1823), and N. Artsybashev (1826), among others. Such investigations, in spite of the fact that they were in many cases naïve, both philologically and from the historico-literary viewpoint, served to lay a foundation for the study of the *Slovo*. Sometimes they traced vocabulary to the Polish dictionary, frequently they argued from the viewpoint of the poetics of the Ossianic ballads or of the classical epics, but for all this they made real progress in puzzling out the historical and philological essence of the monument.

By the 1830's tentative studies were being made of the *Tale of Igor's Expedition* in connection with oral poetry. In 1830 N. Polevoy's *History of the Russian People* compared the *Slovo* with the Scandinavian sagas. Ten years later Pogodin made the same comparison in a letter to Shevyrov printed in the *Muscovite*. In 1835 M. Maximovich gave a special course in Kiev University on the *Tale of Igor's Expedition* and afterward published a series of articles in which he brought particular detail to bear on the establishment of a connection between style and symbolism in the *Slovo* and in popular poetry, chiefly the Ukrainian. (These and Maximovich's later articles on the *Slovo* are reprinted in the third volume of his collected works, Kiev, 1880, pages 498–660.) In 1836, not long before his death, Pushkin did some intensive work on the *Slovo*. He made a careful examination of

[50] Recently certain French scholars have suddenly shown a belated tendency to return to these long superannuated positions. A particularly striking example of obstinate unwillingness to believe that the *Slovo* is an authentic monument from the past is presented in the articles published by Prof. A. Mazon in the journal he edits, *Revue des études slaves*, in 1938 and 1939. Here the author strives to demonstrate that the *Slovo* is a forgery, written at the end of the eighteenth century, in imitation of the *Zadonshchina* chiefly. The utter baselessness and artificiality of Prof. Mazon's arguments in support of his opinion, his unpermissible straining of inferences and obtuseness of aesthetic sensibility, are revealed throughout his extensive, superficially very erudite, but essentially quite unproductive investigations.

the very successful verse translation done by Zhukovsky in 1817–1819 (not published during Zhukovsky's lifetime), left a number of notes on it, and also began an article on the *Slovo* in which he definitely declared against the sceptical attitude regarding the monument and offered a few explanations of individual passages. Death interrupted his work on the *Slovo*.

In 1844 D. Dubensky published the *Tale of Igor's Expedition* interpreted as an early written monument. This edition, besides giving the text of the *Slovo* and a translation, summed up the results of previous study on the one hand and on the other presented a very detailed grammatical, historical, and literary-historical commentary, drawing upon materials and aids hitherto unexploited by commentators. Dubensky's basic problem was to demonstrate the authenticity of the monument; in his views on the origins of the *Slovo* he anticipated the later work of Vs. Miller, declaring in favor of a South Slavic source.

The work done by Buslayev in the early 1840's represents a marked advance in the study of the *Slovo*. The object of his numerous investigations was to examine the *Slovo* in connection with ancient Russian mythology and folk beliefs. Taking the main tenets of the mythological school as his guiding principle, Buslayev brought the material of folk poetry—Scandinavian, Germanic, and Slavic—to bear, explaining its points of likeness to the *Slovo* in terms of a common basis in primordial mythology. If we disregard Buslayev's perverse theoretical premises, his observations contain much that is undeniably of value to the elucidation of the *Slovo*.

In connection with Pekarsky's publication of Catherine's copy, there appeared in 1866 a first, and in 1868 a second, edition of Tikhonravov's *Tale of Igor's Expedition*. Collation of Catherine's copy with the first printed text of the *Slovo* made it possible for Tikhonravov, through conjectures of a paleographical nature, to introduce a number of emendations into the Musin-Pushkin text and determine at what period the burned copy was written (late sixteenth century, in Tikhonravov's opinion). His commentary on the text compared the *Slovo* with written monuments and with oral literary works, chiefly Great Russian. Notwithstanding the fact that the edition was designed by Tikhonravov as a help for students, it was a real step forward in the study of the monument and exercised an influence on subsequent investigations into the *Slovo*.

Such researches, particularly those of Maximovich, Dubensky, Buslayev and Tikhonravov, in large measure prepared the ground for a thoroughgoing study of the *Slovo* in the 1870's. This was greatly facilitated not only by the appearance at that time of a succession of great literary scholars but by the important accumulation of literary-historical and folklore material available for the elucidation of various problems that arose in the course of studying the *Slovo*. In 1870 the periodical *Zarya* [Dawn] brought out a verse translation by Apollon Maykov. This translation was superior to any previously published metrical paraphrase of the *Slovo,* and retains its value even to the present time. Before setting about his translation, Maykov had made a careful study of the literature of the monument, with special attention to the mythologists, and in the notes to his translation proposed explanations in this vein for a number of difficult passages.

In connection with the triumphs registered in the 1870's by the theory of borrowing, a number of works on the *Slovo* from that period are written in the spirit of this theory. Chronologically the work that ought first to be mentioned here is P. P. Vyazemsky's voluminous *Notes on the Tale of Igor's Expedition* (1875), the preparatory studies for which the author had, however, begun printing back in 1851. Being by nature not strictly a scholar but a learned amateur, Vyazemsky had a weakness for forced analogy and exaggeration in comparisons and parallels, in consequence of which, deductions which would be of interest if taken by themselves are drowned in a mass of uncritical and often superficial pronouncements. In the *Slovo* Vyazemsky sees chiefly a reflection of Greek poetry; the author of the *Slovo,* according to Vyazemsky, was a man well versed in the poetry of Homer and Euripides. Boyan, grandson of Veles, is identified with Homer, the descendant of Apollo; Deva-obida, with Helen, the wife of Menelaus; the path, land, and age of Troyan are echoes of the Trojan war, and so forth. In 1877 Vyazemsky issued his *Investigation of Variant Readings of the Slovo* which, as a piece of scholarship, is about on a par with his *Notes.*

The same year also saw the publication of Vs. Miller's much discussed *Glance at the Tale of Igor's Expedition.* As the motto for this book, V. Miller took a quotation from the *Slovo*: "Maidens sing on the Danube; their voices drift across the sea to Kiev." This motto expresses V. Miller's basic attitude toward the *Slovo* as a derivative work written under the influence of foreign models. As Vyazemsky compared the *Slovo* with ancient Greek poetry, so V. Miller seeks the sources of the *Slovo* chiefly in the Greek; that is, in medieval Byzantine poetry reaching the Russian author through Bulgarian versions, albeit to a certain extent in Bulgarian literature as well. In order to demonstrate the connection between the *Slovo* and the general run of Byzantine creative literature, V. Miller compares it in great detail with the *Adventures of Digenis,* discerning in the two works a community of poetic style. The author of the *Slovo,* in V. Miller's opinion, far from having that naïve spontaneity which Buslayev, for example, saw in him, was a bookman well versed in the Byzantine and Bulgarian literatures. When he mentions pagan divinities, he does so only for purposes of embellishment, transplanting to Russian soil what he found in Greek and Bulgarian mythology. Thus, for example, in V. Miller's opinion, "grandson of Dazhbog" may have been the Bulgarian rendering of an epithet applied in some Byzantine work to some mythical or historical personage, Dazhbog being substituted for Helios or Phoebus (page 76). Noting that the principal Russian god, Perun, is not among the gods mentioned in the *Slovo*, V. Miller explains this omission as due to the *Slovo* author's not having found Perun in his Bulgarian source (page 87), though it is easy enough to refute this observation merely by arguing that the author of the *Slovo* was under no obligation to enumerate all the pagan gods of Rus and that he chose to mention only those that fitted naturally into the context. Considerable value attaches to Miller's commentary on separate passages in the *Slovo* and in particular to his emendations of the first printed text.

Especially noteworthy among the studies that appeared in connection with V. Miller's book, is Alexander Veselovsky's article, "A New Glance at the *Tale of Igor's Expedition*" (*Journal of the Ministry of Public Instruction*, 1887, No. 8). Veselovsky treated the basic positions in V. Miller's book sympathetically, even though venturing modifications of the hypothesis in extreme cases; in particular, he disagreed with V. Miller's assumption of a Bulgarian origin of "Troyan," preferring to derive it from the Byzantine *Deeds of the Trojans*, based on the narratives of Diktys and Daretes. In other cases, as, for example, in explaining Div, or Deva-obida, Veselovsky proceeds not from literary sources but from Russian mythical beliefs. V. Miller, however, continued to insist upon the Bulgarian origin of both Troyan and Boyan (in two articles printed in the *Journal of the Ministry of Public Instruction* in 1877 and 1878). Afterward, or at any rate during the final stage of his scholarly career, V. Miller appears to have renounced his original opinion that the *Slovo* was an imitative work. At all events in the article, "An Outline of the History of the Russian *Bylina* Epos," written in the 1900's and first printed in 1924 in Volume III of his *Outlines of Russian Folk Literature*, he has not a word to say about it, but on the other hand gives a good deal of space to the connection between the *Slovo* and the Russian ballad tradition which preceded it.

In 1878 appeared Potyebnya's *Tale of Igor's Expedition: Text and Commentary* (republished in 1914), which in basic trend was by way of being a refutation of the positions from which Vyazemsky, V. Miller, and to a certain extent A. Veselovsky, had set out. Potyebnya considered the *Slovo* an original work by an individual; he discerned bookish elements in it but objected to the theory that "it was composed in accordance with a ready-made Byzantine-Bulgarian, or any other pattern" (an allusion to V. Miller's point of view), holding, on the contrary, that "we do not know any other Old Russian work permeated to such a degree with elements of folk poetry."

Potyebnya adduced a great number of parallels from Slavic folk poetry, especially Ukrainian and Great Russian, in support of his point of view. Along with this he attempted to uncover mythological elements in the monument. As to the text of the *Slovo*, Potyebnya considers that the extant copy "originated in a rough draft written by the author himself, or from his dictation, having notes in the margin, memoranda, corrections, which put some copyist (perhaps of the late thirteenth or very early fourteenth century) in a quandary as to where to insert them." In addition Potyebnya conjectures that the glosses of one or of more than one copyist have been carried over into the text. All these considerations constrained Potyebnya, besides emending the text, to rearrange it and to omit those passages which he considered marginal notes, interpolations, and glosses. Notwithstanding a number of ingenious conjectures, Potyebnya here naturally could not avoid performing operations on the text of the *Slovo* which are in large part arbitrary and subjective.

Of the works on the *Slovo* appearing in the 1870's, importance attaches to the books of O. Ogonovsky (Lvov, 1876) and A. Smirnov (two installments, Voronezh, 1877 and 1879). In the former all previous attempts at emendation of the text of the *Slovo* were reviewed in detail and new ones were made; the text itself was given a painstaking historical and literary commentary and was compared with works of oral poetry, chiefly Ukrainian. The first installment of Smirnov's book was devoted to a survey of literature on the *Slovo* down to 1876; the survey was made in great detail but unsystematically. The second installment contained extensive commentaries on the text, a survey of the explanations of it given in previous literature, and new emendations and interpretations of difficult passages, while an attempt was likewise made to establish the relationship of the *Slovo* to the North Russian folk poetry and language. The author, in addition, traced the fortunes of the *Slovo* in later Russian literature.

E. Barsov's three-volume work, the *Tale of Igor's Expedition as an Artistic Monument of Kievan Prince-and-Retainer Rus* (1887–1889), is largely a résumé of everything that had been learned about the *Slovo* from the time of its discovery. The third volume, devoted to the lexicology of the *Slovo*, was, however, brought down only through the letter *M*. A fourth volume, which was to have completed the lexicology, never saw the light. In spite of the many defects that critics found to point out in this work (the author's inadequate philological background and consequent lack of critical judgment, the subjective approach to material, involving an exaggeration of the value of certain documents, as, for example, the recently discovered papers of Malinovsky), it is, none the less, thanks chiefly to its wealth of material, a very notable item in the literature of the *Slovo*. Barsov regarded the *Slovo* as a monument representing the retainer school of narrative literature and accordingly attempted to link it with original (chiefly chronicle) and translated works of the martial narrative type. Especially fruitful, in spite of methodological blunders, was the comparison of the style of the *Slovo* to that of the "Account of the Destruction of Jerusalem" by Josephus Flavius. Useful, too, is the dictionary to the *Slovo* that Barsov unfortunately never finished.

As a result of all these studies, the general problems connected with an all-round investigation of the *Slovo* were in large measure not only envisaged but even solved, in so far as the single late and far from correct manuscript of the monument permitted. Numerous later studies of the *Slovo* by scholars both Russian and foreign have been focused chiefly on the clarification of specific individual problems arising in the course of its more intensive scientific examination (the rhythmics and form of the *Slovo*, its relation to the western European epos, its foreign language elements, its obscure passages, and so forth).[51]

The latest attempts to give a critical text of the *Slovo* and a detailed commentary, on the basis of everything accomplished by preceding scholars and by their own researches, are V. N. Peretts' book, *The Tale of Igor's Expedition: A Monument of Feudal Ukrainian Rus in the Twelfth Century* (Kiev, 1926), and A. S. Orlov's *Tale of Igor's Expedition* (Moscow-Leningrad, 1938), which contains, among other things, a critically verified text of the monument, a translation into modern Russian, an analysis of its poetical structure and style as well as of the paleographic peculiarities of the lost manuscript, and a textual and historical commentary.

In May, 1938, the peoples of the Soviet Union solemnized the seven hundred and fiftieth anniversary of this noble monument of the Russian heroic epos. Throughout the Union this noteworthy jubilee evoked the most lively response, both in the form of numerous commemorative meetings and in the form of newspaper and magazine articles and special publications. Virtually all the newspapers in the Union, general and special alike, signalized the jubilee date in their pages. All these notices mentioned the age-

---

[51] See P. V. Vladimirov: "Literatura *Slova o polku Igoreve* so vremeni yevo otkrytiya po 1894 g." (Literature of the Tale of Igor's Expedition from the Time of Its Discovery to 1894), *Universitetskie izvestiya* (University News) (Kiev, 1894), No. 4; N. K. Gudzii, "Literatura *Slova o polku Igoreve* za poslednee dvadsatiletie" (1894–1913) (Literature of the Tale of Igor's Expedition for the Past Twenty Years), *Zhurnal min. nar. prosv.* (Journal of the Ministry of Public Instruction) (1914), No. 2; N. K. Piksanov, "K obzoru literatury *Slova o polku Igoreve*" (Toward a Survey of the Literature of the Tale of Igor's Expedition), *ibid.* (1915), No. 1; V. N. Peretts, "K izucheniyu *Slova o polku Igoreve*: noveyshaya literatura o Slove" (On the Study of the Tale of Igor's Expedition: Recent Literature of the Tale) (1911–1923), *Izv. otd. russk. yaz. i slov.* (News of the Division of Russian Language and Literature of the Academy of Sciences) (1923), Vol. XXVIII. Previous surveys in *op. cit.* by Smirnov and Barsov and also by Zhdanov (*Works*, Vol. I).

less artistry of this "immortal creation of early Russian literature" (*Pravda*) and its lofty patriotic inspiration, in tune with our emotions as Soviet citizens.

Along with jubilee articles of a general character, there appeared a number of special studies of the *Slovo* and new verse translations not only into Russian but into the languages of the brother peoples of the USSR.[52] In connection with the jubilee, exhibitions were organized, the most important being the one put on in the State Literary Museum at Moscow.

The clash between Russians and Polovcians described in the *Tale of Igor's Expedition* was by no means the first nor would it be the last. Rus had been subject to Polovcian attacks for a hundred years, since 1061, and the raids stopped only with the Tartar invasion itself, when the Polovcians were vanquished and partly amalgamated into the Horde.

At the beginning of the twelfth century, Rus took the offensive against the nomads of the steppe and dealt them a series of crushing blows. Vladimir Monomakh won particular distinction for his campaigns against the Polovcians. Between 1103 and 1116 he mounted four expeditions, as a result of which the Polovcians were thrown back across the Don, part of them into the Caucasus. Monomakh's work was continued by his son Mstislav. But with the death of Mstislav (1132), the Polovcians are seen gathering strength again.

In two centuries there were more than forty devastating Polovcian raids into Russian territory, without counting innumerable minor raids. Rus was severely shaken by the attacks. No sort of treaties or agreements insured safety from sudden incursions by the restless nomads. Even marriage alliances between Russians and Polovcians were of no use.

From the middle of the twelfth century, the Polovcians began to assail the Russian lands with particular violence. In 1170, fifteen years before Igor's expedition, a congress of South Russian princes talked of joining forces to fight the enemy. Prince Mstislav Izyaslavich, calling upon the princes to mourn for the land of Rus and for their heritage from their fathers and grandfathers, said of the Polovcians, who were constantly breaking their oaths: "They have already deprived us of the road to Greece, and the salt road [to the Crimea] and the gold road [to the Danube]."

The gravity of the situation was aggravated by perpetual quarrels between

---

[52] The Sovietskii Pisatel publishing house brought out a *Tale of Igor's Expedition,* authoritative text, prose translation, and artistic paraphrases by Russian poets of the nineteenth and twentieth centuries; text, prose translation, and commentary ed. N. K. Gudzii; artistic translations and paraphrases ed. Peter Skosyrev (Moscow, 1938). The same house published I. A. Novikov's *The Author of the Tale of Igor's Expedition* (Moscow, 1938). The state publishing house, Khudozhestvennaya Literatura (Belles Lettres), brought out the *Tale of Igor's Expedition,* translation, introduction, and explanations by Ivan Novikov; general redaction and introductory essay by Professor Gudzy.

the princes, during which they frequently sought help of the Polovcians in settling their personal accounts.

All this was the chief contributing factor in the decline of the principality of Kiev, which, from the second half of the twelfth century, was clearly on the way toward political and economic collapse, so that by the time of the Tartar invasions its glory had long since faded. Ever since the ravaging of Kiev in 1169 by the forces of Andrew Bogolyubsky the great-princely throne and the principality of Kiev had lost their political preeminence. Kiev continued to impress the Russian princes actually only by the conventional semblance of being the traditional center of the Russian state and of Russian culture. In political influence and military might, Kiev was now definitely surpassed by the principalities of Suzdal and of Galicia-Volynia.

The failure of Igor's expedition, both in itself and in terms of the immediate historical setting of the campaign, must have been felt as an occurrence of especial gravity, out of all comparison with previous fiascoes of the Russian princes in their struggle with the steppe. Igor's defeat was unexpected not only to himself but also to his contemporaries. He had acquired a reputation as a Polovcian hater and as the lucky winner in several campaigns against them. Igor's first victory took place in 1174, when he killed many Polovcians and took many captive. In 1183 Igor vanquished the steppe tribes for a second time. In March, 1185, he made ready to assist Svyatoslav, Prince of Kiev, in his campaign against the Polovcians, saying: "God grant we may never refuse to fight the pagans: the pagans are the common enemy of us all." But ice conditions unexpectedly prevented his carrying out his intention.

Two months later, however, Igor and his allies set out against the Polovcians without consulting Svyatoslav of Kiev. The plans of the Severian princes were very far-reaching: the hope was, apparently, to win lost Tmutorakan back from the Polovcians. At least the boyars in the *Tale of Igor's Expedition* who interpret Svyatoslav's "troubled dream" speak of two falcons (that is, Igor and Vsevolod) having flown down from the golden throne of their fathers to seek the city of Tmutorakan or drink of the Don from their helmets.

And all these proud hopes were doomed to be cruelly dashed. The first impact of Igor's troops with the steppe, as we know, ended in victory for the Russians. But close on its heels came a grievous reckoning for them. The Polovcians gathered their forces and attacked. The three-day battle ended in the full rout of Igor's troops. The author of the *Slovo* recalls past battles of the Russian princes with hostile forces but can recall none so bloody as this one.

The defeat suffered by Igor in 1185 was really very serious: all four princes were taken captive, the greater part of their retainers were killed and the rest taken captive like themselves. Never yet, to judge by the chronicle accounts, had one of their campaigns against the Polovcians ended so disastrously for the Russians; never before had Russian princes been taken captive by Polovcians.

After their victory over Igor, the Polovcians rushed in to ravage Russian territory. Not without reason does the author of the *Slovo* say that the seeds sown by Igor sprouted sorrow for the land of Rus. The *Hypatian Chronicle* tells how, after routing Igor, the Polovcians were filled with self-confidence and made ready to invade the land of Rus. A dispute arose among them as to which direction they should move in. Khan Konchak voted for Kiev, where the Polovcians had been defeated, and Khan Bonyak and the other Khan, Gza, insisted upon attacking Posemyo where only women and children remained. This town was ripe for capture by the Polovcians and they could take it "without risk." Failing to come to an agreement, the Khans set out in different directions. On his way to Kiev, Konchak attacked Pereyaslavl and besieged the city. The prince of Pereyaslavl, Vladimir Glebovich, defended himself bravely, but was seriously wounded. From Pereyaslavl Konchak marched upon the city of Rimov, sacked it, took a large number of prisoners, and returned to his own country. Gza attacked Putivl, took it, set fire to villages, even burned down the jail at Putivl, then he too went back to the Polovcian steppes.

Like the chronicle, *The Tale of Igor's Expedition* tells of the shock sustained by the land of Rus following Igor's defeat. After this the "pagans" came victoriously into the land of Rus from all sides. Kiev groaned with sorrow and Chernigov groaned over its calamities. Anguish flooded the land of Rus, sadness flowed full across it. The princes were busy quarreling, and the "pagans" scoured the land of Rus. Svyatoslav of Kiev mourns the destruction of Rimov and the wounds of Vladimir, son of Gleb.

The gravity of Igor's fiasco was accentuated for Rus by the fact that this failure rendered meaningless beyond belief the brilliant victories over the Polovcians by the coalition of Russian princes headed by Svyatoslav of Kiev the year before. The long-awaited reconciliation between the sons of Oleg and the sons of Monomakh had finally taken place, and with their combined forces they had administered a crushing blow to their worst enemies.

Judging from the *Hypatian Chronicle*, Svyatoslav, in alliance with the other princes, had immediately won two more great victories over the Polovcians. After this it might have seemed that the enemy had been rendered powerless, and that the principality of Kiev, which had suffered from ceaseless forays by the nomads, been weakened and deprived of political prestige, might now entertain hopes of a political revival. But these hopes were rudely dashed by the rout of Igor's army, which gave new impetus to Polovcian expansion. This explains the energetic attempt of Svyatoslav to unite several Russian princes for the purpose of liquidating the consequences of Igor's fiasco; it explains also the quick reaction to events that we get in the author of the *Slovo,* who purposes by his talent and the force of his civic loyalty to be of service to the interests of his native land. He had a passionate patriotism for Kiev, was afflicted by her misfortunes, and dreamed of restoring her former authority and her former position as center of the Russian commonwealth. The still recent quarrels between the sons of Oleg and the sons of Monomakh were now a thing of the past to him and he was summoning these and the rest to support a common cause, the defense of the land of Rus, under the leadership of the Kievan prince of the line of Oleg, who had surmounted his former family sympathies and prejudices and was fighting for the common property of the "grandson of Dazhbog," the Russian people.

However, the well-being of the principality of Kiev was for the author of the *Slovo* inseparable from the well-being of the land of Rus as a whole, of the whole Russian people. His patriotic feelings for his native South were combined in him with a patriotism for all Rus, and fed this patriotism. For the defense of Rus against the Polovcians, he called not only upon those princes whose lands were immediately threatened by Polovcian inroads, but also upon those who were safe from these inroads, Vsevolod III of Suzdal, and Yaroslav of Galicia.

As affecting the fortunes of the Kievan principality at the end of the twelfth century, the military catastrophe which overtook Igor must have been regarded by the most farsighted of his contemporaries as a bitter trial, as a sort of final warning to the princes who had been following a policy of isolation and even at times striking up quarrels. The *Tale of Igor's Expedition* was an act of intervention on the part of a poet-citizen in affairs which might, he realized, prove fatal for the land of Rus. Consequently it is with trepidation and with passion that he cries out upon the grievous manifestations of princely separatism which had been the undoing of Rus before, and now threatened it with incalculable misfortune. The seriousness and tensity of the political situation of Kievan Rus, in view of the recrudescence of a danger which had but a moment before seemed past, thus evoked immediately after Igor's expedition, and in striking poetic form, what constituted, to use the words of Marx, "a summons to the Russian princes to unite, on the very eve of the Mongol invasion." [53]

The *Tale of Igor's Expedition* gives a vivid picture of feudal life in Rus in the eleventh and twelfth centuries, especially in its characterization of princes and retainers. Igor and Vsevolod come before us as knights for whom

[53] K. Marx and F. Engels, *Works,* Vol. XXII, p. 122.

honor and fame are the principal motives of conduct. Igor says to his retinue: "Brothers and retainers! It is better to fall in battle than to fall into captivity. I wish to break a lance at the edge of the Polovcian plain; with you, Russians, I wish either to lay down my head or drink my fill of the Don from my helmet." In the words of Svyatoslav, Prince of Kiev, the hearts of the two brothers were "forged of hard steel and tempered in daring." Knightly daring, bravery, warlike courage distinguish Igor, his brother the wild-aurochs Vsevolod still more, and likewise the princes Boris, son of Vyacheslav, and Vseslav of Polotsk. Of Román, Prince of Vladimir-Volynia, Svyatoslav says: "You fly high at heroic deeds, like a falcon soaring in the air, rushing boldly to strike at a bird." Igor's retinue is characterized as an army not interested in the material results of battle alone. It is seeking honor for itself, glory for the prince. And this is twice brought out in the *Slovo*. Vsevolod speaks thus of his retinue: "My men are experienced warriors, they were swaddled to the sound of trumpets, cradled to the sight of helmets, fed from the point of a spear. The paths they know, the ravines are familiar to them, their bows are taut, their quivers are open, their sabers sharpened; they leap like gray wolves in the field, seeking honor for themselves and glory for the prince." When addressing Rurik and David, Svyatoslav says: "Have you not a brave retinue who bellow like aurochs wounded by sabers tempered in the unknown plain?"

In the *Slovo* we find vivid and inspired portraits of historical figures of Old Rus, struck off upon occasion with uncommon success, and literally in but a few words. It required great historical and psychological acumen to sketch a whole group of historical portraits in such a masterly way as the author of the *Slovo* has done, and not portraits of his contemporaries alone but of personages who lived and made their name long before the poet's time. It would be difficult to point to anything in the history of the heroic epos in any country that equals the *Slovo* in the degree to which it reflects actuality.

The author of the *Slovo*, judging from the content of the monument, was a warrior, a retainer, presumably of the Kievan prince Svyatoslav, but he has immediate understanding of more than the warlike deeds of battle-hardened soldiers: he understands a brother's feeling of pity for a war-worn brother, and the sorrow of a mother mourning for a young son drowned, and the devoted love of a wife invoking the forces of nature to aid her husband's return to his own land. He is stern when he speaks of the enemies of his country and when he censures princes who start quarrels, and lyrically tender and compassionate when he speaks of those dear to him, the objects of his very real human interest.

Maintaining a viewpoint well in advance of his time in championing broadly national interests, the author of the *Slovo* surrounds the prince of Kiev with the aureole of political authority over all Rus. He looks disapprovingly on Igor's ruinous undertaking and, with Svyatoslav, grieves over the failure that had cost the Russian people so dear. But since he is aiming not at dissociation of their forces, not at disunion among the princes, but at solidarity in a common aim, he speaks of Igor and Vsevolod in such a way as to call forth the sympathy of other princes with respect to the fate of colleagues who had already paid so heavy a price for not tempering their martial fervor. He gives the courage and daring of both princes their due, emphasizes their knightly intrepidity and the warlike quality of their retainers, and in everything that he says about Igor and Vsevolod and about their fate, strives to inspire sympathy and good will for the ill starred unfortunates and to unite the princes all the more firmly for repulsing the Polovcians. And when Igor succeeds in escaping from captivity, the author rejoices over his return to Rus. It is a satisfaction to the poet's patriotic sense that the brave though unfortunate warrior should have returned from bondage to the princely fold, that, as the *Slovo* says, he should have come straight to Kiev, to Svyatoslav, instead of stopping at his own appanage, and thereby had, as it were, atoned for his highhanded behavior with respect to the senior prince.

The distinguishing marks of the *Tale of Igor's Expedition* as a work of art are graphically demonstrated when we compare it with the *Hypatian Chronicle's* account of the campaign of Igor Svyatoslavich against the Polovcians. The chronicle narrative gives seriatim all the principal facts about Igor's campaign, the destruction of Russian cities by the Polovcians following the rout of Igor's army, and the return of Igor from captivity. It is informed to a considerable degree by the pious Christian attitude, and this piety distinguishes Igor himself first and foremost. Seeing an eclipse of the sun when already on the way, Igor consoles his retinue with the observation that the secrets of God no man knows, but that every portent comes from God, creator of the universe. The victory of the Russians over the Polovcians in the first encounter Igor attributes to divine aid, and the defeat that follows victory he explains as God's punishment for the acts of murder and bloodshed that he has perpetrated in the land of Rus.

The *Slovo* does not aim to give a recital of consecutive moments in Igor's campaign and his return from captivity but primarily at awakening emotions of pity and sympathy for Igor's misfortune and explaining everything that happened in terms of a definite political situation. With this aim in view, the author of the *Slovo* presents a series of shifting lyric scenes in which the factual element is relegated to the background and prominence given to picturesque descriptions of the most dramatic moments in the fate of Igor and his army. The *Slovo* bespeaks a Christian author, but that author does not assign to any one of his personages specifically Christian, let alone pious, feelings and attitudes of mind. It contains more elements of pagan mythology than any other Russian monument.

After hesitating as to how to begin his account of Igor's campaign—whether "according to events of our time," that is, in accordance with the historical narratives of his time, or "Boyan's way," as it might have been sung by a poet now unknown who lived in the second half of the eleventh century and the beginning of the twelfth—the author of the *Slovo* decides to choose the former method rather than aim to keep pace with the bold fancy of Boyan, who, when he wanted to compose a song, "set his thought running up a tree, or along the ground like a gray wolf, or flying under the clouds like a gray-blue eagle." But though verbally refusing to follow Boyan, the author in point of fact does follow in his footsteps, and instead of the traditional war story produces what is simultaneously a passionate lyric ballad and a rousing publicistic pamphlet, constituting himself judge not only of present but of past Russian history, repeatedly digressing from his narrative to lapse into reasoning and reflections. Exact facts do not interest him; he finds it more important to give a general impression of events and make the reader relive and really experience them emotionally. The account in the *Hypatian Chronicle* tells exactly what transpired during the first encounter of the Russians with the Polovcians and, just in passing, indicates that the Russians took prisoners. In the *Slovo*, as in the *Laurentian Chronicle*, we find no details of this first encounter, yet here, described in sumptuous hyperbole, are the fruits of Igor's victory, its rich trophies: pretty Polovcian girls and, with them, gold and all manner of costly textiles, seized in such abundance that bridges of them might have been laid across the marshes and swampy places. Following the notice of their first success against the Polovcians, the *Hypatian Chronicle* gives a fairly detailed description of the battle which ended in defeat for the Russians. The *Slovo* provides almost no exact facts about the battle, but conveys with the utmost artistic expressiveness all the drama, all the extraordinary intensity of the action: "The earth hums, the rivers are muddied, dust covers the fields. . . . From morning until evening, from evening until dawn, the tempered arrows fly, swords clang on helmets, steel lances crash in the unknown field, in the land of the Polovcians."

Like the author of the chronicle narrative, the author of the *Slovo* notes the special bravery of Vsevolod. The *Hypatian Chronicle* says that "Vsevolod showed much courage," that he "fought so hard he ran out of weapons." This restrained praise of Vsevolod accords with the *Slovo's* veritable apotheosis of him in impassioned tones of rapture: like a wild aurochs he stands in the forefront of his troops, rains arrows on the enemy, makes their helmets ring with steel swords. Where this aurochs gallops with his golden helmet flashing, there lie the heads of pagan Polovcians, there Avar helmets are cleft by his tempered sabers. The impression of the tragedy of events is heightened by a comparison with long-ago events from the time of that instigator of princely quarrels and internecine strife, Oleg, son of Svyatoslav, when the property of the grandson of Dazhbog was destroyed, when plowmen rarely called to one another in the Russian land but ravens often croaked, sharing the corpses among them, and jackdaws chattered, flying to the spoil. The land of Rus suffered grievously in the time of Oleg, son of Svyatoslav, but never so grievously as now, nor had a like battle ever been heard of.

For the sake of comparing the *Hypatian Chronicle* account with the *Slovo*, let us also study a narrative moment that is common to both. The chronicle account in very realistic, albeit not entirely unlyrical, detail, tells how Svyatoslav was informed of Igor's defeat: he had got as far as Severian Novgorod, with the intention of spending the whole summer attacking the Polovcians on the Don, when he first learned that his cousins Igor and Vsevolod had set out against the Polovcians by themselves, and it was not pleasant news to him; then, upon reaching Chernigov, he heard of the rout of the brothers, from Byelovolod Prosovich, evidently a participant in Igor's campaign, and with a sigh, as he wiped away the tears, began reproaching the princes whose youthful impetuosity had opened the gates of the land of Rus to the enemies whom he had himself laid low the year before. "But God's will be done in all things," he ended by saying, "I now feel sorrier for Igor, my brother, than I before felt vexed with him." Then Svyatoslav sent word of Igor's rout to the neighboring princes, calling upon them for help against the Polovcians.

This literal account, adhering to the actual facts in the case, takes on under the pen of the *Slovo* poet new poetic and publicistic details. Svyatoslav, though as yet he knows nothing of Igor's defeat, is already oppressed by evil forebodings. He has a troubled dream which presages him no good, though the meaning of this dream is as yet not clear to him. The *Slovo* author employs a device as old as the Bible, one which had been used both in oral poetry and in literary monuments, among them the *Adventures of Digenis*, where the prophetic-dream motif, as we have seen, figured twice— with Amir, then with his wife—and where one dream was interpreted by Amir's "knights" (as in the *Slovo* by Svyatoslav's suite, his boyars), the second by soothsayers. In accord with the whole style of the *Slovo*, Svyatoslav's dream is interpreted not through literal realistic equivalents, as in the *Adventures of Digenis*, but metaphorically: "Behold, two falcons have flown from the golden throne of their fathers to reach the city of Tmutorakan or drink of the Don from their helmets; already the falcons' wings have been clipped by pagan sabers and themselves been enmeshed in iron fetters," and so forth. Then follow Svyatoslav's reproaches against Igor and Vsevolod, in spirit and in purport closely resembling the reproaches which Svyatoslav addresses to these princes in the *Hypatian Chronicle*. But the next brief statement in the chronicle, telling how Svyatoslav urged the Russian princes in Igor's neighborhood to aid in checking the Polovcians, is transformed under the pen of the *Slovo* author into the impassioned "golden word" addressed by Svyatoslav to all the most powerful Russian princes, and thrice interrupted by the lyrical refrain: "for the land of Rus, for the wounds of Igor, bold son of Svyatoslav." [54]

Immediately after Svyatoslav's "golden word" come the author's historical recollections. By analogy, the quarrels of the present princes, who have brought ruin upon the land of Rus, recall to his mind the princes of Polotz, who were guilty of the same sin. First the author speaks of the destruction of brave Izyaslav, son of Vasilko, who, unsupported by the other princes, had fallen two years previously in battle with the Polovcians, then his thought turns to Izyaslav's grandfather, Vseslav, warrior and adventurer, energetic participant in interprincely clashes and quarrels, about whom Boyan composed the refrain: "Neither a crafty man nor a clever man nor a clever bird can escape the judgment of God." And this whole part of the *Slovo* ends with the author's sorrowful exclamation: "Oh, groan for the land of Rus, remembering the olden times and the princes of old!" He regrets that old Vladimir Monomakh, terror of the Polovcians, could not have been kept forever on the hills of Kiev, that the princes of Rus have now divided his banners, and that their standards stream separately to the breeze.

This historical reminiscence and that which accompanies the description of Igor's ill starred second battle with the Polovcians, splitting the description itself into two parts, are, like the author's lyrical outpourings, very characteristic of the composition of the *Slovo*. They illustrate the author's habitual intrusion of his personal evaluation into events as he narrates them.

---

[54] In defining the boundaries of the "golden word" of Svyatoslav, we follow the opinion of the majority of commentators on the *Slovo*, who assume that the "golden word" ends with the third repetition of the refrain: "Bar the gates to the steppe with your sharp arrows, for the land of Rus," etc. But there is also some foundation for the opinion of V. V. Kallash, as first stated in a fine and as yet insufficiently appreciated article, "Nyeskol'ko dogadok i soobrazhenii po povodu *Slova o polk Igoreve*" (Some Conjectures and Reflections in Connection with the Tale of Igor's Expedition), *Jubilee Collection in Honor of Vsevolod Fyodorovich Miller*, ed. N. A. Yanchuk (Moscow, 1900), pp. 316–347. V. V. Kallash thinks that the "golden word" includes only Svyatoslav's reproaches to the princes, ending with the phrase, "trouble and anguish for the son of Gleb," and that the following summons to the princes is to be attributed to the author of the *Slovo*. Kallish doubts whether the prince of Kiev could have addressed other princes, for the most part his juniors and subject to him, as *gospodin* (lord), which implies the dependence of the person using it (p. 546).

The figure of the author thus never leaves our field of vision throughout the tale.

To turn to the title, one naturally wonders why our monument should be designated a *slovo,* or discourse, when farther on the author calls it a "song" and a "tale." The first interpreters of the *Slovo,* who were in bondage to classical poetics, called it a "heroic ballad." The monument's title of *Slovo,* however, is very organic to it, being in the tradition of those typical old Russian titles where *slovo* may be taken to mean an oration, an address to listeners and readers. The *Slovo* too begins as an address. The author calls his listeners or readers "brothers"; that is, just what any Old Russian *slovo* would call them. "Would it not be well for us, brothers, to begin in the old-fashioned way our story of the expedition of Igor son of Svyatoslav?" And this form of address occurs five times more. Having begun the *Slovo* with a salutation, the author also ends it with a salutation, proposing, since the fame of oldtime princes has been sung, to sing that of the young ones, and concluding the whole work with the "amen" common to all Old Russian *slovos.* Thus the author maintains throughout the position of an orator speaking in the first person.

He places so little importance on the literal agreement of his narrative with the historical facts as sometimes purposely to arrange events counter to the order in which they occurred, or might have occurred, but in accord with his poetic design. Thus, in the *Hypatian Chronicle* the eclipse occurred at the Donets, when Igor and his army were already on the march, and when to return home would have been inexpedient from the military point of view, but in the *Slovo* it comes when Igor is still only in process of launching the campaign and consequently when he could easily have let the projected undertaking await more favorable portents. As a result of this shifting of the eclipse, the figure of Igor gains in knightliness. His fearlessness, his scorn of threatening danger, are thereby emphasized. It is not faith in Divine Providence, as in the *Hypatian Chronicle,* that makes him go in spite of evil omens to meet the Polovcians, but his knightly desire to break a lance at the edge of the Polovcian plain, to see the blue Don and to draw water from it in his helmet. At the same time an important artistic advantage is also achieved: the augury of disaster opens the account of the campaign like an overture, to recur in various forms up to the time when Igor's fate takes a more favorable turn.

But if our author moved the solar eclipse ahead of the date given in the *Hypatian Chronicle,* he did just the opposite with the lament of Igor's wife Yaroslavna, whom the chronicle does not mention, postponing it from the time when it would actually have taken place. Yaroslavna laments not at the point in the course of events when it would have been natural for her to lament, not immediately after Igor's capture, when the women of Rus began mourning for their husbands, but considerably later, just before Igor's escape from captivity, and thus the lament becomes a magical incantation evocative of Igor's escape itself. One of the most remarkable creations in all literature for beauty of poetical expression, this lament gains special artistic effect from its precise position in the general structure of the *Slovo*. Igor is saved and brought back to the land of Rus by the all-conquering and victorious power of love as embodied in the person of his grieving wife, lamenting for him on the walls of Putivl like a cuckoo for its mate.

The author of the *Slovo* also violates the chronological sequence of facts when describing the martial exploits and misfortunes of Vseslav, Prince of Polotzk, and apparently does so in order to give central place to his picturesque description of the battle of the Nemiga, where Vseslav suffered defeat.

The *Slovo* is distinguished by profound saturation with imagery and symbolism. Poetical personification, metaphor, simile, parallelism: with all these the *Slovo* is full to overflowing. The most important underlying characteristic of this wealth of poetical embellishment is the indissoluble bond existing between the world of nature and the world of man. Nature here takes a very active part—as friend or as foe—in all the events that occur; the animal and the vegetable kingdoms, the earthly and the heavenly elements, are very animately evoked, now to the sorrow, now to the joy of Igor, of his army, and of everybody mentioned in the *Slovo*. With grim auguries nature attends upon Igor's preparations for the campaign and upon the campaign itself. She strives in every way to prevent Igor's carrying out an undertaking doomed to failure: the sun is dimmed, blocking the prince's way with darkness; thunder warns him, with its roar, of impending ill; birds and beasts give the alarm. Nor do those forces of nature that are unfriendly to Igor slumber: the sinister mythical being, Div, screams a warning to the enemy camps of the approach of Igor; the birds in the trees lie in wait for his undoing; wolves, eagles, foxes, black clouds, winds—all are in league against Igor. But when the Polovcians routed the Russians, the grass drooped in sympathy and the trees bent to the earth in sorrow. Even so had the flowers and trees responded almost a hundred years before to the death of young Prince Rostislav. When Igor escapes from captivity, surrounding nature is eager to help him and gives him a glad welcome. The river Donets cradles him on its waves and spreads green grass for him on its silvery banks, wraps him in warm mists under the shade of green trees and protects him in all manner of ways. In order that Igor may hear the pursuit, the magpies cease jabbering, the ravens cease croaking, the jackdaws fall silent, the woodpeckers by their tapping direct him to the river; the nightingales herald the dawn with glad songs. To the forces of nature, to wind, Dnieper, and sun, grieving Yaroslavna prays for help for her husband.

Nature in the *Slovo* is not dumb, not speechless, but vocal and even talkative: the magpies chatter, the Donets converses with Igor; even inanimate objects utter sounds: the carts screech, the battle standards talk. The whole *Slovo* is filled with sounds, ringing, singing: fame rings out; there is a ring of battle, the spears sing.

The rich and abundant epithets and similes in the *Slovo* are without exception from the world of nature. Boyan is a nightingale, Vsevolod a wild aurochs, the pagan Polovcian a black raven. Boyan runs like a gray wolf along the ground, darts like a blue-gray eagle beneath the clouds. To the gray wolf are also compared the princes, the retinue, and Konchak. The princes are in addition compared to the sun, to the moon, to falcons; the retainers, to those same falcons and to flocks of jackdaws; Yaroslavna, to a cuckoo; Igor, to an ermine, a white goldeneye; Vseslav, to a wild beast; the Polovcians, to a nest of snow leopards. The prophetic fingers which Boyan lays upon the living strings that he may sing a song in praise of the princes are compared to ten falcons released by a hunter upon a flight of swans, and the screeching carts, to a flock of frightened swans.

By the complete organic harmony between the author of the *Slovo* and the elemental forces of nature is explained the presence in the *Slovo* of pagan gods. In giving a general description of the *Slovo*, K. Marx noted that "the whole ballad has a Christian-heroic character, though pagan elements also stand out very prominently."[55] The *Slovo* portrays the Old Russian pagan gods, Veles, Dazhbog, Stribog, Khors, introduces the mythical Div, Deva-obida with the wings of a swan, and Karna and Zhlya, evidently personifications of lamentation and woe. Boyan is called the grandson of Veles, the winds, the grandsons of Stribog, the Russian people, the grandson of Dazhbog. There is no reason to consider these gods of the Slavic pagan Olympus a literary expedient which the *Slovo* author resorted to as eighteenth century poets habitually brought in the names of classical gods; nor is there any basis for thinking that he believed in them as his pagan ancestors had done. It is more correct to suppose that the author was so steeped in poetry that, notwithstanding his connection with Christianity, he could not, and did not wish to, depart from that attitude toward the world about him which went with paganism and which still had a very powerful hold at that time among the general masses. The author of the *Slovo* was under the influence of that animistic perception of nature which characterized not only the culturally backward strata but at times the highest cultural levels as well, especially where they had not lost touch with folk poetry.

[55] K. Marx and F. Engels, *Works*, Vol. XXII, p. 122.

In harmony with the general character of the poetic style of the *Slovo* is its varied and graphic symbolism. Symbolical equivalents are a favorite means of figuratively disclosing facts and events in the *Slovo*. The movement of the Polovcian troops is here symbolized by the image of black clouds striving to hide the four suns; that is, the four princes who participated in the campaign. The battle is symbolically likened now to the sowing, now to a wedding feast, now to the threshing: "The black earth under the horses' hoofs was sown with bones and watered with blood, and it sprouted a crop of sorrow for the land of Rus. . . . Then the bloody wine gave out; then the brave sons of Rus brought the feast to an end: they gave the wedding guests to drink and laid themselves down in behalf of the land of Rus." Thus is the rout of Igor's army at the river Kayala given poetic interpretation. Recalling the rout of Vseslav of Polotzk on the Nemiga, the author exclaims with bitterness: "By the Nemiga sheaves of heads are strewn, and are threshed with flails of steel; life is laid on the threshing floor, and soul winnowed from body." The author concludes this exclamation with a picture that he has used once before: "The bloody banks of the Nemiga were sown not with good seed but with the bones of the sons of Rus." Along with these expanded symbolical pictures are more compressed symbolical images: "To taste the great Don," "to break a spear at the edge of the Polovcian plain," "to drink of the Don from their helmets," "flying in thought beneath the clouds"; "Igor the prince slipped from his saddle of gold and into the saddle of a slave," and so forth. Symbolical elements in large numbers are also present in the similes employed in the *Slovo*.

Indissolubly linked with symbol is metaphor, which attends the exposition of events every step of the way: Igor "armed his mind with fortitude and whetted his heart with courage"; calamity "drives the birds to the trees"; "the song of the nightingale is stilled, the chatter of the magpies starts up"; "bloody rays announce the break of day"; "sadness flowed full through the land of Rus"; "the princes forged sedition against themselves," and so forth.

Another factor in the *Slovo's* saturation with imagery is its wealth of epithet. One of the author's favorite epithets is "golden," with its derivatives: "gold-tipped," "gold-forged," "gilded." Some of the combinations in which this epithet occurs in the *Slovo* have their parallels in oral poetry; for example: "golden saddle," "golden throne," "golden helmet," "golden stirrup." The epithet "silver" also appears frequently in the *Slovo*, in combinations, however, which are not encountered either in other written monuments or in oral poetry: "silver spear," "silvery hair," "with silver streams," "on its silvery banks." Of particular interest for us are combinations of noun and modifying epithet which are paralleled only in works of oral literature, and are not encountered in written monuments contemporary with the

Slovo or of earlier date; for example: "blue-gray eagle," "blue sea," "green grass," "tempered arrows," "fair maidens," "bloody wounds," "sharp swords," "cool dew," "gray wolf," "brave retinue," "black raven," "black cloud," "open plain." [56] The author of the *Slovo* also makes use of metaphorical epithets: "prophetic fingers," "iron ranks," "golden word," "pearly soul," "living strings."

The poetical style of the *Slovo* shows the influence both of written and of oral literature. In many cases it is hard to draw a line between the two. In defining the bookish influences, however, it will not do to go to any such lengths as did V. Miller, who vastly overemphasized the presence of borrowed elements. None the less, the attitude of regarding the *Slovo* as a monument reflecting certain peculiarities of style found in book literature of the author's own time or earlier is not to be dismissed. On this theme we find much of value in existing literature on the question, all the way from Tikhonravov's book to the studies by P. V. Vladimirov, A. S. Orlov, and V. N. Peretts. Suffice it to quote the following parallels. A counterpart to the *Slovo* image: "But Boyan, brothers, would lay his prophetic fingers on the living strings" is found in the *slovo* on the Resurrection of Lazarus: "David would say . . . laying his learned fingers on the living strings. . . . " Corresponding to the images, "darting . . . like a blue-gray eagle" and "flying in thought beneath the clouds," we find in Clement the Slovene: "Like an eagle he soared aloft in thought"; in the "*Slovo* on the Life": For he is young in body but old in mind and lofty in thought, flying in thought beneath the clouds like an eagle"; in the *Testament* of Cyril the Philosopher: "Fly in thought like an eagle through the air," and so forth.

In style the *Slovo* still more closely resembles, particularly in its description of martial episodes, the *Account of the Destruction of Jerusalem* by Josephus Flavius. Thus we read in the *Slovo*: "He armed his mind with fortitude," while in Josephus, Vespasian "possessed his mind with fortitude and stood firm." The *Slovo* continues: "And whetted his heart with courage," and Josephus says: "Whet your souls for vengeance"; in the *Slovo*: "Filled with martial spirit," in Josephus: "Fulfilled with martial spirit"; in the *Slovo*: "There was a rain of arrows"; in Josephus: "And the arrows pelted them like rain"; in the *Slovo*: "They roar like aurochs wounded by tempered sabers"; in Josephus: "They fell to groaning like wounded beasts."

In analyzing the Old Russian rhetorical sermon and saint's life we studied the characteristic peculiarities of their style, noted the presence in them of

[56] See V. N. Peretts, "K izucheniyu *Slovo o polku Igoreve*" (On the Study of the Tale of Igor's Expedition), Chap. 4, "Epithets in the Slovo and in Oral Tradition," *Izv. Otd. Russk. yaz. i slov* (News of the Division of the Russian Language and Literature of the Academy of Sciences) (1925), Vol. XXX, pp. 143–204.

symbolism, personification of abstract concepts, the use of metaphor, the introduction of monologue and dialogue, of rhetorical exclamations and questions into the exposition, the use of the devices of simile and parallelism, antithesis, the rhythmic organization of language as exemplified in repetitions, identical beginnings, series of participial phrases ending sometimes with verbs that rhyme. All these stylistic peculiarities are found in the *Slovo* as well, and a great part of them (symbolical comparison, personification, metaphor, simile, parallelism) were mentioned above. As an example of monologue in the *Slovo,* we have the "golden word" of Svyatoslav; dialogue is represented by the conversation between Svyatoslav and his boyars concerning his prophetic dream and by the conversation between Gza and Konchak. The *Slovo* begins with a rhetorical question, and such questions recur farther on: "What is that noise I hear? What rings in my ears from afar in the early hours before dawn?" and so forth. No less frequent are the rhetorical exclamations: "The brave nest of Oleg slumbers on the steppe. Far has it flown!" or "O far did the falcon fly, preying upon birds, down toward the sea!" "But Igor's brave army shall not rise again!" and so forth. Repetition and antithesis are common stylistic devices in the *Slovo.* As illustrations of the repetition of an identical initial word, the following examples may be cited:

> Already shame has made short work of glory,
> Already force has dealt a blow at freedom,
> Already Div has pounced upon the earth.

> Here lances shall break
> Here swords be dulled.

> Igor sleeps.
> Igor wakes.
> Igor measures the steppes in thought.

Here one's attention is attracted by something which is also common in the rhetorical sermon, the symmetrical arrangement of the parts of the sentence. Symmetrically arranged phrases that end in rhyming or, more exactly, in assonant verbs, also occur somewhat frequently in the *Slovo:*

> Boyan, brothers, did not ten falcons on a flock of swans release,
> But his own prophetic fingers on the living strings did place.

> Prince Vseslav the people judged,
> To princes cities allotted,
> But at night, by himself, turned wolf and prowled.

> With thirst their bows did you warp,
> With anguish their quivers stop.

The peculiarities of the Byzantine rhetorical style reflected in Hilarion and Cyril of Turov and in Russian lives of saints found an indubitable echo in the *Slovo* as well.

It would be possible to adduce many more parallels of like nature from works of learned literature, but however many we brought forward—from the Bible, from the chronicle, from books of a narrative character, from the works of Hilarion and Cyril of Turov—these parallels would merely attest to a community of certain stylistic formulae in the *Slovo* and the works indicated. The picture obtained would be approximately the same as if, in analyzing the work of Pushkin, we should note in his poetic economy, in his phraseology, a series of figures and current formulae which had even before his day become established literary usage. To suspect Pushkin on these grounds of having imitated some predecessor or contemporary would be no more of an injustice than to suspect the *Slovo* author of any sort of conscious imitation.

The *Slovo* has also been compared with a number of monuments of western European literature. Students of Russia and of the Occident (N. Polevoy, Buslayev, Zhdanov, Vladimirov, Abikht, Kallash, Dashkevich, and others) have made numerous comparisons between the *Slovo* and the Scandinavian sagas, the *Song of Roland,* the *Nibelungenlied,* the Germanic poem *Waltharius,* French romances of the twelfth century and earlier, with *The Knight in the Tiger Skin* of Shota Rustaveli, and so forth. But in all these comparisons we find only such general resemblances as may be explained at the outset by the fact that both in the western European monuments and in the *Slovo* we are dealing with the literary heroic epos, which by its very nature, by the underlying social conditions, must of necessity, in so far as we are dealing with work from the feudal period, contain common motives and common stylistic formulae.

The author of the *Slovo* was undoubtedly well versed, too, in Russian oral literature, and this exercised an almost greater influence on him than did learned literature, but unfortunately we cannot precisely define the extent of this influence since we do not know exactly what the oral literature of the eleventh and twelfth centuries was like. In any event it is quite clear that the profound saturation of the *Slovo* with animistic concepts was the result of the author's organic connection with the creative works of oral poetry. Then, as we saw above, we meet in the *Slovo* noun-and-epithet modifier combinations not encountered in corresponding works of written literature, another circumstance which unquestionably attests to a connection between the *Slovo* and the products of folk poetry.

This connection is still further corroborated by individual coincidences between images in the *Slovo* and in folk poetry.

The *Slovo's* comparison of a battle to a feast finds a parallel in one of the *byliny* about Ilya Muromets:

> Alyosha is riding drunk; he sways,
> He slumps on his saddlebow.
> Ilya Muromets spied Alyosha:
> "I told you, Alyosha, I charged you:
> 'Don't you drink green wine,
> Don't eat sweetmeats.'"
> To Ilya Muromets Alyosha makes answer:
> "I'd have been glad not to drink green wine
> And not eat sweetmeats:
> 'Twas a brave lad that got me drunk
> And fed me my fill
> Of the whip, beside the road."

The *Slovo's* likening of a battle to the sowing closely resembles what we find both in White Russian and in Ukrainian song:

> That black that you see is not plowland,
> The open plain of the Turk has turned black,
> Not by plows has the field, not by harrows, been tilled
> But tilled is the field by the hoofs of horses,
> Sowed is the field not with seeds that will sprout:
> Sowed with Cossacks' heads,
> Strewn is the field with Cossacks' black ringlets.
>
> The black furrow is plowed
> And sown with bullets,
> Strewn with white bodies,
> And watered with blood.

The prophetic dream of Svyatoslav in which he sees the destruction of his "golden-roofed *terem*" corresponds to the bride's prophetic dream in one of the wedding laments:

> No sleep for me in the dark of the night,
> No sleep but plenty of dreaming,
> And the dream that I dreamed was unhappy:
> In the house of my father who reared me
> All of the pillars were broken,
> All of the fences were down,
> And the brush had grown thick in between.

Yaroslavna's lament is comparable to the folk wedding laments, where the image of a cuckoo, symbolizing a young woman grieving at separation from her parents, is common. It also resembles a wedding lament in its three-fold lyric prayer for help and its mention of the far-away Danube.

A very close parallel to the account of Igor's escape from captivity, flying like a falcon and killing geese and swans, is presented by the following lines from the *bylina* of Voleg:

> He circled like a bright falcon,
> He flew far out on the deep-blue sea,
> And geese he killed and white swans.

The comparison of Igor, returning from captivity, to the sun resembles what is said of Ilya Muromets in a *bylina*:

> One sun in the sky, one moon;
> One Don Cossack in Holy Rus,
> Ilya Muromets, son of Ivan.

A great many more parallels of this sort could be given. There is much in common between the *Slovo* and folk poetry both in the phonetic organization of its language and in its rhythmic scheme.[57]

There is no reason for narrowly limiting the folk literature which influenced the author of the *Slovo* to the retainer background. We have no data whatever for establishing the existence of specific retainer peculiarities in oral epic or song, or specific poetic principles distinct from those that characterize the creative work of the peasantry. Furthermore the retinue was not strictly a closed social class: offspring of peasants and serfs found their way not only into the junior retinue, a quite frequent occurrence, but also into the senior, becoming boyars. If we are to believe the chronicle legend, Vladimir of Kiev promoted to the senior retinue the fur-dresser's son who vanquished the Pecheneg champion in single combat.[58] It is typical that only the lengthy Russkaya Pravda extends to princes' servants belonging to the junior retinue the wergild of forty grivnas which was imposed for the murder of a free man.

All this must be taken into account in all cases where literary works supposed to have originated in the retainer milieu are under discussion.

As to the problem of our author's connection with the literary and with the folk-poetry tradition, it must be emphasized that he was completely independent and original in his use both of learned and of oral poetry material. The *Slovo* reveals such a high degree of artistic originality that there can be no question of imitation even in separate passages.

In speaking of the poetical style of the *Slovo*, it is necessary to touch upon one of the most complicated questions in its study; namely, the question of

[57] On the relation of the *Slovo* to folk poetry, see *op. cit.* of Maximovich, Tikhonravov, Potyebnya, Smirnov, Barsov. See also Y. Sokolov, "Slovo o polku Igoreve i narodnoe tvorchestvo" (Tale of Igor's Expedition and Folk Creation), *Literaturnyi kritik* (Literary Critic) (1938), No. 5, pp. 84–93.

[58] See M. Dyakonov, *Ocherki obshchestvennogo gosudarstvennogo stroya drevney Rusi* (Outlines of the Structure of Society and State in Early Rus) (Moscow-Leningrad 1926), Pt. 4, pp. 67–75.

rhythmic structure. A number of students (Zhitetsky, Tikhovsky, Abikht, Korsh, Shchurat, Zivers) have thought that the *Slovo* was written entirely in meter and have attempted to divide it into lines. Zhitetsky and Tikhovsky considered the verse structure of the *Slovo* similar to the verse system of the Ukrainian ballad; Abikht compared it to that of the Scandinavian skalds, Korsh, with Russian *bylina* verse; Birchak, with Byzantine church song.[59] Professor Sievers takes Korsh's point of view in the main (*Das Igorlied, metrisch und sprachlich bearbeitet,* Leipzig, 1926).

Frankly, however, none of the attempts to divide the *Slovo* throughout into lines can be recognized as successful. First of all it must be borne in mind that the *Slovo* has come down to us in a very much mutilated copy, which no doubt in large measure destroys its rhythmic structure. But even apart from this, it is doubtful whether the *Slovo* was wholly written in verse: in the first place the large amount of purely historical information that it gives, involving the mention of a great many princes, can hardly have been entirely arranged as lines of verse. The presence in many instances of complex sentences also points to the absence of any continuous poetic rhythm. It would almost be more correct to suppose on the basis of its song phrases that the *Slovo,* like the Scandinavian sagas which, incidentally, it resembles in its wealth of alliteration, is an alternation of prose and verse. Traces of song form are perceptible in the *Slovo* not only in the uniform rhythm of series of symmetrically constructed short phrases, but also in the strophic structure of Yaroslavna's lament and in such refrains as "Seeking honor for themselves, and glory for the prince," "O land of Rus, already you are past the crest of the hill," "By the river, by the Kayala," "For the land of Rus, for the wounds of Igor, bold son of Svyatoslav," "Yaroslavna early raises her lament in Putivl on the ramparts." Finally, the song rhythm of the *Slovo* is sustained by abundant alliteration: *"Truby trubyat v Novegrade"* (The trumpets trumpet in Novgorod); *"S zaraniya v pyatok potoptasha poganyya polky polovetskyya, i rassushasya strelami po polyu, pomchasha kraznyya devky polovetskyya"* (From dawn on Friday they trampled the infidel Polovcian hosts and, scattering like arrows over the plain, took fair Polovcian maidens captive); *"Strely po zemlye seyashe"* (Sowed arrows over the land); *"Porosi polya pokryvayut"* (Dust covers the steppe); *"Se li sotvoriste moei srebrenei sedine?"* (What have you done to my silvering head?) and so forth.

The profound political purpose of the *Slovo,* prompted by the very pressing interests of the historic moment, in conjunction with the fact that it is organically connected with the richest strata of folk creation, set it apart as a work of genuinely national character.

[59] A detailed exposition of the views of the scholars mentioned and a criticism of these views is to be found in the surveys by P. V. Vladimirov and N. K. Gudzy already mentioned.

The greater part of the *Slovo* cannot have been written later than April, 1187, since it mentions as alive Prince Vladimir Glebovich of Pereyaslavl, who died on April 18 of that year. But taking into account that it was presumably written in connection with the Kievan prince Svyatoslav's preparations for his campaign against the Polovcians in 1185, immediately after he had received the news of Igor's crushing defeat, there is every reason to suppose that the main part, ending with Yaroslavna's lament, was written in 1185.[60] Some students, Kallash among them, have very astutely called attention to the fact that the account of Igor's escape and his return to the land of Rus, written in triumphant and joyous tones, is out of keeping with the whole preceding exposition, in which the fate of the land of Rus and of Igor himself is depicted in gloomy and pessimistic colors. Therefore the thought quite naturally suggests itself that when the rest of the *Slovo* was written, describing in sorrowful pictures the ill fortune of Rus and of Igor, wounded and in captivity, Igor's escape had not as yet taken place. As soon as Igor reached Rus, however, in that same year, 1185, the author wrote, in honor of him and of the princes who had not yet returned but who were expected, the concluding section of the *Slovo,* calculated to offset the mood of dejection induced by the telling description of the military fiasco. This concluding section may have been written at the end of 1185 or somewhat later.

If we agree with those scholars who think that the inclusion of Vladimir Igorevich among the eulogized princes could have taken place only after his return from captivity, and this was in the autumn of 1187, then the date of the completion of the *Slovo* must be moved forward to the closing months of that year or the early months of 1188. In this case it is natural to suppose that originally Yaroslavna's lament was placed alongside the lamentations of the wives of the Russian warriors who had been in the rout, and that later on, after writing the concluding section of the *Slovo,* the author shifted Yaroslavna's lament closer to the episode of Igor's escape and thus attained the artistic effect above mentioned.

[60] Cf. V. V. Kallash, *op. cit.,* pp. 347; A. I. Lyashchenko, "Etyudy o *Slove o polku Igoreve*" (Studies in the Tales of Igor's Expedition), *Izv. otd. russk. yaz. i slov.* (News of the Division of Russian Language and Literature of the Academy of Sciences) (1926), Vol. XXXI, pp. 137–146; A. I. Sobolevskii, "K *Slovu o polku Igoreve*" (On the Tale of Igor's Expedition), *Izv. po russkomu yazyku i slovesnosti* (News Concerning Russian Language and Literature) (1929), Vol. II, Bk. I, pp. 183–185. V. A. Keltuyala's hypothesis that the "golden word" of Svyatoslav synchronizes with the campaign against the Polovcians undertaken by Svyatoslav in 1187, is not very convincing. Equally unconvincing is his line of reasoning as to Svyatoslav's orientation in the struggle with the Polovcians being toward the Dnieper River system and Igor's toward the Don basin, and that these two orientations were completely isolated. Such reasoning as this of Keltuyala's is refuted by a mere reference to the testimony of the *Hypatian Chronicle,* where it is recorded under the year 1185 that when Igor was on his campaign against the Polovcians, Svyatoslav himself, in ignorance of it, had gone to Karachev to collect troops from the highlands in order to spend the whole summer attacking the Polovcians on the Don.

In the history of Russian literature previous to or contemporary with the *Slovo* we do not have a single monument which either equals it artistically or even in any measure approaches it. This does not mean that the *Slovo* was necessarily the only thing of its kind in our early literature, however. We have no assurance whatever that there did not exist other monuments which, even if not its equal artistically, were perhaps in some degree similar to it. The fact that the *Slovo* has come down to us at all is, as we have seen, to a great extent the result of chance. It is known in only one copy earlier than the beginning of the nineteenth century. How can we be sure that comparable works of the time have not been lost?

However that may be, even by itself the *Slovo* is a striking index to the height of cultural development and of national consciousness already attained by the Russians at that far distant time, in the first centuries of their existence as a state. The *Slovo* is in any event not inferior in artistic quality to the best examples of heroic epos that the world has produced. Originating as it did in Kievan Rus, common cradle of Great Russians, Ukrainians, and White Russians, it by right belongs equally to all three of these brother peoples.

How valid a literary monument the *Slovo* proved to be, retaining over a long period its poetical and conceptual immediacy, is attested by the fact that two hundred years after its writing it exercised a very powerful influence on the tales of the rout of Mamay, primarily on the *Zadonshchina*. And then, after serving its purpose as an ideological and literary stimulus during the period of the Tartar domination of Rus, it was apparently forgotten, the influence of its poetical elements on certain subsequent monuments of Russian literature being attributable to the reflection of these elements in the tales of the rout of Mamay. The average reader, uninitiate in the historical content of the monument, would have had trouble making head or tail of it, and the esthetic merits of the *Slovo* were not enough in themselves to guarantee its continued literary existence in the olden days. Therefore it is not in any way improbable that other valuable literary monuments, on a level with the *Slovo*, having outlived their usefulness from the viewpoint of thematic immediacy, disappeared irrevocably.

The influence of the *Slovo* on Russian literature recommenced with the publication of its text by Musin-Pushkin in 1800. Thus Radishchev prefaces with a motto from the *Slovo* the unfinished poem, *Songs Sung at Contests in Honor of the Ancient Slavic Gods*, on which he was working in 1800–1802. The influence of the *Slovo* is apparent in the only song that Radishchev finished for this poem, the song of Vseslav, and more particularly in the prose introduction to the poem. Next, traces of the influence of the *Slovo* appear in P. Lvov's poem, *The Tale of Mstislav I, Son of Vladimir* (1808), in Katenin's poem, *Mstislav, Son of Mstislav* (1819), in the novels of A. Veltman, *The Living Skeleton* (1832) and *Son of Svyatoslav* (1835), in Zagoskin's novel, *The Tomb of Askold* (1833), in A. N. Ostrovsky's play, *The Snow Maiden* (1873). Pushkin (in *Ruslan and Ludmila*) and poets of Pushkin's time (Ryleyev, Yazykov) use the figure of the prophetic singer Boyan, suggested by a reading of the *Slovo*.[61] The *Slovo* is reflected in the poetry of our own time as well; for example, in A. Blok's poem, *The New America*, in E. Bagritsky's *Ballad of Opanas*, in B. Lavrenev's story, *The Bloody Knot*.

In summarizing the development of Russian literature during the first century and a half of its existence, when it was bound up with the history of Kievan Rus, we may properly arrive at the following conclusions.

Russian literature during this period—partly through a South Slavic medium, partly by way of its own translations—not only assimilated a number of the important genres of medieval Byzantine literature, but on the basis of them itself produced notable work in genres typical of the European Middles Ages in general. Not all that was achieved by Kievan Rus in the field of literature is extant, but even what is testifies to the fact that early Russian literary culture reached a remarkably high level and created in this very short time outstanding monuments of the literary art just as it created notable monuments in the arts of architecture and painting. An acquaintance with the artistic culture of Kievan Rus convinces us that it showed every sign of being a genuine creative growth, checked by the inroads of barbarians from the steppe and retarded for a time by the outrageous severity of the Tartar yoke. "Ever since this ill fated time, which lasted for about two centuries," wrote Herzen, "Russia has let Europe outstrip her." [62] Owing to the conditions governing cultural and historical development, Old Russian literature, in this as in subsequent periods, was dominated by the ecclesiastical genres, but along with these there also existed a category of secular tales, translated and original. The more or less extensive deposit of ecclesiastico-Christian tendencies on the narrative of the Kiev period binds it in with medieval narrative, the typical examples of which are also not without ecclesiastical elements. The greatest literary monument of the Kiev period, the *Slovo o polku Igoreve* is, more than any other work from the earliest

[61] See V. V. Sipovskii, "Sledy vliyaniya *Slovo o polku Igoreve* na russkuyu povestvovatel'-nuyu literaturu pervoy poloviny XIX stoletiya" (Traces of the Influence of the Tale of Igor's Expedition on Russian Narrative Literature of the First Half of the Nineteenth Century), *Izv. po russk. yaz. i slov.* (News Concerning Russian Language and Literature of the Academy of Sciences, USSR) (1930), Vol. III, Pt. 1, pp. 239–257.

[62] A. I. Gertsen, "O razvitii revolyutsionnykh idey v Rossii" (On the Development of Revolutionary Ideas in Russia), *Complete Collected Works and Letters*, ed. M. K. Lemke (St. Petersburg, 1919), Vol. VI, p. 317.

period of Russian literature, an expression of secular ideology. This same ideology is also implicit in the wide range of narrative material found in the *Primary Chronicle,* material which during the period of its existence apart from the chronicle undoubtedly showed its secular character even more strongly than it does when blended into the general context of the chronicle as compiled by a pious monk.

It is noteworthy, however, that ecclesiastical ideology itself was not characterized during the Kiev period by any such monopolistic and active pretensions to the right of subordinating secular culture to itself as it later manifested, primarily under the influence of the events of the Tartar invasion. During this period the Christian world outlook could still be on good terms with pagan mythology, as is admirably demonstrated by the *Slovo o polku Igoreve.* Religious intolerance toward the non-Orthodox West was as yet far from having attained those proportions which it was to reach later. Evidence of this is found in the *Pilgrimage* of palmer Daniel, who did not avoid associating with members of the Latin church and who accepted the patronage of the Catholic king Baldwin. It is also demonstrated by the intermarriages of Russian princes with the ruling houses of western Europe. Thus, the daughter of Yaroslav the Wise was given in marriage to the French king Henry I and, later on, after the death of her husband, became regent of France; another of his daughters, Elizabeth, married Harold of Norway, a third, Anastasia, married Andrew of Hungary. The son and the grandson of Yaroslav, Vsevolod and Vladimir, were married respectively to a Greek princess and to a daughter of the Anglo-Saxon king. Yaroslav's granddaughter Eupraxia married the emperor of the "Holy Roman Empire," Henry IV. The court of Yaroslav gave domicile to exiles from European states, among them members of ruling dynasties. These connections with foreign courts were undoubtedly one channel through which those international migratory secular subjects in which our *Primary Chronicle* is so especially rich may have drifted into Rus.

The secular literature of the Kiev period, like the ecclesiastical, was fundamentally distinguished by a clearly expressed publicistic and moralistic trend, which contributed appreciably toward producing a national consciousness in the feudal state then in process of formation. To this task not only secular narrative literature (the chronicle, the *Slovo o polku Igoreve*) but also lives, sermons, and pilgrim literature were in large measure dedicated Many of these monuments are characterized by a lyricism which often assumes the form of abstract rhetoric, and which exploits elements of symbolic parallelism and abstraction to the detriment of the living and the concrete. The direct reflection of real life as a rule found no place during the initial stage of the development of early Russian literature. At this time human personality and human relations were almost universally envisaged and elucidated under the aspect of fixed ideological formulae, suggested by the official world outlook of the governing class; the personages who figure in literary works also belong for the most part to the governing class and are exponents of the established religio-moral and political ideas. The private life of a man in its everyday routine and psychological manifestations did not get into literature. Human behavior, like historical events, was ascribed for the most part to the interference of an outside force, good or evil. This interference is least evident in works emanating from the secular milieu, in the *Slovo o polku Igoreve* and in certain chronicle stories, where independent initiative is upon occasion ascribed to man and, within certain limits, the free ordering of his own destiny.

All these peculiarities, from the first, led to a situation where the inner and outer aspects of a man, in the great bulk of literary works as in the products of the icon painter's art, were given the conventional, schematic outlines laid down by a rigid stylistic tradition, extending even to the description of people's deeds and acts and the conditions under which they lived (cf. for example, the stylistic formulae for a battle). Rudiments of the realistic style, though in a very relative sense, are encountered chiefly in apocryphas, but the apocryphas all belong with translated literature and, as works inconsistent with the canonical books, were officially prohibited— albeit this did not prevent their influencing the monuments of original Russian literature in the matter of purely legendary motifs which were felt to contain no opposition to the ideology of the ruling class. To the penetration of the apocrypha into original literature is due in large measure the latter's wealth of poetic elements. An even greater contribution derives from the use in written literature of oral legend, folk tradition, and the artistic methods of the oral epic and song traditions, which were in turn influenced by learned literature.

There can be no doubt that as far back as the Kiev period the Russian people had in essence framed not only the song lyric but also the oral heroic epos relating the exploits of the bogatyrs who protected their native land from enemy attacks and vigilantly guarded its borders. This epos—our *byliny* —remained for many centuries in the popular memory and lives on even now in the memory of the reciters, who pass on to their children and grandchildren the heroic traditions of Russia's past.

Many of the peculiarities of Russian literature in the Kiev period here noted were to persist into subsequent periods of the development of early Russian literature, undergoing some alteration, however, as the historical existence of Old Rus progressed.

Provincial Literature
of the Thirteenth and
Fourteenth Centuries

THE impoverishment of Kievan Rus, beginning at the middle of the twelfth century and culminating in the Tartars' devastation of the south, particularly Kiev, brought on at about the middle of the thirteenth century a considerable decline in literary production there as well. From the middle of the fourteenth century, southern Rus (with the exception of Galicia) becomes, along with the western section, part of the Lithuanian state. In northern and northeastern Rus the literary tradition was meanwhile unimpaired and toward the beginning of the thirteenth century was already being enriched by new monuments rising out of specific political conditions existing in the north. At first the literature of northern Rus was of a provincial character, in keeping with the political decentralization. The later development of feudal relationships there is, however, characterized by an effort among the separate provinces to unite, this effort resulting at the beginning of the sixteenth century in the organization of the Muscovite state in the Volga-Oka basin. Parallel to this progressive concentration of separate states around Moscow, a similar concentration of the provincial literatures was also taking place, gradually uniting them into a Muscovite all-Russian literature which by the sixteenth century was already neutralizing the centrifugal and autonomous tendencies of local literary centers.

In direct continuation of the Kiev literary tradition, we get, besides a number of translated works, the above-studied *Kiev-Crypt Paterikon*, produced at the beginning of the thirteenth century. Clear traces of the Kiev tradition are likewise to be found in other monuments of this and of the immediately subsequent period, from the north and to some extent from the south as well. The most important works falling within the thirteenth and early fourteenth centuries are the *Supplication of Daniel the Exile,* a series of tales connected with the Tartar invasion, and the *Life of Alexander Nevsky.*

TRANSLATED LITERATURE

The thirteenth century was marked by the appearance in Rus of historical compilations devoted to the exposition of Jewish history, a subject which interested the Old Russian reader on account of its direct connection with Christianity. The facts of Jewish history are briefly stated in the so-called *"Historical Paleya,"* which in manuscripts carried the title, *Book of the Genesis of Heaven and Earth,* or *Ochy Paleinye* (Eyes of the Old Testament) *kir Feodora* (of Master Theodore). Its literary-historical value rests on the large amount of legendary and apocryphal material that it contains. Compiled in Byzantium, it apparently reached Rus through a South Slavic translation, presumably not later than the thirteenth century. (Copies are late, the earliest being fifteenth century.)[1] At the same time, in the opinion of Professor Mikhailov and Academician Istrin, northeastern Rus produced the *Explanatory Paleya,* which likewise included an exposition of the fortunes of the Hebrew people, with apocryphal interpolations, but this exposition was honeycombed with attacks on the Jewish religion.[2] The thirteenth century also brought Rus the so-called "Archival" or "Jewish" chronograph previously mentioned, setting forth the history of the Hebrew people from the creation of the world to the destruction of Jerusalem in the time of Vespasian. Besides taking in the historical books of the Old Testament and the *Chronicle of Malalas,* this chronograph also included at considerable length the *History of the Judaic War* by Josephus Flavius.[3]

[1] The text of the *Historical Paleya* was published by A. Popov in *Chtenii Obshchestva istorii i drevnostey rossiiskikh* (Papers of the Society of Russian History and Antiquities) (1881), Pt. 1.

[2] For the text see *"Paleya Tolkovaya,* po spisku sdelannomu v g. Kolomne v 1406 g." (Explanatory Paleya from a Copy Made in the City of Colomna in 1406), *Studies by the Pupils of N. S. Tikhonravov* (Moscow, 1892–1896) Pts. 1–2. The question of the place and time of appearance of the *Explanatory Paleya* cannot, however, be considered as finally settled. Thus Sukhomlinov, Uspenskii, and Zhdanov conjecture that it appeared in the tenth-eleventh centuries in Byzantium; Shakhmatov, however, held that the *Explanatory Paleya* was compiled in Bulgaria in the time of Cyril and Methodius. K. K. Istomin shares Shakhmatov's views as to the origin of the *Explanatory Paleya.* See V. Istrin, *Issledovaniya v oblasti drevnerusskoy literatury* (Studies in the Field of Early Russian Literature) pp. 70–198. This gives the literature on the question. See also V. P. Adrianov, *K literaturnoy istorii "Tolkovoy Paley"* (On the Literary History of the Explanatory Paleya) (Kiev, 1910), pp. 1–39.

[3] On this see V. Istrin, *Khronografy v russkoy literature* (Chronographs in Russian Literature) (St. Petersburg, 1898), pp. 11–12, reprint from *Vizantiiskii vremennik* (Byzantine Chronicle) (1898), No. 1–2.

The same collection that gave us the *Slovo o Polku Igoreve* also contained the *Legend of Rich India* or the *Legend of the Indian Kingdom*.[4] This narrative takes the form of an epistle from the Emperor of India, who is simultaneously Prester John, to the Greek emperor Manuel. It came out in Byzantium in the twelfth century during the Crusades, and circulated extensively in the West in a Latin version. The struggle of the West with the Mahometan East, having its roots in economic rivalry, gave rise to fantastic notions about a rich and powerful Christian kingdom in Asia destined to come to the aid of Christian Europe. On the other hand the monument reflects the motifs of the struggle between Church and state, a fact which lends it a lively pamphlet quality. The *Legend* apparently became known in the Suzdal section of Rus during the first half of the thirteenth century, through the medium of a Serbian translation of the Latin original, and as a result of economic and political associations with western Europe. The immediate occasion for its appearance on Russian soil may have been the events of the Tartar invasion, prompting the Russians, like the Christian West, to rest their hopes on a powerful kingdom of their own faith capable of coming to their aid.

No early redaction of the monument in its original form is extant, but we can get some idea of it from that part of the second redaction of the *Alexandria* which utilizes the text of the *Legend*. Separate copies are not encountered in this country earlier than the second half of the fifteenth century, but upwards of forty-five copies in all are extant from the fifteenth to the nineteenth century. They testify to the constant rewriting that the *Legend* underwent: it was already considerably Russianized even in the thirteenth and fourteenth centuries.

In most copies the *Legend* begins thus: The Greek emperor Manuel sent his emissary to the Indian emperor Ivan with many gifts and with orders to inquire of Ivan as to the size of his army and as to all the wonders of the land of India. Upon arriving in India, the emissary first gave the presents to Emperor Ivan, then started to question him about his country. Ivan, having accepted the gifts and made presents to the emissary in return, bade him tell

4 See N. Batalin, *Skazanie ob Indiiskom tsarstve* (Legend of the Indian Empire) (Voronezh, 1876); A. N. Veselovskii, *Yuzhnorusskie byliny* (South Russian Byliny) (St. Petersburg, 1881). Chap. 6 discusses the *Legend of the Indian Kingdom* in connection with the *bylina* about Duke Stepanovich; the oldest Russian text of the *Legend*, from the fifteenth century St. Cyril-Byelozersky Monastery copy, is published as an appendix to the chapter; V. Istrin, *Skazanie ob Indiiskom tsarstve* (Moscow, 1893) where the text of the *Legend* from the fifteenth century Volokolam Monastery copy, fuller than the Cyril-Byelozersk copy, is reproduced as a supplement; M. N. Speranskii, "Skazanie ob Indiiskom tsarstve," *Izvestiya po russkomu yazyku i slovesnosti* (News of the Russian Language and Literature) (1930), Vol. III, Bk. II. This traces the fortunes of Russian texts of the *Legend*, its relation to Old Russian literature, its connection with oral literature. A modern Russian text of the monument from an early seventeenth century copy is reproduced as a supplement.

Manuel that if he wished to find out about his military power and all the wonders of his country, let him sell his whole land of Greece and come himself and enter his service, and Ivan would make him his second or third officer and afterward Manuel could return to his own land. "Even if you were ten times more exalted," Ivan bade him tell Manuel, "it would be impossible for all your scribes to get my kingdom on parchment [later, 'on paper'] before you died. And what you could get by selling your kingdom would not suffice to buy the parchment, for it would be impossible to give you a complete description of my kingdom and all its marvels."

Ivan goes on to tell about himself: "I, John, king and priest, am king of kings and have three hundred kings under me. I am a defender of the Orthodox Christian faith. My domain is as follows: it takes ten months to walk it in one direction, while in the other you can never reach the end, for it is where earth meets heaven." Then follows an enumeration of the assorted marvels in which the country of India abounds: people who are without powers of speech, horned, three-legged, four- and six-handed, giants nine sazhens tall, people with eyes and mouth on their chests, with dogs' heads, and so forth; extraordinary beasts, birds, plants, stones, among them the phoenix, a bird which is burned to ashes and reborn, and the carbuncle, lord over all precious stones, shining by night like fire. In the land of India there are no thieves or bandits or envious persons, because it is so full of all manner of wealth. It has no venomous serpents, and if any get in they die at once. Many other marvels are also enumerated by Ivan as existing in India.

Next he describes his military campaigns: "When we go into battle twenty crosses and twenty standards are carried before me, wrought of gold, adorned with precious stones, and sprinkled with pearls. The crosses and standards are convoyed by an army of 100,000 horsemen and 100,000 foot soldiers." When the battle starts, a single wooden cross showing the Crucifixion is carried before Ivan to remind him of the Passion and crucifixion of Christ. And there they also carry a golden charger with a handful of earth on it, that we may remember that of earth we were created and to the earth we shall return. And beside it is another golden charger on which rest a precious stone and a costly pearl as a reminder of the power and greatness of the kingdom of India. King Ivan's palace precinct is so vast that to walk around it would take five days. It contains many palaces of gold, silver, and wood, adorned like the sky with stars and roofed with gold. One golden palace is supported by eighty golden pillars three sazhens in diameter and eighty sazhens high, with a precious stone set in each pillar. Every day Ivan dines twelve patriarchs, ten kings, twelve metropolitans, forty-five archpriests, three hundred priests, and so forth, and to wait on table and pass the beakers there are fourteen emperors, forty kings and three hundred boyars; the kitchen is managed by two emperors and two kings, besides boyars and servants. And in India the apostle Thomas lies buried.

In several copies the *Legend* ends with the statement that after telling of the marvels of his country, Ivan sent the Greek emissary back to Emperor Manuel with great honor and many gifts.

One of the Byzantine variants of the *Legend* influenced the Russian *bylina* about Duke Stepanovich, and in turn there are echoes of the verse rhythm of this *bylina* in some copies of our *Legend*. Echoes of the *Legend* are also to be found in some variants of the religious poem, the *Book of the Dove*, and in certain details of the fable epos, as well as in learned literature from the second redaction of the *Alexandria* on.

The Tartar invasion evidently provided suitable conditions for the appearance on Russian soil of a tale Eastern in origin and eschatological in content, the *Legend*, or *Discourse on the Twelve Dreams of Emperor Shakhaish*.[5] This treats of the dreams of Shakhaish and the interpretation of those dreams by the sage Mamer. Later on, the names of the emperor and the interpreter become telescoped in Russian copies and the tale acquires the title, *Legend of the Twelve Dreams of the Emperor Mamer*. The dreams and more particularly their interpretation are very gloomy and disconsolate. What it all comes to is that the evil latter days are at hand when revolt shall prevail throughout the earth, justice disappear, human blood be poured forth, the earth cease to nourish the people with its fruits, brother turn against brother, children no longer honor their parents, corruption and injustice be everywhere instated, and so forth. Thus the eighth dream, in which the emperor sees a fine steed eating grass through two throats, one in front and one in back, is explained by the interpreter in this manner:

Emperor, when those evil days shall come, princes and elders shall render justice by bribery rather than by truth, and having neither fear of God nor shame

[5] For texts and studies of the *Legend*, see A. Veselovskii's "Slovo o dvenadtsati snakh Shakhaishi po rkp. XV v." (Discourse on the Twelve Dreams of Shakhaish from a Fifteenth Century Manuscript) (St. Petersburg, 1879), *Sbornik otd. russk. yaz. i slov.* (Collection of the Division of Russian Language and Literature), Vol. XX, No. 2, reprinted in the *Collected Works* (Leningrad, 1930), of A. N. Veselovskii, Vol. VIII, Pt. 2, and A. Rystenko's *Skazanie o dvenadtsati snakh tsarya Mamera v slavyansko-russkoy literature* (Legend of the Twelve Dreams of Emperor Mamer in Slavo-Russian Literature) (Odessa, 1904), and *Addenda* to the article (Odessa, 1905). See also S. Oldenburg, "K voprosu ob istochnikakh Slova o dvenadtsati snakh Shakhaishi" (On the Question of the Sources of the Discourse on the Twelve Dreams of Shakhaish), *Zhurnal min. nar. prosv.* (Journal of the Ministry of Public Instruction) (1892), No. 11, pp. 135–140; *ibid.*, "Sny Keida, tsarya Kanodzhskogo, i sny Shakhaishi" (Dreams of Keid, Kanozhian Emperor, and the Dreams of Shakhaish) *Istoriko-literaturnyi sbornik, posvyashch. Vs. Izm. Sreznevskomu* (On the Literary History of the Legend of the Twelve Dreams of Emperor Shakhaish) (Leningrad, 1924), pp. 47–54; P. O. Potapov, "K literaturnoy istorii 'Skazaniya o dvenadtsati snakh tsarya Shakhaishi,'" (Legend of the Twelve Dreams of Emperor Shakhaish), *Sbornik statey v chest' akademika A. I. Sobolevskogo* (Collection of Articles in Honor of Academician A. I. Sobolevskii) (Leningrad, 1928), pp. 120–129.

before men, and taking sureties from guilty and innocent alike, shall themselves be condemned to torment and outer darkness.

Known here in a large number of copies from the fifteenth century on, the tale attained its greatest popularity in Rus in connection with increasing public hardships and the expectation of the end of the world and the coming of Antichrist. These expectations were at particularly high pitch here toward the end of the fifteenth century and—among the Old Believers—during the seventeenth century.

Produced in India and closely related to the *Panchatantra* and to its Arabian adaptation *Kalila and Dimna*, the *Legend of Shakhaish's Dreams* evidently reached Byzantium through a Persian version by Bogomil mediation, then passed to Serbia and in the thirteenth and fourteenth centuries to Rus, where it circulated in two redactions.

Probably the tale of *Stephanit and Ikhnilat* was translated here not later than the fourteenth century: it too was of Indian origin, produced around the sixth century after Christ in Sanskrit.[6] This tale, consisting of a conversation between an emperor and a philosopher, used the beast-parable form for imparting precepts to emperors upon the wise governance of their peoples. The immediate working-up of the initial nucleus of the tale on Indian soil was the *Panchatantra* collection, shortly translated into Old Persian. In the eighth century the Persian text was translated into Syrian and Arabic. The Syrian version did not have a very wide circulation, but on the Arabic, ascribed to the sage Bidpaya and entitled *Kalila and Dimna* (the straightforward and the crafty), were based the numerous translations and adaptations of the tale known in the East and in the West.

About 1081 a translation from Arabic into Greek was made by Simeon the Scythian and entitled *Stephanit and Ikhnilat* (the Crowned and the Follower). In the Byzantine version, as in the Arabic, the names in the title are those of two jackals, one of whom, wicked and jealous, sows enmity between the emperor, the lion, and his friend the bull. He persuades the lion that the bull is planning to make an attempt on his life and advises him to kill the traitor, while he convinces the bull of the lion's perfidy and the necessity of rebelling against him. The enraged lion, believing the calumny, orders

    6 For texts of Stephanit and Ikhnilat with preface and notes by F. I. Bulgakov, see *Izd. obshchestva lyubiteley drevney pismennosti* (1877–1878), XVI, XXII (Publications of the Society of Friends of Early Literature), and with preface and notes by A. E. Viktorov, *ibid.* (1881), LXIV and LXXVIII. See S. Smirnov, "Stephanit i Ikhnilat," *Filologicheskie zapiski* (Philological Notes) (1879), No. 3; A. Rystenko, "K istorii povesti 'Stefanit i Ikhnilat' v vizantiiskoy i slavyano-russkoy literature" (On the History of the Tale of Stephanit and Ikhnilat in Byzantine and Slavo-Russian Literature), *Letopis istoriko-filologicheskogo obshchestva pri novorossiiskom universitete* (Chronicle of the Historico-Philological Society at the University of Novorossiisk), Vol. X (1902) and (1910), Vol. XVI; *Kalila i Dimna*, translated from the Arabic by I. Yu. Krachkovsky, izd. *Academia* (Moscow-Leningrad, 1934), for a history of the text of *Stephanit and Ikhnilat*.

the bull killed, but when the calumny is disclosed, destroys the jackal-libeler. This basic narrative scheme is developed through a large number of parables enunciated by the two jackals and forming a cleverly articulated chain of moralistic tales. The basic idea of the narrative is contained in the following aphorism, with which the tale of Akir also closed: "Any man who plots against his friend shall fall into the pit that he makes ready."

The text of *Stephanit and Ikhnilat,* which had already undergone some Christianization in Greece, became markedly more Christian on Slavic soil. In Rus the tale circulated in a large number of copies during the fifteenth and sixteenth centuries, particular interest attaching to the application of its parables and adages to the political situation of the time.

ORIGINAL LITERATURE

THE SUPPLICATION OF DANIEL THE EXILE

The work entitled the *Supplication, Epistle,* or *Discourse of Daniel the Exile* is a very curious, highly publicistic pamphlet, written by an author about whom we have no further knowledge, in the form of an appeal to the prince. This monument, extant in several copies, classifiable into two basic editions, was first examined by Karamzin in his *History of the Russian State,* and has evoked a fairly extensive literature, which has not, however, as yet settled certain controversial questions connected with its chronology, the relationship existing between the editions, and the personality of the author.[7]

The *Supplication* in both editions consists of a high-flown rhetorical appeal to the prince to show favor to the author, who is in need, has been persecuted, is not fitted for military service, but is possessed of unusual intelligence and education and might well assist the prince in the capacity of counselor. To convince his addressee that the epistle comes from a man of great erudition, the author punctuates his appeal with citations and aphorisms taken from the Old Testament, the *Bee,* the *Physiologus,* the *Tale of Akir the Wise,* the chronicle, and several other works of original and of translated literature, as well as with "secular parables"; that is, with adages and

---

[7] The literature on the question to 1914 is treated in P. P. Mindalyov's (or Mindalev) book, *Molenie Daniila Zatochnika i svyazannye s nim pamyatniki* (The Supplication of Daniel the Exile and Associated Monuments) (Kazan, 1914), pp. 11–86. The most recent critical edition of all copies of the monument is to be found in *Pamyatniki drevnerusskoy literatury* (Monuments of Early Russian Literature) (Leningrad, 1932), Pt. 3, pubs. Academy of Sciences USSR, "Slovo Daniila Zatochnika po redaktsiyam XII i XIII vv. i peredelkam" (Discourses of Daniel the Exile from Twelfth and Thirteenth Century Redactions and Their Recastings), prepared for the press by N. N. Zarubin.

proverbs. The essential difference between the so-called "first" edition and the "second," consists in the fact that the second edition contains an opposition-inspired thrust at the boyar class and monastic clergy entirely absent from the "first" edition, which in turn arraigns bad wives more emphatically than the "second" does.

The majority of students assign the appearance of the "first" edition—the *Discourse*—to the twelfth century, that of the "second"—the *Supplication* or *Epistle*—to the thirteenth century. The majority have also decided the question of the date of the original in favor of the twelfth century, though individual students differ as to the exact date within this century, according to which prince they regard as Daniel's addressee. Some have believed it possible to date the original as far back as the eleventh century, in which case the so-called "twelfth century" redaction would be only a revision, while others have conjectured that the *Supplication* may not have appeared until the fourteenth century. Some scholars believe that neither the first nor the second redaction, taken by itself, represents the authentic text of the monument and that the original consisted of elements now found partly in the "first," partly in the "second" edition. In the matter of chronological priority, some give preference to the "first," others to the "second." The chronological priority of the "second edition" was championed as early as 1857 by Buslayev, and has been upheld by many scholars. It has also been adopted by the majority of general courses in the history of early Russian literature.

Out of the aggregate of expressed opinions concerning this enigmatic monument, it would appear that the following may be accepted as beyond dispute. In the first place not one of the copies and neither of the editions gives even a reasonably accurate idea of the original. A work compounded of material so fluid and volatile as maxims, parables, and aphorisms, indubitably laid itself open, under the conditions of Old Russian learning, to very free treatment in the form of all sorts of additions, abbreviations, transpositions, substitutions, and so forth. A study of the known texts of the monument and of its revisions convinces us that this is precisely what it received. In other words, the most plausible course will be to admit that the original included elements both from the "first" edition and from the "second." Granted this, then the next problem will be to establish which of the two editions has kept the larger number of those fragmentary, fugitive elements which made up the original. It is possible to say a priori that it will be the one in which we discern the largest amount of concrete, factual, realistic, as opposed to abstract and generalized, material. What we know about the evolution of Old Russian literary monuments through successive revisions convinces us that this evolution was a progressive leveling out and depersonalizing of the concrete and factual side of a monument as the outer events or subjective life interests that called it forth ceased to excite and interest readers of later generations. Anything of a personal or historical nature tends to be removed from the text, and there remain, sometimes in heightened form, those general matters which may be regarded as having some sort of universal acceptability and validity in terms of the present day, for which yesterday and the evils thereof no longer suffice.

From the viewpoint of concreteness, factual content, and historicity, and likewise the presence of a personal element, everything favors the "second" redaction. From it, and only from it do we get a concrete, rather than a generalized, explanation of those circumstances in the author's personal life which impelled him to write an appeal to his prince. The author is in economic dependence on the boyars and from this he hopes to free himself with the prince's help. This dependence is also the source of all the afflictions and moral degradation concerning which he so energetically and insistently makes deposition to the prince. From the unenviable position in which he finds himself, the discussion of possible means for improving his fortunes— to marry a rich woman or to become a monk—issues logically. Neither course attracts him for reasons which are there and then pointed out. All these concrete traits, indicative of the author's personality, are obliterated in the "first" edition. There the author stands before us in the generalized form of a biblical poor man whose friends have deserted him and who is suffering misfortunes at the hands of we don't know exactly whom; his own social position and that of his enemies is not clear. Without any logical connection a fierce and incoherent diatribe against women bursts into the appeal; a dissertation upon good and evil counselors, likewise having no connection with what has gone before, is immediately followed by a sweeping thrust at bad wives—"For it says in secular parables"—the fourth paragraph of which—"Or, you tell me: marry for a rich father-in-law"—is clearly out of place. The "first" edition also lacks the stern denunciation of monks who lie to God. Instead of all this we get the abstract complaint of an unsuccessful man, reinforced by abundant quotations and aphorisms and by interpolations, such as the story of Joseph the Fair which occurs in one of the variants of this edition. Was it not this divergence of the "first" edition from the "second" which brought about the very change in title from "Supplication," a designation which exactly fitted the original content, to the more general and less explicit designation of "Discourse"? The appropriateness of such a substitution is particularly evident in the light of two variants of the "first" edition which bear the title, *Discourse on Worldly Parables and on the Affairs of Life,* and which go considerably farther than their original toward transforming the monument into abstract teaching and edification. Judging by the fact that in the "first" edition the opposition element has been deleted, the unfavorable reference to monasticism in particular being omitted, while the diatribes against women have been reinforced, its origin may presumably be assigned to the clerical milieu.

Thus we have every reason to suppose that the essential elements of the original have been better preserved in the "second" edition than in the "first." The chronological preference accorded the "first" edition on grounds of its more consistent plan (the opinion of Zhdanov and Mindalev) is unjustified first of all because neither edition of itself exactly reproduces the original, and because a greater harmony of plan would in no wise argue for the greater antiquity of the edition having such a plan. Furthermore, there are no grounds for considering the exposition better ordered in the "first" edition rather than the reverse. The phrase: "Daniel said. 'A brave man, Prince, you can easily get, but an intelligent man comes dear,'" commonly adduced to demonstrate that the "second" edition, which contains it, can therefore not pretend to priority, proves nothing of itself. Regardless of how you may interpret this phrase, there are no grounds for regarding it as necessarily belonging to the redaction rather than to later copies. Incidentally, in the variant of the second edition represented by Tikhonravov's copy, the confusing "Daniel said" is absent. And it cannot be maintained that this omission was due to sagacity on the part of editor or scribe: these words may equally well have been missing in the copy of the "second" edition from which the variant derived.

If we agree to look upon the "second" edition as the one which has retained the greater number of traits of the original, then the appearance of the original must date, as has been pointed out by those who maintain the greater authority of the "second" edition, from the thirteenth century, the reign of Yaroslav, son of Vsevolod, in northern Pereyaslavl (1213–1236), or more exactly, to judge from the concluding words—"Do not, Lord, give the land of our tongue into captivity to those who know not God; let not the barbarians say: Where is their God?"—to the time of the first Tartar inroads into Russian territory (1223–1236).

Of the "second" redaction of the *Supplication* two copies are extant, the Undolsky collection copy, sixteenth century, and the Miracle Monastery copy, seventeenth century, the latter being apparently the more accurate.

In these copies, as in the "first" edition, the *Supplication* begins with a high-flown appeal, addressed for the time being, however, not to the prince but to "brothers," like the *Tale of Igor's Expedition:* "Let us trumpet, then, brothers, on our intelligence as on a trumpet of wrought gold; let us strike the silver organ keys, meaning our wisdom, and let us smite the cymbals of our mind, making music on the divinely inspired psaltery, so that edifying thoughts may set tears flowing for us." The author, as we see, has a very high opinion of his own wisdom. He anticipates the glory that will gather about his name: "Arise, my glory, arise psaltery and dulcimer," he continues, "that I may unfold my prophesying in parables and declare my fame with tongues." This prelude of a general character is followed by a direct appeal to Prince Yaroslav, son of Vsevolod, punctuated by frequent repetitions of the unvarying salutation: "My Prince and Lord!"

First our author strives to inspire sympathy for himself on the prince's part: all those about the prince are warmed by his favor as by the sun; he alone is like grass growing in the shade, on which the sun does not shine and which the rain does not water; day and night he walks cut off from the light of the prince's eyes. All feed as from a fount upon the abundance in the prince's house; he alone thirsts for the favor of the prince like the hart for the water spring; he likens himself to a parched tree standing by the wayside, struck at by passers-by: everyone insults him because he is not protected by the fear of the prince's wrath as by a stout fence.

Then follow the first express, though still general, declarations of social protest: a rich man is known anywhere, even in a strange city, but a poor man walks unrecognized of any even in his own town; a rich man starts to speak and all are silent and his words are wafted to the clouds, but when a poor man starts to speak all cry out upon him, for it is fine clothes that cause a man's speech to be respected. But the author proposes to call attention not to his outward appearance but to his inner qualities: even if he be scant in attire, he is abundant in wit, if he be young in years, he is old in understanding and soars in thought like an eagle through the air. (Cf. "running in thought up a tree, flying beneath the clouds like a blue-gray eagle," and "flying in thought beneath the clouds" in the *Tale of Igor's Expedition*.) Farther on, however, he speaks much more modestly of his wisdom: "If I am not wise, yet have I clothed myself in the vestments of the wise and have worn the shoes of those who have understanding," he confesses, and farther on uses the phrase again in another form. In order to ingratiate himself with the prince, the author flatters him immoderately, unexpectedly employing for this purpose quotations from the Song of Songs in which Solomon showers praises upon his beloved Shulamite. Begging the prince for grace and favor, he projects the relationship between them in idyllic and sentimental terms: "Do not look upon me as the wolf upon the lamb," he says, "but look upon me as a mother upon her babe." This request of Daniel's for motherly sympathy is amplified later on into a plea not to desert him as his mother and father had done—vague indications that some sort of family discord had been one cause of the author's misfortunes. Then and there he lays his cards on the table: if he is not any too brave in battle, none the less he is strong in words, and this admission is accompanied by a number of quotations and maxims the object of which is to show the superiority of intelligent counselors over brave warriors of no great intelligence.

After this the author tells what he has suffered under the yoke of bondage and how he has experienced all the bitterness of servile dependence upon boyars. In this connection he gives us to understand that when he was rich many sought his friendship, but that now in the misfortune that has overtaken him, they have turned from him and, while feigning sympathy, are ridiculing him in their hearts. Complaints about his fate are accompanied by repeated entreaties to the prince expressed in figurative and rhetorical form: "Deliver me, Lord, from poverty like a bird from a snare, and wrest me from my beggary like a chamois from a net, like a wild duck borne in the talons of a falcon," or: "When you are eating your fill of varied meats, think of me eating dry bread; when you are gladdened by mellow wine and clothed in your fine raiment, think of me lying in a coarse unwashed garment; on your soft bed think of me lying under a single rag, half dead in winter, pierced by drops of rain as by arrows." Sometimes these appeals terminate in extremely artificial, ornately high-flown phrases: "Turn the cloud of your favor toward the earth of my destitution," or: "None the less hearken unto my voice and place the chalice of your heart under the streams from my tongue, so that the sweetness of words more fragrant than aromatic essences may drip on you."

The prince will perhaps advise him to marry a rich wife, continues the author, but he at once raises decisive objections to this, advancing a number of arguments against marrying a bad wife for the sake of a dowry. He is unsparing in his sharp thrusts at feminine vices, varying the popular medieval diatribes against "bad wives," apparently without even admitting the possibility of marrying anything but a bad wife. He categorically declares against the alternative way out of his disastrous position—to become a monk: he would rather end his life in poverty than take monastic vows and lie to God. Many who have left the worldly life to become monks return again to their worldly ways like dogs to their vomit; at weddings and feasts you will always find iniquitous monks and nuns; they have assumed the form of angels but kept the desires of the flesh; they remain in the clerical order but conduct themselves in an unseemly manner.

Without adequate transition, the *Supplication* goes on to point out that servants who amuse their masters by physical dexterity are the ones who enjoy their favor. Then, having exhausted all arguments in his own behalf, the author decides to bring his discourse to an end lest he fritter away his intellectual riches by much speaking. After quoting a few more aphorisms, and suddenly giving expression to an extreme self-disparagement that is in direct contradiction to all the self-advertisement that has gone before—"Or you may say, Prince, that I have lied like a dog; but good dogs are something that both princes and boyars love"—the author closes his appeal with wishes for the prince's success in all his undertakings, particularly with respect to the barbarian invasion that threatens him.

As a literary type, the *Supplication* is not without analogies in medieval European literature. Scholars have cited as analogous entreaties the poems of two twelfth century Byzantine chroniclers, Mikhail Glika and Theodore Ptokhoprodrom, a supplicatory elegy that the ninth century monk Ermold sent from prison to the son of Ludwig the Pious, the *Proverbs* of some thirteenth century Italian prisoner in Bari, and others. But there are no grounds whatever for supposing that these works had any direct influence on our *Supplication*.

What then was Daniel's social position? The majority of scholars who have touched on this question think that he was a member of the prince's retinue, a courtier. A courtier banished by the prince, the son of his slave woman, thinks Buslayev.[8] Modestov also supposes that Daniel was a member of the junior retinue, a courtier, arguing from his words: "Every courtier should have the honor and favor of the prince." In this connection Modestov sees no contradiction in the fact that Daniel calls himself courtier and at the same time slave of the prince, and son of his slave: "The word courtier need not necessarily signify a man living at the prince's court, his intimate. . . . It probably only means a member of the prince's retinue, possibly of no more than the junior order. And a member of the junior retinue, which was recruited entirely from the lower estate, could even be actually a slave (a manumitted slave) of the prince and call himself by this name because of descent from a slave woman of the prince's."[9]

That Daniel was a courtier is the opinion also of V. M. Gussov, who does not consider it possible, however, to assign him definitely to the junior retinue, since "it is impossible to draw a line of demarcation between the senior retinue and the junior."[10] Keltuyala also speaks of Daniel as a courtier. Mindalyov, who regards the "first" redaction of the monument as the older, thinks that its author belonged to the retinue; as to the "second" redaction, however, he conjectures that it was "no longer" composed "in the retinue but in some different circle," in exactly what circle is not stated. The author

8 *Istoricheskaya khristomatiya tserkovno-slavyanskovo i drevnerusskogo yazykov* (Historical Anthology of Church Slavonic and Old Russian) (Moscow, 1861), p. 638.

9 "O poslanii Daniila Zatochnika" (On the Epistle of Daniel the Exile), *Zhurnal min. nar. prosv.* (Journal of the Ministry of Public Instruction) (1880), No. 11, p. 194.

10 "K voprosu o redaktsiyakh Moleniya Daniila Zatochnika" (On the Question of Redactions of the Supplication of Daniel the Exile), separate reprint from the *Annals of the Historico-Philological Society of Novorossiisk University* (1899), Vol. VIII, p. 29.

of the "second" redaction, according to Mindalyov, "quotes a whole series of excerpts from the Song of Songs, showing no sense of moderation and fawning like a slave who cannot escape the reproach of the name of serf and who is aware of being a man in spite of it. The author is a slave of the prince, son of his slave woman, a member of his household rather than a member of the retinue." [11] More precisely, Mindalyov regards the author of the "second" redaction as a prince's serf. He, this prince's serf, recast the text of the "first" redaction, adapting its contents to fit his station as a serf.

The only writer before Mindalyov to discern a slave in the author of the *Supplication*—in either redaction of the monument—was Shchapov, who mentioned him incidentally in his article, "The Voice of the Russian Church on the Amelioration of the Existence of the Disenfranchised." [12] After speaking of the distressing situation of the serfs in Old Rus and of their grievances against cruel elders and boyars, Shchapov continues in a tone of sympathetic exaltation:

Thus is wafted down to us the bitter, centuries-old complaint of a pathetic exile, a hapless serf of the thirteenth century, from the wild shores of Lake Lach in the Government of Olonetsk. . . . What he wants more than anything else is to transfer his allegiance to his supreme sovereign, to the prince; he would rather renounce all material advantages in the house of his boyar master than live without the comforting and invigorating inner sense of moral freedom. . . . And in answer to this bitter lament of an exile, an Old Russian serf, is heard forthwith the saving and consoling voice of the Church, the voice of Christianity calling for the amelioration of the slaves' lot.

Shchapov's designation of Daniel the Exile as a boyar's slave at the moment of his appeal to the prince seems to us the only correct one: it is suggested by the text of the *Supplication* itself. Having said that he would rather serve the prince even in beggar's raiment than serve the boyar splendidly attired, Daniel continues:

Improper is a golden bangle in the nose of a swine, and costly raiment upon a serf. Even if a kettle were to have golden rings in its handles, its bottom would not escape blackness and burning; and so it is with a serf: let him be ever so haughty and insolent, he will not escape his reproach, the name of serf. [13]

To take these words in an allegorical sense would be an unjustifiably strained interpretation. The fact that they are intended literally is quite clear from the immediate context: Daniel is complaining that he has been in dire need and has suffered under the yoke of slavery; he has experienced in his own person the evil of it. It would be better to serve in the house of the prince in

---

[11] *Op. cit.*, pp. 343–344.
[12] First printed in 1859 in Kazan as a brochure with the above title; reprinted in A. P. Shchapov's *Works* (St. Petersburg, 1906), Vol. I, pp. 1–15.
[13] Quotations from the Miracle copy.

beggar's attire than at the boyar's court in splendid raiment, for just as a gold bangle would be improper in the nose of a swine, so would costly raiment be improper on a serf; even if you should put gold rings through the handles of a kettle the bottom of it would still remain black and burned. So too a serf: no matter how haughty and insolent he is, he will not escape his reproach, the name of serf. He would rather drink water in the house of the prince than mead at the court of a boyar; rather receive a roasted sparrow from the hands of the prince than a shoulder of mutton from the hand of a bad master, for often has his bread of slavery tasted like worm-wood in his mouth, and he has mingled his drink with tears. In serving a good master you may hope to gain your liberty some day, but in serving a bad master, you can only sink still deeper into slavery.

The meaning of this whole tirade is perfectly clear, it is neither ambiguous nor allegorical: Daniel is a boyar's serf who finds his serf's office with some pitiless boyar hard to bear. He is asking to become the prince's serf in the hope of winning promotion with him and in time becoming his free retainer. As testimony to the prince's generosity, Daniel says: "For all turn to you and obtain deliverance from affliction: poor orphans, left by the rich to drown, turn to you as their kindly intercessor." The word for "orphan" in Old Russian meant not only what it still means now but also a slave, a servant, a serf. "Poor" meant, among other things, a peasant of the poorest sort, an insignificant person, a man of no account. Thus, when he speaks of orphans and the poor left by the rich to drown, Daniel may have had in mind literally serfs and dispossessed people exploited by the rich and taking refuge under the prince's protection. This, as it were, justified his own appeal for the prince's intercession. In calling himself the prince's slave and the son of his slave woman (this is not in the "first" redaction), Daniel for once is evidently not simply utilizing a quotation from the Psalter, but denoting his own actual social position. Expressions such as: "Or you may say, Prince, that I have lied. But what of it? If I had known how to steal, I would not have bothered you thus," and: "Or you may say, Prince, that I have lied like a dog; but good dogs are something that both princes and boyars love," come much more naturally from the lips of a serf than from those of a free man.

The assertion that Daniel was a serf, however, at once gives rise to a natural doubt as to whether a serf back in the thirteenth century could have possessed the erudition and the gift for literary exposition that Daniel possessed. Again Modestov pointed out that an education so extensive for that time as Daniel's could, in the twelfth and thirteenth centuries, have been possessed, princes and clergy apart, only by the prince's retainers, and that we must therefore positively assert that Daniel was a member of the prince's retinue. But such an assertion rests on purely theoretical premises which can in nowise be regarded as incontestable. If we did not know the biography of Lomonosov, we might assert quite as categorically that he could not have been a peasant, and on the same purely theoretical grounds on which we would repudiate Daniel's serfdom. If Lomonosov was an exception to the rule, then Daniel may also have been such an exception. In the overwhelming majority of cases we do not know the biographies of our early writers and on that account cannot judge of their social extraction. But we do know that in ancient times rich men sent their serfs to school, chiefly to prepare them to become church functionaries. Theodosius, prior of the Crypt Monastery, was the son of a serf (a bailiff). It is possible that Daniel, too, was given an education in the expectation that he would devote himself to an ecclesiastical career. Not without reason is monasticism mentioned as one of the ways out of servitude that the prince might propose to him.

It must not be supposed that the serf in old Rus was a creature so disfranchised and depersonalized that all possibilities of a career in life were closed to him. A serf could acquire property both real and personal, pass it on as a legacy; he was subject to the public laws and to public legal actions. Often serfs were entrusted with separate branches of farm management, became stewards, village bailiffs, field superintendents, police inspectors, head grooms, and so forth.[14]

Such were the perspectives that opened out for a serf and evidently inspired in Daniel those pretensions which he addressed to Yaroslav, son of Vsevolod. And there is no reason why Mindalyov should see a discrepancy in the fact that the Daniel of the "second" edition while calling himself a slave of the prince, at the same time appropriates to himself the traits of retainer and courtier. ("Every courtier ought to have the respect and favor of the prince.") The point is that the boyar's serf, Daniel, has hopes that once he has been made prince's serf he may come into his own as courtier, counselor and collaborator in affairs of state.[15]

It is possible that Daniel was not born a serf but got into this position through debt. Such a hypothesis seems to be suggested by his complaint that acquaintances and relatives sought his friendship as long as everything was all right with him, and turned away the moment misfortunes befell him. But at the same time there is no reason for thinking that in the past he had belonged to the prince's retinue; we find no indications of this in the *Supplication*, yet such indications would have come naturally to the author's lips

[14] M. Dyakonov, *Ocherki obshchestvennogo i gosudarstvennogo stroya drevney Rusi* (Outlines of the Structure of Society and State in Early Rus), 4th ed., pp. 88–89.
[15] For more details see N. K. Gudzii, "K kakoy sotsial'noy srede prinadlezhal Daniil Zatochnik?" (To What Social Milieu Did Daniel the Exile Belong?), *Collection of Articles Dedicated to Academician A. S. Orlov* (Leningrad, 1934), pp. 477–485.

if he had been asking for restoration to a position which he had formerly occupied.

However that may be, the essential fact for us is that Daniel appears as exponent of the attitudes of the unfree and dependent man, here stated in literature for the first time, and most graphically.

An insistent and impassioned appeal to the prince for deliverance from slavery and indigence, the *Supplication* is at the same time a vicious satire on persons and on orders which make for human oppression and breed social and moral injustice. Being extremely impressionable and reacting very sharply to the ills about him, the author of the *Supplication* exposes all those whom he considers to blame for common ills and for social injustice, be they boyars, monks, or women. Carried away by his passion for withering sarcasm and very much inclined to humor, he is at times unsparing even with himself, likening himself to the barren fig tree and to the prodigal son, and his mind to a night raven among the ruins, and not protesting even against the possibility that the prince may compare him to a lying dog. But neither self-contempt nor pride can disturb the basic motif which runs through the whole *Supplication*. This motif is a passionate and persuasive defense of human personality and human dignity as separate from social and proprietary position, and is inspired by an unshakable conviction that a man's worth and his right to consideration and respect are determined primarily by his intellectual qualities. In no work of the preceding period of Russian literature does the personal element declare itself so vigorously and persistently and so much as a matter of principle as it does in the *Supplication*. And nowhere is it supported in any such degree by the championship of intelligence and culture in their struggle against human stupidity and social disorder as in the *Supplication*. From this point of view Daniel may be regarded as a sort of thirteenth century intellectual attempting to break a path for himself with the exclusive aid of his literary talent and his intellectual gifts.

Belinsky gave a very apt characterization of him. He wrote:

Whoever Daniel the Exile may have been, one may with reason infer that he was one of those personalities who, to their own undoing, are too intelligent, too gifted, know too much, and, unable to hide their superiority, offend the selfish mediocrity of others; whose hearts ache and are consumed with jealous desire for things alien to them, who speak where they would better have been silent, and are silent where it would be to their profit to speak; in a word, one of those personalities whom people first praise, then harry to death, and, finally, having killed them, start in again to praise.[16]

Nowhere in the text of the *Supplication* does it appear that Daniel was ever banished, and thus there would seem to be no warrant for his designa-

16 *Complete Collected Works* of V. G. Belinskii, edited, with notes, by S. A. Vengerov (St. Petersburg, 1903), Vol. VI, p. 380.

tion, "the exile." Hence there seems adequate justification for Academician Istrin's conjecture that our Daniel was later confounded with another Daniel, concerning whom there exists a chronicle item under 1378 to the effect that he was exiled to Lake Lach, something which is also mentioned, as we know, in the *Supplication*, whither this item found its way obviously not earlier than the end of the fourteenth century.[17]

TALES OF THE TARTAR INVASION

The Tartar yoke, of more than two centuries' duration, was a terrific calamity for the Russian people. "This yoke," wrote Marx, "not only crushed, it outraged and withered the very soul of the people which had become its victim."[18]

To the Russian people which shouldered the burden of Tartar domination had fallen the lot of saving European culture from destruction and attrition. "To Russia a high destiny was ordained," wrote Pushkin. "Her boundless plains swallowed up the Mongol armies and halted their invasion at the very edge of Europe; the barbarians did not dare leave an enslaved Rus at their rear, and returned to their Oriental steppes. Formative culture was saved by torn and gasping Russia."[19]

The Tartar invasion of Rus was reflected in a number of narrative works of a homiletic and biographical character. The minds of Old Russian bookmen, overwhelmed by the severity and suddenness of the terrible catastrophe that had descended upon the land of Rus, sought first of all a religious explanation of events: they interpreted the enslavement of Rus by the Tartars as God's punishment for her sins; God sent victory to the Tartars not out of favor toward them but because he wished thereby to admonish us unto repentance. The more active part played by the Church in a time of universal moral depression helped to fix this view of the reason for the national disaster, the Church rationalizing this disaster in its own interests; the summons to repentance and prayer became at the same time a summons to obedience to the Church and acknowledgement of the efficacy of its leadership. And inasmuch as the Church in feudal society, as later, acted in harmony with

[17] See V. Istrin, "Byl-li 'Daniil Zatochnik' deystvitelno zatochen?" (Was Daniel the Exile Really an Exile?), *Annals of the Historical and Philological Society at the University of Novorossiisk* (1902), Vol. X, p. 73.

[18] Karl Marx, *Sekretnaya diplomatiya XVIII v.* (Secret Diplomacy of the Eighteenth Century).

[19] A. S. Pushkin, *Polnoe sobr. soch.* (Completed Collected Works) (Goslitizdat, 1936), 4th ed., Vol. VI, p. 228.

the interests of the ruling class, its role as spiritual leader was also of convenience to the secular authorities.

The summons to repentance and a moral reordering of life permeated the sermons of a most talented and eloquent preacher, Serapion, who, during the first decade of Tartar domination, was archimandrite of the Crypt Monastery at Kiev, and from 1273–1275 bishop of Vladimir, where he died. With his name are associated five discourses, the first of which he wrote and delivered in 1230, and the rest in the interval between 1273–1275. The first discourse interprets as God's punishment for sins the earthquake and the eclipses of the sun and moon which occurred at Kiev in 1230 and the subsequent ravaging of the land of Rus by the Tartars. In speaking of the merciless ravagers of the land of Rus, Serapion resorts to rhythmic language. They, these enemies,

> our land a desert made,
> our cities captive made,
> churches in ruin laid,
> our fathers and our brothers slew,
> our mothers and our sisters did degrade.

To avert future calamities they must turn to God and renounce piratical usury, rapacity of all sorts, robbery, blasphemy, lying, calumny, defamation, and other works of Satan. The four other discourses of Serapion are also filled with reproaches and arraignments of his flock for all manner of unseemly acts committed by them. Thus, in the third discourse Serapion speaks of the fact that in spite of sundry forewarnings and portents whereby God had sought to put the Russian people on the right road, the people had not reformed, had not started to live better lives, had not cast off their heathen superstitions. In the end God had let fly at us

harsh language, fierce language, language that spared neither the beauty of youth, the weakness of old age, nor the helplessness of infancy; for we had brought down upon ourselves the wrath of our God. Churches of God were destroyed; consecrated vessels were defiled; a saint was drowned; bishops were put to the sword; the bodies of holy monks were thrown to the birds; the blood of our fathers and brothers watered the earth like a flood; the strength of our princes, of our generals, vanished away; our brave men took fright and fled, multitudes of our brothers and children were made captive; our villages were overgrown with brush, and our greatness was laid low; our beauty was destroyed; our wealth fed the greed of others; the pagans inherited the fruits of our toil; our land became the the property of barbarians.[20]

The first clash between Russians and Tartars took place in 1223 in the south, on the river Kalko, where joint Russian and Polovcian forces were

[20] See E. Petukhov, *Serapion Vladimirskii, russkii propovednik XIII veka* (Serapion of Vladimir, Russian Thirteenth Century Preacher) (St. Petersburg, 1888). This also gives texts of Serapion's discourses.

crushed by a Tartar army. In connection with this rout, the Kiev district produced, somewhere between 1223 and 1237, a narrative which then traveled to the north and at the beginning of the fourteenth century took its place in the all-Russian chronicle compilation. In the chronicle compilations it is encountered in a variety of redactions, which may be basically classified as the short and the long. To judge by this narrative, the first appearance of the Tartars produced a staggering impression. Their invasion seems to have been unexpected and they were referred to as an unknown people. In the edition of the tale included in the Laurentian manuscript, we read:

There appeared peoples of whom no one had any proper knowledge as to who they were, whence they came, what language they spoke, of what race they were, or of what faith, and they called them Tartars but some said they were Taumenians and others called them Pechenegs, and said that they were the same peoples of whom Methodius of Patara [author of an apocryphal *Revelation.*—N. G.] testifies that they came from the desert of Yetriyev, which lies between east and north, whither Gideon had driven them and whence they were to come forth at the end of the world.

Thus the appearance of the Tartars in the land of Rus was looked upon as a presage of the end of the world. "God alone knows who they were and whence they came," continues the author; "sages know it no doubt, though we do not, but we have written of them here as a reminder of the misfortunes that befell the Russian princes through them."

Next the author tells of Tartar depredations in the land of Rus and elsewhere, and of the destruction of a whole series of princes, here listed by name.

Of special interest to us are very late variants of the tale of the battle of the Kalko, mentioning, among the princes who perished, Alexander Popovich and seventy brave retainers, or Alexander Popovich, his servant Toropets, Dobryna of Ryazan, Golden Belt, and seventy great and brave bogatyrs. This reference to Alexander Popovich stands as a direct link with the *bylina* on the destruction of the Russian bogatyrs, among them Alexander Popovich and Dobryna.

In chronicle compilations the tale of the battle of the Kalko, originating, no doubt, in the retinue, underwent editorial alteration by compilers chiefly of the clerical milieu, and from this time on reflected those piety and repentance motifs which characterized, among other works, the sermons of Serapion. Thus, in a number of chronicle revisions of the tale, the defeat of the Russians is interpreted as punishment for their sins. These motifs appear in still more pronounced form alternately with excerpts from "Holy Writ," in the description of the Tartars' ravaging of northern Rus, the Suzdal country chiefly and the city of Vladimir, as found in the *Laurentian Chronicle* under the year 1237. Borrowing a quotation from the Psalter, the author exclaims in Serapion's vein:

Lord! the pagans entered into thy property, desecrated thy holy church, laid Jerusalem low as a greengrocer's shed, spread the corpses of thy servants as a banquet for the birds of the heavens, the bodies of thy saints for the wild beasts of the field; spilled blood like water.

In connection with Batu's ravaging of the Ryazan district in the same year, 1237, a composite narrative of Batu's attack on Ryazan was compiled, probably shortly after the event, which stands in close relationship to the story of St. Nicholas Zaraisky and is usually placed immediately after it in the manuscripts. It is known only in texts dating from the sixteenth century or later and is found in late chronicle compilations and in some collections. The absence of anything but late copies of the narrative prevents our reconstructing the original text, individual parts of which appeared at different times.

As given in the diplomatic text published by I. I. Sreznevsky,[21] the content of the tale is as follows:

In the year 6745 (1237 A.D.), the twelfth since the conveying of the wonder-working image of St. Nicholas from Kherson, the infidel king Batu invaded the land of Rus with many Tartar troops and stood at the river Voronezh near the land of Ryazan. And he sent to Great Prince Yury Ingorevich of Ryazan his rascally emissaries, demanding a tithe of everything, princes, people, and horses. When he heard this, Great Prince Yury Ingorevich sent to the city of Vladimir to Great Prince George, son of Vsevolod, asking that he either come himself to aid against the infidel king Batu, or send his army. But George, son of Vsevolod, neither came himself nor sent his army, since he wished to proceed against Batu independently. When Great Prince Yury Ingorevich of Ryazan heard that he was to get no help from Prince George Vsevolodovich of Vladimir, he sent for his brothers David and Gleb and for other princes, boyars, and generals. They began to take counsel as to how they might buy off the infidel Batu with gifts. And Prince Yury Ingorevich sent his son Prince Theodore Yurevich of Ryazan, and other princes, to the infidel king Batu with many gifts and urgent entreaties that he should not make war on Ryazan.

---

[21] *Svedeniya i zametki o maloizvestnykh i neizvestnykh pamyatnikakh* (Information and Notes on Little Known and Unknown Monuments) (St. Petersburg, 1867), XXXIX, pp. 77–90. The tale was published from another and more extensive text by I. Sakharov, *Skazaniya russkogo naroda* (Legends of the Russian People) (St. Petersburg, 1841), Vol. I, Bk. IV, 3rd ed., pp. 46–56. See also I. Dobrolyubov's *Skazanie o perenesenii obraza sv. Nikolaya iz Korsunya v Zaraisk v 1225 g.* (Legend of the Wafting of the Icon of St. Nicholas from Kherson to Zaraisk in 1225) (Moscow, 1891). See also A. I. Sobolevskii, "K slovu o polku Igoreve," (On the Tale of Igor's Expedition) *Izvestiya po russkomu yazyku i slovesnosti* (News of Russian Language and Literature) (1929), Vol. II, Bk. I, pp. 177–181.

The infidel king Batu, crafty and pitiless, accepted the gifts and deceitfully promised not to make war on the country of Ryazan, but then started asking the princes of Ryazan for daughters or sisters for his harem. And one of the Ryazan nobles, incited by envy, told the infidel king Batu that Prince Theodore Yurevich had a wife of royal blood who was very beautiful. King Batu, sly and mean like the infidel that he was, and moved by lust, said to Prince Theodore Yurevich: "Let me see that wife of yours, prince, who is such a beauty." Prince Theodore Yurevich of Ryazan laughed and said to Batu: "It is not meet that we who are Christians should bring our wives to you, an infidel king, for your pleasure. Should you conquer us, then you will be lord over our wives also." But the godless king Batu flew into a frenzy and ordered Prince Theodore Yurevich killed and his body thrown to the beasts and birds to rend. And he killed the other princes, emissaries and soldiers. Only one of the soldiers managed to escape and, seeing the body of his master lying untended, wept bitterly, buried it secretly and hastened to Princess Eupraxia to inform her of the death of her husband. Princess Eupraxia "was standing in her lofty *terem* holding her dear child, Prince Ivan Fyodorovich Postnik, and upon hearing these fatal words so fraught with woe, straightway threw herself from her lofty *terem* to the ground with her son, Prince Ivan. And the impact killed them." (That is, they were crushed to death.) When Prince Yury Ingorevich heard of the death of his son and the other princes and the emissaries, he "began to weep exceedingly and with him the great princess and the other princesses and his brothers. And the whole city of Ryazan wept for many hours."

And when scarce recovered from his great weeping and sobbing, Prince Yury Ingorevich set about mustering his army to pursue Batu and avenge the death of his son. He addressed the following words to his retinue:

Lords and brothers, if we have received good things from the lord's hand, then shall we not bear the evil? It is better that we should buy life for ourselves with death, taste death for God's holy church and for the Christian faith, than be subject to this accursed pagan king. Let us drain the cup of death. For lo, I your brother shall before you drain the deadly cup for the holy church of God and for the Christian faith and for our heritage from our father Great Prince Ingor Svyatoslavich.

After making prayer to God, worshiping at the tomb of his father, saying farewell to his wife and receiving the blessing of the bishop and the entire clerical council, Yury Ingorevich set out against Batu. He met Batu not far from the Ryazan country and fell upon him, and the men of Ryazan joined battle stoutly and manfully. And the carnage was fierce and terrible and many of Batu's regiments were laid low. Batu's forces were so great that the

Russians fought "one against a thousand, two with a countless host" (a typical war story formula).

And the great prince witnessed the slaying of his brother David Ingorevich and other princes and relatives, and in the bitterness of his heart he exclaimed: "O my beloved brothers and dear followers, ornament and support of Ryazan, show your courage and manhood! Prince David, our brother, has drained the cup before us, and shall not we drink this cup?"

The "bold and high-spirited men of Ryazan" changed horses and joined battle with a will. They fought so stoutly and mercilessly that Batu's troops were thrown into confusion, and the great prince rode about through his regiments and fought so bravely and manfully that all the Tartar troops marveled at the strength and courage of the dominion of Ryazan. In this battle were killed Prince George Ingorevich and Prince David Ingorevich and Gleb Ingorevich and Vsevolod of Pronsk, and local princes, and stout generals, and many "bold and high-spirited warriors, the ornament and support of Ryazan. . . . All alike died, one deadly cup they drained." Not one of them returned, all lay dead together.

Then the author goes on to tell about later encounters between the Russian troops and Batu. The rehearsal of these encounters closes with an account of the taking of the city of Ryazan. Batu burst into the city, into the cathedral church, cut down Princess Agrippina, mother of the prince, with her daughters-in-law and the rest of the princesses, but the bishop and the "priesthood" he committed to the flames, burned down the church itself, slew many with the sword, drowned others in the river, ruined the whole city, "all the rare treasures, the wealth of Ryazan and of its kin, Kiev and Chernigov, he seized, and the churches of God he ravaged, and the blood of many upon the holy altars shed, and many others captive led. . . . All alike died, one deadly cup they drained, and none was there to mourn or to lament." After this Batu sets out for Suzdal and Vladimir.

Next comes the most picturesque episode in the story, bringing in the epic bogatyr * Yevpaty Kolovrat, avenger of the insults and injuries inflicted by Batu upon the land of Ryazan.

At the time of Batu's ravages, Yevpaty was in Chernigov with Prince Ingvar Ingorevich collecting the tribute for Yury Ingorevich, Prince of Ryazan. Hearing of Batu's arrival in Russian territory, and learning that he had come in force, Yevpaty left Chernigov with a small retinue and reached Ryazan in no time. He saw the Ryazan country laid waste, the city in ruins, the churches burned, the people slain. And Yevpaty cried out in the bitterness of his soul, and his heart burned within him. He collected a small ret-

* Bogatyr: a legendary man of extraordinary strength and success; a hero of *byliny*, a kindly Russian giant.—ED.

inue, seventeen hundred men who had escaped destruction by the Tartars, and pursued the infidel Batu, desiring to drain the deadly cup equally with his lords, and catching up with him in the Suzdal country, instantly attacked his camp and started to smite him without mercy. The Tartars became "like drunken men." (This is the usual formula in war stories: when the enemy shows confusion under sudden attack, he reels like a drunkard.) Yevpaty and his retinue smote the Tartars so hard that their swords were dulled and then they took Tartar swords and slew the enemy with those. (Again a typical war story formula: when their own swords are blunted, they take enemy swords to cut down the hostile forces.) The Tartars thought that the dead had come to life. Yevpaty showed such courage that even the Tartar king himself feared him. When five men of Yevpaty's army who had been rendered helpless by grievous wounds were captured and conveyed to Batu, the following dialogue took place.

"Of what faith are you and of what land and why upon me such mischief do you wreak?" Batu asks the captives.

They answer: "Of the Christian faith are we, slaves of Great Prince Yury Ingorevich of Ryazan, and soldiers of Yevpaty Kolovrat. Sent were we by Prince Ingvar Ingorevich of Ryazan to you, O mighty king, his respects to pay and honor show and unto you your just dues render; but marvel not, O king: we cannot pour the cup for this great force, the Tartar army."

We have before us a striking example of the rhythmically organized, song form of speech, tinged with irony as in oral poetry.

The king marveled at the shrewd answer of the warriors and ordered his brother-in-law Khostovrul to enter into single combat with Yevpaty. Yevpaty rode at his opponent and hacked him in two and killed Batu's other bogatyrs: some he hacked in two, others he "pinned to their saddles."

The Tartars were at their wits' end and decided to use siege cannon to overcome Yevpaty. With difficulty they killed him, and took his body to Batu. The lords whom Batu had called into council marveled at the "strength and determination and courage of the dominion of Ryazan" and said to Batu: "We have made war on many kings, in many lands, on many campaigns, but never have we seen such bold and high-spirited warriors, nor have our fathers told us of any. These are men with wings, death is unknown to them, so stoutly and manfully do they fight, one against a thousand, two with a countless host."

Batu, looking at the body of Yevpaty, said: "O, Kolovrat Yevpaty, you have wrought terrible havoc upon me with your little band, and have killed many distinguished bogatyrs of the mighty Horde, and many troops have fallen at your hand. Had I such a man in my service, I would clasp him to my heart." The enemy shows respect for his late antagonist and does homage to his courage and manliness. In an access of magnanimity, Batu restores the body of Yevpaty to what is left of his completely exhausted retinue and dismisses them unharmed. Batu manifests, as we see, the characteristic traits of the chivalric attitude toward a vanquished adversary. The enemy upon whom so many troops had been squandered, who had cost the Tartar army so many lives, evokes in the professional soldier a feeling of amazement, rapture, and homage in view of the warlike valor he had shown.

The final episode of the story tells how Prince Ingvar Ingorevich, with whom Yevpaty had been in Chernigov, arrived last in the Ryazan district, saw it laid waste, heard that his brothers had been killed by the impious king Batu. When he reached Ryazan he saw his mother and her daughters-in-law, and kinsfolk, and a multitude of the populace lying dead, the land desolate, the city in ruins, the churches burned down, and found that all the "treasure" of Chernigov and Ryazan had been ransacked from the coffers. Seeing the great and total destruction, Prince Ingvar cried out as pitifully "as the war trumpet sounding forth, as the sweet organ pealing." And after his loud crying and terrible wailing, he lay on the ground as if dead, and was with difficulty brought back to consciousness. In his own person the author inserts some lyrical meditations on the subject:

For who would not lament at such destruction or who would not sob for a people in such a pass, or who would not grieve for the multitude of lords and brave generals and distinguished men who had come to such a sudden and terrible end, or who would not groan over such a taking of captives!

Prince Ingvar Ingorevich gathered up the bodies of the dead, recovered the body of his mother, identified his sisters-in-law. He summoned from surrounding towns and villages such priests as remained alive, and buried his relatives, boyars, generals, and many "bold and high-spirited" men of Ryazan with great lamentation and with the singing of psalms.

The story enumerates the princes who were killed and those who perished in Ryazan. A whole list of names is given: Great Prince Yury Ingorevich of Ryazan, Oleg Ingorevich the Fair, his brother David Ingorevich of Murom, Gleb Ingorevich of Kolomna and Vsevolod of Pronsk

and many other local princes and boyars and generals and the whole army and many bold and high-spirited men, the ornament and support of Ryazan. They lay on the bare ground, on the feather grass, chilled by snow and ice, with no one to care for them, their bodies gnawed by animals and torn by a multitude of birds. For all lay dead together, having drunk of a single deadly cup.

The story ends with an account of how Ingvar Ingorevich set out for the river Voronezh, where Theodore Yurevich had been slain, took his body and brought it to the Church of St. Nicholas of Kherson. Thither, too, were brought the bodies of Princess Eupraxia, and her son Ivan Postnik. All of them were buried there. This is why St. Nicholas came to be called "of Zaraisk," for the building of his church was associated with the Princess Eupraxia's throwing herself from the *terem* with her son and being crushed to death. Ingvar Ingorevich himself returned to Ryazan, where he sat on the throne of his father, Great Prince Ingor, son of Svyatoslav, restored the Ryazan country, built churches and monasteries, gave comfort to strangers, and gathered a populace. "And there was rejoicing among the peasants that God with his mighty hand had delivered them from the impious, misbelieving king Batu."

Such is this unusual war story, this vital response to the incidents of the Tartar invasion. It is undoubtedly based on epic narratives, works of oral poetry linked with the events themselves. The episode of the deaths of Theodore and his wife Eupraxia, reflected in the *bylina* about Daniel Lovchanin, and no doubt the tale of Yevpaty Kolovrat as well, go back to specific historical folk songs.[22]

The story of Batu's descent upon Ryazan is in theme and style a striking example of the war story. For artistry it ranks among the foremost works of this type. It is characterized by a tense and at the same time restrained lyric and dramatic quality. The impression of moving drama produced by the tale is attained not by verbose, rhetorical phraseology, as in later monuments of the sort, but by rendering tragic events with the utmost compression, apparently intentionally. This is true, for example, of the account of the deaths of Prince Theodore Yurevich and his wife, as well as of the account of the exploits and death of Yevpaty Kolovrat. The narrative, which derives basically from a lyro-epic tale, appears consciously to avoid the high-flown and florid bluster of the oral tradition as an impediment to the immediate and genuine expression of feeling. It uses this same extreme compression, restraint, and verbal simplicity in rendering the sorrow of their immediate circle over the death of dear ones.

For our present purposes the following lines may serve as a sufficient example: "When he heard, Great Prince Yury Ingorevich, about the infidel king's murder of his beloved son, blessed Prince Theodore, and of the other princes and the many emissaries, he began to lament vehemently and with him the great princess and the other princesses and his brothers. And the whole city of Ryazan lamented for many hours." Only once under such circumstances does rhetoric intrude itself into the extant text of the tale: Prince Ingvar Ingorevich, upon reaching the ravaged Ryazan country and seeing

[22] See Vsevolod Miller, *Ocherki russkoy narodnoy slovesnosti* (Outlines of Russian Folk Literature) (Moscow, 1879), Vol. I, pp. 315–322. The tale was made the theme of poems by Venevitinov, Yazykov, and Mey.

the multitude of corpses, cries out as piteously "as the war trumpet sounding forth, as the sweet organ pealing," but this stereotyped formula of lamentation is a later addition to the tale introduced not earlier than the end of the fourteenth or the beginning of the fifteenth century, most probably from the tale, *Of the Life and Death of Great Prince Dmitry Ivanovich, Tsar of Rus*. Evidently also in some measure the result of later stratification is the ecclesiastico-religious coloring manifested in the pious speeches of the princes and in author's comment such as: "And God visited all these things upon us for our sins," and, finally, in the use of such adjectives as "orthodox" and "pious" to designate the princes. This is also true of certain peculiarities of style borrowed from the tales of the rout of Mamay and from the tale of Nestor-Iskander on the taking of Tsargrad.[23]

Basically the tale has all the distinctive traits of the early martial style both in phraseology and in imagery. It is permeated throughout by the heroic passion of martial courage; princes and retinue are portrayed in a nimbus of supreme courage which inspires them to meet death undaunted. The image of the "deadly cup" runs through the whole story like a leitmotif. Along with the "orthodox" and "pious" princes we find mentioned repeatedly, with lyric enthusiasm, the "dear retinue," "the ornament and support of Ryazan," "the dominion of Ryazan," the "bold and high-spirited men of Ryazan." By its whole tone the story emphasizes the idealistic conception of the chivalric relationship between a prince and his retinue. The princes invariably look out for their retinue and mourn for retainers who perish in battle, while the retainers wish to "drink the deadly cup equally with their lords." Inspired by devotion for their princes, the "bold and high-spirited men of Ryazan" fight "so stoutly and mercilessly that the earth groans, one with a thousand, and two with a countless host," and when unable to vanquish the enemy, they all die to the last man, having drained a single deadly cup.

Unlike the preceding monuments on the theme of the Tartar invasion, this story sounds no note of repentance. The whole content of the tale invokes not passive submission to the terrible calamity but active resistance. And the end is cheerful and confident: the Ryazan district rallies from Batu's invasion and rebuilds itself; the people of Ryazan rejoice at their deliverance from the "godless, misbelieving King Batu."

Distinct echoes of a rhythmic frame have already been in part indicated above. Still further examples might be adduced. When the Tartars seized Ryazan,

[23] See A. S. Orlov, *Ob osobennostyakh formy russkikh voinskikh povestey* (On Stylistic Idiosyncrasies in Russian War Narratives), p. 2.

Great Princess Agrippina, mother of the Great Prince,
with her daughters-in-law and the rest of the princesses
in the synod church with swords they slew,
bishop and clergy to the flames they threw,
to the holy church set fire,
killed with weapons not a few,
many men and women and children of the town with swords they slew
and others into the river threw;
priests and monks into relics slew,
set the whole city burning too,
and all the store of treasures rare, the riches of Ryazan
and of its kin Kiev and Chernigov they seized;
churches of God they ravaged too
and at the holy altars much blood drew
and led away as captives many too.

Of the princes and warriors who perished in the defense of Ryazan it is said:

And their bodies by beasts were gnawed
And by many a bird were clawed.

All the features noted have won for the story of Batu's descent upon Ryazan high esteem as a monument of our early narrative literature of the martial type, and have earned it the rank of close second to the *Tale of Igor's Expedition*.

Additional narratives having to do with the events of the Tartar invasion are: the *Legend of Batu's Invasion of Rus* (about the destruction of Kiev, 1240), the *Legend of the Murder of Prince Michael of Chernigov and the Boyar Theodore by the Horde* (1245), *Tale of the Murder of Batu* (1247). All these, with the exception of the *Legend of Michael of Chernigov* are, in style, typical war stories. Their general purpose is to bring home the necessity for a union of the dissociated principalities to combat the enemy from without.

The most interesting artistically and also as reflecting the typical stylistic formulae for war stories is the first tale, about Batu's destruction of Kiev in 1240. In the *Hypatian Chronicle* it begins thus:

Batu arrived at Kiev in force, with a great multitude of troops, and the Tartar force surrounded the city and blockaded it and the city was in great distress. And Batu was before the city and his servants besieged the city, and it was impossible to hear for the creaking of his carts, the multitudinous bellowing of his oxen and the neighing of his herds of horses. And the land of Rus was filled with soldiers.

From a Tartar who had been taken prisoner, the Russians learned in detail about the number of Tartar forces as well as about the mightiest Tartar generals and bogatyrs, whose names are listed at this point. Next, Batu's conquest of Kiev is described. Batu set up at the walls of the city a countless number of siege cannon which hammered day and night and beat down the walls. The Kievans went out to the breaches "and there it was possible to see the breaking of lances and the cleaving of shields: arrows darkened the daylight for the defeated." After wounding the governor of Kiev and the thousand-officer Dimitry, the Tartars scaled the walls and remained there all day and all night; but by night the Kievans threw a second fortification about the Church of the Virgin and in the morning the Tartars advanced upon them and fierce carnage between them ensued. The people took refuge, with their belongings, under the arches of the church; the walls of the church fell under the load and the Tartars captured the city. They helped the wounded Dimitry to get out and spared him on account of his bravery.

DISCOURSE ON THE RUIN OF THE LAND OF RUS

Among the thirteenth century monuments connected with the Tartar invasion and produced in northern Rus belongs also the *Discourse on the Ruin of the Land of Rus,* discovered by Kh. M. Loparyov in the early 1890's in a fifteenth century manuscript of the Crypt Monastery at Pskov and at once published by him.[24] It is of very small compass (occupies only forty-five lines in the MS.).

The *Discourse* enumerates the natural and material riches in which, before the Tartar invasion, the "land of Rus, brightest of the bright, fairest of the fair," abounded: numerous lakes, rivers, and locally celebrated springs, steep mountains, high hills, virgin forests, marvelous fields, a variety of wild beasts, birds without number, great cities, delightful villages, monastery gardens, ecclesiastical houses. At that time there were in Rus stern princes, honorable boyars, many dignitaries. The vast areas and the people living upon them were subject to Great Prince Vsevolod, his father Yury, Prince of Kiev, and his grandfather, Vladimir Monomakh, with whose name the Polovcians frightened their babes in the cradle and in whose reign the Lithuanians did not show themselves outside their marshes, and the Hungarians strengthened the stone walls of their city with iron gates so that he might not pass through to them; while the Germans rejoiced that they lived far away beyond the blue sea. Various neighboring tribes paid tribute to Vladimir in honey, and the Byzantine emperor Manuel, fearing lest Vladimir take Tsargrad, sent large gifts to him. So it used to be, but now some malady has befallen the Christians.

[24] See *Pamyatniki drevney pismennosti* (Monuments of Early Literature), (St. Petersburg, 1892), LXXXIV.

Such is the content of the *Discourse on the Ruin*. It is immediately followed by the *Life of Alexander Nevsky*, which here has no title of its own and is not even separated from the text of the *Discourse on the Ruin* by a paragraph indication. On the basis of the fact that in its extant form it deals not with the ruin of the land of Rus but with its might and beauty and that only in the last phrase is there a vague reference to some "malady" of the Christians of that time, the first publisher considered it "only the beginning of a magnificent thirteenth century poem bewailing the ruin of Rus," a poem the continuation of which is lost. According to his hypothesis it was followed by a likewise inextant *Discourse on the Death of Great Prince Yaroslav, Son of Vsevolod,* and then by the *Life of Alexander Nevsky*. Thus the *Discourse on the Ruin* is the first, incompletely preserved, section of a trilogy. Loparyov's hypothesis as to the existence of a second part of the trilogy telling of the death of Yaroslav, son of Vsevolod, is based on the fact that in the manuscript, after the title, *Discourse on the Ruin of the Land of Rus,* we find written: "Concerning the death of Great Prince Yaroslav," with the O (Concerning) afterward altered to *Po,* followed by the *Discourse* proper, nothing at all being said, however, about the death of Yaroslav, son of Vsevolod. N. I. Serebryansky thinks that the *Discourse on the Ruin* is the preface to a nonextant secular biography of Alexander Nevsky, written by one of the prince's retainers and produced shortly after his death.[25]

V. Mansikka also thinks that the *Discourse on the Ruin* is a preface to the *Life of Alexander Nevsky,* assuming that the words spoken by Metropolitan Cyril at the burial of Alexander, "Ruin is already upon us," as found in the *Life,* are the precise locution to which the title, *Discourse on the Ruin of the Land of Rus,* may in some superficial way have become attached.[26] It is very likely that at the words, "Concerning the death of Great Prince Yaroslav," the text is corrupt and ought to read, "Alexander, son of Yaroslav." With such an emendation it becomes clear why the *Life of Alexander Nevsky,* placed immediately after the *Discourse,* does not have a separate title. This title was copied in at the very beginning along with the title of the essay introductory to the *Life*.

Whether the *Discourse on the Ruin* is part of an independent work or only an introductory section to the *Life of Alexander Nevsky,* however, the ending as it stands is obviously defective. In the manuscript, which, like all ancient manuscripts, is without punctuation, the last sentence reads

---

[25] See *Zametki i teksty iz pskovskikh pamyatnikov* (Notes and Texts of Pskov Monuments) (Moscow, 1910), Chap. V, and also *Drevnerusskie knyazheskie zhitiya, obzor redaktsii i teksty* (Early Russian Princes' Lives: Survey of Redactions and Texts) (Moscow, 1915), pp. 155–163, 167–174, 210–213.

[26] V. Mansikka, *Zhitie Aleksandra Nevskogo, razbor redaktsii i tekst* (Life of Alexander Nevsky: Analysis of Redactions and Texts) (St. Petersburg, 1913), pp. 9–11.

thus: "But in these days a malady has befallen the Christians from Yaroslav the Great and down to Volodimer and to the present Yaroslav and to his brother Yury Prince of Vladimir." By "Yaroslav the Great" Yaroslav the Wise is apparently meant, by "Volodimer," Vladimir Monomakh. But if this be the case, it is completely incomprehensible how the beginning of the "malady befallen the Christians," that is, the calamities connected with the Tartar invasion, can date from the reigns of these two princes. Evidently the words: "But in these days a malady has befallen the Christians," constitute a complete independent sentence followed by a new sentence: "From Yaroslav the Great and down to Volodimer," and so forth, which was left unfinished in the manuscript. Perhaps this sentence ended with words to the effect that under all the princes enumerated everything was all right in Rus, and then a statement may have followed as to such and such calamities having afterward descended upon the land of Rus.[27]

Judging by the fact that Yaroslav, son of Vsevolod, mentioned in the *Discourse on the Ruin* is called the present Yaroslav, it was written before 1247, the date of Yaroslav Vsevolodovich's death. Until 1236 he was prince of Pereyaslavl in Suzdal. To him the *Supplication of Daniel the Exile* was addressed. On the basis of this and in view of certain lexical correspondences between the *Supplication* and the *Discourse on the Ruin*, Loparyov expressed himself to the effect that the association of the author of the *Discourse on the Ruin* with Daniel the Exile "had something to be said for it." V. M. Istrin was more categorical about identifying the two authors, proceeding, evidently, from a certain rhetorical community of style between the *Supplication* and the *Discourse on the Ruin*.[28] But there is obviously no serious basis for such an identification since a stylistic comparison of the *Supplication* and the *Discourse on the Ruin* can yield nothing beyond remote resemblances.

Nor are there sufficient grounds for associating the *Discourse on the Ruin* with the *Tale of Igor's Expedition* artistically as, for example, Loparyov and Mansikka have done. The styles of the two works have essentially

---

[27] Kh. M. Loparyov (or Loparev) is inclined to understand by "malady befallen the Christians," the internecine quarrels within the appanage system which proved particularly disastrous at the time of the Tartar invasion. In this case the conclusion of the text of the *Discourse on the Ruin,* from the words: "But in these days a malady has befallen the Christians," to the end, may be regarded as one continuous concluding phrase. But, in the first place the internecine quarrels between the princes began and became a disaster for Rus long before the Tartar invasion, so that it would have been impossible to speak of "the malady" in "these days"; in the second place, the *Discourse* itself describes the time of the princes who preceded Yaroslav, son of Vsevolod, as a time of prosperity for Rus, so that it would be just as impossible to speak of the "malady" as springing from internecine quarrels dating from the time between Yaroslav the Wise and Vladimir Monomakh.

[28] *Issledovaniya v oblasti drevnerusskoy literatury* (Investigations in the Field of Early Russian Literature), p. 232.

nothing in common, and in the matter of poetic qualities the *Discourse on the Ruin* is of course no match for the *Tale of Igor's Expedition*, especially if the fragmentariness of the former be taken into account. It is a combination of bookish rhetoric and oral-poetry song forms. Bookish rhetoric asserts itself chiefly in the enumeration of the riches in which the land of Rus abounds, and in compound epithets such as "brightest of the bright" and "fairest of the fair." From the oral-poetry tradition come, evidently, such combinations as "mountains steep," "hills high," "forests virgin," "princes terrible," "boyars noble," "blue sea." Here the placing of epithets after the nouns they modify is as characteristic as the epithets themselves; it is the usual order in works of oral poetry. Thence, too, comes the epic picture of Vladimir Monomakh. Specifically, he is allotted the same legends (about the Polovcians using his name to frighten their children), which were associated with the name of Román, Prince of Galicia. Mention of the fact that various peoples trembled before Vladimir Monomakh is a commonplace encountered in descriptions of the might of different Russian princes; the statement as to Manuel's fear of him is a patent anachronism, however, since Manuel's reign began eighteen years after the death of Monomakh and he actually sent his embassy and gifts to Prince Rostislav. Thus did folk tradition associate with the name of a popular prince even happenings of a later time.

THE LIFE OF ALEXANDER NEVSKY

The *Life of Alexander Nevsky,* particularly celebrated for his brilliant victory over the Teutonic knights, was written, apparently, by some ecclesiastic at the end of the thirteenth or the very beginning of the fourteenth century on the basis of an inextant secular biography, which appeared, presumably, soon after the death of this outstanding prince (1263) and was composed, most probably, by a Suzdal scholar, possibly connected with Alexander's court. The author of the original redaction of the life held close to his source, introducing so few traits of the hagiographical style that his work ought perhaps to be called a war story rather than a "life" in the ordinary sense of the word. The texts of the Laurentian and of the second Pskov chronicle stand closest to the text of the original redaction, but both are defective, and therefore to acquaint ourselves with this redaction we shall use a very late text, one dating from the middle of the sixteenth century.

The author begins his exposition with the stock disparagement of his qualities as a hagiographer: though "bad, sinful, and unworthy," he has undertaken his task because he had heard of Alexander "from his fathers" and had known him personally. And if his own abilities prove inadequate to the undertaking, he can rely on the blessed virgin and St. Alexander, son of Yaroslav, to help him out. Next, following the pattern for saints' lives, he tells how Alexander was "born in God of a pious father, lover of the poor, and benign withal, Great Prince Yaroslav, and of a noble mother, Theodosia." In stature he was taller than other men, his voice was like a trumpet to the people, his face like unto the face of Joseph in the Bible, his strength was of a piece with the strength of Samson, in wisdom he was equal to Solomon, in courage to the Roman emperor Vespasian. These short, general references complete the character sketch of Alexander. Nothing is said about any specifically noble aspects of his conduct, and the rest of the story deals entirely with Alexander's military exploits and his executive activities.

A certain Andreas, a sword-bearer, came from the west country, desiring to see Alexander's "marvelous stature," as once the Queen of the South had come to Solomon to try his wisdom. When he went back, Andreas reported that although he had traversed many lands and nations, nowhere among kings had he seen such a king, nor among princes such a prince. And hearing this, "the king of a part of Rome, the midnight country, that is, Sweden, said: 'I shall go and capture Alexander's country.'" And having gathered a large army and filled many ships with troops, he came against Alexander "in great force, puffed up with warlike spirit." Arriving at the Neva, "reeling with frenzy," he haughtily sent ambassadors to Alexander at Novgorod with the words: "If you can oppose me, here I am; I shall capture your country." Alexander wept and prayed at the Church of St. Sophia, and having received the blessing of Archbishop Spiridon, set about fortifying his retainers with words "from Holy Writ." He did not stop to get a large force together, but advanced against the enemy with a small retinue, trusting in the Holy Trinity. It is sad to hear—says the author in his own person—that his father Yaroslav, the noble, the great, did not know of the enemy attack on his dear son, that news of it could not be got to him in Kiev, since the hostile army was already at hand; nor could many men of Novgorod be mustered in the time at the prince's disposal.

Alexander had great faith in Boris and Gleb. There was a certain man, a syndic of the Izhora district, by name Belgusich, who had received baptism, and lived a pious life among the pagans. And God sent him a strange vision: when he was on guard he saw a powerful army coming against Alexander, and at sunrise he heard a terrifying noise at sea and noticed a ship in the midst of which stood Boris and Gleb, sailing to the help of Alexander. Of this vision Belgusich informed Alexander, who bade him say nothing of it to anyone, and himself hastened to meet the enemy, "and there was great carnage of the Romans," and Alexander killed a multitude of the hostile army and "laid the imprint of his sharp spear on the face" of the king himself. There six brave men in Alexander's army also distinguished themselves, and their names and exploits are quoted in the *Life*. About this, as the author says, he heard from his lord and prince, Alexander Yaroslavich, and from others who took part in the slaughter. On this occasion there occurred a wondrous miracle reminiscent of what transpired during the battle between the Jewish king Hezekiah and the Assyrian king Sennacherib, when an angel suddenly appeared and slaughtered 180,600 Assyrians and in the morning they were found dead. So, too, in this battle, there were left on the opposite side of the river Izhora many of the enemy troops, slain by an archangel, and those who were spared fled. Prince Alexander returned from his victory "praising God and glorifying his creator."

Two years later his neighbors on the west built a city within Alexander's domains. Alexander at once attacked them and razed the city to its foundations and of the people themselves killed part, took part into captivity, pardoned others and let them go, "for he was merciful beyond measure." The following year, in the winter, he liberated Pskov, which had been taken by the Germans, and set out against the Germans with a large army. His father Yaroslav sent his younger son Andrew and a large retinue to Alexander's assistance. And Alexander himself, like King David of old, had many brave men, steadfast, strong, and full of warlike spirit. Their hearts were like lions' hearts, and they were ready to lay down their lives for their dear prince. With a prayer Alexander joined battle with the Teutonic knights on Lake Peipus. The battle is described in typical war-story style, a style particularly like that of the battle episodes in the calendar readings of the anonymous *Legend of Boris and Gleb*: "It was on Saturday, at sunrise, that the two armies met, and there was terrible carnage, and the crash of spears and their breaking and the clash of swords smiting as they moved over the frozen sea; and you could not see the ice, it was so covered with blood." From an eyewitness the author heard that God's host was seen in the air, coming to the aid of Alexander. "And with God's help he vanquished them, and the enemy forces turned and fled. But they [Alexander's army] smote and pursued as if from the air; there was no place to which they could flee." Here God glorified Great Prince Alexander, son of Yaroslav, before all his troops as he did Joshua, son of Nun, at Jericho. And no man was to be found who would oppose him in battle. And he returned from the victory with great glory, leading captive beside the horses those "who call themselves knights." The people of Pskov, headed by the clergy, came out to meet Alexander, singing songs in honor of the conqueror. And his name was celebrated to the ends of the earth, both to the mountains of Arabia, and to Rome.

Then the Lithuanians multiplied and began to do damage to Alexander's domains. He conquered them and they came to fear his name. Hearing about Alexander, the eastern king Batu desired to see him. Alexander set out for his court by way of Vladimir, and terrible rumors of his approach spread to the mouths of the Volga. The Tartars there used his name to frighten their children, saying, "Alexander is coming," as the Polovcians in the *Discourse on the Ruin* frightened their children with the name of Monomakh. Batu found that Alexander surpassed all other princes and sent him home with great honor. Shortly afterward Batu's general Nevryui devastated the Suzdal district. Alexander restored order there, and for this the author pronounces an extended eulogy upon him, employing quotations from the book of the prophet Isaiah. Then the Roman pope sent cardinals to Alexander with the proposal that he accept the Catholic faith, but Alexander declined this proposal, accompanying his refusal with historical references extending from Adam to the seventh ecumenical council.

Finally the exposition passes to the closing events of Alexander's life. Some sort of "oppression by the pagans" impelled him to betake himself to the Horde that he might by his entreaty avert calamity from his people. On the way back, at Gorodets (near Nizhny Novgorod) Alexander was taken ill and, after receiving the tonsure and being invested with the schema, died. The author mourns the death of his lord in lyric lines. The metropolitan Cyril, addressing the people on the occasion of the prince's death, exclaimed: "My children, apprehend that the sun of the land of Suzdal has already set!" Priors and priests, rich and poor, and all the people wailed: "Ruin is already upon us!" The body of Alexander was carried to Vladimir; the populace, meeting it at Bogolyubovo, sobbed so deeply "that the earth shook." When the metropolitan would have placed the Testament in the prince's hand, Alexander, as though alive, stretched forth his arm and took the Testament himself.

As we see, Alexander Nevsky is represented in the *Life* first and foremost as the ideal prince and warrior, endowed with all positive moral and physical qualities in the highest degree. He is frequently compared to the most prominent biblical personages. Such a picture of the prince is likeliest to have been drawn by an intimate of his, and this picture was undoubtedly already present in the secular biography of Alexander upon which the earliest "life" was based.

The author of the *Life* shows the influence of his sources, among which the Old Testament must be assigned first place. From it he draws quotations; its subject matter he uses for comparisons; finally, he frames separate episodes in imitation of biblical episodes. Such is the episode where the people of Pskov meet the victorious Alexander with a song of praise, an episode written in imitation of the biblical story of the Israelite women meeting David after his victory over the Philistines. The story of the fear which Alexander inspired in neighboring peoples after the Battle of the Frozen Sea, finds its parallel in the words of the Bible to the effect that after his victory over the Philistines, "the name of David was spread through all lands and the Lord made it to be feared of all peoples." In the *Life* are described the exploits of six of Alexander's warriors, who "showed steadfast courage" during the Neva battle, and their names are given. David also had his "brave men," and among them, too, there were six of particular prominence, whose deeds and names are similarly recorded in the Bible, but the resemblance between the two episodes appears not so much in particulars as in the general structure of the narrative. The episode of Alexander's six warriors comes closer perhaps to a story in the *Tale of the Destruction of Jerusalem* by Josephus Flavius, where the names of six champions from the army of the emperor Vespasian are likewise mentioned. From Josephus also comes the comparison of Alexander to Vespasian. In addition we find many expressions and stylistic formulae that the *Life* has in common with the Josephus history. Individual episodes in the *Life* may have come into being under the influence of the *Alexandria* and the *Adventures of Digenis*. Finally, a number of minor episodes and stereotyped formulae in the *Life of Alexander Nevsky* were borrowed from hagiography, both translated and original (the *Lives* of Savva the Consecrate and of Alexis, Man of God, the "Legend" of Boris and Gleb, the calendar readings in their honor, and so on), and from Russian chronicle narratives on martial themes.[29]

In the course of the centuries, down to the seventeenth, the *Life of Alexander Nevsky* was several times rewritten in connection with the general evolution of the hagiographical style in the direction of rhetorical embellishment and ornateness. It was so revised with particular zeal after the council of 1547, called for the purpose of canonizing Russian saints. The influence of the *Life* is apparent in a number of works produced in the succeeding period (the *Life and Death of Great Prince Dmitry Ivanovich*, the chronicle narrative of the rout of Mamay, and so forth).

[29] For more details on the connection between the *Life of Alexander Nevsky* and traditional literature, see V. Mansikka, *op. cit.*, pp. 18–48, and N. Serebryanskii, *Drevnerusskie knyazheskie zhitiya* (Early Russian Princes Lives), pp. 182–191.

THE GALICIA-VOLYNIA CHRONICLE

The most important literary manifestation of the end of the thirteenth century in southern Rus was the *Galicia-Volynia Chronicle*, setting forth events from the beginning of the 1200's down to 1292. It opens with the year 1201 and the heading: "Beginning of the Reign of Great Prince Román, Autocrat of All the Land of Rus, Prince of Galicia," but says nothing about the reign of Román, son of Mstislav, the heading quoted being immediately followed by a eulogy on the deceased Román (died 1205) and his great-grandfather Vladimir Monomakh, after which an account is given of events in Galician and Volynian history subsequent to the death of Román, events centering in Román's sons, Daniel and Vasilko, and then in Vasilko's son, Vladimir. The *Galicia-Volynia Chronicle* was not included as a whole in the chronicle compilation; when mechanically appended to the *Kievan Chronicle* it dropped all entries preceding 1201. Part of these had, however, already been taken for the *Primary Chronicle*; for example, the priest Basil's story of the blinding of Vasilko, Prince of Terebovl, which the style marks as being a fragment of the inextant first part of the *Galicia-Volynia Chronicle*. The whole now missing history of the reign of Román Mstislavich, promised by the chronicler in the heading quoted above, was also, apparently, included in it originally.

In the Hypatian copy, where the *Galicia-Volynia Chronicle* immediately follows the *Kievan*, it carries dates inaccurately computed by the compiler of the digest and absent from the original text, as may be seen, for example, from a study of the unchronologized texts of the chronicle included in later copies (the Khlebnikov and the Pogodin), and as is implied in the emphatic assertion of the compiler of the *Galician Chronicle* himself, that he proposes to give not an annalistic but a chronographic presentation of facts; that is, a pragmatic one, based upon the relationship of events rather than on chronological dates—which he had intended to put at the end of his work, but did not.

Like the *Kiev Chronicle*, the *Galicia-Volynia Chronicle* owes its origin not to the clergy but to the laity. It says little about the facts of Church history and deals chiefly with martial encounters, calamities, seditions, and quarrels, principally those incidental to the reign of Daniel. Descriptions of the princes, their manner of life, the details of court economy, are all presented in the *Galicia-Volynia Chronicle* from the viewpoint of a man of the world who took a lively interest in events and in the fate of princes, and who probably moved in official circles.

The exposition of events in the *Galicia-Volynia Chronicle* falls into two parts. The first and longer of these is the strictly *Galician Chronicle*, dealing with the minority of Daniel and Vasilko, which the boyars—described in negative terms—turned to their own mercenary ends, and then with the reign of Daniel. It was writen, to judge from its characteristic peculiarities of language, by one person. Needless to say, he had at his disposal various sources, among them, probably, the story of the battle of the Kalko, of the carnage wrought by Batu in 1237, and so forth, but all this material has been carefully gone over by a scholar distinguished for his very individual manner of writing, a man not without a taste for poetic imagery nor yet for elevated and artificially florid language. The exposition in this whole first part is coherent, consecutive, only interrupted from time to time by such observations as, "but nothing happened," or: "There was peace." As to the second part of the chronicle, the *Volynian*, which begins with 1262 and tells of events during the reigns of Vasilko and his son Vladimir, it is possible two or more persons had a share in its composition. The treatment is distinctly disjointed in character and toward the end comes to little more than ordinary annalistic entries.

As Academician A. S. Orlov has pointed out, the Hypatian collection, and in particular the *Galician Chronicle* which forms part of it, were influenced in vocabulary and phraseology by the compiled chronograph, as represented by the *Archivistic*, or *Jewish, Chronograph* and the Greek chroniclers. These collections included the chronicles of Malalas and Georgius Hamartolas, the books of the Old Testament, the *Alexandria* and the *History of the Destruction of Jerusalem* by Josephus Flavius, all of which are in some degree reflected in the *Galicia-Volynia Chronicle*.[30]

The first part of the *Galicia-Volynia Chronicle*, carrying the story to the end of Daniel's reign, is of the greater historico-literary interest. The author of this part of the chronicle, as has been said, gives special evidence of literary talent. He loves a fine, distinguished phrase, a vivid image, now and then set off by a rhetorical mounting, an archaic grammatical construction which lends his language an academic solemnity all its own. In displaying his erudition, he sometimes even lapses into an excessive profusion of ornament and a sort of deliberate complexity in his syntactical constructions. At the same time, as judge and apologist of the knightly valor of the princes he is praising, he also hearkened to the songs sung by court singers in honor of victorious princes and evidently wrote under the influence of these as well.

The most finished example of the poetic style of the *Galicia-Volynia Chronicle* is found at the very beginning, in the eulogy of Román and of

[30] A. S. Orlov, "K voprosu ob Ipat'evskoy letopisi" (On the Question of the Hypatian Chronicle), *Izv. otd. russk. yaz. i slov.* (News of the Division of Russian Language and Literature of the Academy of Sciences USSR) (1926), Vol. XXXI, pp. 93–126.

Vladimir Monomakh. Román "with wisdom of mind" walked according to God's commandments, pounced on the pagans like a lion, was as irascible as a lynx, baleful as a crocodile. Like an eagle he crossed the enemy's country, was brave as an aurochs. He vied with his grandfather Monomakh, who wiped out the Polovcians and pursued the Polovcian khan, Otrok, to Abkhazia while the other Khan, Syrchan, was in hiding on the Don. Then Vladimir Monomakh drank from his golden helmet of the Don, having won the whole Polovcian country and driven out the pagan Agars. With this eulogy is entwined a poetical story on the theme of love of country. A Polovcian's memory is awakened by the smell of a grass from his native steppes. After the death of Monomakh, Syrchan sent his singer, Or, to Otrok with the proposal that he return to his native land. Neither Or's words nor the Polovcian songs that he sang for Otrok moved him to return, but when he smelled some wormwood from the Polovcian steppes he burst into tears and said: "Better to lay one's bones in one's own land than to win fame in a foreign one," and returned to his country. To him, the story adds, was born Konchak, who, afoot and carrying a kettle on his back, baled out the Sula.[31]

A. S. Orlov has indicated as stylistic sources for the character sketch of Román the character sketches of Heracles (first book of Malalas), Svyatoslav (*Primary Chronicle*), and Alexander of Macedon (*Alexandria*).[32] In his day V. Miller asserted that the story quoted had no connection with the chronicle and had found its way there from some heroic narrative such as the *Tale of Igor's Expedition*, perhaps even from a no longer extant first part of the *Igor*, and this, in V. Miller's opinion, seemed the more probable in view of the fact that at the very beginning of the *Igor* the author promises to carry his narrative "from old Vladimir [that is, Monomakh] to the present Igor," and that this can scarcely have been a mere empty promise. The story in the *Galicia-Volynia Chronicle* is in fact akin to the *Igor*, in the comparison of Román to an aurochs, the expression, "drank the Don from his golden helmet," and the mention of a Polovcian singer and Polovcian songs and, finally, in the hyperbolical description of Konchak baling out the Sula with a kettle, akin to the descriptions of the might of Vsevolod Yuryevich, who was capable of splashing the Volga out with his oars and baling the Don out with his helmet, and of the might of Yaroslav of Osmomysl and Svyatoslav of Kiev.[33]

---

[31] This story was versified by A. Maykov in the poem *"Emshan,"* but one has only to compare the paraphrase with the original to see how superior poetically the latter is to the former.

[32] *Op. cit.,* pp. 101–102, 104.

[33] *Vzglyad na Slovo o polku Igoreve* (A Glance at the Tale of Igor's Expedition), pp. 140–142.

Even if V. Miller's conjecture (that the analyzed story from the *Galicia-Volynia Chronicle* is a fragment of an inextant section of the *Tale of Igor's Expedition*) be only an ingenious hypothesis in support of which it is impossible to produce any real facts, it is still perfectly possible to accept his opinion that this story was brought over into the chronicle from a group of works very like the *Igor* in poetic style. An echo of the songs composed in honor of Román and his son Daniel is found in this same *Galicia-Volynia Chronicle* under the year 1251:

From there Prince Daniel went to Vizna and crossed the river Narov and released many Christians from captivity and they sang a song in honor of him, and of God who had aided him, and he came with glory to his own land, having followed in the footsteps of his father Great Prince Román, who sharpened himself on the pagans like a lion, and with whom the Polovcians frightened their children.

As we see, this eulogy retains the already familiar comparison of Román to a lion: "sharpened himself on the pagans" resembles "sharpened his heart with courage" in the *Igor*, while the mention of the Polovcians scaring their children with Román's name is an echo of the epic formula applied to Vladimir Monomakh in the *Discourse on the Ruin of the Land of Rus*, written at about the same time. Stylistically the stories of Román and Vladimir Monomakh recall the story of the magician Skomond, dated 1248 and written under the influence of the chronicle of Malalas: "For Skomond was a wizard and a professional sorcerer, and swift he was as a wild animal, for he went about on foot raiding the Pinsk district and other regions; and he died a shameful death and his head was impaled on a stake."

From the earliest lines of the *Galicia-Volynia Chronicle*, the chronicler's predilection for literary language declares itself. What first strikes the eye is the very frequent use of the dative absolute, which, incidentally, is not even once encountered in the *Igor*: "Syrchan stopping at the Don, the fish being lively," "and having taken their whole land and driven out the accursed Agars," "only the fiddler Or remaining with Syrchan," "he not wishing to return," "he being stunned and having burst out weeping," and so forth. The rest of the *Galicia-Volynia Chronicle* is likewise abundantly garnished with dative absolutes, the first part in particular. Here in some cases sentence after sentence in uninterrupted sequence will be constructed with the aid of the dative absolute, as, for example, in the following poetic picture of a prophetic portent: "The army not yet having reached the river Syana, and having stopped in the fields to arm, and the following portent taking place above the army: eagles having approached and many ravens, like a great cloud, the birds playing, the eagles crying and floating on spread wings and throwing themselves about in the air, in such manner as had never been seen before."

Another specifically bookish locution is the use of the expressions "that is" and "meaning" to introduce definitions of various words: "To the Caucasus; that is, to the Hungarian mountains"; "*rex,* meaning king, of Hungary"; "They set fire to their wagons; that is, to their camps, on the Lord's day, meaning Sunday," and so forth.

The author also shows his learning by the use of proverbs, parables, and aphorisms: "Oh, flattery is an evil! As Homer writes: 'Until its detection it is sweet, but when detected it is evil; he who walks in its ways will come to an evil end'— Oh, it is an evil that is worse than evil!" (This proverb is evidently borrowed from some collection; it is not in Homer); "To Mitus, who in the olden days had refused out of pride to serve Prince Daniel, a famous singer was brought in tatters, and as if bound, to recite the words of the Preacher: 'The fury of thy house shall be turned to its own destruction, beaver and wolf and panther shall feast themselves.' This was said as a parable." From the chronicle of Malalas also derives in the last analysis the chronicler's story of the bad night that was perpetrated on the people of Belz. It is built on a play upon words:

On Saturday night Daniel and Vasilko perpetrated a capture round about Belz and Cherven and the whole population was captured: boyar captured boyar, serf captured serf, city captured city, so that not even one village remained uncaptured; as it says in the parable: 'I shall not leave one stone upon another.' The people of Belz call this the bad night because the night played a bad trick on them, inasmuch as they were captured before dawn.

A quotation from Malalas, with the same play on words, is also used in a story of the year 1229 about Daniel's victory over the Hungarians on the Dniester: "Many fell into the river; some were killed, some wounded, some were taken out; as it says elsewhere: 'The river Syrtus played a bad trick on the citizens.' Just so did the Dniester play a bad trick on the Hungarians." In the *Galician* as in the *Primary Chronicle,* proverbs are also sometimes encountered. The centurion Mikula says to Daniel, when he is starting out on a campaign against the Hungarians: "Master! If you don't send the bees out you won't eat honey."

The author of the *Galician Chronicle,* as was said above, pays special attention to military events and to the princes who participated in those events, and enjoys sketching in the details of military life and equipment. Here he made abundant use of war-story formulae and of individual images and pictures deriving in part from the Bible, Malalas, Hamartolas, Josephus Flavius, and the *Alexandria,* or, more accurately, as has been pointed out by Academician A. S. Orlov, from the composite chronograph which had absorbed all these monuments. Thus, after Malalas, the Galician chronicler compares the tourney, the single combat, to a game: "And as the other unsheathed his sword, the one playing against the servant of the king made the play of grasping his shield," or: "The next day the Germans rode out with crossbows and the Russians and Polovcians rode down on them with arrows and the Yatvyazians with spears, and they chased each other about the field as if in sport." He imitates the chronicle of Hamartolas, and perhaps to some extent Josephus Flavius, in describing the arms of the Galician infantry:

Their shields were like daybreak, their helmets being like the rising sun, their spears being held in their hands like so many walking sticks, the archers walking on either side of them and holding their bows in their hands and fitting to them their arrows aimed at the enemy, and Daniel, mounted, ordering the battle.

In the manner of Malalas, or perhaps of the *Alexandria,* he describes the weapons of the Russian armies and the battle armor of Daniel:

For the horses had headpieces and caparison of leather, and the men were in armor, and a great light came from his troops because of their flashing weapons. He himself [that is, Daniel] rode beside the Hungarian king in accordance with Russian custom: the steed under him was something to marvel at and the saddle was of burnished gold, and his arrows and sabers had gold mountings, wrought with such craft as to excite marvel, and his corselet was of a Greek brocade with gold plates appliquéd, and his shoes of green leather embroidered in gold.

"Gleaming arms" and "falcon archers" are mentioned under the year 1231 in the story of Daniel's battle with the Hungarians. Daniel himself is always described in apotheosis. Making use of a biblical image, the chronicler characterizes his hero thus: "For he was bold and brave; from his head to his foot there was no defect in him." When the prince rode up to Galich, the inhabitants of the town rushed out to him "like children to their father, like bees to the queen, like men thirsting for water to a spring." Daniel possesses chivalric ideals as to the conduct of war and as to his duty. To the princes who have decided to avoid battle with the Polovcians, he says, in the style of a speech by Darius from the *Alexandria:*

It befits a soldier to rush into battle and either win victory or fall at the enemy's hand; once I forbade you, but now I see that you are fainthearted. Did I not tell you that tired troops ought not to attack troops in good trim? But what is there to hold you back now? Go forth against them.

To his routed allies, the Poles, who have arrived in low spirits, he addresses the following speech:

Why are you dismayed? Do you not know that there is no such thing as a war without people getting killed? Did you not know that it was men, that it was warriors, you were attacking and not women? If a man is killed in battle, what is strange about that? Some men die at home, too, without honor, but these men died with honor; take heart, advance your arms into battle.

The humiliation experienced by Daniel when he became subject to the Tartars calls forth a sorrowful tirade from the chronicler:

Oh, evil of evils, to pay honor to Tartars! Daniel Románovich, former Great Prince, Lord over the Land of Rus, over Kiev and Vladimir and Galich, with his brothers ruling the other districts, must now kneel and be called a slave, and desire favors, uncertain of his life, beset by dangers. Oh, evil of honoring Tartars! His father was tsar in the land of Rus, conquered the Polovcian land and constantly waged war on other lands; if the son of this man is not treated with honor, then who else can expect to be honored?

In like manner, as A. S. Orlov points out, does Darius in the *Alexandria* bemoan his fate when conquered by Alexander of Macedon.

Finally, battle formulae, deriving in part from the *History of the Destruction of Jerusalem* by Josephus Flavius, are of frequent occurrence. Take, for example, the description of the battle of the Poles with the Tartars:

Then they reached Sudomirya and blockaded it from all sides and fenced in their city and set up battering rams: and what with the battering rams hammering incessantly day and night and arrows coming over from the towers without respite . . . they fell from the runway into the ditch like sheaves; though the ditches were very deep, they were so filled with the dead that you could walk across on a corpse as over a bridge.

In other passages the hurling of slingshot, darts, and stones is likened to rain, the crash of breaking spears, to thunder; the casting of spears and firebrands, to lightning. Sometimes the description of martial exploits is attended by the rhythmic repetition of identical endings:

And you could not hear for the screeching of the carts he had,
the multitudinous bellowing of the oxen he had,
and the neighing of the herds of horses that he had.

His cavalry massed and followed the infantry
calmly into battle,
their hearts made stout for battle,
and bent on battle.

One warrior directed his ten
by taking the horn from that belt of his,
from a distance rushed up, smote the prince of Yatvyaz
off that horse of his;
as he hurtled down to the ground,
his soul, with his blood, seeped forth unto Hades.

The second part of the *Galicia-Volynia Chronicle*—the *Volynia Chronicle* proper—is marked by considerably less picturesqueness of style than the first part; in it we do not find even the figurative poetical language so characteristic of the *Galician Chronicle*. It evidences to a much higher degree than the *Galician Chronicle* the ecclesiastical veneer, obvious, for example, in the extensive eulogy of Vladimir, son of Vasilko, which at one point avails itself almost literally of the eulogy of Vladimir, son of Svyatoslav, in Hilarion's *Discourse of Law and Grace*. However, this eulogy begins with a description of the outward appearance of Vladimir, son of Vasilko, which, after first repeating verbatim the personal description of Prince Román, son of Rostislav, entered in the *Kievan Chronicle* under 1180, goes on to set itself off from the general run of chronicle portraits by its detail and by its striving for an exact reproduction of his distinguishing characteristics: "This Orthodox Prince Vladimir was tall of stature, broad-shouldered, of ruddy complexion, had yellow curly hair, a cropped beard, fine arms and legs; his voice was low-pitched and his lower lip thick." These realistic elements in the description of the prince's outward appearance find their counterpart in the equally realistic and detailed description of the malady (evidently cancer of the lower jaw) which led to his death.

OTHER MONUMENTS OF THIS PERIOD

Another noteworthy provincial monument of the thirteenth century is the *Life of Abraham of Smolensk*. It was written by Abraham's pupil, Ephrem, from the testimony of contemporaries, from the author's own reminiscences, and under the considerable influence of original and translated lives, Nestor's *Life of Theodosius of the Crypt* in particular. Abraham of Smolensk stands out in the *Life* as a great bibliophile, distinguished by his unusual reading, well versed in the "Church Fathers" and conversant with "deep books"; that is, books in which abstruse truths are expounded. He was also skilled in icon-painting, but won his greatest popularity as an outstanding preacher, attracting enormous audiences by virtue of his eloquence and at the same time arousing the enmity of the Smolensk clergy, who pursued him with calumny and abuse. The matter got as far as the court, which was, however, obliged to acquit Abraham—whereafter his fame as an ascetic and a teacher increased still further.

Of itself the figure of Abraham, noted scholar and preacher, is a very good index for judging the high cultural level of Smolensk, where Prince Román had founded a school in which, so the tradition goes, they taught not only Slavonic but Greek and Latin as well.[34]

[34] Texts of the *Life of Abraham of Smolensk* were published by S. P. Rozanov in *Pamyatniki drevnerusskoy literatury* (Monuments of Early Russian Literature) (St. Petersburg, 1912), Pt. 1. On the *Life* see Buslayev, *Istoricheskie ocherki russkoy narodnoy slovesnosti i iskusstva* (Historical Outlines of Russian Folk Literature and Art) (St. Petersburg, 1861), Vol. II, pp. 115–122; V. Klyuchevskii, *Drevnerusskie zhitiya svyatykh kak istoricheskii istochnik* (Early Russian Lives of Saints as a Historical Source) (Moscow, 1871), pp. 52–58.

Of any further growth of the literatures of the northern provinces from the fourteenth century on, comparatively few literary monuments are extant: the critical situation in which Rus found itself under Tartar domination was not very conducive either to the development of a literary tradition or to its conservation. Practically the only thing that went on uninterrupted during this era was chronicle work, leading, in Vladimir, to the formulation of an all-Russian chronicle digest, ending with the year 1305, though collections of precepts such as the *Emerald,* the *Pearl,* and so forth, were also brought together.

The literature of Tver in the fourteenth century is represented by such monuments as the chronicle *Legend of Shevkal,* reflected in the historical folk song about Shchelkan Dudentevich, and the narrative of the murder of Great Prince Yaroslavich of Tver (died 1319) at the Horde, which is permeated with anti-Muscovite tendencies and written under the influence of the legends about the murder of Michael of Chernigov and about Boris and Gleb.[35]

The *Legend of Shevkal* deals with a historical fact narrated in the chronicle under the year 1327. In this year the people of Tver, led by Prince Alexander Mikhailovich, burned alive the Tartar deputy Shevkal (Cholkhan) and his suite as retribution for Shevkal's tyrannical and contemptuous administration of Tver. The ballad says that for this mob justice meted out to the Tartars, "no one was ever brought to trial," whereas we know from the chronicle that the Tartars, with the collusion of the Muscovite Prince Ivan Kalita, made the people of Tver pay dear, bringing ruin upon their city and forcing Alexander to flee to Pskov.

Moscow produced during the first half of the fourteenth century, in addition to the local chronicle, a *Life* of Peter, first metropolitan of Moscow (died 1326), written by Prokhor, Bishop of Rostov, largely with a view to promoting Moscow as a political center.[36]

More marked literary progress was made by Novgorod, which came forward during this period as a major political and economic power. Among Novgorod's fourteenth century monuments are several works which employ legendary and apocryphal elements in full measure. Such is the *Colloquy on the Shrines of Tsargrad* (1321–1323), which describes in dialogue form the shrines of Constantinople, its monuments of art, and its historic past, and comes apparently from the pen of the Constantinople pilgrim-priest, Gregory Kaleka, later Basil, Archbishop of Novgorod. Of a similar character is the *Pilgrim* of the otherwise unknown Stefan of Novgorod (*circa* 1350), which

[35] An early redaction is printed in Macarius' *Chet'i-Minei* under Nov. 22 (Moscow, 1914), *cahier* 3rd. See Klyuchevskii, *op. cit.,* pp. 71–74; Serebryanskii, *Drevnerusskie knyazheskie zhitiya* (Early Russian Princes' Lives), pp. 250–253.

[36] See Klyuchevskii, *op. cit.,* pp. 74–77.

likewise describes the shrines of Tsargrad.[37] Apropos of the characteristic religious "wallet bearers" and "vagrants" of northeastern Rus, first appearing at the middle of the fourteenth century, increasing with particular rapidity in the fifteenth, and reflecting the unrest of the suburban rank and file, there came into being at about the middle of the fourteenth century the *Epistle* from Basil, Archbishop of Novgorod, to Theodore, Bishop of Tver, on the Earthly Paradise, included under 1347 in the third Novgorod and in the first St. Sophia chronicle. As opposed to the doctrines current in Tver as to the existence of Paradise being merely "imaginary," the *Epistle* demonstrates its real existence by a number of legendary-apocryphal records: its location was revealed to the Novgorodians Moislav and his son Jacob, though they did not themselves see Paradise "because it was not given them to look upon that ineffable brightness and upon the rejoicing to be heard there." The Novgorodians also knew where hell was. This story has very close parallels in Western, especially German, legends about heaven and hell, which circulated in the West along with the literature of travel. That a Western legend should have been brought to Novgorod is quite comprehensible in view of trade relations between Novgorod and western Europe.[38]

Of the literary monuments of Pskov dating from this time, most importance attaches to the chronicle narrative about Prince Dovmont (died 1299), written at the beginning of the fourteenth century under strong influence of the ecclesiastico-annalistic and the so-called "idiosyncratic" *Life of Alexander Nevsky* and to some extent under that of the *Prologue* life of Vladimir. The influence of the folk-poetry tradition is also apparent in the narrative. Dovmont stands forth as the heroic defender of Pskov against attacks by Lithuanians and Germans. The narrative is included in the first and second Pskov chronicles under 1265.[39]

Finally the literary productivity of Rostov-Suzdal, manifest as early as the end of the twelfth century in the *Life of Leontius,* Bishop of Rostov, and later in the *Lives* of Isaiah and Abraham of Rostov, and the *Rostov Chronicle,* found fourteenth century representation in the above-mentioned Laurentian

[37] See M. N. Speranskii, "Iz starinnoy novgorodskoy litaratury XIV veka" (From the Ancient Novgorod Literature of the Fourteenth Century) (Leningrad, 1934), *Pamyatniki drevnerusskoy literatury* (Monuments of Early Russian Literature), Pt. 4.

[38] See *Novgorodskie Letopisi* (Novgorod Chronicles), *izd. Arkheograficheskoy komissii* (Publications Archaeographical Commission) (St. Petersburg, 1879), pp. 224–229, and *Polnoe sobranie russkikh letopisey* (Complete Collection of Russian Chronicles), Vol. VI, pp. 87–89; A. Veselovskii, "Epizody o rae i ade v poslanii novgorodskogo arkhiepiskopa Vasiliya" (Episodes on Heaven and Hell in the Epistle of Basil, Archbishop of Novgorod), *Razyskaniya v oblasti russkogo dukhovnogo stikha* (Researches in the Field of Russian Spiritual Verse) (St. Petersburg, 1891), Pt. 6, pp. 91–104.

[39] See *Polnoe sobranie russkikh letopisey* (Full Collection of Russian Chronicles), Vol. IV, pp. 180–183; Vol. V, pp. 6–8. There is a historico-literary analysis of the narrative in N. I. Serebryanskii's *Drevnerusskie knyazheskie zhitiya* (Early Russian Princes' Lives), pp. 265–275.

manuscript of the chronicle (1377) and also in a literary adaptation of the local legend of Peter, prince royal of the Horde, and his descendants, in their relationships with the Rostov princes, against a background of typical folkways and historical details. The *Lives* of Leontius, Isaiah and Abraham of Rostov are interesting among other things for the fact that they point up the direct connection of Rostov with Tsargrad, and the Rostov church's independence of the metropolitanate of Kiev. Thus, Leontius went directly from Tsargrad to Rostov, ignoring Kiev and its metropolitan. As to Prince Peter, he appears to have been an emigrant from the Horde who joined the Orthodox Church through the agency of the local bishop of Rostov. Thus the literature of Rostov shows a tendency toward separatism from the other Russian provinces.

The story of Peter of the Horde tells how in the thirteenth century he deserted the Horde under the influence of tales told by Cyril, Bishop of Rostov, when visiting there. Peter came to Rostov, was baptized, and at the suggestion of the apostles Peter and Paul, who appeared to him in a dream, built a church, for which he bought land of Boris, Prince of Rostov, laying out its boundaries with silver and gold coins by way of a rope (a migratory motif, likewise present in the story of the founding of Carthagena). In Rostov Peter married the daughter of a Horde noble who had settled in Rostov and had embraced the Orthodox faith. The prince was on very friendly terms with Peter, even fraternizing with him. Out of affection he deeded to him and to his descendants many fields and forests and the water of Rostov Lake. At a ripe old age Peter died, having taken monastic vows on his deathbed. He was buried in a tomb at the church which he had built and beside which a monastery had been founded. The descendants of the prince of Rostov, being envious of Peter's descendants, started suit against them first about the land, then about the lake. In both instances the Tartar deputies decided the case in favor of the descendants of Peter. One of the latter afterwards kept the Tartar king Akhmyl from ravaging the Rostov area. Akhmyl's son became ill and was restored to health through the prayer of Prokhor, Bishop of Rostov, and this favorably disposed the "king" to the people of Rostov, whom he refrained from harming in any way, while rewarding the bishop and the choristers most generously.

Akhmyl's attack on Rostov took place in 1322 and to judge from the words: "It was terrifying, brothers, to see his troops [Akhmyl's] and the whole force under arms," the story was written by a contemporary and an eyewitness of the attack, consequently not later than the middle of the fourteenth century. The author of the story was apparently a monk of Peter's monastery who had set himself the problem of demonstrating the juridical incontestability of the right of Peter's descendants and of Peter's monastery to possession of the lands and waters to which the descendants of the prince of Rostov were laying claim. It was a time when the author could practically disregard the authority of the princes of Rostov since this was already strictly limited by the authority of the prince of Moscow.

The story draws a very graphic picture of the relations ultimately established between the Russian clergy and the Tartars: the clergy had been accorded many privileges by the Tartars, hence the picture that we get is of mutually benevolent relations between the Russian Church and Tartar authority.[40]

The provincial literatures of the thirteenth and fourteenth centuries developed, basically, as has been shown above, on the foundation of traditions worked out in the literature of the Kiev period. This is true not only of the Galicia-Volynia literature but also of the literatures of the North Russian centers. Throughout, the monuments of this period show peculiarities of style found in the monuments, original and translated, of the Kiev period, well known during the thirteenth and fourteenth centuries, as well as later, both in the north and in the south of Rus. The theme of the defense of Russian soil from enemy encroachments, which occupied a place of such importance during the Kiev period (the chronicle, the *Tale of Igor's Expedition*) is the fundamental and leading one in the succeeding period as well. The struggle with the Swedes, Germans, and particularly with Rus's most terrible enemy, the Tartars, now takes the place of the struggle with the Pechenegs and Polovcians who had ravaged Kievan Rus, and finds the same live response in literature. The clash of political interests and the rivalry for political precedence which were to appear in fully defined form in the provincial literatures of the fifteenth century, at this time still declared themselves only sporadically and not as yet so insistently. For example, in spite of the fact that at times there had been skirmishes between the Galicia-Volynia principality and other Russian provinces (for example, the principality of Chernigov), the *Galician Chronicle*, like the others, very consistently reflects the concept of the oneness of the Russian forces in their struggle against the common enemies of the land of Rus, the Tartars. The story of the battle of the Kalko ("The Rout of Alets") included in the *Galician Chronicle* tells of a conference of Russian princes in Kiev deciding to make a joint attack on the Tartars before they could reach the Russian provinces. "It would be better for us to engage them on foreign soil than on our own," said the princes.

[40] The story is printed in *Pravoslavnyi sobesednik* (Orthodox Interlocutor) (1859), No. 1, pp. 356–376. On it see Buslayev, *Istoricheskie ocherki* (Historical Outlines), Vol. II, pp. 155–169, and Klyuchevskii, *Drevnerusskie zhitiya svyatykh* (Early Russian Saints' Lives), pp. 38–43.

The Galician chronicler narrates the events of the Tartar invasion not only as immediately affecting the fortunes of the Galicia-Volynia principality, but also in their relation to the destiny of the land of Rus as a whole: he speaks with great sympathy and with sorrow of the Tartars having ravaged the Ryazan and Suzdal districts, the cities of Kozelsk, Pereyaslavl, Chernigov, Kiev. It is very indicative that the murder by the Tartars of Michael of Chernigov and his boyar Theodore should have called forth a sorrowful response from him regardless of the fact that Michael of Chernigov had not only been at odds with Daniel of Galicia on account of his pretensions to the prince-ship of Kiev but had at the invitation of the Galician boyars seized Galich, which Daniel had recovered only through the support of the townspeople, who were loyal to him and disliked the boyars. Notwithstanding all this, resentment against the prince-usurper now gives place with the chronicler to sorrow and indignation that a Russian prince, whether friendly to Daniel or not, should have fallen at the hand of the odious Tartar enemy.

Indicative, too, is the fact that already at the very beginning of the four-teenth century, in Vladimir, on the initiative of the metropolitan Peter, an all-Russian chronicle compilation is being composed, bringing the narrative of events down to 1305, and becoming the general basis for all fourteenth century compilations.

It is essentially significant that in the epoch we have surveyed there should also have appeared such a keen pamphlet-satire as the *Supplication of Daniel the Exile,* trenchantly posing the problem of social inequality and testify-ing to the growth of class consciousness at this time in the depressed strata of Russian society.

Development of Provincial Literatures From the End of the Fourteenth to the Beginning of the Sixteenth Century

FROM the end of the fourteenth century to the beginning of the sixteenth, provincial literatures continued to develop, gradually, however, gravitating toward the most powerful, the literature of Moscow, which by the sixteenth century was already the literature of Russia as a whole. This centripetal trend in literature was a product of that process of political concentration which had liquidated the old-time dismemberment of the Russian lands and had thus proved a progressive factor in the formation of a single Muscovite state.

The Muscovite principality now comes forward as the strongest and politically most influential governing power. A favorable conjunction of strategic, territorial, and economic conditions had contributed to its victory over rival states pretending to hegemony. Substantial aid was also given Moscow during its rise and gradual attainment of political consolidation by the Church, which supported the Muscovite principality as the power most certain to be capable of protecting its interests and guaranteeing its prosperity. Moreover, the clergy (as represented by the monasteries) had long since assumed economic functions: the monasteries were, strictly speaking, estates on a large scale, with their own great farms, their own crafts. It was to the interest of a church so bound up with commercial and financial operations, to further that process of centralization which in the political and governmental sphere had also come about in large measure through commercial and financial developments naturally favorable to the process of centralization.

How far the Russian clergy had already assumed a role of political leadership in Moscow during the first half of the fourteenth century may be seen from a record of the eulogy of Ivan Kalita, 1339, preserved on the last page of a book of Gospel readings from the Siisk Monastery of St. Anthony. The familiar formula of Metropolitan Hilarion is employed for the eulogy, which says of Ivan Kalita that the things he accomplished in the land of Rus were like those that the emperor Constantine accomplished in Byzantium. According to this record, the prophet Ezekiel was specifically referring to Ivan Kalita when he said: "In the latter time there shall arise in the desert lands to the west a king loving truth, giving judgment not for recompense nor as a scandal to heathen lands." [1] It is therefore only logical that attempts should have been made, even as early as the fourteenth century, and made in the metropolitan chancelleries, to compose an all-Russian chronicle digest, and that in the first quarter of the fifteenth century, in 1423, such a digest, known as the *Vladimir Polychron*, should have been produced in Moscow itself, likewise in the metropolitan chancellery, and that on the basis of it, in 1442, the emigrant South Slavic monk, Pakhomius Logothetes, should have composed a chronograph revealing the Muscovite tendency to unification in fully defined form. This work is extant in sixteenth century adaptations, the most important of which is the chronograph in the 1512 redaction, the work of Filofey, an ancient of the Pskov Monastery of Elezar, whose epistle to Great Prince Vasily Ivanovich gave final form to the concept of Moscow as the third Rome.

SECOND SOUTH SLAVIC INFLUENCE.
CLERICAL AND ANTI-CLERICAL MOVEMENTS

The growth of political consciousness evidenced during the second half of the fourteenth century in Rus, especially in Moscow, opened the way for the so-called "second" South Slavic influence on Russian literature. In connection with the political and cultural rise during the thirteenth and fourteenth centuries of the South Slavic states—Serbia and more particularly Bulgaria—after emancipation from dependence on Byzantium, a notable renaissance of literary activity had taken place, expressing itself on the one hand in new translations of Byzantine works and on the other in the composition of *Lives* cast in the form of rhetorically verbose and flowery panegyrics. The now clearly marked political decline of Byzantium prompted official Bulgarian publicity to regard Bulgaria as heir to Byzantine world empire, to

[1] See I. I. Sreznevskii, *Svedeniya i zametki o maloizvestnykh i neizvestnykh pamyatnikakh* (Information and Notes on Little Known and Unknown Monuments) (St. Petersburg, 1879), LXXXVI, pp. 145–148.

call its capital, Tyrnov, the new Tsargrad, and to name the Bulgarian tsars successors to the authority of the Byzantine emperors and autocrats.[2]

As the political strength of individual Russian provinces, Moscow in particular, increased, the South Slavic countries exported to us, along with new translations, the publicistic tenor of South Slavic "imperialistic" literature, and the flowery panegyric style with which monuments, particularly those of a biographical character, were invested.

The infiltration of the new South Slavic literary material, for the most part translated from Byzantine originals (works of the "Church Fathers," lives, historical chronicles, to a certain extent secular narratives),[3] with its new tricks of style and new spelling imitated from the Bulgarian, came about in part through increasingly frequent journeys made in the second half of the fourteenth century by Russian Church functionaries to Constantinople and to Mount Athos, where the possibility was brought home to them of utilizing learned works not only in South Slavic translation but also in the Byzantine originals. But it was chiefly the product of the activity of South Slavic emigrants in Russia, first of the metropolitan Cyprian, apparently a Bulgar (last quarter of the fourteenth and beginning of the fifteenth century), and more particularly of the Serb, Pakhomius Logothetes (fifteenth century), who lived in this country for about fifty years. In connection with the nascent ideology of Moscow as the third Rome, successor not only to the political but to the religious authority of the second Rome, Byzantium, the demand for an extensive development of biographical literature in support of propaganda for the ecclesiastical precedence of Rus became immediate, and South Slavic immigrants proved very desirable and useful, the more so as they readily adapted themselves to the publicistic assignment that had been given them.

For a clarification of the future course of biographical literature, and to explain the intellectual atmosphere in which Russian, and in particular Muscovite, literature was produced during the fifteenth and sixteenth and part of the seventeenth centuries, some introduction is needed to the principal Church factions of the fifteenth century, the ideological and cultural trend of which largely influenced the character of literary development.

From the fourteenth century on, the growth of monasteries in Rus was accelerated. As great landlords, concentrating under their control extensive territory with a numerous peasant population, they represented an imposing

[2] P. Syrku, *Iz istorii ispravleniya knig v Bolgarii v XIV veke* (From the History of the Correction of Books in Bulgaria in the Fourteenth Century), Vol. I, Pt. 1, "Vremya i zhizn' patriarkha Yevfimiya Ternovskogo" (Life and Times of Patriarch Euphemius Ternovskii) (St. Petersburg, 1898), pp. 366–372, 390–391.

[3] See A. I. Sobolevskii, *Perevodnaya literatura Moskovskoy Rusi XIV–XVII vv.* (Translated Literature of Muscovite Rus in the Fourteenth-Seventeenth Centuries) (St. Petersburg, 1903), pp. 1–37.

power. This power in many cases conflicted with the interests of the feudal state as a whole, inasmuch as the clergy was competing with the secular owners of land; that is, the boyars and later the nobility.

The state regarded the economic pretentions of the Church in two lights: on the one hand the Church was a quasi-independent organization that frequently hampered the state, but on the other hand the colonizing activity of the monasteries was advantageous to it.

Josephite monasticism, so named from the head of the movement, Joseph of Volok, prior of Volokolam Monastery (1439–1515), upheld the right of the monasteries to own lands and enrich themselves economically. In his writings, notably the epistles, Joseph defends the legality of the large-scale holding of land by monasteries on the ground that the monasteries were an important force not only religiously but politically.

A different school of ecclesiastical thought was headed by Nil of Sorsky (1433–1508) and the trans-Volga hermits; that is, monks domiciled, like Nil of Sorsky, in monasteries beyond the Volga. They denied the right of the monasteries to own lands and concern themselves with economic enrichment. As Nil of Sorsky and the trans-Volga hermits saw it, the prime duty of a monk consisted in devotion, asceticism, and complete renunciation of those material cares and political functions that the Josephite clergy was proposing to assume. A monk, as the hermits saw it, should be critical of "Writ," which the Josephites were not, having shown themselves incapable of distinguishing the authoritative from the unauthoritative in this "Writ," the inner meaning from the dead letter. At the basis of the teaching of Nil of Sorsky and his adherents lay the mystical, contemplative world outlook which had lately swept Mount Athos and the South Slavic countries and had penetrated to Rus through South Slavic influence.

Nil of Sorsky, like the trans-Volga hermits associated with him, was an exponent, chiefly, of the interests of the boyar class, which had suffered the most from ecclesiastical pretensions, since the economic enrichment of the Church, the extension of its appendages of landed property, had a negative effect on boyar economy and on boyar land tenure. Not without reason were a number of the trans-Volga hermits scions of boyar families, and many boyars supporters of the trans-Volga monks.

These two Church factions joined battle, and in the end victory proved to be on the side of the Josephites, who contrived to come to terms with the secular authority: throughout the sixteenth century their cultural, ideological and literary influence asserted itself to the full. Politically they sided with the nobility and in large measure became its ideologists.

The triumph of the policy of the Josephites, who ultimately compromised, relinquishing a number of their economic privileges and at the same time appreciably strengthening the authority of the great prince of Moscow, afterward tsar, also throws light on the fate of such opposition religious factions as arose in Rus from the fourteenth century on. I refer to the so-called "heresies," which basically had a close connection with the economic situation obtaining in Novgorod, Pskov, and afterward in Moscow.

The first such large-scale religious movement, originating in Pskow and Novgorod and having some repercussions in Moscow, was the so-called "Strigolnichestvo," shearers' sect, associated with the name of a certain Karp, who was apparently a cloth shearer—hence the name of the heresy.

The Shearer heresy was primarily based on the repudiation of the Church hierarchy on the ground that this hierarchy existed "on bribery"; that is, the clerics obtained their places for a price. The fact of the matter was that Pskov, where the heresy originated, was a dependency of the Novgorod hierarchy, and in the person of its city and suburban population had experienced the financial pinch of exactions made by the Novgorod clergy.

A second peculiarity of the Shearer heresy was its denial of the necessity of prayers for the dead. Such prayers were usually accompanied by "deposits for the soul," which often ruined the depositors and hence naturally aroused their opposition.

But the Strigolnichestvo was not so powerful or so pregnant with all manner of events in Church history as another heresy which originated a century later, in the 1470's, in Novgorod. I have in mind the heresy of the "Judaizers," [4] so nicknamed by the principal polemist against it, Joseph of Volok, who refuted its positions in a voluminous work entitled *The Teacher*.

What connection this heresy had with Judaism would be hard to say. In any event it was a purely formal rather than an organic one. Reference is commonly made to the Jew Skharia, who went from Kiev to Novgorod and appears to have been the prime mover in the heresy. The main point is that the earliest partisans seem to have been members of the white clergy,* two Novgorod priests: it is a matter of common knowledge that the heresy won over the white clergy of Novgorod, penetrated to Moscow and enjoyed, if not the public, in any event the private sympathy of Great Prince Ivan III. Patrons of the heretics included Ivan's daughter-in-law, the head of the ambassadorial office Fyodor Kuritsyn and even, as was quite extraordinary considering his official position, the metropolitan Zosima himself.

The heresy apparently received the title of Judaizers because the heretics denied at the outset the divinity of Christ. They asserted that Christ was a man, just like Moses; next they denied the existence of saints, the sanctity of

---

4 It should be noted that the word "Judaize" did not at this period carry the opprobrium that later became attached to it as a result of use in anti-Semitic, reactionary circles.

* Nonmonastic clergy.—ED.

churches and icons and, like the Strigolniks, refused to recognize the Church hierarchy.

Obviously the heresy of the Judaizers was a sort of echo of Protestantism. Elements of Judaism were present to the same extent as in any Western Protestant movement. There is reason to suppose that in this heresy we have an echo of ideas nascent in the epoch of the Renaissance. Its primary purpose was to secularize thought from the traditional dogmas and traditional points of view typical of orthodox religion, and from which western Europe emancipated itself during the period of the Renaissance and Reformation.

Inasmuch as the partisans of the heresy were the white clergy, that is, the lower and middle clergy, then the burghers associated with them, it is quite clear that the propaganda of the Judaizers and the very essence of their teaching reflected the war which the lower and middle clergy in alliance with the tradespeople were waging against the economic domination of the official Church in the person of its higher clergy.

The heresy of the Judaizers found secret and sometimes even open sympathy in Moscow because in repudiating the Church hierarchy and its economic pretensions, the heresy undoubtedly played into the hands of the state, which was itself endeavoring to moderate the pretensions of the Josephite Church where these conflicted with the interests of secular authority. On the other hand any radical falling out with the official Church, which had done so much to further the centralizing tendencies of Moscow and to increase the authority of the Muscovite prince, would be inadvisable. In the end the Josephite clergy came to terms with the state by making numerous concessions, and toward the beginning of the sixteenth century the heresy was liquidated. Many heretics were burned, some exiled, some imprisoned.

From all the above it becomes clear that both the heresy of the Shearers and that of the Judaizers had a social and political background. Engels says in his *Peasant War in Germany* that under medieval conditions "attacks on feudalism in general and attacks on the Church in particular, all revolutionary, social and political teachings must at the same time take on the aspect of theological heresies as well. Social attitudes to be brought under attack must be divested of the pall of sanctity."[5] What Engels says of medieval urban heresies as reflecting the bourgeois opposition, applies in large measure both to the heresy of the Shearers and to that of the Judaizers. He wrote:

Urban heresy, and this was the official heresy of the Middle Ages, was directed chiefly against the priests, whose wealth and political position it also attacked. Just as the bourgeoisie at present demands cheap government, *gouvernement à*

[5] K. Marx and F. Engels, *Works*, Vol. VIII, p. 128.

bon marché, so the medieval burghers demanded first of all a cheap Church, *église à bon marché.*[6]

An acquaintance with the heresy of the Judaizers is essential for our purposes because of the intense agitation that it caused in the minds of Russian society. Monuments tell us that even women marketing argued on religious themes, so important had religious fluctuations become. The heresy of the Judaizers shows that critical element in which the Josephites were deficient, but which informed the practice of the trans-Volga hermits. The leaders of the heretical movement were persons well educated for that time, with a literature of their own. Thus, extant examples of their work include the *Logic* of the learned Jew Maimonides, the *Hexapterix,* astrological works; that is, literature of a sort in any event to broaden the horizon of the Old Russian reader considerably and arouse his critical faculty. Hence the tolerance that the trans-Volga hermits showed toward the Judaizers. The two groups were alike, first, in their negative attitude toward the monastic ownership of land; second, in that critical attitude toward "Holy Writ" which the Josephites lacked. The Josephites were so uncritical in their attitude toward "Writ" as to consider that any document had authority if only it accorded in some degree with their interests. (This was very characteristic of them even later on, in the sixteenth century.) Often they did not distinguish the canonical books from the apocryphal, nor did they have the faculty of systematic argument which results from a critical attitude toward material; that is, they lacked everything that the trans-Volga hermits and the heretics both had.

A substantial result of the struggle between the official Church and the heresy of the Judaizers was the bringing out of a complete codex of the books of the Bible, something which up to that time had not existed in Rus. Since the Judaizers leaned heavily upon biblical texts in their propaganda, it was necessary for their adversaries to possess a reasonably accurate text of the Bible as a whole in order to combat them. This enterprise was carried out by an active opponent of the heresy, Gennadius, Archbishop of Novgorod, between 1489 and 1499, and in this connection he utilized not only old translations of biblical texts from the Greek, but new ones specially made from the Latin and to some extent from the Hebrew and German.

[6] *Ibid.,* p. 129.

SAINTS' LIVES FROM THE END OF THE FOURTEENTH
TO THE BEGINNING OF THE SIXTEENTH CENTURY

At the end of the fourteenth century, Metropolitan Cyprian used the new oratorical style in a recasting of the *Life* of his predecessor, Metropolitan Peter, by Prokhor, Bishop of Rostov, interpolating stereotyped miracles and adding a rhetorical preamble and a panegyric conclusion or eulogy of the saint.

The hagiographer who stands out as having carried the new manner of biographical writing to its logical extreme, however, was a remarkably gifted Russian, Epiphanius (died 1420), a past master in rhetoric, called because of his oratorical talent, the Wise, author of the *Lives* of two saints, Stephen of Permia, and Sergius of Radonezh, and possibly author of the preamble to the *Life of Great Prince Michael Aleksandrovich of Tver*. Particular literary significance attaches to the *Life of Stephen of Permia,* which gave Epiphanius his reputation as an expert and gifted stylist. As appears from the text of the *Life,* Epiphanius knew Stephen of Permia personally, but in spite of this and of the fact that the *Life* was written soon after Stephen's death (1396), concrete biographical facts are comparatively few and seldom go beyond the literary pattern long since set for works of this sort (pious childhood, a taste for godly books, zeal in ascetic practice, fervor in preaching the Christian faith and, finally, a beatific end). Isolated touches of realism and any vernacular elements present are completely submerged by the extreme wordiness of the style.

Stephen's principal accomplishment was the conversion of the Zirani (Komi) from paganism to orthodoxy partly by his own preaching but chiefly through translations of the Scriptures into the Ziranian tongue, Stephen himself having invented a Ziranian alphabet for the purpose.

Only the florid, extremely rhetorical style, in conjunction with numerous digressions and lyric outpourings on the part of the author, made it possible for a life having such a relatively low saturation of concrete facts to attain its quite considerable proportions.

After a lengthy preamble the author begins by telling about Stephen's childhood. Stephen surpassed his many coevals in "mnemonic capability, speed of acquisition, mental acuity, velocity of thought." He was a "very well intelligenced" boy.

This concatenation of newfangled, complicated, highly ornate expressions gives a fair idea of the idiosyncrasies of Epiphanius' style.

Stephen of Permia was the offspring of a man who was a true Christian,

Simeon, a cleric in the cathedral church at Ustyug, and of a mother who was a Christian—in a word, of pious parents, as is usual for a saint. From childhood he showed every sign of seriousness: he did not join the other children at their play, turned away from all childish games and sports, practiced doxologies, worked diligently at reading and writing and devoted himself to all manner of "studies." He grew up in innocence and celibacy. Having read many books of the New and Old Testaments, he was convinced that "our life is short-lasting, quick-passing and transitory, like a river's swiftness or like the flower of the grass." Following this come a few quotations from "Holy Writ" which bear out the idea of the swift passing of life.

While still a youth, Stephen took the tonsure in the town of Rostov and then, with the blessing of the bishop of Kolomna, set out to preach to the Zirani. In the land of Permia, among the Zirani, Stephen followed the ascetic form of life. He had an extremely obstinate struggle with the champions of paganism, who regarded him with distrust and tried in every way to discredit him. In spite of persecutions and threats, however, Stephen devoted himself very energetically to his task. He destroyed the heathen temple, chopped down the "bewitching," that is, the misfortune-bringing, magic birch, and, when this act was not followed by any retribution on the part of the gods, the Zirani were convinced that Stephen had right on his side. Stephen's authority increased still further after his successful contest with the Ziranian sorcerer, Pam, who was his chief opponent. Stephen was so convinced of the justice of his cause that he suggested to Pam that they settle their dispute with the help of "divine justice." First he proposed that they ascend a burning pyre together. Next, having cut two holes in the river ice, he proposed that they plunge arm in arm into one hole and come out through the other. But in each case Pam declined to make the hazardous experiment and so defaulted, leaving Stephen the victor in the contest. The Zirani were about to execute Pam but Stephen pleaded for leniency and it ended with the sorcerer merely being banished.

As has been said, Stephen's principal feat, in the author's opinion, was his invention of the Permian alphabet. Epiphanius speaks very ornately of the magnitude of this feat, bids us consider how many years the Greek philosophers took to assemble and compose the Greek system of writing and for all their labors over a long period of time were scarce able to contrive it, while "Permian writing was by one monk contrived, by one composed, by one fashioned; one hermit, one monk, one recluse, Stephen, I say, a Bishop long to be remembered; one, at one time, not at many times and over many years like those others, but one monk, one man by himself and in retirement, one solitary, one man the help of the one God asking, one man to one God for help appealing, one man to the one God praying and saying"—(Stephen's prayer follows).

Having labored in the land of Permia in the office first of priest, then of bishop; having finally brought the Zirani into orthodoxy, Stephen died happy. And his death is followed by the most rhetorical passages in the *Life*. These are found, first, in the "Lament of the People of Permia," second, in the "Lament of the Permian Church," and third, in the "Lament and Eulogy of the Monk Writing"; that is, Epiphanius himself.

The Permians, upon hearing of Stephen's death, began to weep and wail in heartfelt grief:

Woe, woe is us, brothers, for we have lost a good master and teacher! Woe, woe is us, for we are deprived of a good shepherd and ruler! Oh, why has he been taken from us who was the giver of so much good to us? Oh, why have we lost the purifier of our souls and the sympathizer with our bodies? In the first place, we have lost our kind intercessor and petitioner, who was petitioner for us both to God and to man . . .

The plaint of the Zirani goes on in the same strain for several pages: "Who shall comfort the sorrow that has seized upon us? To whom shall we look up? Where shall we hear sweet words? Where shall we enjoy your edifying conversation? Shall we see you, teacher and master, or shall we never see you more?" and so forth.

Next there is another piling up of epithets: "He alone was bishop among us, was also our lawgiver and legislator, also our baptist and apostle, and preacher, and evangelist, and confessor, priest, teacher, purifier, visitor, director, healer, high priest, guardian, pastor, preceptor, narrator, father, bishop." Nor did the author even here let slip a chance to settle political and ecclesiastical scores with Moscow. As Pam the sorcerer, when endeavoring to arouse the Permians against Stephen upon his arrival from Moscow, is made to say: "Can anything good come out of Moscow? Is it not from there that troubles have come to us, both heavy taxes and tyranny, and bailiffs and officials and overseers?" so in their lament the Permians express sorrow that Stephen—only bishop of Permia—should be buried in Moscow, which had treated him with small respect while alive.

Why has this wrong been done us by Moscow? Was there any justification for it? They have their metropolitans and prelates, while we had only a bishop, and now they have taken him, and we lack even the tomb of a bishop. The Muscovites do not respect you as we do, nor so glorify you; for we even know of some who went so far as to cast an aspersion upon you, and call you, for no reason at all, a rowdy, not apprehending the power and grace of God that resided in you and through you.

The same dislike of Moscow is perceptible in the *Life of Sergius of Radonezh* and in the preface to the *Life of Michael Aleksandrovich of Tver*.

The Permians ask that their teacher be extolled, saying:

The land of Rome extols the apostles Peter and Paul, Asia, John the Theologian; Egypt, Mark the Evangelist; Antioch, the evangelist Luke; Greece, the apostle Andrew; the land of Rus, Great Prince Vladimir, who baptized it; Moscow honors the metropolitan Peter as a new miracle-worker, the land of Rostov, Leontius, its bishop; and you, O Bishop Stephen, the land of Permia praises and honors as apostle, as teacher, as leader, as preceptor, as preacher, because through you she came to a knowledge of the true light.

As we see, the author here employs the eulogy formula first encountered in Hilarion's *Discourse of Law and Grace.*

Here, too, in the plaint of the people of Permia are examples of the metaphorical style:

We honor you as the planter of Christ's garden, for you uprooted the thorns of idolatry from the land of Permia; you furrowed her with preaching as with a plow; as with seed you sowed the teaching of bookish words in the furrows of the heart, whence ears of virtue sprang up, which the sons of Permia harvested with the sickle of faith, binding the edifying sheaves with joyous hands. Drying it as in a drying room of abstinence, threshing it as with flails of patience and storing the wheat as in granaries of the spirit, they thus eat food never failing.

After the laments of the people of Permia and of the Permian church comes the lament of Epiphanius himself. The author feels powerless to choose epithets for praising his hero. He proposes various appellations which might be applied to Stephen of Permia, larding his language with alliteration, but all these appellations prove inadequate for the saint:

But what shall I call you, O Bishop, or what shall I name you, or how call upon you and how address you, or what shall I say of you, or what proclaim concerning you? How shall I praise, how honor, how beatify you, how give an account of you and how braid you a wreath of praise? Whatever I call you, whether prophet, you have interpreted prophecies as if prophesying and, like a prophet, have guessed riddles, and to an ignorant and unbelieving people you have been as a prophet; if I name you apostle, you have done the work of an apostle, like an apostle patterning and conducting yourself, following in the footsteps of the apostles.

The author proposes a long series of possible comparisons, but all of them prove too weak for extolling the feat which Stephen accomplished. Epiphanius outdoes himself in the selection of pompous and portentous words which often sound as though purposely chosen to produce a definite quasi-musical effect. He himself very aptly describes his own eulogistic style in the following words:

Even so I, sinful and foolish, in pursuit of a word for your praising, now a word weaving, now a word breeding; now by a word my respect revealing, and of words a garland making; first picking, then plaiting, then again saying: What more can I call you? Guide to him who has strayed, finder of him who is lost, preceptor of the tempted, leader of the heart-blinded, cleanser of the polluted, recoverer of the rejected, fear of the martial, comforter of the sorrowful, feeder of him who hungers, giver to him who asks, admonisher of the foolish, succorer of the injured, kindly supplicator, faithful intercessor, of pagans the savior, of demons the exorciser, of false gods the consumer, upon idols the trampler, of God the servant, of wisdom the pursuivant, of philosophy the student, of celibacy the exponent, of justice the creator, of books the narrator, of Permian writing the originator?

Such are the idiosyncrasies of the new biographical and narrative style that Epiphanius himself defines as a "braiding of words." With Epiphanius it reached the extreme of ornateness but as a norm would be the model followed to a greater or less degree by many works of the fifteenth and sixteenth and part of the seventeenth centuries, and not by hagiographical works alone. It would be used whenever need arose for the two-edged praise and apotheosis of Russian sanctitude as symbol of the gathering power of the Russian state assembling itself around Moscow.[7]

The *Life of Sergius of Radonezh*, written later than the *Life of Stephen of Permia*, and twenty-six years after the death of Sergius, has the same general characteristics as the earlier *Life* except that "word-braiding" is here used in greater moderation and factual material more generously, perhaps because of Epiphanius' having known Sergius more intimately than he did Stephen. In the second *Life* the vernacular elements are also more noticeable.[8]

One very prolific hagiographer was Pakhomius Logothetes. In addition to other literary work, he wrote or rewrote the *Lives* of numerous Muscovite and Novgorodian saints, their eulogies and liturgies. It is typical, however, that individual works by Pakhomius promoted the interests of Moscow or those of Novgorod according to which city had given him the order. Among his *Lives* of Muscovite saints, the most important are those of Sergius of Radonezh (adapted from Epiphanius the Wise), Metropolitan Alexius and Cyril of Byelozersk; among the *Lives* of Novgorod saints, Barlaam of Khutyn and the archbishops John and Euphemius. Pakhomius specialized in moralistic panegyric; in the matter of rhetorical embellishments he markedly surpassed Cyprian. "The majority of Pakhomius' writings," concludes the author of a special study devoted to him, "are redactions of earlier monuments. It is very typical that in handling these monuments our author either adds nothing to the historical material given in previous redactions or actu-

[7] For the text of the *Life of Stephen of Permia*, see *Izd. Arkheograficheskoy komissii* (Publications Archaeographical Commission) (St. Petersburg, 1897), ed. V. G. Druzhinin. For a literary analysis see V. O. Klyuchevskii's *Drevnerusskie zhitiya svyatykh* (Early Russian Lives of Saints), pp. 92–98.

[8] Published by Archim. Leonid in *Pamyatniki drevney pismennosti* (Monuments of Early Literature) (1885).

ally drops part of the facts out of deference to the requirements of rhetoric." [9]
The traits most characteristic of the oratorical style as used in Byzantine
hagiography all found their reflection in Pakhomius. Ornamental epithets,
similes, metaphors and various figures of speech (hyperbole, personification, tautology, rhetorical questions and exclamations, and so forth) are all
generously represented.[10] To Pakhomius, as above noted, is attributed the
compilation of the chronograph of 1442.

Ideologically, the two principal ecclesiastico-monastic factions, the Josephites and the trans-Volga hermits, constituted the determining factor of fifteenth and sixteenth century lives of saints, even though formally these
lives developed along the lines laid down by ancient Byzantine tradition.
It was the author's party affiliations that determined the purport of a life as
revealed in characterization of the saint and general trend. In some *Lives*
the saint stands out, in principle and in practice, as a partisan of outward,
purely ritualistic piety and "Holy Writ," a critically unintelligent partisan,
generally speaking, often mixing apocrypha and legend, a proponent of the
right of monasteries to acquire wealth in terms of territorial possessions and
capital sums, implacable antagonist of heretics and of all heterodox thinkers,
partisan of secular authority and apologist for the political power of the Muscovite prince. Such were the Josephite fifteenth century *Lives*, that of Paph-
nutius of Borov, for example, written by Bassianus Sanin, brother of Joseph
of Volok. In other lives the cardinal points brought out are the saint's striving
for inner self-perfection, his critical attitude toward "Writ," causing him to
make strict separation of what is dogmatically authentic and authoritative
from what is dubious and unauthoritative; his negative attitude toward
monastic "greed," tolerance for heretics, sympathy for the bonded peasantry,
and, finally, his attitude of reserve toward princely power and secular power
in general, all of which qualities resulted from the close connection of trans-
Volga monasticism with the prince-boyar faction, economically and politically hard-pressed and therefore oppositionally inclined, which was being
squeezed out by the nobles' faction then gradually coming into power and
socially bound up with official Josephism, as was pointed out above. Such is
the type of saint that figures in the *Lives* of Dmitry Prilutsky, Dionysius
Glushitsky, and such others as were composed during the late fifteenth and
early sixteenth centuries among the trans-Volga hermits.

[9] V. Yablonskii, *Pakhomii Serb i evo agiograficheskie pisaniya* (Pakhomius Serb and
His Hagiographic Writings) (St. Petersburg, 1908), p. 238.
[10] For a detailed analysis of the style of Pakhomius, see Yablonsky, *op cit.*, pp. 241–275.

TALES OF THE ROUT OF MAMAY

IN 1380 the battle of Kulikovo took place, a crushing blow dealt the Tartars by a coalition of Russian princes under the leadership of the Muscovite Prince Dmitry Ivanovich. The successful issue of the battle constitutes one of the major political events in Russian history. On the one hand the Russian victory on the field of Kulikovo was the first really serious attempt to liberate Rus from the Tartar yoke, already of more than one hundred and fifty years' duration, a harbinger of complete emancipation from foreign servitude, and on the other it exalted and confirmed the authority of the Muscovite prince, chief organizer of the victory. Folk literature gave quick response to this event in *byliny* about Batu, Kalinetsar, Vasily Ignatevich, Mamay.

Several works of written literature are also associated with the events of the battle. First of all we have a chronicle account, the most immediate reaction to circumstances connected with Kulikovo. This narrative was included in all editions of the fourth *Novgorod Chronicle,* then in the first *St. Sophia* and in the *Resurrection:* it was largely influenced by the *Life of Alexander Nevsky.* Here the center of the stage is already given the Muscovite prince, Dmitry Ivanovich, by whom, in conjunction with his cousin, Prince Vladimir Andreyevich of Serpukhovo, and the two sons of Olgerd, Andrew of Polotsk and Dmitry of Bryansk, the victory over the Tartars had been won.

The narrative tells how, with the support of a traitor, Prince Oleg Ivanovich of Ryazan, and of the Lithuanian prince Yagailo, the infidel king Mamay attacked Rus. Dmitry Ivanovich, head of the coalition organized to oppose the Tartars, reveals himself first and foremost as a religious man:

before setting out on the campaign he prays to God and asks Bishop Gerasim for his blessing.

The clash between Russians and Tartars on the Feast of the Nativity of the Virgin, that is, the 8th of September, resulting in the rout of the Tartars at the river Nepryadva, is described in the regular war-story style. Mamay then suffers another defeat at the hands of Khan Tokhtamysh, flees to Kaffa, the present Feodosiya, and there perishes. Dmitry Ivanovich returns in triumph and laden with booty. Hearing of the tyrannical acts of Oleg of Ryazan, he makes ready to send an army against him. The boyars of Ryazan petition him and he sets his deputies over their city.

The chronicle narrative was followed by other literary echoes of the event, as to the chronological sequence of which some difference of opinion exists. A critical survey of literature on the subject was made by S. K. Shambinago in a special study of narratives inspired by the battle of Kulikovo.[1] The principal results of his research are in brief as follows:

At the very end of the fourteenth century there appeared a short chronicle narrative of the rout, having literary associations with the traditional style and rhetorical embellishments borrowed from chronicle narratives, more particularly from the latest Novgorod redaction of the *Life of Alexander Nevsky*. Names of princes and generals killed were taken from the *Synodikon*. At about the middle of the fifteenth century an expanded chronicle narrative appeared, showing greater rhetoricalness: here epithets are added, tautological locutions inserted, prayers augmented and new quotations from "Holy Writ" added. Further, the expanded edition emphasizes the negative characterization of Oleg of Ryazan, calling him a betraying Judas, a headless-beast-fratricidal-Svyatopolk. Later on, in the fifteenth century, the narrative underwent new revisions.

The literary adaptation of the subject of Mamay's defeat that S. K. Shambinago considers closest chronologically to the brief chronicle narrative is the work traditionally called, on the basis of the title in the oldest copy, *Zadonshchina*, but by him denominated the *Communication*, for the wholly insufficient reason that the first lines of the text of the monument read: "For, brethren, it is better for us to begin our communication in other words." Sources for *Zadonshchina* were the *Tale of Igor's Expedition*, oral accounts, and the chronicle narrative. S. K. Shambinago hypothetically assigns the appearance of *Zadonshchina* to the first quarter of the fifteenth century, chiefly because the oldest copy dates from the end of the fifteenth century. He believes the author of *Zadonshchina* to have been the priest Sophonia,

---

[1] "Povesti o Mamaevom poboishche" (Tales of the Rout of Mamay), *Sbornik otd. russk. yaz. i slov.* (Collection of the Division of Russian Language and Literature of the Academy of Sciences) (St. Petersburg, 1906), Vol. LXXXI, No. 7.

earlier a Bryansk boyar. Shambinago restores the text of the monument by collating the three copies known to him with fragments of the monument found in the second or, preferably, in the third edition of a work known as the *Communication and Legend of the Rout of Mamay,* which used *Zadonshchina* to ornament its own presentation of the subject.

The next, or third, stage in the development of the subject of the battle of Kulikovo, was, according to S. K. Shambinago, the monument traditionally called the *Communication and Legend of the Rout by Great Prince Dmitry Ivanovich,* and called by S. K. Shambinago simply the *Legend.* This is extant in a large number of copies, which S. K. Shambinago divides into four editions.

The first edition, represented by the text found in the *Nikonian Chronicle,* goes back to a rewriting of the chronicle narrative from a special angle. Occasionally it uses the *Tale of Igor's Expedition* and *Zadonshchina,* but to a minimal degree. This version promotes to first place Metropolitan Cyprian, the great prince here assuming an attitude of submission and humility, and showing no personal initiative whatever. His victory is as if foreordained from on high, and the glorification of his own personal qualities and those of Prince Vladimir Andreyevich takes second place. The author of the first redaction, personal pleader for Cyprian, was perhaps a functionary in the metropolitan chancellery. S. K. Shambinago assigns this edition to the beginning of the second quarter of the fifteenth century.

In the second edition, Cyprian's part in events and that of the Muscovite church dignitaries, Metropolitan Peter and Sergius of Radonezh, is far outweighed by the personal initiative of Dmitry Ivanovich. This edition, rhetorically ornate, is greatly augmented by borrowings from *Zadonshchina,* with the purpose of giving greater interest and beauty to the narrative. Basically it goes back to the same protograph of the chronicle narrative as the first edition. S. K. Shambinago dates it as of the end of the sixteenth century, for one thing because it utilized the *Life of Gregory Omiritsky,* the translation of which the author synchronizes with the compilation of Makarius' *Chetyi Minyei;* that is, the 1560's.[2]

The third edition, represented by the greatest number of copies, preserves, with very slight deviations, the same general outline as the second. The peculiarity that distinguishes it from the latter is the substitution of the name Olgerd for Yagailo. S. K. Shambinago interprets this substitution as the editor's deliberate attempt to heighten the moral effect of the narrative. The brothers Olgerdovich, in giving support to the Russian Orthodox cause, no

[2] However, the *Life of Gregory Omiritsky* was translated earlier, as A. V. Markov points out in his review of S. K. Shambinago's study in the *Zhurnal min. nar. prosv.* (Journal of the Ministry of Public Instruction) (1908), No. 4, p. 441.

longer revolt against their brother but against their father himself. Stylistically it is characterized by extreme embellishment: redundant epithets are
added and ornate verbosity makes episodes run longer. Borrowings from
Zadonshchina are even more extensive than in the second edition. It was
composed somewhere between the sixteenth and eighteenth centuries.

Finally, in the fourth edition, as S. K. Shambinago observed, almost all
borrowings from *Zadonshchina* are omitted and the number of episodes increased, with the result that it becomes the longest of the redactions. Moreover it is divided into chapters, each carrying a special heading. In 1674 it
was printed as part of a historical manual, *Synopsis,* work of the Ukrainian
writer, Innocent Gizel, and S. K. Shambinago thinks that its appearance
must date from approximately the time when *Synopsis* was published;
namely, the beginning of the latter half of the seventeenth century.

We also get several adaptations and abridgements of these basic narratives.

Such in sum are S. K. Shambinago's findings as to the history of the rise
and development of narratives about the rout of Mamay. These findings
were reviewed at length by A. A. Shakhmatov,[3] who arrived at the following
conclusions. Toward the end of the fourteenth century, perhaps a year,
perhaps two years after the battle of Kulikovo, the original, inextant, version
of the chronicle narrative of the rout of Mamay appeared. Its place of composition was Moscow. The central figure was Great Prince Dmitry Ivanovich. At the same time the official report on the great prince's campaign
was drawn up. Simultaneously a description of the rout of Mamay, akin in
style to the *Tale of Igor's Expedition,* was composed at the court of Prince
Vladimir Andreyevich of Serpukhovo, glorifying Vladimir Andreyevich and
the Olgerdoviches. (The prince of Serpukhovo had married Olgerd's daughter Elena.) Shakhmatov calls this work the *Tale of the Rout of Mamay.* The
central figures in the tale were Dmitry Ivanovich, Vladimir Andreyevich,
the brothers Olgerdovich, and the general Dmitry Bobrok (a Volynian).

At the beginning of the fifteenth century, on the basis of the *Tale of
Igor's Expedition* and the *Tale of the Rout of Mamay,* Sofonia's *Communication (Zadonshchina)* was composed. During the first half of the fifteenth
century, or perhaps even by the end of the fourteenth century, the early
chronicle narrative found its way into the *Muscovite Chronicle* and was
there amplified and revised on the basis of the official report and the *Tale
of the Rout of Mamay.* In 1423 the narrative was included in the metropolitan's all-Russian digest, undergoing on this occasion only trifling
changes. Next the narrative was included in the Novgorod digest of 1448,

[3] See *Otchyot o 12-M prisuzhdenii premii mitropolita Makariya* (Report on the Twelfth
Award of the Metropolitan Macarius Prize) (St. Petersburg, 1910), pp. 79–204.

which presently became model on the one hand for the fourth *Novgorod,* and on the other for the first *St. Sophia Chronicle.* At the beginning of the sixteenth century the metropolitan's chronicle digest was composed: for this a legend of the Don rout was compiled on the basis of the narrative in the *Muscovite Chronicle,* the *Tale of the Rout of Mamay,* and the *Communication* of Sofonia (*Zadonshchina*). This legend is given more or less in full in the Tolstoy and the other separate copies (belonging, by S. K. Shambinago's classification, to the third redaction). A. A. Shakhmatov also disagrees with S. K. Shambinago's assertion that the text included in the *Nikonian Chronicle* was the first edition of the *Legend.* Its considerable resemblance to the text of the chronicle narrative is, according to Shakhmatov, a retroactive manisfestation connected with the fact that in the Nikonian digest interpolations are of common occurrence. Nor is it a valid argument in favor of the chronological priority of the text in the Nikonian digest to assert that this text shows minimal influence of *Zadonshchina,* since the influence is demonstrably almost as great on this as on the other editions, and may be explained as due to the influence of *Zadonshchina* on the basic, inextant edition of the *Legend,* restorable by isolating the passages that the first three editions have in common.[4]

Zadonshchina is extant in five copies—from the fifteenth, sixteenth and seventeenth centuries (three exemplars), the oldest of which, the Byelozersk-St. Cyril, 1470,[5] lacks the end. Unfortunately all copies are plainly defective. At times they show the carelessness and scant literacy of the copyist. Not one of them reproduces the original with any exactitude. Attempts have been made by scholars to construct a diplomatic text of *Zadonshchina* on the basis of published copies. One such attempt was made by Sreznevsky, a second by Shambinago. In what follows we shall proceed from the text as reconstructed by S. K. Shambinago.

Zadonshchina, like the *Tale of Igor's Expedition,* begins with an introduction in which the author invites the "brothers, friends, and sons of Rus" to gather together and join word to word, to make glad the land of Rus and cast grief upon the eastern land, into the lot of Shem (Byzantine chronographs and Russian chronicles regard the eastern peoples as descendants of Shem, one of the sons of Noah), to proclaim the victory over Mamay, and

---

[4] The first edition of the *Legend* is printed in Vol. XI of the *Full Collection of Russian Chronicles (Nikonian Chronicle),* the others in *op. cit.* by Shambinago. The third edition is also printed in *izd. OLDP, Skazanie o Mamaevom poboishche* (Legend of the Rout of Mamay) with preface by Shambinago (St. Petersburg, 1907), where the old illustrations are reproduced.

[5] The latest edition (facsimile) is that of P. K. Simoni in *Pamyatniki starinnogo russkogo yazyka i slovesnosti XV–XVIII vv.* (Monuments of Ancient Russian Language and Literature of the Fifteenth-Eighteenth Centuries) (Petrograd, 1922), Pt. 3.

render praise to Great Prince Dmitry Ivanovich and his brother Prince Vladimir Andreyevich. Then, in imitation of the *Tale of Igor's Expedition,* the author continues:

And let us tell the tale like this: for it is better for us, brethren, to begin communicating our eulogy of Great Prince Dmitry Ivanovich and his brother Prince Vladimir Andreyevich, great-grandsons of Vladimir, Prince of Kiev, in words other than those used in eulogistic tales of the present day. Let us begin our communication in accord with the facts and the *byliny.*

Here, as in many other passages of *Zadonshchina,* it is difficult to determine what to regard as corruptions in the text due to the copyist and what to attribute to the author's clumsy, purely superficial imitation of the style of the *Igor,* without any attempt to make sense of his rhetorical tinsel. In the same mock-rhetorical manner, with the same careful, backward look at the *Tale of Igor's Expedition,* he next mentions "wise Boyan":

We shall not be lifted off the earth in thought; we shall mention the times of early years, shall praise the wise Boyan, skilled harpist of Kiev. For that wise Boyan, laying his golden fingers on the living strings, sang the glory of the princes of Rus: of Rurik, the first prince, of Igor Rurikovich, of Vladimir Svyatoslavich, of Yaroslav Vladimirovich.

This eulogy is called forth by the fact that Dmitry Ivanovich and his brother Vladimir Andreyevich "had courage and zeal for the land of Rus and for the Christian religion," that they "armed their minds with their strength, sharpened their hearts with courage and were filled with martial spirit, appointed for themselves brave captains in the land of Rus, remembering their great-grandfather, Great Prince Vladimir of Kiev."

And we shall meet in other passages this literal borrowing from the *Tale of Igor's Expedition,* with an addition typical of the epoch: "And for the Christian religion."

After mentioning Boyan, the author addresses the lark: "O lark, the joy of fair days! Fly up to the blue clouds, sing the glory of Great Prince Dmitry Ivanovich and his brother Vladimir Andreyevich. Here no storm has borne falcons from the land beyond the forest to the Polovcian plain."

Parallel to the account in the *Igor* of Russian troops preparing for the campaign, we find in *Zadonshchina* an assembling of Russian troops: "Horses neigh on the Moskva; drums beat at Kolomna; trumpets blare at Serpukhovo; glory rings throughout all the land of Rus: in marvelous array the standards rise on the bank of the great Don; the embroidered banners wave." The men of Novgorod stand by St. Sophia and speak as follows: "We shall get there too late, brothers, to aid Great Prince Dmitry Ivanovich." Then, like a flock of eagles, the Russian armies flew down from the north.

After this comes one of those negative parallelisms also typical of the *Igor*:

No, it was not eagles flying in a flock, it was all the princes of Rus riding in company to the aid of Great Prince Dmitry Ivanovich, and they spoke as follows: "Lord, great Prince, already the pagan Tartars are invading our fields and taking our patrimony from us; they stand between Don and Dnieper on the river Mecha."

In response to this appeal, Dmitry Ivanovich says to Vladimir Andrey-evich:

"Let us go, brother, beyond the swift river Don; let us obtain a miracle for our lands, an old men's tale, a memory for the young, and try the bravery of our men, and infuse the river Don with blood, for the land of Rus and for the Christian faith."

The locution is the same as that found in the *Igor* except for the fact that the *Igor* portrays not the "Christian faith" but "the wounds of Igor, bold son of Svyatoslav."

In general *Zadonshchina* is distinguished from the *Igor* by its much thicker veneer of Christianity, evidences of which are minimal in the earlier work.

The author of the *Igor* would have preferred to let Boyan sing of Igor's campaign and he compares Boyan to a nightingale. The author of *Zadon-shchina* likewise addresses the nightingale: "O nightingale! Would that you might sing the glory of these two brothers, Olgerd's two sons, Andrew of Polotzk and Dmitry of Bryansk [that is, the two princes who recognized the authority of the Muscovite prince and received their appanages from him]. For these are brave sons, born on a shield, swaddled to the sound of trumpets, cradled to the sight of helmets, fed from the point of a spear, and given drink from a sharp sword in the Lithuanian land."

As is not difficult to see, the author of *Zadonshchina*, in his effort to imi-tate the style of the *Igor*, makes use of images which are, strictly speaking, indefensible from the viewpoint of sense. In actual fact how could anyone drink from a sharp sword? But the picturesqueness of the images in the *Igor* so captivated the author of *Zadonshchina* that he did not always discriminate as to their meaning.

As Vsevolod in the *Slovo* proposes to Igor that he saddle his swift horses, saying that his own are already in trim, "saddled at Kursk," so Dmitry in almost the same words proposes to Andrew of Polotzk: "Saddle, brother Andrew, your swift horses, and mine are ready, saddled before yours."

Like the participants in Igor's campaign, the participants in that of Dmitry Ivanovich are beset by ominous portents of nature: strong winds come up from the sea; they drive a great cloud to the mouth of the Dnieper, against the land of Rus. From the cloud bloody streaks shoot out, and blue light-nings quiver through them. There will be clamor and great thunder between

Don and Dnieper, and men's bodies will fall on the field of Kulikovo and blood will be shed at the river Nepryadva.

The ominous shrieks of birds and beasts of which we read in the *Igor* are also heard in *Zadonshchina*: "Already their misfortunes have driven the birds to the shelter of the clouds; ravens often croak and jackdaws chatter, eagles give cry, wolves howl menacingly, and foxes bark over the bones."

Russians meet Tartars on the field of Kulikovo. "On the field of Kulikovo mighty clouds came together, and from them blue lightnings often flashed and great thunderclaps resounded." It is the sons of Rus fighting the "pagan Tartars" for the great offense done them; the golden armor of the Russians flashes; their steel swords ring on the helmets of the Orientals.

In the *Tale of Igor's Expedition*, Igor's brother Vsevolod is compared to an aurochs; in *Zadonshchina* Russian soldiers are compared to aurochs: "It was not the bellow of aurochs in the morning by the great Don on the field of Kulokovo—it was the roar of mighty generals, the warriors of Great Prince Dmitry Ivanovich, stricken and cut down by pagan Tartars.

The order of events in *Zadonshchina* is the reverse of that in the *Igor*: in the *Igor* it is first victory for the Russians then defeat; in *Zadonshchina* it is the other way round: the Russian armies first suffer defeat, then, rallying, deal the Tartars a crushing blow.

After telling of the Tartar victory, the author says, again in the manner of the *Slovo*, that in the land of Rus at this time: "Plowmen do not call out, nor do trumpets blare; only the ravens croak often; the cuckoos give voice, waiting for human corpses." The birds chirp plaintive songs over the defeat of the Russians. Princesses and boyar women and the wives of all the generals lament for their slain husbands.

Parallel to the passages in the *Tale of Igor's Expedition* dealing with the lament of the Russian women and later with that of Yaroslavna, *Zadonshchina* carries an account of the lament of the generals' wives, one of whom beseeches the Don to "waft back" her lord, just as Yaroslavna besought the Dnieper. The women of Kolomna, rebuking the river Moskva for "wafting" their husbands to the Polovcians' land, address this question to Dmitry Ivanovich: "Can you, Lord Great Prince Dmitry Ivanovich, bail Dnieper out with your oars or dam the Don with bodies of Tartars?" Here it is imitating Svyatoslav's appeal to Vsevolod-Great-Nest in the *Tale of Igor's Expedition.*

The decisive clash between Russians and Tartars takes place when the reserve comes out from ambush, the regiment of Dmitry's cousin Vladimir Andreyevich, whom *Zadonshchina* describes in almost the terms used to describe Igor's brother Vsevolod in the *Slovo.*

Together with General Dmitry, the Volynian, who rallies princes and boyars about him, Vladimir Andreyevich hurls himself upon the Tartars. Like falcons the Russians swoop down, up gallops Dmitry the Volynian with his troops, attacks the great Tartar army; steel swords clash on Oriental helmets. The Russian army cut off the Tartar field with their war cry and lighted it with their gilded armor.

In the *Slovo* the black earth was sown with the bones of the sons of Rus; in *Zadonshchina*: "The black earth under the horses' hoofs was sown with Tartar bones and watered with their blood." The mighty armies engaged, trampled hills and meadows. Rivers, streams, and lakes were muddied. The sons of Rus plundered the Tartar treasure, carrying off to their own land the enemies' horses, camels, silk stuffs, gold, silver, stout armor, and costly pearls. "Already the Russian women are playing with Tartar gold," as in the *Slovo* the Gothic maidens clinked the Russian gold.

Zadonshchina ends with the statement that Dmitry Ivanovich stood on the field of Kulikovo, by the river Nepryadva, and his brother Vladimir Andreyevich and his generals with him, by the bones of the fallen Russian soldiers, and pronounced a eulogy upon them.

Although being, as indicated above, so largely an imitation of the *Igor*, *Zadonshchina* is not without poetic merits; that it is characterized by vivid artistic imagery may be seen both from the foregoing discussion and from such a picture as:

Then the hawks and falcons and white gyrfalcons tore loose from their gilded perches, tore off their silken fetters, circling up to the blue sky, ringing their little gilded bells over the swift Don: they will strike at many flocks of geese and swans, and the Russian bogatyrs will strike at the great forces of the pagan king Mamay.

For all its dependence on the *Slovo*, however, *Zadonshchina* does not once follow the *Slovo* where it displays pagan elements. Not once does it mention pagan deities, and of the mythical beings present in the *Slovo* imports only Div, and, as appears, for example, from the meaningless phrase: "Div cries in the land of Rus beneath the Tartar swords," even he was brought in quite mechanically, without any attempt to explain his mythological nature, as certain other expressions in the *Slovo* are mechanically and pointlessly carried over—such as the word "steel" in the combination "steel riverbanks." On the other hand, in accord with the role that the Church had started to play at this time, the ecclesiastico-religious trend stands out in *Zadonshchina* very prominently. Several times Dmitry Ivanovich speaks of the struggle with the Tartars as being not only in behalf of the "land of Rus," but also "for the Christian faith" and even "for the holy churches." Before the battle he prays to God and to the Virgin. The princes Boris and Gleb protect him.

Zadonshchina also differs considerably from the *Slovo* in the matter of ideology. The concept of the land of Rus is here already associated with the concept of the Muscovite principality, with its Great Prince Dmitry Ivanovich rallying the Russian princes around him to do battle with the Tartars. It is very indicative that, in contradiction of historical fact, the author of *Zadonshchina* should say: "All the Russian princes came to the aid" of the Muscovite prince, whereas we know that this was not the case, and that Oleg of Ryazan, as well as Yagailo Olgerdovich of Lithuania, was in league with Mamay against the coalition of princes headed by Dmitry Ivanovich. It is also typical that the princes Dmitry Ivanovich and Vladimir Andreyevich should three times be called great-grandsons of Prince Vladimir Svyatoslavich of Kiev, this artificial genealogy quite evidently being introduced with a view to enhancing their authority.

Thus *Zadonshchina* distinctly reveals that Muscovite tendency which in course of time would become stronger and stronger, until in the sixteenth century it would attain monopoly. We need not wonder at finding a Ryazan priest the enunciator of this tendency: as the chronicle account testifies, Dmitry's victory had forced Oleg and his family to flee Ryazan while it brought Dmitry the request of the Ryazan boyars that he settle his deputies there. The author of *Zadonshchina*, who before becoming a priest in Ryazan had probably been a boyar attached to Dmitry of Bryansk, member of the coalition against Mamay, avoids on the one hand gratuitously compromising the already compromised prince of Ryazan when he leaves his alliance with Mamay against Dmitry unmentioned, while on the other he reveals his own allegiance to the Muscovite prince, to whom the Ryazan district had declared full loyalty.

The *Legend* shows in still greater degree the ecclesiastico-political bias and the Moscovite tendency, inasmuch as it appeared in Moscow and later than *Zadonshchina*.

NARRATIVE OF THE LIFE AND DEATH OF GREAT PRINCE DMITRY IVANOVICH, TSAR OF RUS

Thematically the narrative, *Of the Life and Death of Great Prince Dmitry Ivanovich, Tsar of Rus*, belongs with the tales of the rout of Mamay. It was apparently composed shortly after the death of Dmitry Ivanovich (1389); at any rate it was already present in the Novgorod digest of 1448. It is characterized by that high-flown rhetorical and flowery style which began to be fashionable in this country at the end of the fourteenth century and in which the *Life of Stephen of Permia* was written. The set forms of hagiographical eulogy are here combined with elements from the war-story style of which prototypes are to be found in the *Life of Alexander Nevsky* and the chronicle account of the rout of Mamay. In ideological trend the narrative anticipates the *Stepennaya Kniga,* the aim of which was to endow the founders of the Muscovite state with the twin attributes of piety and sanctity.

The narrative begins with a statement to the effect that Prince Dmitry was born "of pious and honored parents." It next mentions the prince's ancestors—as was later to be the practice of the *Stepennaya Kniga*—his grandfather Ivan Danilovich Kalita, consolidator of the land of Rus, and that "fruitful branch and lovely flower of the garden planted by God, Tsar Vladimir, the new Constantine," baptizer of the land of Rus, and also the princes Boris and Gleb. Dmitry was reared "in piety and glory" and "loved God from the time he was in swaddling clothes." He was early left an orphan. His father died when Dmitry was in his ninth year. Shortly afterwards his mother also died, and he assumed "the scepter of dominion over the land of Rus." While still but a youth he "was diligent in spiritual matters and kept from idle talk," always consorted with "good" people, avoided bad people. He always hearkened with emotion to Divine Scripture, was solicitous for the churches of God, guarded the land of Rus with his courage; he was endowed with understanding, was dreaded, and vanquished many enemies in battle. He threw splendid walls of defense about the city of Moscow and was renowned throughout the world; "like a cedar in Lebanon he increased and like a phoenix in the woods he flourished."

When Dmitry was sixteen he married Princess Avdotya, and the whole land of Rus rejoiced at this marriage. The spouses lived purely, striving for their souls' salvation, walked not "after the flesh," and conducted themselves "like a pilot crossing the waves against the wind, guided by a Providence from on high."

And his fame increased like that of the sainted Great Prince Vladimir. The land of Rus flourished during his reign as aforetime the promised land of Israel had flourished. With dread of his power he fenced in the whole land of Rus; from the east unto the west his name was glorified; from sea to sea, from the rivers even unto the ends of the earth his fame was exalted. Neighboring kings marveled at him; his enemies were filled with jealousy.

The jealousy of Dmitry's enemies, leading them to incite Mamay against him, is given as the reason for the Tartars' attack upon Rus. First Mamay dispatched his general Bigich against the Russians with a large army and many princes of the Horde. Dmitry, with the help of God and the Virgin, won a brilliant victory over them in the Ryazan district. Then, put to shame, Mamay himself attacked Dmitry. Having prayed to God, Dmitry gathered his nobles and all the princes of Rus over whom he held sway, summoning them to defend the Orthodox faith. The nobles and princes replied that they were ready to lay down their lives for him, the tsar of Rus. After again praying to God and "with the great and sainted bishop and wonder-worker Peter, intercessor for the land of Rus, to aid him," Dmitry advanced against Mamay.

At this point the battle itself is described in the war-story clichés already familiar to us:

And meeting like mighty clouds, their weapons flashing like lightning on a rainy day, the armies fought hand to hand, and blood flowed down the valley, and Don River flowed mingled with blood, while Tartar heads rolled like stones, and the bodies of the pagans were hacked down like oak trees; moreover, many of the faithful saw God's angels helping the Christians.

The religious cast of the narrative is in evidence every step of the way. God and Dmitry's kinsmen Boris and Gleb helped him vanquish the enemy; the unbelieving Mamay perished without a trace; peace came to the land of Rus; the neighboring peoples, hearing of Dmitry's victory, "all bowed beneath his hand" and the schismatics and rebels who had dwelt in his realm all perished.

Next comes an ornate eulogy of Dmitry's piety: like the prophet David it was his custom to love the innocent but pardon the guilty. As in the Book of Job, he

is like a father to his people, eyes to the blind, feet to the lame. He is a pillar and a sentinel and a standard, judging his subjects to the knowledge of all, having received his governance over mankind from Divine Providence; putting right all manner of worldly confusion, a high-soaring eagle, a fire to scorch ungodliness, a bath that cleanses of pollution, a threshing floor for purity, a wind blowing away the chaff, a bed for those who are weary in God's work, a trumpet for sleepers, a peaceful governor, a crown of victory, a port for the mariner, a ship for wealth, weapons against the enemy, a sword of wrath, a wall inviolable, a net for the wicked, a firm stair, a mirror for living, doing everything with God's help and ruling in God; a lofty mind, a humble spirit, peace in time of storm, a deep of understanding; he confirmed the princes of Rus each in his province, and kept order and harmony among his nobles.

He offended none, loved all equally, instructing the young with precepts, extending his hand to the needy. He may not have been a scholar, but the books of the spirit he had in his heart.

This bombastic eulogy gives still another beautiful example of that "braiding of words" which also typified Epiphanius the Wise. Passing over several equally pompous eulogies to the pious prince, let us proceed to the account of his death. He dies in the same pious and Christian manner in which he had lived. As his end draws near, he gives a complete set of instructions to the princess, his sons, his boyars. Then comes an enumeration of the appanages which as a father he leaves to his sons.

The account of the death of Dmitry Ivanovich is followed by a description of his wife's lament, in which elements of learned rhetoric are combined with tricks of style typical of the oral folk lament.

At sight of the dead prince, the princess "burst into bitter weeping, shed scorching tears from her eyes, her heart on fire within her, and beat her breast with her hands, like a trumpet announcing the battle and like an organ sweetly pealing." Next follow prolonged laments having a distinct artistry of expression:

How could you die, my beloved, and leave me a lonely widow? Why did I not die first? How could the light of my eyes be extinguished? Where have you gone, treasure of my life? Why do you not speak to me? My beautiful flower, why did you fade so early? O fruitful vine, no longer do you yield fruit for my heart and sweetmeats for my soul. Why, my lord, do you not look up at me or speak to me? Have you already forgotten me? . . . My sun, you have set too soon; my beautiful moon, you have waned too early; star of the east, why have you gone into the west? . . . Where, my lord, are your fame and honor, where your sovereignty? Do you not hear, my lord, these poor words of mine? Do my bitter tears not move you to pity? The beasts of the field return to their lairs and the birds of the air fly to their nests, and it is not well, my lord, that you should have left your house.

A comparison of these lamentations with those voiced by Gleb in the anonymous *Legend of Boris and Gleb* when he learns of his father's death, will at once make clear the extent of advance in rhetorical pomp and circumstance represented by our narrative.

After telling of the prince's burial and of the universal lamentation attending it, the author in his own person exclaims passionately:

Oh, what a terrifying prodigy, brothers, and how passing strange! What a fearful and awe-inspiring vision! Hear me, heaven, and prompt me, earth. How can I write or how speak of the death of this great prince? From grief of soul I am tongue-tied, my lips are stopped, my throat is mute, sense plays me false, my sight is dim, strength fails me.

Next, like Epiphanius the Wise in the *Life of Stephen of Permia*, the author seeks figures from biblical history with whom he may compare Dmitry and cannot find his equal. Neither Adam, nor Noah, nor Abraham and Isaac, nor even Moses will bear comparison with Dmitry. Like Epiphanius he varies Hilarion's formula, paraphrasing the passages about different lands praising their patron saints to read that the whole land of Rus praises Dmitry.

The narrative ends, as is usual for Old Russian lives, with a request that Dmitry pray for the land of Rus there in heaven, and also that he forgive the author for his clumsiness and unreason: with such words as were at his disposal he had been powerless to render Dmitry Ivanovich due praise.[6]

We see how a narrative about a layman is here turned, essentially, into the life of a saint. The author even calls Dmitry a saint directly: "And pray, saint, for your kin and for all the people," though Dmitry was canonized neither then nor later. His princely authority is likewise put on a high pedestal and given an aura of sanctity. Here we already have in germ that apotheosis of the great prince's, later the tsar's, authority, which will assume its most striking forms in the sixteenth century and be employed with particularly telling effect in the political practice of Ivan the Terrible.

It is not so much a matter of Dmitry Ivanovich, the man, being given a halo of sanctity, however, as of the Muscovite prince commanding special respect, the prince who will take the title of Tsar, "Great Prince of all Rus, Lord of all the Land of Rus." So viewed, the narrative *Of the Life and Death* played an extremely important part in propagandizing the political monopoly of the Muscovite principality.

TALE OF THE TAKING OF TSARGRAD

In 1453 Constantinople was taken by the Turks, an event which exercised an enormous influence on the development of Russian political and religious ideology. Rus, particularly Moscow, observantly watching the progressive political decline of Byzantium, had more and more been emancipating itself from the reverence traditionally surrounding the state which had earlier acted as religious patron to Rus and had formerly been the unquestioned cultural authority. The Florentine Union of 1439, consummated by Byzantium with Rome in the hope of obtaining support from the western states, and actually making the Byzantine Church subject to the Roman pope, definitely discredited Greek Orthodoxy in the eyes of the official representatives of Russian piety and at the same time exalted Russian Orthodoxy.

In a polemic monument composed in 1461 and bearing the title, *Discourse Selected from Sacred Writings in Latin,* some unknown author, apropos of the events of the Florentine Union, speaks of the land of Rus and of the Muscovite great prince, Vasily Vasilyevich, as the custodians of genuine Orthodoxy, using such ultrabombastic and pretentious expressions as:

And now in the latter times, God-enlightened land of Rus, it behooves you and your people to rejoice in the universal subsolar radiance of true Orthodoxy

[6] The narrative is printed in Vol. IV of the *Full Collection of Russian Chronicles,* pp. 349–357, and also in Vol. VI, pp. 104–111.

in faith, arrayed in the illumination of piety, having the cloak of God upon you—the radiant grace of God—your arms filled with flowers blooming in God's sight —God's temples, holy churches shining like stars in the sky, nay, gleaming like the rays of the sun, adorned in splendor and glorified with selections from sacred song—under the dominion of the God-chosen, God-beloved, God-respected and God-enlightened and God-sent man who governs you in the righteous way of God-appointed law, and the divinely wise student of sacred rules, blessed zealot for God and furtherer of the true Orthodoxy by his piety, petitioner to the Most High in true faith, the God-invested and greatly ruling, faithful and pious Great Prince Vasily Vasilyevich, God-crowned in Orthdoxy, Tsar of all Rus.[7]

In an epistle to Basil III, dating from the beginning of the sixteenth century, the monk-ancient Filofey wrote that up to that time there had been two Romes: the first Rome fell because of its own impiety; the second Rome, that is, Byzantium, fell by constraint of the Agars; but the third Rome—Moscow—was to stand fast, and there would be no fourth Rome.

This concept of Moscow as the third Rome, already in germ during the second half of the fifteenth century, of Moscow as heir to world empire in the sense in which Byzantium had formerly been so considered, was on the one hand conditioned by the thought trend of a whole series of literary monuments, and on the other fostered by that pompous, solemn style which was a counterpart to the solemnity and monumentality of the conception itself of Moscow as heir to the political and religious culture of Byzantium.

One literary repercussion to the conquest of Constantinople was the *Tale of the Taking of Tsargrad* written by a certain Nestor-Iskander. This was a detailed description of all the military alarms and excursions that attended the conquest of Constantinople by the Turks.

Nestor-Iskander was by origin Russian and Orthodox, but having lived in Turkey since childhood and been converted to Islam (the Mahometan name Iskander corresponds to the Orthodox Alexander), he took part in the siege of Constantinople, though secretly sympathizing with the Greeks as Christians. He evidently made day-by-day notes on the siege of the town, and upon entering it along with the Turkish army supplemented them by items obtained from the defenders of Constantinople as to what had gone on inside the town during its siege. Later these notes were revised by some scholar and filled in with items about the founding of Tsargrad derived chiefly from the chronicle of Georgius Hamartolas, and with interpolations of an ecclesiastical character (prayers and portents) and prophetic predic-

---

[7] A. S. Pavlov, *Retsenziya na trud A. Popova "Istoriko-literaturnyi obzor drevnerusskikh polemicheskikh sochinenii protiv latinyan"* (Critique of A. Popov's Work, Historico-Literary Survey of Early Russian Polemical Works Directed Against the Latins) (Moscow, 1875), printed in *Otchet o 19-m prisuzhdenii nagrad gr. Uvarova* (Report on the Nineteenth Award of the Count Uvarov Prize) (St. Petersburg, 1878), pp. 293–294.

tions as to the subsequent fate of Tsargrad. The result obtained was a narrative informed with a definite religio-political tendency.[8]

The popularity of the narrative in Rus was conditioned by the fact that official ideologists of the Russian empire had brought this empire to regard itself as heir to the Byzantine political and religious tradition. The narrative contains the prophecy of Leo the Wise about a "blond" people destined to deliver Tsargrad from the power of the infidels. And here, by the simple substitution for *rusyi* of the similar *russkii*, we get the interpretation that the Russian people is to be the deliverer of Tsargrad.

The narrative begins with an account of the founding of Tsargrad by the emperor Constantinus Flavius in the fourth century. After a conference with his nobles, Constantine decides to set up his residence in Byzantium. While the city is building, a portent appears: suddenly a serpent emerges from its hole and at the same instant an eagle swoops down, seizes the serpent and carries it aloft. The serpent winds itself about the eagle. The emperor and all the people watch in consternation for what will happen next. The eagle, after soaring high aloft, falls to earth, for it has been vanquished by the serpent. The people come to the eagle's rescue and kill the serpent. The emperor in great consternation convokes scholars and sages to interpret this portent for him. And they interpret it in the following manner: this place will be called the Seven Hills, will be famed and exalted above all other towns in the world. But in the end this town will be conquered by infidels. The eagle is the symbol of Christianity, the serpent, of Moslemism. That the serpent vanquished the eagle means that Moslemism will vanquish Christianity, but just as the people killed the serpent and liberated the eagle, so, later on, shall the Christians take Tsargrad and rule in it.

A long period of time elapses and the prophecy is fulfilled: the infidel king Mahomet, son of Amur, who up to that time had been in accord and at peace with the emperor Constantine, attacked Tsargrad. (The last Byzantine emperor, like the first, bore the name Constantine.) The number of the Turks enormously exceeded the number of Greeks besieged in the city. It was very difficult for the Greeks to defend themselves, for "one fought with a thousand, two with a countless host." The Greeks fought back with extraordinary strength and energy, however. The author gives us all the details of the siege of Tsargrad and tells of an endless number of attacks attended by enormous losses on both sides, though chiefly on the Turkish.

[8] See G. P. Bel'chenko, "K voprosu o sostave istoricheskoy povesti o vzyatii Tsar'grada," *Sbornik statey k 40-letiyu uchenoy deyatel'nosti akademika A. S. Orlova* (On the Question of the Composition of the Historical Tale of the Taking of Tsargrad, from the Collection of Essays for the Fortieth Anniversary of Academician A. S. Orlov's Career as a Scholar), pp. 507–513.

Here is one of the battle descriptions, written largely in the traditional war-story style:

The Turks, hearing the great ringing of bells, again set countless sackbuts and trumpets and big drums going, and there was great and terrible slaughter. From the detonation of cannon and harquebuses and from the bell-ringing and from the wails and shrieks on both sides, and the clash of weapons that flashed like lightning, as well as from the weeping and sobbing of the townsmen and women and children, you would have thought that earth and sky had met and that both were swaying, and it was impossible for one man to hear what another said: for the wails and shrieks and the weeping and sobbing of the people and the bursting of the cannon and the ringing of the bells all coalesced into one sound and it was like a great roar. Furthermore, from the many fires and from the shooting of cannon and harquebuses on both sides, a thick cloud of smoke formed and covered the city and the army so entirely that no man could see with whom he was fighting, and many died from powder smoke. So did they hack and harry each other at every wall until the darkness of night parted them.

The Turks left for their camp and started to collect the dead, while the besieged Greeks slept like the dead, leaving only a few watchmen on the walls.

Even such a battle picture is enhanced when the author adds this lyric exclamation:

What tongue can impart or describe the misery and terror? On both sides bodies fell from the ramparts like sheaves and their blood flowed like rivers along the walls; moreover, what with the wailing and shrieking of both armies and the weeping and sobbing of the townsfolk and the ringing of the bells and the clang and flash of weapons, you would have thought that the whole city was being ripped from its foundations; and the moats were filled to the top with human bodies so that the Turks could walk across them, as up a stair, and fight: the dead were a bridge and a stairway for them to the town. Likewise all the streams around the city, and their banks, were filled with corpses, and blood flowed from them in a mighty stream.

The emperor Constantine showed particular courage and bravery, firmly refusing to abandon the city in spite of the exhortations of the nobles, of the patriarch and of General Zusteneya. He fought the enemy courageously and with his own hand inflicted great losses upon them.

But at this point the following portent occurs: at the moment when the emperor and the patriarch entered the "great church," that is, St. Sophia, flame leaped from the temple, surrounded the dome, rose heavenward and then disappeared. This was as a testimony to those present that God's grace had definitely abandoned Tsargrad, and that the city's days were numbered. But even this failed to make Constantine abandon the city. Finally the Turks took complete possession of Tsargrad. In this connection the author gives himself up to sorrowful reflections on the fate of the "seven-hilled." Constantine goes forth to meet the conquerors; they kill him, cut off his head and present it to Mahomet. Mahomet expresses great sympathy for Constantine and respect for his bravery. After kissing the head, he dispatched it to the patriarch to be mounted in silver and gold and fittingly preserved. Riding into the conquered town, Mahomet "slid from his horse and fell on his face to the ground, took dust and sprinkled it on his head, giving thanks to God." Before the assembled people and the clerics Mahomet made a speech that showed him to be a magnanimous sovereign: "I say unto you, Anastasius [the name of the patriarch] and to your whole retinue and to all the people: from this day let no one fear my wrath, or to be killed or taken captive."

The Turkish sultan sits on the throne of the Byzantine emperors but when all predictions as to the fate of this city have been fulfilled, concludes the author, then the prediction of Leo the Wise shall also be fulfilled, that a blond race shall conquer Ishmael (the Mahometans), take Tsargrad, and rule in it.[9]

The fall of Constantinople must have given new wings to Muscovite semi-official thought and color to the notion that Byzantium's lost religious and political values were destined to be reconstituted on Muscovite soil. This, in sum, was the publicistic purport of the narrative of Nestor-Iskander.

TALES OF THE BABYLONIAN EMPIRE AND LEGEND OF THE PRINCES OF VLADIMIR

During the latter half of the fifteenth century, other stories were also composed in Moscow on the theme of the political succession of Rus to the Byzantine heritage. Such are the tales of the Babylonian empire and the natural sequel to these tales, the *Legend of the Princes of Vladimir*.

The tales of the Babylonian empire deal with the founding of the new Babylon by Nebuchadrezzar and with the Byzantine emperor Basil's later acquisition from Babylon of the insignia of imperial rank.

These narratives were composed in Byzantium to give basis to the concept of Byzantium's heirship to the historical world empire of which Babylon had earlier been looked upon as the center. The tales of the Babylonian empire apparently reached Rus at the end of the fifteenth century, precisely

[9] The narrative as given in the oldest copy, early sixteenth century, was published by Arch. Leonid in *Pamyatniki drevney pismennosti* (Monuments of Early Literature) (St. Petersburg, 1886), LXI.

when the idea of Moscow as the third Rome was in process of germination. No doubt it was on Russian soil that a Russian came to be mentioned as one of the active participants in obtaining for the Greek emperor Basil the insignia of imperial rank. It is very curious that a tendentious tale, originating on Byzantine soil and having nothing to do with the current situation in Rus, should have been adjusted to fit the Russian political situation and made to justify Moscow's pretensions to a place in world history.

The first narrative of the Babylonian empire tells how the Babylonian emperor Axerxes sent out into the woods all those afflicted with leprosy, with a view to protecting Babylon from the spread of the infection. Relatives kept in touch with the exiles, bringing them everything needful to sustain life. When Axerxes died, the people in the wood, learning that there was no emperor in Babylon, conspired to go back to the city, since they saw at the moment no obstacle to their return. And they find a boy under a pine tree, give him the name Nebuchadrezzar, and take him with them to Babylon. In the meantime the princes and nobles had convened to determine who should be emperor. It was decided that he should be emperor upon whom a horn of myrrh, hanging above the city gates, should boil up and spill over. And when Nebuchadrezzar rode past it, the horn boiled up and spilled its contents on his head. This was the sign that he was to be emperor of Babylon. They took the boy to the imperial palace, arrayed him in costly garments, gave the scepter into his hand and seated him on the imperial throne.

Notwithstanding his youth, Nebuchadrezzar was very wise and brave. When he meditated founding a new Babylon, he gathered princes and nobles and bade them build the new city with seven walls of seven versts. Exit and entrance were through a single gate about which a stone snake was sculptured. Nebuchadrezzar ordered that the snake symbol be put on every object in the city: on weapons, on bridles, on saddles, on temples, on spoons, on plates, on all vessels, and on all kinds of cattle.

Nebuchadrezzar took an empress of the imperial family and had by her Prince Basil. Nebuchadrezzar was the terror of all his enemies. He was invincible, the more so since he possessed a self-operating sword which he set in motion upon encountering the enemy. The tale describes one of Nebuchadrezzar's battles. The weight of power was on the side of Babylon throughout. But the victory was consummated when the emperor himself entered the battle. The self-operating sword, the asp-serpent, burst from its scabbard and hacked the enemy without mercy.

Nebuchadrezzar reigned many years. Just before his death he commanded that the automatic sword be immured in the city wall and not taken out until the end of the world, predicting, in the contrary event, the inevitable destruction of Babylon.

Upon learning that the terrible Nebuchadrezzar was no more, a number of kings moved powerful forces against Babylon, where Nebuchadrezzar's son Basil had begun his reign. Basil went out to meet the enemy but the weight of power was against him, and he decided to violate his father's prohibition, extract the automatic sword from the wall and set it going. But the sword leaped from Basil's hands and began to move about not only among the enemy but through the Babylonian army as well, and killed all the Babylonians, while the serpents depicted on all objects suddenly came to life and devoured the Babylonians to a man. Even the big stone serpent carved on the city gate came to life.

From that time forth Babylon was a scene of complete desolation. Weeds encompassed it, and of the famous and mighty city no memory remained.

The second narrative tells how the insignia of imperial rank, originally in Babylon, passed to the Byzantine emperor; that is, it gives quasi documentation for the passing of historical world empire from Babylon to Byzantium.

The Byzantine emperor Leo, whose Christian name was Basil, sent emissaries to get the insignia from three retainers, Ananias, Azarias, and Misailas, whose relics reposed in Babylon. Basil at first planned to send two emissaries, a Greek and an Abkhasian, but on the advice of his attendants sent a third retainer as well, "a Slav of the Russians." Thus a Russian, too, took part in obtaining the insignia of imperial rank from Babylon. The emperor and his army followed the emissaries and halted fifteen leagues from Babylon while the retainers set out for the city itself. They walked very slowly, and since the path was narrow, "with great difficulty." Along the way there grew a "great grass like a thistle." This grass extended for sixteen versts around Babylon. In it were all manner of reptiles and serpents. But "by God's will" the retainers reached Babylon unscathed on the third day and, having the good fortune to get past the sleeping serpent, went up a staircase of eighteen steps to the top of the city wall and by a second staircase descended to the city. On this staircase, as also on the first, they found three inscriptions: in Greek, in Abkhasian, and in "Slavonic and Russian." These inscriptions were encouraging to the emissaries, counseling them not to fear the serpent and to advance boldly.

Upon reaching the city, the emissaries went first of all to the tomb of the three retainers to pay their respects and receive a sign. On the tomb they espied a goblet of wrought gold studded with pearls and various precious stones. The goblet was filled with myrrh and frankincense. The emissaries drained the goblet and became "cheerful." Then they fell asleep, and when they waked up and would have taken the goblet along with them, a voice was heard from the tomb forbidding them to do so and bidding them go to the imperial palace and take thence the insignia of imperial rank. The emissaries did as they were bid. They took the crowns of Nebuchadrezzar and his queen and a document written in Greek explaining the provenance of the crown, and other treasures. After this they set out for another palace where they saw various precious things and a carnelian casket containing the imperial purple. There, too, they saw chests full of gold, silver, and precious stones, and a golden goblet. All this they took away with them. Then they went to the church again, to the tomb of the three retainers, again drank from the goblet that stood on the tomb, again had a cheerful feeling, went to sleep, and, upon awakening, started back. On the return trip one of the emissaries, the Abkhasian, stumbled, fell on the snake and roused it. It set up an extraordinary hissing. The emissaries were panic-stricken, fell on the ground and long lay as if dead, but afterward regained consciousness and went to the place where the emperor Basil was to have awaited them. But there they found complete confusion. The hiss of the serpent had been so devastating that an enormous number of Basil's troops had fallen dead. Only a small part had managed to escape, along with Basil himself. The emperor Basil had given up all hope for the retainers and rejoiced greatly when he saw them safe and sound. The retainers turned over to Basil the booty which they had taken in Babylon. Basil gave part of this booty, the precious stones and the gold, to the patriarch, while retaining the imperial regalia himself. Thus the Byzantine emperor became the legally qualified representative of historical world monarchy since he possessed the material insignia of imperial dignity which were the manifestation of this power.

Thus, to confirm the idea of Byzantine world monarchy, a legend was built up which told of the concrete and actual transfer of the symbols and tokens of imperial rank from Babylon to Byzantium.

Neither of these narratives, based on migratory fairy-tale motifs, has been preserved in a Greek text, in spite of the fact that they undoubtedly originated in Byzantium; on the other hand, to judge from various echoes in the literatures of the West, they were popular in medieval Europe. However, the fact that the acquisition of the insignia of imperial rank is discussed only in Russian tales and stories suggests that the mention of the Babylonian crown was not primordial to the group of cognate stories. Mention of this was obviously essential in connection with the developing idea of Moscow's heirship to the legacy of Byzantium: some copies of the second tale say that "the carnelian casket with all the imperial insignia" passed into the possession of Prince Vladimir of Kiev. From this it is only a step to the direct transference of the Byzantine regalia to the Muscovite great princes.

The end of the fifteenth or the beginning of the sixteenth century saw the composition here of the *Legend of the Princes of Vladimir,* a direct development of, and sequel to, the narratives of the Babylonian empire. On this *Legend* were based the *Epistle* concerning the crown of Monomakh written by the monk Spiridon-Savva during the reign of Great Prince Vasily Ivanovich in the first quarter of the sixteenth century, as well as cognate articles in the *Genealogy of the Great Princes of Rus,* and later chronicles. The *Legend* acquired special popularity during the reign of Ivan the Terrible, first officially crowned tsar in 1547.

It begins with Noah and carries the account down to Augustus Caesar, who, when "organizing the world," sent his own brother Prus to the banks of the Vistula, to the country which was thereafter called the land of Prus. (In antiquity it was populated by Prussians; that is, Lithuanians.) Rurik, invited to be prince of Rus, was a descendant of the Roman Prus, and consequently of Augustus Caesar. Hence the habitual declaration of Ivan the Terrible that his family traced its descent to Augustus Caesar.

Thus a legend built up on Russian soil links the Muscovite great princely family with a representative of the oldest world monarchy, with Augustus Caesar.

The author of the *Legend* tells how a certain Novgorod governor, Gostomysl, as the end of his life drew near, bade the people of Novgorod send a wise man to the land of Prus and invite a prince from there. The Novgorodians obeyed him and from the land of Prus came a prince by the name of Rurik, a direct descendant of Augustus ("being of the family of the Roman emperor Augustus"), and was made their prince. With him came his brothers Truvor and Sineus, who also became princes in the land of Rus. In the course of time, the Russian prince Vladimir, son of Vsevolod, descendant of Great Prince Vladimir in the fourth generation,[10] decided to attack Byzantium, quoting as precedents the campaigns of Oleg and Vseslav Igorevich. He gathered his nobles "skillful and wise and prudent," together with a large army, and set out for Thrace, on the outskirts of Tsargrad. Having captured many of the inhabitants of Thrace, he returned with rich booty. The emperor in Tsargrad at that time was the pious Constantine Monomakh, who was then carrying on a war with the Persians and the Latins. He called his imperial council together and despatched Neophitas, Metropolitan of Ephesus, and other emissaries to Vladimir, son of Vsevolod, giving them "a life-giving cross from that same life-giving tree on which the Lord Christ was crucified," the imperial crown from his own head, a carnelian casket "in which the Roman emperor Augustias had taken delight," then the mantelets which he wore on his shoulders, a chain of Arabian gold, and many

---

[10] In some copies of the *Legend,* Vladimir, son of Svyatoslav, appears in place of Vladimir, son of Vsevolod.

other valuable gifts, and all this he sent to Vladimir with the request that the latter refrain from making war on Byzantium. "Accept from us, devout and faithful prince, these gifts of honor, which are sent to confirm your family line and your progeny's imperial destinies in perpetuity, for fame and honor, and unto the coronation of your free and autocratic empire," said Constantine to Vladimir, son of Vsevolod.

Vladimir accepted the gifts, was crowned with Constantine's crown, and thenceforth was himself called Monomakh:

And from that time Great Prince Vladimir, son of Vsevolod, was called Monomakh, Tsar of Great Russia, and thereafter Great Prince Vladimir continued for the rest of his life in peace and friendship with the emperor Constantine. From that day to this, the great princes of Vladimir have been crowned with the imperial crown which the Greek emperor, Constantine Monomakh, sent when he confirmed the Russian great-princedom.

The imperial regalia that had been conveyed out of Babylon thus completed their third and last journey: they settled down with the Russian princes, who by this token were accepted as heirs of the Byzantine empire. To such a tendentious fiction did legend resort in order to substantiate the rights and authority of the Muscovite autocrats who had made good their supremacy in fair fight with the appanaged princes and the boyar opposition. In the process historical facts were distorted: Constantine Monomakh died when Vladimir, son of Vsevolod, was only about two years old. This chronological discrepancy was not noted until the later chronicle compilations, where Constantine Monomakh was replaced by Alexius Comnenus.

However, there existed no historical confirmation of the *Legend's* statement that since the time of Vladimir, son of Vsevolod, the Russian princes had been crowned with Monomakh's crown, and to get around this difficulty several copies tell how Vladimir Monomakh, just before his death, bequeathed the imperial regalia to his son George, with instructions that he guard them as his soul or as the apple of his eye, handing them down from generation to generation until such time as God should raise up an emperor-autocrat worthy to possess the Russian dominion, and that until that time the descendants of Monomakh should not be invested with the imperial regalia nor crowned emperor.

The date of writing of the *Legend* has been more precisely fixed by I. N. Zhdanov as falling between 1480 and 1523. In 1523 it was already included in the *Epistle* of Spiridon-Savva. Previous to 1480 it was apparently not yet in existence, to judge from the fact that the monk Bassianus did not use it in his epistle to Ivan III at Ugra in 1480. This epistle, written by a learned man, counselor and confessor to Ivan III, discusses the heroic history of

Ivan's ancestors and would naturally have utilized the *Legend* had it existed at that time.

The actual rise of the monument, and its ideological content, I. N. Zhdanov associates with the South Slavic influence on Russian literature first manifest at the end of the fourteenth century and primarily developed by such politically useful South Slavic immigrants as Cyprian and Pakhomius Logothetes. These writers adapted the autonomistic tendencies of the Balkan Slavic states to the current political situation in Moscow. Both in Serbia and in Bulgaria there existed fictitious royal genealogies, tracing the kingly line back to the Roman emperors as justification for national aspirations to political independence of Byzantium. Thus Serbian scholars established the kinship of the Nemanyi to Constantine the Great and to the family of Augustus Caesar. The Bulgarian tsars, the Asens, also claimed to be of Roman descent. But the author of the *Legend* showed even greater boldness and directness: he pointed straight at Prus, the brother of Augustus, as founder of the Russian princely family. Zhdanov advances the hypothesis that this author may have been no other than Pakhomius Logothetes himself, the man who worked so hard to develop and consolidate the Muscovite political ideology.

For the relations that the *Legend* represents as existing between the Russian prince Vladimir and the Greek emperor, Constantine Monomakh, Zhdanov has the following explanation. During the fifteenth and sixteenth centuries there had circulated in Rus a folk-poetry legend about Vladimir's war with the Greeks. This legend was akin to extant *byliny* of the Vladimir cycle and appears to have been an echo of the epic tradition about Vladimir Svyatoslavich's campaign against Kherson. The ancient *bylina* about Vladimir's war with the Greeks is not extant in its original form and is known only through learned fifteenth and sixteenth century adaptations, one of which deals with Vladimir Vsevolodovich's war with Constantine Monomakh. Later on, the legend of the transfer to Rus of the Byzantine imperial regalia was combined with the translated tale about Emperor Leo (Basil) obtaining the imperial paraphernalia from Babylon. This combination was reflected in monuments of written literature and also in oral works.

Thus, in one ballad, the Terrible boasts at a banquet:

> As a tsar I have reason to boast:
> I brought the regalia from Tsargrad,
> Put on the imperial purple,
> Took the mace of empire in hand—
> I intend to drive treason from Moscow.[11]

[11] *Pesni* (Ballads), collected by P. N. Rybnikov, 2nd ed. (Moscow, 1909), Vol. I, p. 212.

In another ballad, composed in connection with the conquest of Kazan, the Terrible says:

> In passing I took Kazan,
> Brought Tsar Simeon under my power,
> Took off his imperial purple,
> Conveyed it to stone-walled Moscow,
> Christened the purple in Moscow,
> This purple upon me I put,
> Whereupon I became the Tsar Terrible.[12]

The end of this ballad has the following variant:

> This purple upon me I put,
> Whereupon I became the priest-tsar,
> Tsar Ivan Vasilyevich the Terrible.[13]

Here, as we see, the insignia of imperial dignity are transferred to Moscow from Kazan, and the crowning of the Terrible as emperor is itself connected with the conquest of Kazan.

The transfer of the imperial regalia to Moscow for Ivan the Terrible is also the subject of a folk tale about Borma the Sot, or Fyodor Borma, which exists in several variants and is directly dependent on the tales of the Babylonian empire. According to the Samar variant, Tsar Ivan Vasilyevich shouts: "Who will go get me from the Babylonian empire the crown, the scepter, the orb, and the little book that goes with them?" On the third day Borma responds to the tsar's call, and with his comrades sets out by ship for Babylon, which presents the same scene of desolation as in the written narratives. The folk tale likewise emphasizes the serpents but adds the "tsar-wench," a one-eyed giant, and his sister, with whom Borma lived for twenty years and by whom he had a son. He gets what the tsar had charged him to get, shrewdly outwits everyone and departs for Rus, where he arrives after a good thirty years' absence. As his reward for obtaining the treasure he requests that the Terrible authorize him to drink for three years without money and without price in all pothouses.

According to another variant, retold by E. Barsov, it is from Tsargrad that Borma sets out for Babylon after the imperial purple, the crown, the staff, and the scepter—at the behest of the "top people" of that place. With the help of an unknown person calling himself "Truth," he finds his way to Babylon. In the temple of St. George the Victor and Demetrius of Salonika, he finds the imperial regalia, and on a carpet which a girl at the temple hands him, sails back to Tsargrad. "But in Tsargrad there had been great bloodshed; the Orthodox faith had collapsed, there had ceased to be an Orthodox

12 *Pesni* (Ballads), collected by P. V. Kireyevsky (Moscow, 1864), Pt. 6, pp. 98–99.
13 *Ibid.*, p. 95.

emperor." And Borma went to Rus, to Kazan, "and there placed the purple and the crown from the city of Babylon on the head of the Terrible and Orthodox Tsar Ivan Vasilyevich, who had brought low the empire of Prokhodim, pagan tsar of Kazan."

As we see, the oral tradition in all cases arrogates the imperial regalia from Babylon to Ivan the Terrible, who consummated the process of Moscow's political apotheosis.[14]

TALE OF THE WALLACHIAN GOVERNOR DRACULA

As a footnote to the practice of Moscow autocrats in the last quarter of the fifteenth century, we get the *Legend of Governor Dracula*. Dracula, Governor of Wallachia, a "Christian of the Greek faith," had the reputation for being an extraordinarily cruel and crafty man. His very name, Dracula, the author tells us, meant "devil." The tale lists a succession of incidents exemplifying a perverted cruelty that often had no practical justification whatever.

Once when some Turkish emissaries appeared before Dracula and, as was their custom, did obeisance to him without removing their fezzes, he commanded that their fezzes be nailed to their heads by way of confirming their custom. In a fury the Turkish sultan attacked Dracula in force; Dracula collected such soldiers as he had, fell on the Turks by night and wrought much havoc among them, but, being in no position to hold out against the superior forces of the enemy, turned back. He made a personal examination of the soldiers who returned with him and any upon whom he found wounds

[14] An exhaustive analysis of the tales of the Babylonian empire and the *Legend of the Princes of Vladimir* is given in I. N. Zhdanov's study, *Russkii bylevoy epos* (Russian Bylina Epos) (St. Petersburg, 1895), pp. 1–151, where the literature of the question is also cited. See also A. N. Veselovskii, "Skazaniya o Vavilone, skinii i sv. Graale" (Legend of Babylon, the Tabernacle, and the Holy Grail) *Sbornik otd. russk. yaz. i slov.* (Collection of the Division of Russian Language and Literature of the Academy of Sciences) (St. Petersburg, 1896), Vol. LXIV, No. 6. As a supplement to Zhdanov's book, texts of the tales and of the *Legend* are given. The tales of Babylon had previously been published from other manuscripts by Pypin in *Izvestiya II otdeleniya akad. nauk* (News of Division II of the Academy of Science), III, pp. 313–320; by Kostomarov in *Pamyatniki starinnoy russkoy literatury* (Monuments of Ancient Russian Literature), II, pp. 391–396, and by Tikhonravov in *Letopisi russkoy literatury i drevnosti* (Chronicles of Russian Literature and Antiquity), I (1859), Smes', pp. 161–165; III (1861), Smes', pp. 20–33. For a list and retellings of Russian fairy tales reminiscent of the tales of the Babylonian empire, see Zhdanov, *op cit.*, pp. 1–12, and D. K. Zelenin's collection *Velikorusskie skazki Permskoy gubernii* (Great Russian Folk Tales of the Permian District) (Petrograd, 1914), pp. 525–526. See also F. V. Miller, "K skazkam ob Ivane Groznom" (On Folk Tales About Ivan the Terrible), *Izvestiya otd. russk. yaz. i slov.* (News of the Division of Russian Language and Literature of the Academy of Science.)

inflicted from the front he rewarded lavishly, while any whose wounds turned out to have come from behind he ordered impaled as deserters from the field of battle, saying: "You are not men, but women." The Turkish sultan, learning of the rough justice he had meted out to his own soldiers, was afraid of him and made no attempt at pursuit, but sent an emissary to him with a demand for tribute. Dracula received the emissary with great honor, showed him all his possessions and said that he would not only agree to pay tribute to the sultan but was ready, with his whole army and all his treasure, to enter the service of the sultan, provided the latter did not harm him or his army in any way while in the country. The sultan gladly accepted Dracula's offer, loaded him with all manner of distinctions and appointed overseers upon him. But Dracula, after proceeding for five days through Turkish territory, suddenly turned back and captured towns, villages, and a multitude of people, part of whom he chopped in two, part burned, part impaled, and thus annihilated them completely, not even sparing babes at the breast, and moreover laid waste the whole land, but the Christians he repatriated in his own territory. Then he ceremoniously dismissed the Turkish overseers, saying: "Go and tell your king what you have seen: I have done him what service I could. And if my service suits him I shall be glad to go on serving him in so far as I am able." Nor had the humiliated sultan any way of getting back at Dracula.

Dracula so hated evil in his own district that he would put to death anyone guilty of any offence whatever, of theft, of brigandage, or even of so much as an untruth—whether a powerful noble, or a prelate, or a monk, rich or poor. He had on his domains a well where the water was cool and sweet, and many paths led to it from various lands and many passers-by drank water from that well. Near the margin Dracula ordered a large gold cup to be placed for people to drink from and afterward put back where it belonged. And no one ever dared to steal that cup.

Once Dracula gave orders that all the aged, the sick, and the poor in his whole land be summoned. When they appeared before him in a countless multitude, expecting some great favor from him, he commanded that they be gathered into a large apartment built for the purpose, gave them food and drink in abundance and then asked if they would like to have him free them of all earthly cares and make them want for nothing. Upon receiving an affirmative answer, Dracula gave orders that the whole gathering be locked up and burned, and thus freed forever from poverty and all infirmities.

Another time two Catholic monks came to Dracula from Hungary asking alms. He gave orders that they be separated, and, summoning one of them, showed him, scattered about the courtyard, an enormous number of people impaled on stakes or on wheels, and asked him if he had done well to treat them as he had, considering what sort of people they were. The monk answered that Dracula had done ill to execute people without mercy: it became a ruler to be merciful, and those on the stakes were martyrs. But the other monk, when the same question was put to him, said that as a ruler Dracula was appointed of God to execute offenders and show favor to the virtuous; the offenders had got what they deserved. Dracula gave orders that the first monk be impaled so that he might become a martyr along with those whom he had himself so named, and the other was given fifty gold ducats and dismissed with honor.

Another time a certain merchant from the land of Hungary called on Dracula and at the governor's direction left his cart of goods in the city street in front of a house while he went inside to sleep. As he slept, one hundred and sixty gold ducats were stolen from his cart. The merchant laid his complaint before Dracula, who promised him that the gold would be found that very night and gave orders that a city-wide search be made for the thief, threatening to destroy the whole town if he were not found. At the same time he commanded that the merchant's gold be placed on his cart with an extra ducat added. In the morning the merchant found his money on the cart and, convinced after twice counting it that one ducat had been added, went and informed Dracula of the fact. At that moment they brought in the thief who had stolen the gold, and Dracula turned to the merchant and said: "Go in peace. Had you not told me about the extra ducat, I should have impaled you along with this thief."

Dracula also showed uncommon cruelty toward women who were unchaste or careless about their housekeeping. Once, meeting a poor peasant in a torn shirt, he asked if he had a wife and, upon receiving an affirmative answer, bade him take him to his house. The wife proved to be young and healthy. Dracula asked the man if he sowed flax. The man replied that he did and showed him quite an amount of flax. Rebuking the wife for laziness and negligence, Dracula ordered her hands cut off and her body impaled.

When the servant attending Dracula as he dined amid the corpses on stakes held his nose, unable to endure the stench, and turned his head away, Dracula commanded that he be impaled, saying: "There you will be so high up that the stench can't get to you."

Once an envoy of high rank came to Dracula from the Hungarian king Matthew, a Pole by race, and Dracula had him sit down to dinner with him among the corpses. Beside him lay a large, tall, gilded stake. When Dracula asked him what he thought this stake had been made for, the envoy replied: "It would seem to me, sir, that someone of high rank had offended in your sight and you wished to accord him a death of particular distinction."

Dracula said: "You are right; you are the envoy of a great ruler, and I made that stake for you."

"Sir, if I have committed a crime worthy of death," the envoy managed to say, "do as you wish; you are a just judge: it is not you who will be responsible for my death, but myself."

Dracula smiled and allayed his anxiety: "If you had not answered me as you did, you would certainly have been put on that stake," he said. And, after bestowing honors and gifts upon the emissary, he dismissed him with the words: "Continue to act as envoy between great rulers, for you know how to talk to them, and let the rest learn how to converse with great rulers before they attempt it!"

Dracula's custom was as follows: if an envoy came to him, from a tsar or from a king, "raw" and incapable of guarding against traps, he impaled him, saying as he did so: "It is not I who am responsible for your death but your master or you yourself, so do not have any hard feelings toward me: if your master knowing your illiteracy and lack of intelligence still sent you to me, a great ruler, then it is he who has murdered you; but if you yourself had the audacity to come insufficiently trained, then you have killed yourself."

Some workmen made iron casks for Dracula. These he filled with gold and then lowered them into the river, then ordered the workman killed so that no one might know of his "deviltry" except "the Devil whose namesake he was."

Finally, in a battle with the Hungarian king Matthew, Dracula was defeated, taken captive, and imprisoned at Vyshegrad on the Danube above Budin, while the king appointed another governor for Wallachia. Dracula remained in prison for twelve years, and even there manifested his accustomed cruelty: he caught mice and bought birds, and executed them: some he impaled, others he beheaded, plucked out the birds' feathers and then let them go. He learned how to sew and by this trade supported himself in prison.

When the new governor of Wallachia died, the king offered to reappoint Dracula to the governorship, but only on condition that he embrace the Latin faith. It is with manifest grief that the author tells how Dracula accepted the king's offer and in return for renouncing Orthodoxy received not only the governorship but also the king's sister to wife, and by her he had two sons.

The tale next gives an episode typical of the pride, the extreme self-conceit and sense of his own authority and dignity that did not desert Dracula even after his long incarceration. While he was temporarily domiciled in Budin after his release and before his departure for Wallachia, a certain escaped criminal took refuge in his courtyard and hid there. Pursuers, finding him there seized him, but Dracula at once sprang out with his sword, cut off the head of the bailiff holding the prisoner, and thus released him. When the king demanded an explanation, he received the reply: "Anyone who breaks into the house of a great ruler (that is, in the present case, Dracula) like a robber shall so perish. If you yourself had come to me and I had found this criminal in my house, it would still have been for me to hand him over or to release him." When the king heard this, he burst out laughing, amazed at Dracula's warmth.

Dracula lived ten years longer and died in the "Latin delusion." His end came as follows. The Turks attacked Wallachia; Dracula defeated them and his army pursued and slaughtered them without mercy. In exultation he climbed the hill to get a better view of the slaughter of the enemy. But as he did so one of his attendants disengaged himself from the army, and, thinking that it was a Turk on the hill, killed him with a spear.

The story ends with information regarding the fate of Dracula's family and the appointment of a new governor for Wallachia.

Obviously, the story is very simple in its construction: it is a stringing together of anecdotal incidents from the life of Dracula. The character of the latter combines various, at times contradictory qualities; first of all he is outrageously cruel and crafty, arbitrary to the point of absurdity. But at the same time Dracula is the passionate, albeit stern and strait-laced, guardian of justice and hater of wickedness. Furthermore, he is very quick-witted and can appreciate cleverness and intelligence in others, rewarding them lavishly instead of executing them.

The author, for all his efforts to recount Dracula's actions objectively, betrays signs of a condemnatory attitude when he explains that Dracula's name means "Devil," or when he speaks of "the Devil his namesake," who alone may know of his "deviltry" with respect to the murdered workmen.

He reserves his harshest condemnation, however, not for Dracula's cruelty but for his apostasy from Orthodoxy to Catholicism: "Dracula," he complains, "preferred the pleasures of the temporal world to those of the eternal and everlasting, abjured Orthodoxy and renounced truth, abandoned the light and embraced darkness; alas, he was unable to endure the trials of prison for a season and doomed himself to everlasting torment, abandoned our Orthodox faith and embraced the Latin delusion." Dracula's accidental death at the hand of one of his own soldiers must be interpreted, the story implies, as chastisement for his betrayal of the Orthodox faith. This interpretation of Dracula's fate is part and parcel of the role that traditional Orthodoxy had come to play in Moscow, notably since the Florentine Union.

The historical prototype of Dracula was Vlad Tsepesh, Governor of Wallachia from 1456 to 1462 and in 1476. Whether the story of Dracula is an original or a borrowed work is a moot question. In the early 1840 s, on the basis of the closing section of the story, which says of Dracula's sons: "One son is living at the king's court, another was at the bishop of Vardin's and died during our sojourn, and we saw the third and oldest son, Michael, in Budin on that occasion," Vostokov concluded that the author was in Hungary during the reign of King Matthew. And since in 1482 Ivan III sent his secretary Fyodor Kuritsyn to King Matthew to ratify a peace treaty, Vostokov thought it probable that the tale was written, either by Kuritsyn himself or by someone in his suite, on the basis of stories heard from eye-witnesses or from persons in whose memory the recollection of Tsepesh-Dracula was still fresh.[15] But it is obvious that anyone might have seen the sons of Dracula in Budin, that it need not have been a Russian author, and the fact that Fyodor Kuritsyn's trip to Hungary coincided with the stay of these sons in Budin is still an insufficient argument for authorship by Kuritsyn or some member of his embassy. Of many scholars who later worked on the tale, some ascribed it to Russian, some to foreign origin. (Very late Old German texts exist in which Dracula figures.) Specifically, Academician A. I. Sobolevsky conjectured that our tale derives from some fifteenth century German *feuilleton* but that Fyodor Kuritsyn may have been its editor or translator.[16]

The latest student of the tale, A. D. Sedelnikov,[17] rejects the authorship of Fyodor Kuritsyn, who did not return to Moscow until 1486, on the ground that the oldest copy of the tale, dating from 1490, carries textual indications of having been taken from a copy dated February 13, 1486. The chronological difficulty here is all the more obvious as the original from which the 1486 copy was taken must, naturally, itself have had a still earlier date. In A. D. Sedelnikov's opinion, however, the possibility is not precluded of there having been other, unofficial, intercourse between Moscow and Hungary, and other legations to Hungary. The author of the tale may even have been in Hungary at the time of Kuritsyn's mission but have returned to Moscow earlier and by another route. In the form of the tale as such, the investigator sees one of the oldest examples of the "story-letters" which also emanated from ambassadorial circles at a later time.

[15] *Opisanie russkikh i slavyanskikh rukopisey Rumyantsovskogo muzeuma* (Description of Russian and Slavonic Manuscripts in the Rumyantsov Museum) (St. Petersburg, 1842), p. 512.

[16] Perevodnaya literatura Moskovskoy Rusi XIV–XVII vv. (Translated Literature of Muscovite Rus in the Fourteenth-Seventeenth Centuries) (St. Petersburg, 1903), p. 233.

[17] "Literaturnaya istoriya povesti o Drakule" (Literary History of the Tale of Dracula), *Izvestiya po russkomu yazyku i slovesnosti* (News of Russian Language and Literature) II, 1929, pp. 621–659. This includes the literature on the question, a survey of copies of the tale, and a transcript of its oldest, 1490, text after the Byelozersk-St. Cyril Monastery manuscript.

From the end of the fifteenth century down to the seventeenth, the tale of Dracula circulated in a considerable number of copies, evidence of no small popularity. This popularity was undoubtedly due to the fact that the figure of Dracula soon became associated in the mind of the Russian reader with the person of Ivan the Terrible, whose unbridled cruelty and extreme self-will reminded his contemporaries of Dracula. Very indicative from this angle is the fact that the first episode in the tale of Dracula was later attributed to the Terrible. Thus the Englishman Collins, physician to Tsar Alexis Mikhailovich, states in his book on Russia that when Ivan the Terrible received the French envoy, he gave orders that his hat be nailed to his head for that he had not removed it in the tsar's presence. In a copy of the *Dvinsk Chronicle* (the *Kholmogorsk*), dating from the late seventeenth or early eighteenth century, a Dutch engraving is inserted with the following inscription: "Scene showing an embassy to Tsar Ivan Vasilyevich, how he ordered that the hat of one envoy be made fast to his head with iron nails for his insubordination and pride, that he had been indecorous in the performance of his office as envoy."

TALE OF QUEEN DINARA OF GEORGIA

Political and literary intercourse between Rus and Georgia gave rise to a Russian tale about the Georgian queen Dinara, adapted from a Georgian legend concerning Georgia's renowned Queen Tamara. Both the legend and our tale have a groundwork of historical fact. The tale tells how, after the death of the Georgian king Alexander, his wise fifteen-year-old daughter Dinara ascended the throne, refusing to marry. She applied herself to "Divine Writ" and under its influence schooled herself to martial courage. As a bee gathers honey from the flowers, so Dinara ruled her dominion well and tended it with care; as a good pilot steers his ship across the gulf of the sea, so she took pains "to remain at peace."

When news of Alexander's death reached the king of Persia, he made plans to subjugate Dinara's kingdom and stamp out Christianity there. Through emissaries he demanded that Dinara send him tribute in double the amount sent by her father, on pain of being deprived of authority. Dinara sent the Persian king gifts in treble the amount, with instructions, however, to tell him that he was powerless to take away her authority, since she had received it not from him but from God, and that it was not for fear of him she was sending tribute, since she feared only "the true God," whose law she kept and whose favor alone she sought. Upon hearing this, the Persian king refused the tribute and "brutally" dismissed Dinara's emissaries, again threatening to make war on her. Dinara wrote a letter to the Persian king to shame him, saying that it would be no great credit to him to vanquish a girl, "a weak child"; moreover, with the help of God and of the "Virgin Mother of God," she hoped to plant her foot on his royal body and cut off his head and thereby glorify the women of Georgia and put the men of Persia to shame. The Persian king attacked Dinara in force. The Georgian nobles were against meeting him in battle but Dinara heartened them by a long speech and endeavored to arouse their courage. She said:

"But let us hasten against them. Girl that I am, I shall go and shall take on manly courage and put aside womanly weakness, invest myself in manly vigor, and gird my sword about my loins and put on armor of iron, and put a helmet on my woman's head and take a spear in my maiden hand and spring into the stirrup of military command."

The nobles, inspired by Dinara's words, now urged her to take the field against the Persians. Then Dinara walked barefoot over thorns and sharp stones to the monastery, where she made heartfelt prayer to the Virgin for help. Upon coming out of the church, she mounted her horse and, with Christ's name and the Virgin's on her lips, rushed at the Persians, who fled in terror. Dinara and her troops slaughtered them without mercy. Then she cut off the Persian king's head and bore it on a spear into Tavriz, where treasures innumerable were brought her. Dinara imposed a tribute upon the Persians, then returned to her own realm, where she ruled in peace and quiet for thirty-eight years, until her death.

The tale was based on data from the Georgian chronicle narrative about Tamara and on folk traditions concerning her. This material was recast on Russian soil, apparently by a Muscovite scholar from the diplomatic corps. The time of writing was undoubtedly late fifteenth or early sixteenth century: our diplomatic relations with Georgia began just at the end of the fifteenth century, and information about Dinara-Tamara may have been obtained from Georgians coming to Rus after the Georgian mission to Ivan III. Moscow's interest in Georgia and Georgian history in the late fifteenth and early sixteenth centuries seems all the more natural since at that time the Moscow government was fighting for possession of territories to the southeast. In style and content the tale of Dinara resembles war stories of the Tartar and immediately post-Tartar period. The blending of martial themes and pious mood places it in the same category with the life of Alexander Nevsky, the tales of the rout of Mamay, and Nestor-Iskander's narrative of the taking of Tsargrad, while its expressed idea of imperial authority as God-given, relates it to the tendentious publicism that took its rise in the fifteenth century. Nor are such expressions as "brutally," "woman's form," "took courage," "autocrat" (in the feminine) found in the Russian vocabulary earlier than the fifteenth century.

The tale of Dinara, though also included in Russian historical compilations, is known here in a large number of separate copies, the earliest dating from the sixteenth century. It is also reflected in art: there exist illuminated (that is, illustrated) Russian copies from the seventeenth century and an icon of Dinara, also seventeenth century. In painting this icon the icon-painter presumably identified Dinara not with Tamara but with the tenth century Dinara who was looked upon by the Georgians as a saint.[18]

[18] For the text of the tale see *Pamyatniki starinnoy russkoy literatury* (Monuments of Ancient Russian Literature), II, pp. 273–276. For a study of it, M. N. Speranskii's "Povest' o Dinare v russkoy pismennosti" (Tale of Dinara in Russian Literature), *Izvestiya otd. russk. yaz. i slov.* (News of the Division of Russian Language and Literature of the Academy of Sciences, USSR) (1926), Vol. XXXI, pp. 43–92. This also gives the literature of the question.

Novgorod Literature

BACK in the Kiev period, and later as well, Novgorod was a very noted center of learning, but in early times Novgorod's written works were, from a purely literary angle, not of a sort to command our attention. The early *Novgorod Chronicle* was chiefly factual and contained none of those poetical touches which characterized the southern chronicles. Novgorod's other literature was distinguished by this same predilection for the factual, the documentary and the baldly didactic. During the fifteenth century, apropos of Moscow's clearly defined trend toward subordinating Novgorod to itself, Novgorod produced a series of works of a legendary-narrative and biographical character which aimed to cast an aura about its historical and religious past. The Novgorod archbishops Euphemius and John did a good deal in this direction. The majority of legends concerning Novgorod's past center about the popular name of the Novgorod archbishop Ilya-John (1163–1186). With this name are associated the legends of the signs from the icon of the Virgin, of the Monastery of the Annunciation, of John's trip to Jerusalem on a devil and, finally, the tale of the Novgorod burgomaster Shchil.

LEGEND OF THE SIGNS FROM THE ICON OF THE VIRGIN

In the *Novgorod Trefologion,* or *Paterikon,* this legend—known all told in a very large number of copies, and included in the chronicle—begins a long way back. After Yaroslav the Wise, having requited Svyatopolk for the murder of Boris and Gleb, transferred his residence from Novgorod to Kiev, "the people of Novgorod, for their great service to him and their exceeding virtue and the help that they had been to him against his enemies, were accorded autonomy." They were permitted to take from Yaroslav's family a "ruling prince of their own choosing, whichever they preferred," and to pay a fixed tribute, from the first never increased by the princes. The enjoyment of such privileges by the people of Novgorod excited the jealousy of many towns. Then, through the "man-slaying Devil's" false representations, the people of Novgorod were gradually vanquished by despotism and arrogance. Novgorodians became treaty breakers, but the princes, too, began to break their "given word" occasionally. To bring the people of Novgorod to reason, a miraculous sign was sent them in warning of threatened disaster: during the reign of Andrew Bogolyubsky, three icons of the Virgin shed tears in sign that the Virgin was trying to persuade her son to have mercy on the people of Novgorod. Then Andrew Bogolyubsky mounted a punitive campaign against the Novgorodians for driving out his army, but God, to prevent bloodshed and to protect the city of which he was patron, visited a sickness upon the prince. "But nothing can cure an unchastened mind," says the author of the *Legend*. As cruel Pharaoh, though punished by God through Moses with many wounds, still did not renounce his wicked and brutish undertaking until drowned by the wrath of God, so too this prince Andrew did not give up his plans, but, breathing spite, sent his son with the whole army of the Suzdal area and many Russian princes—the author enumerates more than seventy—so that "practically the whole land of Rus was united for the destruction of that one city," envied for its wealth and its free government. The author bursts into reproaches against the allied princes for forgetting that they were all "of consanguineous family and spiritually related through holy baptism, wherefore the Russian family is wholly one."

In contrast to their enemies, who are shown in a negative light, the people of Novgorod are described very sympathetically and positively. Having nowhere to expect help from, they pinned all their hopes on God and on the Virgin, since they were very pious, zealously frequented the churches of God, and were "generous and kind" to the poor. Help came to them through the fervent prayer of their archbishop John before the image of the Saviour. When the people of Novgorod had reached the point of complete exhaustion in their struggle with the enemy, John heard a voice from the icon before which he was praying, and it bade him go to the Church of the Redeemer on Ilyinka Street, take the icon of the Virgin that was there and set it up on the city wall facing the enemy forces. Then deliverance would come to the people of Novgorod. The Lord, says the *Legend*, glorified the image of his Mother "in order to shame the iconoclasts, and affirm the Orthodox icon-worshipers to be of greater faith." John, having convoked the assembly, sent the first deacon to get the icon, but it refused to move from its place. Then the archbishop went himself and celebrated a Te Deum before the icon, whereupon it moved of itself and was taken and placed on the city wall, facing the besiegers. But the latter not only did not give way but started to attack still more vigorously, shooting arrows at the image of the Virgin itself. Then the icon turned its face toward Novgorod and shed tears, which John collected in his vestment. And finally the Lord became wroth with the men of Suzdal, and sent darkness upon them and they began to slaughter and kill one another, while the men of Novgorod pursued them, taking captives and great booty.

The passionate attachment of the Novgorod author for his city stands out with particular sharpness if his account is compared with what is said about this same event by the Suzdal chronicler, who, while not denying the miraculous help given by the icon of the Virgin to the people of Novgorod, asserts that God chastised and humbled them at the hand of the *orthodox* Prince Andrew for oath-breaking and for pride, but in his mercy delivered their city.[1]

LEGEND OF THE MONASTERY OF THE ANNUNCIATION

This legend tells how when the two brothers, Ivan (the future Archbishop Ilya) and Gregory, scions of a noble and wealthy family, were building a stone church for the Annunciation Monastery, which they had founded, they ran out of silver. The brothers then prayed to the Virgin, who appeared to them in a dream and promised to give them silver in abundance. Outside the monastery gate the next morning they found a beautiful horse with a golden bridle and a saddle with gold mountings, and on the two sides of the saddle two "chests." Removing these, the brothers found them to be filled with gold and silver; then the horse disappeared. Ivan and Gregory understood that the gold and silver had been sent them by the Virgin: it enabled them to finish the church and adorn it in all manner of ways and

[1] The *Legend* (in the short version) is printed in *Pamyatniki starinnoy russkoy literatury* (Monuments of Ancient Russian Literature), I, pp. 241–242, and elsewhere. For an analysis of it see Buslayev's article, "Mestnye skazaniya vladimirskie, moskovskie i novgorodskie" (Local Legends of Vladimir, Moscow and Novgorod), *Letopisi russkoy literatury i drevnosti* (Chronicles of Russian Literature and Antiquity), IV, "Issledovaniya" (Analyses), pp. 18–23.

to buy several villages for the monastery as well. After so doing they both took the tonsure and became successive archbishops of Novgorod.[2]

This legend is based on the chronicle item about Archbishop Ilya and his brother having built, in 1170, a monastery and church of the Annunciation, the *Legend* thus merely moving the founding of the monastery back to the period before Ivan became a monk.

TALE OF JOHN OF NOVGOROD'S TRIP TO JERUSALEM ON A DEVIL

From this tale we learn that once upon a time John confined a devil in a vessel of water. When the devil began begging John to let him out, John agreed to, but only on condition that the devil, in the course of the night, ride him to Jerusalem, to the tomb of the Lord, and back again. The devil changed into a horse, conveyed John to Jerusalem, waited while the archbishop prayed at the tomb of the Lord, and then, tired and out of countenance, got him back to Novgorod the same night, warning him, however, not to tell anyone of his excursion lest the devil bring "temptation" upon him and he as a result be convicted of wantonness, insulted, and set adrift on a raft on the Volkhov. However, once when in converse "with honored priors and most proficient priests and with God-fearing men," John told of a trip to Jerusalem on a devil, not, however, as if it had happened to him, but as the experience of some other person, a certain John. And from that moment, "with the sufferance of God, the devil began to make trial of the saint." Townspeople repeatedly noticed a wanton coming out of the archbishop's cell; town authorities coming to John's cell for his blessing saw there a woman's necklace, sandals, and a woman's dress. Both the people and the authorities were perplexed and outraged by all that they had seen, reflected that it was unseemly for a loose liver to occupy the episcopal throne and resolved to banish John from Novgorod. As the populace approached his cell, the devil came forth from it in the form of a lass. In vain they pursued her—she was not to be caught. When John, wondering what could be causing the uproar outside his cell, went out to the people, the assemblage insulted him in all manner of ways, refused to listen to his explanations, and was resolved to put him on a raft and let it float down the Volkhov. The devil began exulting, but "divine grace" and the saint's prayer proved stronger than the devil's artifice: the raft, though no one was pushing it, floated not downstream but up, and thus the devil was put to shame. Repenting their act, the populace, accompanied by the clergy, set off up the Volkhov and, begging John's forgiveness, besought him to turn back. John returned to Novgorod.[3]

The tale utilized the migratory legendary motifs of catching a devil in a vessel and of riding on a devil. Both motifs were quite widely diffused in the international literature of East and West. The first motif evidently goes back to the Hebrew Talmudic legend about Solomon sealing devils up in a vessel. It was also reflected in Byzantine biographical literature, particularly the paterikons. (Cf. the tale of Father Longinus in the *Hermitage Paterikon*.) In original Russian literature it occurs not only in the story about John of Novgorod but also in the *Life of Abraham of Rostov* and in the story of the ancient who asked the hand of the tsar's daughter, whence it passed over into folk tale. The second motif—a ride on the devil—is most frequently encountered in Western legends, though we find close parallels in Byzantine paterikons as well. It appears in Gogol's tale, "The Night Before the Nativity." The fairy tale about Borma, already studied, tells how a lion, out of gratitude to Borma for rescuing him from a serpent, raced him home on his back in three hours, and then, like the devil in the tale about John, adjured him not to tell anyone of this ride, threatening him with death if he did. But Borma likewise boasted about his ride and only by craft escaped the infuriated lion's vengeance.

The legends about John of Novgorod presumably appeared after the opening of his "relics" (in 1439). They were included as separate episodes in the life of John of Novgorod composed in the late 1470's or early 1480's, evidently by Pakhomius Logothetes.[4]

TALE OF SHCHIL, BURGOMASTER OF NOVGOROD

This tale was written by some ecclesiastic on the basis of an oral legend composed somewhat under the influence of paterikon and prologue stories, and apparently came out at the end of the fourteenth century, apropos of Shchil's having built, in 1310, in the suburbs of Novgorod, a church of the

[3] *Ibid.*, pp. 245–248.
[4] See V. Klyuchevskii, *Drevnerusskie zhitiya svyatykh kak istoricheskii istochnik* (Early Russian Lives of the Saints as a Historical Source), pp. 127, 161–164; V. Yablonskii, *Pakhomii Serb i yevo agiograficheskie pisaniya* (Pakhomius the Serb and His Hagiographical Writings) pp. 109–114.

Intercession. Composed at the middle of the fifteenth century, the legend was repeatedly revised down to the end of the seventeenth century, going through six redactions; in the eighteenth century it penetrated to the chapbooks and then into folk story. First we learn that Archbishop John refused to consecrate the church built by Shchil on account of his being from Rostov. At John's command Shchil lies down in a coffin, which sinks into the earth; John gives orders that Shchil be depicted on the wall of the church as sojourning in hell. The deliverance of Shchil from hell and the consecration of the church that he had built were consummated only after Shchil's son had celebrated a triple "forty-days" Requiem in forty Novgorod churches. Shchil was apparently a monk from Rostov. His burgomastership was most probably the invention of the author, who would have found it inconvenient to exhibit a monk as a Rostovian. Also at variance with historical fact is the bringing in of Archbishop John as consecrator of the church, this very popular name being substituted for one much less popular in Novgorod, that of Archbishop David, in whose time Shchil actually built his church. The writing of the tale is directly connected with the Novgorod church's energetic defense of its right to emolument in the form of deposits "for the soul." Propaganda in support of the efficacy of prayers for the dead was all the more imperative for the Novgorod church inasmuch as in the fifteenth century it was still combating the after effects of the heresy of the Shearers, who had denied the necessity both of such prayers and of contributions to the Church in connection with the commemoration of the dead.[5]

Another popular name in Novgorod tradition is that of Archbishop Moses, twice incumbent of the archiepiscopal cathedra, from 1325 to 1329 and from 1352 to 1359. Moses' second term of office was marked by very strained relations with Moscow, then endeavoring to curtail the ecclesiastical independence of Novgorod. The life of Moses written by Pakhomius Logothetes to suit the people of Novgorod tells how Sergius, Ivan III's Muscovite appointee to the Novgorod cathedra, arrived in Novgorod, entered the church where Moses was buried, and ordered the tomb opened that he might see the "relics" of Moses. The priest stationed at the tomb made refusal, saying that it might only be opened by the archpriest. "Hearing this," the account continues, "Sergius assumed a haughty air by reason of his

[5] Special study of the tale: I. P. Yeremin's "Iz istorii russkoy povesti. Povest' o posadnike Shchile" (From the History of the Russian Tale: The Tale of Burgomaster Shchil), *Trudy komissii po drevnerusskoy literature Akad. nauk, SSSR* (Studies of the Committee on Early Russian Literature of the Academy of Sciences, USSR) (Leningrad, 1932), I, pp. 59–151. This also gives texts of the tale in various redactions and the literature of the question.

office and the fact that he had come from Moscow. And he said arrogantly: 'Who wants to look at that son of a serf!'" Thereupon he marched out of the church and from that hour his mind began to fail and "his faculties to decay" until he reached a state of total dementia. He would come out of his cell "foolishly," unpunctually, without his archiepiscopal vestment, and would sit by the church where Euphemius was buried, or sometimes by the gate of St. Sophia. And after spending ten months in Novgorod in this condition, he was returned to Moscow. This fate befell him because instead of honoring God's saint, his equal in office, he had cast reproach upon him. The account ends with the words: "So are the proud requited both now and world without end." [6] According to a Novgorod folk tradition incorporated in the chronicle, Sergius was chastised by Archbishop John "for riding on a devil." The Pskov variant states that Sergius was chastised by the Novgorod prelates buried in the Church of St. Sophia for that he assumed the Novgorod cathedra during the lifetime of the Novgorod archbishop Theophilus, who had been conveyed to Moscow. The Moscow variant tells quite a different story about the fate of Sergius: according to this variant the Novgorodians took Sergius' wits away by sorcery for that he had contradicted them. [7]

There is some resemblance between the Novgorod tradition about Moses and the Novgorod tradition, entered in the chronicle under 1462, about a visit of Ivan III, before the subjugation of Novgorod, to the Church of the Transfiguration in the Khutyn Monastery where the "relics" of the Novgorod saint Barlaam lay. When the great prince wished to open the tomb of Barlaam, flame suddenly leaped from it and almost burned the prince, who then fled in terror from the church. In token of this event—according to tradition—there remain to this day the flame-scorched wooden door and Ivan III's walking stick.

LEGENDS ABOUT THE END OF NOVGOROD

When Novgorod's loss of freedom became an accomplished fact, back-dated tales and legends on the theme of the city's latter end appeared in Novgorod literature. For the most part they attribute Novgorod's subjuga-

[6] See Buslayev, "Lektsii iz kursa istorii russkoy literatury" (Lectures from a Course on the History of Russian Literature), *Letopisi russkoy literatury i drevnosti* (Chronicles of Russian Literature and Antiquity), III, pp. 72–78.

[7] See V. Klyuchevskii, *Drevnerusskie zhitiya svyatykh* (Early Russian Lives of Saints), pp. 151–152.

tion by Moscow to the grievous transgressions and impieties of the Novgorodians. Entered in the chronicle under 1045 is the following story about an icon of the Saviour done by Greek icon painters for Great Prince Vladimir Yaroslavich's Church of St. Sophia. The painters' orders had been to represent the Saviour with his hand outstretched in blessing. When the bishop of Novgorod entered the church after the icon's completion, he noticed that the Saviour was depicted not with his hand outstretched but with his hand closed. Three times the icon painters did the hand over, but each time it closed up afterward. And on the third day the icon painters heard a voice from the image: "Painters, O painters! Do not paint me with my hand open; paint me with my hand closed, for in this hand I hold Great Novgorod; and when this hand of mine opens, then shall Novgorod come to an end."

Under 1471, in the same chronicle, occurs an entry concerning the portents which preceded the subjugation of Novgorod by Ivan III: a strong wind sprang up and broke the cross on St. Sophia, and blood appeared on two of the tombs; then the Kherson bells on St. Saviour's at Khutyn started ringing by themselves, while in the nunnery of St. Euphemia tears repeatedly flowed in streams from the eyes of the icon of the Virgin. The life of popular Mikhail Klopsky, a partisan of Moscow and an opponent of the Lithuanian party, tells how, upon meeting Archbishop Euphemius, he said to him that now there was rejoicing in Moscow: a son had been born to the great prince, who "shall be heir to his tsardom and a terror to all lands, shall seize Novgorod the Great and change all our customs, and shall take much gold from you and convey you to a cell in his city." [8]

In the *Solovetsk Paterikon,* or in the life of Zosima and Savvatius, composed in the late fifteenth or early sixteenth century, the following story is told about Zosima. When Zosima, having betaken himself to Novgorod to complain about the oppression of the Solovetsk Monastery by the townsfolk of Dvinsk and the boyar stewards, called on the celebrated Novgorod boyar Martha, she refused to receive him and even ordered him sent away. Zosima shook his head as he left Martha's house and said to the disciples accompanying him: "The time is at hand when those that dwell in this house shall no longer walk in the courtyard, and the doors of the house shall shut and not open and their courtyard shall be deserted." However, Martha repented and got Zosima back so that she might receive his blessing, and invited him to dine with her. Sitting at table, Zosima thrice saw a terrible vision: before him sat six headless boyars. His head drooped and he could not go on eating. The vision was shortly fulfilled: Great Prince Ivan Vasilyevich,

[8] *Pamyatniki starinnoy russkoy literatury* (Monuments of Ancient Russian Literature), IV, p. 45.

"autocrat of all Russia," attacked Novgorod in company with all his brothers and the Russian princes, and "all the Tartar kings and princes in his service" and with his whole army, and a battle took place at Shelona and some of the Novgorodians were killed, others taken captive, while some at the prince's command were beheaded. The six boyars whom Zosima had seen headless at the feast were among those taken whose heads were chopped off.[9]

The life of Barlaam of Khutyn tells of the following miraculous vision seen by Sexton Tarasius in the Church of St. Saviour's. At midnight, when the sexton was in the church on some errand connected with his office, all the candles on the lusters and on the candlesticks came alight and the church was filled with fragrance. At this time Tarasius, not in a dream but with his waking eyes, saw St. Barlaam, who was buried in the church, come forth from his tomb. And for three hours Barlaam prayed tearfully and passionately to Christ, to the Virgin, and to all the saints, while the sexton remained in great terror. Having prayed, Barlaam approached Tarasius and said to him: "The Lord God wishes to destroy Great Novgorod. Go up, brother, to the very top of the church, and you will see the destruction of Great Novgorod which the Lord will bring upon the city." When the sexton went to the top of the church, he saw a terrible prodigy: Lake Ilmen had risen high above Novgorod and threatened to engulf it. In terror the sexton told Barlaam what he had seen. Barlaam explained that God wished to drown Novgorod in Lake Ilmen as punishment for the manifold sins of the people and for the iniquity and unrighteousness that they had done. After again standing for three hours in prayer, Barlaam a second time commanded the sexton to go up to the top of the church and see what God would do to Novgorod. And the sexton saw a multitude of angels shooting arrows of fire that fell on the multitude like a heavy rain from the clouds, on men, women, and children, while in front of each human being stood his guardian angel holding a book and reading from it God's decree. If a person was to remain alive, his guardian angel anointed him with a brush of holy oil from a chalice, and straightway this man was healed of his deadly wound; but if a person was doomed to die, his guardian angel went away downcast without anointing him, fearing to disobey the decree of his Master. Having learned what was going on outside the church and having finished his prayer, Barlaam this time explained what the sexton had seen as follows: in response to the prayers of the Virgin and all the Saints, God had spared his people from drowning but would send a plague upon them, that they might repent. And there would be plague for three years. This actually happened.

[9] See Buslayev, "Novgorod i Moskva," *Istoricheskie ocherki russkoy narodnoy slovesnosti i iskusstva* (Novgorod and Moscow, Historical Outlines of Russian Folk Literature and Art), II, pp. 270–271.

When at Barlaam's command the sexton went to the church top for the third time, he saw a great cloud of fire above the city, which, Barlaam explained, signified that after the three years' plague there would be a great fire in Novgorod: the whole merchants' quarter would burn and a multitude of people be consumed; for the present, however, the Virgin and all the saints had prevailed upon her son and saved the city from inundation. Then, having at last concluded his prayers to God, the Virgin, and all the saints, Barlaam reentered his tomb, whereupon the candles and the lusters went out of themselves.[10]

Another and evidently later redaction of the monument says that after the lusters and candlesticks lighted up, the sexton (here his name is Prokhor) saw three men enter the church, shining like the sun, and was asked where Barlaam slept. When the sexton answered that Prior Barlaam had died more than three hundred years before, the men insisted that he show them the tomb of the prior and, approaching it, commanded Barlaam in the name of Christ to rise from his grave and depart from the church, since "in punishment for the increase of iniquity, for its sins, the Lord God wished to destroy Great Novgorod and plunge it beneath Lake Ilmen." But, upon hearing this, Barlaam said tearfully and passionately: "My lords, say to the Master, to the Lord God and our Saviour Jesus Christ: if, Lord, for its great transgressions you destroy Great Novgorod with its multitude of people, then destroy me also; but if, Lord and lover of mankind, you spare the multitude of the people of Great Novgorod, men and women and their children, then save me with them, Lord. How, my lords, can you bid me leave the people of my native land in a moment of such affliction and desert my native land?" In reply to the men's warning that Barlaam's refusal might anger God, Barlaam said: "I know the all-gracious Saviour; he will not scorn us, his servants, who have prayed to him night and day in faith and with contrite hearts." For the rest, this redaction conforms in general to the foregoing in its presentation of events, adding that there actually was plague in Novgorod thereafter for three years, from 1506 through 1508, and then a great fire.[11]

It is very indicative that even the ultimate collapse of Novgorod politically, failed to weaken the city's hold on certain ideas or the latent opposition to Muscovite supremacy which asserted itself in attempts to command recog-

[10] For the text see *Pamyatniki starinnoy russkoy literatury* (Monuments of Ancient Russian Literature), I, pp. 283–284. Cf. A. S. Orlov, "Videnie ponomarya Tarasiya-Prokhora" (nach. XVI v.) (Vision of Sexton Tarasius-Prokhor—Beginning of the Sixteenth Century), *Chteniya v Obshchestve istorii i drevnostey* (Paper Read before the Society of History and Antiquities).
[11] See Buslayev, *op. cit.*, pp. 271–274.

nition as sole genuine continuator of the traditions of the Christian Church
and guardian of Christian sanctitude. This attitude is clearly typified by
Novgorod's production of such works as the *Tale of the White Cowl of
Novgorod,* the *Legend of the Tikhvin Icon of the Mother of God,* and the
Life of Antonius the Roman.

TALE OF THE WHITE COWL OF NOVGOROD

This tale, the closing events of which are associated with the Novgorod
archiepiscopate of Vasily (1330–1352), appeared not later than the middle
of the sixteenth century. Its author was most probably the translator (interpreter) Dimitry Gerasimov, active collaborator with Gennadius, Archbishop of Novgorod, in the collection and translation of the books of the
Bible, a man who had traveled on ambassadorial affairs and gone to Rome
on the matter of the composition of paschal tables.

The tale is preceded by an epistle from Dimitry to Archbishop Gennadius
in which the author tells of his safe arrival in Rome, where he had been
charged to look up a document about the white cowl. This document he
had obtained with great difficulty since it had been carefully concealed "for
shame." Jacob, the librarian of the Roman Church, out of sympathy for
Dimitry and in deference to his urging, had informed him that the Greek
original of the tale of the white cowl, brought to Rome by pious Greeks
after the fall of Constantinople, had been destroyed by the Roman authorities, and that only a Roman translation of it had been preserved, and that
secretly. This translation Dimitry begged of the Roman librarian and was
now transmitting in Russian paraphrase to Gennadius.

The tale itself begins by telling how in the reign of Constantine, successor to Maxentius, wicked persecutor of Christians, the persecutions had
diminished considerably. But in the third year of Constantine's reign, seizing upon the fact that the Roman bishop Silvester had christened some
"man of the emperor's family," the Jew Zambrius undertook his persecution
and roused Constantine, from whose wrath Silvester hid himself in a secret
place. Meanwhile, in the seventh year of his reign, Constantine was smitten with leprosy, of which neither magicians and sorcerers could cure him,
nor the most skillful physicians. Finally the emperor was advised to try
bathing in the blood of newborn babes. When three thousand babes had
been collected, the emperor started off for the Capitoline, there to bathe
in their blood. But when he heard the wailing and groaning of the mothers,

Constantine was filled with compassion for them and renounced his intention, preferring to die of his ailment rather than murder children. That same night the apostles Peter and Paul appeared to the emperor and as a reward for sparing the children promised to give him "the means of salvation." They bade him summon from hiding Silvester, who would show him the "font of salvation"; after washing in it, the emperor would be cured of his ailment and inherit eternal life. In return, Constantine was to give Silvester the means to revive the Orthodox Church throughout the world. Presenting himself in response to the emperor's summons, Silvester baptized Constantine, who was then completely restored to health. The emperor began to honor Silvester as a god and named him pope. The Christian faith prospered in Rome, while the pagan was subjected to all manner of persecution. Constantine wanted to place the imperial crown on Silvester's head but the pope humbly refused it, and then under instructions from Peter and Paul, who appeared to Constantine in a vision, the emperor in a church ceremony laid on Silvester's head a white cowl. Obtaining from the emperor the golden charger on which the imperial crown had rested, Silvester laid upon it the white cowl, which he kept in the church in a "place of honor" and wore only on great ("our Lord's") holidays. He left instructions that after his death his successors should do the same. In the thirteenth year of his reign, Constantine decided that it was unseemly for the temporal authority to be located at the established seat of the spiritual authority and, turning Rome over to Pope Silvester, transferred his own residence to Byzantium, where he founded Constantinograd.

After the death of Pope Silvester all Orthodox popes and bishops paid great honor to the cowl, as Silvester had instructed. And so quite a time passed. But the adversary of the human race, our enemy the Devil, worked upon a certain emperor, Carol by name, and upon Pope Formus, and taught them "to deceive the Christian race with their false words and teachings," and they turned aside from the Orthodox faith and rent asunder "the union of the pious Holy Apostolic Church." (The reference is to the separation of the churches, with which, however, Pope Formus had no connection.) They both disliked the white cowl and refused to show honor to it. The cowl was hidden in a side chapel of the church; then the new pope wanted to burn it, but God prevented this and they decided to send the cowl to far lands across the sea and revile and destroy it there. While the cowl was still on its voyage, a certain "envoy," Indrik, attempted to dishonor it and was punished by an evil death. At a command from on high, the keeping of the cowl was entrusted to another "envoy," Jeremiah, who was secretly an adherent of the Christian faith. Five days later a storm came up and the ship sank, and all those on board perished except Jeremiah, who, clinging to a board and holding tight to the coarse cloak in which the cowl was wrapped, was saved by two shining men who walked on the sea as on dry land. With the cowl Jeremiah returned to Rome and told the pope everything that had happened. The pope was terrified when he heard the story and ordered the cowl placed on a golden salver in the church, but, as before, did it no honor. Then at God's command an angel appeared to the pope in a dream, sternly commanding him on pain of death and eternal fire to send the cowl to Constantinople. The pope dared not disobey. Upon entering the church the next morning, he beheld a terrifying prodigy: the cowl raised itself to the height of a man and then settled back into its place. In great consternation the pope took the cowl in his hand and, placing it in a vessel and sealing it up, sent it to Constantinople to the patriarch Filofeus, a very pious man.

At this time there appeared to Filofeus, in a vision by night, a shining youth, who, after telling the patriarch the story of the cowl, bade him send it, upon its arrival in Constantinople, to the land of Rus, to Novgorod, for Vasily, the archbishop of that place to wear, "for it is there [in Novgorod] that the Christian faith now exists in its true glory." The patriarch, attended by the whole ecclesiastical synod, received the cowl with great honor, and it gave forth fragrance and miraculously healed the patriarch of an illness, and he accorded it a place of honor in the Church of St. Sophia until the emperor should advise with him as to what to do with it next.

But the Roman pope, having dispatched the cowl, repented of the act and demanded its return, but the patriarch with imprecations and reproaches refused the pope's request. Upon reading Filofeus' reply and learning that the patriarch had received the cowl with honor and was planning to send it to Novgorod, the pope flew into a rage and fell ill: he therefore disliked Rus for abiding by the Christian faith. Grievous and repulsive ailments afflicted him and a great stench proceeded from him and a multitude of worms infested his body. He got to the point where he talked all manner of nonsense, howled like a wolf or a dog, and ate his own uncleanness. Such was his latter end.

Meanwhile the patriarch attempted to keep the cowl in Constantinople, thinking to wear it on his own head. But in a vision there appeared to him two shining strangers, who turned out to be Pope Silvester and Emperor Constantine, and they forbade him to make plans to retain the cowl since in a short time Constantinople would be taken by the Agars (Mussulmans) as a punishment for man's increasing transgressions, and all its shrines desecrated, as had been foretold at the founding of the city. (The author evidently has in mind the introduction to Nestor-Iskander's *Tale of the Taking of Tsargrad*.) "For the old Rome," says Silvester, "fell from glory and from the Christian faith through pride and self-will; in the new Rome, that is, in Constantinograd, by constraint of the Agars the Christian faith shall likewise perish; but on the third Rome, that is, on the land of Rus, the grace of the Holy Spirit shall shine. And all lands, Filofeus," Silvester continues, "along with all Christendom, shall in the end come to be absorbed into the single empire of Rus because of its Orthodoxy. In the old days, by decree of the earthly emperor Constantine, the imperial crown of this imperial city was bestowed on a Russian tsar; this white cowl shall now be given by decree of the heavenly emperor Christ to the archbishop of Great Novgorod, and this circlet [the cowl] is more honorable than that [the imperial crown] because it is the imperial crown of the archangelic and spiritual order." Silvester tells Filofeus to send the cowl to Novgorod without delay. As grace had been withdrawn from Rome, so it would also be withdrawn from Constantinople, "and all that is sacred shall be transmitted by God to the great land of Rus in his good time and the Lord shall exalt the Russian tsar to rule over many tongues, and many foreign tsars shall be under his power, and the patriarchy of this imperial city shall likewise be bestowed upon the land of Rus in God's time and the country shall be called shining Russia, God having so willed it."

Awaking in terror, Filofeus wept much, mindful of what he had heard about the white cowl and about the coming fate of Constantinople, and in the morning, after the liturgy, he honorably dispatched the cowl to Novgorod to Archbishop Basil along with many gifts and with "consecrated" vestments. Basil, too, fell asleep at that same time and in a dream saw an angel wearing a white cowl. The angel explained to him the origin of the cowl, which he and his successors were to wear henceforth, and bade him go in the morning to meet it. In solemn state, with the whole church synod and a multitude of people, Basil met the Greek bishop who had brought the cowl to Novgorod. And from that time the white cowl was the established head-covering of the archbishops of Novgorod. Then people from many towns and kingdoms began to come to Novgorod, and marveled as at a prodigy when they saw the archbishop of that place wearing the white cowl, and told of it in all kingdoms and all lands.[12]

The tale of the white cowl, in basing the idea of the inheritance of spiritual power on the inheritance of the material symbols of that power, proceeded from the same tendentious premises as the tales of Babylon and the *Legend of the Princes of Vladimir*, written on the theme of the inheritance of temporal power.

The position assumed by our tale is clearly one of compromise. At a time

[12] The text of the tale is printed in *Pamyatniki starinnoy russkoy literatury* (Monuments of Ancient Russian Literature), I, pp. 287–303.

when Novgorod had been subjugated by Moscow, it was too late to lay claim to the Byzantine political inheritance: this inheritance it concedes to the "Russian tsar"; that is, to the Muscovite prince, but the right to the ecclesiastical legacy, as we see, Novgorod reserves for itself. A strong indication of the meaning of this veiled compromise is the hint, thrown out as it were in passing, that inasmuch as the white cowl is "the imperial crown of the archangelic order," it is, in a literal sense, "more honorable" than the imperial crown. By this innuendo, the tale, which emanated from ecclesiastical circles, establishes not only the unquestionable authority of the Novgorod Church, but also the superiority of "hierarchy" over "empire" —a tendency which was promoted in its most acute form more than a century and a half later by the patriarch Nikon in his losing struggle with Tsar Alexis Mikhailovich. Therefore it was not without reason that the Moscow Synod of 1666–1667, which deposed Nikon, qualified the tale of the white cowl as a "false and untrue" writing and stigmatized its author, Dimitry the Interpreter, as a man "who wrote whatever came into his head."

Our tale was based on a spurious document (the so-called "Gift of Constantine," *Donatio Constantini*), apparently fabricated in the eighth century to further the interests of the papacy in its struggle with the secular authority for privileges. The tale of the white cowl, with respect to events preceding Constantine's removal to Byzantium, essentially does no more than repeat what is said in the spurious Catholic document. The exposure of the false document was undertaken by the Italian humanists in the fifteenth century, but Catholic theologians did not definitively cease to defend its authenticity until the nineteenth century.

LEGEND OF THE TIKHVIN ICON OF THE MOTHER OF GOD

This legend, originating in Novgorod at the beginning of the sixteenth century, during the tenure of Archbishop Serapion, resembles the tale of the white cowl in purport. The story is assigned to the year 1383, sixty years before the fall of Constantinople. At this time there appeared in the precincts of Novgorod, on Lake Ladoga, an icon of the Mother of God which had "by the benevolence of God" left Tsargrad in order not to be taken by the Agars. Fishermen casting for fish in the lake saw the icon sail through the air above the watery gulf and then float away: it appeared several times in the neighborhood of Tikhvin. Residents of localities where it paused built chapels and churches to the Virgin. Finally the icon came to rest at Tikhvin, where it was received with due solemnity by clergy and populace and where a church of the Assumption was then built. Presently the Virgin herself appeared in a miraculous vision to a certain God-fearing man, to direct that on the church erected to her not an iron cross, as had been proposed, but a wooden one be installed. In the reign of Great Prince Vasily Ivanovich, a stone church was built in honor of the Virgin: this was consecrated by Archbishop Serapion in 1515; the Tikhvin Monastery was founded at the same time.

Later the Tikhvin icon was identified with the icon of "the Roman Mother of God," which had been painted, so tradition tells, by order of the patriarch Herman, who dispatched it to Rome at the time of the iconoclasts. After one hundred and fifty years it returned to Byzantium and subsequently migrated to the precincts of Novgorod. Thus, like the white cowl, the Tikhvin icon is associated not only with Byzantium but also with Rome.[13]

LIFE OF ST. ANTHONY OF ROME

It was likewise in the sixteenth century that the tradition about St. Anthony of Rome coming to Novgorod during the twelfth century took literary form. In 1597, when Antonius' relics were opened, this tradition and other sources became the basis for a life composed by a monk of his monastery and known in a manuscript of the late sixteenth or early seventeenth century. Legend states that Antonius was born in Rome of "Christian parents" and was brought up in the Christian faith, to which his parents adhered in secret, since Rome had fallen away from the Christian faith and into the "God-abominated" Latin heresy. After the death of his parents, Antonius distributed a part of their wealth among the poor and the rest, along with some costly church vessels, he put into a cask, then threw the cask into the sea, and departed for a remote wilderness, hiding from the heretics in caves and in clefts in the earth. In the wilderness he found monks "living and laboring for God," and he abode there twenty years in constant prayer and fasting. Then, at the instigation of the Devil, princes and popes started to persecute the monks living in the wilderness, whereupon they dispersed to escape persecution. Antonius made his way to the seashore and there con-

[13] See Buslayev, "Novgorod i moskva," *Istoricheskie ocherki* (Novgorod and Moscow, Historical Outlines), Vol. II, pp. 276–280; S. Kulakovskii, "Sostav skazaniya o chudesakh ikony bogomateri-Rimlyanyni" (Composition of the Legend of the Miracles of the Icon of the Roman Mother of God), *Sbornik statey v chest' akademika A. I. Sobolevskogo* (Collection of Articles in Honor of Academician A. I. Sobolevsky), pp. 470–475.

tinued his ascetic practices, remaining all the time on one rock. Once, when he was standing on the rock, a violent agitation was set up and the rock sailed out to sea like a ship and found its way to the river Neva, then to Lake Ladoga, from the lake sailed up the Volkhov and stopped at a small village on the river. Antonius learned the Russian language, and continued to live on the rock, remaining in prayer day and night as before. Then, at the urgent request of the archpriest, he founded on the spot where the rock had come to rest a church of the Nativity of the Virgin.

A year after Antonius' arrival in the precincts of Novgorod, fishermen casting for fish around Antonius' rock pulled in, along with the fish, that same cask which Antonius had once thrown into the sea and would have kept it for themselves, but by court decree the cask was awarded to Antonius. With the gold and silver in the cask, a richly adorned stone church and a monastery were built, Antonius becoming prior and remaining in this office for sixty years, until his death.[14]

Buslayev in his time called attention to the fact that, according to the life, church vessels of foreign workmanship were found in the cask and furthermore that the inscriptions on them were "in the Roman language." This detail, in Buslayev's opinion, is one more indication of the presence in olden times, in the eleventh and twelfth centuries, of a Western influence on our art. The best example of this influence is the so-called "Kherson" gate at Novgorod with its Latin inscriptions: this was built in the twelfth century by German workmen and afterward brought to Novgorod. Also among the artistic curiosities of Novgorod are the magnificent western European enamels with which the legend of Antonius the Roman was associated.

A study of the literary tradition in Novgorod during the fifteenth and sixteenth centuries brings out the fact that the literary culture which had manifested itself there as far back as the eleventh century not only did not subsequently decline but up to the time of the political collapse of Novgorod continued to gather momentum. This culture, developing parallel to the general culture of a city economically in contact with the West and under the influence of Western trends in religious thought, expressed itself also in a notable development of the *bylina* epos, reflecting the stormy political situation of Novgorod, its manner of living, trade practices, and so forth.

The learned literature of Novgorod responded with special fervor to events in any way associated with the political fate of the once free city now gradually losing its liberty and independence. "Few epochs in our history

14 The text of the *Life* is printed in *Pamyatniki starinnoy russkoy literatury* (Monuments of Ancient Russian Literature), I, pp. 263–270. Concerning the *Life*, see Buslayev, *Istoricheskie Ocherki* (Historical Outlines), II, pp. 110–115, and Klyuchevskii, *Drevnerusskie zhitiya svyatykh* (Old Russian Lives of Saints), pp. 306–311.

have been surrounded by such a swarm of poetic legends as the fall of the free city of Novgorod," writes Klyuchevsky. "It was as though 'lord Great Novgorod,' feeling his life pulse slackening, shifted his thoughts from the court of Yaroslav, where his voice was now silent, to St. Sophia and other local shrines, evoking from them traditions of the olden time."[15]

[15] *Drevnerusskie zhitiya svyatykh* (Old Russian Lives of Saints), p. 162.

Literature of Pskov

PSKOV, being for the greater part of the time up to its final amalgamation with Moscow politically and culturally dependent on near-by Novgorod, did not show any such intensive and diversified literary productivity as did Novgorod. But in Pskov, too, cultural interests were at notably high pitch, as may be seen both from the rise there of such a characteristic social-religious movement as Shearerism and from the extent to which a specific Pskov literature was developed.[1]

Like Novgorod, Pskov after its fall was, even as early as the sixteenth century, making an effort to perpetuate in literature the most important events of its historic past. Vasily-Barlaam, priest-monk of Pskov, wrote a series of lives reviving old traditions about local Pskov saints. Chronicle writing, initiated not later than the thirteenth century under the influence of Novgorod's chronicle activity, had by the end of the fifteenth and the beginning of the sixteenth century gathered momentum, and went on uninterrupted for some time even after the subjugation of Pskov by Moscow. In the first and second Pskov chronicles, the nearer we get to the sixteenth century the more often do we find, in place of short, dry entries, extended narratives and separate pieces having a tinge of lyricism and showing the stylistic influence of martial narratives. Take, for example, the description of the battle below Orsha in the first Pskov chronicle, which reflects, by way of the tales of the rout of Mamay, turns of style found in the *Tale of Igor's Expedition*:

---

[1] See A. A. Pokrovskii, *Drevneye pskovsko-novogorodskoe pismennoe nasledie* (Early Pskov-Novgorod Literary Legacy) (Moscow, 1916).

A great battle between the Muscovites and Lithuania took place below the town of Orsha, and the women of Orsha screamed and wailed at the sound of the Muscovite trumpets, and a great din and roar arose from the embattled Muscovites and Lithuanians; and the Muscovites smote the Lithuanians: Russian princes and boyars with fine, brave fighting men, sons of Rus, smote the mighty Lithuanian army, and Muscovite spears crashed and steel swords rang on Lithuanian helmets on the field of Orsha. Then God withdrew his aid from the Muscovites, and the pagan Lithuanians took many generals, Ivan Andreyevich and Prince Michael Golitsa, and other princes and boyars and bold sons of boyars, but some fled to Smolensk and others to the impassable rivers.[2]

As Novgorod tradition exalted St. Sophia, Pskov tradition celebrated its own shrine, the Church of the Trinity; an aureole was also cast about its two most prominent historical figures, Princes Vsevolod Mstislavich and, more particularly, Dovmont. The *Tale of Dovmont,* mentioned above, underwent a number of hagiographical adaptations in the sixteenth century.[3]

TALE OF THE TAKING OF PSKOV

Pskov's most remarkable literary monument is the tale of the subjugation of Pskov in 1510 by the Muscovite prince Vasily Ivanovich, included in the first Pskov chronicle under a title of its own: *The Taking of Pskov, How Great Prince Vasily Ivanovich Took It,* and written by a Pskovan living at the time the events took place.[4]

The tale, written with great lyric afflatus, contains a large number of elements of spoken Russian. It begins by pointing out that, from the beginning of the land of Rus, Pskov had never been anyone's property and the inhabitants had lived as they chose. The prince of Moscow had subordinated many appanaged principalities to himself but Pskov had remained inviolate. It was protected by strong walls with a multitude of men behind them. This was one thing that checked the Muscovite prince. Another was the fear that the Pskovans might go over to Lithuania. Therefore he "craftily" kept peace with the people of Pskov and the latter swore an oath on the cross that they would give allegiance to no one else. The Muscovite prince sent his princes to Pskov on the recommendation of the Pskovans themselves,

[2] See *Polnoe sobranie russkikh letopisey* (Full Collection of Russian Chronicles), IV, p. 290.
[3] A detailed analysis of these may be found in N. Serebryanskii, *Drevnerusskie knyazheskie zhitiya* (Early Russian Princes' Lives), pp. 275–283.
[4] See *Polnoe sobranie russkikh letopisey* (Full Collection of Russian Chronicles), IV, pp. 283–288.

but it sometimes happened that he sent deputies of his own choosing. These prince's deputies would commit acts of violence, rob the people of Pskov, bring false accusations against them, and the people of Pskov would send their burgomasters to the great prince with complaints against their oppressors, and this happened many times. One such deputy, Prince Ivan Mikhailovich Repnya, made things particularly hard for the Pskovans.

When in October, 1510, Great Prince Vasily Ivanovich came to his patrimony, to Novgorod, the people of Pskov sent their envoys to the prince with gifts, and the envoys petitioned him against Repnya: "We have been insulted by your deputy," they said, "by our prince, Ivan Mikhailovich Repnya, by his men and by his deputies, by the constabulary and by their men." The great prince replied that he wished to favor and protect Pskov, his patrimony, as his father and grandfathers had done, promised to run the matter down and in the event of his culpability punish Repnya, and then he dismissed the envoys. But presently Repnya himself came to the great prince and in turn made complaint against the people of Pskov. When, subsequently, a deputation was again dispatched to Novgorod to Prince Vasily Ivanovich, the envoys were fraudulently arrested.

A certain merchant, Philipp, who was in Novgorod at that time, upon learning how the prince of Moscow was using the envoys from Pskov, abandoned his wares, returned to Pskov and told how things had gone with the complainants. Then fear and trembling seized upon the people of Pskov. Their throats were parched with grief and sorrow, their lips were dry. More than once the Germans had attacked Pskov but never had Germans caused the people of Pskov such grief and sorrow as they now felt. And the Pskovans gathered the town assembly (*veche*) and began to take counsel as to whether they should defend themselves against the sovereign, or shut themselves up from him in the city. But they recalled their oath on the cross and reflected that they might not raise their hand against their sovereign; they also recalled that the burgomasters and boyars and foremost citizens remained in the prince's hands as hostages, and they sent a fast messenger to make tearful petition, leaving nothing unsaid, to their sovereign, Prince Vasily Ivanovich, that he take pity on his ancient patrimony, and to say that they, poor orphans, who had before been importunate, would now remain obedient.

But this appeal of the Pskovans failed to move Vasily Ivanovich. He sent them his clerk, Tretyak Dolmatov, who demanded of them compliance with two wishes of Prince Vasily Ivanovich: first that they give up their assembly and take down their assembly bell; second that Pskov accept two deputies whom the great prince should himself appoint. And if they agreed to comply, they should go on living as of old; but if they refused to carry out the aforesaid two wishes, then it should come to pass as God might put in their lord's heart. His forces were great and to refuse to submit to the sovereign's will would mean bloodshed.

The Pskovans, weeping bitterly, asked to be given until morning to think it over. "How did their eyeballs not drop out along with their tears? How was their heart not torn up by the roots?" exclaims the author of the tale in his own person (an expression already familiar to us from *Digenis-Akritas* where the mother of the maiden abducted by Amir, in complaining to her sons, likewise speaks of Amir's having "pulled up the root of her heart").

In the end the Pskovans humble themselves and decide to do the will of the sovereign. In the morning they turn their assembly bell over to Tretyak Dolmatov and bid farewell to their freedom. They do this because they are well aware of the uselessness of making any show of resistance whatever.

"On the 13th of the month of January, on the day sacred to the memory of the holy martyrs Yermil and Stratonik, the Pskovans lowered their assembly bell from the Holy Church of the Primordial Trinity and, looking at the bell, began to weep for the days of old and for their freedom."

That same night Tretyak conveyed the assembly bell to the great prince in Novgorod. After that, governors of the great prince came to Pskov and put the people under oath, and a week later the great prince himself came to Pskov, and the people met him three versts from the city and, bowing to the earth before him, said in response to his salutation: "Hail to you, our sovereign great prince, tsar of all Rus." After receiving the archbishop's blessing, Vasily Ivanovich went to Trinity where they chanted a Te Deum for him and proclaimed the length of days. Then the great prince summoned the burgomasters and their sons and the boyars and merchants and people of means, saying: "I desire to bestow my favor upon you." And when the people of Pskov had one and all gathered in the prince's courtyard, the great prince commanded that police officers be put over the burgomasters, boyars, and merchants of Pskov, while the "minor people" were told that the sovereign's concernment did not extend to them but that if it should in future, he would take them unto himself.

And that same night, taking with them only their small belongings and abandoning all the rest, the propertied men of Pskov and their wives and children went to Moscow; the wives of those envoys who had earlier been arrested in Novgorod were also deported; in all, three hundred families were carried off. "Then the glory of Pskov was snatched away and made captive not by men of another faith but by men of their own faith; who will not weep and sob thereat?" the narrator asks sorrowfully.

Next the story gives the lament of Pskov for its lost freedom, employing images from the Bible,

O most glorious city, Pskov, the great: why do you mourn and lament? And the fair town of Pskov made answer: "How should I not mourn, how should I not lament and grieve at my desolation? For a many-winged eagle swooped down on me, its wings filled with lion's claws: from me are taken my three cedars of Lebanon; my beauty and wealth and my children are ravished away, God permitting because of our sins; and the land they desolate made, our town in ruin laid, my people captive made, my markets up did spade, some with horse dung overlaid, our fathers and our brothers from us parted, and to a place where our fathers, grandfathers, great-grandfathers never their home had made, our fathers and brothers and friends they conveyed, our mothers and our sisters to outrage they betrayed. And many men in the town turned monk, and women nuns, and to convents retired, unwilling to go forth captive from their city to other cities."

Here, as we see, is an example of rhythmically organized language broken up into lines having verbal rhymes.

The fall of free Pskov is interpreted by the tale as God's chastisement for sins: "It was our self-will and disobedience one to another that brought all this evil upon us."

The great prince began distributing among his boyars the villages of the deported Pskov boyars, and in addition to his two deputies he also set up in Pskov his clerks, provosts, and overseers and ordered them to sit in court with the deputies and bailiffs "to guard the laws. And what with the deputies and bailiffs and clerks of the great prince, the Pskovans' code, their kissing of the cross, flew up to heaven, and falsehood began to walk among them and great evil came to be among them; no allowances were made for the people of Pskov, though the unfortunate Pskovans knew not the Muscovite law." And many other constraints did Moscow put upon Pskov, and there was nowhere the Pskovans could go to escape them, "unless the earth should open, or unless they should fly straight up."

In spite of the fact that the author of the tale is convinced of the inevitability of the fall of Pskov and is inclined to regard the tragedy of his native city as heaven's just revenge for the Pskovans' many transgressions, he cannot reconcile himself to the craft and cruelty shown by the Muscovite prince toward townspeople who had manifested complete submission and full loyalty to him. The voice of protest is here raised against Muscovite wrongs much more strongly than in any of Novgorod's anti-Muscovite literary works. While imitating the lamentations of Jeremiah and Ezekiel, and also the first discourse of Serapion of Vladimir, and while following traditions rooted in Western and Byzantine literature, the author of the *Tale of the Taking of Pskov* expressed with great lyric power his own grief and that of the conquered and enslaved city. His work was, however, only a continuation, literary development, and adaptation of the chronicle reaction to the event which in the first Pskov chronicle precedes the tale itself under the same year, 1510, and is occasionally even more vocal in protest than the tale. It begins with the statement: "In the year 7018, on the 24th day of the month of January, Great Prince Vasily Ivanovich came to Pskov and changed the usage of Pskov and violated the old-time agreement, forgetting the given word of his father and his grandfather and the grant of favor to the people of Pskov and the kissing of the cross." Next it quotes the hypocritical, "soft" words of the prince in his letter to the Pskovans: "Verily I, Great Prince Vasily Ivanovich, desire to favor you, my patrimony, as of old, and I wish to visit the Church of the Holy Trinity, and I wish to administer justice to you," and then with references to the Apocalypse and to the Gospels, the Muscovite great prince is identified as the forerunner of Antichrist, whose kingdom is destined "to be enlarged" and his misdeeds "to be multiplied." [5]

Like the monuments which have for theme the championship of Novgorod and its political and religious privileges, so the corresponding monuments of Pskov emanated from boyar circles and from the related circles of the higher clergy, who were equally interested in keeping their domains from being swallowed up by the centralizing Muscovite nobiliary state in process of formation.

[5] *Ibid.*, p. 282.

Literature of Tver

TVER, Moscow's rival for political priority during the fourteenth and fifteenth centuries, produced a series of literary monuments which reflect in some measure the political consciousness of the upper sections of Tver society. First of all must be noted the fairly intensive development of chronicle writing in Tver as early as the end of the thirteenth century, leading to the formation of an all-Tver chronicle compilation by the beginning of the fifteenth century.[1] In 1406, as was indicated above, the so-called "Arsenian" redaction of the *Kiev Crypt Paterikon* was produced within the precincts of Tver. In the fifteenth century the early fourteenth century tale of the murder at the Horde of Michael Yaroslavich, Great Prince of Tver, was recast in the new flowery rhetorical manner.[2] Also composed in the fifteenth century, during the reign of Prince Boris Aleksandrovich, was the life of Great Prince Michael Aleksandrovich (died 1399).[3] The second of these two works is of particular interest. In establishing the genealogy of Michael Aleksandrovich and tracing his lineage back to St. Vladimir Prince of Kiev, as the *Stepennaya Kniga* was later to do in connection with other princes as well, the author of the life aspires to render him honor "so that it may be known of all from what God-planted root such a God-planted

[1] On the Tver chronicle see A. N. Nasonov, "Letopisnye pamyatniki Tverskogo knyazhestva" (Annalistic Monuments of the Tver Principality), *Izvestiya Akad. nauk, SSSR, Otd. gumanitarnykh nauk* (News of the Academy of Science USSR, Division of the Humanities) (1930), pp. 710–772.

[2] See *Polnoe sobranie russkikh letopisey* (Full Collection of Russian Chronicles), Vol. VII, pp. 188–197.

[3] *Ibid.*, Vol. XV, pp. 463–470.

scion had sprung." Both works, written by Tver patriots, were intended to glorify the princes who had fought for the independence of the Tver principality.

EULOGISTIC DISCOURSE OF THE MONK THOMAS ON BORIS ALEKSANDROVICH

The idea of the heirship of Rus and the Russian princes to the Byzantine ecclesiastical and political legacy as a consequence of the Florentine Union and the Turkish conquest of Constantinople, found literary expression in Tver before finding it in Moscow. In about 1453, that is, at about the time of the fall of Constantinople, the monk Thomas composed an extended *Eulogistic Discourse on the Orthodox Great Prince Boris Aleksandrovich*, a very elaborate panegyric on the prince and principality of Tver, written under the influence of such works as the *Life and Death of Dmitry Ivanovich*, the *Life of Alexander Nevsky*, the anonymous *Legend of Boris and Gleb*, the tales of the rout of Mamay, Metropolitan Hilarion's *Discourse of Law and Grace*, and so forth, and also influenced by "Holy Writ" and the works of the "Church Fathers." The author was a contributor to the Tver chronicle, a fact which declares itself, among other things, in individual passages of his discourse written in the typical chronicle manner. Shakhmatov conjectures that Thomas was court chronicler, compiler of the new edition of the Tver chronicle digest.

The discourse falls into six sections.

The first section is the eulogy proper, given partly in the author's own person, partly in the persons of the Byzantine emperor John, the patriarch, and the twenty-two metropolitans who gathered at the Florentine council—to which Boris Aleksandrovich had also been invited, but had sent the boyar Thomas to represent him and carry his message. Throughout, the author gives Boris the title of "ruling autocratic sovereign" and compares him with the most outstanding historical personalities—with the emperors Augustus, Leo the Wise, Ptolemy Philologus, Constantine I, Justinian, and even with Moses and Joseph from the Bible. The whole district of Tver rejoices that "God should have given them such a sovereign and shepherd and true lover of Christ and God-ordained successor to the ancestral throne." In imitation of the life of Alexander Nevsky, it is said of Boris Aleksandrovich:

The glory of his name was exalted in distant lands, and many people in distant lands and kingdoms heard of this sovereign and straightway came with rejoicing, desirous of seeing him, saying to themselves with glad and shining faces: God be praised for establishing a carefree existence in the glorious land of Tver and under the strong sovereign authority of Great Prince Boris Aleksandrovich.

The emperor John, sighing from the depths of his heart, rendered praise to God for having given such a prince to the land of Rus, and such a helper to every Orthodox believer in the Christian religion. The patriarch praises the prince of Tver in the words of Metropolitan Hilarion and declares that "such a prince had never been heard of in Rus." The metropolitan of Rhodes likewise says: "We have not heard of another such prince in Rus as Great Prince Boris." The other metropolitans also speak ecstatically of Boris Aleksandrovich. Then the author himself again comes forward with praises for the prince: "God spread the heathen peoples over the lands and they settled in the villages of Great Prince Boris Aleksandrovich, and had it been possible the whole world would have made its abode in that promised land." Comparing Boris to the "just" Tiberius Caesar, the author says:

But Tiberius forbade his people to come before him in fine raiment and shining gold ornaments, while this autocratic sovereign, Great Prince Boris Aleksandrovich, did not so, but made countless gifts to his people and bade them come before him, in his palace, fair and resplendent, and he himself put on his imperial crown.

Subsequent passages in the *Discourse* tell how Boris Aleksandrovich routed the Muscovite army which Kolychev had led against Boris' nephew, Prince Ivan Yuryevich, about Boris' architectural activities, particularly about his building of churches and monasteries, towns, and even of Tver's citadel, and in connection with all this the author remarks that the "building done by Great Prince Boris Aleksandrovich shone like a morning star and a splendid crown, but Great Prince Boris Aleksandrovich truly deserves the crown of empire." Next something is said about the trials which God had sent upon Boris "in love" and "so that he should not exalt himself" and which Boris endured with Christian humility. The trials were grievous, for "a great man's trials must also be great." A particularly great misfortune was the fire of 1449, when Tver was burned to the ground. Finally, utilizing excerpts from the Tver chronicle, the author, alternating narrative with new eulogies, tells of various events in the reign of Boris Aleksandrovich, particularly of his helping the Muscovite prince, Vasily Vasilyevich, in his struggle with Dimitry Shemyaka. The only extant copy of the *Discourse* breaks off with an unfinished sentence.

In 1485, in the reign of Boris Aleksandrovich's son Michael Borisovich, the principality of Tver was amalgamated with Moscow. The *Discourse* of Thomas then not only lost its political and literary immediacy, but became in the eyes of Moscow an odious production, which apparently explains its being extant in a single copy and in a manuscript of very modest format at that, apparently the property of some private person.[4]

THE JOURNEY OF AFANASY NIKITIN TO INDIA

The journey of Afanasy Nikitin, merchant of Tver, included under the year 1475 in the second St. Sophia chronicle and there entitled *A Journey Across Three Seas*,[5] is one of the most interesting monuments in Tver's literature. In contrast to the traditional pilgrim, the devout churchman setting out for the "Holy Land" with religious aims, Afanasy Nikitin, a layman, an enterprising and energetic merchant, planned his journey to the unknown East with purely practical mercantile ends in view: to sell his goods there at a profit and with the money he made import foreign goods into Rus. He had originally planned to go to Persia, attaching himself, along with a few others from Moscow and Tver, to the suite of an ambassador to Ivan III who was returning to Samarkand. On the way, this side of Astrakhan, one of Afanasy's ships was captured by Tartars, the other was wrecked. He was compelled to continue his voyage to the Caspian Sea on the ambassador's ship, but from there took the overland route through Derbent and Baku to Persia and then to India. On the way back, somewhere short of Smolensk, Afanasy died. His journey had lasted from 1466 into 1472.

The traveler talks chiefly about India in his work, describing the everyday life and outdoor nature of that country in very great detail, though upon many occasions introducing fantastic elements as well. Orderly arrangement is not a distinguishing mark of Afanasy's exposition, and repetitions are of frequent occurrence. The style of the *Journey* suggests diary entries which the author, a man with no special training, was either incapable of,

[4] The text of the *Discourse*, with introduction, was published by N. P. Likhachev in *Pamyatniki drevney pismennosti*, CLXVII (Monuments of Early Literature) (St. Petersburg, 1908). A review by Shakhmatov of Likhachev's work (St. Petersburg, 1909), is appended to *Otchyoty o zasedaniyakh obshchestva lyubiteley drevney pismennosti* (Minutes of the Meetings of the Society of Friends of Early Literature) for 1907–1910 (St. Petersburg, 1911). See also Ya. Lurie, "Rol' Tveri v sozdanii russkogo natsional'nogo gosudarstva" (The Role of Tver in the Creation of the Russian National State), *Uchenye zapiski Leningradskogo gosudarstvennogo universiteta* (Scholarly Notes of Leningrad State University), No. 36, Seriya istoricheskikh nauk (Historical Science Series), Pt. 3, 1939, pp. 85–109.

[5] See *Polnoe sobranie russkikh letopisey* (Full Collection of Russian Chronicles), Vol. VI, pp. 330–358. A study of the *Journey* was made by I. I. Sreznevskii: "Khozhdenie za tri morya Afanasiya Nikitina" (Journey Across Three Seas of Athanasius Nikitin), *Uchenye zapiski II otdeleniya Akademii nayk* (Learned Notes of Division II of the Academy of Sciences), Bk. 2, Pt. II, 1856, pp. 225–307.

or did not get around to, putting in order. Afanasy's language is artless in the extreme; his sentences are of the utmost simplicity syntactically. Church Slavonic words and locutions are almost entirely absent, but on the other hand Persian, Arabic, and Turkish words occur in considerable numbers, a symptom of the singular internationalism that was his by nature in spite of his strong love of country. The account is factual and businesslike, with only rare lyric digressions expressive of the author's sorrow at being cut off from his native religion and his native land.

Here is a sample of Afanasy's description of India:

And this is an Indian country, and the people all go about naked, and their heads are uncovered, and their breasts are bare, and their hair plaited in one braid, and all have thick bellies, bring forth children every year, and their children are many, and the men and women are all black; wherever I go, many people follow me and stare at the white man. And their prince wears a silken scarf (*fata*) on his head and another at his loins. And the boyars among them go with a *fata* on their shoulders and another at their loins; and the servants of the prince and of the boyars attach a *fata* round the loins and carry a shield and a sword in their hands, and some carry spears and some knives and some sabers and some bow and arrows, but all are naked and barefoot, and black, and the women walk about with their heads uncovered and their breasts bare and boys and girls go naked to the age of seven.

To Afanasy Nikitin it seemed extraordinary that the women should go with their heads uncovered. In Rus, both then and later, this was considered a sin and a disgrace.

Arriving at the city of Alyand, Afanasy saw the Gukuk bird, which flies by night and cries "gukuk," and any roof it lights upon, there the man will surely die, and if anyone attempts to kill it, fire flashes from its beak. And monkeys rove at night and catch fowls. They live on hills or on rocks, and some live in the woods, and they have a monkey prince. They go attended by their army and if anyone offends them, they complain to their monkey prince and he sends his army against that person and, upon reaching the town, this army will pull down the houses and kill the people. And the army these monkeys have is very great and they have their own language and they bring forth many children and any children who resemble neither father nor mother they cast on the highways and people catch them, teach them every sort of handicraft, and some they sell, but by night, so that they will not know how to find their way back, and some they teach to dance.

Afanasy goes to Beder, one of the chief cities of India. The country there is very populous, "the villagers extremely naked, but the boyars extremely wealthy and luxurious." The boyars are carried on silver beds. Before them are led horses in gold harness. Three hundred men follow behind on horseback and five hundred on foot, and ten trumpeters and ten pipers; the sultan goes out hunting with his mother and his wife, and attended by ten thousand horse and fifty thousand foot, and two hundred elephants are led, adorned in gilded armor. Before the sultan go one hundred trumpeters, one hundred dancers, and three hundred ordinary horses in golden harness, and one hundred monkeys.

To what extent this luxurious picture of the sultan's turnout corresponded to the actuality would be hard to say. In all probability Afanasy described this triumphal procession very approximately, rounding out the figures and sometimes exaggerating them.

This is also true of the description of the sultan's palace. It has seven gates, and in the gates are seated one hundred guards and one hundred scribes. They enter the name of any person who goes in; they likewise enter his who goes out. Foreigners are not admitted into the town, and the sultan's palace is "very wonderful, everything in it carved and gilded and to the last stone cut and ornamented with gold most wonderfully." In his palace are divers vessels. The town is guarded at night by a thousand police officers; they are mounted and in armor, and each carries a torch.

Actually such luxury and monumentality can scarcely have existed in India. Elements of invention and legend here declare themselves very plainly.

And of creeds there are in India eighty and four. Everyone believes in But, that is, Buddha (except the sultan and his attendants, who appear to have been Mahometans). And one creed will not drink, eat, or marry with another, and some eat lamb, fowl, fish, and eggs, but no creed eats cattle.

In another passage, as the result of other observations, Afanasy affirms that the Hindus "eat no meat, neither cow flesh, nor mutton, nor chickens, nor fish, nor swine, though of pigs they have a great many." They eat twice a day but do not eat at night. Wine they do not drink, nor honey-water, nor mead. With Mussulmans they neither eat nor drink. Their fare is poor. They always eat with their right hand and take nothing with their left on any account; knives they do not use; spoons they do not know. He who must travel boils gruel for himself on the way, and for this reason anyone setting out anywhere on a journey takes a stone pot with him.

Afanasy travels from place to place in his efforts to trade. But trade is bad, there are no trade goods that the Russians would want. He complains:

The Mussulman dogs have lied to me and said that there was plenty of our goods but there is nothing for our country. . . . Pepper and colors, these are cheap: those who convey merchandise by sea pay no duty and the people who bring it to us will pay no duty, but the duties are many and the pirates on the sea are many.

Once he went to the city of Junir to sell a stallion which he had bought for a hundred rubles, but he had a great many vexations in connection with this stallion: the khan took the stallion from him and having heard that he was no Mahometan but a Russian, said: "I will give you the stallion and a thousand pieces of gold if you will become of our faith and worship Mahomet, but if you do not become of our faith and worship Mahomet, I shall take the stallion and take a thousand pieces of gold upon your head."

The khan gave Afanasy four days to consider. This occurred during the fast before our Saviour's day, and the lord took pity on Afanasy because of his holy festival, and did not let him perish at Junir among the "infidels." Just on the eve of our Saviour's day there came a man from Khorasan; that is, a man belonging to the ruling tribe of India, and Afanasy bowed to the ground and besought him to intercede to prevent his being converted to the Mahometan faith or having his horse taken from him.

Afanasy's plea was granted. He was excused from accepting the Mahometan faith and his stallion was returned to him. In the end he sold it at a profit, but arrived at a conclusion painful for himself and for his fellow-countrymen: "Now, Christian brethren of Rus, whoever of you wishes to go to the land of India, let him leave his religion in Rus and, calling upon Mahomet, proceed to the land of Hindustan."

While abroad Afanasy frequently experienced temptation. It was hard for him as a Christian to get on with "Mussulmans." Sometimes he could not help giving way to sceptical reflections. He says, for example: "But God knows the true faith, and the true faith is to acknowledge only one God and invoke his name in every place in spirit and in truth." But for the most part he holds strictly to the Orthodox faith and is greatly troubled at not having an opportunity to practice Christian observances. He exclaims:

O true believing Christians! He who voyages much through many lands will fall into many sins and lose his Christian religion. I, Afanasy, servant of God, have grown neglectful of religion: already four great fasts and four great days have gone by and I, sinful man, do not know which is great day or fast, nor do I know Christmas or any other holidays, neither Wednesday nor Friday do I know; books I have none: my books were taken from me by those who robbed us.

The grief of Afanasy is all the stronger because he loves his country and knows of none better: "May God preserve the land of Rus," he prays. "God preserve it. There is no country like it in the world. May the land of Rus stand firm!"

The journey ends with a lyric reflection by the author:

After much thinking, I was grieved and said to myself: Woe is me, accursed that I am. I have strayed from the true path and know not which way to go. Lord God Almighty, creator of heaven and earth, turn not thy face from thy servant, for I am thy creature. Lead me not from the path of truth but set me on the right road.

Curiously enough, the prayer that Afanasy wrote into his original in traditional Church Slavonic breaks off into a Mahometan prayer in Arabic, and such is the prayer with which the *Journey* ends.

The *Journey* of Afanasy Nikitin, while a work of very great value from the historico-archaeological viewpoint, inasmuch as Afanasy anticipated by several years Vasco da Gama's voyage to India, is also of no small literary-historical value as a sort of harbinger of descriptive literature and at the same time as an index to the cultural and economic level of Tver on the eve of its subjugation by Moscow.

The *Journey* is also interesting for the distinctness with which it reveals the unusual personality of the author. He stands before us first and foremost as a daring, determined, very enterprising, inquiring and observant man. The journey on which he is embarking with a view to commercial profits is a difficult and hazardous one. Serious calamities overtake him almost at the outset but do not make him turn round and go back: his willful and stubborn nature will not permit him to give up the goal he has set himself; the lot of a man who has failed in an undertaking is not to his mind, and, surmounting great hardships and deprivations, he seeks new successes in new places. In passing, he attentively scrutinizes the unknown country and the unknown people, their manners, customs, their culture, and jots down what he sees and hears.

A man of settled traditions and devotion to his religion and his country who did not depart from these traditions in spite of temptations to do so, he was at the same time intellectually capable of understanding a strange religion and recognizing what was good in it, if only the fact that it taught people to recognize one God and to call upon him. Such a breadth of initiative and outlook, existing in company with Afanasy Nikitin's natural conservatism, is of itself a manifestation extraordinary for his time and his background, and consequently arresting.

Literature of Smolensk

IT was at the beginning of the fifteenth century that the principality of Smolensk finally lost its independence and became part of the Muscovite state. From of old, Smolensk had been known for its scholarship—to which its proximity to the West had contributed. As evidence of this scholarship, as above noted, we have the *Life of Abraham of Smolensk,* composed in the first half of the thirteenth century by Abraham's disciple Ephraim. Both Abraham, who, to judge from the *Life,* possessed a large library of ecclesiastical literature, and the author himself were very well read men. However, the literary product of Smolensk, in view of the early separation of this principality from the other Russian states, is extant only to a very limited degree.

TALE OF MERCURIUS OF SMOLENSK

The most important monument of Smolensk literature known to us from the period under discussion is the legendary story of Mercurius, savior of Smolensk from destruction by the Tartars. It is evidently based on an oral folk tradition arising out of the fact that during the invasion of 1237–1238 the Tartars did not get as far as Smolensk and thus the city escaped devastation. The story tells of an attempt by the Tartars to seize Smolensk, but this version of the event is unsupported by historical evidence. We have two redactions of the story, the second of which is further classifiable into four subsidiary redactions.

As given in the first and older redaction, apparently produced not earlier than the end of the fifteenth century, in connection with the establishment of the worship of Mercurius at that time, the content of the tale is, in summary, as follows.

In Smolensk there lived a pious youth named Mercurius, "flower of seemly living, shining from prayer and fasting like a star divinely made manifest to the whole world." He often went to the monastery of the Exaltation of the Cross to pray for the world. At that time the infidel king Batu took the land of Rus captive and approached Smolensk with a great army, halting thirty versts from the city, burning churches and killing Christians. The people of Smolensk continued in great grief, praying at the cathedral church for the sparing of their town. And there occurred at this time "a divine revelation to the citizens." At the Crypt Monastery outside the city, the Virgin appeared to the sexton (cf. the similar episode of the Virgin appearing to the sexton in the life of Alexis, man of God) and bade him summon Mercurius. When Mercurius came in response to the summons, the Virgin bade him avenge the Christians and vanquish the infidel Batu and all his host. At the same time she told Mercurius that after his victory he would be approached by a man "fair of face" to whom he was to hand over all his arms, and this man would cut off his head. Carrying his head in his hand Mercurius was to make his way back to town, where he would die and his body be laid in the Church of the Virgin.

Her words bring tears and expressions of grief from Mercurius: he feels that a man so accursed and dissolute as himself will not have the strength for so difficult a task, and asks if the Virgin could not use some heavenly power to conquer the infidel king. But he cannot disobey the Virgin and, having received her blessing, leaves the church in full armor, mounts a "doughty" steed that stands nearby, and attacks Batu and vanquishes him, galloping among the troops "like an eagle flying through the air," while Batu, seized with fear and consternation, departs from the city, gets as far as Hungary and there perishes.

As the Virgin had predicted, Mercurius is afterward confronted by a "fair warrior," to whom he bows and turns over his weapons, and this man cuts off his head. The headless Mercurius arrives at the Mologin Gate of the city, carrying his head in one hand and reining his horse with the other. A girl, seeing him headless, starts "foolishly to upbraid him," but he lies down by the gate and dies, and his steed disappears. The archbishop of Smolensk comes with the crosses and a multitude of people to take the body of Mercurius but it will not yield itself to him and so lies unburied for three days. On the fourth day, after keeping vigil all night in prayer that God reveal to him this mystery, the archbishop looked through his window and saw coming out of the church the Virgin, together with the archangels Michael and Gabriel, "in great brightness, like unto the rising of the sun," and saw her go to the place where Mercurius lay, take his body in the skirts of her robe, bear it to the cathedral church and lay it in the coffin where it lies to this day, working miracles and giving forth fragrance like a cypress tree.

The essential differences in the second redaction, in the text chronologically nearest to the first redaction, are as follows. The story begins with an extended introduction telling of the Virgin's special patronage of Smolensk and of the acts of violence perpetrated by the Tartars in the land of Rus. Here, put into the mouth of a country sorrowful as a widow, is a lament for the ruin of the land of Rus. Mercurius was a Roman by extraction, of princely family, and of the Greek faith. In his youth he had come to Smolensk in the service of "the autocrat of that city." Instead of directly addressing the sexton and then Mercurius, the Virgin speaks through the icon. Mercurius gladly obeys the command of the Virgin, attacks the enemy (the miraculous steed is here absent), kills a powerful giant and many Tartars. Mercurius' head is cut off not by a "fair warrior" but by a "fearful barbarian," son of the giant whom Mercurius had slain. There is no mention of the girl who scolded the headless Mercurius upon his arrival at the city. The people of Smolensk bury him in the Church of the Virgin without the intervention of the Virgin herself. Some time later Mercurius appears to the sexton of the church at the icon as in life, wearing the accoutrements of war, and bids him tell the townspeople to hang his weapons, spear and shield, above his tomb. If ever an enemy attack should be made on the city, let prayer be made to God, to the Virgin, and to himself, and his weapons borne forth, and the enemy shall be put to shame. The townspeople did as Mercurius had commanded, and to this day his weapons may be seen above his tomb.

This edition probably dates from the very beginning of the sixteenth century. In it the exploit of Mercurius of Smolensk is compared with the exploit of the Byzantine St. Mercurius of Cesarea, whose fate, even to the Virgin's charging him to advance against "Julian the law-breaker" and his beheading after the victory, is shown to be similar to the fate of his Smolensk namesake. This establishes beyond doubt the influence of the Greek life on our story, which seems all the more natural in view of the fact that the Church's commemoration of Mercurius of Smolensk, who obviously never actually existed, was set for the same date as the commemoration of Mercurius of Cesarea.

The episode of Mercurius carrying his own head most probably originated under the influence of many similar Western Catholic legends of saints, chief of them the legend of Dionysius Areopagiticus.

Such legends are also known on Mussulman soil, particularly among the

Crimean Tartars, who may, however, have borrowed them from a Christian source. The motif of a man carrying his own severed head is also found in oral legends of the Smolensk and Pskov provinces. In one Smolensk record, oral legend directly mentions Mercurius carrying his head after it had been cut off in his battle with the Lithuanians.

The attribution of Roman ancestry to Mercurius of Smolensk must apparently be explained as due to the same motives that produced the Novgorod legend about Antonius coming to Novgorod from Rome. In both cases we are dealing with an attempt to link local sanctity with early Christian tradition.[1]

[1] On the tale see Buslayev, "Smolenskaya legenda o sv. Merkurii i rostovskaya o Pyotre, tsareviche Ordynskom," Istoricheskie ocherki (The Smolensk Legend of St. Mercurius and the Rostov Legend of Peter, Tsarevich of the Horde, Historical Outlines), II, pp. 155–198; A. Kadlubovski, Ocherki po istorii drevnerusskoy literatury zhitii svyatykh (Outlines of the History of the Literature on the Lives of the Early Russian Saints) (Warsaw, 1902), pp. 44–107; P. Mindalyov, "Povest o Merkurii smolenskom i bylevoy epos" (Tale of Mercurius of Smolensk and the Bylina Epos), Sbornik statey v chest' D. A. Korsakova (Collection of Articles in Honor of D. A. Korsakov) (Kazan, 1913), pp. 258–280; L. T. Beletskii, "K literaturnoy istorii povesti o Merkurii smolenskom" (On the Literary History of the Tale of Mercurius of Smolensk), review of Mindalyov's article, Zhurnal min. nar. prosv. (Journal of the Ministry of Public Instruction) (1914), No. 12, pp. 356–370; P. Mindalyov, "Otchyot na retsenziyu L. T. Beletskovo" (Answer to L. T. Beletskii's Review) ibid. (1915), No. 4, pp. 422–425; L. T. Beletskii, "Literaturnaya istoriya povesti o Merkurii Smolenskom" (Literary History of the Tale of Mercurius of Smolensk), study and texts, Sbornik otd. russk. yaz. i slov. (Collection of the Division of Russian Language and Literature of the Academy of Sciences) (Petrograd, 1922), Vol. XCIX, No. 8; N. Gudzii, "Motiv usechennoy golovy v tatarskoy legende ob Azise" (The Motif of the Severed Head in the Tartar Legend of Asiz), Izvestiya Tavricheskoy uchenoy arkhivnoy komissii (News of the Tavriz Scholarly Archive Commission) (1920), No. 56.

Literature of Murom-Ryazan

THE districts of Murom and Ryazan, which at first formed a single Murom-Ryazan principality, had already become separate entities by about the 1130's. At the end of the fourteenth century, by decree of the Khan, Murom passed under the control of the great prince of Moscow, and by the beginning of the fifteenth century, Muscovite deputies were already installed there. The principality of Ryazan kept up the struggle with Moscow much longer, not being finally subjugated until 1520. In spite of the fact that the political fortunes of Murom and Ryazan had long been divorced, the literatures of the two cities possess much in common. Moreover, Buslayev, having in mind the tales of Peter and Fevronia, of the Unzhensk cross and of Juliania Lazarevskaya (see below), observed that "to the lot of Murom preeminently fell the literary development of the ideal character of Russian woman." [1] This statement might well include Ryazan. We recall the attractive figure of Princess Eupraxia in the tale of Batu's attack upon Ryazan. The Tartar invasion of the Ryazan district also inspired the celebrated historical ballad about Avdotya of Ryazan, who unselfishly penetrated to enemy territory and brought all Russian captives back to Rus. Yes, even Fevronia herself, of whom we shall speak presently, was a native of the Ryazan district.

Another characteristic of numerous literary monuments of Murom-Ryazan is their saturation with folklore, particularly fairy-tale, elements.

---

[1] *Istoricheskie ocherki* (Historical Outlines), Vol. II, p. 245.

TALE OF PETER AND FEVRONIA

The most outstanding literary work that Murom-Ryazan produced is without doubt the tale of Peter and Fevronia. In manuscripts it is called now the *Tale of the Life,* now the *Life and Existence,* now simply the *Life.* Peter, Prince of Murom, and his wife Fevronia (so they were called monastically, though their secular names had been David and Eufrosinia) died in 1228, and probably an oral legend about them was composed shortly afterward. In 1547 the Moscow ecclesiastical council canonized them as "new miracle-workers." It is possible that the definitive literary formulation of their life dates from this time, no known copies being earlier than the sixteenth century, but there can be no doubt that not only the oral legend on which the learned tale about them is based, but also the tale itself was in existence prior to their canonization. It hardly seems likely that a work which so departs from the canon for saints' lives would have been written directly on the basis of oral legend in connection with the canonization, or even on the occasion of the final establishment of the official canon for their life. No statement is made concerning religious acts of the saints, who were, incidentally, laymen, and, to judge from the story, not even in close contact with the church before taking monastic vows. Properly speaking, the tale gives no indications as to the particular services to the church for which Peter and Fevronia were accounted saints. The very style is far removed from the grandiloquence, rhetorical embellishment, and abstract verbosity so typical of biographical works in general and of fifteenth and sixteenth century lives in particular. The language is distinguished by simplicity and by its closeness to the idiom of speech. Abundant dialogue, partly cast in the form of riddle and answer, or of wise sayings, lends extreme animation to the whole narrative. The bare, didactic scheme here gives place to an interesting story with a richly developed plot, saturated with folktale elements and at the same time informed with ethological details from actual life.

It may therefore well have been that, for the requirements of canonization, hurried use was made of a life story written earlier and previously circulated in manuscript. In the fifteenth century Pakhomius Logothetes composed a service for Peter and Fevronia. In it, believers are invited to extol "Peter the Pious, who was healed of the haughty snake, together with Fevronia." It is very possible that the first literary adaptation of the oral legend also dates from this time. According to a hypothesis advanced by V. F. Rzhiga, the final literary adaptation may be assigned to a sixteenth cen-

tury writer of Ivan the Terrible's time, Yermolay-Yerazm. But incontroverti-
ble data in support of such an assignment are few.

The content of the tale is as follows.

In Murom reigned as an "autocrat" Prince Paul, whose wife, at the
instigation of the Devil, had been having carnal relations with a serpent,
which appeared to her in its own natural form but to the people of the
household in the semblance of the prince. The wife made no secret from
her husband of the fact that she had been ravished by the serpent, and her
husband in order to compass the reptile's destruction advised her to pretend
to be fond of it and find out from it what there was that could bring about
its death. This the wife did, and the serpent told her that it would die "by
the shoulder blade of Peter, by the sword blade of Agrik."[2] When Paul
informed his brother of the serpent's words, Peter knew that he was the
Peter destined to kill the serpent. Directed by a boy who miraculously appeared to him in church, he found in a chink in the altar wall the sword of
Agrik and slew the serpent, after first taking precautions not to confuse it
with his brother. But the serpent's blood spurted up into Peter's face and his
body became covered with scabs and ulcers of which no one could cure him.

Hearing that there were many physicians in the Ryazan district, Peter
had himself conveyed thither. A certain youth of his suite, in searching for
a physician, came to the village of Laskovo and, entering a house unnoticed,
found a girl there weaving linen cloth while a hare hopped about in front
of her. Catching sight of the youth, the girl said: "It is not well for a house
to be without ears or a dwelling without eyes." Not understanding these
words, the youth inquired of the girl where the master of the house was,
and received the answer: "The master of the house is my father, but he has
gone with my mother to mourn on mortgage. I also have a brother, but he
has gone to look through his legs at death." The youth, perceiving that he
conversed with a wise virgin, asked her to interpret her sayings. The girl
explained that if she had a dog, it would have heard a stranger approaching
and would have barked; if there had been a child, it would have seen him
and said a strange man was coming, and he would not have found her un-
prepared for guests. The ears of a house are the dog, the eyes of a dwelling
the child. As to the girl's parents having gone to mourn on mortgage, it
meant that they had gone to escort a corpse and mourn, so that when they
themselves came to die others would do the same for them. And her brother,
who was, like her father, a tree-climber and in the wild-bee business, had
gone to collect honey from tall trees and that he might avoid breaking his
neck was looking down between his legs, where death lay in wait for him.

[2] Agrik or Agrika, was a legendary bogatyr who possessed an infinite number of weapons,
among them a sword of steel.

Amazed at this wise answer, the youth asked the girl to tell him her name. She said that her name was Fevronia and in turn asked her caller who he was and why he had come. Upon learning what errand had brought him to the village, Fevronia bade him convey the prince to her and promised that he should be cured if he showed kindheartedness and humility. When Peter had been conveyed to Fevronia's house and they asked her where the physician was who should heal the prince, she said that she was herself the physician and that she would cure him if he would marry her. Upon hearing Fevronia's terms, Peter thought: "How can I, being a prince, take to wife the daughter of a tree-climber?" but, exhausted from illness, he sent word to Fevronia that he would agree to marry her. Upon receiving the prince's answer, Fevronia prepared a medicament, which, having blessed, she dispatched to the prince, bidding him first take a thorough bath, then anoint his body with this medicament, leaving only one scab untouched.

Peter, as he set out for the bath, thought to try Fevronia's wisdom and sent her a little bunch of flax proposing that from it while he was at the bath she weave a shirt, trousers, and a towel. In answer to this proposal, Fevronia bade them take the prince a splinter of firewood so that while she was cleaning the flax he might make her a loom for weaving it. But when Peter refused to make a loom out of so small a piece of wood and in so short a time, Fevronia for her part also refused to make clothes for a grown man out of a small bunch of flax in the same length of time. Upon hearing Fevronia's answer the prince praised her. When he had bathed and anointed his body except for the one scab, Peter recovered, but, having recovered, reconsidered his promise and decided that it was impossible for him to marry Fevronia "on account of her having no family name," of which decision he had her informed, at the same time sending many presents. But Fevronia refused the presents, saying that the prince had broken his word, but that there was one who made the truth his care and he would do as he saw fit.

Meanwhile, having returned to Murom, Peter suffered a recurrence of his malady: from the untreated scab new scabs spread and little by little covered the prince's whole body. He again betook himself to Fevronia and once more asked her to cure him. Fevronia, "holding no ill-will," said to the prince's servants: "If the prince will be my husband, verily he shall be healed." This time Peter confirmed by oath his promise to marry Fevronia and as before she sent him the medicament, with which he anointed his scabs, this time not leaving even one of them untreated, and he was as well as if he had never been ill. With all ceremony he took Fevronia back to his patrimony, to Murom, and there married her. And the two of them lived in all piety; soon Paul died, and Peter became sole autocrat of the city of

Murom. But his boyars, at the instigation of the Devil, took a dislike to Fevronia by reason of their wives, because she was not of boyar family. Once a servant who had been waiting on her carried the report to Peter that she did not leave the table properly: before rising she gathered up the crumbs like a starving woman. Peter, wishing to ascertain the truth of this, bade Fevronia dine at the table with him and when she started putting the crumbs in her sleeve as usual, opened her hand and in it saw sweet-smelling incense and frankincense. After that he made trial of her no more.

Some time later, the boyars came to Peter and in a rage declared to him that they did not wish to have Fevronia rule over their wives and that if he wished to remain autocrat among them let him take another wife and dismiss Fevronia after first settling great wealth upon her. But Peter, as was his custom, meekly suggested that the boyars consult Fevronia herself and hear what she had to say. The boyars, beside themselves with rage, got up a banquet to which they invited Fevronia; when drunk they began to make bawdy remarks, "like dogs barking," and in the name of the whole town and in their own besought Fevronia to grant them what they were about to ask of her. She agreed, and the boyars with one voice proposed to her that she accept a fortune and depart for wherever she chose. She made no attempt to go back on her word but in turn proposed that they also grant her what she should ask. The boyars gladly agreed and Fevronia asked them to give her her husband Prince Peter, whereupon, with the malign intention of setting up another autocrat (and each thinking to become autocrat himself), they replied: "If he himself consents, we have nothing to say." Peter did as the Gospel teaches and, setting at nought his princely power, sailed away from Murom with Fevronia down the Oka.

During their voyage there was a certain man on board ship, and his wife was with him; and this man, by instigation of the Evil One, looked with desire upon Fevronia. But she, apprehending his wicked thoughts, bade him dip water from one side of the boat and drink it and then dip water from the other side of the boat and do likewise. When the man had done this, Fevronia asked: "Which water was sweeter?"

And he answered: "It is the same water and it tastes the same."

Then she said: "Woman's nature is also the same. Yet you leave your wife and hanker after someone else's." And realizing that Fevronia had the gift of clairvoyance, the man was afraid after that to think impure thoughts about her.

At the approach of evening, the travelers went ashore: Peter began to feel distressed over the loss of his patrimony, but Fevronia consoled him with the assurance that God would not leave them destitute. Peter's supper was prepared on the shore and the cook drove two little trees into the ground and hung the kettle on them. After supper Fevronia, catching sight of these trees, blessed them and said: "May these saplings be great trees by morning, with twigs and leaves." By morning Fevronia's words had come true.

Then, just as Peter and Fevronia were planning to continue their journey, nobles came out from Murom beseeching Peter to return, since many boyars had perished in an internecine struggle for power and such as were left alive wanted Peter and Fevronia to rule in Murom as before. Peter and Fevronia returned and ruled over their province like an affectionate father and mother, loving all equally.

When they felt that death was approaching, they began asking God to let them die at the same time and, having decided to be buried in one coffin, had it made for them out of a single stone, giving orders that only a partition should be put in. Then they took monastic vows. And just as Fevronia was finishing the embroidery on a chalice cover for the Church of the Virgin, Peter sent word to her that he was about to die, and suggested that she die at the same time. Fevronia asked to be given just long enough to finish her cover. Peter sent back word: "I will wait for you a little longer." Finally, sending for the third time, he said: "I want to die now and I shan't wait for you." Fevronia had only the robe of the saint left to do on the cover, but, moved by her husband's urgency, she stopped sewing, stuck her needle in the cover, twisted the thread on it and sent Peter the message that she was now ready to die with him.

After the death of Peter and Fevronia their people put the bodies in separate coffins, arguing that it is improper for husband and wife to sleep together after taking monastic vows, but on the following day the bodies of the two turned up in the common tomb which they had previously prepared. Their people tried a second time to separate Peter and Fevronia, but again the two rejoined each other, and after that no one dared part them more.

Peter and Fevronia are first shown us in the personal relationships that led to their marriage, after which we get an ideal love which never grows less, no matter what outward obstacles malicious people may put in its way. This inexhaustible power of love finds its highest expression when the spouses, unable to contemplate the possibility of one surviving the other, die in the same day and hour and refuse to be physically separated even after death, notwithstanding the attempts made to part them. The embodiment and exponent of the active principle of love in the story is Fevronia. As compared with her husband Peter, she is a much more volitional and emotionally gifted nature. By her creative faculty of love and the beauty of her spirit she awakens an answering emotion in the passive and spiritually rather commonplace nature of Peter. She is the orderer of her own fate and of that

of the man she loves, while he is her obedient slave, loving her for her superiority to himself and subject to her in all things. A simple peasant girl,
daughter of a poor tree-climber, she first overcomes the class prejudice which
makes the prince unwilling to marry her on account of her extraction, then
wins a victory over the pride of the boyars and their wives who cannot reconcile themselves to the fact that a peasant girl has become their princess. The
antiboyar tendency of the tale also asserts itself when the boyars yield in
the end to the sovereign power of the prince.

The tale of Peter and Fevronia abounds in folklore motifs: the serpent-
werewolf, appearing in connection with a married woman who coaxes it to
tell her what can bring about its death, the marvelous sword of steel by
which the serpent perishes, the wise maiden talking in riddles and counter-
ing unfulfillable demands with demands of her own equally incapable of
fulfillment, miraculous transformations, such as the transformation of bread
crumbs into frankincense, the obtaining of her husband as most precious
of gifts when she is banished. By way of parallel to the tale of Peter and
Fevronia, Buslayev cited the ballads of the *Elder Edda* about the battle of
Sigurd with the serpent Farnir and about the union of this hero with a wise
maiden, and explained the likeness of the Russian tale to the Scandinavian
ballads and to the Serbian fairy tale of the maiden who outwitted the tsar,
as due to their having had a common source back in the prehistoric epoch.
A. Veselovsky, working from the theory of borrowing, was inclined to explain the plot of our tale as the result of borrowing from the Germano-
Scandinavian legends, comparing it to the saga of Ragnar Lodbrok in particular. But the Russian tale has no greater similarity to foreign folklore
material than it has to the material of Russian folk poetry, where we find
—in fairy tales, *byliny*, riddles—all the above-mentioned basic folklore
motifs.[3] To some extent these motifs are also present in learned literature
(for example, the motif of riddles and unfulfillable demands). The episode
of Fevronia's shaming the man on the boat who had looked upon her with
desire is similar to the analogous episode of the shaming of Igor by Princess
Olga of which we read in the life of Olga included in the *Stepennaya Kniga*.

How popular the tale of Peter and Fevronia was in its time is best evidenced by the fact that it is extant in approximately one hundred fifty copies,
classifiable into four redactions, the third of which reflects certain typical
tricks of style found in secular tales of Peter the Great's time. In addition it
includes as friend and adviser of Peter the governor Eustratius. Judging
from the fact that such a friend and adviser is also present in the ancient

[3] See P. V. Vladimirov, *Vvedenie v istoriyu russkoy slovesnosti* (Introduction to the History of Russian Literature) (Kiev, 1896), pp. 130–131, 144–146; S. V. Savchenko, *Russkaya
narodnaya skazka* (The Russian Folk Tale) (Kiev, 1914), pp. 44–46.

legends of various peoples, it is conceivable that this personage already existed in the oral legend of Peter and Fevronia. The tale was reflected in folk poetry and its plot is largely utilized in Rimsky-Korsakov's famous opera, *The Legend of the City of Kitezh*.[4]

In summarizing our study of provincial literatures from the end of the fourteenth to the beginning of the sixteenth century, we arrive at the following general conclusions. Russian literature during this period continued and carried deeper the provincial tendencies observable in the preceding period. Many of its monuments are associated with the local political interests of various provinces fighting for the right to develop along independent paths. Specific examples are the literary monuments of Moscow, Novgorod, Pskov, and Tver. But for the protection of local interests the necessity was also clearly recognized for a unification of the Russian lands, particularly if the Tartar yoke was to be thrown off. Recognition of the necessity for unifying the Russian forces to defend Rus from outside enemies, so clearly expressed in the chronicle and still further emphasized in the *Tale of Igor's Expedition*, was never absent from the minds of forward-looking exponents of Russian government and Russian culture, literary culture in particular. The feudal fragmentation of Rus not only did not destroy the sense of unity possessed by the Russian people as a whole but, on the contrary, strengthened it, thanks to the painful lessons taught by history. In the main the dispute was only as to which state should unite the land of Rus and act as its spokesman. Moscow and Tver contended for political priority, Novgorod for ecclesiastical priority. When Byzantium started down the road to political collapse and then completely lost its independence, the Russian people as a whole began to regard itself as heir to the political and ecclesiastical legacy of Byzantium (cf. Nestor-Iskander's *Tale of the Taking of Tsargrad*), but it was only later, at the beginning of the sixteenth century— by force of the unfolding of the historical process—that the title of "third

---

[4] Three variants of the tale are published in *Pamyatniki starinnoy russkoy literatury* (Monuments of Ancient Russian Literature), I, pp. 29–45. On the tale see Buslayev, "Pesni drevney Eddy o Zigurde i Muromskaya legenda," *Istoricheskie ocherki* (Ballads of the Ancient Edda about Sigurd and the Murom Legend, Historical Outlines), I, pp. 269–300; A. Veselovskii, "Novye otnosheniya legendy o Pyotre i Fevronii i saga o Ragnare Lodbroke" (New Relationship of the Legend of Peter and Fevronia and the Saga About Ragnar Lodbrok), *Zhurnal min. nar. prosv.* (Journal of the Ministry of Public Instruction) (1871), No. 4, pp. 95–142; V. F. Rzhiga, "Literaturnaya deyatel'nost' Yermolaya-Yerazma" (Literary Activity of Yermolai-Yerazm), *Letopis' zanyatii Arkheograficheskoy Komissii* (Chronicle of the Studies of the Archaeographical Commission) (Leningrad, 1926), Vol. XXXIII, pp. 112–147, 170–173, 181–186. For an extended review of V. F. Rzhiga's study, see Yu. Yarovsky's "K voprosu o literaturnoy deyatel'nosti Yermolaya-Yerazma, pisatelya XVI veka" (On the Question of the Literary Activity of Yermolay-Yerazm, Sixteenth Century Writer), *Slavia* (1929), Vol. VIII.

Rome" was applied to Moscow, and even then not by a Muscovite but by a Pskovan—Filofey, an ancient of the monastery of Eleazar at Pskov.

The literary awakening that began here at the end of the fourteenth century with the easing of the Tartar yoke, met the publicistic demands of the current Russian situation by making use of South Slavic works. The publicistic tenor penetrated much more deeply into literature than it had done in preceding epochs. It expressed itself in glorification of the idea of a Russian state and nation which should by its oneness neutralize all private provincial quarrels and differences of opinion. The Church played no small part in reinforcing this idea, in the person, chiefly, of its Josephite wing. South Slavic mystico-contemplative literature gave a start in the critical direction to the thinking of the Josephites' antagonists, the trans-Volga hermits, who, like the heretics—the Shearers and the Judaizers—constituted an opposition to contemporary political and social practice. That an eccleciastical cloak should have been used to mask the purely publicistic double life of the literary releases of all schools of thought at this time need not surprise us: this was a perfectly natural thing in the Middle Ages, particularly the Russian Middle Ages.

In appropriating for a number of its monuments, especially lives of saints, the pompous and elaborate style so fashionable in South Slavic literature during the thirteenth and fourteenth centuries, Russian literature from the end of the fourteenth to the beginning of the sixteenth century was only exploiting elements of rhetoric and panegyric already present in it during the Kiev period, and, so viewed, these stylistic peculiarities were not in principle a new manifestation. This literature did not break with the traditions of the period immediately preceding or with those of Kievan literature. The style of Hilarion's eulogistic discourse, of annalistic and war narratives, of saints' lives is palpable in the corresponding literary genres of this time as well. And when it became necessary for Muscovite literature, then in the earliest formative stage, to find literary means of expression for its triumph over the Tartars in 1380, it went for help in modeling the style of the tales of the rout of Mamay all the way back to the *Tale of Igor's Expedition*.

At the beginning of the sixteenth century, when Moscow had finally gathered about itself the once independent provinces, literary production in them could no longer draw upon those ideological and political stimuli that had previously typified the various provinces and hence naturally began to decline and lose its individuality. As the provincial literatures merged with the general stream of Muscovite all-Russian literature, they were themselves utilized by Moscow, which, by virtue of its unifying tendencies, assimilated the accumulated stock of literary monuments, gradually erasing from them the traits of provincial separatism and adapting them to the steadily tightening ideology of the all-Russian Muscovite empire, the "third Rome." Local traditions, as, for example, those of Murom-Ryazan, still underwent literary revision, but in a spirit no longer inconsistent with the general trend of Muscovite literature.

Literature of Russia
as a Whole in the Sixteenth
and Seventeenth Centuries

THE first decade of the sixteenth century brought to completion Moscow's absorption of separate feudal-patrimonial provinces into a single Russian (Muscovite) state under the central authority of an autocratic tsar supported by a bureaucratic nobility and committed to an energetic campaign against the great feudal princelings and boyars who stood out for old forms of feudal fragmentation.

From the historical point of view, this merging of detached Russian provinces into a single governmental unit headed by the Muscovite autocrat was indubitably a positive and progressive manifestation. Moscow's role in the evolution of the Russian commonwealth was very successfully defined by the once noted Russian historian, Zabelin, in the course of an attempt to combat the position that envisaged Moscow as a despotic power suppressive of the free development of Russian provincial centers. He wrote:

For example, we do not find any historical grounds whatever for the now widespread view that makes it practically obligatory to regard the Muscovite period of our history with a certain squeamishness, almost with animosity. . . . When out of the welter of sectional autocracies, undefined, revolving without plan, and consequently without any single common aim, there arose a fully articulated, active, sharply defined type of autocracy, only then, and by means of that active type, were all the common aims and problems of national development perceived. The people so understood this new phase of its existence. The only elements that could not grasp it were those sectional spheres of interest which continued to pursue their own sectional ends as before, having no conception whatever of the aims of the nation as a whole. In this sense Moscow stood as the emblem of common aims; she held firmly to those aims, kept them to the fore, and her history demonstrates that these aims were essential since they were broadly national. . . . The advantage of the Moscow form over its predecessors, the small-scale sectional forms of autocracy, consists of course in its unity; in unity there is strength, if nothing more; strength has at least enabled us to reach our present position.[1]

Here, in terms of conditions prevailing in Rus at that time, is a situation analogous to that set forth by Engels as maintaining in connection with the victory of kingly power over feudal opposition in western Europe: "That in all this general confusion the kingly power was the progressive element," wrote Engels, "is perfectly obvious. It was the representative of order in disorder, the representative of a formative nation as over against parcellization into rebellious vassal states."[2]

In discussing the effect of the struggle between boyars and nobles upon the course of social thought in sixteenth century Russia, Plekhanov, too, uses an analogy from medieval political practice in western Europe: "A case in point," he writes, "is France, at one time the classic land of feudalism. In their struggle with the feudal lords, the French kings likewise leaned on the third estate, which stood to profit by a strengthening of the monarchical power at the expense of the power of the landowning aristocracy."[3]

The Josephite clergy, an important political force antagonistic in economic practice to the interests of the nobiliary monarchy, in the end made no particular difficulty about compromising with the temporal authority, and found ways of reconciling its interests with those of the social ruling power, the nobility. In opposition to this clearly defined political and social situation, we get the great boyars and their supporters, the monastic faction which had inherited the traditions of the trans-Volga hermits.

The continuing political struggle between different factions within the ruling class of Muscovite society found expression in numerous monuments permeated with a quite undisguised publicistic tendency and having a sharply defined political aim.

Part of these monuments contain no specifically literary elements in the sense indicated in the introduction to this book; part of them contain such elements only in a proportionately very slight degree. Both are to be regarded chiefly as cultural-historical monuments, but a general knowledge of them and of the trends of social thought conditioning them is necessary for an understanding of the intellectual atmosphere in which properly literary monuments took their rise and which they reflected in subject matter and in theme.

[1] Iv. Zabelin, *Opyty izucheniya russkikh drevnostey i istorii* (Experiments in the Study of Russian Antiquities and History) (Moscow, 1873), Pt. II, pp. 109–110.

[2] F. Engels, "O razlozhenii feodalizma i razvitii burzhuazii" (On the Decline of Feudalism and the Development of the Bourgeoisie), *Proletarskaya revolyutsiya* (Proletarian Revolution) (1935), No. 6, p. 157.

[3] G. V. Plekhanov, *Istoriya russkoy obshchestvennoy mysli* (History of Russian Social Thought), 2nd ed. (Moscow-Leningrad, 1925), Vol. I, p. 115.

TRENDS OF THOUGHT IN THE FIRST HALF OF THE SIX-
TEENTH CENTURY AND THEIR LITERARY EXPRESSION:

Works of Maxim the Greek and of Metropolitan Daniel

The struggle between the Josephites and the trans-Volga hermits in the
ecclesiastical-social sphere achieved expression as early as the first decade of
the sixteenth century through such spokesmen as Prince Vassian Patrikeyev
and Maxim the Greek on the one hand and Metropolitan Daniel on the
other. Vassian Patrikeyev, having embraced monasticism and become the
disciple and zealous follower of Nil of Sorsky, stepped forward as the energetic opponent of monastic ownership of land, and also as antagonistic to
the merciless persecution of "heretics." For his various activities, among them
a revision of the *Pilot Book,* Vassian was condemned by the ecclesiastical
synod in 1531 and banished to the Josephite monastery of Volokolam, where,
apparently, in the course of time he died. The year 1518 brought the arrival
from Athos of Maxim the Greek (1480–1556), who, before taking the
tonsure on Athos, had long resided in Italy, associated with the humanists
there, and, even if without gaining command of the finer points of Renaissance thought, had none the less acquired a very extensive theological and
philological education. Though summoned to Moscow by Great Prince
Vasily Ivanovich to make translations and to correct the books in his library,
the primary object being a translation of the *Explanatory Psalter* from the
Greek, he soon became involved in the politico-ecclesiastical disputes and
clashes that were still raging at this time in Rus, and produced a large number of works revealing him as preacher, publicist, and castigator of the various
ecclesiastical and social disorders that he discerned in the life about him. In
his opinions and pronouncements, if we disregard his outspoken hostility
toward "heretics," he sided with the trans-Volga hermits and was, in particular, on very intimate terms with Vassian Patrikeyev and other representatives of the boyar opposition. His critical attitude toward the texts he
corrected, and also toward aspects of Russian ecclesiastical and socio-political
practice which had the patronage both of the Josephite party and of the
temporal authority, brought persecution upon him: he was thrice condemned, and passed the years from 1525 to 1551 in imprisonment first in
the Volokolam Monastery, to which Vassian was also subsequently banished, and then in the Page's Monastery at Tver, from which he was released
only five years before his death, though he had several times previously
sought permission to return to Athos.

In his works—dogmatic, polemic, moralistic, publicistic—Maxim the Greek revealed himself as a very unusual writer, expressing himself passionately on any subject upon which he and his constituency became aroused. Possessing great literary talent and a much better education than his Russian contemporaries—not alone the Josephites but the trans-Volga hermits as well —he advanced the culture of the written word itself to a marked degree by employing methods of literary craftsmanship that he could only have acquired in the West, and in this respect his works made a concrete contribution to the further development of specialized literary culture. At the same time the critical spirit and intellectual acuity, the strict logic with which he argued his ideas, and, in consequence, the structural harmony and consistency of Maxim the Greek's work, were assimilated by his pupils and the continuators of his literary tradition, being inseparable from the high qualities of his literary art as a whole. He gives practical instructions on how to write and on how to distinguish a person who has talent for writing from one who has not. Of anyone planning to make books his profession, he required a knowledge of grammar, rhetoric, and the other "formal" sciences. To test those desiring to devote themselves to translation or to the correction of books he composed sixteen Greek hexameter and pentameter poems. Only aspirants who showed that they understood these examples did he recommend treating with full confidence and consideration.

Maxim the Greek speaks with high approval and respect of the extensive development in Paris of the philosophical and theological sciences, which anyone so desiring may pursue free of charge. He is enraptured that they teach there not only sciences associated with theology but also all manner of "external" sciences, that thither flock from all directions to study the literary sciences and the "arts" both the children of simple folk and the children of princes and tsars, and that all of them upon finishing school and returning to their own country will become an ornament to their native land and also advisers, experienced leaders, and helpers in any good work that needs doing. This is what Maxim the Greek thinks those Russians who boast so much of their nobility and their great wealth ought also to be to their fatherland.

Along with instructional and polemic discourses and epistles in the traditional form, Maxim the Greek wrote highly emotional works of moral philosophy in the form of apostrophes to his own soul, or colloquies between mind and soul, conceived in the form of Platonic dialogues. Wedged here and there into the discussion will be a lively polemic against contemporary social evils and prejudices, against usury, astrology, and so forth. Dialogue form also clothes a debate on the monastic life between Philoktimon (the money grubber) and Aktimon (the poor man) as well as a dispute between Maxim himself and the fundamental positions of the apocryphal book,

Lucidarius. Also encountered in Maxim the Greek are short, lyrical, panegyric sermons as well as meditations shot through with impassioned accusation, such as the discourses on the "insatiable belly" or on the "delusiveness of dreams." The moral is sometimes drawn not by the author in his own person but by the Virgin or even by the ambo which priests ascend to preach. In the *Discourse Setting Forth at Length and with Sorrow the Disorder and Indecorum of Tsars and Authorities of the Latter Age,* Maxim the Greek unmasks covetous and unjust rulers who oppress their subjects, representing Rus allegorically in the guise of a widow weeping disconsolately by the road with wild beasts all about her. She complains of her utter defenselessness, of her lack of devoted subjects to look after her, of the money grubbers and usurers in whose power she now finds herself. "I traveled along a difficult and sorrowful road," writes Maxim the Greek, "and I saw a woman sitting by the wayside, her head bent in her hands, weeping bitterly and disconsolately. She was clothed in black raiment, as becomes a widow, and round about her were lions, bears, wolves, and foxes." To the traveler's inquiry as to who she was, and how to address her, why she was sitting by this desolate road, and what was the cause of her grief, the widow at first refused to reply, since her grief was not only difficult to put into words, but incurable by any human means. The traveler, however, continued to insist that the widow reveal to him her sorrow and thereby lighten it, and moved by his entreaties she stated that she was known under various names—authority, and power, and dominion, and lordship. Her real name, however, the one which combined all those enumerated, was Basilia (that is, empire), but many, misunderstanding it, and administering the affairs of their subjects in a manner unworthy of her, instead of being tsars had become torturers and thereby were both dishonoring her and laying up great trials and afflictions for themselves, when God should recompense them as their folly deserved.

Having heard these words, the traveler fell at the woman's feet, beseeching her forgiveness for having previously failed, through inadvertence, to accord her the honor due a tsar, and asked her to explain to him in more detail the cause of her sorrow. Then she, apprehending that the traveler, actuated by an unfeigned love for the human race, desired to learn her fate in order to turn it to men's advantage, told in detail, with references to "Holy Writ," what had caused her such grief: all lovers of pleasure and lovers of power had been eager to become her subjects, but very few people of the sort who would really have looked after her and have brought about for dwellers upon earth a state of affairs worthy of her father and of the name she bore; the greater part of her subjects, a prey to greed and usury, tormented in every way those under them. Next come vigorous accusations directed against the mighty, and in conclusion Basilia explains why she is sitting alone by the desolate road, with wild beasts all around her: the desolate road and the wild beasts that are rending her symbolize the accursed latter age, already deprived of pious rulers, its tsars striving only to widen their boundaries, and for that purpose arming one man against another, making one to offend against the other and rejoicing to see the slaughter of the faithful.[4]

A very energetic adversary of Vassian Patrikeyev and Maxim the Greek, a stubborn persecutor of the traditions of the trans-Volga hermits, and of the trends, still not definitely checked in spite of physical destruction, that had been in one way or another bound up with the "Judaizers," was Daniel, who occupied the metropolitan cathedra from 1522 to 1539. An ardent disciple of Joseph of Volok, he went even farther than his teacher in his "crafty use of divine wisdom" against his opponents. Though very diplomatic by nature and outwardly amiable, he did not scorn any means toward the attainment of the goal he had set himself—to make the Russian Church even more Josephite than it already was—and, removing heterodox incumbents, he appointed to archiepiscopal chairs and to priorships his own adherents and partisans. Toward secular authority, in the person of Great Prince Vasily III, he showed a sycophancy so extreme as to verge on direct breach of the ecclesiastical canons. Of his work, sixteen discourses are extant and a series of epistles which he himself gathered into a separate collection. Both deal with questions of dogma and ritual, and also with questions of moral conduct. Like a typical Josephite, Daniel leans on a wide range of "Godly or sacred writings," including under this head all ecclesiastical literature which gave no evidence of a critical attitude, and putting canonical "Holy Writ" on the same footing with apocryphas and even with spurious books at variance with Christian dogma. In contrast to what we get in the writing tradition of the trans-Volga hermits, Daniel's works are distinguished neither by harmony of form and logical consistency nor by inner unity.

Of special interest to the literary historian are Daniel's works on themes having to do with moral conduct. Unlike the works on dogma and ritual, with their traditional scholarly style, those on themes of everyday living are written in lively, frequently picturesque language. Here, along with bitter attacks on a manner of living unsympathetic to Daniel, we now and again get pictures from real life and rather striking portraits of the perpetrators of

[4] The works of Maxim the Greek (incomplete) were published in three parts in Kazan in 1859–1860. In 1910–1911 a translation of this edition into modern Russian was brought out at Sergiev Posad. On Maxim the Greek, see V. Ikonnikov, *Maksim Grek i evo vremya* (Maxim the Greek and His Time), 2nd ed. (Kiev, 1915), and also V. F. Rzhiga's "Opyty po istorii publitsistiki XVI veka: Maksim Grek kak publitsist" (Experiments in the History of Publicism in the Sixteenth Century: Maxim the Greek as Publicist), *Trudy otd. drevnerusskoy literatury* (Works of the Division of Early Russian Literature) (1934), I, pp. 5–120. In both these studies see also the general literature on the question.

sins particularly repellent to a strict churchman brought up in the traditions of a conservative, if sometimes purely external, ethic of asceticism. As precursors to Daniel's discourses it is possible to point out certain anonymous Old Russian discourses on drunkenness, and discourses from the *Emerald* on different themes from everyday life. The lack shown by the Josephites and their writers, particularly Daniel, of that "academic," so to speak, verbally disciplined, culture which the trans-Volga hermits and their disciples had, was counterbalanced from a purely literary angle by a freedom and daring in the use of language thanks to which the writers in the Josephite camp were not afraid to introduce into their works vernacular expressions crude from the scholarly purist's point of view, and, at times, realistic images and everyday details suggested by the life about them. Such tendencies could not fail to result in the penetration into the literary process itself of realistic elements which declared themselves more and more emphatically as time went on.

These rudiments of a realistic style appear frequently both in Daniel's discourses and in his epistles. Thus, in the third discourse, where he rebukes the man who is indifferent to the traditions and precepts of the Church, he writes:

When you hear Divine Scripture read or someone expounding the Divine Scriptures, you stop up your ears like an asp, being beguiled of Satan; and when you hear people congregating in the church of God for prayer and supplication, you make off like a wild animal, and slink away like a serpent, and bark at the brethren like a dog, and wallow in filth like swine in the mud. . . . You eat and drink all the time, like cattle, and slander the brethren like Satan. And when, out of shame, you do enter the church of God, you are hardly inside before you yawn and stretch and cross one leg over the other and stick out your hip and fidget and make faces like a boor.

In the twelfth discourse, where he attacks libertines, Daniel says:

Moreover you eat all the time like cattle, and drink day and night, many times even to the point of vomiting, so that your head aches and your wits wander . . . and your pride and boastfulness increase and you roar like a lion, and are sly as a devil, and stream to devilish spectacles like a herd of swine.

Such a libertine, for greater success in his amorous quests commonly becomes a great dandy and man of fashion. Daniel describes him in this same twelfth discourse in the following picturesque terms:

A great job you make of pleasing your wantons: you change your garments, put on a costume, boots of bright scarlet and exceeding small so that your feet are cramped by their tightness; you are groomed and glossy; you gallop and snort and neigh like a stallion. . . . You do not shave the hair from your body with a razor but pluck it out by the root with pincers and are not ashamed to make women jealous by transforming your man's face into a woman's. . . . Moreover you wash your face much and rub it; you make your cheeks scarlet, beautiful, shining, as if you were getting yourself ready to eat, like some marvelously prepared dish.

Such a dandy also gets it from Daniel for his predilection for buffoonery, for playing on dulcimers, reeds, and pipes, and for the buffoons themselves.

In discussing the indifferent attitude of gentry and rich folk, addicted to idleness and wasteful luxury at the expense of their ill used peasantry, Daniel, in the sixteenth discourse, draws the following picture of a boyar's kitchen:

Day after day the cooks crowd into the kitchen, and beautify themselves, and change their clothes and wash their hands and brace their leaves and sharpen their knives and pile on wood and kindle a fire and put kettles over it and set up frying-pans and pots, and make ready to glut the belly with food.

Such a spendthrift and disorderly manner of living reduces a man to stealing, ravishing, robbing, cheating, borrowing and not repaying, breaking his oath, and committing many another sin (thirteenth discourse). "Whence come these ruinous costs and debts?" asks Daniel in the fifteenth discourse.

Are they not from pride and senseless expenditures, and to wife and children are they not slavery and bail and orphaning and sobs and despair and tears? Always entertainments and food, always feasts and spectacles, always baths and reclining. . . . Everyone is too lazy to learn an art; all avoid manual work. . . . All deride the tillers of the soil. . . . All paint their faces and put on motley and appear in costume, and give all their attention to these things and no longer look up to heaven, they all scoff, all jest, all gossip and talk slander.[5]

Daniel's works were later held in high repute by the Old Believers, and presumably constituted one of the influences under which the language of their leader, Archpriest Avvakum, rich in elements of realism and of colloquial speech, took form.

Through the efforts of Metropolitan Daniel, the tenets of the Josephite Church were stabilized, and these tenets very largely determined the direction taken by Russian literary thought during the years that followed, the more so since, almost immediately after Daniel, the metropolitan see was for more than twenty years (1542–1563) occupied by that active and very enterprising exponent of Josephite ideology, Metropolitan Macarius. Movements in opposition to the official Josephite Church cropped up even during this period but were quickly and decisively liquidated through administrative intervention by the Church. Thus in 1554 the ecclesiastical council condemned Artemius, prior of the Trinity Monastery of St. Sergius, and the boyar's son, Matvey Bashkin, a member of his circle. Both were conversant with the teaching of the trans-Volga hermits and apparently were

[5] On Daniel's literary activities see V. Zhmakin, *Mitropolit Daniil i yevo sochineniya* (Metropolitan Daniel and His Works) (Moscow, 1881). Selected works are reproduced as an appendix.

also in touch with German Protestantism, Matvey Bashkin in particular. With all the rest, Bashkin's conscience was disturbed by the existence of slavery among us, and he granted manumission to such of his slaves as wished it. To his confessor he said:

In the book of Acts it is written: The whole law is summed up in the words, "Love your neighbor as yourself"—but we hold Christians as our slaves. Christ called all men brothers, but among us some are bondmen, some fugitive, some subject to the *corvée,* some in total servitude. But I thank my God that all who were full bondmen to me I have released so that now, sir, I hold my people of their own free will: if it suits a man let him stay, if not, let him go where he will.

Artemius was sentenced by the tribunal to banishment in the Solovetsk Monastery, and Matvey Bashkin to life imprisonment in the Volokolam Monastery, but Artemius soon succeeded in escaping to Lithuania, where he became a zealous champion of Orthodoxy.

Protestant free thought was carried still farther by a fugitive slave, afterwards a monk, Theodosius Kosoy, against whose teachings the learned monk Zinovius of Otensk wrote two complete books: *Testimony of Truth* and *Protracted Epistle.* Theodosius Kosoy denied the Trinity of the Godhead, the ecclesiastical hierarchy, formal ritual, churches, monasteries, icons, ecclesiastical mysteries, fasts, and civil authorities and wars as well: "All people are one in God: Tartars and Germans and all other languages," he asserted. Condemned in 1554 to imprisonment in a Muscovite monastery, Kosoy, like Artemius, fled to Lithuania.

The free thought of Theodosius Kosoy may be compared to the plebeian and peasant heresy, of which Engels said in contrasting it with burgher heresy:

Of an entirely different character was heresy which gave direct expression to peasant and plebeian needs and which was almost always combined with uprisings. While sharing all the demands of burgher heresy regarding priests and the papacy and the restoration of the early Christian ecclesiastical order, it at the same time went infinitely farther. It demanded restoration of the equality that existed among members of the early Christian commune, and the recognition of this equality as the norm for the civil community as well. From the equality of sons of God, it deduced civil equality and in part even equality of possessions. The equalizing of nobility with peasants, of patricians and privileged townsfolk with plebeians, the abolition of the *corvée,* of agrarian rights, of taxes, of privileges and the doing away with at least the most crying property distinctions—these were the demands put forward with more or less precision as necessary deductions from the teaching of early Christianity.[6]

All three of these freethinkers had many followers and adherents, part of whom were condemned by the council of 1554—testimony to the fact that

---

[6] K. Marx and F. Engels, *Works,* Vol. VIII, p. 130.

the spirit of criticism and inquiry was still fairly strong in Rus at the middle of the sixteenth century notwithstanding the dominance of official Josephite ideology, which had established itself and vanquished its opponents through the use of strict punitive measures.

PUBLICISTIC LITERATURE IN THE SIXTEENTH CENTURY:

Works of Ivan Peresvetov, A. Kurbsky, Ivan the Terrible

What chiefly determined the character and content of publicistic literature from the 1540's on was the struggle between the rising nobility and the boyars, whose rapid political and economic decline was followed by complete loss of former social privileges after the founding of Ivan's bodyguard in 1564.

The outstanding ideologist for the nobility during the Terrible's epoch was Ivan Peresvetov, who had come to Rus from Lithuania in about 1538 and who achieved prominence during the latter half of the 1540's as author of several publicistic tales and petitions to Ivan the Terrible. In both he revealed himself as the apologist of the autocratic Muscovite state, supportive primarily of the interests of the nobility and organized on the basis of a well regulated official and military machine. His works reflect such writings as Nestor-Iskander's *Tale of the Taking of Tsargrad*, the *Tale of Dracula,* and the historical works of western Europe. In the *Legend of the Emperor Constantine,* which describes the pernicious influence of the Byzantine boyars on the emperor Constantine and on the destinies of Byzantium, Peresvetov depicts allegorically the domination exercised by the boyar party during the Terrible's minority. Here, as in his other works, Peresvetov appears as the partisan of imperial "terror": "When an emperor is mild and gentle with his empire," he says, "its wealth declines and his fame decreases. When an emperor rules in terror and in wisdom, his empire broadens and his name is known in all lands."

In his first *Petition* to Ivan the Terrible, Peresvetov, quoting the governor of Volotz, makes direct mention of boyar domination in the Russian empire:

Thus speaks the governor of Volotz concerning the Russian empire, that the nobles of the Russian tsar are growing rich and lazy and weakening his empire, and that when they call themselves his servants because they ride forth on his service in gala attire, well mounted and well attended, but fail to stand firm in behalf of the Christian faith and play the deadly game against the enemy fiercely, they lie both to God and to their lord.

The *Legend of Sultan Mahomet* presents in thin disguise a complete political program anticipatory of the later governmental reforms of Ivan the Terrible, in particular the founding of the bodyguard. The *Legend* begins with a description of the fate of Byzantium. Constantine, the last Byzantine emperor, was a humane and gentle ruler. These qualities in the emperor were exploited by the boyars, who robbed him of strength and power, with the result that Byzantium was conquered by the Turks. Sultan Mahomet, conqueror of Byzantium, considered that the most important concern of the state was justice. This justice he had found in the books of the Greek Christians when he took Constantinople, but Mahomet's governmental practice was entirely different from Constantine's. First of all he narrowed down to almost nothing boyar power and boyar privileges, allotting important prerogatives to the army and abolishing the system of administrative machinery whereby the administrator took for his own use the taxes and imposts that he levied on the population: all taxes were to go directly into the treasury, and the administrative official was to receive a fixed salary. The matter of fines was similarly managed and thus injustice ceased to prevail in the state. Mahomet, realizing that an emperor's power and fame rest with his troops, took pains to build up a model army and patronized it in every way.[7] He kept forty thousand Janizaries about his person, to whom he paid a salary and gave "dates every day." Mahomet took stern and pitiless measures to eradicate all law-breaking, on the principle that "like a bridle-less horse under an emperor, so is an empire without terror." Mahomet valued his subjects not for the degree of their nobility but for the quality of their services, especially military services: "We are all sons of Adam," he said. "He who serves me faithfully and withstands the enemy fiercely, shall be best in my eyes." Preoccupation with the "deadly game" is the highest merit of a soldier.

Mahomet is, finally, the enemy of slavery, which he abolishes in his state, because "in any empire where the people are enslaved, there the people lack courage nor are they bold in battle with the enemy." To put it in the words of Comrade Stalin, Peresvetov propagandized for a "powerful and well organized nobiliary military bureaucracy."[8] Peresvetov's works are written in plain, energetic Russian, almost entirely free from Church Slavonic elements, and are without the quotations from "Holy Writ" customary among his contemporaries.

Before coming to Rus, Peresvetov had lived long in the West—in Hungary, Czech-land, and Poland, and his publicistic views had evidently taken form

[7] In the first *Petition*, Peresvetov says, in the words of Peter, Governor of Volotz: "To maintain an army is like a falcon to rear and keep of good cheer and on no account let sad thoughts come near."

[8] Stalin, *Marksizm i natsional'no-kolonial'nyi vopros* (Marxism and the National-Colonial Question) (1939), p. 17.

under the influence of Western political ideas, as has been convincingly demonstrated by V. F. Rzhiga. In Europe at that time the rising kingly power was successfully battling the feudal orders, and the monarchical principle was everywhere victorious. The exceptions were Hungary, Czech-land and Poland, precisely where Peresvetov had served, but even in these countries attempts had been made toward the consolidation of the monarchy, and projects for reform in military finance very similar to those that Peresvetov recommended in connection with the current Russian situation had been set up. The concept of the ideal monarch as sage and philosopher that he adopted was common among European humanists. His high opinion of the Turkish political and social structure was likewise prompted by Turkey's great popularity in western Europe, particularly in western Slavdom.[9]

Another work emanating, to judge by its tenor, from the same nobiliary milieu as Peresvetov's writings was the *Tale of a Man Who Loved God*, addressed to Ivan the Terrible and directed chiefly against the boyars, who were represented as having bewitched the tsar.[10]

The boyar party in turn put forward no less a publicist than Prince A. M. Kurbsky, a prolific writer, author of letters to the Terrible and of a *History of the Great Prince of Moscow* written during the 1560's and 1570's in Lithuania, where, as a traitor to his country, he had taken refuge from the wrath of the Terrible after losing a battle in Livonia. The literary significance of Kurbsky's letters to the Terrible and of his pamphlet history resides in the striking originality of his style, revealing him as a skilled orator and a dialectician capable of combining language emotional to the point of passion with harmony and strict formal logic of structure.

In his first letter to the Terrible, sent through his servant Basil Shibanov,[11] Kurbsky accuses the tsar of cruelty to the boyars, hurling invective at him, largely in the form of rhetorical questions and exclamations:

[9] On Peresvetov see V. F. Rzhiga, *I. S. Peresvetov, publitsist XVI v.* (I. S. Peresvetov, Sixteenth Century Publicist) (Moscow, 1908). Printed as a supplement to the book are all Peresvetov's works except the *Legend of Peter, Governor of Volotz*, which is a variant of the first *Petition* and is reprinted in *Uchenye zapiski Kazanskogo Universiteta* (Scholarly Notes of Kazan University) (1865), Vol. I, Pt. I, pp. 21–27. See also S. A. Shcheglov, "K voprosu o sochineniyakh Ivana Peresvetova" (On the Question of the Works of Ivan Peresvetov), *Zhurnal min. nar. prosv.* (Journal of the Ministry of Public Instruction) (1911); V. F. Rzhiga, "I. S. Peresvetov i zapadnaya kul'turno-istoricheskaya sreda" (I. S. Peresvetov and the Western Cultural-Historical Background), *Izv. otd. russk. yaz. i slov. akad. nauk* (News of the Division of Russian Language and Literature of the Academy of Sciences) (1911), Bk. 3, pp. 169–191; G. V. Plekhanov, *Istoriya russkoy obshchestvennoy mysli* (History of Russian Social Thought), 2nd ed., Vol. 1, pp. 115–128.

[10] For the text of the tale, see Buslayev's *Istoricheskaya khrestomatiya tserkovno-slavyanskogo i drevnerusskogo yazykov* (Historical Anthology of Church Slavonic and Old Russian), Cols. 877–882.

[11] This has, of course, been very finely paraphrased by A. Tolstoy in his poem "Basil Shibanov."

Why, Tsar, have you struck down the mighty in Israel and delivered to various deaths the generals God gave you and spilled their victorious saintly blood in God's churches at the Lord's feasts and stained the thresholds of the churches with their martyr's blood? And why have you contrived, against those who wish you well and would lay down their lives for you, unheard of tortures and persecutions and deaths, slanderously accusing Orthodox Christians of treasons and sorceries and other unseemly things, and striving zealously to turn light into darkness and call sweet bitter? Of what crime are they guilty in your sight, O tsar, and how have they angered you, Christian protector? Did they not destroy proud kingdoms and by their manly courage make subject to you in everything those to whom our forefathers were formerly in bondage? Were not strong German cities given to you by God through their careful planning? Is this the way you requite us, poor wretches, by destroying us root and branch?

Kurbsky next enumerates all the persecutions that he has suffered at the hands of the Terrible, beginning this section of the letter with such exclamations as: "What evil and persecution have I not endured at your hand! And what miseries and calamities have you not brought upon me!" And also concluding his reproaches to the tsar with vigorous exclamations: "Those whom you have slain, standing before the throne of God, implore vengeance upon you; those of us whom you have imprisoned or unjustly banished from your sight cry to God from on earth day and night!" This letter of his, "wet with tears," Kurbsky vows he will have laid in his coffin against the Last Judgment.

Upon receiving, in answer to his elegant and effectively composed letter, the Terrible's singularly verbose, disjointed, and muddled epistle interspersed with immense quotations, Kurbsky wrote a reply which, in pointing out his correspondent's shortcomings as a writer, superbly defines the difference between his own literary style and that of the Terrible:

Your magniloquent and clamant letter I have received and fathomed, and have perceived that it was belched forth out of uncontrollable rage in venomous words, in a manner unworthy not only of a tsar so great and universally famous, but even of a poor common soldier; the more so since it is raked together from many sacred discourses, and this with much fury and truculence, giving no indication of lines or strophes, as is customary with experts and scholars when they feel moved to compress much reason into few words; nor does it so compress, but rather is it prolix and involved beyond all measure, whole books being included and whole proverb collections and epistles!

Kurbsky wonders how the Terrible could have made up his mind to send such a clumsy letter to a foreign land where there were people expert "not only in the grammatical and rhetorical but also in the dialectical and philosophical sciences." Dobrolyubov wrote:

Kurbsky was unconvinced by Ivan's arguments. He had a different *point d'appui*—the sense of his own worth. He could not even lift his gaze sufficiently to give proper interpretation to the Terrible's treatment of Shibanov; no, let Shibanov suffer; it was proper that he should, and what happened to Vashka Shibanov was none of Prince Kurbsky's business. But any such treatment of himself, Prince Kurbsky, aristocrat and valiant leader, he would not brook: on his own behalf and that of his fellow aristocrats, he would take vengeance on Ivan by publicity, by a history.[12]

Kurbsky inherited the best literary traditions of his teachers, the trans-Volga hermits and Maxim the Greek. He was not ideologist for the appanaged "regiment of princes" that dreamed of a return to the forms which had existed in the days of its ancestors; he did not deny the historical role of the Muscovite state, but was striving to preserve some part of his former prerogatives and to give official form to the governmental footing of large landowners. Even such a position on the part of this descendant of the princes of Yaroslav was, in terms of the political situation of that time, however, already not a program of today but of yesterday and was therefore obviously doomed to failure, the more so since, showing through Kurbsky's outwardly very harmonious, emotionally charged, and logically convincing language was his necessarily subjective, personal, and finally, in many ways, prejudiced appraisal of the actions and policies of his mortal enemy. This prejudice stands out with particular prominence in the *History of the Great Prince of Moscow*.

Kurbsky's resentment against Ivan was the stronger for his consciousness of being one of those princelings hounded by the Terrible who were, like the tsar himself, descended "from the family of Vladimir the Great," of which fact the disgraced prince also took occasion to remind his persecutor. "This reminder," says Plekhanov, "shows that the quarrel between Kurbsky and Ivan was not merely a quarrel between an official and his sovereign. It appears also to have been in some measure a quarrel between two branches of this same 'family of Vladimir the Great.' In other words, in the person of Kurbsky there spoke not only the disaffected 'noble'; in his person there also spoke and perhaps still more strongly, who knows? a descendant of the princes of Yaroslav who had been insulted by the powerful prince of Moscow."[13]

The Terrible had been brought up in the Josephite literary traditions.

[12] N. A. Dobrolyubov, "O stepeni uchastiya narodnosti v razvitii russkoy literatury" (On the Degree of Participation of Nationality in the Development of Russian Literature), *Complete Collected Works*, ed. P. I. Lebedev-Polyanskii, Vol. I, pp. 224–225.

[13] The latest edition of Kurbsky's works, ed. G. Z. Kuntsevich, Vol. XXXI of *Russkaya istoricheskaya biblioteka* (Russian Historical Library), is *Sochineniya knyazya Kurbskogo*, (Works of Prince Kurbsky), *Original Works* (St. Petersburg, 1914), Vol. I. On Kurbsky see A. Yasinskii, *Sochineniya kn. Kurbskogo kak istoricheskii material* (Works of Prince Kurbsky as Historical Material) (Kiev, 1889); G. V. Plekhanov, *Istoriya russkoy obshchestvennoy mysli* (History of Russian Social Thought), 2nd. ed., Vol. 1, pp. 138–147. The quotation is from p. 141.

Extremely conscious of being sole autocratic ruler, he obstinately believed himself the descendant of Augustus Caesar and, according to Josephite doctrine, God's vicar upon earth. He was convinced that all his subjects without exception were his slaves. "I am free to show favor to my slaves and I am also free to execute them!" he wrote Kurbsky. In his writings, and particularly in his two letters to Kurbsky he showed the typical stylistic peculiarities of his teachers, the Josephites. Alongside magniloquence and bombast and a predilection for pompous Church Slavonic sentences, at times very disjointed as to syntax, the vernacular would slip into his writing, a coarse term of abuse, a prosaic detail from everyday life, a picturesque expression, as we have seen happen with Metropolitan Daniel. Thus phrases like the following are wedged into the archaically bombastic style of his first letter to Kurbsky: "Why, dog, do you write and complain to me after committing such an enormity? What will your advice be good for when it stinks worse than dung?" Or: "Why do you boast, dog, so proudly, like other dogs and traitors, of your courage in battle?" And from then on the epithets "dog," "dog's" are frequently applied by the Terrible to his enemies. In response to Kurbsky's threat that he is not going to show the tsar his face until the Last Judgment, the Terrible writes: "Who wants to see any such Ethiopian face?"

The Terrible's second letter, possibly under the influence of Kurbsky's upbraidings, was written much more concisely than the first, much more simply and clearly, almost in the language of conversation. In it we meet, for example, such colloquial sentences as: "But how was Kurlyatev better than I was? Buy his daughters all manner of trinkets, well and good, but let my daughters be cursed even after their death. But enough of this. You have caused me more trouble than could ever be written down." Or: "But you will say that I did not bear her loss patiently and did not remain true to her—but we are all human. Why did you take the musketeer's wife?" In 1577 the Terrible captured Volmar, whither Kurbsky had fled, and in this same second letter, written shortly after his military success, he indulges in ironic exultation over the fugitive prince:

But you wrote that you were annoyed at our sending you to far-off towns as if in disgrace, yet now, by God's will, we have with our own gray hair advanced even farther than your far-off towns and our horses' hoofs have traversed all your roads into Lithuania and out of Lithuania and we have dismounted and drunk the water of all those places, so that Lithuania can no longer say there is anywhere that our horses' hoofs have not been. And where you hoped for peace from all your troubles, in Volmar, even there, to your retreat, did God lead us; and there by the will of God we overtook you and then you had to move far-off-er still.

Even greater irony, conjoined not with pride but with a show of humility, informs the Terrible's epistle to Cosma, prior of St. Cyril's Monastery at

Byelozersk, and the brotherhood, written in about the year 1578. To this monastery the Terrible had banished the disgraced boyars and there they had violated the strict monastic rule and settled down to a free and easy existence differing little from the life they had led in the outside world. The epistle was written in reply to a request from Cosma and the regular monastic brotherhood that the highborn monks who were forgetting themselves be steadied by a stern imperial admonition. Referring back to this, the Terrible begins his epistle with a bombastic but envenomed mock disparagement of himself as an admonisher:

Alas, sinner that I am! Woe unto me, accursed! Ah me, vile that I am! Who am I to venture to such a height? For God's sake, lords and fathers, I pray you give over any such undertaking! I am unworthy to be called your brother, but, in the words of the Gospel, make me as one of your hirelings; in this capacity I fall down before the honored soles of your feet and pray: for God's sake, give over any such undertaking.

According to the epistle, the light of monks is the angels, the light of laymen, the monks, and therefore it is for the monks to enlighten their prodigal lords, rather than for him, the tsar, "a stinking dog," to teach or admonish anybody. They have a "great lamp" in Cyril, founder of the monastery; let them look without ceasing upon his grave and take light from their teacher. He himself, the tsar, having sometimes visited their monastery and there eased his "vile" heart and "accursed" soul, had decided that when the time came he would take the tonsure there and receive Cyril's personal blessing on that occasion. Therefore he already felt himself half a monk, and this consciousness, in spite of the unworthiness he had just mentioned, gave him a right to reason with and instruct the prodigals, and, abandoning the pompously archaic Church Slavonic with which he had begun his epistle, he passes over into colloquial for his attack on the odious boyars Sheremetev, Khabarov, Sobakin, and the already deceased Vorotynsky: "And what name do the brethren call Sheremetev by? He has ten slaves living in his cell, eats better than the brothers who eat in the refectory. . . . Yes, Sheremetev's rule is good, keep it; the way of Cyril is not good, leave it." Vorotynsky and Sheremetev have more honor in the monastery than St. Cyril himself: "And here is a church to Vorotynsky and none to the miracle-worker; Vorotynsky is of the church and the miracle-worker out back of it. And at the Last Judgment Vorotynsky and Sheremetev will stand higher than he because Vorotynsky has a church and Sheremetev a law that are stronger than those of St. Cyril."

The boyars in the monastery give themselves over to gluttony and all manner of excesses, denying themselves nothing:

And now Sheremetev sits among you in his cell like a Tsar and Khabarov calls upon him, and so do some of the monks, and they eat and drink as if in the outside world; and Sheremetev, as if for a wedding or a birth, distributes fruit-jelly pastries through the cells, gingerbreads and spiced vegetables; and behind the monastery is a courtyard and in it are stores of all manner of baked things; and you say nothing to him of such great and pernicious monastic indecorum.

In a monastery there ought to be equality and brotherhood, regardless of the social extraction of the monks, the Terrible insists, whereas at the present time there is nothing of the sort in St. Cyril's monastery. "But is it the way of salvation," asks the tsar, "when a boyar becomes a monk and does not shave off his rank, and a serf does not escape his serfdom?" Along with his reproaches to the dissolute monk-boyars, the Terrible expresses his vexation at being bothered with complaints about them. "And for whose good is it?" he asks resentfully, "for the good of that ill tempered dog Basil Sobakin? . . . Or of that devil's son Ivan Sheremetev? Or of that fool and parasite Khabarov?"

The Terrible's epistle, as we see, besides being of interest for its style, is also of value as a monument giving a telling sketch of everyday life in one of the most important monasteries.[14]

Even before Kurbsky, in 1553–1554, boyar interests had found a champion in the unknown author of a publicistic pamphlet entitled "Conversation Between Saints Sergius and Herman, Wonder-Workers of Balaam Monastery." The basic idea of the pamphlet is in brief that the tsar ought to govern not with the aid of the "unburied dead," the monks, but with the aid of the boyars chiefly, and ought not to give excessive privileges to the soldiers. This bespeaks an opposition directed both against the Josephite-court-noble party in the clergy and against the army, which was basically just as much recruited from the nobles.[15]

[14] For Ivan the Terrible's letters to Kurbsky, see *Russkaya istoricheskaya biblioteka* (Russian Historical Library), Vol. XXXI, pp. 9–102, 117–124. The epistle to St. Cyril's monastery at Byelozersk is given in full in *Akty istoricheskie* (Historical Acts), Vol. I, No. 204, pp. 372–394. On the Terrible as writer, see I. N. Zhdanov, "Sochineniya tsarya Ivana Vasil'-evicha" (Works of Tsar Ivan Vasilyevich), *Works* of I. N. Zhdanov, Vol. I, pp. 81–170.

[15] The text of the "Conversation" (*Beseda*), with introduction by V. G. Druzhinin and M. A. Dyakonov, is printed in *Letopis' zanyatii Arkheograficheskoy komissii* (Chronicle of the Studies of the Archaeographical Commission) Pt. X, pp. l–xxiv, 1–32. See G. V. Plek-hanov, *Istoriya russkoy obshchestvennoy mysli* (History of Russian Social Thought), 2nd ed., Vol. I, pp. 129–137; G. P. Belchenko, *K voprosu o sostave i ob avtore Besedy prep. Sergiya i Germana* (On the Question of the Composition and the Author of the Conversation of Saints Sergius and Herman) (Odessa, 1914), which also gives the literature of the question. See also A. D. Sedelnikov, "Dve zametki po epokhe Ioanna Groznovo, 2: Iz kom-mentariya k besede Valaamskoy" (Two Notes on the Epoch of Ivan the Terrible: From a Commentary to the Balaam Conversation), *Sbornik statey k sorokaletiyu uchyonoy deyatel'-nosti akademika A. S. Orlova* (Collection of Essays for the Fortieth Anniversary of Academician A. S. Orlova's Career as a Scholar), pp. 167–173.

LITERARY WORKS THAT EXALTED AND CONSOLIDATED MUSCOVITE POLITICAL AND ECCLESIASTICAL TRADITIONS: Chronicle Compilations, *Chetyi Minyei* of the Metropolitan Macarius, *Stepennaya Kniga*

At about the middle of the sixteenth century, Moscow embarked upon a series of large-scale literary undertakings directed toward a summing up of the past from the viewpoint of official Muscovite ideology, in the first place as a means of throwing a nimbus about that past, in the second to demonstrate the continuity and consecutiveness of the culturo-political and ecclesiastico-religious process in its unfolding from the beginning of the Russian state and the Russian church down to that day.

In this connection mention should first be made of Moscow's far-reaching and intensive development of the chronicle. Setting out from such all-Russian metropolitan chronicle compilations as the *Vladimir Polychron* and the *Chronograph* of Pakhomius the Logethete, extant in the redaction of 1512, Muscovite clerks cooperated to produce in the 1540's several typical Muscovite chronicle compilations clearly expressive of the Muscovite centralizing tendency. Just as Moscow had gathered the autonomous Russian provinces about itself politically, so in a literary way it brought together the autonomous chronicles, those of Kiev, of Rostov-Suzdal, of Novgorod, of Tver, and so forth, with a view to representing the history of the once politically independent Russian districts as organically antecedent to the history of the united Muscovite state. Having arrived on the historical scene later than the other principalities, Moscow possessed no chronicle compilations of its own and in the chronicle compilations that it organized did not start including items from its own history until the fourteenth century. Individual notes of political separatism, still to be heard in the old metropolitan compilations, were now more or less skillfully toned down, and the idea brought forward was of a God-preserved and God-ordained Muscovite empire headed by autocrats who traced their line to the Roman emperor Augustus.

Most important among the Muscovite compilations are the *Resurrection Chronicle*, bringing events down to 1541,[16] and the *Patriarchal*, or *Nikonian*, *Chronicle*, which ends with 1558 [17] and was evidently an adaptation and extension of the *Resurrection Chronicle*. The title of both collections is associated with the name of the patriarch Nikon, owner of the copies, one

16 Published in Vols. VII–VIII of the *Full Collection of Russian Chronicles.*
17 *Op. cit.,* Vols. IX–XIV.

of which he donated to the Resurrection Monastery. In both chronicles the Muscovite state is regarded as the patrimony of the Muscovite lords, sole orderers and owners of the land of Rus. Dry factual entries are here interspersed with lengthy articles written in an elevated and solemn style which fully accords with the solemnity of the idea of the imperial power of the Muscovite absolute monarch. With the *Nikonian Chronicle* belongs the *Lvov Chronicle,* so called after its first publisher. This carries events down to and including the year 1560.[18] The legend, tale, discourse, and epistolary material contained in these chronicle collections is of considerable interest to the literary historian.

The Nikonian and Lvov chronicles were continued to include events from the last years of Ivan the Terrible's reign. In the 1560's and 1570's an enormous historical compilation, profusely illustrated, was composed. This was based chiefly on the Nikonian compilation and is therefore sometimes called the *Illuminated Nikonian Compilation.* It is not extant in its entirety and was never fully completed, but the surviving portion runs to ten thousand sheets (about twenty thousand pages) with sixteen thousand illustrations. It begins with the creation of the world and goes down to the 1560's. This was the most grandiose of the chronicle enterprises, aiming, as it did, to depict full length and in all solemnity the greatness of the Muscovite empire, to which, in the opinion of the authors of the digest, the whole previous history of mankind had led up. The compilation was later elaborated into the so-called *"Imperial Book,"* likewise never carried to completion.[19]

The subsequent stormy incidents of the peasant wars and foreign intervention rocked the sumptuously built edifice of the Muscovite empire to its foundations and undermined its official conception of history. Traditional

[18] *Op. cit.,* Vol. XX.
[19] Published in Vol. XIII of the *Full Collection of Russian Chronicles.* On the Moscow chronicle compilations see I. A. Tikhomirov, "Obozrenie sostava moskovskikh letopisnykh svodov" (Survey of the Composition of the Moscow Chronicle Compilations), *Letopis zanyatii Arkheograficheskoy komissii* (Chronicle of the Studies of the Archaeographical Commission) (St. Petersburg, 1895), Pt. 10, pp. 1–84; review of this work by A. A. Shakhmatov in *Otchyot o 40-m prisuzhdenii nagrad gr. Uvarova* (Report on the Fortieth Award of the Count Uvarov Prizes) (1899); V. S. Ikonnikov, *Opyt russkoy istoriografii* (Experiment in Russian Historiography), Vol. II, Bk. 2, pp. 1137–1274; A. E. Presnyakov, "Letopisnoe delo v XV i XVI vv." (The Manuscript Profession in the Fifteenth and Sixteenth Centuries), in *Istoriya russkoy literatury do XIX v.* (History of Russian Literature Up to the Nineteenth Century), ed. A. Gruzinskii (Moscow, 1916), pp. 248–270; *ibid.,* "Moskovskaya istoricheskaya entsiklopediya XVI v." (A Moscow Historical Encylcopaedia of the Sixteenth Century), *Izv. otd. russk. yaz. i slov.* (News of the Division of Russian Language and Literature of the Academy of Sciences) (1900), Bk. 3, pp. 824–876; *ibid.,* "Zametki o litsevykh letopisyakh," (Notes on the Illuminated Chronicles) *ibid.* (1901), Bk. 4, pp. 295–304; V. N. Shchepkin, "Litsevoy sbornik imp. rossiiskogo istoricheskogo muzeya," (Illuminated Collection in the Imperial Russian Historical Museum), *ibid.* (1899), Bk. 4, pp. 1345–1385.

chronicle-writing lost its meaning and thereafter went into a marked decline.

Simultaneously with the unification of Russian chronicle literature, a unification of ecclesiastico-instructional literature took place. The initiator and guiding spirit of this project was the metropolitan Macarius, who had also taken a prominent part in the organization of the chronicle project in Moscow.

The year 1552 marks the completion of Macarius' labors on the composition and redaction of a grandiose twelve-volume collection of products of Russian ecclesiastico-religious scholarship, both translated and original, which had circulated in numerous manuscripts. This collection, known under the name of the *Grand Chetyi Minyei*, exists in three copies, the fullest of which (about twenty-seven thousand pages, large size) is the copy that was destined for the Cathedral of the Assumption in Moscow.

Macarius' work was based on the old translated Greek *Chetya Mineya* which had by degrees, especially since the beginning of the sixteenth century, broadened its scope to include, in addition to biography, material drawn, chiefly, from instructive and eulogistic discourses, and, in part, of Russian origin. But up to Macarius' time not all the Chetyi Minyei dates had been filled in and, to fill them, Macarius drew first upon detached lives, translated and Russian, which for various reasons, chiefly their bulk, had not been included in the pre-Macarian Minyei. Besides these he used biographical material from the older, the so-called "plain," *Prologue* and from the new, or "rhymed," *Prologue*, transmitted to us from Byzantium by way of the South Slavs not earlier than the fifteenth century and containing lives that bulked larger than those carried by the "plain" *Prologue*. All this material was subjected to fresh redaction, chiefly stylistic, in the spirit of that pompous rhetoric which first got a foothold here in lives of saints, and the destined function of which was to bestow luster and grandeur upon Russian sanctitude.

The same panegyric cast of style was used in writing the lives of saints canonized at the councils of 1547 and 1549 and those canonized earlier whose lives had not as yet been written.

In the sixteenth century, particularly from the end of the first half, biographical literature is noticeably on the increase. The definitively established quasi-official concept of Moscow as the "third Rome," focal point of Orthodox sanctity, put forward by the ideologists of the Muscovite autocracy, created the primary incentive for supplementing the roster of saints, special glory of the land of Rus, and reexamining the supply of ascetics ready to hand, saints who had enjoyed reverence in separate provinces previous to the merging of these provinces into a single Muscovite state. At the instance of Metropolitan Macarius, both councils assumed the complicated task of canonizing new saints, promoting local saints to full Muscovite sainthood, and decanonizing any provincial saints who, upon scrutiny of the pertinent material, failed to meet the requirements. And this overhauling and ordering of the Russian-Orthodox Olympus necessitated the writing of new lives or the revision of old ones. Revision embraced both thought and style: it was obligatory that all hagiographical material be clothed in that panegyric-ceremonial style which was sign and symbol of the court-autocratic tendencies that had triumphed. The urgent need for getting new lives written and, on the other hand, the absence in many cases of adequate material for the purpose, resulted in the modeling of new lives on lives already existent of saints similar in type or even in name to the saints requiring biographies. As in the preceding age, so now, lives reflected sometimes the official ideology of Josephism, sometimes the opposition ideology of the trans-Volga hermits.

Macarius originally intended that his collection should consist exclusively of biographical literature but, later on, as the work progressed, it absorbed "Holy Scripture," patristic literature, homiletic and didactic works, and so forth; in a word, any spirituo-religious literature available, provided its religious or political trustworthiness was not suspect. In detached instances, however, even apocryphal works found their way into the Macarian *Chetyi Minyei*, if they existed under some title other than that given them in the indexes of "repudiated books." The outward monumentality of the work was designed to symbolize the monumentality and grandioseness of the idea of the Muscovite Orthodox empire.[20]

Associated with the *Chetyi Minyei* was a work which took final form shortly after it (in 1563), the *Book of Degrees of the Imperial Genealogy,* composed, apparently at the instance of Macarius, by the imperial confessor, the priest Andrew, monastically known as Athanasius, successor to Macarius

---

[20] Publication of the *Grand Chetyi Minyei* by parts and cahiers was carried on by the Archaeographical Commission from 1868 to 1917. The material for September, October, and April was printed in full; for November, from the first of the month to the 25th; for December, the first through the 24th and the 31st; for January, the first through the 11th. The rest of the material has not yet been published. There is a description of the *Grand Chetyi Minyei* by A. V. Gorsky and K. I. Novostruev—"Opisanie Velikikh Chet'ikh Miney," *Chteniya v Obshchestve istorii i drevnostey* (Description of the Grand Chetyi Minyei, Papers Read Before the Society of History and Antiquities) (1884), I, and (1886), II, with preface and supplement by E. Barsov, incomplete—as well as one by Archimandrite Joseph—*Podrobnoe oglavlenie Velikikh Chet'ikh Miney* (Detailed Table of Contents of the Grand Chetyi Minyei) (Moscow, 1892). On it see V. Klyuchevskii, "Velikie Chet'i Miney, sobrannye Vserossiiskim mitropolitom Makariem" (The Grand Chetyi Minyei, Collected by Macarius, Metropolitan of all Rus), *Otzyvy i otvety* (Reviews and Answers) (Moscow, 1914), third collection of articles, pp. 1–20; M. N. Speranskii, *Istoriya drevney russkoy literatury i Moskovskii period* (History of Ancient Russian Literature, Moscow period), 3rd ed. (Moscow, 1921), pp. 161–172; *ibid.*, the September *Chetyi Minyei* in the Pre-Macarian Corpus," *Izvestiya otd. russk. yaz. i slov.* (News of the Division of Russian Language and Literature) (1896), Bk. 2, pp. 235–257, and the "October *Chetyi Minyei* of the Pre-Macarian Corpus, *ibid.* (1902), Bk. 1, pp. 57–87.

in the metropolitan cathedra. The material was classified according to the generations of the great princes and presented in the pompous rhetorical style, the purpose of the book being to offer a history of pious Russian rulers functioning in unison with outstanding representatives of the Russian Church, metropolitans and bishops by preference. In the *Stepennaya Kniga,* biography habitually passes over into hagiography, the style of hagiography asserting itself even in the treatment of princes or top church hierarchs who not only did not achieve sainthood, but, especially in the case of princes, were in no wise distinguished for Christian piety. Though utilizing for the most part available chronicle literature and borrowing from it many facts of a purely historical character, the *Stepennaya Kniga* so embellished its material stylistically as to produce the effect of one continuous high-flown and flowery panegyric in praise of Russia's rulers through Ivan the Terrible, to whom the seventeenth and final degree of the book is devoted.

The whole style is of a piece with the long drawn-out title: *Book of Degrees of the Imperial Genealogy of the Illustrious God-ordained Scepter-Holders Who Rule in Piety the Russian Land, and Who, Like the Groves of Paradise, Were Planted of God by the Water Springs and Given to Drink of Orthodoxy and Made to Grow in Wisdom and Grace, Who Were Irradiated by the Glory of God Like a Luxuriant Orchard Which Is Fair with Leaves and Flowers, Abounding in Fruit Mellow and Full of Fragrance, Which Is Great and Tall, and Productive of Numerous Progeny, Spreads Magnificent Branches and Is Extolled for Virtues Pleasing to God,* and so forth.

And in what follows, this high-flown style is maintained, as we have said, regardless of what prince is under discussion and whether he had or had not been canonized. For example, this is how the item about Great Prince Yaroslav, son of Vsevolod, begins: "Of a noble root the fruitful and unwithered branch, of an imperial stock a seed productive of Russian autocrats, was this Great Prince Yaroslav," and so forth. The degree devoted to Ivan Kalita begins thus: "This noble, God-appointed heir and blessed inheritor of the noble realm of the God-loving Russian empire, Great Prince Ivan Danilovich, called Kalita, grandson of the blessed Alexander, was the tenth degree from the apostolic St. Vladimir I, thirteenth from Rurik," and so forth. The seventeenth degree, set apart to Ivan the Terrible, begins with a rhetorical introduction which discusses the importance of prayer and then tells of the "joyous imperial birth" which was consequent upon the heartfelt prayer of Ivan's parents:

Here too is seen the virtue of prayer and how it made the imperial sterility of the autocrat Basil Ivanovich to flower, and how a son was born to him and an heir to the empire, the present anointed tsar and great prince, of the most pleasing

name of Ivan, lord and autocrat of all Russia and conqueror of many other languages and empires, who is the seventeenth degree from St. Vladimir I, and
twentieth from Rurik.

To show how the *Stepennaya Kniga* revised its sources stylistically, let
us take the first article in the twelfth degree: "Of the life and deeds of the
blessed and praiseworthy Great Prince and Russian Tsar Dmitry Ivanovich,"
and compare it with its source, the tale *Of the Life and Death of Great
Prince Dmitry Ivanovich, Tsar of Rus,* which occurs in almost literally coinci-
dent texts in the fourth Novgorod, first St. Sophia, Resurrection and Nikonian
chronicles. Even the first words of the source: "This Great Prince Dmitry,"
are in the *Stepennaya Kniga* expanded to: "This God-glorified and praiseworthy Great Prince Dmitry." To the information that Dmitry was grandson
of Ivan Danilovich is added: "Great-grandson of Great Prince Daniel
Aleksandrovich of Moscow, great-great grandson of Great Prince and wonder-worker Alexander Yaroslavich Nevsky" and, in the conventional "degree"
manner, it is pointed out that he was the twelfth degree from Vladimir and
fifteenth from Rurik. The source's phrase: "He was reared in piety and
glory with all manner of spiritual admonitions and in the fullness of these
came to love God," takes on this aspect in the *Book of Degrees*: "And he
was reared in true piety and in upright good repute with all manner of
spiritual admonitions: and in the fullness of these came to love God and
was obedient to his parents, and to the end continued to order his life in
accordance with God's will." The source says of Dmitry that when his father
died, "he left a young son, about nine years old," instead of which we read
in the *Degrees*: "This God-beloved son and heir of his, Great Prince Dmitry,
being then young, was parted from this honored parent at about the age of
ten, though in wisdom he was as mature as if he had been a thousand."
Further rhetorical amplifications of the same sort are introduced into the
original tale and many biographical details are also added.

As we have seen, the tale *Of the Life and Death* is, even without this, generously supplied with pompous rhetoric, but not sufficiently, it would seem,
to suit the compiler of the *Degrees,* who strove to saturate his narrative with
still further "fine wordage."

Like the Muscovite chronicle compilations and the *Chetyi Minyei* of
Macarius, so the *Stepennaya Kniga* set itself the task of extolling and glorifying to the utmost the historic past and the present of Muscovite Rus,
primarily by glorifying and extolling the rulers as having acted in full accord
with the Church.[21]

[21] The *Stepennaya Kniga* was published under the editorship of P. G. Vasenko in Vol.
XXI of the *Full Collection of Russian Chronicles.* Many studies have been devoted to it,
but as a literary-historical monument it has scarcely been investigated at all; even its immediate sources have not really been studied, and no work has actually been done beyond

There is a very close connection between these monuments of sixteenth century official Muscovite literature and such nonliterary enterprises of the mid century as the *Domostroy* (House Orderer), the *Stoglav* (Book of a Hundred Chapters), and the *Azbukovnik* (ABC of Knowledge), which are permeated throughout with the same official ideology as the monuments which may be classified as literary. There was not only an organic connection between the two but also a mutual interplay of ideas. The *Domostroy*, aiming to regiment human behavior down to the smallest detail in the religious, socio-governmental, and domestic spheres, the *Stoglav*, constituting a digest of the enactments and decisions of the ecclesiastical council of 1551 on various questions relating to religious and secular life, the *Azbukovnik*, striving, in the form of an encyclopaedic dictionary, to invest with authority the system of knowledge and opinion obligatory for the right-thinking reader—all proceeded from full reliance on the religio-political and moral principles of Moscow, the "third Rome" that had been erected on the assumption of their being indisputable and unshakeable. There could be no question of critically revaluating these principles in the slightest degree but only of lifting the general structure and everyday routine of life to that ideal norm which had been prescribed once and for all in hard and fast, sacrosanct traditions. Hence the blueprint worked out in the *Domostroy*, which provided down to the last detail a positive religious, moral and practical life pattern to aid the family, under the headship of the master of the house, the father and husband, in orienting itself by the rule of monastic communities, hence, too, the *Stoglav's* open criticism of manifestations in Russian life that conflicted with the ideal worked out and officially decreed for it.

For an understanding of the intellectual atmosphere in which conservative Russian literary works took their rise not only during the sixteenth century but for part of the seventeenth as well, a knowledge of the *Domostroy* will provide particularly abundant material. Whoever the author may have been (most probably Archpriest Sylvester of the Annunciation, with whose epistle to his son Anfim the monument itself ends), he reflected very fully in his own person that system of ideas, norms, and principles that Moscow

---

the most general indications not so much as to its connection with, as its resemblance to, the material of the Macarian *Minyei,* the genealogical lists, the *Legend of the Princes of Vladimir,* the chronographs, and the lives of the Serbian kings and archbishops. The latest detailed investigation of separate problems arising in connection with the study of the *Stepennaya* is P. G. Vasenko's *Kniga Stepennaya tsarskogo rodosloviya i evo znachenie v drevnerusskoy istoricheskoy pismennosti* (Book of Degrees of the Imperial Genealogy and Its Significance in Early Russian Historical Literature), (St. Petersburg, 1904), Pt. 1; *ibid.,* "Sostavnye chasti *Knigi Stepennoy Tsarskogo Rodosloviya* (Component Parts of the Book of Degrees of the Imperial Genealogy), *Letopis zanyatii Arkheograficheskoy komissii* (Chronicle of the Studies of the Archaeographical Commission), (1908), Pt. 19, pp. 1–51. See also V. S. Ikonnikov, *Opyt russkoy istoriografii* (Experiment in Russian Historiography), Vol. II, Bk. 2, pp. 1308–1338. Here the literature of the question is also given.

had worked out, taking itself as focal point of Orthodox sanctity and custodian of the highest social and political values. Great importance also attaches to the *Domostroy* as an objective presentation of the life of the well-to-do Russian family, whose interests are the author's chief concern. Beginning with instructions as to the duty of honoring tsar and prince, as to religious observances, as to how a husband should train his wife, children, and servants, and how conduct himself as a householder, and ending with detailed culinary formulae, the *Domostroy* embraces all sides of life in the matter of basic general principles and daily routine. Though genetically linked with traditional medieval "guides for living," both Western and Eastern, and also with previous Russian testaments (instructions), chiefly from father to son, it at the same time bore the living imprint of the age when it was written. Later it would evoke Russian imitations, and even be clothed in poetic form.[22]

The problems of unification which Muscovite Rus had set itself were aided in their solution by the introduction here of book-printing. The first print shop in Moscow was opened in 1563; the first printers were Ivan Fyodorov and Peter Mstislavets, the first printed book an *Acts of the Apostles,* which came out in 1564. Later, even during the seventeenth century, service books were the chief thing printed: only through the help of the printing press did the united Muscovite church succeed in bringing uniformity to the chaotic Russian literature of worship.

HISTORY OF THE EMPIRE OF KAZAN

Apologetics for the power and greatness of the Muscovite empire and of its head, Ivan the Terrible, also characterize the popular monument (preserved in as many as two hundred copies) entitled the *History of the Empire of Kazan,* or the *Kazan Chronicler,* which sets forth the fate of the empire of Kazan from its founding by Volga Bulgars to its conquest by the Terrible in 1552. While including a large amount of historical material, the *History* is at the same time a work of considerable interest from a purely literary point of view. Though the manner of describing battle scenes and even

[22] Texts of the *Domostroy* are published in *Vremennik obshchestvennoy istorii i drevnostey* (Chronicle of Social History and Antiquities) (1849), the "Konshin" edition; more accurately reprinted by A. S. Orlov in *Chteniya obshchestva istorii i drevnostey* (Papers of the Society of History and Antiquities) (1908), and separately and *ibid.* (1882), Bk. 2, "Zabelin" redaction. The latest work on the *Domostroy* (incomplete) is A. S. Orlov's "Domostroy," *Issledovanie* (Investigation) (Moscow, 1917), Pt. 1. This also gives the literature of the question.

individual episodes was chiefly borrowed from Nestor-Iskander's *Tale of Tsargrad,* the tales of the rout of Mamay, the later chronicles, and the Bible, and to some extent from the story of the Georgian queen Dinara, as well as from the *Chronograph,* the *History* at the same time reflected the pompous style of works of the Macarian period and also made extensive use of the methods and style of oral poetry.

Presumably the *History* appeared between the years 1564–1566. Its author, to judge from his own statement, was a Russian who had been captured by Kazanians, had passed twenty years in captivity, and when the Terrible took Kazan had entered his service. In the introduction to the *History,* he himself calls it a "fine, new and pleasing tale." And the work does indicate a writer with poetic taste and a fondness for figurative language and literary elaboration. Here, for example, is the form in which he gives us the lament of the empress of Kazan, who had been removed from the city of Sviyazhsk to the Russian border: "Woe unto thee, woe unto thee, bleeding city, woe unto thee, a city cast down; why art thou still proud and haughty? Already the marriage crown has fallen from thy head as from a poor woman widowed and destitute. Thou art slave, not master. And thy imperial renown is past and ended, thou hast fallen helpless like a beast without a head." And from this he draws a moral indirectly in apologia of the Muscovite government: "The bulwark of any empire is a wise tsar, not its protecting walls; armies with mighty generals can stand firm without a wall."

Next the empress recalls the former greatness of Kazan, something of which she is made particularly aware by its present tragic situation: "Where now are the royal feasts that you knew in other days? Where are your grandeurs? And where are the lancers, and princes, and mirzas of your days of beauty and greatness? And where are the gayety of young women and fair maidens and the songs and dances? All that was yours has now vanished and perished." Once rivers of mead and streams of wine had flowed in Kazan. But now the people are pouring blood and tears, conquered by Russian might. The lament ends with the following rhetorical exclamation: "Woe is me, my lord; now I shall take a swift-flying bird that speaks the language of men, and it shall be a messenger from me to my father and mother and carry them news of what has befallen their child."

A style resembling that of *Alexis, Man of God,* is used to portray the sadness of Empress Anastasia after seeing the tsar, her husband, off on his campaign against Kazan: she returned to her chamber "like a swallow to its nest, with great grief and sorrow and much mourning . . . and, like a bright star going under a dark cloud, covered herself with sorrow and grief in her chamber, and stayed there and shut all the windows and would not look upon the light of day until the tsar should return victorious."

The *History* describes very explicitly the acts of violence perpetrated in Russian territory by the Kazanians. It was presumably from these passages that a celebrated writer of the epoch of "Disorder," Avraamy Palitsyn, drew his graphic description of the acts of violence and fury perpetrated in Rus, so he says, at the time of the second pretender.

It is in the typical, already familiar, style of Nestor-Iskander's *Tale of the Taking of Tsargrad* that the author depicts the repeated assaults attending the siege of Kazan:

And from the roar of cannon and harquebus, and the clashing and ringing of many weapons, and the weeping and sobbing of the townsmen and women and children, and the great shrieking and wailing and whistling, and the neighing and stamping of the horses of both armies, there arose such a mighty uproar and such a fearful clangor that it could be heard to the Russian border, three hundred versts away. And it was impossible for one to hear what another said, and a murk of greenish fumes rose aloft and completely covered the city and the Russian army, and night was as bright as day from the light of the fires, and unseen was its darkness, while summer day was like dark autumn night from the smoke fumes and murk.

And this is how the women of Kazan lament when finally convinced that they have lost their independence: "O hills, cover us! O mother earth, open your lips speedily and swallow us, your children, alive that we may not see this bitter death that has come suddenly upon us all! Let us flee, let us flee, women of Kazan, that we may escape death!" To this counsel of flight other women of Kazan reply: "Guests not a few have come upon us and are giving us the same bitter cup of death to drink that we have often drawn for them; from their hands must we now take and drain that same bitter draught of death ourselves." With the motif of the "deadly cup" we are already familiar through the tale of Batu's attack upon Ryazan.

The bravery and martial fervor of the Russian troops are very graphically described:

The Russian troops swooped swift as famished eagles and hawks upon the ruins, and leaped like hinds over the hills and through the streets of the town, and scoured up and down like wild beasts in the wilderness, and roared like lions to confound their prey, tracking down the people of Kazan.

Finally there is a very picturesque description of the apotheosis that awaits the Terrible upon his return from the conquest of Kazan. The whole population of Moscow, headed by the clergy, the legates, and all the gentry, go out to meet the tsar:

And when they saw their autocrat they swarmed like bees about their queen, and with great rejoicing lauded and thanked him, calling him a great conqueror and all the while shouting, "Long life!" and bowing to the ground before him. He advanced serenely through the midst of the populace on his imperial steed with much majesty and great acclaim, the populace on either side bowing; and all his people were pleasured by the splendor and fame with which he shone upon them; for his imperial majesty was clothed cap-a-pie as for bright Easter Sunday, in armor and silver raiment, with a gold crown on his head set with great pearls and precious stones, and the imperial purple about his shoulders, and even on his feet nothing visible but gold and silver and pearls and precious stones—and no one had ever seen such precious things anywhere, and the minds of all beholders were amazed by them.

Likewise sumptuously arrayed, likewise adorned with gold and precious stones were the most noble boyars who rode behind the Terrible. Next comes a graphic description of the way the populace of Moscow feasted its eyes upon the Terrible's procession:

Some of the people of Moscow climbed to the churchtops and to the battlements and the palace roofs and looked on their tsar from there, while some ran to meet him farther out and clung to some elevation or other to look; yes, they did everything possible in order to see him; maids in waiting and the wives of princes and boyars whom modesty did not permit to leave their houses and depart from their homes to attend this great spectacle—for it is expedient that they remain in and live like caged birds—leaned out of doors and windows and looked through little chinks, and had much pleasure of this wonderful sight, while keeping their good name untarnished.

As we see, the author of the *History* spared no pains in his effort to present the Terrible in all the splendor and magnificence with which the official ideology had endowed him.

The Russians' subjugation of Kazan and final settlement of accounts with the once menacing Tartar power constituted a crowning triumph for the imperial policy of Moscow. We have already seen how popular ballad associated the Terrible's very coronation with the fall of Kazan. And this is why such a halo is thrown about the Terrible and his military undertaking, and about his eminent comrades at arms as well. Not without reason did the Terrible on the eve of the Kazan campaign, when taking council with "his golden brothers," with the "local princes," with the "great generals" and the "noble lords," enumerate the deeds of his ancestors, descendants of Augustus Caesar, and say: "I am by God's grace tsar and their heir. I have just such generals, great and renowned and strong and brave and skilled in military matters, as they had."

Elements of the oral-poetry style appear in such epithets as rivers "of mead," "mother earth," "virgin" field, maidens "fair," horses "goodly," turret chambers "lofty," and so forth.

An echo from oral poetry, as A. S. Orlov points out, is also audible in such expressions as "family and clan," "unwelcome guests," meaning enemies; "a heap of gold," meaning riches; "drinks crimson wine and pleasant mead," and also in the description of the Terrible's triumphant entry into Moscow, which recalls poetic details from the *bylina* about Churil Plenkovich.

Notwithstanding the *History's* general solemnity of style, it never for a moment suggests that flowery verbal craftsmanship, in the sense of the traditional "braiding of words," which we find in the *Stepennaya Kniga*. Pretentious words here encountered, such as "man-made," "cattle-grazing," "eye-delighting," "fulmination," "abscondence" are, comparatively speaking, very rare. On the other hand expressions from everyday colloquial speech occur: "ringing with all their might," "old and few," "not bad fighting," and others.

Thus the *History of the Empire of Kazan*, for practically the first time after a long lapse, brings into a scholarly work elements from oral poetry and folk speech. Here the determining factor was perhaps that the *History* did not emanate from official circles as did the monuments just surveyed, but was a product of personal initiative on the part of some scholar not committed to the established stylistic patterns of Muscovite scholarly centers.[23]

Under the influence of battle scenes from the *History of the Empire of Kazan* and from the tales of the rout of Mamay, a Pskov monk wrote, at the end of the sixteenth or the beginning of the seventeenth century, the *Tale of the Attack of the Lithuanian King Stephen Batory in the Year 7085 [1577] on the Great and Famous Town of Pskov*. But unlike the monuments mentioned as having influenced it, the *Tale of the Attack* is embellished to excess with bombastic rhetoric in the taste of the *Stepennaya Kniga*. In it occur, one after another, florid words such as the following: "town-fortification," "good-healthiness," "brave-good-victorious," "cleverly-stone-enclosed," "stipulatory," "high-thinking," and so forth. Lithuania is called "haughty-aggressive." An epithet will occur in various forms, all having the same meaning; thus, for example, Batory is here "all-proud," "much-proud," "high-proud." Tautological combinations constantly appear in the tale: "They become wise in the humility of wisdom"; "they strengthened themselves with adamantine strength"; "their wickedly plotted plots," "of wisely-intelligent intelligence," and so forth.

[23] The *History of the Empire of Kazan*, ed. G. Z. Kuntsevich, is published in Vol. XIX of the *Full Collection of Russian Chronicles*. For a study of it see G. Z. Kuntsevich, *Istoriya o Kazanskom tsarstve, ili Kazanskii letopisets* (History of the Empire of Kazan or the Kazan Chronicler) (St. Petersburg, 1905). See also V. S. Ikonnikov, *Opyt russkoy istoriografii* (Experiment in Russian Historiography), Vol. II, Bk. 2, pp. 275–291. This also gives the literature of the question. An analysis of the poetic style of the *History* in relation to its sources is made in A. S. Orlov's article "O nekotorykh osobennostyakh stilya velikorusskoy istoricheskoy belletristiki XVI–XVII vv." (On Certain Stylistic Peculiarities of Great Russian Historical Belles-Lettres in the Sixteenth and Seventeenth Centuries), *Izv. otd. russk. yaz. i slov.* (News of the Russian Language and Literature of the Academy of Sciences) (1908), Bk. 4, pp. 344–346. See also *ibid.*, "Khronograf i Povest' o Kazanskom tsarstve" (The Chronograph and the Tale of the Empire of Kazan), *Sbornik statei v chest' akad. A. I. Sobolevskogo* (Collection of Articles in Honor of Academician A. I. Sobolevsky), pp. 188–193.

The apotheosis of the Muscovite empire as prime owner of all Russian territories, heir of Rome and of Byzantium, along with the apotheosis of the Terrible as a ruler pious almost to the point of saintliness, are here carried to their extreme expression. Similarly hyperbolical, though negative, terms are used to draw the picture of his adversary Stephen Batory, who is likened to the "untiring asp," the "evilly venomous serpent," and compared with devils and "insatiate" tormentors.[24]

LEGEND OF THE KIEV BOGATYRS

The Terrible's conquest of Kazan, and shortly afterward—in 1556—of Astrakhan, was presumably the occasion for the composition, in the latter half of the sixteenth or at the beginning of the seventeenth century, of a very curious monument deriving directly from the *bylina* tradition in point of style. Until our own time it was known in two copies.[25] One of these, formerly Barsov's, dates from the first half of the seventeenth century and has the title: *Legend of the Kiev Bogatyrs: How They Went to Tsargrad and How They Vanquished the Tsargrad Bogatyrs and Won Honor for Themselves*. The other, an eighteenth century copy, formerly Buslayev's, is entitled *Legend of the Seven Russian Bogatyrs*. Both copies derive from a nonextant common original, but in the older copy—Barsov's—the original text of the monument and its *bylina* character are better preserved than in the Buslayev copy, with the aid of which, however, certain gaps and defective readings in the first copy may be restored.[26]

The *Legend* has a regular *bylina* beginning, which we quote from the Buslayev copy (it is lacking in the Barsov):

> In the capital city of Kiev,
> At Great Prince Vladimir's dwelling,
> A noble banquet was set
> For many princes and boyars
> And for mighty and strong bogatyrs.

[24] The tale was published by O. Bodyanskii in *Chteniya v Obshchestve istorii i drevnostey* (Papers Read Before the Society of History and Antiquities) (1847), No. 7, Smes'. An analysis of its style is given in *op. cit.* by A. S. Orlov, pp. 362–368.

[25] One more—unpublished—copy of the *Legend* is now known, evidently from the beginning of the eighteenth century; it is preserved in the A. M. Gorky MS. collection of the Institute of World Literature, Academy of Sciences of the USSR (Moscow).

[26] The latest edition of the two copies, ed. P. K. Simoni, is in "Pamyatniki starinnogo russk. yaz. i slov., XV–XVIII stoletii," (Monuments of Ancient Russian Language and Literature of the Fifteenth-Eighteenth Centuries), *Sbornik otd. russk. yaz. i slov* (Collection of the Division of Russian Language and Literature of the Academy of Sciences) (Petrograd, 1922), Col. C, No. 1.

At the height of the feast, Vladimir (using the language in which Moscow clerks wrote documents) says to "Ilya Muromets and his companions":

> You may not know, bogatyrs,
> That Emperor Constantine's sending against me
> From Tsargrad forty-two bogatyrs
> And bids them demolish Kiev.
> And you'd better not scatter on quests just now
> But stay and look after the town of Kiev
> And all of my patrimony.

The bogatyrs make supplication to the prince to let them go forth into the "virgin field"; they will procure "direct information" and get him a "good foreign language" (that is, a captive Mussulman noble) and so bring fame to their ruler, gain honor for themselves, and strike terror into many of the Horde. Next comes an enumeration of Vladimir's bogatyrs:

1. Ilya Muromets, son of Ivan
2. Dobrynya Nikitich
3. The nobleman Zaleshanin, "gray suit, gilt buttons"
4. Alyosha Popovich
5. Shchota Elizynich
6. Sukhan Domentyanovich
7. White Mace, "decorated with red gold, set with precious pearls, and in the midst of the mace a stone that flashes fire"

Of these, Shchota Elizynich (in the Buslayev copy, Glapir) and White Mace do not figure in any biliny known to us and were evidently brought over into the *Legend* from some fairy-tale source.

In spite of the prince's having forbidden them, as a precaution against the arrival of the Tsargrad bogatyrs, Vladimir's bogatyrs don their armor and set forth. On the way, Ilya Muromets says to his companions that it will be better for the Russian bogatyrs to go and meet the Tsargrad bogatyrs and with the help of God defeat them than to await them in Kiev. Twelve versts from Tsargrad, when crossing the river Smugra (probably the river here meant is the Ugra, on which the battle between Ivan III and the Tartar khan Akhmat took place), our bogatyrs meet twelve cripples, with whom they exchange clothes and who confirm the report that the Tsargrad bogatyrs intend to take Kiev and make the prince and princess prisoner and "lay all" the bold bogatyrs "prostrate under the sword." Upon hearing this, Ilya Muromets expresses a desire "to lay down his head for his lord's cup and offer up prayers for his great bread-and-salt."

Leaving horses and all accoutrements at the Smugra, the bogatyrs set out for Tsargrad in cripple garb. Arriving at court when the emperor was at table, they stood before the "red window" and began to beg loudly for alms.

The emperor heard them and, guessing that they were Russians, ordered his table companion Tugarin Zmeyevich to ask the cripples in and let him get news of Kiev. Ilya Muromets gave the emperor to understand that his band had come from Great Prince Vladimir. Bogatyr Idol Skoropeyevich, sitting across from the emperor, joined in the conversation. In stature he was "goodly beyond ordinary"; between his eyes "you could fit an arrow," between his shoulders, a great seven-foot rule; his eyes were like cups and his head like a beer kettle. He was terrible to look upon. He inquired as to how many bogatyrs Vladimir had, their stature and "prowess," and particularly as to whether there was a bogatyr named Ilya Muromets in Kiev and what he was like. Upon learning from Ilya that Ilya Muromets was of the same stature and appearance as himself (that is, Ilya Muromets) the monstrous Idol, according to the Buslayev copy, said "with a laugh": "'If he is really no larger than that, this Ilya Muromets, I shall set him on the palm of one hand and smash him flat with the other,'" and he urged Emperor Constantine to send the Tsargrad bogatyrs to Rus without further delay to take the prince and princess captive, lay the bold bogatyrs of Kiev prostrate under the sword and obtain gold and silver. This was too much for Alyosha Popovich and, just as the prudent bogatyr nobleman, Zaleshanin, had predicted, he spoke his mind: "If you bogatyrs come to Kiev you will never get out again, but Tartar heads will roll and the hot blood of Tsargrad bogatyrs be spilled."

The diplomatic Zaleshanin, seeing Idol's gorge rising, strives to divert attention from Alyosha Popovich's sally and explains his flare-up as due to the emperor's mead having gone to his head. Robbing the Tsargrad bogatyrs of the horses which the tsar had ordered brought out to show the cripples, they chopped off the Tartars' heads and sped out of Tsargrad to the river Smugra: "It was not birds or nightingales singing or warbling early in the leafy grove, but bogatyrs shouting at the top of their bogatyr voices, and the steel maces of Ilya Muromets and his companions whistling, and Tartar heads flying off; one good horse apiece they took and, having mounted, rode off out of town and down to the river Smugra." Meantime Alyosha Popovich alone remained in Tsargrad long enough to tell the tsar that the pilgrims would await the Tsargrad bogatyrs at the Smugra and give an account of themselves in the open field, and then he too galloped to the Smugra, where the Russian bogatyrs don their bogatyr armor and all their bogatyr harness and join battle with the promptly arriving Tartar force and the forty-two Tsargrad bogatyrs. In this struggle the whistling and shouting made the wood draw back, the grass droop flat, goodly horses fall on their haunches, poor horses cease to be.

Idol Skoropeyevich and Tugarin Zmeyevich are thrown into panic by the

Russian bogatyrs and Ilya Muromets at once takes them alive, but the rest of the Tartar force and all the Tsargrad bogatyrs are wiped out. The bogatyrs convey Idol and Tugarin to Tsargrad. Of Idol they make a parting gift to the Tsar but Tugarin they decide to take along with them in order to "have something to show the prince." In response to the entreaty of Tugarin's mother not to take her son away, Ilya Muromets promises to return him to Tsargrad alive and well after the bogatyrs have got credit in Kiev for his capture and showed him to Prince Vladimir. Sending on ahead of them nobleman Zaleshanin, a "lodger" at the prince's court (this was a court rank in the Muscovite state) to prepare the ground for their favorable reception, the truant bogatyrs ride into Kiev, where the prince, as was the custom of the Muscovite tsars, presents them with fur coats, gold "chains" and pay, and promises to reward them still further for the "great task accomplished and for their service as bogatyrs." When Vladimir questioned Tugarin as to the news, Tugarin replied as he could only have done if addressing the autocrat of Moscow: "Why, my lord, do you ask news of me? Do you not, my lord, possess a patrimony greater than all the Hordes and do bogatyrs bolder than yours exist in any land?" At a feast in Vladimir's hall, Ilya makes petition to the prince in the servile style typical of sixteenth century Moscow: "My lord, Prince Vladimir Vseslavich! Show mercy and favor to us your servants," and beseeches him to let Tugarin return to Tsargrad. Vladimir grants this request, and the bogatyrs accompany Tugarin as far as the border and then set him free.

As is easily seen from this summary, the *Legend* reflects forms of political and social life characteristic not of Kievan Rus, the supposed setting, but of fifteenth and sixteenth century Muscovite Rus. The *Legend* was evidently produced under the influence of the social awakening associated with Ivan the Terrible's conquest of Kazan. This event put life into the long cumulative concept of Moscow as heir of Tsargrad, and the geographical position of Tsargrad as described in the *Legend* (not across the sea, but across the steppes) is immediately reminiscent of Kazan. Another thing that takes us to Kazan is the naïve combination in a single town of Emperor Constantine on the one hand and the Tartar troops and Tartar bogatyrs in Constantine's service on the other. As popular ballad confused Tsargrad with Kazan, associating the Terrible's triumph over them with his being crowned emperor, so the *Legend* substitutes one town for the other in capitalizing on a recent historical event, the final destruction of the Tartar empire.

A. N. Veselovsky, in analyzing the *Legend*,[27] advanced the hypothesis that it represents some scholar's retouching of the record of a primitive *bylina* from the eleventh century period of Polovcian-Russian, Polovcian-Byzantine

[27] *Yuzhnorusskie byliny* (South Russian Byliny), pp. 356–374.

clashes, but Vs. F. Miller, in a work devoted to the study of the *bylina* cycle built around Ilya Muromets and Alyosha Popovich,[28] quite correctly pointed out that among known *byliny* we do not find even compressed or distorted descendants of Veselovsky's hypothetical *bylina*. Furthermore, the *Legend* itself had no circulation among the people and is known only in single copies. In relating the rise of the *Legend* to the sixteenth century and regarding it as a naïve popular response to political ideas circulated concerning the Moscow court both by the clergy and by Muscovite statesmen, Vs. Miller very plausibly conjectures that it was written by some literate person on the basis of two *byliny*, one about Ilya Muromets and the pagan Idol, the other about Alyosha Popovich and Tugarin Zmeyevich, with the help of traditional *bylina*, and, to some extent, fairy-tale, motifs and situations. To the author's independent invention must be ascribed his introduction among the Tsargrad bogatyrs of Tugarin Zmeyevich, who nowhere figures in the *byliny* along with Idol, both appearing in various *bylina* plots, but never simultaneously. Obviously the author's own ingenuity is also responsible for the presence of the Mussulman giant, Idol, enemy of Orthodoxy, as a bogatyr at the court of the Orthodox emperor Constantine and his consort.[29]

Thus there is every reason to suppose that the author of the *Legend*, who utilized *bylina* tradition so freely in his composition, was even farther removed than the author of the *History of the Empire of Kazan* from those official scholarly centers where tendentious Muscovite literature was framed, yet he too developed the official ideology in his work.

LITERATURE OF THE EARLY SEVENTEENTH CENTURY:
The Epoch of "Disorder"

The end of the sixteenth and the beginning of the seventeenth century were signalized in Russian history by the tempestuous events traditionally denominated the "Disorder" and characterized by tense class struggle. During this epoch the peasantry first makes its appearance as a major influential factor, having been reduced by the cumulative exploitation of serfage to the economic straits so glaringly exemplified at the time of the terrible famine of 1601–1603.

The gravity of the material situation of the peasantry was enhanced after

[28] *Ocherki russkoy narodnoy slovesnosti* (Outlines of Russian Folk Literature) (Moscow, 1910), Vol. II, pp. 87–168.

[29] See Vs. Miller, *op. cit.*, pp. 139–143, 145, 147, 153.

the death of the Terrible by aggravated competition between the great feudal boyars and the official nobility, the middle and small landowners who, in the long run, came off victors in the struggle. But the victory of the nobility, with some support from the merchant class, only intensified the economic crisis of the peasantry, on whose further pauperization the well-being of the victors depended. In an effort to escape from famine and bondage, peasants fled en masse to the woods at the southern outskirts of the Muscovite state, often even going beyond the boundaries of Moscow and organizing in new localities as free Cossacks. These malcontents of the Muscovite regime gave active support to the pretenders, one of whom posed as the supposedly rescued Demetrius, son of Ivan the Terrible, the other masquerading as Peter, a purely fictitious son of Theodore Ivanovich, and both actually adventurers, creatures of the Polish aristocracy. The pretenders utilized the dissatisfaction of the rebellious masses of the people for their reactionary ends, but tricked the people and left an evil memory in their minds. The peasant mass put forward an energetic leader in the fugitive slave Ivan Bolotnikov, who appeared at the walls of Moscow in 1616. Civil turmoil within the state was greatly complicated by Polish and Swedish intervention, which only collapsed when Minin and Pozharsky organized their defense against the intruders.

The profound social upheavals resulting from the "Disorder" would naturally be a great shock to the shapely and pompous ideology of the sacrosanct "third Rome" which official Moscow had been building up through the fifteenth and sixteenth centuries and which by the middle of the sixteenth century had been regarded as definitively established and beyond criticism, let alone abrogation. The grandiose edifice erected with such assurance was indeed shaken to its very foundations. And it is only natural that the political crisis and the concomitant crisis in the realm of ideas should have evoked an intensive literary response, expressing itself in numerous works [30] directed toward explaining and rationalizing these momentous historical events, and produced not only in Moscow but also in provincial centers, in Novgorod, Vladimir, Nizhny Novgorod, and elsewhere.

Tales, Legends, and Lives relating to the epoch and written partly in the heat of events, partly during the two decades immediately following, reflected, on the one hand, reactions to social and political upheavals of the turn of

[30] The most important of these were published in Vol. XIII of the *Russkaya istoricheskaya biblioteka* (Russian Historical Library), "Pamyatniki drevney russkoy pismennosti, otnosyashchiesya k Smutnomu vremeni" (Monuments of Early Russian Literature Dating from the Epoch of "Disorder"), 2nd ed. (St. Petersburg, 1909). A general study and survey of the monuments of the epoch of "Disorder" may be found in S. F. Platonov's book, *Drevnerusskie skazaniya i povesti o Smutnom vremeni XVII v. kak istoricheskii istochnik* (Early Russian Legends and Tales About the Seventeenth Century Epoch of "Disorder" as a Historical Source), 2nd. ed. (St. Petersburg, 1913).

the century and on the other the surge of patriotism occasioned by the tense struggle with the interventionists. The authors of these works were almost exclusively representatives of the propertied classes in Moscow society —boyars, nobles, higher and middle clergy and, less frequently, officials. In works by this last group, for example, in the *New Tale of the Illustrious Russian Tsardom,* written at the end of 1610 or the beginning of 1611, in all probability by some clerk, in the form of an anonymous letter, we encounter an explicit antiboyar tendency. The author expresses indignation at the boyars first of all because they had connived at the Poles taking over and establishing themselves in Russian territory, devastating and ravaging it, violating and dishonoring women. The boyars were "well-wishers" of the Polish king, the "vile adversary" Sigismund, and his son Ladislaw, and the "rascals among ourselves, land agents and justices," better termed "land-devourers and crooks. . . . Their minds on utter madness bent, support to the enemy they lent." In the eyes of the author, the one figure about whom they would do well to unite in protest against the Poles and their boyar patrons was the patriarch Hermogen, "a great pillar, firm adamant, a stout soldier of Christ." If we had possessed more such unshakable pillars, thinks the author, so much evil could never have been wrought "by those soulless wolves, our open enemies both foreign and domestic."

The response of the peasant mass to events of the epoch of "Disorder" found expression in ballads and *byliny*. These speak with most sympathy of Kseny Godunov, of the popular hero, Prince Michael Vasilyevich Skopin-Shuisky, and of Minin and Pozharsky, and with hatred of the "dog-and-thief" pretender, "Grishka-rastrizhka," Marina Mnishek, "the lass Marinka, wicked heretic," the "accursed peoples," the "wicked Poles" and the Polish king Sigismund, and of the "vile dogs," the "skew-eyed, fat-bellied" boyars. On the one hand Skopin-Shuisky is instated as a hero of the Vladimir cycle and on the other our favorite *bylina* hero, Ilya Muromets, assumes traits suggested by the epoch: he calls himself an "old Cossack," at times a "Don Cossack," takes the part of the insurgent "poor" and opposes Vladimir. The old enemies of the land of Rus, the Tartars, are now replaced by the Poles, under the name of "pagan Lithuania." A sixteenth century historical ballad includes in its cast of characters historical personages from the epoch of "Disorder." [31] No extant written monuments of the epoch reflect the peasant opposition. Works emanating from the peasant ranks were naturally tracked down and destroyed by government censorship. Government documents mention "sheets" emanating from Bolotnikov's camp in the village of Co-

[31] See Vs. Miller, "Otgoloski Smutnogo vremeni v bylinakh" (Echoes of the Epoch of "Disorder" in Byliny), *Ocherki russkoy narodnoy slovesnosti* (Outlines of Russian Folk Literature), Vol. II, pp. 265–358.

lomna. In a letter written by the patriarch Hermogen, 1606, we read this about Bolotnik's proclamations: "They write their accursed sheets to Moscow and order the boyar serfs to kill their boyars and the boyars' wives, and promise them patrimonies and estates . . . and plan to give them boyarship, and generalship, and district authority, and clerkship."

One is struck by the literary and intellectual traditionalism of the great majority of works from the epoch of "Disorder," their rigorous dependence upon the fixed models and molds of previous literature as set by the sixteenth century scholarly practice of Moscow. In almost everything written at the time, we are profoundly aware of an "edifying style," a pompous rhetoric to which factuality and truthfulness are constantly sacrificed. Curiously enough, certain authors who had been eyewitnesses of and even participants in events prefer to describe them not from personal observation and recollection but from written sources. It is also characteristic that the description of real facts is here constantly and copiously intertwined with the traditional fantasying of various miracles, visions, portents, and so forth. Instead of seeking a pragmatic explanation of events, authors were for the most part content to regard them as chastisement for manifold sins and as a lesson to offending Tsars and boyars and to the Russian people as a whole. The persons most frequently named as concretely to blame for the calamities are Boris Godunov and Pseudo-Demetrius I. Only rarely, for example by the clerk Timofeyev or Avraamy Palitsyn, is disunity advanced as the cause of these events, or social negligence, political apathy, what Palitsyn calls "insane reticence" before the tsar, in other words servility to authority and stupid submission to evil and injustice.[32]

Rhetorical emotionalism and the "braiding of words" are already present in one of the earliest works of the epoch, a tale of the year 1606, included in the so-called *Other Legend* and evidently from the pen of a monk of the Trinity Monastery of St. Sergius, a bitter enemy of Boris Godunov and zealous partisan of Vasily Shuisky. A glance will suffice, for example, to show how a metaphor first encountered in the anonymous *Legend of Boris and Gleb* looks as here applied to the tsarevich Demetrius: "And he [Boris Godunov] gave orders to break off that young and fair-flowering twig, to reap the pious tsarevich Dmitry, like an unripe ear, and consign an innocent child to death as you might sacrifice a lamb," and so forth.

The tale is embellished with numerous compound epithets such as "evil-inflamed," "bravehearted," "stonyhearted," "devil-beloved," "goodly-flowering," and so forth. In it we continually encounter emotionalized rhetorical

[32] See A. Yakovlev, "Bezumnoe molchanie" (Insane Silence), *Sbornik statey, posvyashchennykh V. O. Klyuchevskomu* (Collection of Articles Dedicated to V. O. Klyuchevsky) (Moscow, 1909), Pt. 2, pp. 651–678.

exclamations, questions, apostrophes, and comparisons, quotations from "Holy Writ" and from the "Church Fathers." Even the traditional war formulae are embellished:

Like two clouds that draw water and darken to shed rain upon the earth, so did these two armies fall upon one another to shed human blood, and did cover the earth, one desiring to conquer the other. And there was a noise like thunder, not from heavenly but from earthly clouds, the rumble of cannon, while flashes as of lightning quivered in the dim darkness and cannonballs whistled through the air, and arrows from countless bows; like sheaves men fell on the battlements. And again the two armies met and there was great slaughter; they fought hand to hand and there arose a wailing and a tumult of human voices and such a clash of weapons that the earth itself trembled and it was impossible for one to hear what another said. And the battle was very terrible, like the fearful and terrible struggle of old between Great Prince Dmitry and Mamay on the Don.

The style of the tales of the rout of Mamay, evidently well known to the author, gains added decorativeness under his pen:

As bright falcons in pursuit of gray ducks or white gyrfalcons clean their beaks to peck, and their sharp claws to pierce the flesh, and straighten their wings and stretch their shoulders for the killing of birds, so do the Christian defenders of the Orthodox faith, the generals with their Christ-loving troops, array themselves in armor against the favorite of Satan and his devil-beloved army, take weapons and shields into their hands.

The fall of enemy corpses is hyperbolically likened to the laying of bridges over the ground, the felling of trees, and the mowing of grass: "And they spanned the earth with human corpses as with a bridge. . . . They felled a human corpse as if it were cypress wood and laid a bridge nine versts long or more. . . . Vasily Ivanovich Shuisky . . . with fury in his heart cleverly and most bravely attacked from the right, with his picked troops, the army of Satan's favorite and cut it in two and mowed the enemy down like grass." On the left Ivan Ivanovich Godunov "bravely and manfully attacked and felled them like chopping a path." The same figures are also utilized for the expanded metaphor combined with antithesis seen in the following example: "This is the selfsame Boris who formerly felled great fair-flowering trees such as cypresses, and reaped with his merciless sickle many other things as well, such as meadow flowers and leafage of fig trees; see where he finds himself now, a man dispossessed and in disgrace."

The author's rhetorical emotionalism is particularly manifest when he lashes out in indignation; for example, at the dead Otrepyev:

Ah, woe and abomination unto you, so accursed that even the earth revolts against keeping your excommunicate heretical corpse, and the air is unfriendly to fertility, the clouds refusing to give rain, unwilling to wash your evil-accursed body, and the sun refusing to shine and warm the earth, so that frost has fallen on all the crops and has robbed wheat and grapes of germinal power until your stinking corpse shall have been plunged into the earth.[33]

Rhetoric still more pompous is to be found in a little story about the pretender's appearance and his sack of Moscow in 1611–1612, the *Lament for the Captivity and Final Destruction of the Muscovite State*. The beginning of this *Lament* is distinguished by special rhetorical flourish:

At what point shall we begin to lament, alas, such a collapse as has befallen illustrious, resplendent Great Russia? From what brink shall we rear the gulf of tears of our sobbing and groaning? Oh, what disasters and sorrows has our eye been deemed worthy to see! We beseech attentive listeners: O people called by Christ's name, sons of light, children of the Church, born in vital immersion! open the ears of your thoughts and feelings and together let us sound the organ of words, blow the trumpet of lamentation, wail to the living and inaccessible light, to the King of Kings and Lord of Lords, to the ruler of the cherubim, with pity in our hearts, and beating our breasts and saying: "Ah, alas, woe! how can such a tower of piety have fallen? How can the vineyard planted by God have been laid waste, the tendrils of which lifted to the clouds its thick leafage of fame, and the ripe clusters of which yielded an inexhaustible supply of sweet wine for all?

and so forth. Of the pretender the *Lament* says:

There arose a forerunner of God's adversary, the Antichrist, son of darkness, kinsman of ruin, from the rank of monk and deacon, and he cast away his former bright angelic rank and tore himself from Christianity like Judas from Christ's pure angelic person and fled to Poland and there filled his heart with the commandments of innumerable impious heresies,

and so forth. As also in the *New Tale*, we here find outcries against the Poles and against "domestic enemies"—the Moscow boyars—and a genuflection to the patriarch Hermogen.

The *Lament's* unknown author reveals both knowledge of literary language and artistic talent: thus, though not an eyewitness of the events described and hence forced to work chiefly from documents distributed to the towns by the Moscow government, he was not content to render the documents in plain language but gave them an original working over into the rhetorical phraseology customary at the time. The *Lament* was probably written in some provincial town for the instruction of local residents. The fact that the author, without having witnessed the events for himself, found it possible to tell others about them shows that he was better acquainted

[33] See also A. S. Orlov, *O nekotorykh osobennostyakh stilya* (On certain Peculiarities of Style), pp. 368–371, and M. A. Yakovlev, "Inoe skazanie" (The Other Legend), *Povest o krest'yanskom dvizhenii nachala XVII veka* (Tale of the Peasant Movement at the Beginning of the Seventeenth Century), *Uchenye zapiski Leningradskogo Gosudarstvennogo pedagogicheskogo instituta im. M. N. Pokrovskogo* (Scholarly Notes of the Leningrad M. N. Pokrovsky State Pedagogical Institute) (Leningrad, 1938), Pt. 1, pp. 183–232, faculty of language and literature.

with these events than the rest, through reports and official documents. If so, he may very well have been a member of the local administration, or of the clergy, who received and kept the documents distributed by the government. As to the time of composition, no data appear in the work itself, but since we know by analogy from other facts that the author used documents distributed from Pozharsky's camp in April, 1611, it follows that the monument cannot be earlier than 1612, and we may further assume that it dates not from the end but from the middle of the year, since, by the end of 1612, news of the liberation of Moscow had already got about, whereas the author of the *Lament*, when asking God for mercy on "the remnant of the state," does not yet know of the liberation of the capital.

One very popular work on the "Disorder" was the *Legend* by Avraamy Palitsyn, which is extant in its full form in a large number of seventeenth and eighteenth century copies and parts of which are included in the *Chronograph*. In addition to the complete *Legend*, constituting the most extensive work on the theme of the "Disorder"—seventy-six chapters all told —two earlier redactions of the first six chapters are known, the so-called "Zabelin" and "Academy," each preserved in a single copy. The two are very similar as to text and apparently came out in 1611–1612 and before Michael Fyodorovich's election as tsar, to judge from the narrative. In the longer edition we get, in the first place, a revision both as to style and content of the six chapters that had been written earlier (in many instances the note of accusation audible in the original editions is considerably toned down) and in the second an amplification and continuation of the factual history of events to the final months of 1619, ending with an account of Ladislaw's attack on Moscow. Palitsyn finished work on the book in 1620, to judge from his own autograph dating.[34]

Palitsyn was a very prominent functionary of the epoch, gifted with extraordinary intelligence and powers of observation, and consequently his book makes an extremely valuable contribution to the history of the "Disorder." But it is also of great interest from the viewpoint of literary style. For his time Palitsyn was an exceptionally good writer with a fine mastery of

[34] The rather extensive literature that has been devoted to Palitsyn and his *Legend* is reviewed in *op. cit.* of S. F. Platonov. The Zabelin and Academy redactions of the *Legend* are the subject of an article by P. G. Vasenko, "Dve redaktsii pervykh shesti glav 'Skazaniya' Avraamiya Palitsyna" (Two Editions of the First Six Chapters of Avraami Palitsyn's Legend), *Letopis' zanyatii arkheograficheskoy komissii za 1919–1922 gg.* (Record of the projects of the Archaeological Committee, 1919–1922) (Petrograd, 1923), Pt. 2, pp. 1–38. See also studies devoted to the Zabelin edition in particular: P. G. Lyubomirov, "New Edition of Avraami Palitsyn's *Legend*," *Sbornik statey po russkoy istorii posvyashchennykh C. F. Platonov* (Collection of Articles on Russian History Dedicated to S. F. Platonov) (St. Petersburg, 1922), pp. 285–293, and P. G. Vasenko, "The Zabelin Redaction of the First Six Chapters of Palitsyn's History," *Sbornik statey v chest' A. I. Sobolevskogo* (Collection of Articles in Honor of A. I. Sobolevsky), pp. 100–102.

literary language, capable of producing a striking picture on occasion and of rising to heights of publicistic passion and genuine eloquence. In all this he frequently transcended the traditional "fine-wordage" and ponderous oratory, though in general adhering to them in the same degree as other writers of his time. If in battle scenes he followed established literary formulae in the main, and in descriptions of visions and miracles the patterns of hagiography, in other descriptions and in personal expressions of opinion he showed genuine talent and originality as a writer. In demonstration of the foregoing statement suffice it to quote the following attack on those in high places from the Academy redaction of the *Legend,* a passage considerably toned down in the final edition:

And many of us to this day live by foul usury and maintain pothouses to tempt the whole world; by extortion and promises we build churches of God and beautify them with images, while in the courts and on the roads and at our gates creatures made in God's image and protected, like ourselves, by God's angels are always lamenting and sobbing to obtain mercy and justice! But we do not hearken to their voices and order them beaten on face and breast and, sin of sins, break their bones with the rod and condemn them to bonds and prison and the stocks and the yoke . . . nor do we hear the voice of the poor man begging and shivering with cold at our gates, not asking for a golden ten-ducat piece that he may fill his belly but desiring only a single loaf to allay his hunger and a cup of cold water to quench his thirst. But not for such as these has our table been laid, but for those who have great gifts to bring: gold and silver, damasks and velvets, and pearls and precious stones, and wine from overseas, and birds and beasts and cattle, and all manner of woven stuffs, and varied foods.

The extreme realism of the picture of the moral savagery of people at the time of the "Disorder" drawn by Palitsyn, somewhat under the influence, however, of the "Kazan Chronicler," surpasses anything of the sort found in previous literature.

In describing these painful events of Russian history, Palitsyn represents himself as an irreproachable patriot, whereas he is known to have been in communication with the Poles and frequently to have acted in their interests. Motives of personal gain played a large part in the behavior of this pragmatically unscrupulous man.

Typical of many tales of the epoch of "Disorder" is the insertion of lines of verse into the prose text, apparently with a view to making the exposition still more flowery and high-flown. Such lines are encountered as early as the *Tale of the Noble Life of Tsar Theodore Ivanovich,* written in 1603 by Patriarch Job, and afterwards in the *Other Legend.* We are here dealing with the initial stage of our art of verse, still presyllabic, characterized by uneven lines, absence of caesura and, for the most part, by verbal rhyme, sometimes replaced by assonance or consonance. At this stage the prose text is in most cases interrupted by two or three lines of verse. A further step was taken by Palitsyn, who upon two occasions introduced into his *Legend* (in Chapters 45 and 47 of the finished text) a complete series of consecutive lines of verse largely held together by nominal rhymes and assonances, for example, in the following passage from Chapter 47:

> Out past the monastery they went to get their wood
> And then returned to town not without shedding of blood.
> With blood they bought their curds and faggots of wood
> And with it they prepared their daily food.
> To martyr's deeds by greens they were incited
> Thereby each other's enmity excited.
> Wherever the young brush had been cut down
> There valiant men lay slaughtered on the ground,
> Wherever some young withy had been clipped
> There lay a human corpse by vultures stripped.[35]

One of the most interesting monuments of the period in point of style is a work with a lengthy title starting: *The Tale in This Book Is of Former Years: Concerning the Beginning of the Imperial City of Moscow,* and so forth, and to which the versified epilogue gives the title *Annalistic Book.* It was written, as the title indicates, in 1626. The author was earlier thought to have been Sergey Kubasov, compiler of the *Chronograph,* then the tale was attributed first by Klyuchevsky and then by Platonov, in his study of "Disorder" narratives, to an intimate of Tsar Michael Fyodorovich, Prince I. M. Katyrev-Rostovsky, though later on Platonov came to doubt Katyrev-Rostovsky's authorship and reopened the question of attributing it to Kubasov.[36]

Whoever may have been its author, the *Annalistic Book* was written in the reign of Michael Fyodorovich, by which time the epoch's exceptional events were already in the past and a relatively objective view of them established. This more or less objective attitude toward bygone events asserts itself to a marked degree in the *Annalistic Book.* Its author had no occasion, as did writers of the tempestuous epoch itself, to work excessively on the

[35] On rhymes in tales of the epoch of "Disorder," see N. P. Popov, "K voprosu o pervo-nachal'nom poyavlenii virsh v severo-russkoy pismennosti (On the Question of the First Appearance in Verse in North Russian Literature), *Izvestiya otd. russk. yaz. i slov.* (News of the Division of Russian Language and Literature of the Academy of Sciences) (1917), Vol. XXII, Bk. 2, pp. 259–275; V. P. Adrianova, "Iz nachal'nogo perioda russkogo stikhos-lozheniya" (From the Initial Period of Russian Versification)—apropos of N. P. Popov's article—*ibid.* (1921), Vol. XXVI, pp. 271–276

[36] See his article "Starye somneniya" (Old Doubts) in *Sbornik statey v chest' M. K. Lyubavskogo* (Collection of Articles in Honor of M. K. Lyubavsky) (Moscow, 1917), pp. 172–180. See also A. M. Stavrovich, "Sergéy Kubasov i Stroganovskaya letopis'" (Sergéy Kubasov and The Stroganov Chronicle), *Sbornik statey po russkoy istorii, posvyashchennykh S. F. Platonovu* (Collection of Articles on Russian History Dedicated to S. F. Platonov) (Petrograd, 1922), pp. 285–293.

feelings of his readers, to advance this idea or that, to demonstrate his views. His task, as he saw it, was the plain presentation of facts: he was content to describe events seriatim, and rarely even expressed his opinion on events and personages. For vital and descriptive language, the tale ranks higher than almost any other of the "Disorder" legends. At the same time it is practically free from their multitudinous moralizings and quotations from "Holy Writ." The few ecclesiastical phrases found in the work are to the point, and merely testify that the author was a learned man. From the historical side, the *Annalistic Book* is interesting in that it gives for the first time an integrated description of the epoch as a whole. All previous works on the subject had lacked articulation—even Palitsyn's *Legend* did not possess inner unity. Palitsyn did not give everything equal attention or write from a single point of view, whereas this author gives all events practically the same amount of study. He does not go into detail, does not undertake the description of trivialities, but sketches all the chief moments of the epoch consecutively and in admirable proportion, albeit briefly.

The *Annalistic Book* begins by telling of Tsar Ivan the Terrible and ends with an item about the election of Michael Fyodorovich as tsar. After this come six lines of rhymed verse, then a chapter entitled "Brief Description of the Muscovite Tsars, Their Appearance, Age, and Dispositions," and after that more verse, this time thirty lines.

As above stated, the tale attributed to Prince Katyrev-Rostovsky is distinguished by originality of poetic style, but for this originality, as Academician A. S. Orlov has pointed out,[37] it leaned heavily on a translation made in Rus in the fifteenth century of Guido de Colonna's new Latin version of the *Trojan History*. A. S. Orlov arrives at the conclusion that our tale was almost half made up of rhetorical and lexical material provided by the Russian translation of the *Trojan History*. At the same time it reflected the traditional stylistic peculiarities of Russian war stories[38] and of sundry other works of the preceding period.

Let us take, for example, the description of spring, the "fair season" of spring, which the author purposely describes with lyric zest in order to contrast the joyous awakening of nature with the arrival in Rus of that "rapacious wolf," Dimitry the Pretender:

Already winter is past, and the time has come when the sun, performing its zodiacal circuit, arrives in the constellation of the Ram, when night and day are equal and the festival of spring is celebrated, and the season of glad resurrection

---

[37] "Povest' kn. Katyreva-Rostovskogo i Troyanskaya Istoriya Gvido de Kolumny" (Tale of Prince Katyrev-Rostovsky and the Trojan History of Guido de Colonna), *Sbornik statey v chest M. K. Lyubavskogo* (Collection of Articles in Honor of M. K. Lyubavsky), pp. 73–93.

[38] See A. S. Orlov, *O nekotorykh osobennoctyakh stilya* (On Certain Peculiarities of Style), pp. 371–375.

begins, making the air radiant with brightness. When, the snow having melted and the breeze blowing gently, in widened streams the sources flow, then the farmer starts and plows and a pleasant furrow draws, and for aid upon God the giver of increase calls; grass springs up and fields are clothed in green and trees put on new leaves and everywhere fruits deck the earth, and the birds raise a sweet caroling that through God's care, through his love of mankind, all manner of comfortable things may ripen for man's solace.

This picture was suggested to the author first by the Russian translation of the *Trojan History* of Guido de Colonna, where we read: "It is the time when the sun has already reached the height of its zodiacal course and is already descending into the constellation of Cancer, when, in accord with God's ordering of the stars, the return of the summer sun is celebrated, for then the days arc longer"; secondly, the reference to farmers stems from the *Discourse on New Sunday and on Spring* by Gregory the Theologian or possibly from Cyril of Turov's *Discourse on the Sunday After Easter* which, as above pointed out, was itself strongly influenced by the discourse of Gregory the Theologian. To increase the expressiveness of the picture, the author has recourse to alliteration: *"I vo prostrannye potoky istochnitsy protekayut, togda ratai ralom pogruzhaet, i sladkuyu brazdu prochertaet, i plododatelya boga na pomoshch' prizyvaet"* (In widened streams the sources flow, then the plowman sinks his plow into the earth, runs a nice furrow, and calls for help upon God, the giver of the harvest).

Side by side with battle scenes reminiscent of the old martial formulae ("And the air was disturbed by the running of horses, and men could not recognize one another for the obscuring of their faces by the dust that whirled through the air," and so forth), we continually encounter pictures fundamentally borrowed from Guido de Colonna; the following, for example: "And so the battle seethed fiercely, arrows flew through the air like lightning and sword blades flashed like moonlight, and there were great losses on both sides and the bodies of the dead dropped hither and yon" (cf. Guido de Colonna: "Wherefore the battle then seethed fiercely . . . and savage war was unleashed upon them and many were the corpses of the dead that fell hither and yon; through the air whistled many arrows"). A common formula in our tale: "They reach the fields and pursue with the mouth of the sword" (that is, they pursue at the point of the sword—Latin, *"in ore gladii"*) is the exact counterpart of a formula used by Guido de Colonna.

In the concluding chapter, where portraits are drawn of tsars and their children, our tale says of the tsar's daughter Xenia, that she was "a girl of marvelous intelligence, fair in her fresh beauty, very white . . . with scarlet lips, great black eyes of brilliant brightness; when she was sad and tears welled from her eyes, then her eyes shone with the greater brilliance . . .

suffused with youthful whiteness. . . . Goodliest among all women . . . truly surpassing in all matters." In Guido de Colonna, Hecuba was "a woman of marvelous skill," Andromache was "fair in her fresh beauty . . . shining with young whiteness, had eyes that shone with great brilliance, red cheeks, scarlet lips . . . was goodliest among all and truly surpassing in all matters." Of Polyxena, Guido says that "streams of tears flowing from her eyes were dimmed by her eyes' brilliance."

Thus the *Annalistic Book* is fundamentally as typical a learned work as the monuments of the epoch of "Disorder" above surveyed. Definitely present, though to a lesser degree than in the latter, is the usual rhetoricism, exemplified in complicated word formations such as "hold-in-possession," "beneficently-calming," "benignantly-imbecile," "Scythian-Trojandom," and "blood-rulers," and in impassioned exclamations imitative, among other things, of the style of Kurbsky's epistle to the Terrible, as, for example: "O illustrious Tsar Boris! or, rather, ungrateful wretch! Why did you attempt such a soul-destroying deed and have such ambitious desires? Why did you betray to bitter death an innocent child, son of the tsar, and sever the imperial line of the Russian state?" (Cf. Kurbsky's: "Why, tsar, did you slay the mighty in Israel and betray to various deaths the generals given you by God?" and so forth.)

The author's rhetoric also asserts itself in his proclivity for metrical patterns, present not only at the end of the work in the form of concluding verses but used as embellishment here and there throughout the tale, as we have also seen done in the *Other Legend* and in the *Legend* of Avraamy Palitsyn:

> And he ordered the people of his party on those of the other to prey,
> And to death betray,
> Their houses destroy,
> And the generals God gave him guiltless to slay,
> And fairest cities in ruin lay,
> And the orthodox peasants in them pitilessly slay.

As we see, the rhymes here, as in practically all the lines of verse scattered through the text, are exclusively verbal, in contrast to the lines at the end where nominal and adjectival rhymes are used.[39]

The literary merits of the *Annalistic Book* gave it wide popularity in seventeenth century Moscow society. It was not only copied entire but extracts from it were often included in compilations on the "Disorder" and even copied into peerages by way of preface. In the copying it frequently under-

[39] For further details see N. Gudzii, "Zametki o Povesti kn. Iv. Mikh. Katyreva-Rostovskogo" (Notes on the Tale of Prince Ivan Mikhailovich Katyrev-Rostovsky), *Sbornik statey v chest A. I. Sobolevskogo* (Collection of Articles in Honor of A. I. Sobolevsky), pp. 306–309.

went revision. Thus, there exists a copy of the second edition of the tale where it is divided into chapters. Each event is given a separate chapter, and since the accounts of individual events had been kept brief and compressed, the division results in a fragmentariness distinctly detrimental to unity and artistic effect. The second edition also brings in a didactic element and frequently introduces quotations from "Holy Writ." Shortly afterward the tale underwent substantial revision at the pen of official Muscovite historians. There is reason to think that this official revision was undertaken at the order, and under the personal supervision and direction, of the patriarch Philaretes and on this account bears the title, *Manuscript of Philaretes*. That the *Annalistic Book* should have been the work chosen as basis for the official work is explained primarily by the fact that it was the first book to give a well proportioned and integrated survey of all events of the epoch and, secondly, that it was written by an intimate of the patriarch. Nevertheless there were certain things about the tale that did not suit Philaretes; for example, its unsympathetic attitude toward Tsar Basil Shuisky, which is consequently canceled out in the manuscript by a series of official eulogies, while Tsar Basil is represented in a very sympathetic light. The style itself seemed too simple and in the *Manuscript of Philaretes* was therefore frequently embellished with rhetorical locutions.

Along with tales and legends embracing longer or shorter sections of the epoch, there are also extant from this period works devoted to separate episodes or to the fate of separate personages who took an active part in events. Of the latter works those of greatest literary-historical interest are the tales about Basil Shuisky's nephew, Prince Michael Vasilyevich Skopin-Shuisky, an outstanding general especially distinguished for his victories, in conjunction with the Swedish general Yakov Pontus Delagard, over the armies of Pseudo-Demetrius II. While preparing for his forthcoming campaign against the Poles in April of 1610, he was suddenly taken ill at a banquet at the house of I. M. Vorotynsky, for whose son he had been invited to act as godfather, and two weeks later, in his twenty-fourth year, he died. Obstinate rumors explained Skopin's death as due to poison administered by the "godmother," Mariya, daughter of Malyuta Skuratov and wife of Dmitry Shuisky, uncle of Michael Skopin, who was jealous of the fame and popularity of his nephew. Skopin's body was buried with solemnity in the Cathedral of the Archangels in Moscow.

Of two extant tales about Skopin-Shuisky, the first tells "of the birth" of the prince and of his exploits, and then very briefly of events following his death, and the second about his "death and burial." On the evidence of a number of stylistic coincidences, it seems probable that both tales were written by a single, now unknown, author, the first about eight years later than the second: the first tale, in describing the battle of Kalyazin, quite obviously borrows from the corresponding section of Avraamy Palitsyn's *Legend* and consequently cannot have been composed before 1620, date of the completion of Palitsyn's work. The second tale, judging from the fact that it is an immediate echo of the death of Skopin and contains many reliable details, was written shortly after the event—apparently not later than 1612. Subsequently the two tales in abbreviated form were joined into one and inserted in the *Chronograph*.[40]

The first of the two, "on the birth" of Skopin, is written, in the main, according to the set forms for saints' lives and martial tales, and is of no particular literary-historical interest, unlike the second, which, for all its copious hagiographical rhetoric, shows very strongly the influence of an oral ballad, composed, no doubt, immediately after Skopin's death.

After beginning the tale "of the death and burial" in the *Stepennaya Kniga* vein, with a genealogy of Michael Skopin, tracing his family through Alexander Nevsky to Vladimir Svyatoslavich and then to Augustus Caesar, the author tells of Skopin's coming to Moscow from the suburb of Aleksandrovo for the christening at Prince Vorotynsky's. There his fellow sponsor Mariya, "a fierce serpent with an evil eye, like a fierce beast," upon the advice of wicked traitors and bad counselors, plotted "a wicked traitorous plot" to ensnare Skopin, "as a lynx casts its spell on a bird in the wood." Next, utilizing the oral *bylina,* though disregarding its meter and importing certain bookish elements, the author continues:

And after the ceremony there was to be a festive banquet, and with diabolical craft the malefactress Princess Mariya, the godmother, offered a goblet of punch to the godfather and bowed low and wished her godson Alexis Ivanovich well. And in that goblet, in the punch, was prepared a fierce, deadly potion. And Prince Michael Vasilyevich drained the goblet without knowing that the evil potion was fierce and deadly. And all too late Prince Michael felt sick to the heart and left the christening feast before it was over and sent word to his dear mother Elena Petrovna. And as soon as he entered his princely house, his mother looked him over and gazed straight into his eyes; and his eyes were bright and troubled and his face was terribly flushed and the hair on his head quivered.

The style of *bylina* poetics is also used to render the "piteous word" of Skopin's mother: "Child of mine, my son, Prince Michael Vasilyevich, why have you left the christening feast early and in haste? Was it that your God-given godson did not accept baptism gladly? Or were you denied your ancestral place at the feast?" and so forth.

[40] Published by A. Popov in *Izbornik slavyanskikh i russkikh sochinenii i statey, vnesennykh v Khronografy russkoy redaktsii* (Collection of Slavic and Russian Books and Articles Carried in the Russian Redaction of the Chronograph) (Moscow, 1869), pp. 379–388.

After this the style of the tale again becomes bookish and remains so to the end, only occasionally retaining the traits of the oral epic. Skopin-Shuisky dies in spite of the aid of Swedish doctors. Everyone laments for him from the beggars to Yakov Pontus Delagard, the tsar, and the patriarch. They have trouble finding a coffin that will hold the body of Skopin "because he was great of stature." At the demand of the populace, who had collected in great numbers, Skopin was buried not in the Miracle Monastery, as had been proposed, but in the Cathedral of the Archangels where tsars and great princes were buried. As in the life of Alexis, Man of God, and several Russian lives written under its influence, so here there is mention of the funeral chant being inaudible for the wailing of the populace and of the fact that not a single person was to be seen not weeping, with the result that the church floor was flooded with streams of tears. The threnodic laments of Skopin's mother and his wife, written under the influence of the analogous lament of Princess Eudokiya for Prince Dmitry Ivanovich, are given. Basil Shuisky also laments bitterly. Returning from the funeral, he went into his chamber and "fell prostrate on his imperial golden table, choking with bitter sobs and wetting the table with his tears and the tears dripping from the table onto the floor." After the funeral Skopin's mother and wife lament just as inconsolably: "They fell prostrate on their table, weeping bitterly and choking, groaning and wetting the table with their tears, and swift as a river the streams of their tears poured from the table onto the floor, and they remained without food until morning." Old women also weep, "like daws," and widows, "like swallows." The tale ends with an account of an icon-painter's vision foretelling the death of Skopin-Shuisky.

Thus the tale exhibits a manifest discrepancy in style resulting from the use of bookish and oral-poetry material in combination. Such a combination, as the author of a special study of tales and ballads about Skopin-Shuisky [41] correctly concludes, is justified, since Skopin was neither saint nor tsar and since elements of martial heroism took the foreground in his story, wherefore material for the narrative was necessarily drawn not alone from the hagiographical tradition of the *Stepennaya Kniga* but from popular song as well.

From the foregoing survey of the most characteristic works of the epoch of "Disorder," it becomes apparent that in the main they continued the literary tradition established at the middle of the sixteenth century. But along with this we also find elements of innovation. These consist in an en-

[41] A detailed analysis of both categories is given in V. F. Rzhiga's article, "Povest i pesni o Mikhaile Skopine-Shuiskom" (Tale and Ballads About Michael Skopin-Shuisky), *Izvestiya po russkomu yazyku i slovesnosti* (News of Russian Language and Literature) (1928), I, pp. 81–133.

deavor to comprehend the present time historically on the basis of preceding events, in a heightened interest in and attention to the human individuality of those participating in events and, finally, in the stylistic peculiarities exemplified by a number of monuments. These peculiarities most frequently represent a striving for maximum picturesqueness and ornamentation. This is achieved by the use of poetical methods derived from a source of Western origin as in the *Annalistic Book* attributed to Katyrev-Rostovsky, or by the introduction of *bylina* material as in the tale "of the death and burial" of Skopin-Shuisky, or, finally, by experiments in versification as in a whole series of tales from this period.

To what has been said about the style of tales of the epoch of "Disorder," must be added some mention of the striking poetic similes, comparisons, and characterizations which we encounter in articles on the "Disorder" included in the second edition of the *Chronograph,* 1617, and very possibly from the pen of Terentius,[42] archpriest of the Cathedral of the Annunciation in Moscow. The fact that tales with poetic embellishment were used to fill out the *Chronograph,* a practice observable, incidentally, in Siberian seventeenth century chronicle writing as well, is of itself an interesting indication as to how new literary material was taken over bodily into Russian historical compilations.

TRADITION AND INNOVATION IN THE CULTURE AND IN THE LITERATURE OF THE SEVENTEENTH CENTURY

Events at the end of the sixteenth and the beginning of the seventeenth century gave a rude jolt to the economic structure of the Muscovite state and also to the harmonious finality of the self-perpetuating Muscovite ideology. The victory of the propertied class and the consolidation of the suburban element resulting from the epoch of "Disorder" contributed very largely toward bringing about a secularization of culture in the Muscovite state; cultural and trade relations with the West, greatly expanded at this time, likewise did much to further this secularization, first in the realm of purely routine and practical affairs, then in the realm of literature as well. The Church, which had, like the state, been rocked to its foundations by the "Disorder" and had attempted at the close to win an independent position

[42] Cf. P. G. Vasenko, "Zametki k stat'yam o Smute, vklyuchennym v Khronograf redaktsii 1617 g." (Notes on Articles About the Disorder Included in the Chronograph in the 1617 Redaction), *Sbornik statey po russkoy istorii, posvyashchennyi S. F. Platonovu* (Collection of Articles on Russian History Dedicated to S. F. Platonov), pp. 248–249.

for itself, yielded, after a period of frenzied resistance, to the overwhelming power of a state with fundamentally secular aims and objectives. As traditional Byzantine principles relaxed their hold on the culture of Muscovite Rus, the ecclesiastical element in literature also lost importance, little by little giving way to a secular element, now largely fed by material imported, belatedly, it is true, from the West, chiefly through the medium of Poland and Czech-land.

Russia's intercourse with Poland in particular gained importance during the epoch of "Disorder," largely as a result of the military clashes that took place between them. Intercourse was indirectly carried on both then and later through the Kievan litterateurs who had long since been coming to Moscow, but who became a fixture there after the consolidation of the Ukraine with Moscow in 1654. In the Ukraine, which had been politically dependent upon Poland and subject to Polish influence in the realm of culture, an intensive literary development is observable as early as the sixteenth century, not only in ecclesiastical polemic on burning questions of the day but in various purely literary genres as well, notably the lyric and the drama. Numerous schools had been founded there by ecclesiastical brotherhoods as seats of what may be termed middle education, while Kiev's Mohila "collegium," an academy founded by Peter Mohila in 1631, already ranked with the higher schools of neighboring Poland. There, in addition to the theological and philosophical disciplines, the literary sciences were taught and works in verse produced, the so-called "school" dramas, along with numerous manuals on poetics. Alumni included many of the great scholars who worked in Moscow, among them Epiphanius Slavinetsky, Simeon Polotsky, Demetrius of Rostov, and later Feofan Prokopovich, aide and apologist of Peter I. Kiev scholars were not regarded with full confidence in Moscow, where they were suspected of Latinist leanings, which was, of course, partly the case, but none the less their labors and literary efforts were utilized to the full. With their help the foundations of a school system were laid in Moscow after attempts toward this end with the aid of Greek immigrants had failed.

In 1648 the boyar F. M. Rtishchev set up, in a monastery expressly founded for the purpose near Moscow, under the auspices of the Church of St. Andrew, a school "to give enlightenment in the liberal sciences in a monastery of the Russian order," where, besides the Slavic and Greek languages, the literary sciences, including rhetoric and philosophy, were offered. The teachers here were scholars especially called from Kiev, among them the well informed and widely read Epiphanius Slavinetsky. Epiphanius was apparently also the founder of a Greek school at the Miracle Monastery in Moscow. To Simeon Polotsky, who reached Moscow in 1664, is ascribed the founding of a Latin school at St. Saviour's Monastery. Even if these schools were not all fully organized educational institutions and did not command any very impressive number of students, none the less they undeniably gave a serious impetus to the further development of intellectual and, indirectly, of literary culture in Muscovite society.

From the very beginning of the activities of Kievan scholars in Moscow, the question arose as to whether the Latin or the Greek system of education should be introduced and for a long time the answer to this question is seen to have hung in the balance. In 1682 Simeon Polotsky's pupil Silvester Medvedev was charged with organizing a school at the St. Saviour's Monastery. This school, which continued in existence for about five years without reaching the level of the type of elementary school maintained during the sixteenth and seventeenth centuries in the Ukraine by ecclesiastical brotherhoods, was Latin in orientation. Almost simultaneously the enthusiasts for Greek education founded in Moscow a "typographical school," which was equally shortlived. When it came to establishing higher schools in Russia, however, the decision was in favor of the Greek trend: in 1687 a Slavic-Greek-Latin academy was founded in Moscow, headed by two scholars imported from Greece, the brothers Ioanniky and Sophrony Likhuda.

Thus Russia's unsolved school problem of the preceding period finally reached its solution. The very circumstance that this problem took such acute form as it did in the seventeenth century and the fact that it was worked out, beyond doubt made for progress in the general development of the literary process here as well.

Also characteristic of seventeenth century literature is the fact that participation in it by new, democratic strata, chiefly of artisans and tradespeople, and likewise the emergence of a new reading public from these strata, resulted in the admission of folk poetry on a much larger scale than had been the case in the sixteenth century; on the one hand records of works of oral poetry first make their appearance, and on the other oral poetry exerts a much more palpable influence on learned literature than before. Old tradition, however, does not give place to the new without a struggle, and throughout the century this struggle, or in some cases the interaction and parallel existence of tradition and innovation, is still very clearly apparent.

Thus we note a very substantial overhauling of historical literature during the early years of the seventeenth century. The *Chronograph* of 1512 is superseded by a new edition, the second, dating from 1617. Taking the old *Chronograph* as a foundation, the author of the new *Chronograph* fills in with items of western European history drawn from recently translated Polish chronicles by Conrad Likosten, Stryikovsky, Martin Belsky. The same material was utilized by the author of the third redaction of the *Chron-*

ograph (1620). The mere fact that the history of the West is here placed on a sort of par with biblical, Byzantine and Russian history is ample evidence of our having recognized at the beginning of the seventeenth century the role of the West in the process of world history. We saw above that the *Chronograph,* second edition, paid a good deal of attention to the artistic side of writing, as is especially evidenced by the articles it includes on the "Disorder." With the same view to freshening up the material in a purely literary way, some articles in the first edition are here replaced by new translations and new revisions of works earlier translated in this country. Thus, for example, the old translation of the *Trojan History* is replaced by the most recent, made from Guido da Colonna's Latin version, written in the style of the tales of chivalry and accompanied by illustrations.[43]

But in spite of all this, we still continue to encounter practically throughout the seventeenth century patently hopeless attempts to continue the tradition of sixteenth century chronicle writing almost without change. Such belated attempts include both the *History of the Tsars and Great Princes of the Land of Rus,* written by the clerk Fyodor Griboyedov at the end of 1660, and the so-called "Lakhutin" *Stepennaya Kniga,* composed in 1670 by Tikhon, a monk of the Zheltovod Monastery of St. Macarius. Both authors use to some extent the factual material from the West utilized in the second and third editions of the *Chronograph,* but in their conception of history still continue to hold stubbornly to the ideological positions of Moscow, the "third Rome." Nor is there any marked departure from this conception in a book popular for almost a century, and brimming with fabulous inventions, the *Synopsis,* written by Innocentius Gizel, archimandrite of the Kiev-Crypt Monastery (1674).

One of the literary genres most popular in fifteenth and sixteenth century Muscovite Rus, namely, saints' lives, continues developing for the first half of the seventeenth, under the pen of Macarian scholars, along fundamentally the same lines as those laid down for it back in the middle of the sixteenth century. The traditional "fine wordage" and abstract panegyric style, made up for the most part of generalizations, will throughout the seventeenth century continue to be used for writing lives which merely vary the general scheme prescribed for hagiography in the Macarian period. In imitation of the *Chetyi Minyei* of Macarius, analogous collections were composed in 1627–1632 by Herman Tulupov, a monk of the Trinity Monastery of St. Sergius, and in 1646–1654 by a priest of the suburban church of the same monastery, Ioannus Milyutin, in collaboration with his sons. Both

[43] On the second and third editions of the *Chronograph,* see A. Popov, *Obzor Khronografov russkoy redaktsii* (Survey of Chronographs in Russian Redaction) (Moscow, 1869), Pt. 2, pp. 67–229.

collections consist almost exclusively of lives, legends, and monuments of a historical nature, and both give appreciably more lives of specifically Russian saints than do the *Minyei* of Macarius.

It should be noted, however, that the farther the seventeenth century advances the more frequently are lives rounded out with concrete and genuine biographical material, clear evidence that stereotyped schemes are being rejected and attention brought to bear on individual peculiarities in the life and behavior of the subject.[44] At the end of the century, printed format, making them widely known, was given the *Chetyi Minyei* of Demetrius of Rostov, which carried one step farther than the Macarian *Minyei* the collecting, editing and systematizing of accumulated biographical material. The principal source of this work—the *Minyei* of Macarius—was not, however, the only one used by Demetrius of Rostov: it is supplemented by Western Latin and Polish sources—the collections of Surii, of the Bollandists, of Skarga.

LIFE OF JULIANIA LAZAREVSKAYA

Among seventeenth century lives which depart from the established pattern and make an effort to round out the narrative with genuine biographical facts, the place of first importance belongs to the *Life of St. Juliania Lazarevskaya* (died 1604), written as early as the 1610's–1620's by her son Kalistratus Osorin, a boyar of Murom. This is not so much a saint's life as a tale, even a sort of family chronicle, from the pen of a secular author who was thoroughly acquainted with the details of the life he was writing, and who presented them affectionately, rather than with the cold, stereotyped rhetoric of an outsider. The *Life* does not entirely lack common traditional elements: as usual the Devil appears as an active force, visiting grievous misfortunes upon Juliania's family (with his connivance two of her sons perish), twice pursuing and frightening Juliania herself and only retreating thanks to the intervention and aid of St. Nicholas; miraculous elements also occur, albeit only to a very slight degree. The ideal of Juliania's life is, in the last analysis, asceticism, to which she devotes herself with particular zeal after the murder of her sons. Step by step she renounces physical contact with her husband, emphasizes fasting, spends more time at prayer and at work, sleeps on sharp stakes, puts hazelnut shells and sharp potsherds in her shoes, and

---

[44] On lives of the saints of the post-Macarian period, see V. O. Klyuchevskii, *Drevnerusskie zhitiya svyatykh* (Early Russian Lives of the Saints), pp. 297–357.

finally, after the death of her husband, stops going to the bath. In the meanwhile she passes her whole life, from childhood to the grave, in unceasing
toil and in caring for the moral and physical well-being of her peasants,
whom she feeds during the terrible years of famine by denying herself and
her family the very necessities, giving until she has nothing left to give.

During her years of wealth, of material prosperity, she, a boyar with
plenary powers, full orderer of the lot of her "slaves," invariably protected
her "subjects," interceded and made excuses for them even when they
caused her great anxiety, and by so interceding evoked the reproaches of
her husband and his family, who generally dwelt on peaceful and affectionate terms with her. Distinguished by unusual gentleness, meekness, and
consideration for others, Juliania refused the services commonly rendered
a mistress in her own house by the servants, would not, for example, let
them take off her shoes, but removed these herself. Juliania's delicacy of
feeling and sincere consideration for others also assert themselves in matters
of detail such as this: on Saturdays and Sundays, when she entertains at
dinner in her house priests, widows, orphans, and the members of her household, she drinks one goblet of wine not because she, a devotee of the ascetic
life, likes wine, but in order not to hurt the guests' feelings by abstaining.

The essential point about Juliania as a new type of saint-heroine is that
she leads a pious life by exertions carried on not in a monastery but in the
world, in the setting of everyday cares and worldly bustle that go with her
duties as wife, mother of thirteen children, and mistress of a large and complicated estate. The traditional saint's biography, showing a life lived from
childhood exclusively under the influence of the Church, does not fit Juliania: during the years before her marriage, she could not attend church
because of the distance and thus lived for quite a time outside its direct
influence. But even afterward ill health and again the distance long kept
her from attending service, and she consoled herself with the thought that
"home prayer" is also efficacious. After the loss of her two sons, she tried to
persuade her husband to permit her to retire to a convent, but convinced by
his argument that "black robes will not save us if we live unmonastically,
nor white robes destroy if we do what is pleasing to God," she remains in
the world, merely ceasing to live with her husband after the flesh. Even at
the approach of death she does not embrace monasticism as Peter and Fevronia, for example, and other saints had done.

The thought that runs through the whole life as its fundamental thesis
is that salvation and even sainthood may be attained without shutting one-
self up in a monastery but by living the secular life piously, in toil and
unselfish love for others. From this it would appear that the author of the
Life came from that same boyar milieu which had swelled the ranks of the

trans-Volga hermits in their repudiation of the ritualistic worship of God and the self-contained formal monastic order of life.[45]

ARCHPRIEST AVVAKUM AND HIS WORKS

A very striking and indicative example of seventeenth century literature in its evolution toward realism is found in the works of the leader and inspiror of the sect of Old Believers, Archpriest Avvakum, particularly in the *Life* of himself that he wrote during the years 1672–1675.

The figure of Avvakum as a writer and as a historical character who epitomized Old Rus and who, at the same time, broke new paths for literary development, is so typical that a somewhat extended treatment both of the man and of the historical setting in which he moved is indicated.

At the middle of the seventeenth century, upon the initiative of the patriarch Nikon, certain reforms were introduced into the religious ritual of the Russian church, and in this connection a rectification of the service books was undertaken. The substance of the reform was the reconciliation of Russian church ritual and Russian service books with the ritual and service books of the contemporary Greek church, these differing at some points from Russian practice. The consolidated Russian nobiliary state, after emerging victorious from the economic and social crisis signalized by the epoch of "Disorder," set about regularizing various matters of governmental procedure, and at the same time of procedure in the ecclesiastico-religious sphere as well, inasmuch as the latter was at that time, as before and after, very closely connected with the machinery of government and subserved its interests. In consequence, we get in the 1640's a circle of "zealots for piety" organized with a view to raising the religious and moral level of the Russian church in the person of pastors and congregations and to giving harmony and decorum to the disordered and fussy church service. At first this group included both the future agents of reform and its subsequent opponents. Among the members we find both Nikon, then archimandrite of New St. Saviour's, and the provincial archpriest Avvakum. So long as they concerned themselves with problems touching the elevation of decorum and piety, the members of the circle were of one mind in theory and practice, but as soon as Nikon, promoted patriarch, and supported by the tsar and his confessor

<hr />

[45] An abridged edition of the life of Juliania Lazarevskaya is printed in *Pamyatniki starinnoy russkoy literatury* (Monuments of Early Russian Literature), I, pp. 63–67. A detailed retelling and analysis of the long edition is given in Buslayev's "Ideal'nye zhenskie kharaktery drevney Rusi" (Ideal Women Characters of Early Rus), *Istoricheskie orcherki* (Historical Sketches), II, pp. 238–268.

Stephen Vonifatyev, decided to go farther, radically reforming traditional Russian ritual on the model of contemporary Greek ritual, unanimity among members of the circle was at once shattered. Like a bolt from the blue fell Nikon's "memorial" reducing the number of bows to the earth during the Lenten prayer of Ephrem Syrus, and substituting three fingers for the two approved by the Stoglav council on pain of excommunication. Avvakum was profoundly shocked and troubled by this decree. So were the other provincial members of the circle and Avvakum's friend Ivan Neronov, archpriest of the Kazan Cathedral in Moscow.

The idea of bringing the Russian church into full accord with the Greek was essentially both a politic and a practical one from the viewpoint of secular and ecclesiastical supporters alike.

Tsar Alexis Mikhailovich considered himself successor to the Byzantine emperors and as such not only the guardian of ancient piety but also heir to the dominion of the Greek emperors. As far back as the fall of Constantinople, semiofficial publicity had, as we know, affirmed the preordained role of the Russian people as emancipator of Constantinople from the rule of the Turks. Alexis Mikhailovich assumed that either he or his successors would carry out the historic mission of winning the Byzantine capital back from its Turkish conquerors. For the success of this undertaking, it would be helpful to remove any discrepancies between the Russian church and the Byzantine.

If the reform was justified by considerations of secular policy and therefore seemed advisable to the guardians of such interests, and chiefly so to Tsar Alexis Mikhailovich, then it was equally handy for the executors of church policy, and primarily so for Patriarch Nikon. The middle of the seventeenth century brought to a conclusion the process whereby the church had gradually lost its relative independence and had become subordinate to the nobiliary Muscovite government. In order to elevate the authority of the church in the state and restore former privileges, it would be necessary to seek support from some power theoretically mightier and more influential than the domestic Russian church organization.

Thus the heads of the administrative aristocracy and of the ecclesiastical both had reasons of their own for being interested in the reform. The first to oppose it were the middle and lower clergy, reflecting in essence the social protest of definite strata of the population: the tradespeople and the peasantry. With both, this category of the clergy was very closely bound up economically. Social antagonism lurked, with all the rest, in the hostile attitude of the lower ranking clergy toward the princes of the church who exploited them by burdensome levies. With Nikon's accession to the patriarchal throne, burdens increased and were further complicated by an intensified system of espionage and pure policing that extended to the clergy of rural and urban parishes alike. All these oppressive measures emanated from the official state church headed by the patriarch, and protest against this church inevitably entailed protest against the reform that it had put through. Opposition to the state church was simultaneously opposition, albeit for the most part unconscious, to the state as well, inasmuch as the forms taken by church organization were merely a product of the general policy of the nobiliary state.

Divine service for the common run of the clergy resolved itself into the mechanical performance of memorized rituals and the pronunciation of verbal formulae learned by rote. These rituals and formulae of themselves, regardless of their inner content, possessed in the minds of the professional servants of the church the magic power of an incantation which would lose its significance if departed from in the slightest degree. The power and the saving efficacy of the old ritual were verified and confirmed in their eyes by the fact that Russian saints, the glory of the Russian church, had won God's favor by communicating with him through precisely this same old ritual that was now being tracked down and trampled under foot. To admit the irregularity of this ritual, or to doubt it, was, for the champions of the old, tantamount to doubting the sanctity of the ascetics, ornament of the land of Rus. The new ritual came from Greece, from that same Greece which two centuries before, so tradition asserted, had, for deviating from true piety, been punished by God and delivered over to the infidels. For two centuries official church publicity had taught that the true and only preserver of Orthodox piety was the Russian church, now obliged to recognize the higher authority of the Greek church. Morever, inasmuch as the reform was linked to foreign tradition, even though in no wise the product of Western influence, but on the contrary produced by conservative tendencies, it was regarded by champions of the fixity and inviolability of the nation's past as due to the influence of the Catholic West, the more so as Nikon had corrected the service books by Venetian editions.

Such were, in sum, the determining causes of hostility to the reform on the part of the common clergy, who were the first to react to it. The higher black clergy, with individual exceptions, accepted Nikon's innovation without protest and in a number of cases even gave it energetic support. This attitude on the part of princes of the church may usually be attributed to the fact that the interests of this stratum of the clergy not only did not suffer by the reform but on the contrary profited. The best demonstration of this is the fact that the Russian hierarchs who judged the subsequently deposed patriarch had at first supported Nikon's fundamental position as to the precedence of the priestly order over the imperial.

The reaction against Nikon's reform, originally headed by the common clergy, soon found sympathizers in various social groups that had felt the pinch of the nobiliary government's regime. The first to side with the defenders of the old was a fairly large section of the urban bourgeoisie—the tradespeople. Ruined by intolerable assessments, exploited by governors, seeing in Nikon one of their most powerful adversaries, placed in circumstances of cutthroat competition with foreign traders enjoying numerous privileges in the Muscovite state, the tradespeople were ripe for just such an active expression of political protest as they registered in their sympathetic attitude toward the schism. This political protest was the more significant that, in view of the accelerated growth of urban centers in the seventeenth century, the tradespeople represented an impressive social force. They were also joined by the musketeers, whose economic affiliations were in part with the tradespeople, in part with the peasantry.

Later the schism was also joined by the peasantry, who had become completely enserfed to the landowner by the middle of the seventeenth century and been reduced to destitution. Ordinarily they did not concern themselves with disputes on such questions as old and new ritual, but before long the Old Belief became for the peasantry, as for all dissatisfied social groups, a standard about which to rally in protest against governmental oppression.

The schism was further joined by a certain section of boyardom. The boyars as a class had even in the seventeenth century been unable to recover from the blow dealt them by Ivan the Terrible in the sixteenth. Due to the direction that history had taken since the "Disorder," they had been definitely relegated to the background by the power having political and economic influence in the state, the nobility. Scions of highborn boyar families gravitated toward the schism as being a movement in opposition to the regime they hated.

The temporary combination in an Old Believer opposition of different classes held together by no community of economic or social interests is analogous to the situation that arose in Germany in the sixteenth century at the time of the peasant wars that attended the Reformation. Of this situation Engels wrote in his *Peasant War in Germany*:

The multiform, mutually conflicting aims of knights and burghers, peasants and plebeians, princes seeking sovereignty, of the lower clergy, the secret mystic sects and the learned satirical literary opposition, found in them [Luther's theses. —N. G.] for the first time a common expression and organized about them with astounding swiftness. This overnight alliance of all opposition elements, however shortlived it may have been, revealed at a stroke the vast combined strength of the movement and gave it a powerful impetus.[46]

[46] K. Marx and F. Engels, *Works*, Vol. VIII, pp. 156–157.

The genuine economic and class basis of the religious struggle brought on by Nikon's reform is also well illustrated by another quotation from the same book by Engels:

And at the time of the so-called "religious" wars of the sixteenth century it was a question first and foremost of quite positive economic class interests; these wars, too, had a basis in class struggle, like the later civil crises in England and France. If this class struggle bore at the time a religious imprint, if the interests, requirements, and demands of separate classes were concealed under the cloak of religion, this does not alter matters in the least and is easily explained in terms of the age.[47]

Archpriest Avvakum was the most striking and the most influential leader of the Old Believer opposition and the most talented and prolific writer produced by the schism. Avvakum's great literary gift and his extraordinary manner of writing made his works an outstanding manifestation of Old Russian literature, quite apart from the thought content, which for us has only a historical interest. Turgenev was enraptured by Avvakum's "Moscow colloquial" and contrasted it with the book language of other seventeenth century writers. In Turgenev's words, Avvakum "wrote a language that every writer should study without fail." [48] "The language and also the style of Archpriest Avvakum's letters and Life remain unsurpassed as examples of the fiery and impassioned language of a fighter," says A. M. Gorky, adding: "and in general there exist in our old literature things that will bear study." [49]

A man of tremendous temperament, fanatically stubborn in his championship of the Old Belief, undergoing terrible sufferings in the course of the struggle, dooming his family to them, and ending his days at the stake, Avvakum's span of life was filled with all manner of experiences and, at times, with inhuman hardships. These are the chief subject discussed in his Life, the first attempt at autobiography in Russian literature, and source of the following biographical details.

Avvakum was born in 1620, or, more probably, in 1621, in the village of Grigorovo in Nizhegorod Province. Not long before her death, his mother married Avvakum to the orphaned Anastasia Markovna, daughter of the late village blacksmith. The wife became her husband's spiritual companion, heroically sharing his sufferings, and heartening him on life's hard road. For reasons unknown, but probably in consequence of youthful evidence of the stubbornness of his "fiery" spirit, Avvakum was driven from his own village and took up his abode in the village of Lopatitsa, also in the province

[47] Ibid., p. 128.
[48] A. L(ukanina), "Moe znakomstvo s I. S. Turgenevym" (My Acquaintance with I. S. Turgenev), Severnyi vestnik (Northern Herald) (1887), No. 2, p. 234.
[49] O literature (On Literature), 3rd ed. (Moscow, 1937), p. 143.

of Nizhegorod. There in his twenty-first year he was ordained deacon and two years later, priest.

From the first years of his ministry, Avvakum devoted himself zealously to his work: he taught, strictly admonished his spiritual children, and at times joined battle with the oppressor-officials. For this he was repeatedly beaten, his property destroyed, and he himself finally again driven out. With his wife and newborn son he tramped his way to Moscow to the archpriests Stephen Vonifatyev and Ivan Neronov, they reporting on him to the tsar, who first heard of him at that time. With a document from his spiritual fathers, Avvakum returned to his old place, where he found his house demolished and his farm in rack and ruin. No sooner had he succeeded in repairing the damage than persecutions again rained down upon him. The boyar Sheremetev came near drowning him in the Volga for making short shrift of some buffoons and for refusing to bless his shaven-faced son; another authority almost shot him. Ultimately he was driven out of Lopatitsa for the second time; again he set out for Moscow, and there received an appointment as archpriest at Yuryevets-on-the-Volga. This was in the eleventh year of his priesthood. But at Yuryevets he only lasted eight weeks: the priests, the peasants, and the peasant women, one and a half thousand persons—in Avvakum's words—beat him in the middle of the street with cudgels and handspikes, stamped on him and threw him under the corner of a house as good as dead. Only the intervention of the authorities saved the archpriest from death. This mob justice overtook Avvakum, as he says, because he had restrained the priests and peasant women from their "whoring ways," and probably because of his too strict collection of the patriarchal taxes.

Going again to Moscow, without his family, in 1652, he was appointed priest in the Kazan cathedral, the incumbent of which was his spiritual father and friend Ivan Neronov. Avvakum arrived in Moscow at exactly the moment of Nikon's election to the patriarchate and himself supported his candidature before the tsar. Presently, however, he became involved in the struggle against Nikon's innovations, and for this was penalized with imprisonment in the monastery of Andronicus. As he says in the *Life*, they put him in chains, starved him, pulled his hair, poked him in the ribs, spat in his eyes, then took him to the patriarchal court where they exhorted long but fruitlessly and were about to unfrock him when the tsar intervened in his behalf.

After this, Avvakum and his family were exiled to Siberia, to Tobolsk: he was thirteen weeks on the way. This was in 1653. In Tobolsk he won favor with the local archbishop and was appointed archpriest in the Church of the Ascension, but even here he led a very troubled life. During his year and a half in Tobolsk, five denunciations were lodged against him. Then he had a skirmish with the archbishop's scribe, Ivan Struna, as the result of whose denunciation Avvakum was sentenced to exile on the Lena, afterwards commuted to exile in Dauria on the border of Mongolia. For Avvakum and his family this was the beginning of a life full of toilsome wanderings, constant sufferings and privations, a life of hunger and cold; frequently he was under threat of death. The general on location in the region, Athanasius Pashkov, under whose command Avvakum had fallen, worried him in all manner of ways, beat him, starved him in chains in prison and oppressed him beyond measure, and even without this his situation would have been terrible. Hunger and hardship killed two of his sons. Of all this, Avvakum gives a detailed account in the *Life*.

With the purpose of getting Avvakum to make peace with the official church and of thereby removing an influential opponent who had succeeded in winning popularity for himself, the tsar in 1663 summoned him to Moscow. On the way, to quote Avvakum's words, he "cried aloud in every town and in every village, in churches and in market places, preaching the word of God and teaching and unmasking ungodly deceit." In Moscow both the tsar and the boyars, who had already broken with Nikon, received Avvakum "like an angel of God" and strove by cares and attentions to make up to him in every way possible for the sufferings he had endured in Siberia. They promised him posts of honor and made him gifts of money and in return the authorities only asked that he hold his peace. For half a year Avvakum practiced self-restraint, looked after church matters, from time to time scolded "recreants," but, seeing that "church work naught availed but rather tumult prevailed," in the end gave up "and again began to grumble," sending the tsar a petition requesting him to "seek after the old piety." The tsar and the authorities, convinced of his obstinacy, passed from kindness to anger, the more so as he was vigorously starting to gather about him the malcontents created by Nikon's innovations. It was decided to banish Avvakum and his family to the far north, to Pustozersk, but after they had started, in view of the extreme difficulty of the road in winter, banishment to Pustozersk was commuted by decree of the tsar to banishment in the less distant Mezen.

A year and a half later, in March of 1666, in connection with a convocation of the synod at which the question of the struggle with the Old Believers was brought up for settlement, they conveyed Avvakum and his two sons to Moscow, leaving the rest of his family at Mezen. At Moscow they kept him for a year and a half, trying in every way to overcome his obstinacy, alternating physical means of persuasion with arguments and admonitions. But neither chains and imprisonment in monastery jails nor efforts at conciliation succeeded in breaking Avvakum's will, and along with his comrades at arms in the struggle against Nikon's adherents he was defrocked by the synod, anathematized, and in August of 1667 sentenced to imprisonment in Pustozersk. Here he was confined for fifteen years in a cell in the district jail under the most terrible conditions. But the rigors of existence did not prevent Avvakum's energetically carrying on the struggle. In fact it was here that his literary career really began. In the Pustozersk jail he wrote the greater part of the works through which he kept in touch with his followers. Avvakum's place of exile became a place of pilgrimage for his adherents, zealots of the Old Belief. Avvakum refused to give up. Soon after the death of Alexis Mikhailovich, he wrote his son Theodore Alekseyevich a petition in which he made the young tsar fear for the fate of his father, whom he represented as a prisoner in torment for conniving at the Nikonians. This petition was apparently brought up against him when the decision was finally made to settle with Avvakum and his associates. On the 14th of April, 1682, along with the priest Lazarus, the monk Epiphanius, and the deacon Fyodor, he was burned at the stake "for grand treason against the imperial house."

Of Avvakum, besides his autobiographical *Life*, known in three redactions, there are extant more than fifty works of varying character and length. Here are colloquies, for the most part on questions connected with contemporary church practice, and commentaries on biblical books, and testaments, and polemics on questions of dogma, and theological works and notes on persons and events connected with Avvakum's life, and, finally, petitions, epistles, and letters. Everything that Avvakum wrote is directly linked with his struggle in behalf of the Old Belief and with his sermonizing on the inviolability of the old tradition in religion, morals, and everyday conduct.

The guiding principle of his religious behavior is best formulated in these words of his own: "I keep them even unto death as I received them; I shall not shift the eternal boundaries. That which was laid down before our time, let it so remain to all eternity!"

But Avvakum, who had given the summons to die "for a single *A*," was less than any of his contemporaries, whether partisans or opponents, a man merely of the dead letter, an abstract scholastic defending the letter for its own sake.

Avvakum's striking originality as man and as writer consists precisely in his combination of traditional modes of thinking with the direct expression of actual feeling and a vital instinct for life as lived in the circles for which the "fiery" archpriest was spokesman. Hence the many "heretical" pronouncements, especially in the polemic against deacon Fyodor, which, if viewed objectively, are irreconcilable with the dogma and institutions of traditional Orthodoxy; hence, too, the boldness of his literary method, making him a true innovator, the iconoclast of time-honored literary standards. Avvakum's powers of innovation are shown first of all in his transformation of the traditional Life, with its stylistic and thematic stencils, into a sharply polemic autobiography, into a narrative not about some outside saint but about himself. Old Russian literature had known nothing of the sort before Avvakum. The ancient scholar had been trained to show contempt for his own personality; he would have considered it pride and sacrilege to write his own life and to make his own personality the center of attention and the means of edification. If before Avvakum we occasionally find some writer telling about himself, as, for example, in the *Testament of Vladimir Monomakh*, the *Supplication of Daniel the Exile*, the old-time pilgrimages, in letters, still, in all these instances the autobiographical moment is on the one hand merely adventitious and not the prior problem, while on the other the author's appraisal of his own personal importance is much more modest and unassuming than with Avvakum. The boldness of Avvakum's approach is due to his extremely high opinion of himself and his consciousness of enormous spiritual superiority over ordinary people. Thus, in the fifth petition to Tsar Alexis Mikhailovich, Avvakum tells of a vision that had come to him during Lent when he lay on his bed for ten days without taking nourishment and reproaching himself that on such great days he was drifting "rudderless" and merely reciting prayers by the rosary. In the second week his body became greatly enlarged. First his tongue was enlarged, then his teeth, next his arms and legs, finally the whole of him broadened and lengthened and covered the whole earth, and then God placed within him the sky and the earth and all creation. "Can't you see, autocrat?" he continued. "You reign supreme over the land of Rus alone, but to me the son of God made subject during my imprisonment both sky and earth." Small wonder that in the consciousness of such enormous power Avvakum did not shrink from arguing and disputing with the Son of God himself. After he had been severely beaten at Pashkov's orders for interceding in behalf of two widows, this, he says, is what flashed through his mind: "Son of God, why did you permit him to beat me so sorely? Look you, I was championing widows consecrate to you! Who shall judge between me and thee?" he asks in the words of Job. "When I lived as a thief you did not so chastise me, but now I do not know in what I have sinned."

In his works, especially the *Life*, Avvakum repeatedly points out how God's power miraculously saved and sustained him in his misfortunes: the harquebus aimed at him did not shoot; he and his family were not drowned; his guardian angel miraculously satisfied his hunger with tasty morsels during his imprisonment; in response to his prayer the ice broke, a hole formed, and he quenched his thirst, and so forth. Avvakum speaks of himself as a man endowed with supernatural ability to heal the sick—both man and beast—and those possessed by devils. The *Life* abounds in items about such cures.

Thus did Avvakum exalt himself in his own eyes, counting himself the appointed of God and teacher of the faithful.

Though Avvakum had taken upon himself the mission of prophet and emissary of God, he was not a monk. He was a family man, an affectionate father, living the secular life and not given to preaching monastic asceticism, even though traditionally giving the monastic life preference over the secular. His own religious instinct affirmed not the principial renunciation of life in the world but the permeation of that life in all its routine details with religion. This secular element in Avvakum largely predetermined the liberties he took with the traditional forms of literary creation. Not only in content but in form, the *Life* and Avvakum's other works are an extraordinary manifestation of individuality.

The first thing that commands attention in Avvakum's works is his colloquial Russian, either injected into the literary language, Church Slavonic, or, in most cases, completely crowding it out. Avvakum himself characterized his language as "plain speech" and "babble"; that is, free and easy talk. In the preface to the third edition of the *Life*, he thus forewarns his readers and listeners: "And if it be plainly told, do not, for God's sake, condemn our plain speech, for I love my natural Russian and am not wont to deck what I say with philosophic rhymes, for God does not hearken to fine words but looks to our matter." To Tsar Alexis Mikhailovich he says: "Look, Mikhailovich, you are a Russian, not a Greek. Speak your native tongue; stop setting it at nought in church and at home and in proverbs." And notwithstanding the fact that Avvakum does not draw any clear line of demarcation between Russian and Church Slavonic, as may be seen from the way he juxtaposes them, none the less it is evident that he preferred everyday, artless, domestic speech to the pompously high-flown language of the learned.

Avvakum's daring use of the spoken idiom was not confined to elements already admitted into documents, into juridical and domestic monuments, but extended to dialect peculiarities from the speech of his native Grigorovo, among them such an idiosyncrasy as the postpositive article (a demonstrative pronoun following a noun). The infiltration of the spoken language is also observable in other monuments of seventeenth, and, as we have seen above, even of sixteenth century literature; for example, the writings of Metropolitan Daniel or Ivan the Terrible, but nowhere to such an extent as with Avvakum. Nor in this respect did he leave any immediate literary successors, unless perhaps the monk Efrosin, who wrote a tract against self-conflagration—Epistle in Confutation of the Newly Invented Method of Suicidal Death, written in 1691 and evidently indebted for its vernacular elements to Avvakum's bold start. Avvakum begins the story of his life in pure Church Slavonic but soon shifts to spoken Russian, with only a sprinkling of Church Slavonicisms, these being used unalloyed only in quotations from "Holy Writ," with which the *Life* and his other works alike abound. Scriptural quotations are not only adduced by Avvakum in argument and illustration of his various pronouncements but are frequently put into the mouths of persons mentioned in the *Life*, himself included.

In striking contrast to his Church Slavonic quotations are the vulgarisms in which Avvakum's writing abounds. These occur chiefly in the abusive epithets which he showers upon his adversaries, in the forthright description of physiological functions, and in extraordinary combinations made up of words belonging to different stylistic categories, such as: "The kingdom of heaven itself is ready to drop into your mouth," or: "Christ has more of that keen lash in store," and so forth.

The implicit reason for Avvakum's use of the vernacular in his works is that all these works, regardless of their outward form, were, in tendency, primarily didactic and polemical and furthermore addressed to the audience at large of his fellow believers. Even the *Life* is as saturated with polemicism as with the didactic elements usual to this genre. Polemic passages in the *Life* are not confined to detached incidental phrases; the work begins with a long polemic introduction followed by two short polemic articles—on the Communion and on the disposition of the fingers. The impassioned polemic intensity of Avvakum's whole tone relieved him of any hesitation on the one hand about ascribing to his adversaries negative qualities which were incompatible with their position in the church, and which sometimes they may even not have possessed, and on the other hand about training the most practiced profanity upon them. Nikon, as Avvakum describes him, is a "long-nosed, fat-bellied he-wolfhound, a wolf in sheep's clothing," a "hellhound," a "fox," a "fig of Antichrist," a "swindler." Though patriarch, he leads a dissolute life, keeps mistresses, a fact of which Avvakum speaks in quite frank and highly realistic terms. Of Paul, Metropolitan of Krutits, Avvakum says in one place that he "did not live after the spirit, was always peddling pancakes and flatcakes; for while studying to become a priestling he had also learned to lick plates at the courts of boyars." He sets Hilarion, Archbishop of Ryazan, over against the biblical Melchizedek, who "did not crave Rhine wines, and Italian, and vodkas, and strained wines, and beer with cardamom, and raspberry and cherry mead, and all manner of untinctured strong waters," and addresses him after this manner: "And who are you? Bethink yourself, Yakovlevich, you priestling! He seats himself in his carriage, blows himself out like a bubble on the water, perched there on the cushion, with his hair dressed like a girl's, to go and show his mug on the public square and inspire love in Uniate Wallachian nuns. Alas, alas, poor wretch! There will be none to weep for you." Avvakum also heaps energetic abuse on Nikon's supporters as a body. They are "dogs," "pagans," "fat bellies," "fat faces," "robbers," "voluptuaries," "fornicators," "drunkards," "fools," "wry noses," "murderers." After at last losing hope of Tsar Alexis Mikhailovich's giving support to the Old Belief, Avvakum started in to use him just as ill as he used the rest of Nikon's adherents. Sketching with malicious delight the infidel emperor Maximian's lot in hell and thereby clearly alluding to the fate of Alexis Mikhailovich himself, he exclaims: "Poor wretch, poor wretch, foolish little emperor! What have you brought upon yourself? Very well, let the earth swallow you! Enough of this torturing of Christians!"

In his polemic fervor and extreme indignation at his adversaries, Avvakum repeatedly bombards them with the most shrewdly aimed threats. Upbraiding the Nikonians for religious intolerance, he indulges in the following reflections: "It is amazing how they refuse to come to their senses! By fire and knout and gibbet they expect to establish the faith! Which, then, of the apostles so taught?—I do not know. My Christ did not instruct our apostles to teach that fire and knout and gibbet were the way to bring men to the faith." But this theoretical religious tolerance did not prevent Avvakum's behaving in exactly the opposite manner himself. While at liberty, he repeatedly asserted that the only methods by which he could get religion and piety were blows and main force, and, especially in the *Life*, gives instances when he employed them: "I was always like that, accursed that I am, quick to anger, primed for a fight," he says apropos of a beating he administered to his wife and the serving-woman.

He frequently expresses regret that he cannot induce the tsar to execute the "heretics" or cannot himself take stern measures with his enemies. To Alexis Mikhailovich he addresses the following plea: "Stop torturing us, then! Take those heretics who are destroying your soul and burn them instead, the filthy dogs. . . . and let us, who are your own sort, go free. It would certainly serve them right!" To the "Nikonian dogs," Avvakum addresses this exclamation: "Just give me time—I'll stamp on your necks in fine style, you'll see, for Christ Jesus, our Lord." In another place, he writes: "Just give me time, dogs, you shall not escape me; I hope to Christ I get my hands on you! Then I'll squeeze the juice out of you!"

If toward those whom he considered enemies of God, heretics, Avvakum was implacable, showering indiscriminate abuse upon them, toward his fellow believers, and even toward those of his enemies whom he regarded as only temporarily astray and capable of being put right, he could be, and was, extremely considerate and even tender in his treatment. In addressing them he used such epithets as "darling comrade," "my darling child," "my light," "infant in the church," "little dove," "little hen pigeon," "little cuckoo." To persons whom he particularly respected and to martyrs for the faith, Avvakum sometimes sent missives gotten up in the pompously flowery Church Slavonic form. Thus the letter to the four "maritime fathers" begins with the words: "Four-horse chariot of the fiery course"; one letter to F. P. Morozova, E. P. Urusova, and M. G. Danilova begins with the following salutation: "multiple-eyed cherubim, six-winged seraphim, flaming archangels, army of the heavenly hosts, triple unity of threefold Godhead, servants of the faith: Theodora in Eudokiya, Eudokiya in Theodora and Mariya in Theodora and Eudokiya." Another letter to Morozova and Urusova has a lofty pompousness of style reminiscent of the acathists: "Alas, Theodosia! Alas, Eudokia! Two spouses unloosed from the traces, two sweetly chirping swallows, two olive trees, and two lampstands set up on earth before God! . . . O great luminaries, sun and moon of the land of Rus, Theodosia and Eudokiya, and your children, shining like stars before the Lord God! O two dawns, lighting the whole subcelestial world!" and so forth. But all these lofty encomiums do not prevent Avvakum's upbraiding Morozova when she is at fault in his sight as her father-confessor. In response to her complaint that her son had received supreme unction from a Nikonian priest, Avvakum writes his correspondent in stern admonition: "Enough of this puking, now, for Christ's sake! . . . A fine nun you make, bad cess! But who are you?—Not Theodosia, not that saintly martyr? You have not yet gone a verst of the way to sainthood!" On another occasion in connection with Morozova's complaint against Fyodor, the Fool of God, and her request that he be excommunicated, Avvakum lectures her still more vigorously:

Ouch! Alas! Woe! My poor, poor spiritual authority! Here's a peasant woman telling me how I ought to pasture my flock in Christ! She herself is perfectly filthy, but she will clean others; she herself is blind, but here she is showing the way to people who can see! Stop and think! Why, you don't know what you are clucking about! . . . You dumb, stupid, hideous woman, dig your eye out with a shuttle the way Mastridia did; better to enter upon life with one eye than to have two eyes and be cast into Gehenna. And do not wear that three-cornered headdress; make a cap that will cover your whole face—that three-cornered thing of yours might bring me bad luck.

Avvakum recalls with lyric cordiality not only people who had been kind to him but even a dog which had visited him in the Bratsky prison, and the dear little black hen that laid two little eggs each day and so fed his starving children. The episode of the hen, brought in just after the story of their terrible journey from Dauria to Rus, is the sort of characteristic genre picture that gives the *Life* its easy narrative character and sets it so apart from the regular canonical form of Life.

This quality of unrestraint is also borne out by the frequent occurrence of irony, sarcasm, and pleasantry in Avvakum's works. With the Nikonians in mind, he writes: "I shall again tell of my troubles, of the kindnesses and favors you have done me these twenty years past." He apostrophizes himself in the following words: "You loved, archpriest, of the great to be friend; love, then, and suffer, poor wretch, to the end." After telling about sending two epistles by the priest Lazarus, to the tsar and to the patriarch, Avvakum goes on to say: "And for all this they sent us presents: In Mezen they hanged two persons of my household, my spiritual children." In prescribing for his spiritual daughter Yelena a long penance, he addresses her as follows: "Well, little sister Yelena, here is a little pie for you from ourselves and Malanya; eat it for your health: observe the penance for seven years." And this is followed by an indulgent pleasantry for Yelena's encouragement:

My darling friend, dear little Yelena! Now see you weep nicely before your candle to the Virgin so that she shall speedily purify you. And you may be sure that I shall not desert you: you weep there, and I shall weep here. A friendly affair, how can I abandon you? If it kills me I'll keep up with you. Yelena, ah, Yelena! Have no communication with those sisters, for they are pure and saintly. But consort with me, for, being scabby myself, I do not fear your mange, as I have much of my own! The raspberries reached me. I shall eat, for I am a catechumen; you are a catechumen: we are not shocked at each other, being birds of a feather. Have you noticed?— The zemstvo loafers do not condemn one another. Nor shall we.

Closely related to these examples are those locutions of Avvakum's in which he uses certain words for the express purpose of giving a sentence the common touch. In speaking of his struggle with the devils that had possessed his brother, Avvakum writes: "I spent the whole winter night stewing over him." He concludes a reference to the Hebrews' persecution of their prophets, Christ, and the apostles, by saying: "And they made a great stew over it." On Alexis Mikhailovich he expresses himself thus: "He frisked about a good deal in this life, the late lamented, like a goat capering over the hills, chasing the wind," and so forth.

To add liveliness to his discourse, Avvakum brought in proverbs, aphorisms, and adages, frequently rhymed: "If no athletes had striven, no crown had been given"; "Whose mind is on God's service set, must for self feel no regret"; "Though a sea passed his throat, on a crumb he would choke"; "Better empty ravings than rovings through the streets"; "But what did you get from them, soul? Oh, a sack and a crock and bast shoes for my feet, to make three"; "Peasant women have long hair but are short of wit"; "The bear is shedding cow's tears"; and so forth.

The same purpose is served by dialogue, in which the *Life* and Avvakum's other works abound. His dialogue is not of the conventional sort typical of old lives and tales but adds real touches of life to the portrayal of his personages. A brief retort will sometimes bring out essential traits of character. The archpriest and his wife and children on their way back to Rus from Siberia tramp for five weeks over bare ice. With them are a few others, as exhausted as themselves. The archpriest's wife tramps along, tramps along, until she slips and falls. Then another weary person trips over her as she lies there and falls on top of her. Both scream and flounder but can not get up. When her husband reaches them, the archpriest's wife asks: "How long, Archpriest, are these sufferings to last?"

"Markovna, till our death," Avvakum replies. And these words, decisive and hopeless as a judge's sentence, are capped by the meekly submissive and courageous answer of the archpriest's wife:

"So be it, Petrovich; let's be getting on."

Returning to Rus from exile, looking about him and seeing that "the winter of heresy is at the door," Avvakum was troubled and in doubt as to whether he should preach the word of God or hide himself, since he was bound by his wife and children. His wife, seeing her husband look troubled, came up to him "decorously" and asked the cause of his grief, and when he told her what the matter was, heartened the archpriest to do the heroic thing: "I, and the children too, give you our blessing. . . . Get you gone, get you gone to church, Petrovich—unmask the whore of heresy!" Avvakum's doubts were at an end and he resumed his fiery and incessant preaching. These two extracts from the *Life*, for all their verbal compression, give, as nothing else could, the whole power and passion of the nature of the irrepressible archpriest's companion and friend, who fearlessly shared with him all the burdens of his stormy life.

One idiosyncrasy of Avvakum's religious attitude was his habit of conceiving abstract religious entities and characters from the Bible and from Church history in concrete terms of everyday human life, as was also largely done in apocryphal literature. Hence his tendency to give material form to objects of discourse traditionally regarded by Christians as conceptual and abstract. This attitude is reflected in certain peculiarities of his style. God, as Avvakum imagines him, is an "old wonder-worker"—a being "of benign craft," ordering the destinies of the world by diplomacy. In connection with the dogma of the Incarnation of Christ, Avvakum says: "By sagacity God got the better of that Devil, brothers; he outwitted him as a fisherman catches a fish on a hook."

The snake that tempted Eve is thus described by Avvakum: "It had legs and it had wings. It was a fine animal, handsome, stole its cunning from no one." The comment on Adam and Eve after their fall is in this vein: "Oh, my dears, there was no one they could blame; the Devil got them into trouble, but they did their share too. The sly landlord gave them to eat and to drink and then hustled them out. The drunken man rolls in the street, robbed, and no one takes pity on him. . . . They waked up with a drunken head-ache, and all in a mess: Adam's beard and mustache were caked with vomit, and his head was spinning from the wassail bowl." To God's question: "What have you done?" Adam replied: "It was the wife that you created for me." To this answer Avvakum gives the following interpretation: "In plain language: 'Why did you make such a foolish woman for me?'" Upon Eve's excuse: "The serpent beguiled me," the following comment is made: "There you have it: like husband, like wife; both were sots, but you can't expect children to be good for long, they get bored except just around meal times." Cain's sacrifice was not acceptable to God because Cain offered a "measly little loaf that was no use to him," while Abel gave his "best ram." Of Noah he says: "The dear old man drank himself happy, and then took off his breeches, and lolled around naked." Sarah, who "baked pies" for the Holy Trinity, said to God when he told her that she was to bear a son: "Why, I am a *baba* * ninety years old; how can this be?" Likening himself to a beggar going about through the city streets, collecting alms under the windows and then portioning them out to his "ecclesiastical nurseries," Avvakum con-tinues: "Of the rich man, the emperor Christ, I shall beg a slice of bread from the Gospel; from the apostle Paul, from the rich merchant, a crust of bread; of Chrysostom, of the trader, I shall receive a morsel from his dis-courses; of King David and of Isaiah the prophet, of the tradesmen, I shall get a quarter-loaf each. And, having filled my wallet, I shall give them to you, dwellers in the house of my God." Of St. Nicholas it is said that he "spat in the teeth of Arius, the dog," and to this is added the observation: "He was a zealous man, the dear departed." All references to the Bible and to church history, and the morals to be drawn from them, are given a nega-tive slant as applied to the activities of the contemporary church.

Still more definite form is taken in Avvakum's imagination by the constant object of his struggle—the Devil. When driven by Avvakum out of his brother, he sits on the window, hides in the corner, runs under the stove. Acting through a certain Philip, he beats and tears Avvakum "like a spider's web"; he vexes him by playing on balalaikas and rebecs, knocks his rosary out of his hands, in the church sets a table in motion, lifts the lid of a coffin and stirs the dead man's shroud, at the altar makes the vestments and sur-

* *Baba*: a married peasant woman.—ED.

plices fly from place to place. The weapons for struggle with the Devil are holy amulets, which alone frighten him and paralyze his power over man. "You do not bring the Devil to reason with a stick, like a peasant," says Avvakum. "What he fears are holy water and sacred oil, and he flees quite away from the cross of the Lord."

All the indicated peculiarities in Avvakum's works are imparted to them by a realistic method of writing which is part and parcel of the archpriest's own individuality. Even his aesthetics, as revealed in the curious chat on icon-painting, are not inconsistent with Avvakum's realistic tendencies. Having cultivated "refinement of feeling," he protests against the fashion that had struck root in our icon-painting of representing sacred personages "as if alive . . . after the manner of the flesh. . . . They paint the image of Emmanuel the Saviour," he reproaches, "with the face plump, the lips red, the hair curly, arms and muscles thick, the fingers dimpled, and likewise the legs with thick hips, and altogether make him look like a German, big-bellied and fat, except that no sword is painted at the hip." Avvakum's protest was called forth by the fact that the new painting, which penetrated to us in the second half of the seventeenth century under the influence of western European baroque, was, in the first place, by its very origin Western Catholic and therefore "heretical"; was, in the second, in terms of conservative Russian manners and traditional Russian life, not realistic but highly conventional, as conventional as the representation of the newborn Christ with a full beard, something which Avvakum pokes fun at in the name of common sense.

That history should have singled Avvakum out as the most influential and the greatest champion of the old religious order is due to these same features of his personality. Old Rus, with its backward forms of culture and social existence, found in him the most striking personification of its religious life. As a cultural-historical type, Avvakum was very representative, reflecting in his behavior a long historic epoch, which, though doomed in the course of things to destruction, would go on defending its pattern of culture and manners long after he was dead. Avvakum's marked possession of the attributes of a fanatical demagogue-champion with a psychic obsession—subject to hallucinations, and on that account inclined to appropriate to himself the qualities of a miracle-worker under the special protection of Divine Providence—determined that infectious influence on the rank and file of his followers which brought him such wide popularity. His struggle with Nikon was largely prompted by the personal animosity which he, like many other representatives of the lower and middle clergy, cherished for the omnipotent ecclesiastical favorite who had alienated from participation in church policy even those who had backed his appointment, among them Avvakum. An ambitious and dictatorial nature, Avvakum could not reconcile himself to the role of obedient executor of the orders of the all-powerful patriarch who had abruptly and in haste shattered the traditions built up through the ages—the more so since the provincial archpriest's dull, slow-moving and uncritical mind and his conservative psyche could not keep up with the whirlwind of innovations which Nikon's leadership had loosed upon the Russian church, ossified in its immobility.

No sooner had Nikon promulgated his first reforms than Avvakum's "heart shivered and his legs shook"; he felt "that the winter of life was approaching" and, in order to warm his shivering heart and take shelter from the Nikonian winter, he lighted those bonfires into which his despairing proselytes flung themselves by the thousands. The loud and importunate "Nikonian uproar, like a whirlwind," troubled his soul and was more than ears lulled by the tranquil assurance of fables about the splendid and holy bygone days of Rus could bear. There was no doubt in his mind that "before Nikon, the apostate, everything in our Rus, under pious princes and tsars, had been Orthodox, pure, and immaculate, and the church unrebellious." The indisputability of the old-time Orthodoxy was for him demonstrated by the saints reared in it who had brought glory to the land of Rus. At the Stoglav council in Tsar Ivan's time, the "standard bearers" Gury and Varsonofy, wonder-workers of Kazan, and Philip, prior of the Solovyetsk Monastery, had given the support of their authority to that old faith which "Antichrist's forerunner," Nikon, was now "breaking down and destroying." The zeal shown by the heads of the Greek clergy in the affairs of the Russian church could not fail to offend Avvakum, brought up to the traditional attitude of condescension and disdain for those whom he regarded as yesterday's beggars today impudently making themselves at home in the Russian church and creating courts and tribunals in a foreign country as if they belonged there.

The West, with its world culture, "German customs," and experimental science, was rapidly gaining ground in Rus. All this was undermining the foundations of the olden time and its religious, social and economic usages. Nikon and his closest adherents were not less hostile than Avvakum himself to the "fascination" of the West, but the elements of self-criticism manifest in the reform, shattering the idyllic concept of the infallibility of antiquity, and undermining its fundamental authority, at the same time indirectly paved the way for an even more radical revision of all the traditional bases of Russian life. The summoning of learned monks from Kiev for the business of correcting the service books, monks who brought with them if not the content of contemporary Western scientific thought, at least its methods and—above all—a respect for the hitherto "ill-thought-of" intellect, was of itself already a danger signal for the mental stagnation characteristic of Old Testament Muscovite usage. A typical well read but uncritically minded person, able to reel off by heart enormous numbers of quotations from the books of "Holy Writ," Avvakum zealously preserved the letter even where it represented an erratum. This he did, apparently, not because the letter was dear to him of itself but because to move an *a* suggested a lack of confidence in antiquity and threatened this same "divinely guarded" past with extinction. Toward science, which was attempting to comprehend the letter and rise above the superstitious worship of it, his attitude was keenly negative and antagonistic. "Do not seek rhetoric and philosophy, nor eloquence," he taught, quoting Gregory of Nyssa, "but live according to the true and wholesome word, for a rhetorician and philosopher cannot be Christian." He is decrying Plato, Pythagoras, Aristotle, and the other philosophers of antiquity whom he knew through references in the *Chronograph*. He speaks of himself with evident satisfaction as an unlearned simpleton, and unskilled in any learned subtleties: "I am neither a rhetorician nor a philosopher nor skilled in dialectics and logistics; I am a simple man and replete with ignorance." Pigs and cows that predict bad weather by grunting and lowing, know by what instinct tells them more than the almanac and zodiac experts, rational swine, who measure sky and earth but know not the hour of their own death.

Though a brilliant literary figure and daring innovator in the province of style, and temperamentally a very extraordinary individual, Avvakum as a thinker was altogether the exponent of an outlived tradition that contended long and furiously with the irrevocable unfolding of the historical process—something which neither the belated preaching of the fiery archpriest nor the efforts of his partisans and adherents after him could reverse.[50]

[50] The great majority of the presently known and in part hitherto unpublished works of Avvakum were printed under the editorship of Ya. L. Barskov and P. I. Smirnov in *Pamyatniki istorii staroobryadchestva XVII v.* (Monuments of the History of Old-Believerism in the Seventeenth Century) (Leningrad, Academy of Sciences SSSR, 1927), Bk. I, Pt. 1. See also *Zhitie protopopa Avvakuma, im samim napisannoe, i drugie yevo sochineniya* (Life of Archpriest Avvakum Written by Himself, and Other Works by Him)— ed. with introduction and commentary by N. K. Gudzy (Academia, 1934). This also gives the literature on the question.

Translations from
Western Narrative Literature

IN the seventeenth century, particularly during the latter half, an increase is observable in translated narrative literature from the West, deriving chiefly from Polish and Czech originals and in some degree influencing the development of the original Russian tale.

Out of this literature, works still bearing to a marked degree the stamp of ecclesiastical ideology are in the minority, while the majority are purely secular both in style and in subject matter. Translated monuments of the former type to which particular importance attaches include such collections of moral tales as the *Great Mirror (Speculum Magnum)* and the *Deeds of the Romans (Gesta Romanorum)*. To the second category belong the *History of the Seven Wise Men,* and a good many tales and romances of chivalry, comic stories and anecdotes, *novelle,* fables. Most of these works of narrative literature are based on migratory subjects current in both East and West. Part of the material was contributed by Byzantium, which had long kept Rus supplied with its literary products.

In the West, among the culturally more advanced, all the works enumerated had long since been supplanted by creations showing higher artistry or had undergone a literary metamorphosis bringing them up to the higher level. Among us they served at first as reading material both for the best educated strata, consisting primarily of the clergy and the feudal aristocracy, and, to judge by the language of extant seventeenth century copies, for certain democratic strata as well. (Cf. the seventeenth century copy of the tale of Bova—Bevis of Hampton—discussed below.) Apparently they were at once reflected to some extent in folklore: in religious poetry, *bylina,* and fairy tale.

Translators of story material with a pious tinge were for the most part learned monks who had emigrated to Moscow from Kiev and other parts of the Ukraine to work in the Foreign Office. Such translators were not always equipped to cope with their problem: they either had insufficient knowledge of the Russian literary language, so that the vocabulary and syntax of the original, particularly a Polish original, sometimes slipped over into the translation, or else were insufficiently grounded in the language of the original and confused the meaning, or, finally, could not figure out how to render in the Russian usage of that time terms, concepts, and customs peculiar to Western culture, with a resulting incongruity between original and translation that to the next generation of cultured eighteenth century readers sounded naïvely helpless and comic.

GREAT MIRROR: *Speculum Magnum*

The collection known as the *Great Mirror* was translated in Moscow in 1677, having been approved the year before by the late Tsar Alexis Mikhailovich. The translation was made from a Polish original bearing the title, *Wielkie Zwierciadlo prsykladów*, a second or third edition of which had come out in Crakow in 1633. Somewhat later a second translation was made that had a special circulation in manuscript. This translation, to judge by the copy of it once in Buslayev's possession, painstakingly written and very finely lettered, had been intended for print, yet it was never actually printed. The Polish original of the *Great Mirror* derived from a Latin text entitled *Speculum Magnum Exemplorum*, composed in 1605 by the Jesuit Johannus Major. In translating the Latin collection into Polish, several additions were made on the basis of Polish sources. The *Speculum Magnum Exemplorum* was in turn an adaptation, enlargement, and systematization of a medieval Latin collection, *Speculum Exemplorum*, printed in 1481 in the Netherlands. In all these stages of its development the *Mirror* was intended primarily as a collection of examples (*exemplorum*) to aid in elucidating and illustrating sermon texts. This had been its role in the West and also in the Ukraine.

The Polish text of the monument contained over 2,300 stories; the Russian translation included less than half the text of the original.

In content and tenor the *Great Mirror* was in many ways similar to the traditional *Chetyi Minyei*, prologues and paterikons of an earlier period.

In some cases where the Russian translator stumbled upon a story found in the Russian prologues, for example, he would leave it untranslated and refer the reader directly to the prologue. In general character the monument was tendentious and didactic, exemplifying the ethics of asceticism. The presence of legendary-apocryphal material and the incredible variety of its stories, however, made the collection entertaining as well as instructive, the more so as it also contained secular tales capable of use, if desired, for illustrating some moral teaching, and an occasional amusing anecdote. In the Ukraine, where no complete translation of the *Mirror* existed, seventeenth century preachers went to the Polish or to the Latin text for stories whereby to enliven the abstract precepts they addressed to their flock.

It should be noted that in Russian translation the Catholic tendency of the collection was toned down (the bishop of Rome was replaced by the ecumenical patriarch, the Roman Church by the Holy Universal and Apostolic Church, son-Catholic by son-Christian, and so forth), the scholarly and critical apparatus of the Polish text omitted, separate articles collated with traditional collections of Byzantine origin such as the *Prologue,* and verses present in the Polish original omitted. The translators took an offhand attitude toward the original, peppered the translation with Polish and Latin expressions, but in a number of cases went out of their way to preserve Russian linguistic peculiarities. In some copies the original is padded out with tales from other, usually translated, sources. There is one instance, however, where an original story found its way into the Russian text of the *Great Mirror,* a story dating from the time of Ivan III: "Of a certain presbyter [Timotheus] who fell into grievous transgression."

In this way a foreign monument, instead of being mechanically transplanted, underwent more or less organic adaptation. Apparently there was good reason that the *Great Mirror* should have been held in high esteem even by Old Believers.

Texts of the *Great Mirror* both Russian and foreign are broken up into separate rubrics defining the basic theme of the tales or "examples" under the respective headings: "Heavenly Glory," "Trials," "Burial," "The Last Judgment," and so forth.

In order to acquaint ourselves with the subject matter of our monument, let us study a few of the included tales.

One of the most popular was the tale of Udon, Bishop of Magdeburg, which enjoyed a wide circulation, even apart from the *Great Mirror,* in various Russian collections and "anthologies" of the late seventeenth and early eighteenth centuries. The tale was written with a view to demonstrating "how wicked it is for a man in high position fast and loose to live, wantonly the property and collections of the Church to squander, those under his authority with the stench of temptation to corrupt, and persons dedicated to the Lord to profane." In Magdeburg there was a student named Udon who had no success at schoolwork in spite of being repeatedly beaten by the teachers. Once, "following a severe beating," he went after school to the Church of St. Mauricius and there began praying earnestly and tearfully to the Virgin and to Mauricius that he might get understanding. While the youth prayed, he fell asleep, and as he slept the Virgin appeared to him and said that she would answer his prayer by bestowing upon him not only understanding, but, after the death of the present bishop, the Church of St. Mauricius as well, for the "faithful tending" of it, and if he should do his duties well, he would receive a great reward, but if badly, he would die soul and body. And sure enough, from that time on, Udon astonished everyone by his success in his studies and by his wisdom, and two years later, when the bishop of Magdeburg died, Udon was chosen to take his place. At first he conducted himself piously but after awhile began to forget what the Virgin had told him, and to give himself up to worldly pleasures, squander what was in the church treasuries, profane women and girls, violate nuns, and in general "incline himself to every sort of iniquity" so that all came to hate and loathe him. Once, when he was passing the night with the prioress of a nunnery, he heard a terrible voice from on high: "Cease from wantonness, Udon, for already you have played the wanton too long." But thinking that it was a hallucination, he laughed at what he had heard and, in spite of the fact that the voice was thrice repeated, went on living the same profligate life.

Three months later a certain monk prayed in the Church of St. Mauricius that the Lord either rid the land of Udon or reform his manner of living. The prayer was heard and a terrific vengeance meted out to Udon, clear to all people, "but chiefly to rulers of the church" who disgraced their office. A wind blew out all the lamps in the church: the monk was terror-stricken and became as if dead. Then two youths approached with two great lighted candles, then two more, who spread a carpet and set up two thrones. Next, some sort of warrior came forth with a naked sword, saying in a loud voice: "All saints, wherever your relics may be, arise and come to the tribunal of God." A great number of saints assembled, disposing themselves in the church "according to their rank, which is to say, according to their virtues"; then the twelve apostles appeared with Christ at their head, and the Virgin attended by a multitude of "very good-looking" maidens. Christ and the Virgin seat themselves on the thrones and then Mauricius, patron saint of the church, appears with 6,666 warriors. At Christ's command Udon is brought into the church, having been "snatched from the prioress' side." Mauricius wrathfully rebukes him for his disreputable behavior, Christ orders that Udon's head be cut off, and then the whole assemblage disappears.

Subsequently regaining consciousness, the monk lighted a candle and saw the severed head of the bishop lying at a distance from the body and the floor of the church stained with blood.

The same day a priest who had been Udon's subordinate was on a journey and, ordering his servants to go on ahead, fell fast asleep with the horse's bridle tied to his wrist. In a dream there appeared to him a multitude of unclean spirits with trumpets, with drums, with staves, with swords, and other weapons. And when they had all assembled they seated the Prince of Darkness high on a throne, and with howling, applause, and laughter began to shout aloud: "Stand back, stand back, for here is Prince Udon our beloved already approaching!" After this the demon torturers brought before their prince the soul of Udon in its bodily form, bound in fiery fetters of iron. Satan mocked at him and bade that he be tormented and starved, and his mouth stuffed with toads and all manner of reptiles. Then they gave him burning sulphur to drink and took him to the "bath," whence an all-devouring flame rose sky-high. Emerging from it like red-hot iron, he stood before the Prince of Darkness, who asked him with a smile: "Did you have a nice bath, my prince?" Then, seeing himself consigned to total perdition, Udon began cursing the Devil, and God, and all creation: "A curse upon you, Devil, and all your crafty and evil spirits, and all your license and mischief-making and all your power; cursed be God who created me, cursed be the earth which bore me, cursed be my parents, who begat me, cursed be every creature in heaven and on earth!"

Upon hearing this blasphemy, the devils rejoiced that Udon was so "very perfect" at "singing their refrain," and in order that he might learn this refrain still better, threw him into the abyss of hell. They decided to throw the priest in along with him because he had been adjunct to Udon in his iniquities. But at that moment the priest awoke and took to his heels while the horse, in alarm, started galloping, and wrenched his hand from the socket. With great difficulty the priest got astride and upon returning to town told of his vision and to prove the truth of his words showed his injured hand. Thereupon the townspeople threw Udon's body into the swamp, where the "beasts of hell" welcomed it with dancing and frolicking, rending it in all manner of ways and nibbling at it with their teeth, but as people living in the neighborhood had many filthy tricks played on them by the demons, the body of Udon was recovered from the marsh, burned and thrown into the river Elbe, whereupon the fish that frequented the river swam out to sea and only came back after strenuous prayers on the part of the inhabitants.

At the spot where Udon's head had been cut off, the marble floor of the church soaked up the blood of the offending bishop. This spot was covered by carpets but whenever a new bishop was installed these were taken up so that the newly installed bishop might see the blood and fear to die the death of Udon. The story ends with the following words: "These things were truly done by the Lord to bring fear and trembling upon the bishops of that church and all loose-living authorities, that, hearing of them, they might tremble in soul and body and dread the terrible throne of God, his fearful and awful judgment."

The tale of Udon is a very typical example of medieval religious legend having a strong demonological cast. As we can see, it is shot through with arraignments of moral laxity and of malfeasance on the part of members of the higher clergy. Not by accident did this tale circulate separately here in an enormous number of copies. Its wide popularity in Russia demonstrates that here too it was made a vehicle for exposing vices to which our clergy was likewise addicted.

Typical of the Catholic origin of the *Great Mirror* is the role assigned the Virgin as benefactress of the human race. Unlike Byzantine legend, Western legends in which the Virgin figures are often characterized by such refinement of plot, attention to psychology, and relative freedom and boldness in thematic treatment as at times to resemble secular *novelle*. Take, for example, the story of how the Virgin delivered a certain youth from amorous temptation, motifs from which were used by Pushkin in his romance of the poor knight. A certain young warrior, fair and chaste, was, through the instigation of the Devil, inflamed with passionate desire for his mistress, whereby he lived in torment for a whole year. Then, casting shame aside, he told his lady of his passion, but, being an honorable woman, she received his declaration coldly, and his sufferings were only increased. In tears he sought the aid of a certain hermit-monk to whom he was in the habit of going for advice. The hermit bade the youth pray and render the angels' praise to the Virgin a hundred times during the year, assuring him that he would then be granted the desired relief. The youth did so, and at the end of the year mounted his horse and set out for the neighboring church to make his customary prayer. As he left the church he saw a lovely woman, of a beauty transcending that of all other women, and she was holding his horse's bridle. "Is my beauty to your liking?" she asked him, and he replied: "Never saw I such a woman."

"Would it please you to be my betrothed?" the woman again asked.

"Even a tsar would count himself blessed, if so be he might become your betrothed," replied the youth. Then the woman said:

"I desire to become your betrothed. Approach me." And giving him her hand to kiss, she continued: "Now is our betrothal sealed, and later in my Son's presence we shall be wed." By these words the youth knew her to be the Virgin. And from that hour he was so quit of his passion for his mistress that she too marveled at it. When the youth informed the saintly man of all that had happened, the latter, marveling at the compassion of the Virgin, told him that he hoped to be present on his wedding day. As the youth's hour of death drew near, the monk appeared to him and asked if he were suffering. "Now I suffer," he replied and straightway gave up the ghost, that he might attain to the promised marriage in heaven and eternal bliss.

Into the *Great Mirror* anecdotal *novelle* taken from life and secular in mood also found their way. One of these, entitled: *There Is No Wrath Greater Than a Woman's, nor Obduracy and Intractability More Hardened and Indomitable*, tells the following. Once when walking in the field with his wife, a husband remarked that the field was well mowed, but his wife out of contrariety retorted: "It is not mowed but sheared," and obstinately held her ground. Her husband lost patience, in his rage threw her into the water, but even when drowning and past speech she managed to reach her hand out of the water, cross her fingers to indicate scissors, and thus insist to the end that the field was not mowed but sheared.

Another story tells how a certain Henrikh, a nobleman and wealthy, had a wife who notwithstanding the fact that she was kindly by nature was, like other women, unable to refrain from malignant gossip and censure. Once she started censuring Eve for disobedience. The husband had long tried to persuade his wife to cease speaking ill, but since she would not hearken he determined to test her own obedience and forbade her to bathe in a filthy cesspool that existed in the yard. At first the wife laughed, but when walking past the forbidden pool she always stopped. In the end she so longed to try it that one day she left the bath and bathed in the pool. The husband was told, caught his wife in the act and took away her clothes.

As to the first anecdote, the preface to the *Speculum Magnum Exemplorum* points out the necessity of making clear when explaining such anecdotes that the events related in them came about through the Devil's interference in men's affairs.[1]

The *Great Mirror* was contributory to the formulation here in the seventeenth century of a very popular, lavishly illustrated collection, the so-called *Synodikon*, which became during the seventeenth and eighteenth centuries

[1]Extracts from the oldest copy of the *Great Mirror* are given in *Izd. Moskovskikh vyshikh zhenskikh kursov seminarii po drevnerusskoy literature* (Publication No. 9 of the Moscow College Courses for Women's Seminaries in Early Russian Literature), "Iz Velikogo Zertsala" (From the Great Mirror). Concerning the monument, see P. V. Vladimorov, *Velikoe Zertsalo, Iz istorii russkoy perevodnoy literatury XVII v.* (From the History of Russian Translated Literature of the Seventeenth Century) (Moscow, 1884); *ibid.*, "K issledovaniyu o Velikom Zertsale" (Toward a Study of the Great Mirror), *Uchenye zapiski kazanskogo universiteta po istoriko-filologicheskomu fakul'tetu* (Scholarly Notes of the Historio-Philological Faculty of Kazan University) (Kazan, 1885).

a sort of people's book, even passing over into chapbook literature. At this time the commemorative listing of the deceased customary in the old syn-odikons is relegated to the background while first place is given to disserta-tions and stories, largely borrowed, demonstrating the necessity of commem-orating the deceased, or simply to interesting stories of a religio-moralistic character.[2]

The *Great Mirror* also exerted an influence on oral poetry, leaving its imprint in religious verse and popular legend.

Closely related in character to the *Great Mirror* was the collection *Radiant Star,* which contained stories of the miracles of the Virgin and was translated here in 1668 from a White-Russian original. This also circulated widely in seventeenth and eighteenth century copies.

DEEDS OF THE ROMANS: *Gesta Romanorum*

A collection informed with the secular element to a more pronounced degree than the *Great Mirror,* very popular especially in the Middle Ages, and entitled in the Latin text *Gesta Romanorum,* contains stories of a pseudo-historical character, in which the Roman background so predominates as to give the collection its name. This work had taken form in western Europe, under the pen of some unknown author, apparently as early as the thirteenth century. It was based on migratory tales that had come to the surface at one time or another either in the West or East, and stemmed specifically from the fifteen stories already constituting a popular medieval collection dating from the eleventh century, the *Disciplina Clericalis* of Peter Alphons, which provided illustrative material for preachers just as the *Gesta Roman-orum* primarily set out to do, almost all stories being accompanied by moral-istic interpretations in terms of Christian doctrine.

Numerous manuscript copies of the monument are extant in the West from the fifteenth century on, almost no two of which contain exactly the same selection of tales. From the fifteenth to the eighteenth century various printed editions of the monument also appeared in the West. In Russia the *Deeds of the Romans* was translated from a Polish printed edition first brought out at the middle of the sixteenth century and entitled *Historye Rzymskie.* (Apparently no manuscript texts of the monument existed in

---

[2] See E. V. Petukhov, "Ocherki iz literaturnoy istorii Sinodika" (Outlines of the Literary History of the Synodikon), *izd. O-va lyubiteley drevney pismennosti CVIII* (pub. 108 of the Society of Friends of Early Literature) (St. Petersburg, 1895).

Polish.) From what edition of this the Russian translation was made has not as yet been precisely determined but there is reason to suppose that it derives from the Cracow edition of 1663. In one of the Russian copies of the *Deeds* there is an indication that the translation, "from a new Polish printed book," was made in 1681; in two others the date of translation is given as 1691. Notwithstanding a number of textual variants in existing Russian copies of the monument, there are grounds for supposing that they represent a single Russian translation. This supposition is borne out by the fact that different Russian copies observe the same chapter arrangement, show the same deviations from the Polish original, and that all copies reveal characteristic lexical correspondences in the rendering of specific Polish words, including identical mistranslations. The presence of textual variants in Russian copies is probably due to individual copyists having compared the existing translation with a Polish text. The number of tales included in Russian copies of the *Deeds* varies but never exceeds thirty-nine. This corresponds to the number of tales included in the Polish text, which used only a cut version of the Latin original, where more than a hundred and eighty stories are given. In other respects besides the marshaling of material, Russian copies also practically coincide with the Polish original. Divergences are limited to the Polish text's omission of one tale found in all Russian copies, *Moral: Beware of Sweets,* and the fact that the first story in the Polish text, *In Disparagement of Empty Praise,* exists in only two Russian copies. The translation of the collection was apparently made in White Russia, to judge from the prevalence of Polish syntactical usages in it. Some stories found in Russian copies of the *Deeds of the Romans* had been known in translation even before the appearance here of the collection—the tales of Apollonius of Tyre, of Alexis, Man of God, Eustaphius, and Pope Gregory, for example—but the author of the collection instead of using the earlier translations, made a new one in each case.

To get some idea of the subject matter of *Deeds of the Romans,* let us study the tale of Pope Gregory, one of the broad general cycle of legends about an incestuous hero stemming from the Oedipus-Telephus-Perseus myth. To this cycle belong the eastern and western European medieval legends of Judas the betrayer, the Russian tale of Andrey Kritsky, the Serbian ballads about Nakhod Symeun, the Bulgarian tale of Paul of Cesarea, the Coptic history of Tsar Amenios, the Armenian fairy tale of the "River Wanderer," and finally a French eleventh and twelfth century romance, the *Life of Pope Gregory the Great.* This last passed, with trifling omissions, into the Latin *Gesta Romanorum,* thence into the Polish *Historye Rzymskie,* and later into the Russian translation of the collection.

The content of the tale as given in the *Deeds of the Romans* is as follows.

In the lands ruled by Rome there dwelt a king named Parcus (in the Latin text, Marcus), and he had a son and a daughter whom he loved dearly. As he lay dying, the father charged the son to look after his sister and give her in marriage when the time came. After the king's death the son conceived a passion for his sister and tried to persuade her to enter into carnal relations with him. Notwithstanding his sister's obstinate refusal, the brother insisted on having his way and soon the princess conceived. When the brother learned of this, he was greatly distressed, but the sister consoled him as best she might and then advised him to confide the whole matter to an aged knight whom the late king had especially trusted. On the advice of this knight, the young king announced to his suite that he was making a pilgrimage to the Holy Sepulchre and in their presence entrusted his sister to the care of the aged knight. The latter conveyed her to his house and made known to his wife the secret reason for the princess' visit. When a son was born to the latter, the knight offered to summon a priest to christen the child, but the princess forbade him. She ordered a little boat made and in it bade them place the infant, together with fifty pounds of gold, a hundred pounds of silver, and a note stating the child's origin and the fact that he had not been christened. When all this had been done, the child was lowered into the sea. At this moment a messenger arrived from the Holy Land and reported that the king had died there and was being brought home for burial. And the king was scarcely buried when a messenger arrived from the prince of Burgundy with a proposal of marriage for the princess. The latter declined it, saying that she intended to die unwedded. The prince was furious and attacked her territory and laid it waste.

In the meantime the child's boat floated in toward a monastery, just as the prior was walking along the seashore. He rescued the boy and, after reading the note, christened him, named him Gregory, and turned him over to a certain fisherman to rear. When Gregory was seven years old, the prior took him to the monastery for instruction in reading and writing. The boy made rapid progress in his studies and was beloved of all the monks. Once when Gregory struck the fisherman's son and the latter complained to his mother, she, being irritated, disclosed to Gregory the fact that he was not her son but a foundling. Notwithstanding the prior's attempts to dissuade him, he decided to leave the monastery. After reading in the note then given him by the prior that he was the son of brother and sister, Gregory took ship and set out for the Holy Land to atone for the sin of his parents. On the third day of his voyage a mighty storm arose and drove Gregory's boat to the city where his mother lived. For a price he promised to rid the queen's land of the Burgundian prince and did indeed win a brilliant victory. On the advice of the governor of the city, the princess married her deliverer.

Gregory had a habit of retiring before meals to his own room and tearfully reading the note that had been placed with him in the chest. Gregory's tear-rimmed eyes attract the attention of the princess; in his absence she finds the note, reads it and discovers the terrible truth. Gregory then takes to the road in beggar's raiment with the intention of atoning for his sin. He reaches the house of a fisherman, who, upon learning that the stranger is seeking a place suitable to do penance in, conveys him to a crag sixteen miles from the shore and there locks him into an "empty chamber" and then throws the key into the ocean. So incarcerated, Gregory spent seventeen years. Then a pope died in Rome and after his death a voice from heaven was heard saying: "Seek out the holy man named Gregory and consecrate him pope." Long did the emissaries seek the holy man indicated but all in vain. By chance they found their way to the house of the fisherman who had locked Gregory up, and told him of their failure. The fisherman recalled having locked someone named Gregory in the crag and told them. Then the fisherman caught a fish and in it found the key to the crypt where Gregory was. In company with the messengers, the fisherman set out for this crypt and showed them the entrance to it. Gregory was found alive, and at the request of his discoverers set out for Rome, where he was installed pope in the Cathedral of Peter and Paul. Word of the new pope's saintliness reached his mother and she betook herself to him as a penitent. After hearing the sinful woman's confession, Gregory revealed the fact that he was her son, and then appointed her prioress of a nunnery. Thus were St. Gregory and his mother, it says at the end of the tale, cleansed of their sins. In extreme old age they departed this world unto the Lord.

Next comes the following "explication" of the tale. The king is Jesus Christ, who entrusts the sister, that is, the soul, to the brother, that is, to man, since all the faithful are brothers of Christ, while the soul is God's sister. But the soul is joined to the body and therefore the body is sister of the soul. Only then does the body show respect for the soul when it refrains from treating it contrary to the will of God, and so forth.

As has been said, the tale of Pope Gregory was known in a Russian translation preserved in several seventeenth and eighteenth century copies, even before the *Deeds of the Romans* appeared in Russian. The text of the tale later underwent some curious adaptations. Thus, in an eighteenth century collection belonging to Professor M. I. Sokolov and now preserved in the Moscow State Historical Museum, there is a copy written in epic language and folk-tale style. Here and there in it we encounter passages in *bylina* form. In another eighteenth century copy our tale was revised as to style and expanded in the vein of fashionable romances of the epoch of Peter the Great.[3] A writer of the latter half of the seventeenth century, Simeon of Polotsk, versified it and included it in his collection the *Flowery Plesaunce*. Finally, the tale of Pope Gregory[4] was reflected in Ukrainian and White Russian folk literature, in religious verse and oral legend.

In the West, narrative material from the *Deeds of the Romans* was reused by such eminent writers as Boccaccio and Shakespeare. In Rus, as was also the case with other works of medieval literature, the *Deeds of the Romans* did not in the main undergo rewriting by outstanding literary artists. An exception is the tale of Tsar Jovinian, which had also existed in separate copies apart from the collection under the title *Tale of the Emperor Aggeus and How He Was Afflicted by Pride*. First, it passed over into the folk legend of the proud rich man; secondly, it served as a source for Garshin's *Legend of Aggeus the Proud* and for an unfinished play by Leo Tolstoy on the same subject.[5]

HISTORY OF THE SEVEN WISE MEN

One of the most popular books of antiquity and the Middle Ages was the *History of the Seven Wise Men*, which circulated in numerous translations and adaptations both in East and West and was known here in a large number of copies. The *Seven Wise Men* was native to India, its origin on Indian soil being confirmed by Persian and Arabic translations, though the book itself has not been preserved there. In oriental versions it appears under the title *History of the Wise Man Sindbad*, or Sindababa. Later on, the book was translated into Syrian, Hebrew, Greek, and other languages. From the Hebrew, and probably not later than the thirteenth century, was made the Latin translation entitled *Historia septem sapientum Romae*, which became the basis of numerous European adaptations in different languages and

[3] See "Drevnosti" (Antiquities), *Trudy Slavyanskoy komissii moskovskogo arkheologicheskogo obshchestva* (Works of the Slavic Committee of the Moscow Archaeological Society) (Moscow, 1902), Vol. III, "Protocols," pp. 4–5.

[4] See N. K. Gudzii, "K istorii legendy o pape Grigorii" (On the History of the Legend of Pope Gregory), *Izvestiya otd. russk. yaz. i slov.* (News of the Division of Russian Language and Literature of the Academy of Sciences) (1914), Bk. 4, pp. 217–256.

[5] The Russian text of the *Deeds of the Romans* was published from practically the worst of the existing MSS., likewise a very late one, by the Society of Friends of Ancient Literature (St. Petersburg, 1877–1878); literature of the work: N. Oesterley, *Gesta Romanorum* (Berlin, 1872); S. L. Ptashitskii, *Srednevekovye zapadnoevropeiskie povesti v russkoy i slavyanskoy literaturakh* (Mediaeval Western European Tales in Russian and Slavic Literatures), I; *Istorii iz Rimskikh Deyanii* (Stories from the Deeds of the Romans) (St. Petersburg, 1897); F. Buslayev, "Perekhozhie povesti i rasskazy" (Travels of Tale and Story), *Moi dosugi* (My Leisure Hours) (Moscow, 1886), Pt. 2, pp. 358–372.

where both the constituent material and the names of characters were altered. During the first third of the sixteenth century there was a printed Polish translation, made from the Latin by a bachelor of Crakow university, Jan z Koszyczek.

A detailed analysis of the language of Russian copies of the *Seven Wise Men* made it possible for Professor Murko, who traced the course of the work through the various Slavic literatures, to verify Pypin's conjecture that it had been translated into Russian from Polish, and furthermore, on the basis of two mistakes repeated in all the highly varied Russian copies, to assert that there had been but a single translation. There can be no question of translation in the literal sense, however. This was rather a rewriting of a Polish text, and at that not of the regular printed one deriving from Jan z Koszyczek's translation, as Murko conjectures, but of some other text, probably in manuscript, deriving from a second Polish translation which had become incorporated with the *Deeds of the Romans,* as happened in many western European manuscripts, whereas Jan z Koszyczek's translation had no connection with the *Deeds of the Romans.* To this hypothetical Polish manuscript original it is also necessary to trace not only the title of the Russian copies—"History," "Book," or "Tale" of the seven wise men—which replaces the *Historya . . . o Poncyani cesarzu rzymskim* of the old Polish printed editions, but the change in the emperor's name from Pontsian to Eliazar, phonetic alterations in the names of the seven wise men as given in the old printed Polish texts, and certain other peculiarities.

Professor Murko sets the number of Russian copies of the *History* at forty, but to this figure must now be added copies listed in catalogues of Russian manuscript collections that have come out since Murko's study. The oldest manuscript of the *History,* once belonging to Professor Bauze and destroyed during the burning of Moscow in 1812, dated from 1634. It is permissible to assume with Murko, even if on inadequate factual grounds, that the translation of the book dated from a still earlier time—the end of the sixteenth century—and was made, as an analysis of the linguistic peculiarities of certain manuscripts of the *History* would appear to show, in White Russia, whence it reached Moscow and points farther north by way of Novgorod.

In Russian copies the *History of the Seven Wise Men* consists fundamentally of fifteen stories, the assembling of which is motivated by two introductory chapters where the following story is told. In Rome there ruled an emperor named Eliazar, by whom his wife had a son Diocletian. The queen suddenly fell ill and, dying, asked the father to give her son every care, avoid causing him offense through a new wife, and send him abroad to study. Upon the advice of his boyars, he sent his son to school to the Roman wise men at the age of seven. After a while, at the urgent request of his nobles,

Eliazar married again. The new wife, upon learning that the emperor had a son who had been sent abroad to study, was greatly troubled and began thinking how she should bear a son herself to be Eliazar's successor, and should kill the emperor's son who had gone to school to the seven wise men. And upon a time she asked her loving husband to have the prince return from abroad since she was as yet childless and looking upon him would give her joy and through this joy she might herself conceive. The emperor agreed to carry out his wife's request, the more readily as seven years had already passed since he had parted from his son, and sent an emissary to fetch Diocletian. Divining by the stars, the wise men find that the moment Diocletian appears before the emperor and utters one word, he will die an evil death. The wise men are troubled and, although disobedience means death, prefer suffering death themselves to dooming the prince to death. Seeing his teachers troubled and learning the cause of their grief, Diocletian started to scan the stars himself and saw in them that he would escape with his life if for seven days he spoke not a word. Seven days he would be led to execution and each time one of the wise men would save him from death by telling some tale, and on the eighth day he would speak for himself and in turn save all of them from execution. Diocletian has a prophetic dream which forewarns him that the threat upon his life will come from his step-mother.

Upon arriving at the emperor's palace, the son receives all his father's words of welcome in silence, thereby causing Eliazar great perplexity. The stepmother herself undertakes to talk with the prince, conducts him to her chamber and, captivated by his beauty, tries to tempt him, but the prince resolutely declines her insistent proposals, whereupon, after rending her dress and tearing her face until it bled, she began to call loudly for help, beseeching protection from Diocletian. In response to her cry, the emperor came running, and, believing his wife's false accusation, commanded that his son be led off to the gallows. At the request of his nobles, who wished to prevent the emperor's doing anything rash in anger, Eliazar postponed the youth's execution until the morrow. In order to incline the emperor to part from his son the more readily, the wife told him a story the point of which was that the emperor ought to take care not to be deceived lest he suffer for his credulity. Convinced by his wife's story, the emperor confirms the decree for his son's execution, whereupon the first wise man comes forward and tells his story, the moral of which is that one ought never to put too much confidence in a woman, and the emperor postpones the execution. Thus, in the course of seven days, the stepmother and the seven wise men, turn about, tell fourteen stories, the effect of which is to make Eliazar hesitant about deciding his son's fate. Finally, on the eighth day, Diocletian himself opened his lips, accused his stepmother of amorous relations with a youth, who might be found among her maids in waiting disguised as a girl, and told his father how his stepmother had tried to entice him into adultery. The emperor then decided to execute his wife. But first Diocletian told a lengthy tale about a certain knight who attempted to drown his son in the sea. In this tale, utilized by Boccaccio in the eighth *novella* for the tenth day, the prince makes a prediction as to his own fate, which is duly fulfilled. The father turns his empire over to his son, but consigns his wife and her lover to a lingering death.

As specimens, let us quote the stepmother's first tale and the tale of the first wise man.

There lived in Rome, the stepmother's story says, a rich man who owned a beautiful garden, and in the garden was a fine big tree which bore fruit every year. Once when he went into the garden, the master noticed that under the old tree a very fine young one had shot up, and summoning the gardener, remarked to him that the little tree, when it got its growth, would be finer than the old one. The gardener agreed with him. Another time when he came into the garden, the master gave orders for trimming the branches of the old tree so that they should not cut off the sunlight from the young one. Next the master ordered that the old tree be cut down entirely because, being tall, it kept the breeze from reaching the young tree, but when this had been done, the young tree, deprived of nourishment from the old, dried up; the poor and the helpless who had fed on the fruits of the felled tree started to curse the master of the garden. As the stepmother interprets the story, the old tree and the young symbolize the emperor and his son. The son tries to seize his father's empire and plots against his life. The inability of sun and breeze to get to the young tree signifies that the son wishes to steal his father's glory, and when he does steal it, many of the mighty attach themselves to him and begin to meditate the death of the emperor, and then the son ascends the throne, and intelligent people start to curse those who deterred the emperor from hanging his son. Therefore the emperor ought to speed his execution.

In reply to the empress's tale, the first wise man tells a story about a noble dog and a falcon.

In a certain place there lived a brave knight who had a son and loved him dearly. Three nurses were put in charge of the child. One fed him, another bathed him, a third rocked his cradle. That knight had a dog and a falcon to which he was very much attached on account of their unusual qualities. Once the knight and his wife went to a banquet, leaving their son in the care of the nurses, the dog, and the falcon. When the child fell asleep, the nurse who was rocking him went outside, stationing the dog and the falcon by the cradle. The dog fell asleep and at that moment a grass snake crawled toward the cradle, intending to sting the child. The falcon waked the dog, and the dog did battle with the snake, tore it to pieces and deluged the room with its blood. During the fight the cradle was upset and fell on top of the sleeping child; the dog, after settling with the snake, lay down beside the fallen cradle. Coming into the room and finding it all deluged with blood, the dog lying beside the overturned cradle, and the child nowhere to be seen, the nurses concluded that the dog had devoured the infant. They ran to the house where the knight and his wife were guests and told the wife of the disaster. The knight's wife shrieked aloud and told her husband what the nurses had told her; the knight took his sword and coming to his house cut down the dog as it rushed out joyfully to meet him. But upon lifting the cradle he found the child sleeping unharmed, then discovered the snake that the dog had torn to pieces, and started to mourn bitterly and lament that he had deprived himself of so true a friend by believing the words of his wife. "So shall it be with you, Emperor," the wise man ended his tale, "you will weep inconsolably for your son if you hang him through relying on the words of your wife."

The *History of the Seven Wise Men* suited the taste of the Russian reader because it coincided in tendency with the discourses on "evil women" which were so widely diffused through Old Russian literature. It was reflected in folk tale, and during the late eighteenth and early nineteenth centuries received literary treatment.[6]

WESTERN TALES (ROMANCES) OF CHIVALRY

(About Bova-Korolevich [Bevis of Hampton], Peter of the Golden Keys, Emperor Otto, Melusine, Basil Goldenhair, Bruntsvik, Apollonius of Tyre)

Western adaptations of European tales, as we saw above, had been in-filtrating into Russian literature through the southern Slavic countries,

[6] A very incomplete and careless edition of one of the Russian copies of the *History* was prepared by F. Bulgakov, *izd. obshchestva lyubiteley drevney pismennosti* (Publication of the Society of Friends of Early Literature) (St. Petersburg, 1878–1880). On the monument itself, see A. Pypin, *Ocherk literaturnoy istorii starinnykh povestey i skazok russkikh* (Sketch of the Literary History of Ancient Russian Tales and Folk Tales), pp. 251–260; F. Buslayev, "Perekhozhie povesti i rasskazy" (Travels of Tale and Story), *Moi dosugi* (My Leisure Hours), Pt. 2, pp. 313–328; M. Murko, "Die Geschichte von den sieben Weisen bei den Slaven," *Sitzungsberichte der Kaiserlichen Academie der Wissenschaften, Phil. Hist. Klasse* (1890), Vol. CXXII. On the connection of the *Istoriya semi mudretsov* (History of the Seven Wise Men) with folklore, particularly the Russian, see I. N. Zhdanov, *Russkii bylevoy epos* (Russian Bylina Epos), pp. 152–192.

Serbia chiefly, since long before the seventeenth century. Examples include the *Legend of the Indian Empire,* which appeared here in the thirteenth century, the Serbian *Alexandria,* and the *Trojan History* of Guido de Colonna, which had been circulating in Rus since the fifteenth century. At the end of the sixteenth century, in the so-called "Poznan" collection, we encounter, translated into White Russian from "Serbian books," tales of Tristan and Lancelot and Bova (Bevis), and a tale of Attila translated from the Polish.

"Serbian books" must apparently be taken to mean not Serbian texts but only books imported into Serbia and actually written in Italian. As early as the end of the sixteenth century the personal names Bova and Lukoper occur in Rus, evidence that the tale of Bova was at that time already popular on Russian soil, though possibly as yet only through oral transmission. By the first third of the seventeenth century, at the latest, the tale was known here in written form as well, to judge from the fact that it is mentioned in the 1640's by the imperial gentleman-waiter Ivan Begichev. The Italian printed text from which the White Russian translation preserved in the Poznan manuscript was made, goes back to a French text composed in the twelfth and thirteenth centuries. Russian texts of the tale trace their origin to the White Russian translation represented by the text of the Poznan manuscript. From the sixteenth century to the nineteenth, about fifty Russian copies of the tale of Bova, classifiable into several redactions, are preserved. In the eighteenth and nineteenth centuries chapbooks were made up on the basis of manuscript texts (more than two hundred in all) and popular "comic sheets" in upwards of sixty editions. During the nineteenth and twentieth centuries eight records of oral folk tales about Bova were made.

The plot of the story as given in Russian manuscript texts is, in broad outline, as follows. King Guidon, who ruled the illustrious town of Anton, sends his servant Licharda to King Kirbit, or Kirbich, to act as matchmaker for him with the latter's daughter Militrice. Militrice refuses to become Guidon's wife, because she loves King Dodon, but, in compliance with her father's wishes, does marry Guidon. Three years later a son, Bova, is born to them. After a certain passage of time, Militrice sends Licharda to Dodon, inviting him to invade their kingdom and help her do away with Guidon. Dodon murders Guidon and becomes the husband of Militrice. The boy Bova seeks safety in flight, but the pursuit overtakes him; Militrice puts her son in prison and decides to poison him with some bread rolls which she herself has kneaded with serpent's tallow, but through the help of a serving-woman, Bova escapes poisoning, gets out of prison, and flees to the seashore, where some merchant captains pick him up: he gives them to understand that he is the son of a sexton and a laundress. Upon reaching the kingdom of Armenia, the captains turn Bova over to the Armenian king Zenzevey, who is captivated by Bova's beauty; Bova tells him the same story about being the son of a sexton and a laundress. Zenzevey's daughter Druzhnevna falls in love with Bova, only later finding out that he is a king's son. Then Bova has a succession of varied adventures. He beats the powerful armies of the suitors to Druzhnevna's hand, King Markobrun and Lukoper, bogatyr warrior, son of Tsar Saltan Saltanovich, in addition to which he slays Lukoper in single combat. Falling into the hands of Saltan Saltanovich, who had decided to exact the death penalty of Bova for the murder of his son, Bova wins the affections of Saltan's daughter Milchigria, or Malgiria, who proposes that he marry her, after first going over to the "Latin faith" and believing in the "god of Akhmet."

Saltan Saltanovich consents to his daughter's marrying Bova but the latter refuses to change his religion and for that is put in prison and left to starve. Escaping from prison, he arrives at the kingdom of Markobrun, who had abducted Druzhnevna, takes her away with him, and then defeats the army of Markobrun which had been sent in pursuit of him. But Markobrun has a mighty bogatyr, Polkan, who has dog's legs to the waist but from the waist up is just like other people. Releasing him from prison, Markobrun sends him against Bova. In his first encounter with Polkan, Bova suffers defeat but afterward the two make their peace, fraternize, and defeat Markobrun's army, which had been besieging the city of Kostel, whither Bova was bound with Druzhnevna and Polkan. All three then continue their journey and on the road Druzhnevna bears two sons. Next, having left Druzhnevna and her sons in the care of Polkan for a short time, Bova returns to find neither Druzhnevna nor the children, while Polkan lies dead, mauled by a lion. Deciding that both Druzhnevna and the children must have perished, he goes to the kingdom of Saltan Saltanovich to marry Milchigria. But there Bova meets Druzhnevna and her sons. Along with them he sets out for the city of Anton. Dodon and Militrice he condemns to death and then settles down quietly in his kingdom with Druzhnevna.

This story varies in individual copies: new details are introduced, episodes are transposed, additional secondary personages are brought in. The tale becomes more or less Russianized. Not only were individual expressions in the original incomprehensible to our translators, with the result that an epithet applied to Bova's mother, *meretrix* (adulteress), was converted into the proper name Militrice, and *castello* (castle) into Kostel, the name of a city, but the fine points of chivalry as practiced in western Europe were also beyond them and chivalry was interpreted in terms of the more familiar bogatyr way of doing things. In Russia the hero of the tale was endowed with attributes in the pious tradition, its personages were sometimes called,

Russian style, by name and patronymic (Kirbit Verzaulovich, Militrice Kirbitevna, Zenzevey Adarovich, Saltan Saltanovich) and had fixed epithets attached to them. Thus Militrice, whose traits are those of the typical "wicked woman," is called throughout the tale "most beautiful," though she is clearly a thoroughgoing villainess.

Isolated copies of the tale of Bova show a pronounced Russian fairy-tale influence. One of these, from the seventeenth century, conducts the narrative from the very beginning in Russian fairy-tale style: "Once upon a time, in a certain empire, in a great realm, in a celebrated city, in Anton, there dwelt an illustrious king named Guidon." In addressing Licharda, Guidon says: "Ah, Licharda, my servant, if you would do me a true and faithful service, go you to the town of Dementian to the goodly and illustrious king Kirbit Verzaulovich, as my emissary, as my matchmaker." Nor did Licharda "disobey his master, but took the letter and bowed low and rode off to the town of Dementian to the goodly and illustrious king Kirbit Verzaulovich." Upon arriving at Kirbit Verzaulovich's court, Licharda "entered the king's palace and placed the letter on the table in front of the king," and so forth, all in the same singsong, fairy-tale style, with the usual repetitions and retardations, and with folk-poetry epithets: "clear field," "white hands," "goodly bogatyr horse," "dear child," "merchant captains," "sharp spear," "sugary lips," "the deadly business of war," and so forth. At the voice of Bova, waves rise and the ships roll. He kills fifteen thousand warriors at once by waving a broom. The bogatyr Lukoper had a "head . . . like a beer kettle, and the eyes of the goodly man were a span apart, and between his ears you could lay a tempered arrow, and between his shoulders a sazhen measure, and no one under the sun was a match for him." The goodly bogatyr horse upon which Bova rode out to meet Lukoper, "stood fastened by twelve chains, buried in the earth to the knees, and behind twelve doors"; the bogatyr monster Polkan, who could do seven versts at a bound, had, before his encounter with Bova, been imprisoned behind thirty locks and thirty drawbridges. The tale depicts the sword of steel, magic potions. Every so often, details peculiar to the Russian manner of life and the Russian background find their way into it: at the feast the "beautiful queen broke up the swan"; upon setting out for battle, Bova "fetched sand for Druzhnevna and sprinkled it on her heart"; Zenzevey and Markobrun "rode forth with their hawks to the creek for a bit of diversion"; Bova walked down "to the creek for diversion and shot geese and swans." Women making a request of a man fall at his feet. Bova repeatedly asks help of the "gracious Saviour" and the "immaculate Virgin," king Zenzevey attends (stands at) the "church singing" on Sunday. The action takes place in "palaces," in "golden-roofed halls," in the "rear [women's] apartments," in the "cabin courtroom" where sits the "peasant burgomaster" Oryol (Italian, "Orio"), who speaks in Russian proverbs: "All women have long hair but short wit." In a description of a house, "cote," "stable," and "sideboard" are mentioned; people play on dulcimers and on balalaikas.

In the sixteenth and seventeenth centuries the tale of Bova was known in boyar circles and among the nobility. In 1693 it is mentioned among the "recreational books" of Tsarevich Alexis Petrovich. In court circles during the first third of the eighteenth century, the tale of Bova acquired the characteristics of a "history" of gallant adventure. During the second half of the eighteenth century, in the same circles, it was transformed into a fairy tale about knights and bogatyrs, with allusions to political events of the epoch occasionally tucked in. Through a parallel development, the story of Bova had by the seventeenth century already made itself at home among merchants, townsfolk, and peasants, little by little losing its foreign flavor and acquiring, to an ever increasing extent, traits imparted by folklore. By the beginning of the eighteenth century, it was generally assumed to be a favorite Russian folk tale and was so treated by Radischev and Pushkin, and later by Populist writers. The Russian chapbook story of Bova served not only the peasantry but the urban lower middle class and the merchants as well. A number of variants on the chapbook tale (from the 1850's to 1918) are saturated with elements typical of the petty bourgeois sentimental-domestic tale. As early as the beginning of the nineteenth century there were "portraits" of Bova in the garb of an Old Russian knight; in the middle of the nineteenth century Bova was frequently depicted in company with the favorite characters of Russian folklore, Ilya Muromets and Ivan Tsarevich. For a long while previously, *byliny* and religious verse had reflected the tale. The wide popularity of Bova among the people in a way justified the closing lines of the tale as found in the copy from which the above quotations were taken: "And Bova's fame shall endure henceforth unto all generations."[7]

---

[7] I have borrowed the information as to the fortunes of the tale of Bova on Russian soil from an as yet unpublished dissertation on this theme by V. D. Kuzmina, which investigates all known manuscript and chapbook texts, "comic sheets," and literary adaptations. An old study of the tale, with two texts of it as a supplement (the White Russian from the Poznan collection, and a Great Russian one), exists in A. N. Veselovskii's *Iz istorii romana i povesti* (From the History of Romance and Tale) (St. Petersburg, 1888), Pt. 2, pp. 229–305, and Appendix, pp. 129–172, 237–262. The second published Great Russian text of the tale, analyzed above, is given in *Pamyatniki drevney pismennosti* (Monuments of Early Literature) (1879), Pt. 1, pp. 45–79, reprinted by B. I. Dunayev in the series *Biblioteka staro-russkikh povestey* (Library of Old Russian Tales) (Moscow, 1915). For chapbooks and a discussion of them, see D. Rovinskii's *Russkie narodnye kartinki* (Russian Popular Prints) (St. Petersburg, 1881), Vol. I, pp. 76–115; Vol. IV, pp. 142–151; Vol. V, pp. 109–112. On fairy tales about Bova in Russian folklore in general, including *byliny* and religious verse, see A. N. Veselovskii, "Pamyatniki literatury povestovatel'noy" (Monuments of Narrative Literature) in Galakhov's *Istoriya russkoy slovesnosti* (History of Russian Literature), 3rd ed., Vol. I, pp. 460–461.

After Bova the next most popular translated Western tale was that of Peter of the Golden Keys, which usually bears the title: *History of the Brave and Illustrious Knight Peter of the Golden Keys and the Beautiful Princess Magilene*, and goes back to a fifteenth century French romance about Peter, Count of Provence, and the beautiful Magelona, daughter of the king of Naples. The romance made the round of all the countries of Europe and through the medium of a Polish text reached Russia in the late seventeenth century. It is mentioned in 1693, along with the tale of Bova, among the "recreational books" of Tsarevich Alexis Petrovich. There are as many as thirty registered Russian copies of it all told.

The story is, briefly, as follows. Peter, son of a French prince, sets out as a knight unvanquished in the lists for the kingdom of Naples where dwells the incomparable beauty, Princess Magilena. In Naples, without revealing his name to anyone, he defeats in a tourney all defenders and is given the nickname of Knight of the Golden Keys because to his helmet, to distinguish him from his rivals, he had attached two golden keys. Peter's bravery and his good looks are too much for Magilena and she falls in love with him. Magilena's nurse, who had at first tried to dissuade her from marrying Peter, later on, when Peter has revealed his origins to Magilena and to her, and she is convinced that the two aspire to an "honorable legal marriage," encourages their intimacy. Thrice Peter presents Magilena with costly rings, while she gives him a golden chain set with precious stones. Then Peter fights a second victorious tourney, after which he informs Magilena of his desire to go to his parents and receive their blessing. At the request of Magilena, who is distressed at the prospect of parting from him, Peter decides to take her with him and they depart from the kingdom of Naples secretly. On the seashore the exhausted Magilena fell sound asleep with her head on Peter's knees, and he, forgetting his promise to respect the princess's virtue, entertained unchaste thoughts about her and, unfastening her dress, took from her neck the knot containing the three rings he had given her, and set it down beside him. A raven flew past and mistaking the knot for meat made off with it. It looked to Peter as though the raven had dropped the knot on an island, and he got in a boat and rowed toward the island but was carried out to sea by a storm and picked up by ship captains who conveyed him to the Turkish sultan.

Peter lived for a long time at the sultan's court in great honor, never ceasing to think of Magilena and tortured by his separation from her. He prays for her and reinforces his prayers by giving alms to poor Christians. In the meanwhile, waking up and not finding Peter beside her, Magilena, after a long search for him, goes on alone in deep sorrow, finally reaches the country where Peter's parents live, and there builds a monastery, a church of Peter and Magilena, and a hospital, where she nurses sailors suffering from "seasickness." She spends her days in prayer and fasting. Once some fishermen catch a pike in which they find the knot of rings that Peter had given to Magilena. They take the rings to Peter's parents who decide that their son has been devoured by fishes and tell Magilena, who identifies Peter's rings. But Peter himself, having obtained from the sultan permission to visit his parents and having received on this occasion many valuable gifts, after a series of adventures finds his way, exhausted and ill, to Magilena's monastery. She recognizes him first and cares for him. After Peter's recovery, sumptuous wedding festivities lasting a whole month are held, attended by his parents and several kings from overseas. The Turkish sultan releases Peter from his promise to return to Turkey and sends him rich gifts. Peter lived with Magilena in love and harmony to the age of eighty. After his death his son reigned as gloriously as his father had done.

Traces of the Polish original are few in the Russian translation; [8] folk-speech ways are occasionally in evidence. At the beginning of the eighteenth century the tale of Peter of the Golden Keys was twice made the subject of dramatic adaptation, once as a prose work, which became part of the repertoire of Tsarevna Natalya Alekseyevna's theater and of which only an insignificant fragment is extant, a second time in verse. Such attention to a plot dealing with a hero who, among other things, went abroad to complete his studies is apparently to be explained by the identity of his name with that of the Russian tsar who had symbolically unlocked Russia's way to

[8] No Russian manuscript texts of the tale of Peter of the Golden Keys have as yet been published. On them, see A. N. Pypin, *Ocherk literaturnoy istorii starinnykh povestey i skazok russkikh* (Sketch of the Literary History of Ancient Russian Tales and Folk Tales), pp. 236–237; *ibid.*, "Dlya lyubiteley knizhnoy stariny" (For Lovers of Literary Antiquity) *Sbornik obshchestva lyubiteley rossiiskoy slovesnosti na 1891 god* (Collection of the Society of Friends of Russian Literature for 1891) (Moscow, 1891), pp. 247–250. For extended extracts from the tale, taken, however, from eighteenth century copies and evidently refurbished in the eighteenth century, see V. I. Rezanov's article, "Iz istorii russkoy dramy" (From the History of Russian Drama), *Izvestiya otd. russk. yaz. i slov.* (News of the Division of Russian Language and Literature of the Academy of Sciences) (1906), Bk. 4, pp. 165–244; see also "Neposredstvennyi istochnik romana o petrezlatykh klyuchey" (Immediate Source of the Romance of Peter of the Golden Keys), *op. cit.*, (1911), Bk. 4, pp. 144–150.

Texts of the dramatizations are given in I. A. Shlyapkin's book *Tsarevna Natalya Alekseyevna i teatr yeyo vremeni* (Tsarevna Natalya Alekseyevna and the Theater of Her Time) (St. Petersburg, 1898); *Pamyatniki drevney pismennosti* (Monuments of Early Literature, CXXVIII), pp. 7–8, and in G. P. Georgievskii's article, "Dve dramy Petrovskogo vremeni" (Two Dramas of Peter the Great's Time), *Izv. otd. russk. yaz. i slov.* (News of the Division of Russian Language and Literature of the Academy of Sciences) (1905), Bk. I, pp. 215–255. See also I. M. Badalich, "Ob odnom dramaticheskom pamyatniki Petrovskovo vremeni, *Akt ili deistvie o Petrezlatykh klyuchey* (On a Dramatic Monument of Peter the Great's Time, The Act or Action of Peter of the Golden Keys), *ibid.* (1926), Vol. XXXI, pp. 231–266. For chapbook texts of the tale and a discussion of them, see D. Rovinsky, *op. cit.*, Vol. I, pp. 115, 122; Vol. IV, pp. 152–153; Vol. V, pp. 109, 113–114. The folk tale about Peter is given in E. R. Romanov's *Byelorusskii sbornik* (White Russian Collection) (Moghilev, 1901), No. 3.

communication with Europe. Starting at the beginning of the eighteenth century, the tale also went through a lengthy series of chapbook editions and popular lithographs. At the end of the eighteenth century it was twice translated here from the French. In the nineteenth century a fairy-tale adaptation of it was recorded.

Several copies are also extant of another tale popular in the literatures of Europe, that of the Roman emperor Otto, which likewise derives through Polish translation from a sixteenth century French romance. The Russian translation of the tale was made in the 1670's. It tells how the emperor Otto, led by his mother's false accusations to suspect his wife Olunda of unfaithfulness, banishes her and her twin sons. In the wood, as Olunda slept, a monkey made off with one of her sons, a lioness with the other. But both sons, as it turns out, are rescued. One of them, called Lion, because he had been taken off by a lioness, the mother herself finds, and later on this son rescues his brother, christened Florens, and his father Otto, both of whom had been seized by the sultan of Egypt. Otto makes his peace with Olunda, Lion marries the daughter of the king of Spain and becomes his heir, while Florens, who had become king of England, marries the sultan's daughter, who, as a preliminary, accepts baptism along with her father.

The tale of Otto was extremely voluminous and included many episodes of the knightly adventure type. It is known here in seventeenth and eighteenth century manuscripts and also in an abbreviated form which omits personal names and usually bears the title: *A Very Edifying and Touching Tale of an Empress and Her Two Sons and a Lioness*. This redaction of the tale was printed here with illustrations in 1847 from a manuscript of 1720. At the beginning of the eighteenth century the tale was twice dramatized. One of the dramatizations, derived from the full edition of the tale, was produced in Tsarevna Natalya Alekseyevna's theater, the other, derived from the abridged edition, became part of the repertoire of the school theater of Peter the Great's time.[9]

Manuscripts containing the tale of Otto commonly include also the *True Tale of the Princess of Altdorf*, who produced twelve sons at one birth and

[9] Russian MS. texts of the complete tale of Otto have not been published. On them see A. N. Pypin, *Ocherk* (Sketch), pp. 238–239, and I. A. Shlyapkin, *Tsarevna Natalya Alekseyevna i teatr yeyo vremeni* (Tsarevna Natalya Alekseyevna and the Theater of Her Time), p. xxxv. This also gives a detailed resume of the tale with a large number of quotations from it (pp. xxxii–xlii) and the text of the play *Komediya Olundina* (from the repertoire of Natalya Alekseyevna), pp. 21–27. The abridged text of the tale (of the empress and the lion) is published from a nineteenth century copy in *Pesni* (Plays), collected by P. N. Rybnikov, 2nd ed. (Moscow, 1910), Vol. III, pp. 239–244. The text of the school drama on the theme of the tale and a study of the play are given in S. A. Shcheglova's publication, "Neizvestnaya drama Petrovskoy epokhi o tsaritse i l'vitse" (An Unknown Drama of the Petrovian Epoch About an Empress and a Lioness), *Trudy komissii po drevnerusskoy literature* (Works of the Committee on Early Russian Literature) (1932), I, pp. 153–229.

decided to drown eleven of them. The prince rescues the children, gives them out to nurse, and later introduces them to his family, including his wife. The princess repents and receives absolution.[10]

Simultaneously with the tale of Otto, a translation was also made here of the tale of Melusine, which goes back to a fourteenth century French romance likewise widely read throughout Europe. A Polish translation was made from the German, and a Russian translation from the Polish. The tale deals with the sorceress Melusine, who for disobeying her father was doomed each Saturday to turn into a being half human, half snake. She could be released from this metamorphosis only by finding a husband who could make up his mind to marry her in full knowledge of this idiosyncrasy of hers. Count Raymond of Puata proved to be such a man; by agreement he did not see his wife on Saturdays. Melusine brought Raymond success and wealth. But, breaking his promise at the instigation of his brother, and spying on Melusine of a Saturday, when she was performing her occult ablutions, Raymond lost her forever. With a mournful cry she left her husband's house and from that time Raymond's good fortune ceased. Tradition adds that thereafter when any misfortune threatened Raymond's descendants, Melusine appeared three days in advance on the tower of the castle that Raymond had built at Puata.

The tale is based on the widely diffused folk-poetry motif of the union of a man with a fairy woman, also known in Russian fairy stories. The tale is known here in more than twenty copies and, like the tale of Otto, was dramatized for Natalya Alekseyevna's theater and made the subject of popular prints.[11]

To the seventeenth century also belongs the translation of a tale entitled in one copy the *Parable Showing How Inadequate It Is for Marriageable Girls and Young Widows Desirous of Entering Upon Matrimony to Speak Ill of Their Suitors and Dishonor the Messengers Sent by Them. A Fictitious Tale About King Basil of the Golden Hair from Czech-land and His Polymestra, the Beautiful Princess of France.*[12]

The content of the tale is as follows. In olden times, in the German em-

---

[10] See A. N. Pypin, *Ocherk* (Sketch), pp. 241–242.

[11] The text of *Melusine*, from a seventeenth century copy, was printed in the publications of the Society of Friends of Early Literature (St. Petersburg, 1882). On it see A. N. Pypin's *Ocherk* (Sketch), pp. 230–233; F. Bulgakov, "Istoriya o Melyuzine" (Story of Melusine), *Pamyatniki drevney pismennosti* (Monuments of Early Literature) (1880), Pt. 2. pp. 73–80; I. A. Shlyapkin, *op. cit.*, pp. xliv–xlvi (information as to copies of the tale) and 31–32 (the preserved fragment of the play on Melusine); D. Rovinskii, *op. cit.*, Vol. I, p. 482; Vol. IV, pp. 354–355.

[12] The tale was published from the eighteenth century copy of the antiquarian Pogodin by I. A. Shlyapkin in *Pamyatniki drevney pismennosti* (Monuments of Early Literature) (St. Petersburg, 1882). Another copy of it—also eighteenth century—is preserved in the Tikhonravov collection (Lenin All-Union Library), No. 324.

pire, in Czech-land, in the town of Prague, there ruled a king named Mechi-slav (later on he is called Mstislav and Stanislav), who had a son named Basil. Basil was "very pious and extremely good-looking, and his hair shone like gold, and because of his beauty his father nicknamed him Goldenhair." When the time came, Basil's father began to look about for a bride for him, but Basil learned from a merchant, also named Basil, that King Charles of France had a comely daughter named Polymestra whose beauty surpassed that of Basil Goldenhair, while her intelligence equaled his. The son asked his father to dispatch "polixars; that is to say, matchmakers" to King Charles, but the father tried to discourage his son's intention of suing for Polymestra's hand, arguing that since the French kingdom was great, illustrious, and rich, while the Czechish was small and poor, nothing but shame could come of the suit. Basil insisted, however, and his father gave in and dispatched emissaries to France "with great gifts" and the proposal of marriage. Both Polymestra and her father were in a fury as they gave audience to the match-makers. The daughter was so extremely exasperated that she smashed to bits the valuable cup sent her by Basil, with his proposal of marriage inscribed on the bottom. She also pronounced the following "ultimatum": "The bread shall not be grated, the hemp shall not be trod, the shoe shall not be put on the foot: bast sits down with a person who has shoestrings; a slave's son wishes to take the daughter of a king; this shall never be: a slave's son shall not take a king's daughter."

The infuriated Basil then started to plan how he might take vengeance on the princess and at the same time win her. Having received the blessing of his father and mother and taking his valuables with him, he embarked for France. He is accompanied by the merchant Basil and thirty "noble lads, sons of senators and knights," all of whom he gets to take the name Basil. He decides to pass as servant of the merchant Basil. Upon arriving in France, Basil Goldenhair sends the merchant Basil to the king with rich gifts while he himself stays on the ship and plays on the dulcimer so "very marvelously" that everyone in the city and at the king's court starts to dance. The king asks the merchant Basil to summon the marvelous musician to the palace, but the merchant suggests that the king himself do this, since in the king's presence he does not dare give orders to his servants; Prince Basil haughtily refuses to do the king's bidding, since he is not his slave and does not wish to be ruled by him. And only at the third summons, after receiving the ring from the hand of the merchant Basil as proof that his "lord" commands him to appear, does Prince Basil set out for the palace. He consents to play the dulcimer there only at the command of his "lord." His playing first makes everyone dance, then puts everyone to sleep. At the request of the princess the king buys Basil Goldenhair of his "lord," paying the full asking price set by the merchant: "Put him on a golden carpet and heap him from head to foot with red gold pieces; that is his price." The golden carpet and the gold pieces are carried off to the ship.

Basil Goldenhair lives at Charles' court in high honor, his only task being to divert the king and the princess by his playing. For the ten thousand pieces of gold that Charles had paid for him, he builds near Charles' palace a luxurious palace of his own, better than the king's, and takes his thirty lads into his service. Twice the princess plies Prince Basil with liquor in her room in an effort to get him to tell who he is, for she suspects that he is "not of lowly birth." Twice Basil pretends to be drunk and, upon leaving, asks to have someone accompany him home and carry his dulcimer, which he is afraid of breaking. Both times the princess sends maids in waiting with Basil and he entices them into his palace, captivating them by his beauty. On one of the maids he bestows a gold ring, on the other a gold chain. The princess, having heard from her two maids about the splendor in which Basil lives, accompanies him home the third time herself, disguised as a maid. Upon arriving, Basil takes the princess to his bedchamber, strips her and beats her with a lash, saying as he does so: "Here is how your loaf does not get grated, nor the hemp trodden, nor the shoe put on the foot; see how bast sits down with a person who has shoestrings; a slave's son wishes to take the daughter of a king, quoth she, but now the king's daughter has herself paid a visit to the slave's son." From these words Polymestra learns that the marvelous dulcimer player is Prince Basil. After beating the princess and chiding her for scorning him when he had sent his matchmakers to her, and then caressing her, Basil makes his revenge complete by ravishing her. The princess then asks Basil to marry her, saying that unless he does, she will take her own life to wipe out her disgrace. Now that he has had his revenge, Basil promises to make her his wife and bestows a wreath of gold upon her.

After telling the merchant Basil how he had treated the princess, Prince Basil sailed back to his own country. He left nailed to the gate of his palace a sheet of paper on which he had written who he really was and how he had treated the princess in revenge for her insulting behavior to him. The sheet was brought to the king and he forced his daughter to make full confession of how Basil had used her. After this, King Charles thrice sent emissaries to Basil beseeching him to marry his daughter, and only after the third time did Basil accede to Charles' request, go to France, and marry Polymestra. They lived in love and concord. After the death of Charles, and of his father, Basil became king of France and king of Czech-land. Two sons were born to him, one of whom was given the French kingdom, the other, the Czechish. Basil and Polymestra died at a ripe old age, leaving a goodly memory after them in the minds of their subjects.

Thus did Basil win the hand of the fastidious beauty, having first taken pitiless vengeance on her and likewise on her father for the disdain that they had shown him. Upon every possible occasion Basil derides those who had once insulted him. The king he puts in an utterly foolish and ridiculous position by getting him to interpret the dreams that he pretends to have had after the visits of Polymestra's two maids and Polymestra herself. Each time he "dreamed" about a doe, each better than the one before, with whom he has the same experience that he actually had with the princess' two maids and the princess herself, and each time the king reassures him by saying: "Your dream is a good one provided it comes true." And only when he has had his fill of vengeance and thereby wiped out the insult, does Basil take Polymestra to wife and thus obtain what he had set out after.

The original of the tale has up to the present not come to light. Judging chiefly by the content, the tale probably originated in Czech-land, but there is no reason to think that it came to us through a Polish translation as its publisher I. A. Shlyapkin thought and as almost all who have expressed themselves in any way about the tale have reiterated: there are no obvious Polisms in the Russian text, Shlyapkin's statement to the contrary notwithstanding. Furthermore the word *rezhi*, which probably goes back to the Czechish *říše*, leads one to postulate a Czechish original. There is more justification for the general description of the tale given by Shlyapkin in an introductory note to the edition:

This cleverly told tale bears traces of epic creation as found the world over: three times they ply the hero with liquor, three times he makes presents to the girls who see him home, three times messengers are sent, three times one and the same dream is told, thirty young men accompany the hero, epic repetitions are of constant occurrence, and so on. The subject itself, a quest for a bride, is one of the greatest favorites in all folk creation. So is the magic flute that sets everyone dancing. Consequently, the tale, being very close both in invention and in methods to the usage of Russian folk fantasy, could easily take on purely Russian locutions and a full-length Russian adage. The moral lesson with which the tale begins, itself bears the stamp of folk humor.

A. N. Veselovsky adduced a whole series of fairy-tale parallels, Russian and otherwise, to the tale of Basil Goldenhair, and arrived at the conclusion that the chief interest of our tale lay "in the wealth of fairy-tale motifs or rather in the way it runs completely true to fairy-tale form. This is simply a fairy tale masquerading as literature." [13] In a number of motifs the tale of Basil Goldenhair impinges upon the *byliny* about Solov Budimirovich and

[13] See A. N. Veselovskii, "Zametki po literature i narodnoy slovesnosti," I (Notes on Literature and Folk Literature, I), *Sbornik otd. russk. yaz. i slov.* (Collection of the Division of Russian Language and Literature of the Academy of Sciences) (St. Petersburg, 1883), Vol. XXXII, No. 7, pp. 62–80.

Basil Okulevich, a fact which has led students to postulate some Western prototype common to the tale and the *byliny* or, more convincingly, to discern the partial influence of this prototype on the assembling of separate motifs in the *byliny* indicated.[14]

At the beginning of the eighteenth century our tale was again rewritten, receiving the title: *History of the French Son*.[15]

From a Czechish source is also derived a tale very popular in its own country, that of Bruntsvik, translated here in the latter half of the thirteenth century, without doubt from a Czechish original. It is based on a thirteenth century German story about Reinfried of Braunschweig, given verse form in Czech-land during the fourteenth century and then in the next century turned back into prose again to form two folk books—about Shtilfried and about his son Bruntsvik. Only the book about Bruntsvik was translated into Russian. The story teems with the varied marvels Bruntsvik saw and the adventures that befell him.

After his father's death he had become king of Czech-land, but his craving for knightly exploits leads him to embark with thirty companions on a seven-year voyage, leaving his young wife at home. He suffers shipwreck, and one by one all his companions perish; a faithful old servant wraps him in a horsehide and a bird picks him up in its "foot" (claw) and bears him to far-off lands. While wandering over the mountains, Bruntsvik meets a lion and helps it to vanquish a ten-headed, fire-breathing dragon. From that moment the lion refuses to leave Bruntsvik. Accompanied by the lion, Bruntsvik sails for a certain town inhabited by monsters, people with one leg, one eye, dogs' heads, and so on. Olimbrius, the king of that place, had eyes front and back, and eighteen fingers on each hand. The king promises to help Bruntsvik get back to his own country if he will free the king's daughter Afrika, who has been abducted by a dragon-basilisk. After conquering, with the lion's help, the monsters guarding the gates of the fabulously rich and beautiful city where the basilisk lives, Bruntsvik next conquers, with the lion's cooperation, the incalculable number of reptiles and snakes that inhabit the city and then even the eighteen-tailed basilisk itself. After this he restores to her father the beautiful Afrika, who has two snakes' tails for legs

14 See M. G. Khalanskii, *Yuzhno-slavyanskie skazaniya o kraveliviche Marke v svyazi s proizvedeniami russkogo byelogo eposa* (South Slavic Legends of Prince Mark in Connection with Compositions of the Russian Bylina Epos) (Warsaw, 1894), Vol. II, pp. 321–334; Vs. F. Miller, *Ocherki russkoy narodnoy slovesnosti* (Outlines of Russian Folk Literature) (Moscow, 1897), Vol. I, pp. 212–216. A review of the question of the genesis of the *bylina* about Solov Budimirovich is given in A. I. Lyashchenko's "Byline o solov'e Budimirovich i saga o Garal'de, Sertum bibliologicum" (The Bylina about Solov Budimirovich and the Saga about Harald), *Sbornik v chest prof. A. I. Maleina* (Collection in Honor of Professor A. I. Malein) (Petrograd, 1922), pp. 94–136.

15 Published by S. F. Eleonskii in *Chteniya obshchestva istorii i drevnostey* (Papers of the Society of History and Antiquities) (1915), No. 3, *Smes'* (Miscellany), pp. 13–39.

and takes the form of a snake by day but at night assumes human aspect. Against his will Bruntsvik takes Afrika to wife, but afterward, finding the sword of steel, uses it to slay Olimbrius's whole kingdom, the king himself and his daughter Afrika, whereupon, in company with the lion, he takes ship for his own country. On the way Bruntsvik has many adventures, sees much of marvel, but though his life is often in danger, the sword of steel sees him through safely. Bruntsvik reaches his own country after the seven years that it had been agreed his wife was to wait for him, and she is now about to remarry. Changing into beggar's raiment, Bruntsvik makes his way unrecognized into his own house and there sees his wife by her bridegroom's side. Throwing into her wine cup the ring that she had given him at parting, he leaves the banquet. From the ring and from the inscription left by Bruntsvik on the gate of the house, they know who the stranger was who had left their midst. The bridegroom sets out in pursuit of Bruntsvik, but perishes along with his companions, smitten by the sword of steel and mauled by the lion. After a time Bruntsvik returns to his house once more and celebrates his reunion with his wife by giving a banquet to the whole town and bestowing lavish presents upon all. On the royal coat of arms which had formerly shown an eagle, a lion was now depicted, by Bruntsvik's order, alongside the eagle. After passing thirty years in perfect felicity, Bruntsvik dies. His two sons succeed him. The lion is incapable of facing life without its master and in grief goes to his tomb and dies.[16]

The return of a husband to his wife, after a stipulated period, in the guise of a vagrant, when the wife is about to marry another, the wife's recognition of her husband by a ring dropped into a glass of wine, and finally the husband's settling with the bridegroom, are all of them motifs found in the widely diffused plot hinging on a husband at his wife's wedding. They are specifically present in the numerous variants of the *bylina* about Dobryna Nikitich and Alyosha Popovich.

Mention was made above of the fact that several tales included in the *Deeds of the Romans* exist also in translations made independently of the translation of the collection itself. Among these belongs still another tale very popular here and known in a large number of separate copies, the story of *Apollonius of Tyre*, which derives from a nonextant, third century Greek romance of which Latin adaptations were later made, these being the source from which western European and Slavic versions of the tale

---

[16] Russian texts of the tale were published by M. Petrovskii in *Pamyatniki drevney pismennosti* (Monuments of Early Literature) (1888)—here a historico-literary study of the tale and a Russian translation of the Czechish text are also given—and by Yu. Polívka in her publication *Czech Academy of Sciences, Kronika o Bruncvikovi v ruské literatuře* (The Chronicle of Brunsvik in Russian Literature) (Prague, 1892). In making the latter edition, the publisher had a large number of MSS. at her disposal.

are drawn. The plot was used by Shakespeare and Lyly. The text found in the Polish *Deeds of the Romans* was translated from the Czechish. Apparently the Russian translation which circulated in separate copies was also made from the Czech.

The tale of *Apollonius of Tyre* has all the typical features of the ancient Greek romance. In it amorous intrigue is joined to fabulous adventure; the recognition motif leads to the inevitable denouement and makes the two ends meet.

The tale begins by telling how King Antioch, who reigned in the city of Antiochius, which he had built, fell in love, after his wife's death, with his daughter, she being the only woman of them all whose beauty equaled that of his dead spouse. Notwithstanding his daughter's obstinate refusal, Antioch enters into amorous relations with her. In order to drive off suitors, he makes the winning of her conditional upon the guessing of a riddle. Anyone who fails to guess the riddle will be put to death. Accordingly, all the many kings' and emperors' sons who aspire to the hand of Antioch's daughter are beheaded, for not one of them can guess the riddle propounded to him. The only suitor to succeed in guessing it was Apollonius, King of Tyre. The purport of the riddle was that the king was living with his own daughter. The enraged Antioch denied the correctness of the solution. With the threat of death upon him, Apollonius took to flight. A high price was put on his head. He retired to the city of Tarsus, where he had ingratiated himself with the citizens by help given them in time of famine. But not feeling secure in Tarsus, he sails away, suffers shipwreck, is rescued by a fisherman, and finds his way to the land of Cyprus. There, attracted by his playing and dancing, the king's daughter, Luchnitsa, falls in love with him. He becomes her teacher, and afterward, preferring him to the other suitors for her hand, and learning that he is king of Tyre, she marries him.

After some time, Apollonius finds out from ship captains calling in at Cyprus that Antioch and his daughter have been killed by lightning. He makes ready to go to his own land, to Tyre, intending to leave his pregnant wife temporarily at her father's, but the enamored Luchnitsa insists that her husband take her along. "O great King Apollonius!" she says: "O beloved, dearest to me in all the world! . . . I want to be with you always: if happiness comes, let us rejoice together; if misfortune awaits you, let us go through it together; with you I am even ready to die." Apollonius yields to his wife and together they set out for Tyre. On board ship Luchnitsa, with great difficulty, gives birth to a daughter, and afterward her body goes completely numb so that they think she is dead. In the meantime a fierce storm rises and the shipmasters, assuming a corpse on board to be the cause, entreat Apollonius to lower the dead woman into the sea. Though it gives him great pain, Apollonius has no choice but to yield to the entreaties of the shipmasters and they lower his wife, in her costly raiment, into a dory, having first placed under her head two thousand gold ducats and a note saying: "This queen is the daughter of a great king; for her many tears have been shed and there are many who now grieve." The boat bearing Apollonius' wife is driven ashore at the city of Ephesus. She is revived and becomes priestess to a pagan "goddess," living in ceaseless distress over her separation from Apollonius. His daughter, named Tarsia, Apollonius conveys to Tarsus for her upbringing. Tarsia's governess, envious of her beauty, plans to kill her, but pirates abduct Tarsia and sell her into a brothel, from which she is redeemed by the prince of the city to which the pirates had conveyed her.

Twenty years after the fatal voyage, still grieving inconsolably for his wife, Apollonius comes to Tarsus, where they inform him of the death of his daughter. The new grief impels Apollonius to set forth on another journey, and he vows to himself that he will not leave the ship for ten years. But at this point news reaches him of Tarsia, who is marrying her rescuer the prince, and later on, in Ephesus, Apollonius meets his wife. They all set out for Tyre. The inhabitants of Antiochius beseech Apollonius to become their king. The king of Cyprus gives half his kingdom to his daughter Luchnitsa and the other half to his granddaughter Tarsia. Apollonius becomes the father of a son, to whom, after living happily to a ripe old age, he turns over his kingdom.

The narrative is saturated with impassioned dialogue, chiefly put into the mouths of Apollonius, his wife, and daughter. The work also passed over into chapbook literature.[17]

Narrative reaching us from the West during the seventeenth century was of a very different quality from the narrative material to which we had been accustomed in Rus up to that time. First of all it was narrative of a purely secular nature, informed by mundane interests and expectations. Amorous intrigue is its invariable stock in trade. The hero wins the heart and hand of his beloved only after he has accomplished his quota of knightly deeds. To the lovers, love means not only joy but suffering as well. Everything imaginable is put in the way of their happiness and felicity, but they overcome all obstacles. Their lives are filled with sudden catastrophes and mis-

[17] Of the numerous Russian copies of the tale in its separate form, only one (eighteenth century) has been published—by N. S. Tikhonravov in *Letopisi russkoy literatury i drevnosti* (Chronicles of Russian Literature and Antiquity), Vol. I, pp. 1–33. Here may also be found historico-literary information about the Russian texts. See also M. Murko, "Die russische Übersetzung des Apollonius von Tyrus und der Gesta Romanorum, *Archiv für slavische Philologie*" (1891), XIV, pp. 405–421.

fortunes; they are long separated without hope of meeting, but after under-going many deprivations and dangers, they are united never more to part. Constancy in love is a distinguishing trait of the heroes of Western chivalric romance. as introduced to the Russian seventeenth century reader. This constancy distinguished Bova and Druzhnevna and more especially Peter and Magilena and Apollonius and Luchnitsa. It was also shown by Basil Goldenhair, notwithstanding his stern method of getting even with Poly-mestra for insulting him. Faithful love also triumphs in the tales about the Roman emperor Otto and about Bruntsvik. Peter and Magilena, Apollonius and Luchnitsa speak of their love for each other as love had never been spoken of before in Old Russian literature, where authors had generally avoided dwelling on romantic situations, at best only stating them. It was also an innovation that love and success in love should be made the aim of the hero's life and its *raison d'être*.

At the same time the behavior of the lovers does not depart from the tra-ditional ethics decreed by Old Russian patriarchal usage: an affair of the heart is crowned by "legal" marriage, succeeded by a long, happy, and harmonious wedded life. Characters in Western tales frequently had pious dispositions—take, for example, Peter and Magilena; in other cases, the tale of Bova, for instance, the hero was endowed with piety on Russian soil. The element of marvel, of the supernatural, found in numerous tales, also struck a note familiar to the Russian reader; it checked with that element of marvel which existed so abundantly in old translated tale, saint's legend, *bylina*, and fairy tale alike, and this fact led to its being emphasized in Russian adaptations. (Cf. again the tale of Bova.) Thus, in the new, it was possible at times to recognize the old and familiar things which had for centuries held a place in the moral and artistic consciousness of the Russian who liked something interesting to read.

COLLECTIONS OF ANECDOTES AND COMIC STORIES, FABLES, AND SO FORTH

During the seventeenth century, especially the latter half, translations were made here from the Polish and, to some extent, from the Latin and German of sundry secular narrative miscellanies made up of anecdotes, instructive or entertaining, jokes, fables, and, at times, indiscreet *novelle*. Russian seventeenth century manuscripts include copies of the so-called *Apothegms,* a collection, in four books, of sayings and stories connected with edifying actions and incidents of one sort or another from the lives of celebrated philosophers, eminent men, "honorable women and girls of discretion." Similar collections in Poland trace their origin to the *Apothegms* compiled at the end of the sixteenth century by Rey of Naglovits in imitation of numerous similar collections circulating in western Europe, particularly those brought together by Petrarch and Boccaccio. The original of the Russian translation was the Polish collection of Benyash Budny, first printed at the beginning of the seventeenth century and in the course of the century several times reprinted. In the eighteenth century this translation came out in printed editions in Moscow and in St. Petersburg, the earliest dating from 1711. Stories from the *Apothegms* were utilized in such eighteenth century publications as the *Sensible and Witty Comrade,* Kurganov's *Letter Writer,* satirical journals of the time, Chulkov's *Mocker,* and so on.

Let us quote, by way of example, an *Apothegm* story about Socrates. A certain madcap kicked Socrates in passing. When those about Socrates expressed surprise that he did not hale the rascal into court, Socrates said: "If a donkey had kicked me, would you have advised me to hale it into court?" The philosopher, not desiring to go to law with the numskull, meant by this that he saw little difference between a fool and an animal and that it was no more suitable to take the law on a scatterbrained fellow than on a dumb brute. Then several sayings of Socrates are given: "A thing done in haste is seldom done well"; "It is hard to work without hope of gain"; "A victory without an opponent is small fame," and so forth.[18]

In 1680 a translation was made from the Polish of some "humorous tales," the *Facetiae* or *Polish Miscellany,* which went back in the last analysis to the popular western European collections, in Latin, of Poggio Bracciolini, Heinrich Bebel, Frischlin, and Melander, and to analogous Italian, French, and German adaptations of them. A product of urban bourgeois literature, the *Facetiae* told, frequently with details very indiscreet from the contemporary viewpoint, and in jocular, often satirical, form, various happenings from the lives of simple-minded peasants, pleasure-loving ecclesiastics, and, more particularly, reckless and resourceful women.

Let us quote from the translated *Facetiae* two tales on the theme of womanly cunning. The first of these tells how a woman taught a bear its letters. A certain priest was falsely accused to the squire, who laid a heavy fine on him. The lord said he would only remit the fine if the priest taught a bear its letters. The distressed priest told his wife of the lord's verdict and she at once came to his aid. First she fed and tamed a bear, and afterward took a book, put pancakes between the leaves and taught the bear to turn the

---

[18] A few stories from a seventeenth century manuscript of the *Apothegms* are printed in Buslayev's *Istoricheskaya khrestomatiya* (Historical Anthology), Cols. 1387–1390.

leaves looking for pancakes and purr as it did so. When the lord saw the bear turning the leaves of the book and purring, he was so amused that he remitted the priest's penalty, saying as he did so: "A wife is a cunning creature, more prone to wiles than her husband." This facetia is a variant of the story about how Eulenspiegel in Erfurt taught a donkey its letters.

The second story tells how a wife commemorated her late husband. As his end drew near, a peasant enjoined his wife to sell a bullock after his death and spend the proceeds on a mass for his soul. The wife, seeing her husband at death's door, wept exceedingly and promised not only to carry out his instructions but to sell something of her own as well. When her husband died, the wife led the bullock to town to sell it, taking the cat along too. Of the butcher who wanted to buy the bullock she asked only one groschen, but stipulated that along with the bullock he buy the cat, for which she asked four gold ducats. The butcher considered this a high price for the cat, but paid it in order to get the bullock. Upon receiving the money, the woman laid by for herself the four gold pieces that were her proceeds from the cat, and used the groschen which she had got for the bullock to buy a mass for her husband's soul.[19]

Separate facetiae were subsequently used in such eighteenth century collections as *Merry Old Soul, Laughing Democritus,* Iv. Novikov's *Adventure of Ivan the Merchant's Son,* and so on.

With the *Facetiae* are associated several *novelle* from Boccaccio's *Decameron,* translated, apparently, from the Polish and at approximately the same time, the story of Griselda among them.[20]

In the roster of translated *novelle* of the seventeenth century should also be included the *Tale of Prince Baltasar,* which narrates in very frank terms the amorous adventures of women who hoodwink their husbands, and is known in a single Russian copy of the late seventeenth or early eighteenth century. The inextant or as yet undiscovered Western original of the *Tale of Baltasar* was apparently based on an Oriental folk tale. On Russian soil the story assimilated to some extent the elements of the oral-poetry style and was padded out with quotations from popular exhortations on the subject of evil women.[21]

---

[19] Texts of seventeenth century Russian translations of the *Facetiae* are printed in *Pamyatniki drevney pismennosti* (Monuments of Early Literature) (1878–1879), I, pp. 94–152, and in *Letopisi russkoy literatury i drevnosti* (Chronicles of Russian Literature and Antiquity), Vol. V, *Smes'* (Miscellany), pp. 56–89.

[20] See Pypin, *Ocherk literaturnoy istorii starinnykh povestey i skazok russkikh* (Sketch of the Literary History of Ancient Russian Tales and Folk Tales), pp. 276–278.

[21] The text of the tale is published in full as a supplement to N. K. Piksanov's book *Starorusskaya povest* (The Old Russian Tale), pp. 86–92. A study of it (uncompleted), giving considerable excerpts, may be found in I. N. Zhdanov's "Povest o koroleviche Valtasare i byliny o Samsone-Svyatogore" (The Tale of Prince Baltasar and the Byliny about Samson-Svyatogore), *Works*, Vol. I, pp. 842–869.

In place of the old-time *Stephanit and Ikhnilat,* we now had new Euro-peanized animal epos collections: Aesop's fables, twice translated from the Polish, in 1609 and 1675, the *Pageant of Human Life,* translated from the German or from the Latin by A. Vinius in 1674, and the fables of Lokman (in conjunction with two stories from Saadi's *Gyulistan*) in a late seven-teenth century translation from the German.[22] Finally, among translations made from the Polish during the latter half of the seventeenth century should be mentioned Ovid's *Metamorphoses* and a new rendering of the *History of the Judaic War* by Josephus Flavius.[23]

Such was the multifarious narrative material from the West that reached Rus in translation during the seventeenth century. A distinctive feature of this material, or more exactly of its fortunes here, was its extremely rapid "popularization," gaining for it a much wider circle of readers than previous literary material had been able to command. Outward manifestations of this popularization are the language of a number of the tales, rich in folklore elements, notations found on various story manuscripts indicating owner-ship by members of democratic strata, and finally the fact that tale, novel, facetia, relatively soon after translation, passed over into chapbook, fairy tale, religious poem or folk legend.

[22] See Pypin, *Ocherk* (Sketch), pp. 169–179.
[23] See A. Sobolevskii, *Perevodnaya literatura Moskovskoy Rusi XIV–XVII vv.* (Trans-lated Literature of Muscovite Rus in the Fourteenth to Seventeenth Centuries), pp. 96–97, 183.

Influence of the East

TALE OF ERUSLAN LAZAREVICH

IT was apparently at the beginning of the seventeenth century that the very popular tale of Eruslan Lazarevich, or Uruslan Zalazorevich first came out here: the oldest copy likewise dates from the seventeenth century. This tale goes back to an inextant Eastern original and is, presumably, the record of an oral retelling of a Turkish adaptation of two episodes from the Persian epic, Firdusi's *Shah-Nameh* (tenth century), interwoven with Eastern fairy-tale motifs. The central figure of the *Shah-Nameh* is Rustem, in the Turkish adaptation perverted into Arslan (lion), whence our Uruslan and later Eruslan, with the patronymic Zalazorevich, then Lazarevich, an adaptation from Zal-Zar, the Persian name of Rustem's father.[1] To judge from the application to Eruslan Lazarevich and his son of such expressions as "he went Cossacking in the open country" and "you are young, and have gone Cossacking early," our tale was composed among the Cossacks, who had, during the sixteenth and seventeenth centuries, repeatedly come to blows with Eastern peoples. From the earliest period of its existence here, the tale of Eruslan so far took on the traits of Russian life and became so closely linked with Russian folklore that we may justly count it among original works on borrowed subjects, as we do the tales of Oriental origin about Karp Sutulov and the unjust trial discussed below.

[1] On Eastern sources of the tale see I. V. Stasov, "O proiskhozhdenii russkikh bylin" (On the Origin of Russian Byliny), *Vestnik Yevropy* (Messenger of Europe) (1868), No. 1, pp. 171, ff., or *Collected Works* (St. Petersburg, 1894), Vol. III, pp. 948–985; O. Miller, "Il'ya Muromets i bogatyrstvo kievskoe" (Ilya Muromets and Kievan Bogatyrdom) (St. Petersburg, 1869), pp. 43–49; Vs. Miller's *Ekskursy v oblast' russkogo narodnogo eposa* (Excursions into the Province of the Russian Folk Epos) (Moscow, 1892), pp. 152–171; G. N. Potanin, *Vostochnye motivy v srednevekovom yevropeiskom epose* (Eastern Motifs in the Mediaeval European Epos) (Moscow, 1899), pp. 286–347.

432

In the oldest surviving copy the plot of the tale is as follows. Zalazar Zala-zorevich, uncle of Tsar Kirkous Kirkodanovich (Persian, "Keikaus") had a son Uruslan. "And Uruslan from his tenth year would go out on the street, and take hold of a boy's arm and pull it off or take hold of his leg and break it off." The princes and boyars and "powerful merchants" respectfully make complaint to Kirkous about Uruslan, saying that he "does not play nicely with their children." Uruslan gives ear to the reproaches of Zalazar, with whom Kirkous had brought the matter up, asks his father to build him a "palace of stone near the sea," put in it a saddle, a Tesmian bridle and a steel sword, and says he will live in that palace, but that if Tsar Kirkous should call him to service, he will not come. Uruslan took up life alone in the palace built for him, began to "stroll out from the palace down the curved shore, and, moving noiselessly along the creeks, learned to shoot geese and swans and in this way to feed himself." When he stretched the bow, it was like the Horde getting in motion, but when he shot, it was like a mighty thunderbolt crashing from the clouds. His father's aged groom Ivashka brings him the horse Arasha (Persian, "Rakhsh"), and upon receiving it, Uruslan lays a "Circassian saddle" upon it and betakes himself to the steppe, where a great army is drawn up, that he may "try his bogatyr shoulder." The army, as it turns out, is that of Tsar Kirkous and it is headed by Urus-lan's father. The army is fighting Prince Danilo the White. After receiving his father's blessing, Uruslan goes alone against the enormous host of the enemy and cuts it to pieces, but spares and releases Danilo inasmuch as he had appealed for mercy and had promised never again to plot against Tsar Kirkous and Prince Zalazar. He forgives Kirkous for banishing him, but none the less refuses to enter his service, though promising to help should need arise; he also refuses to accept any reward. Riding on and encountering the Russian bogatyr, Prince Ivan, Uruslan defeats him in single combat, fraternizes with him, and after vanquishing Feodulazmei, gives Prince Ivan the latter's beautiful daughter to wife.

Then, hearing from Ivan's wife that somewhere on the steppe there rove two princess sisters more beautiful than herself who even have maids to bring them water, and that there exists a man more daring than Uruslan, by name Ivashko the White of the Glade, and that he guards the Indian border, Uruslan, eager though he was to find these two princesses and make trial of his strength against Ivashka, decided first to visit his aging parents, but, upon reaching the kingdom of Kirkous, found it desolate. Perfidious Danilo the White had ravaged it and taken captive Kirkous, Zalazar and twelve bogatyrs. Uruslan dashed away on Arasha to Danilo's realm and found the captives in prison and blinded. From his father Uruslan learned that sight could be restored to him and the others by rubbing their eyes with the fresh liver and warm blood of the Green Tsar of the fiery shield and flaming spear. With the help of a sorceress maiden, transformed into a bird, Uruslan finds his way to the realm of the Green Tsar. Here he comes upon a scene of great carnage, in the midst of which lies the enormous human head of a bogatyr done to death by the Green Tsar, and under it a sword which, the head says, is the only thing that can slay the Green Tsar. Some time later, having served with the Green Tsar, Uruslan returns to the head, it rolls over, he picks up the sword and with it kills the tsar, then takes the liver and blood. After returning to the kingdom of Danilo the White and killing him, Uruslan heals Kirkous, Zalazar and the twelve bogatyrs. Then, having conducted them all to the kingdom of Kirkous, Uruslan "rode out into the open field Cossacking."

After many days he found the white tent with poppies of red Arabian gold in which dwelt the two princesses whom Ivan's wife had praised. Taking "to his couch" first the older sister, then the younger, he cut off the older sister's head because she had said that the Indian tsar had a guard, Ivashko the White of the Glade, who was bolder than Uruslan. From the sisters he learns that the king of India has a daughter who is much more beautiful than either of them. Having met Ivashko the White of the Glade and vanquished him, Uruslan rides on to the court of the Indian king and makes petition to enter his service. In the Indian kingdom he kills a "monster with three heads" that had dwelt in the city devouring one person each day, and that was preparing to devour the king's daughter on the morrow. At the bottom of the monster's lake he finds a precious stone the like of which did not exist in the whole land of India. As a reward for slaying the monster, Uruslan receives the king's daughter in marriage. On his wedding night, however, he deserts her: he had learned from her that in the City of the Sun there reigned a queen many times more beautiful than herself, and he sets out in search of the new beauty, bidding his wife if she bears a son to place on his hand a ring made from the precious stone that he had dredged from the lake, and if a daughter, to make her an earring of this stone.

Having reached the City of the Sun, Uruslan proceeded to live with the queen, who told him that there was no one in the whole world more beautiful than herself. He forgot his wife, the daughter of the Indian king, but in the meantime she bore him a son, likewise named Uruslan, and a bogatyr like his father. When he was twelve years old, he wished to "play at the sport of kings," but the "royal children of good stock and the children of great princes" began plaguing him and calling him a bastard. He complained to his mother and she told him whose son he was and where his father had gone. Choosing a good horse, the young Uruslan rode off in quest of his father. When they meet, Uruslan senior does not succeed in unhorsing him until the second round. By the stone in the ring he identifies his antagonist, then reveals himself to him. The son rebukes his father for having left his lawful wife to live with a woman to whom he is not married, and his father replies: "I am indeed at fault in this, but every man wants to enjoy himself while he is young, yet every age lasts but for a season; now it all seems useless to me nor do I intend to act thus in future." And leaving his unwedded wife, Uruslan Zalazorevich followed his son back to his legal wife in the kingdom of India. The Indian king gave him half his kingdom. From that time forth he lived "serenely" with his wife. To the king of India he made subject many cities and many kingdoms, emperors and kings and powerful bogatyrs and bold men. The young Uruslan did not remain long under his father's roof, but astride the knowing Arasha "roamed the open country—Cossacking," to "make trial of his bogatyr shoulder." [2]

As will appear even from this résumé, our tale is almost entirely written in the spoken language of the people, albeit employing certain Turkish words (*tebenki, kutas, tegilyai, saadak*), is permeated throughout with elements of Russian folklore, borrowed in generous quantities from *byliny* and fairy tales, and in turn exercised an influence on Russian fairy tales, particularly those about Ilya Muromets, separate episodes in *byliny* about Ilya deriving from a source in common with the *Tale*. Epic repetitions, rhythmic sentence structure, set formulae of speech, and fixed epithets all came into the tale from the folklore tradition. The Russianization of the tale is also shown in its social coloration. Besides being called by given name and patronymic, the characters, Uruslan in particular, adhere to Russian custom in their behavior. Prince Ivan, with whom Uruslan fraternizes, is a Russian bogatyr. Of himself Uruslan says that he is a "Russian" and a "Christian." He is not only a respectful son, but a pious man who prays to God in a crisis. When about to do battle with Ivashko the White of the Glade, he says, in reply to the latter's threat: "Brother Ivashko! Both of us are still in God's hands: God will help one of us against the other." After telling how Uruslan pierced Ivashko with a spear, the tale adds: "And then his fate was sealed: God did not confirm his boast." Curiously enough, the tale closes with the traditional colophon: "Now and evermore, world without end. Amen."

Elements of folklore and of Russian custom stand out still more prominently in later copies of the tale, for example, the copy in the Pogodin

---

[2] The copy upon which this retelling is based is in the V. M. Undolsky collection and comes from a miscellany which once belonged to a well known literary figure of the seventeenth century, Karion Istomin. Published by K. S. Tikhonravov in *Letopisi russkoy literatury i drevnosti* (Chronicles of Russian Literature and Antiquity), Vol. II, Bk. 4, Sec. 2, pp. 100–128.

seventeenth and eighteenth century archives,[3] where we find by collation with the Undolsky copy substantial changes in the order of episodes and a good many new details in the plot development itself. The following sentence will perhaps give some idea of the way folklore and custom enter into the style of this copy:

Nor does a stout falcon swoop down on geese and swans as Eruslan Lazarevich swooped down on mirzas and Tartars: he beat down and slew and unhorsed 170,000 mirzas and Tartars, but serving-people and boys in their ninth year he converted to the Christian faith and bade them kiss the cross in loyalty to Tsar Kartous and ordered them to abjure their Tartar faith . . . but having taken Prince Danilo the White, he banished him to a monastery and ordered him tonsured.

After Eruslan's victory over the "three-headed monster" in the lake, the tsar, whose name is here given as Bartholomey, comes out to meet him with the archbishop and "with the whole synod, and with crosses and with icons, with princes and with boyars and with all Orthodox Christians." When Eruslan's wife Nastasya Bartholomeyevna bore her son, she "gave him the baptismal name Ivan and the appellative Eruslon Eruslonovich."

Notwithstanding its Eastern origin, the tale of Eruslan Lazarevich also has a good deal in common with the Western romances of chivalry reaching us in the seventeenth century. It resembles them first in the wealth and variety of its fabulous-adventure elements. Ingrained in Eruslan as in the heroes of Western romances is the chivalric ideal of honor and nobility. In refusing the reward which Tsar Kirkous offers him for vanquishing the army of Danilo the White, Eruslan says: "Lord Tsar! I must choose one or the other: either amass riches or make my name as a bogatyr." Coming upon the bogatyr, Prince Ivan, asleep, Eruslan refrains from killing him. When Eruslan falls asleep, Ivan in turn thinks to himself: "It would be dishonorable for me as a bogatyr to kill a man in his sleep." Nor is Eruslan indifferent to amorous adventures, even though they play a less important part in his biography than they do with the heroes of Western romances, and though his love is not dyed with the deep and lasting emotion which Peter of the Golden Keys or Apollonius of Tyre entertained for the women they loved. Yet Eruslan, like his Western colleagues, finds a calm haven and complete happiness only beside his "lawful" spouse.

During the eighteenth century and down to the second decade of the twentieth, we get an uninterrupted succession of chapbook adaptations of the story of Eruslan, and popular prints based on it.[4] With the eighteenth

---

[3] Published by N. I. Kostomarov in *Pamyatniki starinnoy russkoy literatury* (Monuments of Ancient Russian Literature), II, pp. 325–339, and reprinted by B. I. Dunayev in the series *Biblioteka starorusskikh povestey* (Library of Old Russian Tales).

[4] See D. Rovinskii, *Russkie narodnye kartinki* (Russian Popular Prints), Vol. I, pp. 40–76; Vol. IV, pp. 27–34, 135–142; Vol. V, pp. 114–119.

century we begin to get literary adaptations also. Pushkin utilized in *Ruslan and Lyudmila* the episode of Ruslan's encounter with the bogatyr head. Finally, it inspired a fairy tale and is reflected in a Ukrainian charm against snake bite.[5]

[5] See B. and Yu. Sokolov, *Skazki i pesni Byelozerskogo kraya* (Folk Tales and Ballads of the Byelozersk Region) (Moscow, 1915), No. 115, and S. I. Savchenko, *Russkaya narodnaya skazka* (The Russian Popular Tale), pp. 52–53.

Original Russian Historical and Genre Narrative, Chiefly from the Latter Half of the Seventeenth Century

THE seventeenth century, particularly the latter half, is marked in Russian literary history by a notable development of narrative literature. In some works we still detect old, outworn motifs, and identify superannuated themes and plots thickly glossed with Christian piety, shot through with elements of marvel and legend, and perpetually reverting to the Devil's machinations as cause of all evil. In other cases the traditional themes are found in combination with a new, previously unexploited motif, sentimental love, still interpreted in the old-fashioned way as demoniac possession, but occupying a place of far from old-fashioned importance in the hero's life and in his destiny.

Historical narrative, departing from the well worn themes of the martial tale, with its ingrained qualities of supernaturalism and hyperbole, contains, as do many works in other genres, conspicuous elements of realism both in language and in treatment.

At this time we also begin to get narrative entirely free from any taint of piety, marvel, or the related ecclesiastical outlook on things, and informed by a purely secular attitude toward events and facts that is a far cry from the old established ethics. Moreover satire and parody now come into being, and are trained not only upon administrative practice but also upon the conduct and habits of church functionaries, nay more, upon the church service itself.

Each of these varied narrative developments is directly dependent on the social background that gave rise to it and the interests of the class that it served. The purely secular narrative without ecclesiastical bias, satire, and

438

parody are the creative product of the suburban "rank and file," the petty official nobility, the more forward-looking of the peasantry and, at times, even of semiecclesiastics who had in one way or another felt the pinch of church regulations. It was largely writers from these social strata who brought over into narrative literature the oral-poetry style and those folklore details which are frequently present even in works otherwise showing all the earmarks of literary antiquity.

Written entirely in the spirit of lingering tradition, except for the extensive infiltration, in many cases, of folklore elements, are a series of tales unmasking the "wicked woman," favorite object of scholarly attacks even during the earliest period. Thus the *Legend and Colloquy of a Wise and Affectionate Father . . . and His Son . . . Concerning the Wickedness of Women*,[1] written, to judge from the numerous references to "Holy Writ," by some ecclesiastic in the spirit of medieval discourses against "evil women," sets forth very graphically and picturesquely, though with unconscionable prolixity, the manifold vices of women. Though the son attempts to parry his father's angry thrusts at the female sex by quoting passages from "Holy Writ" mentioning good women, the father is not to be shaken and makes every effort to argue his son out of marrying. Before marriage a girl pretends to love her future husband, but, once married, she deceives him:

If he happens to be out of the house, she sits by the window, swaying this way and that, and is never still: she leaps and dances and moves her whole body, taps her sandals, waves her arms, and dances like the depraved adulteress Herodias, shakes her hips, vibrates her bangles, nods her head, sings with her voice, talks with her tongue, puts on many changes of devilish raiment, and often looks out the window, behaves like Herodias, and makes herself attractive to many youths and does everything to coax them to her side.

Substantially the same "evil woman" whom the fanatical misogynist-ecclesiastic so sternly unmasks, appears in two erotic tales, the *Parable of the Old Man* and the *Legend of a Young Man and a Girl*.[2] Both these tales, profoundly saturated with folklore elements, were penned by literate laymen

[1] Published in *Pamyatniki starinnoy russkoy literatury* (Monuments of Ancient Russian Literature), II, pp. 461–470.

[2] For texts, see *Pamyatniki starinnoy russkoy literatury* (Monuments of Ancient Russian Literature), II, pp. 453–454, as published by V. N. Peretts, Kiev *Universitetskie izvestiya* (University News) (1907), No. 8, pp. 77–80; Kh. Koparev's brochure, "Skazanie o molodtse i devitse, vnov' naidennaya eroticheskaya povest narodnoy literatury" (Legend of the Youth and the Maiden, a Newly Discovered Erotic Tale from Popular Literature), *Pamyatniki drevney pismennosti XCIX* (St. Petersburg, 1894), and the supplement to V. I. Dreznevski's article, "Skazanie o molodtse i devitse po spisku XVII v. v biblioteke Akademii nauk" (Legend of the Youth and the Maiden from a Seventeenth Century Copy in the Library of the Academy of Sciences), *Izv. otd. russk. yaz. i slov.* (News of the Division of Russian Language and Literature of the Academy of Sciences) (1906), Bk. 4, pp. 79–89 (reprinted in N. K. Piksanov's book, *Starorusskaya povest* (The Old Russian Tale), pp. 81–85.

and not only do not condemn women no better morally than the "wicked woman" depicted in the colloquy between father and son, but seem intended by their authors to invite the reader's full approval.

The theme of the "wicked woman" also occupies an important place in later tales about Solomon, protagonist of ancient apocryphas already discussed. In seventeenth century narrative recastings,[3] likewise reflecting to a high degree the oral-poetry element, he unmasks his erring mother Bathsheba and then his wife, who in one version was abducted by Kitovras, in another by the Indian tsar Por. These also tell how while still a child he astounded those about him by his wisdom, created law courts and became tsar over the peasant children. In this respect the tales about Solomon resemble the tale of the merchant Dimitry Basarga and his son Dobrosmysl (or Borzosmysl),[4] which also depicts a wise boy, and shows him getting his father and his father's traveling companions out of trouble by expert guessing of riddles, and cutting off the head of the infidel tsar Nesmeyan Gordyaevich and becoming tsar in his place.

Side by side with works depicting the "wicked woman," however, we get a seventeenth century tale about two "good women," not saints or nuns like the heroines of previous Russian literature, but ordinary women of the world. I refer to the Murom *Legend of the Phenomenon of the Unzhensk Cross*, which deals with two devoted sisters, separated by a misunderstanding between their husbands but reunited after the death of both husbands. To judge from the introduction, the tale was based on an earlier legend "written on a small parchment in crude language such as villagers speak." This tale in the vulgar idiom had with the approval of Church authorities been done over in literary ("artful") form by some scholar and is extant in this revision.[5]

Once upon a time, says the story, there were two sisters, Martha and Marya, nobleman's daughters, one of whom married a man named John from the province of Murom, the other a man named Login from the province of Ryazan. John was noble but poor, Login was of less distinguished birth, but rich. At a banquet at the home of some relatives the husbands had a quarrel on the subject of office holding by right of birth, ceased to meet, and forbade their wives to see each other or even exchange letters. A long time

[3] Published in *Letopisi russkoy literatury i drevnosti* (Chronicles of Russian Literature and Antiquity), Vol. IV, pp. 112–153.

[4] Texts of the tale in two redactions are published in *Pamyatniki starinnoy russkoy literatury* (Monuments of Ancient Russian Literature), II, pp. 347–356. See also V. N. Peretts's publication in the Kiev *Universitetskie izvestiya* (University News) (1907), No. 8, pp. 58–67.

[5] The *Legend* in two variants is published in *Pamyatniki starinnoy russkoy literatury* (Monuments of Ancient Russian Literature), I, pp. 55–59. On it, see Buslayev, "Ideal'nye zhenskie kharaktery drevney Rusi" (Ideal Woman Characters of Early Rus), *Istoricheskie ocherki* (Historical Sketches), II, pp. 245–251.

passed, then John and Login both died on the same day and at the same hour. Meanwhile the sisters grieved separately, neither knowing that the other had lost her husband, and simultaneously each thought of now going to live with her supposedly surviving brother-in-law. Both acted upon this thought. Simultaneously, accompanied by their servants, each started out for the other's house, met, but at first did not recognize each other, then, as recognition dawned, kissed with tears of joy, meanwhile grieving over the misunderstanding between their husbands that had sundered them for so long. Next we are told how an angel miraculously appeared to Martha and Marya in a dream and gave them gold and silver. Upon awakening, the sisters turned these over to three ancients who had come "at God's command" from Tsargrad, and who then made a cross of the gold and a shrine of the silver. The cross was set up in the church of the archangel Michael at Murom and proceeded to work many miracles.

As Buslayev pointed out, the *Legend* conforms to the icon-painting style of that time, where symbolism and a strict but naïve symmetry held sway. The heroines of the *Legend* are women whose whole lives are a series of symmetrical events. They both marry at the same time, their husbands both die in the same hour, simultaneously the sisters think of living together, simultaneously start out and, finally, at one and the same time have an identical dream and afterward find in their sleeves, one, gold, the other, silver.

Also traditional in theme are two tales about the Byzantine emperor Michael III,[6] composed, to judge from the language, which frequently resembles that found in works of oral poetry, in the same "depressed" social milieu as the above-mentioned later tales about Solomon.

STORY OF THE DON COSSACKS' DEFENSE OF AZOV

Among seventeenth century historical narratives, special literary interest attaches to the tales about Azov.

In 1637 the Don Cossacks took the city of Azov from the Turks. This they did without the cognizance of Tsar Michael Fyodorovich, who was then at peace with the Turkish sultan Murad. Immediately after the taking of Azov, Murad made ready to win it back, but in 1640, in the midst of his preparations, died. In the following year, 1641, the new sultan, Ibrahim I,

---

[6] Published as an appendix to M. N. Speranskii's study, "Evolyutsiya russkoy povesti v XVII v." (Evolution of the Russian Tale in the Seventeenth Century), *Trudy otdela drevnerusskoy literatury* (Works of the Division of Early Russian Literature) (1934), Vol. I, pp. 137–170.

marched on Azov, and besieged the city. Notwithstanding the enormous superiority of the Turkish forces, however, a four months' siege of Azov proved unsuccessful, and after twenty-four assaults it was raised. The Azov episodes inspired a number of literary works, apparently composed immediately after the event. Representative examples are the historical narrative of the taking of Azov by the Don Cossacks in 1637 and the documentary and poetical (to use A. S. Orlov's terminology) tale of the defense of Azov in 1641. The latter, extant in four redactions, takes the form of a report to Tsar Michael Fyodorovich, cast in a poetical mold to some extent influenced by *byliny* and by the tales of the rout of Mamay. Later on, apparently in the last quarter of the seventeenth century, based to some extent on the above-mentioned narratives about the taking and the defense of Azov, and, as A. S. Orlov suggests, under the influence of Cossack ballads of the Razin cycle, there came into being a fabulous (to use A. S. Orlov's terminology) *History of the Taking of Azov and of Its Defense Against the Turkish Tsar Ibrahim by the Don Cossacks*.

Let us make a study of one of the earliest redactions of the "poetical" tale of the defense of Azov. This tale shows greater artistry than others of the Azov cycle.

The narrative opens with a statement to the effect that in 1641 a written report of the siege was delivered to Tsar Michael Fyodorovich by Hetman Naum Vasilyev, Captain Fyodor Ivanov, and twenty-five Cossacks who had endured the siege with them. The "report" begins with a detailed description of the armed force that the Turkish sultan Ibrahim brought against Azov. The size of the Turkish and allied armies is indicated in the following picturesque terms: "Where our open steppe had been, there sprang up in an hour, so many were their troops, a great forest, dark and impenetrable. And what with the size of the Turkish army, and the horses galloping about, the ground under the city of Azov settled and the river Don overflowed its banks." The Turkish cannonading was as fierce as "thunder" crashing "from the sky" and lightning flashing, and the fire and smoke from it rose to heaven so that the sun itself was dimmed and darkness set in.

The Turkish sultan sends four emissaries who "fluently" address the Cossacks in the following words:

O people of God the heavenly king, no one led or sent you into the wilderness; like eagles soaring you fearlessly fly through the air, like lions fierce you roar in the wilderness. The Don Cossacks free and wild, our near neighbors, are of unsettled habits, crafty dwellers in the wilderness, wicked assassins and merciless brigands! Your eyes are hungry, your bellies unfilled. But have you thought upon whom you are heaping these colossal insults, this terrific barbarity? Here you defy one mighty ruler, the tsar of Turkey, while as yet not recognized by Rus as holy-Russian bogatyrs.

This unique peroration, alternating praise with vituperation, is followed by a rebuke to the Cossacks for taking the "dear heritage" of the sultan, the city of Azov, and a concluding demand that they clear the city that same night. The Cossacks will be permitted to take along all their gold and silver without let or hindrance. But if they refuse to obey the order, then on the morrow not one of them shall be left alive. There is no one in the world mightier than the Turkish tsar and the Cossacks have not as many hairs on their heads as there are Turkish troops before the city of Azov. Nor can the Cossacks expect help or relief from the Muscovite empire: no bread will be sent them from Rus. But if "fierce, free, Don" Cossackdom wishes to serve the Turkish tsar and bring him "their guilty robber heads" then the tsar will forgive the Cossacks for all their "former barbarity" and their present taking of Azov. He will confer great honor upon them, enrich them with vast and uncounted wealth, clothe them in costly raiment, and give them bogatyr patents bearing his royal golden seal. And people of all ages in Tsargrad shall bow to the Cossacks and shall call them the "noble, picked Cossack knights of the illustrious Don," and all the Mussulman and Greek and Persian hordes shall call them holy-Russian bogatyrs because, though their forces were small—five thousand troops—they did not tremble before the dread and invincible forces of the Turkish tsar, three hundred thousand strong.

In reply to this speech, the Cossacks declare that they know the "strength and pride" of the Turkish tsar and that they have long been expecting a visit from the Turks. The Turks say that they have three hundred thousand troops, but this does not frighten the Cossacks, who trust in God, the Virgin, and the holy saints, and in their comrades dwelling in the cities on the Don: from these they will receive succor. They continue:

And we are by birth slaves of the lord tsar of the great and illustrious Christian empire of Moscow, and our time-honored appellation is: Don Cossacks free and fearless. We shall fight him, your Turkish tsar, like a miserable swineherd; we, the free Cossacks, will make death the price of our lives. Where your great armies now stand there shall many Mussulman corpses of you be laid low by us Christians. . . . Your Turkish tsar in his foolish pride is no better than a mad dog. He professes to be God on high and by his titles puts his madness on record, the Mussulman!

And next, in true *Rout of Mamay* style, the Cossacks say:

Where now his great army roars and boasts in our fields, there before the city you shall tomorrow lie just so many corpses, brought low by our hand. Long have blue-gray eagles given cry in our land and black ravens croaked along the quiet Don, and wild beasts, the gray wolves, kept up a howling, while on our hills the brown foxes bark, awaiting your Mussulman corpses.

As to the Turks' alarming them by the assertion that no provisions will be sent them from Rus nor relief given them, the Cossacks themselves entertain no hopes of aid from that quarter: "And furthermore we ourselves know," they say, "how much valued we are in Rus, in the Muscovite state, and we know without being told how much use they have for us there." In Rus the Cossacks are less esteemed than a "stinking dog." They had fled thence "from eternal slavery, from bonded serfdom, from boyars and from government nobles." There will be no one in Rus to grieve for the Cossacks; everyone there would be glad of their speedy end; provisions have never come to them from there, but by the Lord the Cossacks have been fed on the steppe with all manner of beasts and with the fish of the sea. And here in passing they make mock of the Turks: "And we lure ourselves beautiful women from you in Tsargrad and get the pick of them, and with them we beget ourselves children that are also yours."

In spite of the insults that the Cossacks have endured from the Muscovite state, they respect it, for it is "populous, great, and extensive, and shines forth among the many states and the Mussulman, Persian, and Greek hordes like the sun in the sky." They honor the Muscovite tsar even though they took Azov against his will and expect the death penalty for having done so, honor him for being "owner of many states and hordes, with many Mussulman tsars as good as Ibrahim, the Turkish tsar, serving him, the great lord, in eternal slavery." The power and greatness of the Muscovite tsar are lauded in the Cossacks' reply almost to the limits of hyperbole. The Cossacks declare themselves his slaves; as Orthodox Christians they cannot serve the infidel tsar of Turkey, and ironically tell the emissaries what they propose to do to him:

As soon as the siege of Azov-town is lifted, we shall cross the sea and visit him, your tsar, before Tsargrad, and we shall take a look at the architecture of his Tsargrad and its beauty; there we shall talk everything over with him, the tsar of Turkey, provided he, the tsar, takes a fancy to our Cossack speech. To him, the tsar, will we serve our Cossack harquebuses and our sharp sabers.

The Cossacks refuse to enter into any negotiations with the pashas. They go so far as to remind them of a fifteenth century incident, the Turks' conquest of Tsargrad, when Emperor Constantine was murdered and countless thousands of Christians were slain and the thresholds of the churches stained with their blood. The Cossacks express a desire to reconquer Tsargrad, murder Tsar Ibrahim "with all his Mussulman pagans," and say that not until then can there be any talk of peace. After making a good many other caustic and insulting remarks to the messengers, comparing the "Mussulman" religion to a mad dog, promising on the morrow to regale the Turks on what "God has sent us lads in Azov," and finally calling the messengers themselves dogs, the Cossacks suggest that they go back and in future keep away from them "with their stupid talk."

Then the siege of the city is resumed. Assaults by the Turks alternate with sallies by the Cossacks. The Turks suffer enormous losses. As ransom for the bodies of their soldiers, the Turks offer the Cossacks a large sum of money, but the Cossacks refuse it. "We don't sell dead bodies to anyone," they answer. "We don't want your gold and silver; what we want is enduring fame. You dogs will not get so much as a chessman out of us Cossacks in Azov until we lads have cleansed our weapons by regaling all you Mussulmans on nothing less than what you have given us: a siege." In their decisive battle with the Turks, the Cossacks are fighting "for the Church of God, for the whole Muscovite state, and in the name of the tsar."

Twenty-five bitter assaults have been sustained by the besieged Cossacks; they are already almost worn out: their legs tremble under them, their hands will scarcely hold a weapon, their lips are deadly pale, their eyes seared with powder. Only one resource remains to them, their patron saint, John the Baptist, but instead of praying to him even now, they merely deplore their approaching end, and in expectation of it bid farewell to Tsar Michael Fyodorovich, the ecumenical patriarchs, the metropolitans, and so on, down to all Orthodox Christians, then to their native woods and fields, the Black Sea, the river Don. Their farewell to nature is particularly lyrical:

Farewell, dark forests and green oak groves. Farewell, open country and quiet creeks. Farewell, blue sea. Farewell, our lord, quiet Don Ivanovich; no longer will our hetman lead his terrible army along you, nor shoot wild beasts in the open country, nor catch fish in quiet Don Ivanovich.

But unexpectedly, when the Cossacks had completely despaired of their lives, the Turks precipitately broke camp and fled from their positions before Azov to the Black Sea, where the greater part of them perished in the bustle and panic. Most redactions of the tale attribute this panic-stricken flight of the Turks to the intervention of some heavenly power that aids the Cossacks and saps the strength of their enemies. The tale concludes:

Our small band and free Don Cossackdom were the instrument of bringing upon Ibrahim the eternal contempt of all lands, of tsars and kings, and giving our Orthodox Lord Tsar Great Prince Michael Fyodorovich, autocrat of all Russia, glory and enduring repute in the eyes of all Mussulman and Greek hordes, and our hetman Naum Vasilyev and his whole terrible and glorious Don army honor and eternal fame. And we are glad to serve the Lord Tsar of Moscow, not sparing our heads, faithfully and truly, world without end, Amen.

The tale is based on factual material; it sets forth with great accuracy and detail all the alarms and excursions of the siege of Azov, gives a detailed enumeration of the military forces participating in the siege, and also of the types of firearms at the disposal of the besiegers. How reliably the tale reports the circumstances, down to the estimated numbers of the Cossack and Turkish forces, may be demonstrated on the testimony of the Turkish traveler Evlia-Effendi, who was among the Turkish troops. His statements are in complete agreement with what we find in the tale. Various Russian historical documents relating to the events of the siege likewise admirably exemplify the factual reliability of the narrative.[7] But this factual material is given a lyric heightening proportionate to the tense drama of the besieged Don Cossacks' situation. The daring, courage, and warlike prowess of the heroes of Azov are sketched in almost legendary terms. The Cossacks are true knights, fearless, strong in mind and body, epic bogatyrs, manifesting prodigies of courage, with small forces stubbornly defending the beleaguered city against countless enemy troops. The magnitude of the Cossack exploit and its extraordinary character determine the epic cast of the narrative, which was composed under the influence of oral ballad poetry, and took over its typical inversions ("mountains terrible," "tents Turkish," "trumpets great," "eagles soaring," bogatyrs holy-Russian," "Azov-town," "Don-river," and so forth), very frequent use of apposition ("began they, the Turks," "you, thieves stupid," "enriched he, the lord," "from him, the great lord," "from him, the tsar Turkish," and so forth), folk-poetry epithets ("Steppe open," "open country," "forest dark," "women beautiful," "eagles blue-gray," "ravens black," "Don quiet," "oak groves green," "quiet creeks," and so forth).

The legendary prodigiousness of the event as described in the tale dictated a return to the traditional forms of the war-story style, with its introduction of the supernatural into battle scenes. The pointing up of the destructive ravages which a small Cossack army wrought in the enemy camp, with its enormous troop concentrations, is itself a method familiar from the old war stories. From them too come the descriptions of the extraordinary din and uproar produced by the enemy's trumpets, castanets, and drums; of the plaints about extreme weariness and fatigue, under which legs give out, lips are parched and bleeding, voice and hearing fail; and, finally, the mention of aid given the Cossacks by heavenly powers, now in the form of two young youths or two "young peasants" in white raiment, now in the form of a woman "fair and beautiful," in shining raiment, hovering in the air between John the Baptist and St. Nicholas. Sometimes the intercession of heavenly powers is revealed by the appearance of tears on an icon or in a

[7] On this see N. I. Sutt's special investigation of the "poetical" tale in "Povesti ob Azove" (Tales About Azov), *Uchenya zapiski kafedry russkoy literatury Mosk. Gosud. pedagogich. instituta* (Scholarly Notes of the Chair of Russian Literature of Moscow State Pedagogical Institute) (Moscow, 1939), Pt. 2, pp. 3–49.

church lamp. One edition of the tale says that the hetmans and Cossacks plainly saw "flowing from the image of John the Baptist, from dry wood, many tears, like a stream"; another edition says that they saw "in the churches of God lamps full of tears shed by the wonder-working icons."

One arresting feature of the tale is its mingling of the pompous archaic style with the vigorous spoken idiom, something that was to occur later on in the writings of Archpriest Avvakum. On the one hand we get the traditional impassioned and ecstatic phrases about the greatness and power of the Muscovite state, the Russian tsar, the Orthodox faith, and a rhetorical farewell to the Russian people from the tsar down to all Orthodox Christians that resemble the farewell lamentation of Boris in the anonymous *Legend;* on the other, vernacular reproaches and home thrusts launched at Moscow boyars and nobles and above all at the Turks, thrusts that surpass even Avvakum's writing in irony and sarcasm.

Like the Azov cycle as a whole, our tale was composed in democratic Cossack circles and accordingly constitutes an extraordinary example of their creative work. While reflecting the energetic protest of the Cossacks against the economic domination of the wealthy upper classes of Moscow, it at the same time reflects no less truly the world outlook of that part of Cossackdom which considered as inviolable and immune to criticism the foundations on which, as personified in the tsar and the Orthodox Church, the governmental and religious practice of Moscow rested.[8]

8 For texts of the tales about Azov (the "folk-tale" version excepted) see A. S. Orlov's *Istoricheskie i poeticheskie povesti ob Azove (vzyatie 1637 g. i osadnoe sidenie 1641 g.)* (Historical and Poetical Tales About Azov [Its Taking in 1637 and the Siege of 1641]) (Moscow, 1906). See also *ibid., Skazochnye povesti ob Azove, "Istoriya 7135 goda"* (Fabulous Tales About Azov, History of the Year 7135) (Warsaw, 1906), including text of the "folk-tale" story of Azov; *ibid., Ob osobennostyakh formy russkikh voinskikh povestey* (On the Stylistic Idiosyncrasies of the War Narratives) where various passages relate the style of the tales about Azov to the traditional war-story style. For a restored text of the "poetical" tale about Azov, on the basis of all available copies, see N. I. Sutt, *op. cit.,* pp. 50–67. The above quotations come from this text.

In the category of seventeenth century historical narrative also belong the Siberian chronicles, the Stroganov, the Esipov, and the Remezov, which appeared in the 1620's and 1630's and tell of Yermak's conquest of Siberia (St. Petersburg, Archaeographical Commission, 1907); on them, see S. V. Bakhrushin, *Ocherki po istorii kolonizatsii Sibiri v XVI i XVII vv.* (Outlines in the History of the Colonization of Siberia in the Sixteenth and Seventeenth Centuries) (Moscow, 1927), pp. 1–35. Greatest literary interest attaches to the Stroganov and Remezov chronicles, owing to the large number of folklore motifs entering in. This is particularly true of the Remezov chronicle: see S. V. Bakhrushin, "Tuzemnye legendy v *Sibirskoy istorii* S. *Remezova"* (Native Legends in the Siberian History of S. Remezov), *Istoricheskie izvestiya* (Historical News) (Moscow, 1916), Nos. 3–4, pp. 3–28. The Esipov Chronicle is markedly traditional in its use of the elaborate rhetorical style. To its author, Savva Esipov, may perhaps also be attributed the martial tale of an attack by Tartars and Kalmyks in the 1630's on Siberian cities, notably Tara and Tyumen. The text of the tale and a study of it may be found in M. N. Speranskii's "Povest' o gorodakh Tare i Tyumeni" (Tale of the Cities of Tara and Tyumen), *Trudy komissii po drevnerusskoy literature* (Works of the Committee on Early Russian Literature), I, pp. 13–32.

TALE OF GORE-ZLOCHASTIE

The remarkable verse *Tale of Gore-Zlochastie* (Woe-Misfortune): *How Woe-Misfortune Caused a Youth to Turn Monk,* ranks as a major work of world literature. It is extant in a single copy from the first half of the eighteenth century but apparently came out at about the middle of the seventeenth century. It literally starts from Adam:

> By the will of Lord God and our Saviour
> Jesus Christ the Almighty,
> from the dawn of the human era . . .
> At the dawn of this life corruptible
> created He heaven and earth,
> created God Adam and Eve,
> bade them in holy Paradise to dwell,
> gave them this sacred command:
> not to taste of the fruit of the vine
> that grew on the great tree of Eden.

Adam and Eve broke God's commandment and tasted the fruit of the vine and for so doing were banished from Paradise and made to dwell on the earth where they were told to grow and multiply and subsist by their own labors. And from Adam and Eve is mankind descended:

> To paternal teaching unreceptive,
> To its mother's wishes not submissive,
> To friendly counselors deceptive.

For all these transgressions the Lord became wroth at the human family and sent upon it great calamities and afflictions in order to make men humble and bring them to the "way of salvation."

This exposition is followed by the story of the hero himself—a youth. His father and mother undertook to teach him, to put him on the right path, and instructed him in the traditional norms of worldly conduct, the observance of which would enable the youth to guard against the temptations with which the ways of human life are sown:

> "Go not, child, to feasts and celebrations;
> Do not sit thee in the higher place;
> Drink not, child, two beakers at one time!
> Nor let your eyes rove, child, where'er they will—
> Do not be tempted, child, by good fair-women,
> Daughters with fathers!
> Do not lie down, child, in a place deserted;
> Fear not the wise man, fear the fool,
> Lest fools for you lay snares,
> And lest they strip you of your costly clothes."

And the youth's parents teach him more things of the same sort, in the style of the precepts in the *Domostroy*. But youths will be youths and turn a deaf ear to the advice of their parents and attempt to live as they think best and as they please:

> The youth was young and foolish at that time,
> His mind unripe, his reason undeveloped—
> He felt ashamed his father to obey
> Or to his mother's wishes deference pay,
> Preferred to live his life as pleased his fancy.

As he acquired money, he acquired friends, and

> His honor like a river flowed—
> Folk fastened to the youth in friendship's name
> And members of his family became.

One of these friends grew particularly attached to him, declaring that he was his "sworn brother" and pressing him to come to the tavern yard. There he brought him a goblet of green wine and a mug of heady beer and advised him to lie down and sleep where he had drunk, relying upon his sworn brother to sit beside him and look after him.

The heedless and confiding youth trusted to his friend, drank himself insensible, and where he had drunk there lay down and slept.

The day passes; evening draws on. The youth awakes and sees that he has been stripped to the skin, is covered only with rags, that a brick has been placed under his unruly head, and that his "dear friend" has disappeared. The youth arrayed himself in the tatters that had been left him, spoke ironically of his "great life" and of the inconstancy of his friends, decided that it would be disgraceful to show himself in such a state to his father, his mother, his relatives and friends, and went to a far-off foreign land, where he happens in on a banquet the first thing. The banqueters receive him very affably because he conducts himself "according to the written instruction," and seat him at the oaken table—

> Not in a great place and not in a small,
> They seat him in the midst of the hall
> Where the merchants' sons are seated.

But the youth sits joyless at the banquet. Those present remark on it and ask him the cause of his sorrow. He frankly tells them that he is being punished for "disobedience to his parents" and asks them to teach him how to live. The "good people" take a hand in the youth's destiny and, just as his parents had previously done, give him a series of salutary practical precepts to help him get on his feet again:

> "In a foreign land be not haughty,
> Submit to friend and foe,
> Bow to old and young,
> Don't call other people's affairs to attention,
> And what you hear or see do not mention."

The youth listens attentively to the counsels of the good people, goes on to another foreign country, and there begins to live "wisely." He acquires greater wealth than before and wishes to marry. Having sought out a bride, he plans a banquet, invites the guests, and then, "through God's sufferance and the Devil's agency," makes the fatal mistake that is to cause all his future misfortunes. He boasts that he "is making a better living than before . . . but a boastful word is always rotten." Gore-Zlochastie overhears the youth's boast and says:

> "Boast not, young man, of your fortune,
> Don't brag about your wealth—
> I, Gore, have known people,
> Both wiser and smarter than you,
> That I, Gore, have outwitted:
> Great misfortune befell them—
> Till death with me they contended,
> Disgrace their misfortune attended—
> They could not elude me, Gore,
> Until their very life ended."

That is the first misleading impression that Gore-Zlochastie introduces into the youth's mind. Afterward Gore appears to him in a dream and whispers bad advice in his ear, tells him to cease mending his ways, to renounce his betrothed, drink up all his possessions and tramp the wide world naked and barefoot without any worries. It frightens the young man by telling him that his wife will poison him for his gold and silver, and cozens him with the promise that Gore will leave him at the tavern, that it will not pursue a naked man, "for to the naked, the barefoot, robbery is an empty threat."

The youth did not give credence to this dream, whereupon Gore-Zlochastie appears to him again, in the form of the archangel Gabriel, and sketches the advantages of the free life of the naked and barefoot, who is not beaten, nor tortured, nor banished from paradise. To this dream the youth did give credence, drank up his possessions, cast aside his merchant's dress, put on tavern sackcloth and took to the road, bound for parts unknown. On his way he came to a river and on the other side of the river were ferrymen and they demanded a fee of the youth for their services and he had nothing to give them. The youth sits the whole day until evening by the river with nothing to eat, and in despair decides to throw himself into the swift stream in order to escape his grievous lot, but Gore, barefoot, naked, girded with a bast thong, leaps from behind a rock and restrains the youth. It reminds him of his disobedience to his parents, demands that the youth obey and bow down to it, Gore, and says that then he will be ferried across the river. The youth does as he is bid, begins to feel cheerful and, as he walks along the bank, starts singing a song:

> "My mother bore me free from care,
> With a comb arranged my curly hair,
> In costly garments dressed me fair
> And shading her eyes stood back to look at me there:
> 'Say does my child look well in costly garments?—
> In costly garments he is something no money could buy!'"

The ferrymen liked the youth's song, ferried him gratis to the other side of the river, gave him food and drink, dressed him in peasant clothes and advised him to go penitently back to his parents. The youth sets out for his own country, but Gore pursues him yet more assiduously:

> Like a stout falcon the youth took wing—
> Like a white gyrfalcon Gore flew after him;
> Like a blue-gray pigeon the youth took wing—
> Like a gray hawk Gore flew after him;
> Like a gray wolf the youth took the field,
> But Gore with swift hounds sped after.

It is impossible to escape from Gore-Zlochastie, which now teaches the youth to live in wealth, to kill and rob, so that he may be hanged for it or cast into the river with a stone tied to him. Just in time the youth bethinks himself of the "way of salvation" and goes to a monastery to be shorn a monk, while Gore stops outside the holy gates and from that time forth ceases to pester him.

In no Russian work previous to this do we find the destiny of an ordinary layman and the principal stages of his life set forth. Old-time narratives featured either ascetics and saints, or—more rarely—historical personages, whose lives, or more precisely, whose "legendary lives," are described in the traditional style of conventional ecclesiastical biography. The *Tale of Gore-Zlochastie* deals with the fate of an unknown youth who breaks time-honored precepts and pays a heavy price for so doing. The youth is rescued from total perdition by the "way of salvation" which leads him to a monastery, at the walls of which the Woe-Misfortune which had dogged his footsteps leaves him. The youth had taken a notion to scorn old-time manners and morals, had decided to live "as he pleased," paying no heed to parental prohibitions, hence all his calamities. He very nearly got back on his feet again after his first fall from grace, began—on good people's advice—to live as his parents had taught him, but was too conceited, felt too confident of himself and of the success he had achieved, boasted, and was at once seized upon by the relentless Gore-Zlochastie, which broke his stubborn will, transformed him into a pitiable, lost man.

The picture of Gore-Zlochastie, of doom, of fate, given in our story is a very notable literary image. Gore simultaneously symbolizes an outward force hostile to man and an inner state of man, a spiritual bankruptcy. It is, in a way, his double. The youth, having on impulse transgressed the boundaries set by the pious past, has now no curb on his impulses, and can no longer achieve salvation under the traditional conditions of secular life from which he had dared to depart, but only in a monastery, where he is forbidden any manifestations of independent initiative, even such as were permitted by the strict forms of *Domostroy* practice. Such was the terrible penalty that the youth brought down on his own head by transgressing the commandments of his fathers and thinking to live "as he liked," not as the sacrosanct past had ordained. For the time being, victory is on the side of the latter, of the past; for the time being, the past triumphs over the awakening individualistic impulses of the younger generation. This is the fundamental idea brought out in a tale which describes with exceptional talent the fate of "children" at the turning point between two epochs.

It is typical, however, that the story does not treat the monastic life as an ideal or even as a norm, but as a sort of specific for the man who cannot adjust his secular life to the rules laid down by old established tradition. Withdrawal to a monastery is for the youth the painful but only way out of the failure he has made of life. Not without reason does the title promise a tale of how Gore-Zlochastie, an evil force, got a youth into its power and caused him to turn monk. The monastic life, not long since treated as the best and highest form of existence, to which every pious person ought to aspire, is shown in our tale as the lot of the sinner, of the man driven to it to atone for grievous errors. An author who reasoned in this manner is more likely to have come from a secular than from a monastic milieu. This supposition is borne out not only by the whole style of the story, permeated as it is with secular folklore elements, but by the image of Gore-Zlochastie itself, ill fate, as distinguished from the traditional enemy of mankind, the Devil. The tale reflects the life of the conservative merchant class, and very probably the author himself belonged either to this or to the related class of tradespeople in general.

Oral-poetry elements color the *Tale of Gore-Zlochastie* almost all the way through. What first strikes the eye is its practical identity in metrical form with *bylina* verse; what next arrests attention is the presence of *bylina* commonplaces such as happening in upon a banquet and boasting at a banquet. Other links with *bylina* verse are its manner of repeating individual words

("Trust to, trust to me, your sworn brother"; "and thence set forth, set forth the youth to a foreign land"; "at the hand, at the right hand," and so forth), its use of tautological combinations ("He sorrows in grief," "steal-rob," "feed-eat," "family-clan," and so forth), and the employment of fixed epithets ("fierce winds," "unruly head," "swift river," "green wine," "oaken table," and many others). In style the *Tale of Gore-Zlochastie* also has a good deal in common with the oral lyric ballad, this coinciding in many respects, however, with the *bylina* style.

But side by side with these elements from the oral-poetry tradition, clear traces of the learned tradition may also be detected. These are first manifest at the very beginning of the story, in the introduction setting forth the coming of sin upon earth in consequence of Adam and Eve's breaking God's commandment not to taste of the fruit of the vine. They are likewise present in the closing lines. Both the beginning and the end relate the tale to the saint's life genre. The learned tradition is further represented by certain typically bookish epithets.

The youth's misfortunes, Gore-Zlochastie's getting him into its power, are shown to have been the result of his drunken debauch. Gore itself says: "But my nest and patrimony are among the frequenters of pothouses." Many works had been written in this country on the theme of the pernicious effect of intoxicating beverages. Manuscripts of the *Discourse of the Philosopher Cyril, the Slovenian* were known in Rus as early as the fifteenth century. This work took the form of an appeal "to all men: to the priestly order, to princes and boyars, to servants and merchants, to rich and poor, and to women." The hop itself is the preacher, and employs such proverbs and sayings as: "Lying long will no goods get but woe from which there's no escape. Asleep your prayers you cannot say nor fame and honor gain; sugary morsels do not eat, the mead cup do not drain, lest you into disfavor fall and unseen of the prince remain. Those who displease the prince are jailed, his lash is on their shoulders laid, sorrow and grief in their hungry loins tintinnabulate," and so forth. Many works in prose and verse, apparently based on the *Discourse of the Philosopher Cyril* were promulgated during the seventeenth century on the subject of the hop vine, alternate of the apocryphal grape vine, which is also mentioned in the *Tale of Gore-Zlochastie*. Examples are the *Tale of the High-Minded Hop and the Low-Minded Drunkard,* the *Tale of How Vinous Drinks Came to Be,* a parable of the hop, a legend of the origin of distillation, *Discourse on the Lazy, the Drowsy, and the Drunken,* and so forth. In several of these works, as in the *Discourse of the Philosopher Cyril,* the hop itself tells of the misfortunes that it causes its devotees. Thus, in the *Tale of the High-Minded Hop,* it declares to a confirmed drunkard who has sobered up:

"If a rich man takes a fancy to me, I drive him to sorrow and folly, and he shall walk in torn garments and broken shoes, and start asking people for loans. . . . If a wise workman clever at his trade seeks my friendship, I take away his skill and ability and sense, and do as I like with him, and make him as one of the crazed."

A large number of ballads about woe, Great Russian, Ukrainian, and White Russian, are preserved in later recordings.[9] In one group, the motive of woe is worked out as applied to woman's lot, in another it is linked with the figure of a goodly youth. In both groups we find many correspondences with this tale not only in the matter of separate situations but also as to poetical formulae and individual expressions. It is, however, very difficult to determine with certainty where ballads influenced the tale and where the influence was in the opposite direction. The fact that we possess a considerable ballad tradition connected with the theme of woe, while the tale is extant in only one copy, evidence of its having had no wide popularity, fosters the supposition that oral poetry's influence on the tale was more pronounced than the tale's influence on oral poetry.

So extensive a penetration of folklore into book literature as we see in our tale could have occurred only in the seventeenth century, when popular poetry was little by little beginning to work itself free of the ban which for centuries had been imposed upon it by the Church. The whole history of

[9] *The Tale of Gore-Zlochastie* has been published several times. The best edition is that of P. K. Simoni in *Pamyatniki starinnogo russkogo yazyka i slovesnosti XV-XVIII stoletii* (Monuments of Ancient Russian Language and Literature of the Fifteenth and Eighteenth Centuries) (St. Petersburg, Academy of Sciences, 1907), 2nd ed., Pt. 7. The text is supplemented by a metrical reconstruction of the monument. On the story see Buslayev, *Tale of Gore-Zlochastie, Istoricheskie Ocherki* (Historical Sketches), I, pp. 548–643. The author quotes a large number of parallels from Russian and western European literature, but as opposed to Pypin and Kostomarov, who considered the story a scholarly work, Buslayev on insufficient grounds regards it as an oral work akin to the devotional poems. A. V. Markov takes the same general view in his article "Povest' o Gore-Zlochastii," in *Zhivaya starina* (The Living Past) (1913), Pts. 1, 2. The latest student of the tale, V. F. Rzhiga, in "Povest' o Gore-Zlochastii i pesni o Gore" (The Tale of Gore-Zlochastie and the Ballads About Woe) (*Slavia*, 1931), Pt. 1, pp. 40–66; Pt. 2, pp. 288–315, after analyzing in very great detail the oral and learned elements in the tale, rearrives at its learned origin. He also suggests that the ballads about Woe applying to woman's lot influenced the story, while those in which a goodly youth figures were influenced by it. See also A. I. Sonni, "Gore i Dolya v narodnoy skazke" (Woe and Fate in the Popular Tale), *Kiev Universitetskie izvestiya* (Kiev University News) (1906), No. 10, pp. 1–64, especially pp. 59–64. Judging from a printed statement, P. K. Simoni (in a report given before the Institute of Literature of the Academy of Sciences) is inclined to date the *Tale of Gore-Zlochastie* as of the end of the sixteenth or the very beginning of the seventeenth century. In his opinion the tale was a fledgling of Novgorod culture and its author the Muscovite archpriest Terentius, who was, to quote P. K. Simoni, a brilliant representative of the literary school, a great connoisseur and lover of the language of folk poetry (see *Sovietskii fol'klor* [Soviet Folklore] [1936], Nos. 2–3, p. 459). Without knowing P. K. Simoni's argument in defense of his hypothesis, it is difficult to express a definite opinion about it. We know the archpriest Terentius among other things as author of articles on the "Disorder," included in the second edition of the *Chronograph*. But the style of these articles has little in common with that of the *Tale of Gore-Zlochastie*.

Russian literature up to this point will not yield a single example possessing so rich a vein of oral poetry material as is found in this tale.

TALE OF SAVVA GRUDTSYN

A youth who attempts to deviate from the code bequeathed by pious antiquity and who pays for the experiment by being shorn a monk is likewise the central figure in another work, extant in several copies from the seventeenth century and later. In one of these copies it is entitled: *The Very Marvelous Tale of What Happened in Ancient Times and Years to Thomas Grudtsyn, Merchant of Great Ustyug, His Son Savva, How He Gave a Deed Against His Person to the Devil and How He Was Delivered Through the Compassion of the Holy Virgin of Kazan.* In another copy the title runs thus: *A Very Miraculous and Astonishing Tale of What Happened (When for Our Sins There Was Persecution of Christians by the Russian State Through the Impious Heretic Grishka Otrepyev, a Recreant Monk) in the Town of Kazan, to a Certain Merchant Thomas Grudtsyn, His Son Savva.*

Savva Grudtsyn was the son of staid and pious parents. According to the story, his father, the rich merchant Thomas Grudtsyn, had, in 1606, been compelled by events of the "Epoch of Disorder," to move from Ustyug to Kazan, whence he made trading trips to various places down the Volga, even calling in at Persia. He likewise trained his son in the merchant's trade from childhood. Some time later, when setting out for Persia, Thomas directed Savva to sail with the merchant fleet to Soli-Kamska. Upon reaching the city of Oryol in that province, Savva stopped at an inn kept by a good friend of Thomas's. In the same city dwelt an aged and wealthy citizen by the name of Bazhen II, a friend of Savva's father, married for the third time and to a young woman. When he learned that Savva was living in Oryol, his affection for the latter's father moved him to insist that the youth come and stop at his house. Savva gladly accepted the offer and lived at Bazhen's house quite content. But the Devil, that "detester of the good," awakened in Bazhen's wife wanton feelings toward the youth, "for it is woman's nature to snare young men's minds to love-making." Savva yields to temptation and abandons himself to unbridled passion, recking neither of Sundays nor holidays. On the eve of the Feast of the Ascension of Christ, however, as though pierced "by some arrow of the fear of God," Savva refused to go near Bazhen's wife, for all her persistent urging. Then, blazing with anger, the woman plotted to get the youth to drink a magic potion. Her plot succeeded.

After he had drunk the potion, Savva's "heart was filled with anguish and pain for the woman"; while she, pretending to be completely indifferent, accused him to her husband, who was obliged, albeit with regret, to show him out of the house. Savva returns to the inn and grieves so inconsolably that "his great suffering makes the beauty of his face to fade and his flesh to waste away." The host of the inn, feeling great sympathy for Savva and not knowing the cause of his woe, consults a sorcerer about him.

One noon, going outside the city to take his mind off his troubles by a stroll, Savva thought to himself that if any man, or even if the Devil himself, could give him back his lost love, he would enter the Devil's service. At that moment he heard a voice from behind calling him, and when he turned he saw, running at top speed to catch up with him, a youth, or more exactly, the Devil, "who is always scouring about, seeking to destroy human souls." Saying that he was Savva's kinsman, a member of the Grudtsyn-Usov family, he proposed that he consider him his friend and brother and rely on him for help in all matters. Savva was delighted with his unexpected relative, but refused to confide to him the cause of his sorrow, whereupon the Devil said that he knew the reason himself: Bazhen's wife had cooled toward him. Savva promised to recompense his kinsman lavishly if he would help him win back the heart of Bazhen's wife, but the Devil replied that his father was immeasurably richer than Savva's father, and therefore he had no need of riches; for his services he asked only "a little sample of his handwriting." Suspecting no harm and not properly grasping what was in it, Savva without hesitation put his "handwriting" on the document, never guessing that thereby he was renouncing Christ and committing himself to the Devil's service. Giving directions for finding him, the Devil bids Savva betake himself to Bazhen, who will be delighted to receive him again into his house. Amorous relations between the youth and Bazhen's wife are resumed: rumors of her son's wayward conduct reach his mother in Kazan and twice she sends him reproachful letters adjuring him to return home, but Savva scoffs at his mother's letters and pays them no heed, abandoning himself as before to his wanton ways.

Some time later, the Devil takes Savva for a walk outside the city, and having explained that he is not Savva's kinsman but a tsar's son, conducts him to a certain hill and from there shows him a splendid city in his father's kingdom. Brought before a throne on which the "Prince of Darkness" is seated in all his splendor, Savva, at the Devil's suggestion, bows to Satan and gives him the "handwriting," even now not suspecting what it is all about. Upon returning from the kingdom of Satan, he resumes his dissolute life.

In the meantime Thomas, Savva's father, returns from Persia and, upon learning from his wife of his son's conduct, sends him a letter urging him to return to Kazan, but when Savva pays no more attention to this letter than he had to his mother's, his father decides to go to Oryol in person and get his son out of there; the Devil, however, upon learning of Thomas's intention offers Savva a trip to various cities, which Savva readily accepts. In the course of a single night the Devil and Savva reach the city of Kozmodemyansk on the Volga, eight hundred and forty versts from Oryol, and, after stopping there for a short time, make another night journey to the village of Pavlov Perevoz on the Oka. There Savva chances upon a certain holy monk clothed in rags, who bemoans his downfall and informs him that his traveling companion is the Devil and that Savva has betrayed himself to Satan. But the Devil, gnashing his teeth, calls Savva away and, having by threats and persuasion constrained him to disregard the words of the ancient, sets out with him for the city of Shuya. Savva's father, having meanwhile vainly sought his son in Oryol, returns in great grief to Kazan, where, a short time afterward, he dies.

At this moment Tsar Michael Fyodorovich decided to send his army to Smolensk against the Polish king. In Shuya they were recruiting soldiers. Savva, upon the Devil's advice, enters military service and with the Devil's aid is uncommonly successful at the business of war. Arriving in Moscow, Savva wins universal favor by his military talents and becomes known to the tsar himself and to his suite. He takes quarters on the Sretenka, in Zemlyan town, in the house of the centurion of musketeers Yakov Shilov, who shows a great partiality for him, as does his wife. Once Savva and the Devil reach Smolensk in a night, for three days spy out the enemy's fortifications there and then show themselves to the Poles and flee in the direction of the Dnieper; the water parts before them and they pass through the river dry-shod, while the Poles pursue them to no purpose. Soon Savva and the Devil, along with the Muscovite regiments under the command of Boyar Shein, again set out for Smolensk, where Savva engages in single combat three Polish giants, whom he defeats; then everywhere that he and the Devil appear in aid of Russian troops, the Poles take to flight with enormous losses. The traitor Shein is very much distressed by Savva's successes and uses all manner of threats to get him to leave Smolensk and return to Moscow, to the house of the centurion Shilov.

We are now approaching the denouement. Savva falls grievously ill and, when Shilov's wife insists, summons a priest to confess him. During the confession there appear in the sick man's room a crowd of devils headed by Savva's "brother," who now appears to him not in human form as heretofore but in his "beastly" devilish shape. Gnashing his teeth and showing Savva the "handwriting," he threatens him with dire retribution. The confession is carried to its conclusion in spite of all this, but afterward the Devil begins to torment Savva mercilessly. Shilov notifies the tsar of the inhuman sufferings of his lodger, and the tsar orders that two watchmen be set to guard Savva lest, beside himself with suffering, he throw himself into the fire or into the water. The tsar himself sends him food every day.

Then once, having fallen asleep after being uncommonly tormented by the devils, Savva dreamed that, as if awake, he prayed to the Virgin for help, promising to fulfill a vow that he would make to her. When he awoke, he told Centurion Shilov that he had dreamed he saw approaching his bed a "woman radiant and shining in ineffable brightness" and, with her, two men with gray hair. Savva conjectured that it had been the Virgin accompanied by John the Theologian and Peter, Metropolitan of Moscow. The Virgin promised to cure Savva of his ailment if he would embrace monasticism, and bade him go to Kazan Cathedral, which is on the square in Moscow by Ragmarket Row, on the feast day of her Kazan icon, saying that at that time, before all the people, a miracle would be performed upon him.

The tsar was told of Savva's vision and ordered that on the feast day of the icon of the Virgin of Kazan the sick man be brought to the Kazan Cathedral. The tsar attended the service in person. During the singing of the cherubim chant, a voice like thunder came from on high bidding Savva enter the church and promising him restoration to health. And at that moment the "document that had contained Savva's renunciation of God" dropped from the top of the church, as smooth as if it had never been written on, and Savva leaped from his carpet as if he had never been ill and rushed into the church to give thanks to the Virgin for his salvation. He distributed all his goods to the poor and then sought the Miracle Monastery, embraced monasticism, and passed the rest of his life in fasting and perpetual prayer.

In style the *Tale of Savva Grudtsyn* is a unique mingling of elements from the old narrative tradition, lives of the saints in particular, with elements of literary innovation. The basic idea of the tale is the salvation of a sinner through prayer and penitence. Here, as of old, the origin of all evil is the Devil, and he is vanquished by the intervention of divine power. The conduct of the man who has fallen into sin is not so much the consequence of qualities in his own nature as the result of outside forces acting upon him for evil or for good. Personal initiative on the part of the hero does not enter in, being completely subordinated to elements outside him. Even the "handwriting," a motif in use as far back as the apocryphas, is not a conscious act on Savva's part, but purely mechanical behavior, since the youth has no inkling as to the consequences implicit in this "handwriting," while up to the time of Savva's illness the Devil appears to Savva in human form, masking his devilish nature most adroitly. Woman figures in our tale as an instrument of the Devil—that is, when prompted by the Devil, she leads the

inexperienced youth into temptation and then carries her disgraceful lib-
ertinism beyond all bounds. If the voice of religion and conscience is still
audible to Savva in restraint of profligacy on the eve of a great feast, nothing
sacred remains to Bazhen's wife, nothing for which she can be moved to
sacrifice her uncontrollable passion. The ebb and flow of love itself are
regulated not by the lovers' inner impulses but by a magic potion or the
Devil's taking a hand. In this respect the tale of Savva Grudtsyn is as weak
psychologically as most other biographical and narrative works of Old Russian literature.

And at the same time such outcroppings of the new style as we have
already noted to some extent in the *Life of Juliania Lazarevskaya* are plainly
observable. Side by side with the elements of fantasy and legend revealed in
Savva's relations with the powers of evil and his divers supernatural adventures and successes, in the description of Satan's realm, and finally in the
sinner's miraculous cure and his release from the Devil's power, we find an
effort being made to limn concrete aspects of the epoch in all possible detail, even down to introducing actual historical personages, Tsar Michael
Fyodorovich, Boyar Shein and Semeon Streshnev, the gentleman-waiter *
Vorontsov, the centurion of musketeers Yakov Shilov, and also actual localities and even streets. The very family of Grudtsyn-Usov is no mere fiction;
it actually existed: several rich representatives of the merchant class living in
Veliky-Ustyug and in Moscow during the seventeenth century bore this
name. Further, a great many of the ethological and historical details noted
in the story correspond almost exactly to the historical actuality of the period
when the action of the tale unfolds. The epoch it reflects is defined from
the outset by facts given in the body of the narrative. Thomas Grudtsyn
moved from Veliky-Ustyug to Kazan in 1606. The Smolensk campaign in
which Savva takes part in company with the regiments of Boyar Shein,
occurred in 1632–1634. Thus the tale approximately covers the first half of
the seventeenth century. The time of writing, to judge from certain factual
details given in the narrative, fell in the later 1660's or the early 1670's.
This dating is further confirmed by the primary resemblance of the tale of
Savva Grudtsyn—with its motif of the miraculous aid of the Virgin in destroying the "handwriting," picturesque demonological fantasy, forceful
depiction of forbidden love and its vicissitudes (something previously unknown to Russian literature)—to that twin, as it were, of the *Great Mirror,*
the *Radiant Star,* translated into Russian in 1668. The motif of selling the
soul to the Devil for success in love, and subsequent deliverance from the
powers of evil by the good, or heavenly, powers, basis of folk traditions about

---

* The Russian word is *Stolnik* (Table-setter), an official rank under that of a boyar, analogous to the modern *kammerherr* or groom of the chamber (German, *tafeldecker*).—ED.

Dr. Faustus, is, however, present in a number of works of medieval literature, particularly in the popular Byzantine legend of Euladius (*The Miracle Done by St. Basil, Archbishop of Cesarea, on the Bewitched Page*). We also find points of contact between our tale and such Byzantine works then known in Rus as the legends of Proterius and Theophilus, and also in numerous Russian legends about "wonder-working" icons of the Virgin.

Its saturation with historical items, use of actual historical names, and mention of definite geographical localities as well as its association of events with a documentally attested family name would seem to invite the conjecture that real facts in connection with the amorous infatuation of some Grudtsyn may have gone into its writing. Such a dramatic episode and the psychic disturbances evidently associated with it may have combined to suggest to the author his interpretation of the facts in traditional terms as outcome of a pact with the powers of evil. To judge from the pious tone of the tale as a whole and from its finale, the author was a clerical personage, belonging perhaps to the clergy of the Kazan cathedral in Moscow and therefore interested in seeing miracles performed by the Kazan icon of the Virgin.[10] Another argument for the tale's having been written by a cleric is the presence in it of author's comments in the spirit of conventional ecclesiastical ethics. Needless to say, the author's conversance with the life of the merchant class in no way contradicts this hypothesis, since a cleric might, like anyone else, have been reasonably well informed as to merchant customs.[11]

TALE OF FROL SKOBEYEV

In striking contrast to the tales of Gore-Zlochastie and Savva Grudtsyn both as to language and as to content is the *History of the Russian Noble-*

[10] Cf. the accounts, very similar in theme to the *Tale of Savva Grudtsyn*, about miracles of the Kazan icon of the Virgin, printed by V. N. Peretts in "Iz istorii starinnoy russkoy povesti" (From the History of the Ancient Russian Tale), *Kiev Universitetskie izvestiya* (Kiev University News) (1907), No. 3, pp. 29–32. *Op. cit.*, pp. 24–28, gives stories from the *Great Mirror* that resemble our tale.

[11] Five seventeenth and eighteenth century copies of the *Tale of Savva Grudtsyn* have been published: in *Letopisi russkoy literatury i drevnosti* (Chronicle of Russian Literature and Antiquity), Vol. II, *Materialy* (Materials), pp. 61–80; in *Pamyatniki starinnoy russkoy literatury* (Monuments of Ancient Russian Literature), Vol. I, pp. 169–190 (two copies); in *Pamyatniki drevney pismennosti* (Monuments of Early Literature) (1880), Pt. 3, pp. 43–66, and in V. V. Sipovskii's book, *Russkie povesti XVII–XVIII vv.* (Russian Tales of the Seventeenth and Eighteenth Centuries), pp. 22–38. See M. O. Skripil, "Povest' o Savve Grudtsyn" (Tale of Savva Grudtsyn), *Trudy otdela drevnerusskoy literatury* (Works of the Division of Early Russian Literature) (1935), II, pp. 181–214, and (1936), III, pp. 99–152. Here the literature of the question is also given. Debatable points in M. O. Skripil's work are his derivation of the tale from the Byzantine tradition exclusively, and, more particu-

man Frol Skobeyev, which recounts the adventures of a rogue and cheat. The hero, a poor nobleman, makes very successful provision for his own material well-being by fraudulently marrying Annushka, daughter of the wealthy and influential gentleman-waiter at court, Nardin-Nashchokin. Neither Frol nor Annushka gives a single backward glance at tradition or shows the slightest symptom of any such spiritual tragedy as that experienced by the youth in *Gore-Zlochastie* when he broke away from the past.

By bribing Annushka's governess, Frol, in girl's clothes, gains admission to an evening party at Annushka's, during which, again with the aid of the governess, he gets the girl off by herself and takes advantage of her inexperience to seduce her. He not only escapes scot-free but makes a profit out of this escapade: Annushka on parting from him presents Frol with several gold pieces, "and from that time on the starveling Skobeyev made money and began to live luxuriously and give banquets to the rest of his fellow noblemen." Elated by his success, Frol meditates marrying Annushka, whom her parents at this juncture summon from their Novgorod estate to Moscow "so that nice young men, gentlemen-waiters' sons, may seek her hand in marriage." He hastens to Moscow, bound and determined to get what he wants: "If it costs me my life," he tells his sister, "I don't intend to give Annushka up: I shall come out of this either a colonel or a casualty!" Again through the help of the nurse, he gets in touch with Annushka, who gives him twenty rubles. Profiting by the fact that a carriage was to be sent for Annushka to take her on a visit to her aunt in a nunnery, he fraudulently obtains a carriage from his patron the gentleman-waiter Lovchikov, to "inspect a bride," gets the coachman drunk, and drives Annushka not to the nunnery but to his own apartment and then marries her.

When, by decree of the tsar, proclamation is made of the disappearance of Nardin-Nashchokin's daughter, and her abductor ordered to return her on pain of death, Frol informs Lovchikov that he has abducted Annushka and married her, and asks him to intercede, threatening in the contrary event to implicate him in the affair, since by giving his carriage Lovchikov had been an accessory to the abduction. Lovchikov had no alternative but to help Frol out and to this end arranged a meeting with Annushka's father in his own presence. With the audacity of an adventurer consciously taking a gamble, and governing himself accordingly, Frol notifies Nardin-Nashchokin that it was he who had abducted his daughter, and asks forgiveness. The despairing father is about to make immediate complaint to the tsar, but Lovchikov saves Frol by recommending to Nardin-Nashchokin that he first consult his wife. Gradually the father's heart softens, and out

larly, his attempt at a sociological interpretation in treating the author of the tale as an ideologist of the merchant class in seventeenth century Russia.

of concern for his daughter's future he not only refrains from lodging a complaint against Frol but asks the tsar to absolve his son-in-law of guilt. Frol makes expert use of the parents' sympathy for their daughter, has her pretend to be deathly ill when Nardin-Nashchokin's servant comes to call on her, asks them to give her their blessing if only *in absentia,* and then, after the parents have sent a valuable image, bids Annushka get up, notifying them that the parental blessing has put her on her feet. Luck is the rogue Frol's constant companion, and he not only comes dry out of the water, but all the better for it. Annushka's parents provide the young couple with abundance of food so that the "thief" and "dog" Skobeyev shall not starve their daughter. And "already Frol Skobeyev began to live luxuriously and to go everywhere like a person of quality, and they were greatly amazed that Skobeyev should be cutting such a dash and being so bold about it."

Frol the swindler and sneak ends his life as a man whose worth, in the eyes of his circle, leaves nothing to be desired, and about whose past no one knows or in any event remembers. His wealth secures him honor and respect. Annushka's noble parents in the end make peace with the son-in-law whom they had so recently despised as a thief and a rogue, receive him with honor and make him heir to all their possessions. Frol personifies the triumph of that pragmatic approach to life which was becoming so typical of the petty official nobility then elbowing its way to the top rungs of the social ladder. The author himself makes no attempt to conceal his generally sympathetic attitude toward the hero and toward his success in his life career.

And Annushka is a match for Frol in the liberties she takes with ancestral covenants and time-honored precepts. As a mere formality, she reproaches her governess after Frol has had his way with her: "What a trick to play on me, you damned fool! That wasn't a girl in there with me but someone of the masculine sex, our fellow townsman Frol Skobeyev!" But when the governess, pretending that she had never suspected there was anything wrong, proposes to repay him for the "filthy trick" he had played by shutting him up in a "privy place," Annushka, who has already managed to take a liking to her seducer, refuses to try to get back at him, briefly giving as the motive for her decision: "What's done is done! I can't undo it!" Moreover, she keeps Frol there for three days, during which time he "continually made merry with Annushka"; then she gives him a generous present and lets him go. Annushka does not withdraw her favor or her money from Frol even after she leaves for Moscow, and it is on her initiative that Frol takes her off in the carriage supposed to have been sent from the nunnery by her aunt. She does not experience even a shadow of remorse in fleeing from her parents' home; she has no pity for her elders, her father and mother, to whom she well knew her action would come as a shock, and later, in pretending to be ill, cooperates with her beloved in deceiving them.

Nor is Annushka's governess any better than they are: though of the older generation, she is none the less utterly lacking in moral principles, a mercenary procuress, backing Frol because he pays her for her services.

The author does his characters to a turn, especially Frol Skobeyev. Frol's combination of impudence, cynicism, and officiously calculated considerateness is exhibited in a masterly manner. To Lovchikov's question as to whether he is married and whether he has got himself a rich girl, Frol replies: "As yet there is no wealth in sight but as to the more distant prospect, time will tell," and at once proceeds to threaten his patron with personal hostilities if he refuses to help him out. When they bring the image from the Nardin Nashchokins, Frol and Annushka kiss it, set it up in a suitable place, and Frol directs that Annushka's parents be thanked for not "abandoning their erring daughter." In his father-in-law's house he quietly and uncomplainingly swallows insults and answers humbly and submissively to the insulting appellations lavished upon him by the rich old man whose pride and self-esteem have been wounded.

Annushka's parents, as they waver between the emotions of anger and pity for their daughter and in the end make their peace with her, are also characterized in an extremely lifelike manner and with verisimilitude.

The tale is of great interest for its underlying realism and psychology. Here the characters act not as motivated by those forces from without, God or the Devil, which commonly determined the behavior and destinies of people in works of Old Russian literature, but as motivated by a free agency within themselves, deriving from their characters and natural qualities; they are not the objects of some activating and directing force outside them but the subjects of action, independently ordering their own lives and, to the extent of their abilities and practical skill, building their own worldly happiness. The tale is also interesting for its lively humor. How priceless that last page is, with its transcript of the conversation between old Nardin-Nashchokin and Frol Skobeyev, who has come with Annushka to dine at his father-in-law's house! How subtly and adroitly it renders the condescending and disdainful attitude of the high-born gentleman-waiter toward his undesirable son-in-law; how well it shows the gradual mollification of the outraged father and his growing solicitude for the fate of the young spouses! How neatly aimed are passing phrases such as the remark that Nardin-Nashchokin addresses to the servant by whom—in token of his blessing *in absentia*—he is sending the valuable image to the pretended invalid Annushka: "And tell that rogue and thief Frolka not to squander it!" Shrewd, too, is it to mention the fact that when several carts plentifully loaded with provisions arrive at Frol's apartment, and a list along with them, Frol accepts the gift "without paying any attention to the list." But perhaps the most effective of all is Frol's quietly cynical reply to Nardin-Nashchokin's condemnation of him for abduction of his daughter: "My dear sir, such is the judgment already passed on it by God!"

The very language in which the tale is written differs radically from the traditional language of previous monuments. It resembles that found in secular tales of Peter the Great's time and at the same time makes abundant use of contemporary chancellery-scrivener jargon, first heard at the very beginning of the tale: "In the year 1680, in the Novgorod district, was located nobleman Frol Skobeyev; in that same Novgorod district were located the estates of the gentleman-waiter Nardin-Nashchokin and upon these estates was located his daughter Annushka and lived on them," and farther on, in the same vein: "And Gentleman-Waiter Nardin-Nashchokin was located extremely well on in years." Fashionable foreign words also occur in the tale, such as "publication," "register," "apartment," "person," "banquet," "natural," and such pretentious and equally fashionable expressions as "conceive a passion," "none of my kind offices are acceptable to you," "the evenings of entertainment known as the Christmas holidays," "compulsory love," and so forth. The author apparently strove to write in the language that he thought best suited to the requirements of a story about contemporary high society, but his painful efforts to be fashionable must have seemed naïve even to his better educated contemporaries. He himself apparently belonged either to the chancellery-scrivener class or to the petty nobility, and in spite of undoubted talent was a man of very limited literary training.

In one copy 1680 is given as the date of the action, in another as the date when the tale was written. To judge from the language, however, and from the circumstance that certain facts are referred to as already things of the past ("In those days everybody had the habit of congregating on Ivanovsky Square"; "at that time old people had a habit of carrying natural staves with flattened ends"), the tale must date from the very end of the seventeenth century—the eve of Peter the Great's reforms—or the beginning of the eighteenth century. Tales written in a vein of romantic gallantry—for example, those about Basil Kariotsky and Alexander, Russian nobleman—would within the next few years become the usual thing.

The tale of Frol Skobeyev is a typical example of the picaresque novel, fairly widespread in the West at that time. However, no Western parallels bearing any resemblance to our tale have up to the present been found, nor are they likely to be, inasmuch as its plot situations are more or less generic to this specific historical epoch. Furthermore the family names which figure in the story about Frol—except in one copy where Skomrakov appears instead of Skobeyev, and Nardin-Tsaplin instead of Nardin-Nashchokin—have their counterparts in historical documents of the epoch and are associated with precisely the localities mentioned in the story. This last circumstance suggests the possibility of its having had some basis in fact.[12]

During the last quarter of the eighteenth century, the story of Frol Skobeyev was rewritten by Iv. Novikov as "The Novgorod Girls' Christmas Party That Ended in a Moscow Wedding," included in his book *The Adventure of Ivan the Merchant's Son*. At the end of the 1860's, the dramatist Averkiyev wrote a play on the subject, entitled the *Comedy of the Russian Nobleman Frol Skobeyev and Gentleman-Waiter Nardin-Nashchokin's Daughter Annushka*.

TALE OF KARP SUTULOV

The frankness of subject and the free and easy attitude toward traditional principles that we see in the story of Frol Skobeyev also characterize the *Story of a Certain Rich and Celebrated Merchant Karp Sutulov and of His Prudent Wife: How She Avoided Profaning Her Couch*, evidently dating from the end of the seventeenth century and extant in a single eighteenth century copy.

There was once a very rich and respected merchant by the name of Karp Sutulov, so the story says, who had a very beautiful wife by the name of Tatyana. They lived together in great affection. Once when he left to do some trading in Lithuania, Karp Sutulov requested his dear friend, Afanasy Berdov, likewise a rich and honored merchant, to make his wife Tatyana a loan if she should need money during his absence. Afanasy Berdov willingly agreed to do so. As he left, Karp Sutulov enjoined his wife to be faithful to him. Tatyana, while separated from her husband, arranged frequent banquets for her friends as he had authorized her to do, and in making merry always thought happily about him.

But three years went by, Tatyana's money was used up, and she betook herself to Afanasy Berdov with the request for a loan of a hundred rubles.

[12] Printings of the tale having the greatest scientific importance are those found in V. V. Sipovskii's book *Russkie povesti XVII–XVIII vv.* (Russian Tales of the Seventeenth and Eighteenth Centuries), pp. 59–70, and as a supplement to V. F. Pokrovskii's article "Povest o Frole Skobeyeve" (Tale of Frol Skobeyev), *Trudy otdela drevnerusskoy literatury* (Works of the Division of Early Russian Literature), I, pp. 250–297. This article also gives the literature of the question.

Berdov, however, captivated by her beauty, consented to give her the money only on condition that she pass the night with him. Tatyana, very much embarrassed by this proposal, told Berdov that she could not give him an answer until she had consulted her confessor, her spiritual father. Tatyana's spiritual father, after hearing her story, offered her on the same conditions that Berdov had proposed, two hundred rubles. Tatyana was still more embarrassed and asked him to give her time to think it over, while she herself went to get the advice of the archbishop, who recommended that she refuse the offers of the merchant and of the priest and spend the night with him, for which he promised her a good three hundred rubles. To Tatyana's words: "O great saint, how can I escape burning in the hereafter?" the archbishop replied: "I will absolve you of everything." Then Tatyana made an assignation with the archbishop for two o'clock in the afternoon, with her spiritual father for five, and with Afanasy Berdov for nine.

When the archbishop comes as appointed and hands Tatyana the three hundred rubles, she points out the impropriety of a man who holds such high office in the church retaining his usual garments for an amorous encounter and, after an edifying recital of pious reflections on the subject, suggests that for lack of anything else he change into a woman's chemise, to which he consents with pleasure. While Tatyana is deliberately keeping the archbishop's desires in check, the priest, her spiritual father, knocks at the gate, bringing two hundred rubles with him. Looking out the window, she joyously informs the archbishop that her husband, whom she had been expecting at just about this time, had arrived, and she hides the archbishop in a chest. After first reproaching the priest for his sinful behavior, which carries the threat of eternal torment for both of them, Tatyana distracts him with talk on many topics up to the time when Merchant Afanasy Berdov knocks at the gate. She tells the priest the same story about her husband having arrived and, after reading her spiritual father a salutary lesson, gets him, likewise in a chemise, into a second chest. After receiving a hundred rubles from the merchant, she addresses words of admonition to him as well, then orders her serving maid to knock loudly at the gate and, notifying Berdov that her husband has returned, hides him in a third chest.

In the morning Tatyana betakes herself to the governor of the city and tells him that she had tried to get a loan of a hundred rubles from the merchant Afanasy Berdov but had not found him at home, and asks the governor to lend her this sum with three chests of expensive dresses as security. The governor agrees to lend Tatyana the hundred rubles even without security, but she urges him to take the chests from her house as she is afraid that in her husband's absence they may be stolen with all their contents. When the chests had been conveyed to the governor's yard, the governor ordered them opened, with a view to checking over the expensive clothes stored in them, as Tatyana had requested, but instead discovers the merchant Berdov, the priest, and the archbishop confined there in nothing but chemises and almost dead with shame. Upon learning of Tatyana how the three had come to be in the chests, the governor expressed amazement at her shrewdness and praised her highly for remaining true to her husband. "This is good security of yours, woman, and worth the money!" he added, smiling, and taking five hundred rubles from the merchant, a thousand from the priest, and a thousand and a half from the archbishop, he released them, split the money equally between himself and Tatyana and again praised her for her virtue, "that your husband in his absence you did not forsake, nor any love to these persons make, nor your husband's advisement to you break, wherefore you may great credit take, while your couch remains unsullied." And when her husband returned home and learned from Tatyana of all these occurrences, he "rejoiced greatly over his wife's prudence, over such prudence having been exercised by her."

The story undoubtedly derives from a foreign migratory plot, most likely of Eastern origin (cf. the tale of Arui in the *Thousand and One Nights*), which found reflections in a large number of European literary works, as well as in oral tales, Russian included. Among all the many stories and folk tales, both Eastern and Western, on the theme of clever tricks devised by women to escape the importunities of admirers and place them in highly embarrassing situations, there is, however, not one where the motifs present in the *Tale of Karp Sutulov* are exactly repeated. It is possible that our tale is a literary adaptation from the written record of some *novella* first reaching Rus through oral channels. A potential argument in favor of this is the presence of typical peculiarities of the oral-poetry style, epic repetition in particular, as found in Tatyana's detailed reiteration of the same small talk with each succeeding pretender to her couch, with a resulting retardation of the narrative such as is customary in works of oral poetry.

On Russian soil the borrowed plot underwent considerable Russianization. Not only were Russian first names and family names introduced into the story but even a typically Russian ethological background, with its merchant usage, its city-governor rule, and numerous details characteristic of specific conditions prevailing in Russia. The quotation from the *Discourse on Evil Women* put into Tatyana's mouth, and Tatyana's moral admonitions in the style of ecclesiastical aphorisms are likewise very typical of the Russian cultural background. Linguistically the tale is a combination of Church Slavonic forms and elements from colloquial speech. All this taken together constrains us to regard the *Tale of Karp Sutulov*, notwithstanding its evident derivation from a foreign plot, as an original work of Russian literature to the same extent that we regard, for example, the *Decameron* of Boccaccio, as an original work of Italian literature, regardless of the fact that this collection is almost wholly based on migratory narratives from East and West.

As in the tale of Frol Skobeyev, so here no moral judgments are passed on the facts related. Tatyana stands before us as a virtuous and sensible woman of a practical turn of mind. She is embarrassed but not outraged by the indecorous proposals which her three admirers make to her. While protecting her own honor and that of her husband, she at the same time makes her attraction for these admirers extremely profitable to herself materially. If the author puts pious-sounding admonitions in her mouth, he does so only to heighten the comic effect. The merry merchant's wife tells her spiritual father and the archbishop, in church texts, how they must behave to escape God's stern chastisement, and gets answers to her texts that do credit to the author's gift for humor: the erring archbishop promises the woman that by exercise of his spiritual authority he will absolve her from sin, while the priest declares that in angering him she also angers God. Tatyana's husband expresses, not displeasure with those who had made attempts on his wife's virtue, but only delight at the clever maneuver whereby his wife, without breaking faith with him, had still managed to increase his capital. The sedate governor shows, not indignation at the amorous pranks of his honored fellow townsmen, but only amusement at the fact that they had miscarried. It is very typical that we should find among the personages who conduct themselves so disgracefully not only a merchant but also a priest, who is at the same time spiritual father of the woman whose charms prove too much for him, and even the archbishop himself. Such a frankly offhand attitude toward persons immune to ridicule in the old literature, let alone frivolous mockery, could have found written embodiment only in the seventeenth century, with the slackening of church authority, and even then only in the milieu least committed to official reverence for this authority; that is, most probably, in the democratic society of artisans and traders.[13]

[13] A study of the tale, a detailed analysis of similar plots, and the text itself may be found in Yu. M. Sokolov's "Povest o Karpe Sutulove" (The Tale of Karp Sutulov), *Trudy Slavyanskoy komissii moskovskogo Arkheologicheskogo obshchestva* (Works of the Slavic Committee of the Moscow Archaeological Society) (Moscow, 1914), Vol. IV, Pt. 2, pp. 1–40. The text of the tale is reproduced in N. K. Piksanov's book *Starorusskaya povest* (The Old Russian Tale), pp. 75–80.

TALES OF THE ORIGIN OF TOBACCO, OF THE DEMONIAC
SOLOMONIA, OF THE BEGINNING OF MOSCOW, OF THE
FOUNDING OF THE PAGE'S MONASTERY OF TVER

Demonological motifs, present in the tales about Gore-Zlochastie, about
the hop, and about Savva Grudtsyn, occupy a very large place in a work
which apparently took its rise among Old Believers at the end of the seventeenth century, *Legend from the Book of Pandok About the Forbidden
Blade, the Vile Weed, Which Is Tobacco Grass, Whence It Was and What
Its Origin and How It Became Disseminated Throughout the World.*[14]
This recounts, on the basis of apocryphal legends, the origin of tobacco and
the efforts made to prevent its propagation. The Devil, put to shame by
Christ, who had chained him in hell after the Resurrection, decided to take
revenge by corrupting the elect human family, and for this purpose planted
weeds; that is, the herb tobacco, on the corpse of a "great adulteress, full of
all manner of filthiness," the "accursed daughter" of an erring nun. After
a while a certain physician, at Satan's prompting, chanced on this herb and
thereafter it achieved wide distribution to the undoing of Christians. Under
the auspices of Christ and the Virgin a vigorous campaign is conducted
against the tyranny of the "vile weed" over men.

Demonological motifs find particularly forceful development in the story
of the demoniac woman Solomonia, which is one of the miracles (the twenty-
seventh) of the Ustyugian saints Procopius and John.[15] The action is represented as having taken place in the neighborhood of Ustyug, in 1661. After
her marriage Solomonia is possessed by devils, who cohabit with her and
cause her unspeakable tortures. They steal her away, entice her into the
water, into the forest, carry her up to high mountains, to housetops, ram
her hands and feet into the stocks, prick her, cut her, and when through
torturing and reviling her, leave her there, lacerated, naked, completely
unconscious. They give her no peace even at home: they fling her from
corner to corner, tie her to the rafters, prompt her to kill her father, and
so forth. It is useless for Solomonia to resist them. From her commerce with
demons she conceives "dark-skinned" blue devils. Devils dwell inside her
and once even gnaw through her left side. Solomonia is subjected to all

[14] Published in *Pamyatniki starinnoy russkoy literatury* (Monuments of Ancient Russian
Literature), II, pp. 427–434.

[15] Published in *Pamyatniki starinnoy russkoy literatury* (Monuments of Ancient Russian
Literature), I, pp. 153–161. See also *Zhitie prep. Prokopiya Ustyuzhskogo* (Life of St. Procopius of Ustyug), *Izd. OLDP* (Obshchestva lyubiteley drevney pismennosti) (St. Petersburg, 1893), pp. 143–195; also D. Rovinskii, *Russkie narodnye kartinki* (Russian Popular
Prints) (St. Petersburg, 1881), Vol. IV, pp. 537–543; Vol. V, pp. 206–210.

these devilish tortures because she had been christened by a drunken priest who had only performed half the service. In the end she is delivered from the power of the demons through the aid of the Virgin and of the Ustyugian saints Procopius and John. Solomonia's cure is given with a good many very naturalistic details. Solomonia narrates:

"He came close to me, St. Procopius, and made the sign of the cross on my belly with his hand, while St. John came with a lancet in his hand and slit my belly and took a demon from me and gave it to St. Procopius. The demon began to howl in a great voice and twist in his hand. And St. Procopius showed me the demon and said: 'Solomonia, do you see the demon that was in your belly?' I looked at it— it was black and had a tail; its lips were thick and terrible; and he put it on the floor, the accursed thing, and stabbed it with pokers. St. John began to take more from my belly one by one and give them to St. Procopius; he stabbed them one by one."

Thus were half the devils drawn from Solomonia, and the other half St. John drew out at the tomb of Procopius: "And St. John began to remove demons through the same slit as before, while St. Procopius took and cast them on the church floor and crushed them with his foot." Solomonia was not dismissed until Procopius had looked into her belly and satisfied himself that it was free of pollution.

The demonological elements that are so strongly marked in the story of Solomonia, the interweaving of wild fantasy with touches of extreme naturalism in describing the powers of evil, are apparently due not alone to the influence of Russian folklore but quite as much to Western literary influences reaching us through books such as the *Radiant Star* or the *Great Mirror*. Russian demonology provided no such graphic descriptions of devils and devilish machinations as those found in the tale of Solomonia.[16]

The commingling of hagiographical features and romantic intrigue that characterized the tale of Savva Grudtsyn is also exemplified in a poetical tale about the founding of Moscow composed at the end of the seventeenth century.

From a literary angle this tale is one of the most curious links in the whole chain of tales about the founding of Moscow, tracing ultimate origin to the ecclesiastico-biographical account of the murder of Andrew Bogolyubsky entered as of the year 1175 in the *Hypatian Chronicle*. This account was rewritten at the beginning of the sixteenth century, with the colors laid on particularly thick in descriptions of Andrew's murderers, the Kuchkov brothers. It was next rewritten at the middle of the sixteenth century, for

[16] See Buslayev's article "Bes" (The Evil One), in the collection *Moy Dosugi* (My Leisure Hours), Pt. 2, pp. 1–24. Cf. also F. A. Ryazanovskii, *Demonologiya v drevnerusskoy literature* (Demonology in Early Russian Literature) (Moscow, 1915), pp. 6–8, 71–73.

inclusion in the *Stepennaya Kniga*, where the negative characteristics of the murderers were still further emphasized. Still another adaptation of the story is found in the Nikonian compilation. Soon afterward, in the course of its numerous revisions, the tale of the murder of Andrew Bogolyubsky turned up in connection with traditions about the founding of Moscow, which the early chronicles had called Kuchkovo. A special study of the tale of the founding of Moscow made by S. K. Shambinago[17] distinguished three forms: 1) the *Chronograph* story, 2) the *novella,* 3) the fairy tale.

The first, encountered in historical collections and including dates, appeared at the middle of the seventeenth century.[18] It begins with an introduction which repeats the formula of the hermit Filofey: Moscow, the third Rome. Like the first Rome and the second (Constantinople), Moscow had been built upon blood. It was founded by Great Prince Yury Vladimirovich on the former site of the villages of the wealthy boyar Stepan Ivanovich Kuchka, whom Yury killed for not showing him proper respect. The two handsome sons and the beautiful daughter Ulita he sent to Vladimir, to his son Andrew, who married Ulita. Irked by the unresponsiveness of her ascetic husband, she plots with her brothers and kills him. The motif of murder of a pious husband by a wife with a more passionate nature was here suggested by an episode from the chronicle of Manassius dealing with the murder of the emperor Nikiphorus Foka by the empress Feofania, but the explanation of the murder given in Manassius; namely, the empress's predilection for her husband's rival, is absent from the *Chronograph* story; it does not appear until the next redaction, the *novella.*

The hero of the *novella* is the Muscovite prince, Daniel Aleksandrovich, son of Alexander Nevsky, who reigned in Moscow from 1272 to 1303. To him are transferred events assigned by the chronicle and the chronograph accounts to the person of Andrew Bogolyubsky, so that what is told about him in the *novella* has absolutely no connection with the actual biography of Daniel, who, incidentally, is here prince of Suzdal. The only possible excuse for such a transfer is Daniel Aleksandrovich's sudden and early death. As ancestor of the Muscovite princes he was a very popular personality: he acquired the reputation of being founder of the might of the Muscovite state. In the sixteenth century his life was included in the *Stepennaya Kniga,* and in 1652 his "relics" were opened, this event apparently providing the incentive for writing his tendentious-romantic biography. To this

17 S. K. Shambinago, "Povesti o nachale Moskvy" (Tales of the Beginning of Moscow), *Trudy otdela drevnerusskoy literatury* (Works of the Division of Early Russian Literature), III, pp. 59–98.

18 The *Chronograph* tale has not been published. On copies of it, see *op. cit.* of S. K. Shambinago. For a retelling see I. Zabelin's book *Istoriya goroda Moskvy* (History of the City of Moscow), 2nd ed. (Moscow, 1905), Pt. 1, pp. 36–38.

biography was attached in a purely superficial manner the legend of the founding of Moscow by Daniel's brother Andrew Aleksandrovich.

The story, written in the *bylina* vein, begins by saying that on the site where Moscow was later to be founded, there once stood fine, fair villages belonging to Boyar Stepan Ivanovich Kuchka. And this boyar had two sons, than whom there were no fairer in all the land of Rus. Learning of this, Prince Daniel Aleksandrovich of Suzdal demanded that Kuchka send his sons to court, threatening to attack him and burn his villages if he refused to meet this demand. From fear of the prince the boyar sent him his sons, of whom the prince became very fond; he began showing them favor and promoted one to the office of gentleman-waiter, the other to that of cup-bearer. But with the Devil's connivance the youths were also beloved by Daniel's wife, Princess Ulita Yurevna; the enemy of the human race poisoned her with lecherous passion, and she entered into amorous relations with them. Then the Kuchkov brothers plotted with the princess how they might do away with Prince Daniel. They invited him to go hunting and attempted to murder him then, but Daniel galloped his horse into the thick of the wood and then dismounted, ran along the bank of the Oka and, upon reaching the ford, tried to get the ferryman to convey him to the opposite bank, giving him his gold ring for the service. But, after taking the ring, the ferryman cast off from shore, leaving the prince behind. In the dark autumn night the prince kept running along the bank of the Oka until he came to a hut where a dead man had been buried; here he took shelter and slept until morning.

The Kuchkoviches were worried at having let Daniel slip through their fingers, for they feared his taking refuge in Vladimir with his brother Andrew Aleksandrovich, who would bring his army against them and condemn them to a frightful death and order Princess Ulita hanged on the gates or buried alive.

But as a serpent with venom, so the Devil filled Ulita with malice against her husband and, inflamed by the satanic temptation of wicked desire, she told her lovers that the prince possessed a devoted hound which he had ordered sent in search of him if he should be killed or taken captive in battle with the Tartars. The Kuchkov brothers take the dog with them and when it joyfully finds Daniel they visit a savage death on the prince, stab him through the ribs with swords and spears, cut off his head and conceal his body in the hut. Thus the "pious Prince Daniel was the fourth martyr; he suffered a martyr's death at the hands of his wife's lovers. The first martyrs, Boris and Gleb and Svyatoslav, were murdered by their brother accursed Svyatopolk [Holy-Troop], who deserved the name Pagan-Troop." The Kuchkoviches took Daniel's bloodstained garment back to Suzdal, turned it over to the princess, and proceeded to live with her as before, "in unlawful adultery."

David Tudermiv, faithful servant of the murdered prince, took Daniel's little son and galloped away with him to Vladimir to Prince Andrew Aleksandrovich and told all that had happened. Prince Andrew mourned for his brother, as Prince Yaroslav Vladimirovich had mourned for his brothers Boris and Gleb, and led an army against the Kuchkoviches. They, in terror, fled to their father, Boyar Stepan Ivanovich Kuchka. Upon reaching Suzdal, Prince Andrew ordered Princess Ulita executed with all manner of tortures and consigned her to a horrible death. After that he set out against Boyar Kuchka, took his fair villages and liberties by assault, and executed him along with his sons by all manner of horrible methods. Kuchka's villages and liberties were pleasing to Andrew and "God put it in his heart" to build a city on the site and thus the city of Moscow was founded, and Andrew took up his residence there after setting his son George over Suzdal and Vladimir. After Andrew's death his nephew Ivan Danilovich, son of his murdered brother, became reigning prince of Moscow. The tale ends with an item about the arrival in Moscow of Metropolitan Peter, who prophesied universal fame for Moscow and future world power.[19]

As is easily seen, this tale, too, features the traditional "evil woman," the temptress. In some respects it resembles the story of Prince Bova, which may even have had some influence on certain details of the plot. The motif of the founding of a city "on blood" is a very widely diffused one. It is present in legends of the founding of Rome, Constantinople, and other cities.

Finally, the fairy-tale story gets even farther away from history than the *novella*. In almost all copies Daniel Aleksandrovich is replaced by the fictitious Daniel Ivanovich. Romantic intrigue plays no part in it. To judge from this and also from the fact that the story is more concerned with the founding by Daniel Ivanovich of the Krutits archpriestly house than with the founding of Moscow, the author of the story, which was written at the end of the seventeenth century, must have been an ecclesiastic.[20]

A combination of ecclesiastical motifs with romantic intrigue enters in an original and novel manner into the beautiful tale of the founding of the Page's Monastery of Tver, the appearance of which must be assigned to the end of the seventeenth or the beginning of the eighteenth century. The content of the tale is as follows.

Gregory, beloved page of Yaroslav Yaroslavich, Prince of Tver, is sent out

---

[19] For the text of the tale see I. Zabelin's book *Istoriya goroda Moskvy* (History of the City of Moscow) 2nd ed., Pt. 1, pp. 30–36. On other published and unpublished copies, as well as on the genesis of the tale, see S. K. Shambinago, *op. cit.*

[20] For the text of the tale see I. Zabelin, *op. cit.*, pp. 28–29; S. K. Shambinago's study gives a list of copies.

to collect taxes, and comes to the village of Edimonovo, where he stops at the house of Sexton Afanasy, who has a daughter of uncommon beauty, Xenia by name. The moment he saw her, Gregory fell in love and, thinking to marry her, set about suing the father for his daughter's hand. Having obtained the father's consent and the maiden's, he finished the business he had been charged with, returned to Tver, and asked the prince's permission to marry the sexton's daughter. The prince at first tried to persuade Gregory not to take this step, advising him to marry some rich girl of noble family, but in the end yielded to his page's urgent entreaties and gave his consent to the marriage. That very night the prince dreamed that he went out hunting and that his favorite falcon caught and brought him a dove "of a beauty more exceeding bright than gold." Under the influence of this dream, Prince Yaroslav Yaroslavich makes ready to go hunting and gives orders that all the falcons be taken along.

In the meanwhile Gregory, drawing near the house of his betrothed, sends a messenger to her with the request that she prepare for the wedding, but the bride, foreseeing the future, asks him to wait a little while and tells her parents that the go-between has already arrived and that the bridegroom, who is now diverting himself in the field, will soon be there. Xenia still delays the wedding even when Gregory rides into the yard without having waited to hear from her. At this moment, prolonging his hunt and already in the environs of Edimonovo, the prince saw on the Volga a flock of swans and ordered the release of the hawks and falcons, among them his favorite falcon, which flew to the village and led the prince to Xenia's yard. The bride goes out to meet the prince, calls him her bridegroom, and bids Gregory leave the house, saying: "Get thee from me and make way for your prince, for he is greater than you, and my bridegroom, while you were my go-between." When the prince himself saw a girl "so beautiful that beams of light seemed to radiate from her face," his heart burned for her and he bade Gregory leave and find himself another bride. Gregory left in great sorrow, while the prince and Xenia went to the church and were married.

Not knowing what had become of his favorite page, Yaroslav Yaroslavich was very much troubled and feared for the life of his afflicted and faithful servant. But Gregory, having changed into peasant dress, came, guided by "God's providence," to the river Tverets, fifteen versts from the city, and there took up his abode after building himself a hut and an oratory. Soon after this the Virgin appeared to him in a dream, showed him the site where a church and a monastery were to be built, and foretold the future fame of this monastery and the early death of its founder. With the prince's co-operation a wooden church and monastery were erected and called the Page's, and there Gregory took the tonsure under the name of Gurius. Before long he died, and a stone church was built at the monastery and endowed with villages deeded to it by the princes of Tver.

With the motif of a prince's marriage to a girl of the "lower classes," we are already acquainted through the tale of Peter and Fevronia. The heroine of our tale resembles Fevronia in her wisdom, her gift of second sight, and her piety. One of the copies says of her: "She was a very pious and gentle girl, humble and cheerful and possessed of very great intelligence and walking in all the Lord's commandments." Innovations in our tale are its romantic nucleus, absent from the tale of Peter and Fevronia, and the motif of retiring to a monastery because of bad luck in love. These are signs of arrival at a later stage in the evolution of the narrative genre. Mention should also be made here of the presence of folk-ballad wedding symbolism manifest in the poetical description of falcons chasing a flock of swans and in the winning of a mate with the help of a falcon. Later on, the tale was adapted by several of our secondary nineteenth and twentieth century writers.[21]

Any picture of the development of the narrative genre in this country during the seventeenth century would be incomplete without mention of the first extant records of *byliny* as found in manuscripts of "tales," "legends," and "histories" from that time. As in the *Legend of the Kiev Bogatyrs*, transcribers did not adhere exactly to the traditional *bylina* plots, permitting themselves a certain license in the combination of separate motifs and thus in some measure subjecting the *bylina* material to literary revision. There can be no doubt that these transcription-adaptations were for the most part made in that new democratic milieu which felt most at home with the works of oral poetry.[22]

[21] V. F. Rzhiga has an article on it, "Iz istorii povesti" (From the History of the Tale), *Izvestiya Tverskogo pedagogicheskogo instituta* (News of the Tver Pedagogical Institute) (1928), Pt. 4, pp. 97–116.

[22] See *Russkie byliny staroy i novoy zapisi* (Russian Byliny in Old and New Recordings—ed. Acad. N. S. Tikhonravov and Prof. V. F. Miller) (Moscow, 1894), pp. 1–88; N. S. Tikhonravov, *Pyat bylin po rukopisyam XVIII veka* (Five Byliny from Eighteenth Century Manuscripts) (Moscow, 1891); B. M. Sokolov, "Byliny starinnoy zapisi" (Byliny in Old Recordings), *Etnografiya* (Ethnography) (1926), Nos. 1–2 (1927) Nos. 1–2. The first transcriptions of oral proverbs also date from this time. See P. Simoni, *Starinnye sborniki russkikh poslovits* (Ancient Collections of Russian Proverbs) (St. Petersburg, 1899). A. S. Arkhangelskii in *Iz lektsii po istorii russkoy literatury* (From Lectures on the History of Russian Literature); *Literatura Moskovoskogo gosudarstva kontsa XV v.–nachala XVII v.* (Literature of the Moscovite State in the Late Fifteenth and Early Seventeenth Centuries) (Kazan, 1913), p. 435, assigns to the category of late seventeenth century narratives an extremely interesting monument, *Roman v stikhakh* (Novel in Verse), first printed in full in Sipovskii's book *Russkie povesti XVII–XVIII vv.* (Russian Tales of the Seventeenth and Eighteenth Centuries) but on the evidence of the phrase, "Lyubeznoy nemilago so mnoy v Lafertovo [i. e. v Lefortovo] prosit gulyati," the novel cannot have been written earlier than the eighteenth century, when the Moscow suburb of Lefortovo, named after Peter the First's famous collaborator Lefort, was founded.

Satirical Literature of the
Seventeenth Century

SATIRE, parody, the comic story, chiefly as ridiculing the official classes or anything having to do with ecclesiastical life, were the direct consequence of tendencies latent in the original secular tale as developed during the seventeenth century. Elements of satire and humor may already be detected in the tales about the hop, and are still more evident in the tales of Frol Skobeyev and Karp Sutulov. By the unfolding of the historical process and by class struggle, the emancipation of the democratic strata of seventeenth century Muscovite Rus from the domination of old-fashioned principles and attitudes naturally contributed to the development of satire and parody on the means whereby official Rus in the person of its upper ruling class maintained itself and exploited the economically and politically disfranchised city and country masses.

TALE OF AN UNJUST TRIAL: *Shemyakin Sud*

This tale is based on a plot the details of which are encountered in a number of literary monuments both Eastern and Western. On Russian soil it became associated with the figure of the Galician prince, Dmitry Shemyak, who blinded his brother, the Muscovite prince, Basil II, and was regarded as such an unjust judge that the *Chronograph* in speaking of him remarks, as Karamzin pointed out: "For from this time in Great Russia, *Shemyakin Sud* was applied to all sorts of judges as a term of reproach."

476

In a certain place, says the Russian story, there lived two brothers, tillers of the soil, and one was rich, the other poor. The rich brother for many years made loans to his poor brother but could not "fill in his lack." Once the poor brother came to the rich one and asked for a horse so that he could haul himself some firewood. The rich brother was angry and gave him the horse but did not give him the horse collar. The poor brother hitched the horse to his sledge by the tail, collected the wood and then, driving straight into the board under the gate, which he had forgotten to take out, he struck the horse with the whip, whereupon the horse squeezed through by main force and broke off its tail. The rich brother refused to accept the tail-less horse and set off for town to enter a complaint with Justice Shemyak against his brother; the poor brother walked along after him. Part way to town, the rich brother decided to pass the night in a village at the hut of a priest he knew. The poor brother also went to the priest's house and was given the shelf bed to sleep on. Then the priest and the rich brother started to sup, but did not invite the poor brother. While watching his brother and the priest eating, the poor brother fell off the shelf onto the cradle and crushed the priest's son to death. The priest joined forces with the rich brother and went in his company to make petition to the judge against the man responsible for the death of his son. As the three approached the city and crossed the bridge, a certain resident of the town was conveying his sick father across the ditch under the bridge to the bath. Feeling that the approaching trial boded him no good, the poor brother thought he would commit suicide, and dived head foremost into the ditch, but in his fall crushed the sick graybeard, and himself remained unharmed. As complainant against the murderer, the son of the slain man also betook himself to the judge.

Thinking how he might bribe the judge and finding he had nothing with him, the poor brother picked up a stone from the road, wrapped it in his kerchief, put it in his cap and took his place before the judge. Each time the judge questioned him with regard to the claims of the injured parties the poor brother took from his cap the stone wrapped in the kerchief and showed it to the judge; the judge, thinking that the accused was making him a new promise of gold each time, decided: that the horse should remain with the poor brother until its tail grew in, that the priest's wife should be turned over to him until he begot a child on her and that then this child should be returned to the priest along with his wife, while the son whose father had been killed should throw himself on the murderer while the latter stood under the bridge and crush him as he had crushed the sick graybeard.

Needless to say such a verdict did not satisfy any one of the complainants, and each hastened to get well out of it by paying the poor brother off, alike for the award of the horse and of the priest's wife and for the decision that the old man's son throw himself off the bridge, while the judge, upon find-ing that the kerchief contained not a bribe but a stone, was glad that he had decided just as he had, since a different verdict might have cost him his life.

In the literatures of both East and West, as we have said, there exist a number of works in which, with divers variations, the motifs present in our tale appear. Examples are a Tibetan tale, derived from an Indian original and found in the "Dzanglun" collection, Buddhist legends about courts of law, the Indian folk tale about the Cairo merchant, the German ballad of the judgment of Charlemagne, Italian *novelle* on the theme of shrewd judicial verdicts, and so forth. All this material portrays impartial judges like Solomon, guided in their decisions exclusively by a sense of justice. Typical of many of these foreign tales of just judgments is the motif of cutting off an exact amount of flesh from the defendant, found also, of course, in Shakespeare's *The Merchant of Venice*. It is very indicative that even Rus-sian folk tales representing the poor peasant as a good but unlucky man cruelly exploited by his rich brother, deal with a just judge and contain no hint of satire on judicial obliquity. It is only in the literary adaptation that we get satire on judicial verdicts, with the judge himself appearing as an unjust judge: superficially his verdicts are fair, but in actuality they are dictated solely by mercenary motives. To explain the turn taken by the tale on Russian soil, M. I. Sukhomlinov adduces data from monuments of Semitic apocryphal literature, the *Babylonian Talmud* and the *Book of the Just* which deal with unjust judges. Still earlier, on the basis of the fact that in some manuscripts of the *Shemyakin Sud* there exist indications that the story was "excerpted" from "Polish books" or from "Polish miscellanies," Tikhonravov suggested the possible existence of some Polish original of the Russian tale and in support of his idea adduced one satirical poem by a sixteenth century Polish writer, Rei of Naglovits, where the unjust verdict of a mercenary judge is recounted. However, the complete absence from Russian manuscript texts of any traces of a Polish original and the ethologi-cal Russianization in all copies known to us, not to mention the fact that up to the present no works of Polish literature have been found that fully correspond to our tale, argue against its direct connection with such an original. It would seem more correct to suppose, as Pypin did, that the indicated reference to "Polish books" is due to a misunderstanding and came about through the fact that in the earliest collection containing it, the *Shemyakin Sud* stood alongside some "ludicrous" tales which actually had been translated from the Polish.

Manuscript texts of the tale must apparently be regarded as stemming most immediately from recordings of oral Russian folk tales, which neces-sarily predated the manuscript texts, since, like the Eastern and Western versions of the plot, they deal with a just judge and are not even correlated with Shemyak. Our folk tales were without doubt a reflection of migratory international tales about a just judge. On the basis of them, a literary story was composed which transmuted the didactic material into satire, changing things about so that the narrative turned on an unjust judge. Such an adaptation of a migratory plot is most likely to have been made in the seventeenth century (also the date of the oldest extant copies) when, in connection with the evolution of Russian literature in general, satire, upon the judicial practice of Muscovite Rus among other things, first came into being.

During the eighteenth century the *Shemyakin Sud* passed over into chapbook literature and later on, in the nineteenth century, was given literary treatment by several writers, for example, Polevoy.[1]

TALE OF YORSH YORSHOVICH

Apparently not written earlier than the middle of the seventeenth century, the *Tale of Yorsh Yorshovich* [Ruff son of Ruff], *Son of the Prickler,* or *Record of the Suit Brought by the Bream Against the Ruff in the Matter of Rostov Lake and the Rivers,* takes for its theme the judiciary processes of Muscovite Rus. It is a satirical reaction to the lawsuits about land which had followed thick and fast upon the epoch of "Disorder."

In one copy of the oldest redaction, the tale runs as follows: the "boyar's son," Bream of lake Rostov, and his companions, petition the "fish-lords," great Sturgeon, Beluga, and White Vimba against a "malefactor," the cheat Ruff, son of Prickler. Bream complains that Ruff by breeding in Rostov

1 MS. texts of the tale have been published by: 1) Pypin in Kalachov's *Arkhiv istoricheskikh i practicheskikh svedenii otnoyashchikhsya do Rossii* (Thesaurus of Historical and Practical Information Relating to Russia) (1859), Bk. IV, Sec. V, pp. 1–10; 2) Kostomarov in *Pamyatniki starinnoy russkoy literatury* (Monuments of Early Russian Literature), II, pp. 405–406; 3) Buslayev in *Istoricheskaya khrestomatiya* (Historical Anthology), columns 1443–1446; 4) F. Bulgakov in *izd. Obshchestva lyubiteley drevney pis'mennosti* (Publications of the Society of Friends of Early Literature) (St. Petersburg, 1879); 5) Afanasyev in *Narodnye russkie skazki* (Russian Folk Tales) (1897), Vol. II, pp. 276–279; here also may be found folk-tale variants on the just judge. On the tale see N. S. Tikhonravov, "Shemyakin Sud," *Works,* Vol. I, pp. 308–313; M. I. Sukhomlinov, "Povest o sude Shemyaki" (Tale of the Judgment of Shemaka), *Issledovaniya po drevney russkoy literature* (Studies in Early Russian Literature), pp. 637–671; F. Buslayev, "Perekhozhie povesti i rasskazy" (Travels of Tale and Story), *Moy dosugi* (My Leisure Hours), Pt. 2, pp. 298–313; D. Rovinskii, *Russkie narodnye kartinki* (Russian Popular Prints), Vol. I, pp. 189–192; Vol. IV, pp. 166–176; Vol. V, pp. 148–150 (Rovinski reproduces MS. and chapbook texts of the folk tales). A bibliography of the tale in Russian and foreign literatures is assembled by S. F. Oldenburg in *Zhivaya starina* (The Living Past) (1891), Pt. 3, pp. 183–185.

Lake has deprived Bream and his companions of their "old perquisites." This Ruff had been breeding all over the rivers and lakes; personally he was small, but he had prickly scales like sharp boar spears, and when he met the Breams, he stabbed them in the ribs with his sharp prickles. He scurries about the rivers like a mad dog, whereas the Breams are incapable of a life of constant dodging, do not care to quarrel and have high words with aggressive people, and ask the righteous judges to protect their rights as against Yorsh.

When questioned as to the complaints against him, Yorsh makes reply to the judges that Rostov Lake had from of old been in the possession of his grandfathers and now by right belonged to him, while Bream lived in a vicinity at the bottom of the lake and had previously never shown himself to the world at large. In his defense Yorsh says:

"But I, my lords, Yorsh, by the grace of God, the blessing of my father, and my mother's prayers, was never a rioter, a thief, a robber, or a brigand by nature; no robbery charge has ever been brought against me; I am a good man; I live by my own strength and not by other people's; I am known in Moscow and other great cities by princes and boyars, court gentleman-waiters, and nobles, Muscovite lodgers, clerks, and scriveners, and persons of all ranks: and they pay a high price for me, and boil me with pepper and saffron, and serve me honorably, and many good people eat me when they have a drunken headache and compliment me afterwards" [that is, they express satisfaction at the taste].

Then the judges turn to Bream, who presents in support of his case the witnesses for his side, Whitefish and Loduga. The judge asks Yorsh what he has to say with respect to the testimony of these witnesses. Yorsh replies that there has never been any hostility or disagreement between him and the witnesses, but that their evidence is not to be depended upon because Whitefish and Loduga are "rich people, living on their incomes," while Bream is also an "industrialist"; that is, a well-off man. "These people," says Yorsh, "want to ruin us people of small means without due cause."

As a witness for Bream the celebrated Lady Herring then comes forward, endorses Bream as a good Christian, calls Yorsh a swindler, drunkard, cheat, and mischief-maker. And as to the taste of Ruff, Mistress Herring has no very high opinion: he is known in Moscow not by persons of quality but by tavern idlers, "who have only one coin to spend and for this buy many Ruffs, eat one half and spit out the other and toss it to the dogs." Judge Sturgeon himself can remember sly tricks of Yorsh's that nearly cost Sturgeon his life. Yorsh takes exception to celebrated Mistress Herring because she is related to Bream, but in the end the judges decree that Bream and his companions are justified and that Yorsh is guilty. They turn him over to the plaintiff with instructions to administer the merchants' form of execution for robbery and cheating: to beat him and then hang him in the sun in the heat of the day.

An ending later added to the tale states that Yorsh was in no wise taken aback by this sentence but said to the judges: "'Lord judges, you have judged me not as you ought, but as you were bought. Bream and his companions you corrected, me you have convicted.' Yorsh spat in the eyes of the judges and leaped into the thicket: that was the last they ever saw of Yorsh." So ended this lawsuit.

The tale is a very clever parody on processes of examining testimony and passing judgment in Muscovite Rus. In addition to the judges, the plaintiff, the defendant, and the witnesses, it presents the bailiff Perch, the expert witnesses Bull-head and Sea Urchin, Clerk Sheatfish, examining magistrate Carp, Clerk Groundling, and so forth. Perch is a bribetaker. The judges order him to invest Turbot as expert witness for the induction of Witness Herring, but Turbot buys himself off from Perch "with great bribes," saying as he does so: "Lord Perch! I am not suited to being an expert witness: I have a great belly; I can't walk, and my eyes are small; I can't see very far, and my lips are thick; I can't talk before gentlefolk." The author of the satire-parody was evidently acquainted with the "legal" and "judicial" records kept of law cases as early as the fifteenth century, and also, perhaps, with the Code of Tsar Alexis Mikhailovich. In moral qualities and in conduct, Yorsh is akin to the rogue and cheat Frol Skobeyev. The judges in the story are not on the side of the Yorshes, "men of small means," but of the Breams, rich and influential boyars, who are, perhaps, formally right in their complaints against the insignificant fishlet, but who win the case not because they are right but because they are gentlefolk, people of means, and can bribe the judges. The satire describes the shifty rogue Yorsh with a good deal of art. The author apparently knows exactly where to have him and is not inclined to exaggerate his virtues but at the same time tells with evident sympathy and great glee, in Sturgeon's words, how Yorsh made a laughingstock of the "old peasant," slow-witted Sturgeon, reduced his stoutness considerably, and was very nearly the death of him. In this respect again the author's attitude is highly reminiscent of the attitude adopted by the author of the "history" of Frol Skobeyev.

In the second edition the fishes seeking legal protection are "God's orphans," peasants who have suffered at the hands of the "cheat" and "ugly mug—Yorsh." Here the accusatory tendency is more marked. The complainants against Yorsh are now Bream and Bull-head, who turn out to be "peasants of the Rostov district," while Yorsh is descended from "the boyar offspring of petty boyars." Yorsh says that Bream and Bull-head had been "bondmen" of his father, who manumitted them just before his death "to commemorate his soul." Thus the complaint in this edition comes not from the children of boyars but from peasants. In one of the copies of this edition, Yorsh and his like are called "powers that be" and "moneybags." In later adaptations the tale passes over into a facetious skit abundantly interspersed with rhymes and assonances.

In genre the tale belongs with western European poems of the type of the *Romance of Reynard,* where animals become a vehicle for satire. In this country, of course, plots dealing with the animal kingdom were superbly employed by Saltykov-Shchedrin in his satirical fairy tales. In the tales of the "wise gudgeon" and "Carp-the-Idealist," the characters, as here, are fishes.

Like the *Shemyakin Sud,* the "Record of the suit", of Bream *versus* Yorsh found its way during the eighteenth century into chapbook literature and also passed over into oral folktale.[2]

ALPHABET OF THE NAKED POOR MAN

Russian seventeenth century satire also drew into its orbit a genre which had been popular here from as far back as the twelfth century, that of "explanatory alphabets," works consisting of detached sentences arranged in alphabetical order. Down to and during the sixteenth century, "explanatory alphabets" dealt for the most part in church dogma, moral admonition or church history. Later on, they specialized in material bearing on social life and its abuses, with particular emphasis on material illustrative of the perniciousness of intoxication. In many cases such alphabets were adapted to the purposes of the schoolteacher.

The *Alphabet of the Naked Poor Man,* also known in manuscripts under such titles as *Legend of the Poor and Naked* and *History of the Naked in Alphabet Form,* already belongs in the category of purely satirical works along with such things as the *Alphabet of the Beautiful Girl* or the *Instruc-*

2 MS. texts of the tale of Yorsh are reproduced in Afanasyev's *Russkie Narodnye skazki* (Russian Folk Tales), Vol. I (*Academia,* 1936), pp. 133–135 (*ibid.,* pp. 123–133 gives folk-tale texts of the narrative), and as supplement to I. A. Shlyapkin's article, "Skazka o Ershe Ershove syne Shchetinnikove" (Tale of Yorsh Yorshovich, Son of the Prickler), *Zhurnal min. nar. prosv.* (Journal of the Ministry of Public Instruction) (1904), No. 8, pp. 380–400, and as a supplement to V. P. Adrianova-Peretts' study *Ocherki po istorii russkoy satiricheskoy literatury XVII v.* (Sketches in the History of Russian Satirical Literature of the Seventeenth Century) (Leningrad, 1937), pp. 124–162. See also D. Rovinskii, *Russkie narodnye kartinki* (Russian Popular Prints), Vol. I, pp. 402–405 (eighteenth century chapbook text of the tale); Vol. IV, pp. 271–280; Vol. V, pp. 151–154 (items on printings of MS. copies of the tale, analysis of MS. texts).

tion Administered by a Husband to His Wife Since the Wife to the Husband Ministers. The company in which the *Alphabet of the Naked* is found in manuscript collections, that of satirical tales popular in the seventeenth century, bears out the supposition that it was itself regarded as a work of about the same kind and not as an "explanatory alphabet" in the traditional sense. Fundamentally the *Alphabet of the Naked* consists of a narrative in the first person about the bitter lot of a man, barefoot, naked, and cold, living in Moscow, the details of the text sometimes varying considerably from copy to copy. In general the poor man is described as the son of well-to-do parents, who always had "fritters and hot buttered pancakes and nice pies. . . . My father and my mother left me their house and their estate," he says of himself. In the oldest seventeenth century copy, the hero's ruin is thus explained: "The envy of relatives, the oppression of the rich, the hatred of neighbors, the treachery of talebearers, the backbiting of flatterers conspired to knock my feet out from under me. . . . The object must have been my house, for the rich swallowed it up while my relatives plundered it." In other, later, copies, the misfortunes of the young man are explained as due to his "drinking and squandering it all away," or they are not explained at all, mention of them being accompanied by the uninformative observation: "But it was not God's will that I should possess it," or: "But it was not God's will that I should live on my scant means," and so forth. Even the youth's pitiful personal effects all went to pay debts: "I had some very good bast mats and bast rope, and those too they took for debt," he complains. He has even no land that he could plow and sow. "My land is waste," he says, "and all overgrown with grass; I have nothing to weed it with and nothing to sow, and I have no bread either."

The *Alphabet* is written in rhythmic prose, rhymed here and there, as in the following example:

> "People I see that in wealth do live,
> And to us naked nothing give,
> Devil knows to what end they save,"

or:

> "I cannot find a place my head to lay,
> My boots and my bast sandals break and fray,
> I cannot do a thing to bring in pay."

Adages are also encountered; for example: "How could I even offer him a bribe when I had nowhere to get it from?"; "I would have gone on visits, but was not invited anywhere or to anything"; "I would have stitched on a string of corals for the holiday but was short of funds," and so on. All these peculiarities of the *Alphabet of the Naked,* along with its typical use of colloquial speech, place it on a level with such works of late seventeenth century satirical literature as the *Kalyazin Petition,* the *Tale of Savva the Priest,* and so on (see below). Its general tenor and ethological details also place the *Alphabet* in the latter half of the seventeenth century, and its rise is associated with the suburban milieu, the intra-class attitudes of which it reflects.[3]

TALE OF THE ROOSTER AND THE FOX

Another tale known in Rus during the first half of the seventeenth century, to judge by a documentary reference, was that of the *Rooster and the Fox,* which is extant in prose and verse adaptations in eighteenth and nineteenth century copies, later passed over into chapbook literature and folk tale, and constitutes a satire on outward and formal piety.

Even in the old *Physiologus* the fox was regarded as a very crafty and cunning creature. A fox story related to the *Physiologus* saga is found in a manuscript collection of the latter half of the seventeenth century under the title, *Discourse on Those Who Bear Tales to the Prince About a Friend.* A fierce beast, the lion, was taken ill and all the beasts on earth came to see him, except the fox. And the wolf denounced her to the fierce beast, who sent a fierce servant to bring in the fox and beat her without mercy. The wolf sought to do the fox an ill turn, not knowing that he was making trouble for himself. When the lion reproached her for absenting herself from the bedside of her sick king, the fox made the excuse that she had been scouring the whole country in search of some means of curing the king of his malady, and had with difficulty found a certain peasant woman whose advice was to take the hide from a live wolf and wrap the invalid's head in it, whereupon the invalid would recover. When they started to skin the wolf alive, he began to howl:

"Alas, brothers, may my woes teach you not to bear tales about one another to the prince. Behold the cruel execution done on me, and how I must die in my sins. For such is the fate prepared for one who bears tales about another to the prince: here he shall perish without a trace, and after death his soul shall abide in hell." [4]

The oldest edition of the *Tale of the Rooster and the Fox* is in prose; the versified form did not appear before the beginning of the eighteenth cen-

3 For study and texts of the monument, see V. P. Adrianova-Peretts, *op. cit.,* pp. 10–26.

4 See I. I. Sreznevskii, *Svedeniya i zametki o maloizvestnykh i neizvestnykh pamyatnikakh* (Information and Notes on Little Known and Unknown Monuments) (St. Petersburg, 1876), LXII, pp. 367–368.

tury. In this oldest edition the story begins with the affable fox approaching the tree on which sits the rooster, that is, the cock, praising Christ "in a great, loud voice" and waking Christians from their sleep; she addresses words of flattery to the rooster, suggests that he come down to her, a "reverend woman," and make confession of his sins, which the fox will gladly remit "in this world and in the world to come."

The rooster, although acknowledging his previous sins, at first refuses to come down from the tree because he knows that the fox has a flattering tongue and that her lips are full of guile.

In words from "sacred books," and even shedding tears over the rooster's sins, the fox tries to persuade him of the necessity of confession if he would escape eternal torment and utter darkness. Overcome by the "edifying" words of the fox, the cock himself weeps and starts to come down to her "from tree to tree, from branch to branch, from bush to bush, from stump to stump." Having descended, he perched on the fox's head, and the fox at once put her claws into him, started to grind her teeth, look at him with "pitiless eye, like the Devil looking pitilessly at a Christian," and, as he started to wail in her claws, to reproach him for his various transgressions. In "sacred books" and in "precepts of the holy fathers," it is written: "It is expedient to take one wife to comply with the law, a second for the begetting of children, but he who takes a third, commits adultery; whereas the rooster, "evildoer, miscreant, sorcerer, lawbreaker," keeps many wives, twenty and thirty and more, and for this the fox dooms him to die in his sins.

But the cock tries to parry the fox's reference to "Writ" with another reference to that same "Writ" where it says: "Be fruitful and grow and multiply upon the earth; show every solicitude for widows and orphans, and care for them exceeding well, so shall you be heirs of the kingdom of heaven."

Then the fox prefers a new charge against the cock: he hates his brother, and wherever he meets him fights grievously with him over their jealous wives and concubines and for this he must die. And again, when she, the hungry fox, came to the peasant's yard where the hens were sitting, he screamed and roused the people and they chased her and would have killed her, just as if she had meant to strangle their father and drown their mother; for one hen they would have destroyed her. And now no one can deliver him from the fox's claws, neither prince, nor boyar, nor any other magnate.

The rooster excuses himself by saying: "With whatever master you live, him serve and do his will," and in the Gospels it says: " 'No servant can serve two masters.' "

But neither quotations from "Writ" nor pitiful pleas for forgiveness have any effect on the fox. "You have put your trust," she said, "in your much learning and your ability to answer. But these cannot save you. You are condemned to death."

The fox is now about to "end the cock's life," but the cock, wailing with a loud voice, asks to be permitted to say one last word: the metropolitan of Krutits had made him subdeacon, had praised his voice highly and had invited him to sing a delicate descant from his ambo. The cock promises to pay the fox an annual poll tax, if she so desires, and if she cares to be employed by the church will get the metropolitan to make her wafer baker and she will have a large income over and above the rooster's poll tax of fifty rubles. But the fox sets no store by the cock's promises. "Don't promise me cranes in the sky, just give me a titmouse in the hand. Don't promise me in a year, promise me in the mouth," says she, and eats the cock.

The use of "Holy Writ" for purposes of satire and parody in such ludicrous connections as these plainly testifies to a general collapse of church authority, especially in the milieu from which the tale emanates, that of the office worker or the tradesman. As a Western counterpart to the tale of the rooster and the fox, one of the stories in a Polish collection of Aesop's fables may be cited, where the accuser is the cat, who ends by eating the cock. The tale is a skillful combination of ecclesiastical quotations with elements from vulgar speech and from the oral-poetry tradition.[5]

TALE OF THE DRUNKARD

In a seventeenth century index of forbidden books was included a work briefly styled *About a Drunkard*,[6] which was a parody on old stories of visits to paradise that had been translated from the Greek. It is quite possible that the reference in the index is to the tale known as *Discourse on a Drunkard; How He Entered into Paradise*. The aspirant to residence in paradise is here not a pious, saintly man, every act of whose life makes him worthy of reception into paradise or at least of a vision of it, but a drunkard, a reveler, whose only merit had been that while drinking he praised the lord at every ladleful and, in addition, often prayed to God during the night. When the drunkard died, the Lord bade his guardian angel take his soul and set it down at the gates of paradise. Having done this, the angel went away, and the drunkard began knocking at the heavenly gates. In response to the drunk-

---

[5] For texts and a study of the tale, see V. P. Adrianova-Peretts, *op. cit.*, pp. 163–224.

[6] See A. N. Pypin, "Dlya obyasneniya stat'i o lozhnykh knigakh" (In Explanation of the Article about False Books), *Letopis zanyatii Arkheograficheskoy komisii* (Chronicle of the Studies of the Archaeographical Commission) (Moscow, 1862), Pt. 1, p. 39.

ard's knocking there appear in turn the apostles Peter and Paul, kings David and Solomon, St. Nicholas. All of them refuse to admit the drunkard to paradise, giving as the reason: "Drunkards may not enter here." The drunkard censures all of them, reminding each about his shortcomings, and they retreat in shame from the gates of paradise. Even when John the Theologian, Christ's friend, tries to keep him from entering paradise, the drunkard rebukes him: "But you and Luke wrote in the Gospels: 'Love one another,' for God loves all, but you hate strangers, and you hate me! John the Theologian! Either your hand miswrote, or your words you revoke!" In reply, John the Theologian says to the drunkard:

"You are our man, drunkard, enter with us into paradise," and opens the heavenly gates to him. Upon entering paradise, the drunkard sits down "in the best place." The holy fathers, shocked at his action, ask him what right he had to enter paradise, nay more, seat himself in the best place which they themselves dare not approach. But, unembarrassed, the drunkard replies:

"Holy fathers! you can't talk to a drunkard as you do to a sober man!" And they all said to him:

"Be that place yours, drunkard, now and for everlasting."

The plot of the tale, utilized by Leo Tolstoy, along with other material, in his story "The Repentant Sinner," belongs to the migratory category. We encounter it, with some variations, in a French fabliau and in a German retelling. The former portrays a peasant, the latter, a miller. By making it a drunkard who enters paradise and claims the best place there, the Russian variant gives added satirical and parodic point to the tale, for we now get the triumph of no ordinary sinner but of an addict of that vice which not only in the good old days but even in the seventeenth century entailed hell-fire, from which the only possible escape was through repentance in a monastery. Plainly marked in the tale is the attempt to set over against the churchly preaching of asceticism an assertion of man's right to earthly pleasures, even those that the conventional rules for pious conduct stigmatize as sinful.[7]

---

[7] The text of the tale is published in *Pamyatniki starinnoy russkoy literatury* (Monuments of Ancient Russian Literature), II, pp. 477–478, in Afanasyev's book, *Narodnye russkie legendy* (Russian Folk Legends) (Kazan, 1914), pp. 143–147, by V. N. Peretts in the Kiev *Universitetskie izvestiya* (University News) (1907), No. 8, pp. 71–76. On the tale see A. N. Veselovskii, "Pamyatniki literatury povestvovatel'noy" (Monuments of Narrative Literature), in A. Galakhov's *Istoriya russkoy slovesnosti* (History of Russian Literature), 3rd ed., Vol. I, pp. 497–500.

PETITION OF KALYAZIN MONASTERY

The *Record of the Petition of Kalyazin Monastery*, written in the last quarter of the seventeenth century, exposes, under the guise of a humorous supplication, wayward and drunken practices in a monastery of the Tver eparchy. The lesser monastic brethren of the Kalyazin cloister petition Simeon, Archbishop of Tver, against their archimandrite Gabriel for that he, having forgotten the fear of God and his monastic vows, is plaguing the monks: he has taught the rascally sextons to ring the bells at inopportune times and beat on the boards, and these rascally sextons give the monks no rest day or night. At midnight they call the monks to Church service, whereas the monks are then seated about the bucket, trouserless, clad only in wrappers, and have not yet had time the nightly "cell rule" of nine dippers to tell o'er, the decoction of beer into buckets to pour. The archimandrite is uneconomical with monastery funds, burns much incense and many candles, and thereby has smudged the whole church, while the monks' eyes have been eaten out and their throats choked with lampblack. At the archimandrite's order, one-eyed Falaley had been stationed at the monastery gate with a whip. He refused to let the monks out: "To go to the villages them forbade, the cattle pens to inspect, the calves into the stalls to drive, the broody hens in the cellar to set, the dairymaids to shrive."

Upon arriving at Kalyazin Monastery, the archimandrite had set about "destroying the monastic order, had driven out all the old drunkards." He would have completely emptied the monastery if the authorities in Moscow had not thought to send it new drunkards discovered in other monasteries and in taprooms. The archimandrite chastises the monks mercilessly:

> At Kalyazin our archimandrite does just as he pleases,
> On holidays and workdays great chains on the brothers' necks he places.
> Upon us rods he has broken
> And whips to tatters stricken,
> But though our treasury he has drained,
> Small profit for himself has gained.

Once the monks got the idea of twisting long, thick ropes out of hemp and dragging kegs of beer from the cellar and using them to block their cell doors and keep out the "wakers" who disturbed their beer-drinking. But the archimandrite gave orders that the ropes be so twisted from the hemp that they would be suitable for lashes and ordered that with these lashes the lay brothers beat the monks, and that the monks meanwhile bawl a canon. The archimandrite makes them eat meagre fare, when in their opinion it would be better on fast days to feed them caviar, white vimba,* sterlet soup, pies, pancakes, and other tasty victuals, and give them March beer to go with it.

The monks tried to persuade the archimandrite to live in peace and harmony with them, brew beer with the brethren and get drunk with them, go to church less frequently and not tire them out with services; but the archimandrite, "by birth of the coastal provinces, in temper a Rostovite, and in mentality a Kashinian," would not listen to anything his advisers said and continued to ill-treat them. The brothers contemplate ridding themselves of their strict superior and getting another who will live as they live and not persecute them for their drunken revelry. But in the meantime they request the archbishop to curb the stern archimandrite. The monks declare:

Otherwise, the archimandrite will get it and no mistake. We, your devoted servants, will drive the mules round the bend there, and put our hands to the plowshare, and then start out by shank's mare to another monastery, and where beer and wine we discover there shall we stop over; and when everything's drunk up there, to another cloister fare. And after headache and regret, a third ramble and much grief shall back to Kalyazin come and inspect the barns and granaries here at home.

The petition holds up to very keen and malicious ridicule the state of affairs obtaining in Kalyazin Monastery. It is written in a lively, picturesque colloquial style, with a great number of rhymed lines, and rhymed proverbs and aphorisms, such as: "On our shoulders our bodies lay heavy, and whips make a sleeping-room stuffy"; "turnip, horseradish, and with them, the dirty cupbearer Ephrem"; "To live alone suited his disposition, and munch the dry bread of affliction"; "Of respect for us he had no lack; it lay so smooth all the way down the back that your skin would slip from your shoulders," and so on. The names of Archbishop Simeon and Archimandrite Gabriel mentioned in the petition are not fictitious but real: Simeon was archbishop of Tver from 1676 to 1681, and Gabriel, archimandrite of Kalyazin Monastery at the same time. Consequently the appearance of the *Kalyazin Petition* must be assigned to this period. Judging from the fact that in two copies it is dated 1677, the writing may be more exactly assigned to this precise year. The scenes from the monastic life depicted in the satire were, however, typical not alone of Kalyazin Monastery but of many Russian monasteries during practically the whole seventeenth century and from then on. Not without reason was this proverb composed in connection with monastic habits: "The right-hand clergyman's singing you hear, but the one to the left of the altar is drinking beer." The frank realism with which the petition describes monastic life on the one hand demonstrates very graphically the decay of monastic traditions that had already set in at this time, and on the

* Variety of white fish found in the Baltic.—Ed.

other testifies, as do the two preceding tales, to the growing critical attitude
toward representatives of the Church now prevalent in the suburban or
peasant circles from which the petition apparently emanated, thence passing
in the eighteenth century into chapbook literature.[8]

TALE OF SAVVA THE PRIEST

If the *Kalyazin Petition* gives a satirical picture of the life of the black
or monastic clergy, then the *Legend of Priest Savva and His Great Reputation,* written throughout in awkward verse or, more exactly, in rhymed
prose, tells of life among those of the white urban clergy who earned their
living by the training and tuition of laymen desiring to become priests.
Candidates for priestly office from this contingent were in the majority of
cases of very low grade both from the moral and from the scholarly point
of view. Young men who could scarcely read and write were often ordained
priests, making their scant learning pass muster in the eyes of their inter-
mediaries, their priest-teachers, by bribes and all manner of presents in kind.
A fairly large revenue also came into the patriarchal treasury from aspirants,
since Patriarch Nikon and his predecessor Joseph had established the ruling
that ordinations must take place in Moscow even if the candidate lived
several hundred versts away. Hence the ordinand was subject to double
exactions.

The tale of Priest Savva unmasks a Muscovite priest-professional who
made a fortune by the instruction of candidates for holy orders, but paid
heavily for extreme abuse of his profession and in general for a too negligent
attitude toward the duties of his office.

Priest Savva officiated at SS. Cosmas and Damian, across the Moscow
River, and the people in his parish were all "rich peasants." He never so
much as set foot in the church:

> The people stood and prayed, but he through the law courts strayed,
> Seeking some youth to attract with whom later a deal might be made.
> And he scoured the public square, to seek for candidates there,
> And tried to talk them over, to lure them across the river.
> 'Drop in on me some day as you pass, even if not to stay for Mass
> I am Savva the priest, you see, I think most people have heard of me.
> I'll manage your brothers' ordaining, you won't have a shirt remaining.'

[8] MS. texts of the *Kalyazin Petition* are printed in *Russkii arkhiv* (Russian Archives)
1873), No. 9, pp. 1777–1779, and as a supplement to V. P. Adrianova-Peretts, *op. cit.,* pp.
96–123; the chapbook text is given in Rovinskii's *Russkie narodnye kartinki* (Russian Popular Prints), Vol. I, pp. 405–409; Vol. IV, pp. 280–287.

He keeps the candidates as long as their money lasts and upon sending them home takes a voucher from some to the effect that they will come back to Moscow and bring him wine. His candidates water the cabbages and heat the bath.

Savva's wife warns him to be more circumspect in his behavior, but he refuses to listen and ends up in prison and in chains. While in chains, Savva has a dream. Two angels have come to him and they tell him that he has a great deal of money in his pouch and that they will take care of it for him. At home Savva slept on a feather bed, but in the patriarch's bake-house he waked up on a bast mat. A man with a whip was put in charge of him and came near thrashing him. There was no money in the pouch: those two angels had let it fall out and now he would never get it back from safekeeping. The tale ends with a "droll ditty" to Priest Savva:

Rejoice, rascally Savva, wicked Priest Savva!
Rejoice in the bake-house confined, staying in like a candidate.
Rejoice that your beard has grown, though this can't be said for your mind.

The *Legend of Priest Savva* may be used as documentary illustration of historical facts from the latter half of the seventeenth century. Thus, the *Legend* says that Savva's parish across the Moscow River, Cosmas and Damian, was populated by "rich peasants." This tallies with the facts: the left-bank church of Cosmas and Damian was located in the suburb of Kadashevo, populated by the imperial weavers and craftswomen of the linen guild who enjoyed considerable privileges in the province of trade and were therefore well-to-do. Priest Savva is fairly typical of the actual priests who taught candidates. Finally as to Savva's punishment, confinement on a chain in the patriarch's bake-house, that too is consonant with the actual method of punishing offending ecclesiastics during the latter half of the seventeenth century. The palace of Patriarch Nikon and the episcopal courts had dungeons with iron chains and wooden stocks. In these dungeons penalized ecclesiastics were confined on a chain and, so chained, were made to sift flour for the patriarch's or the bishop's bake-house.

Like the *Kalyazin Petition*, the tale of Priest Savva is written in a lively colloquial style and introduces to an even greater extent the rhymed proverb and aphorism, these giving the tale a folklore flavor. Curiously enough, one of the episodes in the *Legend*, the "Dream of Priest Savva," beginning with the words, "Little did I sleep last night but much I dreamed," is a parody of folk ballads about a youth's or a maiden's dream, beginning with the words: "Last night, my dear, last night I slept, and many things I dreamed," and so forth.[9]

[9] The text of the *Legend* from three copies, and a study of it, may be found in V. P. Adrianova-Peretts's book, pp. 224–238.

PARODIES ON THE CHURCH SERVICE AND ON "HOLY WRIT"

The latter half of the seventeenth century brought satires against social and domestic evils of the time in the form of parodies on the church service, on "Holy Writ" and on saints' lives. The foremost example of this type of thing is the *Holiday Mass of the Pothouse Loafers,* or the *Pothouse Service,* a very witty and malicious arraignment of the "imperial pothouse," parodying an Orthodox Church service, the so-called "little" and "great" vespers, and the stereotyped life of the saint. The author of the parody, unlike his predecessors, the unmaskers of drunkenness, condemns this vice not from an abstractly religious point of view, as a sin punishable by God's justice, but from a practical viewpoint, as a great temporal evil undermining the popular well-being. Thus censure is directed not only at drunkards but at the "imperial pothouse" itself, which, with the furtherance of the tapsters, was enticing and ruining the whole Russian people from priests and deacons to serfs and women. Popular indignation against the propagation of taverns by the government stands out clearly in the parody. Every mention of the tavern is accompanied by very uncomplimentary epithets: the tavern is a "teacher of sin," a "destroyer of souls," an "insatiable maw," "domestic desolation," a "destroyer of the home," a "waster of wealth," a "purposeless existence," the "refuge of malefactors," and so forth. The despotism of the tavern is set forth in quite realistic or, more exactly, naturalistic terms.

The author is well up on all details of the church service, a fact which leads to the supposition that he was an ecclesiastic, most probably a member of the lower clergy. Judging by the words in one text of the *Holiday:* "Rejoice, tavern, blot on Vychegotsk Usolya," the parody came out in the Solvychegodsk district. The copy containing the oldest text of the *Holiday* is dated 1666.

After a short introduction the *Holiday* gives the following invitation: "Let us ring the summons to the little vespers on little goblets, then let us sound on the half-pails of beer, then play the thanksgiving hymns on the lesser forfeits, on rings and skirts and sleeves and trousers and breeches." The author addresses the tavern thus: "Who after drinking himself naked will not remember you, tavern unholy? Who will not sigh for long-hoarded wealth lost all in a single hour? Sorely though he may repent, it shall not be restored to him."

In parody of a prayer from the *Book of Hours:* "Grant, Lord, to keep us this evening without sin," and so forth, we find in the *Pothouse Service* the following lines:

Grant, lord, to stupefy us this evening without fights. I lay me down to sleep, may thy blessing be upon us, seekers and drinkers of the hop, and for getting us drunk thou shalt be praised and thy name exalted by us throughout the ages. Let thy power be upon us, hop, for in thee do we drinkers put our trust.

To the question as to what each may bring to the cheerful pothouse, this is the answer given:

Each man brings thee different gifts with the zeal of his heart: the priest and the deacon bring skullcaps and caps, rosaries and missals; monks their cloaks, cassocks, cowls and wrappers and all the furniture of their cells; clerks drink up their books and translations and ink and all manner of clothes and their brief cases, while wise philosophers exchange their wisdom for folly; office workers worship with their backs on the stove; princes and boyars and governors boast of their position under the influence of mead; gunners and soldiers have bought trouble for themselves and will swell up as they lie on the stove; swordsmen sharpen a sword for their own neck; doctors and charlatans boast to you of calamities; thieves and robbers make merry, while slaves save themselves as, carrying relics in their aprons, they talk fast and spit far.

Parodying the usual stereotyped life of a saint, which starts with a characterization of his parents, usually pious and worthy people, and goes on to tell of his deeds, the author gives us a drunkard's life: "For he was born in many different countries of an unrevered and foolish father and was reared on the bread of affliction." Others were begotten of fine, rich parents and brought up without a care, but upon reaching young manhood began to live not according to parental advice but as they chose. Their parents could not keep them on the right road by any precepts and left them to their own devices.

They were fierce and bold, were neither woodsmen nor farmers, took a certain part of their father's estate and went to the tavern, squandered their estate contrary to God's will, and afterward went poor and hungry . . . but having an insatiable maw, ever desiring to drink themselves tipsy and loll like fools and annoy people with ridiculous talk, picking quarrels and coming to blows and breaking bones, in the extremity of their need enduring hunger and nakedness and all manner of affliction, they had neither soft beds nor warm clothes, nor a pillow under their head, but curling up like dogs found places for themselves on the stove; moreover their bodies were stained with soot, and they endured smoke and fire

and all this not for God but for the satisfaction of their lower instincts: "Had they endured such misery for God's sake, truly they had been new martyrs, and their memory had merited praise."

So does this work parody the canonical life of the saint in terms of a drunkard's.

Throughout his parody the author, by means of puns, plays fast and loose with everything that had enjoyed the highest respect in Old Rus: for "seemly" (holy) things he substitutes "unseemly" (obscene), for "Christian prelates" (*svyatiteli*), "fierce destroyers [*gubiteli*] of Christians," "Christian extortioners" (*lupiteli*), "the three blind men" (*slepiteli*), for wonder-workers "bringers-to-naught," and so forth.

The language of the parody is a combination of intentionally archaized speech with colloquial, conversational, often facetious, language, as, for example: "Glory be to the father Ivanets and to the son Selivanets. Everyone who touches you won't go forth with praise on his lips, but saying: 'Last night I was drunk; in my pouch there was money to spare; this morning when I got up and felt it, not a penny was there.'" We often find proverbs, sometimes rhymed: "Bread, Lord, according to our strength, but a canopy according to our shoulders"; "You can pull by the hand, but more easily by the hair"; "As I shout into the wood, so is it echoed back"; "He had everything, but amounted to nothing"; "Into a forest they can see, but what's under their nose cannot hear"; "To live happily but be of no account"; "Your mother bore you, may the debtor's prison ignore you"; "Who doth a nettle pick shall his hand prick," and so forth. Sometimes the author makes a long string of rhymes as was done in the *Kalyazin Petition*: "Wherever we stay we stink, they say, enough to drive other people away," or: "The house is having fun, the master has been hung; the children whine, a hunger sign, and we, I swear, and no cheating, ourselves go to bed without eating." [10]

There is another interesting monument that calls for study, the *Legend of the Peasant's Son*, emanating apparently from the same milieu as the *Holiday Mass of the Pothouse Loafers*, judging from the fact that here too the author shows conversance with the church service and with "Holy Writ." The language suggests a late seventeenth century dating, although there is a remote possibility that the *Legend* may have appeared during the early years of the eighteenth century.

A father and a mother had a son whom they sent to school to learn reading and writing, but for his great disobedience and laziness the teacher beat and tormented him. Then he decided to stop studying and he set out to earn his living by robbery. He found some companions, with whom he went one night to a peasant's house, knocked on the locked gate and said, as he did so: "Open, windows of heaven, and unto us the peasant's gate." Having got into the yard, the thief continued: "Jesus went up into Mount Tabor with his disciples, and I into the peasant's yard with my companions." Approaching the storeroom, he declared: "Thomas touched Christ's rib, and I the corner of the peasant's storehouse." Having penetrated into the storehouse, the robber found under the bed a coffer of money and a chest of

---

[10] The text of the *Holiday* and a study of the monument are given in V. P. Adrianova-Peretts, *op. cit.*, pp. 27–96.

dresses. He stole all and said: "Bringing of thine own to thee, of all and for all." He found the peasant's wife's shawl and said: "Jesus girded himself with a towel, and I with the peasant's wife's shawl." Finding a loaf of bread in the storeroom, the thief started to eat it, saying: "Receive the body of Christ, taste of the fount immortal" (words pronounced during the Communion service), and so forth.

The peasant's wife, hearing the thief making himself at home in the storeroom, roused her husband: "Get up, husband, there's a thief in our storeroom," but her husband answered:

"That isn't a thief but an angel of the Lord, and he keeps saying godly words." Then the wife quite reasonably objected:

"If it was an angel of the Lord, he wouldn't be taking our fur coats from us and putting them on." The peasant hearkened to his wife, took a birch club and hit the thief on the forehead, but the thief said:

"Sprinkle me with hyssop and I shall be cleansed and become whiter than snow" (quotation from the Psalter).

Terrified, the peasant fell on the bed and started to scold his wife: "You wicked and accursed woman! You have made me commit a sin; an angel I have killed, Christ I have reviled! In future hold your tongue and don't talk to people." Seeing the peasant's lack of wit, the thief found a basin of water under the bed and started to wash his hands, saying as he did so:

"I wash my hands, I go about Thy altar, Lord."

The tale ends with the following paragraph:

And the thief opened the storeroom and called to his companions: "Peace to you who are heavy laden! And what I have done, have gathered, you will help me to bear away." And his companions entered the storeroom and what possessions the peasant had, they took them all and departed and closed the doors after them. And the peasant said: "Clean is my house and pure, and righteous moreover." And there remained to him nothing. Amen.

Thus does the *Legend of the Peasant's Son* introduce a parody on texts from the church service into the framework of a story depicting in comic form the slow-wittedness and simplemindedness of a peasant—a theme also fairly common in western European Facetiae—comic tales.[11]

In the latter half of the seventeenth century there appeared here a parodied *Medical Handbook on How to Cure Foreigners,* provoked by the grudge that

[11] The text of the *Legend* has been published by A. V. Markov, in "Pamyatniki staroy russkoy literatury" (Monuments of Ancient Russian Literature), *Izvestiya Tiflisskikh vysshikh zhenskikh kursov* (News of the Tiflis College Courses for Women) (Tiflis, 1914), Bk. I, Pt. 1, pp. 153–156, and by V. I. Sreznevsky as a supplement to *Svedeniya o rukopisakh, pechatnykh izdaniyakh i drugikh predmetakh, postupivshikh v rukopisnoe otdelenie biblioteki Akademii nauk v. 1902 g.* (Information About Manuscripts, Printed Editions and Other Items Received by the Manuscript Division of the Library of the Academy of Sciences in 1902) (St. Petersburg, 1903), pp. 106–107.

part of the Russian merchant class bore their competitors, the foreign merchants. This *Medical Handbook* is a parody on medical nostrums and oral charms. The very beginning will give a fair idea of its character:

When anyone feels pains about the heart and a heaviness in the belly, the correct treatment is: to get 16 drams of white pavement clatter, 16 drams of fine-ground spring horse-stamping, 13 drams of ferocious bell-ringing, and take the whole over a period of three days on an empty stomach; at noon on the fourth day take and sweat for three days naked in the frost, protected from the hot rays of the sun with seines and dragnets strung together.[12]

To the end of the seventeenth century belongs a rather mild comic anecdote in verse about two stupid, clumsy, obstinate and unlucky clowns, the "peddlers" Thomas and Yerem, who constantly get into scrapes and now and again into a fight.[13]

The examples above quoted practically exhaust the satirical and humorous parody literature of democratic origin that may be regarded as having appeared during the seventeenth century. However, judging from the fact that immediately afterward, during the eighteenth century, this sort of material occupies a very important place in chapbook literature, there must evidently have been more of it, even in the seventeenth century, than the manuscript tradition has transmitted to us. But even what is extant of seventeenth century satire, as produced in "plebeian" circles, will give a fairly clear picture of the development of new literary facts showing a new tenor. It is natural that the democratic strata should have been the milieu to introduce here the satirical genres that ridiculed and parodied the social and ecclesiastical principles basic to Old Rus. The leading role in seventeenth century satirical creation was taken by the suburb in the person of its intelligentsia, particularly the over-burdened clergy and the scriveners. Neither had any reason to be favorably disposed toward the official ecclesiastical order or to the governmental regime of their time. The plebeian intelligentsia shared in this respect the mood of the popular masses and reflected it in their satirical productions. Hence the closeness of seventeenth century satire to oral folk creation, revealing itself in lively, picturesque colloquial language, and in witty sayings and rhymed proverbs. Hence, also, its gravitation toward the realistic manner of depicting life which in general characterizes folk poetry.

And it is no accident that both by its motifs and methods and by its realistic elements, plebeian satire should have been linked with the creative work of the democratic Old Believer opposition that had fought the constituted ecclesiastical and civil authorities. The style of the *Kalyazin Petition*, the

---

[12] For text and study see *op. cit.* by V. P. Adrianova-Peretts, pp. 239–249.

[13] For texts see N. Aristov's article, "Povest' o Fome i Yereme" (Tale of Thomas and Yerem), *Drevnyaya i novaya Rossiya* (Old and New Russia) (1876), Vol. I, pp. 358–368.

Holiday Mass of the Pothouse Loafers, and the *Legend of Priest Savva* on the one hand, and that of Archpriest Avvakum's writings on the other, have a good deal in common notwithstanding the essential differences in psychology and world outlook that separated the authors of the satires and parodies from the author of the *Life* and the epistles to his followers, zealots for the sacrosanct days of yore.

Versification in the

Seventeenth Century

PRESYLLABIC VERSE

IN studying the narrative literature of the epoch of "Disorder," we noted as of fairly frequent occurrence in several stories of this epoch the embellishment of prose with rhymed lines of unequal length, terminating in verbs. This method was however by no means new in principle. It had been used sporadically, as was said earlier, in many monuments of Russian literature, some of them from as far back as the eleventh century. The only unusual thing was the intensiveness of its application, and real innovation came when into two chapters of Avraamy Palitsyn's prose *Legend* were wedged verse passages consisting of several of these uneven lines and having not only verbal but also nominal and adjectival rhymes, while still greater innovation marked the use of this same type of verse in the tailpiece to the *Annalistic Book* ascribed to Katyrev-Rostovsky, where, incidentally, verse is for the first time so called ("Begin in verse the Rebellion's course"). At approximately the same time as Avraamy Palitsyn and the author of the *Annalistic Book* (that is, about the first quarter of the seventeenth century), other verse writers came forward: Prince Sem. Iv. Shakhovsky, author of *Epistle to a Friend*, ending in twenty-six lines of verse; Priest Ivan Nasedka, who wrote a long polemic work, *Exposition on Luther*, which likewise ends with verses; Monk Antonius Podolsky, to whom is ascribed the long *Epistle to a Certain Person*, containing more than six hundred lines of verse, and, finally, Prince Iv. Andr. Khvorostinin, a most fertile author, celebrated as a religious free-thinker, charged with heresy, with negligence of the Orthodox faith, of fasts and other church observances, and also with Latin sympathies. Khvorostinin maintained a very disdainful attitude toward Moscow society, considered himself infinitely superior to his fellow countrymen intellectually, said that "in Moscow people there are none, every man is a fool; there is no one to associate with," and longed to leave Moscow for Lithuania where he hoped to find a cultural background more suited to him. In searching his house, they found in his handwriting "many reproaches concerning all the people of the Muscovite state," among them one to the effect that " 'Moscow people sow the land with rye but all subsist, so to speak, on a lie,' and many other reproachful sayings in verse." For his free thought and for his defiant behavior, Khvorostinin was twice penalized by banishment to a monastery. During the second banishment, in 1622–1623, to the Byelozersk Monastery of St. Cyril, he "steadied down . . . came to his senses," broke with his heresy, was pardoned and returned to Moscow, where shortly afterward, in 1625, he died, having a short time previously gone so far as to be shorn a monk in the St. Sergius Monastery of the Trinity. During the last years of his life, to redeem his past in the eyes of the religious and secular authorities, he wrote several polemical works against heretics, among them a "Preamble set forth in paired lines ending with the same letters" [1]—a verse tract of more than 1,000 lines. It begins thus:

> Beautiful tales of believers
> Humiliate misbelievers.
> As a brightly shining star,
> So great the rewards of the saintly are.
> In the Orthodox faith they were well informed,
> To the godly law of the church conformed,
> The sacred canon rules they kept,
> Heretical teaching and writing refused to accept.
> First principles shone so bright to the good
> That invincible they in their piety stood;
> Fair indeed are the words of their mouth,
> True are their miracles, shining forth.

Unlike later Russian syllabic verse, which strove to observe the balance of lines in individual poems, used only feminine rhyme and consistently marked the caesura, presyllabic verse knew neither balance of lines nor caesura, used feminine, masculine, dactyllic, and even hyperdactyllic rhyme equally, and for it frequently substituted assonances and consonances.

On the question of the genesis of our presyllabic verse, two basic opinions have been advanced. One of these, that of A. I. Sobolevsky, is, in substance, that versemaking took its rise in Rus under the direct influence of Ukrainian poetic practice and was brought to us by emigrants from the Ukraine. In his

---

[1] Printed, with preface by V. I. Savva on the works of Prince I. A. Khvorostinin, in *Letopisi zanyatii Arkheograficheskoy komissii*, 1905, (Chronicles of the Studies of the Archaeographical Commission) (St. Petersburg, 1907), Pt. 18, pp. 40–80.

refutation of Sobolevsky, L. N. Maykov, basing his argument on the fact that attempts at versification were made here even before the appearance in Rus of Kievan scholars, considers that the "first attempts at rhymed verse appeared here spontaneously so to speak, or in any event not as an imitation of West Russian syllabic rhymed verse." [2] On this question Sobolevsky's opinion must be recognized as closer to the truth. Sporadic instances of the use of rhyming lines such as we have observed in Russian literary practice even before the seventeenth century will not serve to explain either as to quantity or as to quality the relatively wide diffusion of versemaking already observable in the first quarter of the seventeenth century; as to the connections of Rus with the Ukraine, such without doubt existed even long before the coming of Kievan scholars to Moscow, and Moscow readers might easily have acquainted themselves with early irregular verses from the Ukraine, for example those of the late sixteenth century writer, Gerasim Smotritsky. [3]

The above examples of early Russian versemaking, on themes of a narrative and polemic nature, are all associated with names of specific writers belonging to the top social strata of Moscow society. Presyllabic verse, which continued to be written all through the seventeenth century (cf. the verses found in Timothy Kamenevich Rvovsky's epistle to Karion Istomin, 1681) and even into the early eighteenth, when the syllabic form had long since been adopted by the higher cultural strata, later broadened its thematic range considerably, even to include love, and came into common use in society at large. Thus, in the seventeenth century, presyllabic verse was the form used for numerous prayers and laudatory religious songs. [4] In it was also written at this time a complete Solemn Mass found in one of the collections belonging to the Miracle monastery in Moscow. [5] In another seventeenth century manuscript collection occurs the following verse eulogy of the hop:

[2] See A. I. Sobolevskii, "Iz istorii russkoy literatury XVII v." (From the History of Russian Literature in the Seventeenth Century), *Bibliograf* (1891), No. 304, pp. 37–60; L. N. Maykov, "O nachale russkikh virsh" (On the Beginning of Russian Verse), *Zhurnal min. nar. prosv.* (Journal of the Ministry of Public Instruction) (1891), No. 6, pp. 443–453; A. I. Sobolevskii, "K istorii russkikh stikhov" (Toward a History of Russian Verse), *Bibliograf* (1891), Nos. 7–8, pp. 102–106; L. N. Maykov, "K istorii o nachale russkikh virsh" (Toward a History of the Beginning of Russian Verse), *Bibliograf* (1891), Nos. 9–10, pp. 113–118.

[3] On presyllabic verse, in addition to the articles previously indicated (on pp. 365 and 368), see introductory essay by I. N. Rozanov to the collection *Virshi, Sillabicheskaya poeziya XVII–XVIII vv.* (Verses: Syllabic Poetry of the Seventeenth and Eighteenth Centuries), Biblioteka poeta, malaya seriya, No. 3 (Poet's Library, Minor Series) (Sovetskii pisatel').

[4] See V. N. Peretts, *Istoriko-literaturnye issledovaniya i materialy* (Historico-Literary Investigations and Materials) (St. Petersburg, 1900), Vol. I, pp. 124–194.

[5] See A. S. Orlov, "Sborniki Zlatoust i Torzhestvennik" (The Collections Golden Mouth and Celebrant), *Pamyatniki drevney pismennosti* (Monuments of Early Literature) (St. Petersburg, 1905), CLVIII, pp. 29–80.

A monarch who takes me for his friend
Will as a foolish farmer end.
An official who makes a friend of me
Shall shortly great misfortune see.
A prior who for me his rank ignores
Will roam with a wallet the threshing floors.
If my friend is an archpriest,
He will become a foolish hedge priest.
If my crony is a priest,
He'll be like a tavern cat, the beast.
If a monk my friendship court,
He will be like a frisky colt.[6]

Inserted in a seventeenth century manuscript just after the *Tale of the High-Minded Hop* is a versified *Discourse on the Lazy, the Drowsy, and the Drunken,* one source of which appears to have been the *Discourse of the Philosopher Cyril, the Slovenian* mentioned above. Individual expressions from the latter work are duplicated in the *Discourse on the Lazy* almost literally:

O my beloved child!
Consider and apprehend the truth;
Be not a sleepyhead nor linger long abed
Like those who often sleep and without measure;
Good you'll not gain nor from evil refrain,
Good fame you'll not share
Nor fair garments wear,
Will drain no goblets sweet,
Your own bread will not eat,
With God and the kind prince you will not be,
Nor pleasure shall you see.[7]

In the manuscript in which the *Tale of Gore-Zlochastie* was found, there occurs a eulogy of the birch rod, likewise written in presyllabic verse:

With the birch the Holy Spirit bids us our children beat:
For the birch does nothing their health to deplete.
The birch will knowledge into a child's head drive,
Teach him his prayers and from all evils shrive.
Birch makes the child his parents to obey;
Birch teaches him his Scripture texts to say.
The birch may hurt but will not break his bones—
It deters him from all sorts of evils at once. . . .
God, we pray thee bless that wood
Which grows the birch for times of need! [8]

[6] Buslayev, *Istoricheskie ocherki* (Historical Sketches), I, p. 570.
[7] *Ibid.*, p. 569.
[8] *Ibid.*, p. 585.

As an example of seventeenth century comic and satirical poetry, Buslayev quotes the poem, "Cup of the Solovetskian Sea," from a collection written not later than the first quarter of the eighteenth century:

Cup of the Solovetskian Sea—
Drink to the health of the company!
The bowl is brimming, they bid us drink
And drown all care at its cheerful brink.
Those who with us stay
Cheerful looks display,
Courteous and kind are they,
"Take the best place," they say,
They use first names alway,
Hand in hand they lay,
Straighten beards that stray,
Mustaches smooth they.
The bowl is brimming, they bid us drink,
And drown all care at its cheerful brink.
Cup of them
Who love all men,
Cup of all
Who love at all!
To others giving,
Itself asking nothing,
It never stands idling.
Each year give
To God his tithe,
Good to attain,
A good living to gain.[9]

In 1698 a whole lawsuit was started over the following amorous epistle, written by an orderly for the colonel's son, Fyodor Tsei, who was in love with the lieutenant colonel's daughter, Yelena Rydel:

To thee my eyes' most glorious light
And to our troth so fondly plight.
Long life, my dear, and mayest thou
Never forget thy righteous vow.
How before God our troth we swore,
Made our exchange of rings and wore
Golden crowns upon our heads,
In those glad, sacred days now dead,
This may you, darling, oft recall,
In your prayers above all.
And I shall truly turn to thee
At every hour in memory.
I so pine for thee
That if it might be

[9] *Ibid.*, pp. 515–516.

> Hence would I take wing
> To you, dear, migrating.[10]

Verse such as this was used for the tales of Priest Savva and of Thomas and Yerem, and for the verse adaptation of the *Tale of the Rooster and the Fox* and for many legends on eighteenth century broadsides.

Side by side with these seventeenth century works in rhyme, there existed also a form of ballad verse exemplified by such works as the *Tale of Gore-Zlochastie*, the ballads from the epoch of "Disorder" taken down in 1619 in Moscow for the English bachelor of arts Richard James,[11] and the ballads of P. A. Kvashnin, written in about 1681.[12]

Among the six ballads written down for Richard James, two are particularly worthy of attention, the one about the princess Xenia Godunov and the one about the death of Michael Vasilyevich Skopin-Shuisky.

The former gives the lament of Xenia, bereft of her parents and on the point of herself becoming a victim of the Pretender:

> There weeps a little bird,
> A little white quail:
> "Alas, that I so young must mourn!
> This green oak they wish to burn,
> My little nest to overturn,
> My little ones to kill,
> To catch me, the little quail."
> In Moscow the princess weeps:
> "Alas, that I so young must mourn!
> For to Moscow is riding the traitor,
> Grishka Otrepyev Rostriga,
> Who wishes me captive to take,
> And into a black nun make,
> A nun in a nunnery.
> But I will not be shorn a nun,
> In a cloister I should die:
> I shall keep my dark cell open,
> And watch the fine fellows go by.
> Oh, our beautiful corridors!
> Who will along you walk,
> Who will live tsar after us,
> And after Boris Godunov?

10 L. N. Maikov, *Ocherki iz istorii russkoy literatury XVII i XVIII stoletii* (Sketches from the History of Russian Literature in the Seventeenth and Eighteenth Centuries) (St. Petersburg, 1889), p. 230.

11 The best edition is that of P. K. Simoni in *Sbornik Otd. russk. yuz. i slov.*, (Collection of the Division of Russian Language and Literature of the Academy of Sciences) (1907), Vol. LXXXII, No. 7, and published separately.

12 Published as a supplement to M. N. Speranskii's article "Iz materialov dlya istorii russkoy pesni" (Some Materials for a History of the Russian Ballad), *Izvestiya Akademii nauk* (News of the Academy of Sciences) (1932), series VII, No. 10, pp. 913–934.

Oh, our dear palace halls!
Who will within you sit,
Who will live tsar after us,
And after Boris Godunov?"

The second ballad tells of the impression produced by the death of M. V. Skopin-Shuisky on the merchant folk of Moscow:

What can have happened in Moscow?
Since midnight the bells have been tolling.
And the Moscow merchants make moan:
"Now are our heads bowed low,
Our general is no more,
Vasilyevich, Prince Michael!
But the princes and boyars flocked
To the Mstislavian prince, Vorotynsky,
And among them the word went round,
And they said the word with a smile:
"High did the falcon soar
But crashed to hard mother earth once more!"
And the Swedish Germans fell weeping:
"Our general is no more,
Vasilyevich, Prince Michael!
The Germans to Novgorod fled
And in Novgorod shut themselves up,
Good-folk a-many low they laid
And the country into a Latin land made.

In both these ballads, as in the others taken down for Richard James, the traditions of oral poetry are combined with learned versification, particularly to be noted in the verbal rhymes.

Bookish elements stand out still more plainly in Kvashin's records, as for example in the following ballad:

My light, my dear, my darling
Would not let me on her gaze,
Or look upon her pretty, beauteous face.
Shall I go out walking in the open fields,
Or shall I find some portrait painter's place
And bid him paint her form on paper fine?
Her beauteous face and person I shall set
In a bright, sunny room.[13]

---

[13] See V. V. Danilov's article "Sborniki pesen XVII stoletiya—Richard Dzhemsa i P. A. Kvashnina" (The Seventeenth Century Ballad Collections of Richard James and P. A. Kvashnin), *Trudy Otdela drevnerusskoy literatury* (Works of the Division of Early Russian Literature), II, pp. 165–180. The author considers both collections the product not of popular, oral, but of individual, learned creation. In particular he demonstrates conclusively that Kvashnin was not the recorder of the ballads but their author, as the MS. shows all the characteristic peculiarities of a rough draft, with corrections, unfinished texts, etc.

SYLLABIC VERSIFICATION

Grafted on Russian versification as practiced in the latter half of the seventeenth century is a precise syllabic form distinguished by lines of equal length (usually thirteen or eleven syllables to the line), caesura in the middle of the line, and paired feminine rhymes. All these characteristics of syllabic versification had been worked out on Polish soil, where the conditioning factor was the nature of Polish stress itself, this always falling on the penultimate syllable; they were afterward taken over into southwestern (Ukrainian) literature, and through this medium were early engrafted upon Russian literature as well.

Syllabic verse was brought here by the learned Kievan monk, Simeon of Polotsk (Petrovsky-Sitnianovich, 1629–1680), who had mastered the methods and content of Latin-Polish scholastic theology and literary practice, and interested himself in versification, back in his student days at Mohila's college in Kiev, where much attention was paid both to the theory and to the practice of poetry. At first Polotsky wrote verses in White Russian, Polish, and Latin; but after his immigration to Moscow in 1663, following the Polish occupation of Polotsk, where he had previously been a teacher (*didasculus*) in the monastery school, he began to write in the Russian literary language of that day. Though a teacher in the School of the Redeemer, the future Slavyano-Greco-Latin academy, and prominent as preacher and as author of polemic works directed against dissenters, Polotsky at the same time strenuously devoted himself to poetical activity, largely as called forth by his position as court poet and instructor to the tsar's children.

Polotsky's official relations with the tsar's court determined his cultivation of the genre of eulogistic and panegyric poems, in themes and in form direct forbears of the stately classical odes of the Russian eighteenth century poets. In 1656, while still at Polotsk, he had written *Meters* in collaboration with some other monks, on the occasion of Tsar Alexis Mikhailovich's coming to Pskov. Later on, after settling in Moscow, Polotsky repeatedly expressed in verse his reactions to the varied events of court life. Here, for example, is how he greeted the birth of Peter I, seeing in him the future deliverer of Constantinople from the power of the Turks:

> The month of May has brought us great rejoicing,
> With young Prince Peter's birth its progress gracing.
> Yesterday glorious Tsargrad by the Turks was taken,
> Today its hopes of freedom gloriously awaken.
> The conqueror has come and he will vengeance give her,
> The imperial city will this day deliver.

> O Constantinograd! Rejoice in exultation!
> Sofia, trim your lamps in celebration!
> This day is born to us an Orthodox tsarevich,
> Great Prince of Moscow, Peter Alekseyevich.

In a series of such accolades, Polotsky lavishes the conventional compliments upon members of the imperial family, bodying forth in stereotyped expressions the flattery and servile adulation which were the accepted thing in western European panegyrics and to some extent became so in the later Russian ode. In conformity with poetic classicism, we encounter in his eulogistic verses elements of ancient mythology and names from antiquity, as, for example, in the following excerpt from a panegyric entitled the "Russian Eagle":

> Athena's skill itself were scarce sufficient—
> So great is Russia's glory past and present!
> Illustrious Homer in his verse unerring
> Could never sing such things as are occurring! . . .
> Let Arion renowned through the deeps of the ocean
> To Russia ride, astride of a dolphin!
> Luring Amphion to visit us with him
> And smite the strings of the lute to his rhythm.

In an improvised conclusion to the voluminous *Well Tempered Dulcimer*, written upon the occasion of the coronation of Theodore Alekseyevich, Polotsky, apropos of the fact that he had succeeded in obtaining admission to the institute of typography, spoke in championship of the dissemination of the printed word:

> I desired to have this dulcimer printed
> That by it the tsar's fame might be augmented
> Throughout all Russia and to Slavs residing
> In far-off foreign lands, in Christ abiding.
> For books will bear the fame to every nation
> Of our illustrious tsar of God's creation,
> And the Russian race still further fame acquire
> By fostering the native versifier.
> Since nothing so promotes fame's propagation
> As printing, which brings wide dissemination
> And even carries fame to future ages
> And overseas, through its prolific pages . . .
> For it is fitting
> That Russia too its fame should be transmitting
> Not by the sword alone but by that nimble
> Type which makes books fame's everlasting symbol.

All these verses on themes chiefly connected with court life or having a bearing on it, as well as two plays, of which more later, were gathered by

Simeon not long before his death (in 1678–1679) into a collection entitled the *Rhythmologion*. At the same time Polotsky compiled another collection as well, the *Flowery Plesaunce*, containing over thirty thousand lines of verse, constituting 1,246 poems on a great variety of themes. These poems were distributed under rubrics of the author's own designation: "Similarities," "Images," "Sayings," "Interpretations," "Epitaphs," "Legends for Pictures," "Tales," "Admonitions," "Accusations," and so forth. Here we even find adaptations of plots of a quasi-historical character, borrowed chiefly from medieval historical collections; for example, stories from the *Speculum Historiale* of Vincent of Beauvais, dealing with the murder of the Lombard King Alboin by his wife Rosamunda, or with the death of Bishop Hatto, who was devoured by mice; ecclesiastico edificatory tales, derived from the paterikons, the *Prologue*, the *Great Mirror*, the *Golden Legend* of Jacques de Voragine, and, possibly, from the *Deeds of the Romans*; moral anecdotes akin to the *Apothegms*, comic tales of the *Facetiae* type, plain jokes, and, finally, satires giving genre pictures exposing various human vices, among them some that the author had observed in contemporary Russian life.

Of particular interest for us are the humorous and satirical verses in which Simeon attempts to sketch ethological aspects of life in a realistic manner. Thus, in the poem "Matrimony," he enumerates the drawbacks of married life, at times utilizing almost verbatim the *Colloquy of Father and Son on the Wickedness of Women*. There it says of woman that in her husband's presence she "complains day and night and gives her husband no peace, gets angry, so that her husband gets no rest from her, and she says: 'Some husbands' wives are well dressed and everyone respects them; but I, poor unfortunate, am a wife despised and ignored and reproached by all!'" And in Simeon of Polotsk the wife

> All night her worried spouse from slumber keeping,
> Plagues him about her troubles instead of sleeping;
> Speaks in querulous tones, her husband chiding
> For insufficiently her needs providing.
> She holds other husbands up as a pattern:
> "His wife has clothes that make me look a slattern,
> His wife is everywhere greatly respected,
> While I, as your wife, am by all neglected."

The *Colloquy* goes on to say of wives: "For a wife wants to be praised, loved, and respected by all; if anyone else is praised, she becomes resentful and takes it as an affront and blows cold over the other's being praised. If her husband wishes to please her, he must like everyone that she likes, and show hatred for anyone to whom she has taken an antipathy." And in Polotsky we find this about the wife:

> For she wishes to have you always fondly gazing,
> The beauty of her face and temper praising.
> If to some other your chance gaze has tended,
> She thinks she has been scorned and feels offended. . . .
> Whomever she likes, you must also favor;
> Always to meet her whims you must endeavor.

However, unlike the *Colloquy* which discusses the "wickedness of women" seriously, Simeon of Polotsk speaks of women in a tone of harmless banter and, in L. Maykov's words, "makes merry over the worries and troubles of family life like an old bachelor who prizes the independence of his single blessedness."

In several poems, Simeon of Polotsk undertakes to expose negative traits of various strata of contemporary society. Thus, in his poem "The Corporation of Merchants," he speaks as follows of the merchants:

> The merchant class can hardly keep from sinning,
> To evil ways their foes are wont to win them;
> Luxury is the rule in merchants' houses,
> And many an evil impulse it arouses.
> Firstly, it's every merchant's deep desire
> To buy a thing for less and sell it higher.

A second sin noted by Simeon of Polotsk in the merchant class is the "lying word" to which merchants are prone to resort, and the false oath, false measurement, and all manner of other deceits and dodges. He enumerates eight deadly sins of which merchants are guilty and concludes the poem with the following impassioned words:

> O savage sons of darkness! Why continue?
> This cozening will but to ruin bring you.
> To outer gloom you will be cast and never
> See the eternal light again forever!
> Put aside the works of darkness, walk in the light,
> Lead the heavenly life, scale the heavenly height!

A comparison of these arraignments with documentally attested facts as to the behavior of Russian merchants at the time when Simeon was writing is convincing evidence that the poem gives a true picture of actual conditions.

A still more striking satirical exposé is found in Polotsky's poem "The Monk," which tallies in many ways with such a work as the *Kalyazin Petition,* with this difference, however, that our author makes his exposé in indignation while the *Kalyazin Petition* is permeated throughout with quiet humor.

After first speaking of the qualities that ought to distinguish the ideal monk, Simeon of Polotsk exclaims:

> But alas the disorder! Good order perverted!
> Monasticism to sensualism all but converted.

Then, after stipulating that he is not going to talk about "honest" monks, deserving of respect, but about the "dissolute," whom "it grieves" him to unmask, Polotsky speaks of the latter thus:

> Laymen are not the only ones who serve their belly,
> Some monks drink just as much and eat as heavily.
> After choosing to lead a life of abnegation,
> Of food and drink they make their chief preoccupation.
> Many are to be seen lying in streets and byways,
> Vomiting drink and unable to open their eyelids;
> Many of these out of harm's way are carted—
> Being half dead, from the people they must be guarded;
> Many, fierce with wine, obscenities bellow,
> Slander and curse, a disgrace to their honest fellows.

After pointing out other vices prevalent among monks, he bursts into this angry tirade:

> Oh, the depravity! Ah, the moral disaster!
> How can it fail to rouse the heavenly master!
> Wolves in sheep's clothing beasts of prey remain,
> Belly-servers naught but their souls' ruin gain.

And then the accusations and reproaches continue:

> They also go about fine robes displaying,
> Their vow of total poverty betraying.
> No bridegroom ever made so fine a showing
> As the heedless monk to his own undoing.
> His aim is often feminine affection;
> Handsome robes, alas! but hide his soul's corruption.
> Such monks a woman brazenly accosting,
> Pick up a friendship, then go drinking, feasting:
> Falsely claim they're related to each other,
> Calling them either sister, aunt, or mother.

The poem ends with an exhortation to monks: let them strive to walk in the footsteps of the sainted fathers of old time, that they may be sharers in their "eternal gladness" up in heaven.

This poem of Simeon Polotsky's is also a reaction to the exposure of actual facts about monastic life made, among other things, in the pronouncements and decrees of the ecclesiastical conference of 1666–1667. There, vices prevalent among both the white and the black clergy were noted: drunkenness, harlotry, fortunetelling, fraud, and even participation in robberies and acts of brigandage. Thus Polotsky's position in making his accusations was the same as that of official Church authority, his point of departure likewise being the traditional conservative notions as to the ideal norms which should govern the conduct of the clergy. These norms were in general dictated by ascetic views of the task of Church and monasteries as propagandized from of old by Russian ecclesiastical publicity with a view to propping up the "somewhat shaky days of yore." Herein lies the radical difference between the position taken by Simeon of Polotsk and the social group to which he belonged and the position taken by the author of the *Kalyazin Petition* and his social set, who were not in the least interested in maintaining the institution of monasticism even in a reformed guise, being intuitively out of sympathy with the institution itself.

In 1680 Polotsky printed his *Rhymed Psalter*,[14] with a versified calendar subjoined. What impelled Polotsky to put the Psalter into verse was the fact that not only in White Russia and in the Ukraine, but even in Moscow itself many had fallen in love with the "sweet and harmonious chants of the Polish versified Psalter" and that those who sang the Polish hymns "understood little or nothing and took spiritual delight merely in their harmoniousness." Working from the Church Slavonic original, he copied the very popular rhymed Psalter of the sixteenth century Polish writer Yan Kokhanovsky. To the influence of Kokhanovsky's psalter are attributable

---

[14] Neither the *Rhythmologion* nor the *Flowery Pleasaunce* has been published in full. A relatively very small amount of material from these two books and from the *Rhymed Psalter* is quoted in Buslayev's *Istoricheskaya khristomatiya* (Historical Anthology), columns 1189–1209, and in the following studies on Polotsky: L. Maykov, "Simeon Polotskii" (*Ocherki iz istorii russkoy literatury XVII i XVIII stoletii* [Outlines of the History of Russian Literature in the Seventeenth and Eighteenth Centuries], pp. 1–162); I. Tatarskii, *Simeon Polotskii, yevo zhisn' i deatel'nost'* (Simeon Polotsky, His Life and Work) (Moscow, 1886); A. I. Byeletskii, *Stikhotvoreniya Simeona Polotskogo na temy iz useobshchey istorii* (Poems of Simeon Polotsky on Themes from Universal History) (Kharkov, 1914). See also Prof. V. M. Peretts' *Otchyot ob ekskursii Seminariya russkoy filologii v Moskvy 1–12 februarya 1912 g.* (Report on the Excursion of the Seminary in Russian Philology to Moscow, Feb. 1–12, 1912) (Kiev, 1912), pp. 96–98. S. P.'s panegyric the "Russian Eagle" (Oryol Rossiiskii) from the *Rifmologion*, is published in *Pamyatniki drevney pismennosti* (Monuments of Early Literature) (Petrograd, 1915), CXXXIII. The calendar appended by S. P. to the *Rhymed Psalter* is reproduced in *Mesyatseslov: Stikhotvoril ieromonakh Simeon Polotskii* (The Calendar: Versified by the Holy Monk Simeon Polotsky) (St. Petersburg, 1882). For a reprint of previously published poems by S. P., see the collection indicated above: "*Virshi Sillabicheskaya poeziya XVII–XVIII vekov.* (Verses: Syllabic Poetry of the Seventeenth and Eighteenth Centuries), pp. 97–119. On the literary work of S. P., see in "Psaltir' Simeona Polotskogo i yevo otnoshenie k pol'skoy Psaltiri Yana Kokhanovskogo" (The Rhymed Psalter of Simeon Polotsky and Its Relation to the Polish Psalter of Yan Kokhanovsky), *Kiev Universtitetskie izvestiya* (Kiev University News) (1896), No. 4, pp. 1–18; A. I. Byeletskii, "Iz Nachal'nykh let literaturnoy deyatel'nosti Simeona Polotskogo" (From the Earliest Years of the Literary Activity of Simeon Polotsky), *Sbornik statey v chest' akad. A. I. Sobolevskogo* (Collection of Articles in Honor of Acad. A. I. Sobolevsky), pp. 264–267; *ibid.*, "Povestvovatel'nyi element v "Vertograde" Simeona Polotskogo" (The Narrative Element in the Plesaunce of Simeon Polotsky), *Sbornik statey k sorokaltetiyu uchenoy deatel'nosti akad. A. S. Orlova* (Collection of Articles on the Fortieth Anniversary of the Scholarly Activity of Acad. A. S. Orlov), pp. 325–334; I. N. Rozanov, above-mentioned preface to the collection *Virshi* (Verses), pp. 48–59.

in particular the variations in meter observable in Polotsky's psalter: here the thirteen-syllable line predominates, but along with it occur fourteen, twelve, eleven syllable lines, and so forth, as well. Some psalms are rendered in mixed meters; finally, twelve psalms are put into Sapphics.

The *Rhymed Psalter* gained a very wide popularity among readers from various strata and was, of course, destined to become, along with the *Arithmetic* of Magnitski and the *Grammar* of Meletius Smotritsky, one of Lomonosov's "gates to learning."

The most eminent immediate successors to Simeon of Polotsk as versifier were his pupil Silvester Medvedev (1641–1691) and Karion Istomin (born in the middle of the seventeenth century, died in the first quarter of the eighteenth). Both, like Polotsky, were monks, both were "correctors" for the press and thus performed a complicated and responsible task in connection with the editing of printed editions; both, finally, succeeded Simeon Polotsky as court poets, but Silvester Medvedev, following in the footsteps of his teacher, was an ardent adherent of the "Western," or Latin, educational traditions, whereas Karion Istomin, brought up in the Byzantine Greek traditions, propagandized in his works, verse included, the Greek principles of education. Having been involved in the political struggle as zealous champion of the interests of Princess Sofia and as associate of her adherent Shaklovit, Medvedev, by order of Peter I, was executed in 1691.

In Silvester Medvedev's literary work as a whole, consisting chiefly of theological polemics, his poetical production did not bulk particularly large.

Extant from his pen are fifteen editions of the "Epitaphion," dedicated to his teacher, Simeon Polotsky, the "Epithalamium" presented to Tsar Theodore Alekseyevich, "Lament and Consolation," upon the death of Theodore Alekseyevich, "Legend for the Portrait of Princess Sofia," and a few other poems, among them those included in his prose works. All were written in a high-flown panegyric style.

Thus, the latest redaction of the "Epitaphion" to Simeon Polotsky begins with the following verses:

> Look, man, with heartfelt pity upon the coffin here,
> For the death of a famous teacher shed a tear:
> As a teacher he had no equal in this land,
> A theologian upright, the dogma to defend,
> A pious man, of use to church and country,
> His preaching profitable to all and sundry,
> Simeon Petrovsky, to all true men endeared,
> For his humility by all admired.

In the lengthy "Epithalamium" the introduction is followed by this address to the tsar Theodore:

Rejoice, O Tsar, elect of heaven,
By God unto us Russians given.
Exult and be thou glad, all hail, Theodorus,
Thou gift of God most precious and most glorious.[15]

Silvester Medvedev was distinctly the inferior of his teacher in poetical talent, confining himself chiefly to adapting the latter's verses to fit various occasions as they arose. The "Epithalamium" in particular is largely an adaptation of several poems found in the *Rhythmologion*. Silvester Medvedev's other poems are likewise in large measure directly dependent on the *Rhythmologion* or on the *Flowery Pleasaunce*. On the other hand, Medvedev also adapted to fit new circumstances verses that he had himself previously written, altering them but slightly and sometimes not at all. Medvedev's inexpertness at versemaking is also revealed in the fairly large number of bad rhymes encountered in his work, such as "Theodore" and "dare," *"supostaty"* and *"uspevati" "negodny"* and *"nedostoiny,"* and so forth.

A much more prolific versifier than Silvester Medvedev was Karion Istomin, one of the most learned men of the latter half of the seventeenth century, author of various dogmatic, homiletic, historical, and pedagogical works, among them such then outstanding schoolbooks as the "Little" and "Large" primers, written for the tuition of Tsarevich Alexis Petrovich and including, incidentally, a good deal of versified material. In content, the poems of Karion Istomin are extremely varied. Among them we encounter acathists, prayers, legends for icons, saints' lives, epitaphs, complete theological tracts, precepts for the rearing of children, such as his *Domostroy*, and, finally, panegyrics relating to various events of court life, these at times running to complete books; for example, the book of complimentary verses presented to Princess Sofia Alekseyevna in 1681. Among these panegyrics is one written as an acrostic and dedicated to Tsarevich Alexis Petrovich. Another book of Karion Istomin's written entirely in verse was *Polis*, where we get a description of twelve different sciences, items on geography and on the sacraments of the church. Like Istomin's primers, *Polis* was provided with illustrations.

15 S. Medvedev's poems are reproduced in part in Novikov's *Drevnyaya Rossiiskaya Biblioteka* (Early Russian Library), 2nd ed., Vol. XIV, pp. 95–111, and Vol. XVIII, pp. 198–199. The "Epithalamium" (Privetstvo brachnoe) is published in *Zapiski Khar'kovskogo universiteta* (Kharkov University Notes) (1912), No. 3, p. 17. On Medvedev see I. Kozlovskii, *Sil'vestr Medvedev, Ocherk iz istorii russkogo prosveshcheniya i obschhestvennoy zhizni v kontse XVII v.* (Silvester Medvedev: A Sketch from the History of Russian Education and Social Life at the End of the Seventeenth Century) (Kiev, 1895), and more particularly A. Prozorovskii, *Sil'vestr Medvedev: yevo zhisn' i deyatel'nost'* (Silvester Medvedev: His Life and Work) (Moscow, 1896), where several of S. M.'s poems were printed for the first time. Selected poems are reproduced in the collection *Virshi: Sillabicheskaya poesiya XVII–XVIII vv.* (Verses: Syllabic Poetry of the Seventeenth and Eighteenth Centuries), pp. 126–136.

For the most part the poems of Karion Istomin produce the impression of having been composed purely mechanically: they rarely show any real poetic inspiration. The stereotyped quality of his versification is sensed with particular force in the numerous panegyrics addressed to persons of the imperial family. Karion Istomin's best and most sapid panegyric is the accolade to Princess Sofia Alekseyevna in which the author champions the propagation of the sciences in Russia, in this connection, as it were, anticipating Lomonosov. The accolade begins with the usual salutation to its subject:

> Noble Sofia Tsarevna,
> Ruling Princess Alekseyevna!
> Virtuous, holy, and eminent virgin,
> For the heavenly life by God first chosen!
> May you through God have peace and prosperity,
> And be preserved to extreme longevity,
> Through you may wisdom our hearts inspire,
> This being our word for the Greek name Sofia.

After having pointed out that Sofia signifies wisdom, the author goes on to expatiate on the importance of wisdom in the existence of man and of the state, shows how it has been exemplified in the achievement of members of the imperial house, from Alexis Mikhailovich on, and beseeches Sofia Alekseyevna to further in every way possible the spread of wisdom in Russia through propagation of the sciences:

> Great Russia's deep desire throughout the ages
> Has been to delve in wisdom's sacred pages:
> Let boys, by school in early youth attending,
> Learn to gather the flowers of understanding;
> To manhood grown, if so habituated,
> They are from every care emancipated . . .
> Let lords for knowledge show an inclination,
> And for it unto God make supplication,
> Give orders that our sciences be perfected
> And by teachers the people in them be instructed.
> Again I pray you, maiden queen discerning,
> Lay the foundations of liberal learning.[16]

[16] Comparatively few of Karion Istomin's verses have been published. See Buslayev, *Istoricheskaya khristomatiya* (Historical Anthology), columns 1299–1301; S. Smirnov, *Istoriya Moskovskoy Slavyanogreko-latinskoy akademii* (History of the Moscow Slavo-Greco-Latin Academy) (Moscow, 1855), appendix, pp. 396–400, *Letopis zanyatii Arkheograficheskoy komissii* (Chronicle of the Studies of the Archaeographical Commission—1862–1863) (St. Petersburg, 1864), Pt. 2, pp. 126–132 (*Domostroy*). Istomin's *Little Primer* (Malyi Bukvar'), composed in 1692 and first printed in 1694, is described in detail by D. Rovinsky, and all verses in it quoted, in *Russkie narodnye kartinki* (Russian Popular Prints), Vol. II, pp. 483–503; Rovinsky also reproduced it in facsimile in *Bukvar', izgotovlennyi monakhom Karionom Istominym, dlya obucheniya tsarevitcha Alekseya Petrovicha, v. 1692 g.* (Primer Prepared by the Monk Karion Istomin for the Teaching of Tsarevich Alexis Petrovich in 1692) (St. Petersburg, 1891). See also I. M. Tarabrin, "Litsevoy bukvar' Kariona Istomina" (Illustrated Primer of Karion Istomin), *Drevnosti: Trudy Moskovskogo Arkheol-*

One very interesting point in connection with Karion Istomin's poetical activities is the fact that he used verse as a means of inculcating knowledge in the minds of pupils. He did so in both his primers and in the book *Polis*. Followers of his in the practical use of versification for pedagogical and methodological purposes were Theodore Polycarp, compiler of the *Primer of Slavic, Greek, and Roman Letters* (printed in 1704) and of the *Trilingual Lexicon* (printed in the same year), and Leontius Magnitski, author of the celebrated *Arithmetic* (printed in 1703).

How widespread syllabic versification became in the latter half of the seventeenth century may be judged from the fact that in 1679 Mardarius Khonykov, reader and librarian of the press, wrote, in collaboration with Simeon Polotsky, a large number of versified legends for the Latin Piscator Bible in the edition of 1674. These legends, partly an adaptation of the Latin text, partly the independent work of Khonykov, were written in thirteen-syllable strophes and come to a total of 3,824 lines.[17] There was no complete Russian edition of the Piscator Bible but editions of separate parts of it existed as did separate pictures from it on biblical subjects. In both we find verse legends borrowed from Khonykov.[18]

Later on, during the first decades of the eighteenth century, syllabic versification was further developed in the work of Peter Buslayev, Feofan Prokopovich, and, more particularly, in that of Antioch Kantemir, who left the best specimens of syllabic verse both as to form and as to content. Then syllabic verse, in consequence of theoretical studies and actual experiments made by Trediakovsky and more particularly by Lomonosov, lost hold and was succeeded by accentual verse. Accentual elements were, however, already present even in the old syllabic poetry, particularly in that of Karion Istomin.

---

ogicheskogo obshchestva (Antiquities: Works of the Moscow Archaelogical Society) (1916), Vol. XXV, pp. 249–330, and A. A. Shemshurin, "O gravirovannom i rukopisnykh litsevykh bukvaryakh Kariona Istomina" (On the Engraved [singular] and Manuscript [plural] Illustrated Primers of Karion Istomin), *Chteniya v obshchestve istorii i drevnostey rossiiskikh* (Papers Read Before the Society of Russian History and Antiquities) (1917), Bk. I, pp. 1–50. Several of Istomin's poems are reproduced in S. N. Brailovskii's study of him, *Odin iz pestrykh XVII stoletiya* (One of the Motley Throng in the Seventeenth Century) (St. Petersburg, 1902).

17 See M. I. Sokolov, "Slavyanskie stikhi monakha Mardariya Khonykova k litsevoy Biblii Piskatora" (Slavic Verses of the Monk Mardarius Khonykov for the Illustrated Bible of Piscator), *Arkheologicheskie izvestiya i zametki* (Archaeological News and Notes) (1895), Nos. 9–10; M. I. Tarabrin, "O sostavitelyakh virsh k litsevoy Biblii Piskatora" (On the Composers of the Verses for the Illustrated Bible of Piscator), *Drevnosti: Trudy slavyanskoy komissii moskovskogo arkheologicheskogo obshchestva* (Antiquities: Works of the Slavic Committee of the Moscow Archaeological Society) (Moscow, 1907), Vol. IV, Pt. 1, *Protokoly* (Protocols), pp. 61–62. Legends for the Piscator Bible are published in full in an appendix to A. I. Uspenskii's study *Tsarskie ikonopistsy i zhivopistsy XVII veka* (Imperial Icon-Painters and Artists of the Seventeenth Century) (Moscow, 1913), Appendix I, pp. 1–51.

18 See D. Rovinskii, *Russkie narodnye kartinki* (Russian Popular Prints), Vol. III, pp. 307 ff.

Beginning of
the Russian Theater and
Russian Dramaturgy

WESTERN European dramaturgy was in large measure an organic out-growth of folk-poetry material. The Western church was in many instances able to adapt this material to its own purposes instead of rejecting it entirely. Such was not the case in Russia. Here the church had long and vigorously persecuted all forms of secular poetry and secular entertainment. This is why we do not get transcriptions of oral poetry in this country until the seventeenth century. And even in the seventeenth century the church still urged its offensive against works of folk creation. Tsar Alexis Mikhail-ovich, destined to become founder of the first secular theater in Rus, himself promulgated very strict edicts against all manner of "entertainments" and their producers, in particular against buffoons or "merry men" who operated puppet theaters, led bears, or diverted onlookers by means of any sort of entertainment.

Archpriest Avvakum tells how, upon encountering buffoons with bears in his own village, he attacked the troupe singlehanded and indignantly drove them off. Avvakum did this in the consciousness that he was performing a task incumbent upon the church in connection with its war on all secular amusements.

Old Russian literature knew no dramatic works. Russian travelers, from the fifteenth century on, sometimes saw theatrical productions in the West: for example, while attending the conference of Florence in 1438–1439, Abraham, Bishop of Suzdal, saw in one of the Florentine churches a mystery of the Annunciation. Upon returning to their native land, travelers described the wonders that they had witnessed, but no attempt was made to transplant even pious dramatic presentations to Russian soil. The only thing in this country even remotely suggestive of church drama was the primitive church "action," intimately bound up with the religious service: such things as the "furnace action," "the journey on the ass," and the "washing of feet."

Here we had the rudiments of drama, but no more, those rudiments which, notably as found in medieval Nativity and Easter mysteries, the West developed into genuine theatrical productions, later to leave the confines of the church, absorb many accessory secular motifs, and so acquire added interest and vitality.

Passing over the church mystery play, which it was already too late to bring into the Russian theater, Tsar Alexis Mikhailovich, who notwithstanding his devoutness had no objections to secular entertainments if they were not made accessible to the people at large, took a notion to found a theater on the contemporary western European model, influenced thereto by no less a partisan of Western culture than the boyar Artamon Matveyev. A document of May 10, 1672, is preserved, from which one may gather that the original proposal was to set up a theater with the means at hand: in the attic of the house of Boyar I. D. Miloslavsky an apartment was finished off "where comedy might be played." At the same time, apparently, negotiations toward the organization of a theatrical company in Moscow were instituted with Pastor Johann-Gottfried Gregori, a resident of the German suburb. Gregori proposed getting experienced assistance from abroad if possible, and to this end Colonel Van-Staden was dispatched first to Courland, then to Sweden, with instructions to find two *régisseurs* capable of "putting on all sorts of comedies" and willing to come to Moscow. While abroad, however, Van-Staden carried on negotiations not only with *régisseurs* but also with separate small troupes, among them the troupe of the then celebrated entrepreneur Felten, and with such famous artists as Anna Paulsen, but for various reasons Van-Staden's negotiations both with the *régisseurs* and with the actors ended in failure and he was only able to bring musicians to Russia.

On the 21st of September, 1672, Gregori, with two German assistants, Jury Gievner and Johann Paltser, and a troupe of sixty recruits from the German younger set, began rehearsing a play written in German on a plot out of the Book of Esther and entitled the *Artaxerxes Action*. (The text has not been preserved.) Simultaneously in the village of Preobrazhensky, a large wooden theater was hurriedly built, a "mansion of comedy" about ninety square sazhens in area. The dimensions of the stage may be roughly judged from the fact that five hundred arshins of cloth went into the draping of the sky. And as other items of expense, among them costumes for the actors, were on the same generous scale, the theater ran to a huge sum.

On the 17th of October, the first showing of the *Artaxerxes Action* took place. This presentation, like those immediately following, was given in German. For Alexis Mikhailovich a Russian translation of the play was prepared, but did not reach him until after the first performance. Later on, when the troupe had come to consist partly of Russian actors, plays were given in Russian. Here, as in the other plays put on in Gregori's theater, women's parts were taken by men. The first Russian secular theater, in contrast to the theater founded by Peter I, was a court amusement intended only for the imperial family and for persons in some way connected with the court. The tsar's wife and daughters were among the spectators, but sat in special latticed boxes, a provision which, in view of the element of levity in the plays, would appear to have been far from superfluous.

After the *Artaxerxes Action,* Gregori produced the plays *Tobias the Younger* (text likewise not extant), *Judith,* the *Piteous Comedy of Adam and Eve,* and the *Small Refreshing Comedy of Joseph.* For some time after the building of the theater at Preobrazhensky, the apartment previously finished off in Miloslavsky's house was used for productions, as was a new apartment in the Kremlin over the palace dispensary. In February, 1675, Gregori died and his work was first taken over by Jury Gievner, who put on a "small comedy" about Bayazetes and Tamerlaine, otherwise known as the *Temir-Aksakov Action,* and the inextant *Yegorev Comedy,* about which nothing further is known to us. Gievner was soon succeeded by a Kievan, Stepan Chizhinsky, who put on two new productions, the likewise inextant comedies *Of David and Goliath* and *Of Bacchus and Venus* and a ballet besides. In January, 1676, Alexis Mikhailovich died and the theater he had founded died with him, as the new tsar, Theodore Alekseyevich, apparently felt no inclination for theatrical entertainment. After a lapse the theater project was revived, though not for long, in the reign of Peter I.

With the exception of the "comedy" of Adam and Eve, which is denominated as "pitiful" and is, in essence, a morality play of the medieval mystery type, all the "comedies" were purely secular in spirit, "refreshing," and "entertaining," in spite of the fact that part of them were on biblical subjects. They are a transplantation to Russian soil of the repertoire which in western Europe was typified by the so-called "English comedies." The brilliant development of the dramatic art in sixteenth century England, which found its highest embodiment in the work of Shakespeare, brought into being a large number of professional actors who toured continental countries, Denmark and Holland chiefly, and finally Germany, where "English comedy" took particularly firm root. In Germany the productions were at first given in English by English actors, but gradually, as English actors mastered the German language and as Germans began to take up acting, the plays came to be given in German. For material the "English comedies" drew upon sacred and profane history, knightly romance, legend, medieval ballad, Italian *novella*, English chronicle, and so forth. Plays of this repertoire dispensed with the moralistic element entirely, bringing emphasis to bear on the element of extrinsic interest, reinforced by various theatrical effects, by music, singing, dancing, striking stage sets. Tragic episodes, presented in the most impassioned manner, here alternated with the cynical sallies of jesters, Gansvursts and Pickelherings, as they were called by the Dutch and the Germans, or "foolish persons," as they were called here. Dramatic passions and unrestrained clowning both passed all bounds. Episodes were heaped upon episodes, often without inner logical connection or regard for the basic principles of dramaturgy. For the most part "English comedy" was epic narrative, classifiable as drama only by virtue of its purely outward symbol, the presence of dialogue. Naturalism was carried to an extreme: sanguinary incidents, murders, were here portrayed in all possible detail, down to the blood, for which bladders of red liquid were used. The acting of these dramas may best be described by quoting what Hamlet had to say of the English comedians of Shakespeare's time: "A robustious periwig-pated fellow tear a passion to tatters, to very rags, to split the ears of the groundlings"; the actors "so strutted and bellowed that I have thought some of nature's journeymen had made men and not made them well, they imitated humanity so abominably."

As early as the 1620's we get German printed editions of "English comedies" and such editions were without doubt the ultimate source of the plays put on here at Gregori's theater, starting with the *Artaxerxes Action*, which had all the characteristics of the "English-comedy" style.

In order to get an idea of the repertoire of the first Russian theater, let us study one of the plays most typical of this repertoire, and of "English-comedy" style, the *Judith*.

The play is a very long one. It is divided into seven acts and each act in turn is divided into "senes" or scenes. There are twenty-nine "senes" in all; in addition we get an entr'acte between the third and fourth acts. The cast of characters runs to about sixty-three. *Judith* is a very detailed rendering in dialogue form of the biblical story of Judith, often with extensive interpolations and additions; the development of the action is extremely slow, being retarded by protracted dialogues often having only a superficial connection with the main plot, which is, in brief, as follows. King Nebuchadrezzar sends against the Jews an army commanded by Colonel Holofernes, to whom he entrusts his own sword. Holofernes makes a victorious advance through Judea as far as the town of Bethel, where he encounters the stoic resistance of the Jewish army and the townspeople. Then Holofernes gives orders to cut off the water supply, and five days later the residents of Bethel, weak from thirst, decide to surrender the town. But at this point the beauty Judith steps forward, appearing for the first time in the fourth act, and in five pious speeches lifts the drooping spirits of the besieged, and promises, with God's help, to deliver them from the hostile armies. After zealously praying to God, she takes her serving-maid Abra and sets out for the camp of Holofernes, hoping to fascinate him by her beauty and then murder him. Holofernes, having heard of Judith's beauty, invites her to banquet with him, and she finally wins his heart, which has also been powerfully heated by wine. When left alone with Holofernes, Judith cuts off his head with his own sword, returns with it to Bethel, and delivers it to the magistrates of the city. To the sound of trumpets and drums, the head of Holofernes is hung on the city wall, while the residents of Bethel in their joy sing a song of thanksgiving to God.

As was usual in the "English-comedy" repertoire, *Judith* mingles scenes of lofty tragic pathos with the comic clowning of "foolish persons" such as Susakim, a soldier of Holofernes' army taken captive by Jewish soldiers, and Judith's serving-woman Abra. A pompously high-flown style is consistently maintained, on the whole, in scenes where serious personages hold the stage, notwithstanding the jarring coinages and awkward locutions occasionally perpetrated by inexperienced translators. Here, for example, is how a Jewish magnate, Salmanasar, declaims in the entr'acte between the third and fourth acts:

"O tormentor! O fierce and for-human-blood-insatiable dog, Holofernes! Was it valiant procedure, was it praiseworthy military custom for you first to invoke to peace, promise clemency, and give assurance of religious freedom, and then in the course of such negotiation deprive of their lands and people those who had trusted to such clemency, those who had submitted, and to put the crowned heads in shackles? O viper! Never yet has the whole world borne his like!"

And the following specimens show the amorous passion that takes possession of Holofernes upon meeting Judith:

"Sit down, O victress over my courage, mistress of my heart! Sit down beside me that you may eat and drink with me, and be merry; for verily as you have single-handed taken possession of my invincible magnanimity, so do you have my clemency entirely at your personal disposal, without intermediary."

Or again:

"Don't you see, lovely goddess, how the power of your beauty has already in part overcome me? I look upon you but I can no longer see; I wish to speak, but my tongue is incapable of great utterance; I wish, I wish, but I cannot; it is not so much by wine as by the power of your beauty that I am brought low."

Side by side with such impassioned utterance we get the vulgar idiom spoken by Abra and more particularly by Susakim, serious and comic constantly rubbing elbows in the play so that the serious speeches of personages of standing alternate with the comic sallies of the "foolish persons." At one of the most tense moments in the action, when Judith is setting out for the camp of Holofernes, this is the sort of dialogue that takes place between her and Abra:

Judith: Abra! Follow me.

Abra: Ah, dear mistress, such fear has come upon me that my heart is like to leap out of my belly.

Judith: What are you so afraid of, stupid?

Abra: Tell me, mistress mine: what are Assyrians like? Are they at all like men?

Judith: But even supposing they were like calves, what is that to you?

Abra: Calves I do not fear, nor men; but what sort of creatures Assyrians are, that I have no way of knowing.

Judith: But if I am not afraid, why should you be?

Abra: Oh! My life is so dear to me, my mother took such a lot of trouble to get me somewhere in the world. If the Assyrians kill me, I won't be able to bring in anywhere near so fine a price at the auction, why I won't sell for five three-kopeck pieces.

Judith: Hush, chatterbox, don't talk such nonsense; say your prayers again and follow me.

Even when Judith bids her put the newly severed head of Holofernes into her sack, Abra does not cease her buffoonery: "Why, I would never have dared to!" she exclaims. "Such a brave soldier as she has cut the head off of! . . . What will the poor man say when he wakes up and Judith has gone off with his head?"

Comedy thickens when the captive Susakim appears on the scene. The Jews threaten to execute him. Naturally, he is very much frightened but, as becomes a jester, attempts to make light of it. When told that his head will soon fly off, he declares: "If the master can make heads fly, then I'll ask him to put wings on my body and, head and body, I'll fly a thousand versts from this place."

When Susakim becomes convinced that execution is inevitable, he pronounces a series of lengthy farewells, with a view to obstructing it momentarily. He bids farewell to his huckstress sister, to his fellow thieves, rogues, sewage carters, and so forth; then to the nine "arts" whereby he had gratified his flesh, to drunkenness, fornication, murder, and so forth; then to his favorite dishes and, finally, to the ravens who would soon peck his body.

Vanea, the officer who has been charged with Susakim's execution, gets bored over this lengthy valedictory, and orders the execution to proceed. But the execution turns out to be a hoax: Susakim is knocked down and struck on the neck with a fox tail instead of a sword until he drops as if dead. Then Vanea and his comrades laugh and leave him. Susakim raises himself gingerly, not knowing whether he is dead or alive. He asks:

"Am I alive or am I dead? Indeed I can't think how to tell for sure whether I am really dead. I am sure I heard life go out of my insides into my right leg and from my leg into my throat, and my soul left through my right ear; only it still seems to me that I can notice light some: here are my stockings and shoes; there's my hat lying; here are my cloak and trousers; only I can't seem to think where my head is."

Susakim looks everywhere for his head and requests that whoever finds it return it to him.

These examples of the combination of serious and comic in one play are typical also of the other "comedies" of Gregori's repertory.[1]

It is very indicative that all the plays put on during Gregori's lifetime were on biblical subjects, while one play, that about Adam and Eve, as above pointed out, went so far as to revive the medieval mystery and morality. From this it would appear that Gregori sought to avoid a too sudden leap from the pious material traditional in Old Russian literature to material purely secular not only in treatment but in theme as well. Only after the audience had become accustomed to foreign entertainment did Gregori's successors decide to put on plays with purely secular plots, and even then they did not eschew biblical themes entirely, as is attested by Chizhinsky's production of *David and Goliath*.

But regardless of whether the plot was religious or secular, the plays in Gregori's repertoire always contained the instructive element to some degree. Moral and religious truth always came out triumphant, getting the better of all manner of evil and dishonest contrivances. At the same time the content of the play was frequently given a bearing on current times, hints of this being concealed in prologue and epilogue, a feature already discarded in western European productions of "English comedies" but retained here. Thus, for example, it would appear from the prologue to *Judith* that the triumph of Judith, of the Hebrew people, over the Assyrians and their colonel Holofernes was associated in this country with a future victory of Tsar Alexis Mikhailovich over the "fierce Mussulmans"; that is, over the Turks.

Dramaturgy as practiced by Gregori and his immediate successors, of brief duration and confined to the narrow limits of the palace household, did not of itself constitute a substantial contribution to the forward progress of Russian literature, but it was, none the less, a first step toward the development of secular dramaturgy and a secular theater, as reconstituted under Peter I,

---

[1] The surviving plays of Gregori's repertory were published by Tikhonravov in *Russkie dramaticheskie proizvedeniya 1672–1725 godov*. (Russian Dramatic Works of the Years 1672–1725) (St. Petersburg, 1874), Vol. I, pp. 78–295. It is noteworthy that the *Judith* staged by Gregori served as source for a verse drama of the same name written in the Petrovian epoch; see P. N. Popov, "Neizvestnaya drama petrovskoy epokhi 'Iudif'" (An Unknown Drama of the Petrovian Epoch, Judith), *Trudy otdela drevenerusskoy literatury* (Works of the Division of Early Russian Literature) (1936), III, pp. 195–253.

and secondly, it is, in a way, part of the general stream of secular literature in that it expounded those lay themes, profane love in particular, that during the latter half of the seventeenth century became, if not predominant, in any case extremely popular here.

Gregori's theater in large measure opened the way for the school drama, first promulgated in Moscow by the already familiar Simeon of Polotsk, who had been adept in the theory and practice of school drama since his days in the Kiev-Mohila college where this form of dramatic production was already firmly established.

The school drama, offspring of German educational institutions, whence its name, appeared in western Europe toward the close of the fifteenth century, during the Renaissance, in connection with the increased interest at that time in the study of Greek and more particularly of Roman classics. At first, for practice in Latin, students memorized and declaimed the comedies of Terence, these being given preference over the harder to understand and less discreet comedies of Plautus. Next, school dramas on the model of the comedies of Terence were composed by the German humanists Reichlin, Melanchthon, Frischlin and others. Gradually Latin was replaced by German, and theatrical production was transformed into an instrument of pedagogical and religious propaganda in the spirit of protestant ideology. Later, the school drama passed beyond the limits of the school and became the property of the public at large.

As a medium for propagating their ideas and as a very convenient means of exerting a pedagogical influence upon youth, the school drama was shortly adopted also by the Jesuits, who exploited it to further the interests of Catholicism and made it general practice in the Jesuit colleges which sprang up during the sixteenth and seventeenth centuries. The strictly confessional character of Jesuit propaganda constrained the Jesuits to avoid using Latin comedies, the comedies of Terence in particular, as models, and to entrust the composition of school plays to teachers in the colleges, who wrote pieces in the spirit of medieval moralities, on plots chiefly from the Bible, from lives of the saints, and later from history. To make more of an impression on the spectators, these plays were pretentiously mounted, various decorative effects being used along with mythological and allegorical accessories. In them figured, on the one hand, the ancient muses, Apollo, Daphnis, Venus, Cupid, and so forth; on the other, such abstract concepts as Heaven, Earth, Hell, Evil, Hatred, Mercy, Enmity, Compassion, not to mention angels and the rest of the heavenly host. The luxuriousness of the productions and the select public in attendance, crowned heads among them, are outward indications of the influence of the Jesuit order. Particular splendor was attained by plays presented in celebration of court events. These panegyric presentations were chiefly given in the Jesuit colleges of Vienna and Paris and were called *"ludi caesarei"*; that is, "imperial presentations."

Though at their peak in Europe during the sixteenth and the first quarter of the seventeenth century, school dramas were still being acted even in the 1780's. At a very early stage special volumes of "poetics" were composed to serve as manuals for the composition of school dramas, these deriving chiefly from the corresponding poetics of Scaliger and Pontano. Theory divided the school spectacle into three principal sections: prologue, plot, and epilogue. Prologue and epilogue had their variations. The plot of the play was commonly developed in not less than three or more than five acts. Each act was subdivided into scenes, the number of which per act must not exceed nine. In Germany and Poland it was customary to write the central part of the play in Latin, the prologue, epilogue, and choruses in the language of the country. The vernacular was also used in the so-called "intermezzi" or "interludes," supplementary scenes from the "life of plain people" inserted between the acts of the play and designed to divert the spectator fatigued by the seriousness of the spectacle itself. The intermezzi contained a good many elements of realism showing promise of further development under favorable circumstances. That the text might be understood by those who did not know Latin, short programs of the spectacles explaining the action in simple language were distributed to the audience. The text of the play was in verse, or at least in rhymed prose.

To Simeon Polotsky, aside from his dialogue *Pastoral Conversations*,[2] may safely be attributed two school dramas in syllabic verse, *On Nebuchadrezzar, the Golden Calf and the Three Children Who Were Unburned in the Furnace*,[3] and the *Comedy of the Parable of the Prodigal Son*.[4] Both are included in the *Rhythmologion*. The former is a literary adaptation of an old-time Muscovite Church ritual, the "furnace action," the latter, of the Gospel parable of the prodigal son repeatedly used by English, French, German, and Polish dramatists. Since this is much the more interesting of the two, alike from the literary, the dramaturgical, and the ideological angle, let us make it the object of our study.

The *Comedy of the Parable of the Prodigal Son* consists of a prologue, six

[2] Published by S. A. Shcheglova as an appendix to the article "Russkaya pastoral' XVII veka" (A Russian Seventeenth Century Pastoral), in the collection *Starinnyi teatr v Rossii XVII–XVIII vv.* (The Ancient Theater in Seventeenth and Eighteenth Century Russia), ed. Acad. V. N. Peretts, *Academia* (Petrograd, 1923), pp. 65–92.

[3] Published by Novikov in *Drevnyaya Rossiiskaya Biblioteka* (Early Russian Library), 2nd ed., Vol. VIII, pp. 158–168, and by Tikhonravov in *Russkie dramaticheskie proizvedeniya* (Russian Dramatic Works), Vol. I, pp. 324–336.

[4] Reproduced by Novikov in *Drevnyaya Rossiiskaya Biblioteka* (Early Russian Library), 2nd ed., Vol. VIII, pp. 34–59, and in D. Rovinskii's *Russkie narodnye kartinki* (Russian Popular Prints), Vol. III, pp. 8–38. Printed by Tikhonravov from the stage manager's MS. copy in *Russkie dramaticheskie proizvedeniya* (Russian Dramatic Works), Vol. I, pp. 296–323.

acts, and an epilogue. It was provided with five intermezzi, references to which occur in the prologue and after each act except the last, but these intermezzi are not extant in the body of the play. Only one intermezzo, extant in a separate manuscript, and dealing with a prodigal and a drunkard, can be regarded as belonging with Polotsky's comedy.

The prologue consists in an address to the audience stating the theme of the play. The first act begins with a monologue by the father, who divides his estate between his two sons and gives them some good advice. He counsels them to trust in God, be guided in life by the principles of piety, and observe the Christian virtues. Both sons reply to their father but reply quite differently. The elder son is the personification of passivity and fixity; he is an exponent of the golden mean, the embodiment of traditional conservatism; the obedient slave of his father, he desires to remain with him to the end of his days, to care for him in his old age. No prospects draw him, nothing tempts him. The father gratefully accepts the elder son's decision, commends his humility and keeps him at home.

But not so the other son: he, too, answers his father politely, and thanks him for planning to give him part of the estate, but for his own part decides to arrange matters differently; he says:

> "My brother dear has chosen at home to tarry
> And seek no fame beyond these boundaries narrow.
> God help him here on thy old age attending
> And all the lovely years of youth so spending.
> My mind is set on doing something higher,
> To spread your fame abroad is my desire.
> Where the sun rises and where sets the sun,
> To all the ends of the earth shall I be known.
> Through me shall the fame of this house be spread
> And joy descend upon thy aging head."

The self-confident youth, bursting the bounds of tradition, can hardly wait to be off down the broad highway to win fame for himself and for his family:

> "No bushel shall hide this candle of mine,
> With the sun I propose to course and shine,"

he declares. And he backs up his desire by arguments that anticipate the idea of natural law, freedom of individual choice, and the self-determination of man:

> "God gave these birds the liberty to soar,
> The beasts full leave to roam the forest o'er.
> May you be pleased, my father, to give me,
> A reasoning being, leave the world to see."

The youth promises that he will return to his father's house enriched in experience and knowledge and that fame and gladness shall redound upon his father. The latter tries to persuade his son to postpone his departure, to obtain the requisite experience in life and then start out. But the father's admonitions are without effect. The younger son replies:

> "Why should I stay at home? Why should I stop to study?
> To enrich the mind by travel is better for anybody.
> Among my set it's the regular thing for a father
> To send a boy abroad and have no bother."

He is referring to the already settled practice of sending young men abroad to carry on their studies. The father is forced to grant his son's request, and lets him go.

However, once he has broken loose, the "prodigal" son immediately plunges headlong into a new life of revelry. Though in urging his father to send him abroad he had made the plea that he wished to enrich his mind by study, once he finds himself on the loose, he forgets his good intentions and tries to take in every pleasure and delight that is to be had in a foreign land far from the watchful supervision of his elders. He has a good deal of money and squanders it in all directions, provides himself with a large staff of attendants, tipples and plays at games of chance with them and, in the end, robbed by his comrades of the bottle, goes bankrupt and arrives at complete destitution.

The fourth act depicts the "prodigal son" hungry and clothed in rags after selling his last suit of clothes. He looks for work and some lord employs him to tend pigs. So here is the youth who had left his father's house with such proud prospects, promising to bring it fame, resolved to shine like the sun, reduced by luxurious living and drunken revelry to a plain swineherd, who eats with the pigs and feels lucky to get a few scraps of their fodder. But the youth does not make a success of his job. He kills a pig, is beaten, and the future looks black. Then, after the manner of the youth in the *Tale of Gore-Zlochastie* who remembers the "way of salvation" and goes into a monastery, so he remembers the house of his father, which he had once so thoughtlessly disdained. Like the prodigal son in the Gospel, he hopes that his father will take him in if only as a servant. But the father gives a banquet in his honor, orders a calf killed for him. And then, as in the Gospel parable, we get the elder son grumbling that for him who had never gone against his father's will not so much as a kid had ever been killed, and the father explaining why he had welcomed his prodigal son with such rejoicing: the elder son had always dwelt with his father and everything that belonged to his father was also his, but the younger had been lost and now was found.

The point of the play is elucidated in the epilogue:

> This shows that youth to age should pay attention,
> And not depend on youthful good intention;
> To elders—that they give youth sound instruction,
> Leave nothing to its immature discretion,
> Above all else let kindness be apparent,
> In kindness is the grace of God inherent,
> In this, too, make yourself God's imitator:
> Give full forgiveness to repentance later.

In other words youth ought not to be self-confident and rely on its own judgment, but older people should instruct youths wisely, and show kindness and lenience when they repent and return to upright ways of living.

At the time when it was written, the play must have created quite a sensation. It gave vital application to a story out of the Bible, retold it to fit questions revolving about relations between the older generation and the younger in those early stages of the Europeanization of our upper social strata. It is possible that an immediate motive for writing the play was the flight abroad in 1660 of the son of the tsar's favorite, Ordyn-Nashchokin, which had been a great grief to the father.

In revamping the Gospel parable, Simeon Polotsky simply did what many another author both before and since has done, took an old plot—biblical ones were particularly favored—and gave it a new interpretation as applied to his own time.

The prime quality of the play is its permeation with the broad humanity that one might expect in so enlightened a figure as Simeon Polotsky. The victory of tradition, the triumph of the fathers, here occurs not in consequence of coercion and the exercise of parental prerogatives, but as a result of the painful personal experience that the younger generation goes through when it turns aside from the path trod by its fathers. Victory is won, the play implies, first of all in view of the advantageous moral and practical foundations on which the old-time tradition for living is erected. The play depicts the father as a moderate and humane conservative, not given to exercising his authority in order to make his son behave as he thinks best. He recognizes youth's right to freedom and refrains from preventing his son's enjoyment of that right. At the same time he receives him with rejoicing when, admitting his mistake, he returns to the bosom of tried and true tradition.

This does not mean, however, that Simeon Polotsky puts a ban on youth's yearning for knowledge and for the enrichment of life through experience. With its longing for knowledge he is most sympathetic and the play is as much an apology for science as it is a defense of ancestral traditions. If the "prodigal son" is ultimately discredited, this is not because he put too much trust in the new culture that had come to us from the West, but because he neglected this culture for those physical pleasures which immediately enthralled him and almost cost him his life.

Both the *Comedy of the Parable of the Prodigal Son* and the play about Nebuchadrezzar are distinguished from the general run of school plays by their simplicity, the absence of any allegorical element, and their proximity to the conditions of real life. The influence of Gregori's repertory was perhaps responsible for some of these qualities.[5]

Later, in the epoch of Peter I and from then on down to the middle of the eighteenth century, the school drama was more vocal than the specifically secular drama concerning political and historical questions of the day and thus became an instrument of publicistic propaganda.

In summing up the development of Russian literature in the sixteenth and seventeenth centuries, it is first necessary to emphasize once more the fact that at this time it was an all-Russian literature. The sixteenth century took over everything produced in Rus during the preceding centuries, collected and combined the literary treasures accumulated in the past, and strove to consolidate and interpret them in the spirit of the dominant idea—Moscow, the "third Rome." Moscow regarded the past as sacred, but conceived of it as in many ways "unreliable" and hence, in spite of its recognition in principle, felt the necessity of examining, testing and, to some extent, even expurgating it. Hence the strenuous effort put into the composition of such all-inclusive learned works as the Macarian *Chetyi Minyei*, the Muscovite chronicle compilations, the *Stepennaya Kniga*, the *Domostroy*, and so forth. All this was not only a summation of the age-old experiment of Russian culture but, in a certain sense, its recension as well. This recension was made, however, in the firm conviction that the foundations of religious and moral existence, laid long ago, were themselves not open to question or subject to change. Any

---

[5] On the history of the Russian drama and the Russian theater in the seventeenth century, consult the following very important aids to study: P. O. Morozov, *Istoriya russkogo teatra do poloviny XVIII stoletiya* (History of the Russian Theater to the Middle of the Eighteenth Century) (St. Petersburg, 1889); V. I. Rezanov, *Iz istorii ruskoy dramy, Shkol'nye deistva XVII–XVIII vv. i teatr iezuitov* (From the History of the Russian Drama: School Dramas of the Seventeenth-Eighteenth Centuries and the Theater of Jesuits) (Moscow, 1910); B. V. Varneke, *Istoriya russkogo teatra* (History of the Russian Theater), 2nd ed. (St. Petersburg, 1914), 3rd ed. (Moscow, 1939); *Istoriya russkogo teatra* (History of the Russian Theater), ed. V. V. Kallash and N. E. Efros (Moscow, 1914), Vol. I; V. Vsevolodskii Gerngross, *Istoriya russkogo teatra* (Leningrad-Moscow, 1929), Vol. I; the collections *Starinnyi teatr v Rossii* (The Ancient Theater in Russia), ed. acad. V. N. Peretts, *Academia* (Petrograd, 1923), articles by V. N. Peretts and S. A. Shcheglova; and *Starinnyi spektakl' v Rossii* (The Ancient Spectacle in Russia), ed. V. S. Vsevolodskii-Gengross, *Academia* (Leningrad, 1928), articles by V. Adrianova-Peretts, V. Peretts, V. Lastochkin, S. Shcheglova, O. Noskova, A. Bulgakov. In it see also the bibliography on the seventeenth and eighteenth century Russian school drama and theater compiled by V. Adrianova-Peretts.

criticism of current conditions made by the ideologists of the Muscovite empire, carried away as they were by faith in its inviolable strength and might, was commonly confined to the condemnation of private infringements of and departures from the standards set for living. A different state of affairs is observable in those strata of Russian society dominated by the ideas which the "trans-Volga hermits" and associated groups had enunciated back in the preceding century. Critical thought, largely abstract, was more operative among them than among their opponents, and was directed not only against disorders in private life; but against the essential religio-moral and social structure of Muscovite Rus as such. Yet for all this, in the matter of political ideology, the opposition groups in Russian society at that time would appear to have lagged behind those with whom they were engaged in a sometimes very bitter conflict. In terms of the unfolding of the historical process during the sixteenth century, the pupils of the "trans-Volga hermits" were political conservatives, while the pupils of the "Josephites" were progressives. The passionate political struggle promoted the flowering in the sixteenth century of the publicistic polemic, and both in this polemic and in actual practice historical right and realism of historic thinking were not on the side of Kurbsky but on the side of Ivan the Terrible and Peresvetov. The realists in politics also leaned toward realism in literary style.

But toward the end of the sixteenth century, Muscovite Rus was undermined by internal social conflicts and entered an epoch of "Disorder" which shook the governmental organism from top to bottom, though without depriving it of the vitality to struggle to reconstitute itself. The seventeenth century was a period of popular movements and popular uprisings. The people, by taking a much more active part in governmental affairs than before, expedited the airing and renovation of Russian culture along lines already worked out in western Europe. Against a stormy background of social strife, the religious element which not long since had been dominant, now, albeit not without a struggle, yielded its position to the secular. In the seventeenth century, especially during the latter half of it, Russia's culture and literature were suddenly enriched by creative art "worldly" in form and content. Medieval Byzantine traditions lost their unquestioned influence and gave place to the traditions of Western culture, not borrowed by Russia mechanically, however, but with due regard to vital needs as dictated by the whole course of national history and by the idiosyncrasies of Russian folkways. As in preceding epochs, so in the seventeenth century, we adopted things of value from foreign culture, other literatures in particular, actively, not passively, in proportion as they met the urgent needs of the time. A translated monument was often Russianized not only in language and style but also in content. The folk-poetry element, though subject to persecution by the church and by temporal authorities even in the seventeenth century, none the less made good its entrance into literature at that time and had a noticeable effect on literary style.

The widespread social protest that sought expression in Old Believerism was founded on superannuated religious and social principles, but even Old Believerism made its contribution in the work of its most brilliant exponent, Archpriest Avvakum, and enriched our literature through its live, picturesque vernacular style and realistic tenor.

Seventeenth century literature left the eighteenth century a legacy in the form of purely secular experiments in narrative, satire, lyric poetry, and dramaturgy. It also laid the foundations of the classical style which was to dominate the eighteenth century. At the same time the seventeenth century built up a literary tradition emanating from those "lower" strata which before had been practically unable to gain a foothold in written literature. This gave rise to a number of works oppositional in tenor and new in their linguistic physiognomy, written by authors of the artisan and trader and, to some extent, of the peasant milieu. In this respect as well, the literature of the seventeenth century paved the way for the literature of the eighteenth, when, along with the court classical style and court themes, a style and themes would also be developed by the democratic social strata, enriching Russian literature with those elements of realism that were to become firmly established here in the nineteenth century.

Russian Transliteration Table

(Based on the new Russian orthography)

This scheme is designed for the convenience of readers who do not know Russian. It is intended primarily for the rendering of personal and place names—mostly nouns in the nominative case.

The aim is to produce words as "normal" in appearance as possible, without the use of diacritical marks, superscripts or apostrophes, but at the same time to approximate the sounds of the Russian words, so that if spoken by an educated American they would easily be identified by a Russian.

Names which are a part of English cultural tradition, such as Moscow, Abraham, Fevronia and Peter, Alexander Nevsky, Michael of Chernigov, are given in their customary English spelling.

Extended phrases or entire sentences involving verb forms and case endings, which occur in footnotes for the convenience of students who know Russian, are given in a somewhat more complex transliteration which is reversible.

Russian		English	
А	а	*a*	
Б	б	*b*	
В	в	*v*	
Г	г	*g*	{except in genitive singular where it is *v*, as in Tolstovo.
Д	д	*d*	
Е	е	(1) *ye*	{when initial, and after ь, ъ, and all vowels, except ы, и: Yekaterina, Izdanie, Nikolayev.
		(2) *e*	elsewhere, as in Lenin, Vera, Pero.
Ё	ё	*yo*	but after Ж and Ш = *o*.
Ж	ж	*zh*	
З	з	*z*	
И	и	*i*	but after ь = *yi*, as in Ilyich.
Й	й	*y*	{in terminal diphthongs, but *i* medially, as in May, Kochubey, Kiy, Tolstoy, but Khoz*y*aistvo.
К	к	*k*	
Л	л	*l*	
М	м	*m*	
Н	н	*n*	
О	о	*o*	
П	п	*p*	
Р	р	*r*	
С	с	*s*	
Т	т	*t*	

531

Russian		English	
У	у	*u*	
Ф	ф	*f*	
Х	х	*kh*	as in Kharkov.
Ц	ц	*ts*	Tsargrad.
Ч	ч	*ch*	Chapayev, Vaigach.
Ш	ш	*sh*	Shakhta.
Щ	щ	*shch*	Shchedrin.
Ъ	ъ	Omit	
Ы	ы	*y*	Mys, Tsaritsyn.
Ь	ь	Omit	
Э	э	*e*	Ermitazh.
Ю	ю	*yu*	
Я	я	*ya*	

Adjectival Endings

Singular	ЫЙ, ИЙ	ый, ий	both simply *y*, as in Dostoyevsky, Grozny.	
Plural	ЫЕ, ИЕ	ые, ие	both simply *ie*.	

The English letter *y* serves both as vowel and as consonant (as it does in English): (1) as a vowel *within* words, as in Mys, Tsaritsyn, and also (2) as an adjectival terminal vowel, as in Khoroshy, Razumovsky, May, Kochubey, Tolstoy, and (3) with consonantal force to soften vowels, as in Istoriya, Bratya, Yug.

Index of Authors

(This index is a translation of
the index in the Russian edition.)

533

Index of Works

A

Accolade to Princess Sofia Alekseyevna, by Karion Istomin, 513

Adventure of Ivan the Merchant's son, by I. Novikov, 430, 465

Adventures of Digenis, 72-78, 149, 154, 165, 217

Alexandria, 63-71, 82, 186

All-Russian chronicle digest, 226, 232

All-Tver chronicle digest, 302, 304

Alphabet of the Beautiful Girl, 482

Alphabet of the Naked Poor Man, 482-484

Annalistic Book ascribed to Katyrev-Rostovsky, 365-369, 372, 498

Annals Which Are Called the Chronicle of the Russian Princes and the Land of Rus, 149

Apocrypha: Acts of the Apostle Paul and Thekla, 37

Apocrypha: Aphroditian's Legend, 35

Apocrypha: Apostle Paul's Revelation, 35

Apocrypha: Ascension of Isaiah, 37

Apocrypha: Colloquy of the Three Prelates, 35

Apocrypha: Creation of Adam and Eve, 39-40

Apocrypha: Gospel of Jacob, 34, 35, 45

Apocrypha: Gospel of Nicodemus, 35, 45

Apocrypha: Gospel of Thomas, 35, 45

Apocrypha: Judgments of Solomon, 43-45

Apocrypha: Legends About the Tree of the Cross, 35

Apocrypha: Martyrdoms of the Three Children and Daniel, 37

Apocrypha: Solomon and Kitovras, 40-43

Apocrypha: The Revelation of St. John the Divine on Mount Tabor, 35

Apocrypha: The Revelation of St. Methodius of Patara, 35

Apocrypha: The Virgin's Visit to Hell, 35, 37, 46-50

Apocryphal legends about paradise, 35

Apocryphal lives of the saints, 35

Apothegms, 428, 429, 507

Arabian Nights' tales, 96

Archival or Jewish Chronograph, 183, 219

Arithmetic of Magnitsky, 511, 514

Artaxerxes Action, 516, 517, 518

Avvakum's petition to Tsar Alexis Mikhailovich, 386, 387, 389

Azbukovnik, 347

B

Babylonian Talmud, 478

Ballad about Avdotya of Ryazan, 314

Ballad about Princess Xenia Godunov, 503

Ballad about the death of Michael Vasilyevich Skopin-Shuisky, 504

Ballad of Oleg the Wise, by A. Pushkin, 130

Ballad of Opanas, by E. Bagritsky, 179

Ballad of The Judgment of Charlemagne, 478

Ballads about Nakhob Symeun, 405

Ballads of P. A. Kvashnin, 503, 504

Ballads written down for Richard James, 503, 504

Basil Shibanov, by A. Tolstoy, 335

Bee, 56, 69, 82, 188

Beware of Sweets, 405

Book of St. Cyril, 39

Book of the Dove, 186

Book of the Genesis of Heaven and Earth (see Historical Paleya)

Book of the Just, 478

Brothers Karamazov, by F. Dostoevsky, 50

Bylina about Basil Okulevich, 424

Bylina about Batu, 244

Bylina about Churil Plenkovich, 352

Bylina about Daniel Lovchanin, 207

Bylina about Dobryna Nikitich and Alyosha Popovich, 425

Bylina about Duke Stepanovich, 184, 186

Bylina about Ilya Muromets, 174, 175, 359, 435

Bylina about Ilya Muromets and the pagan Idol, 357

Bylina about Kalinetsar, 244

Bylina about Mamay, 244

Bylina about Solov Budimirovich, 423

Bylina about the perishing of the Russian bogatyrs, 201

Bylina about the Voleg, 175

Bylina about Vasily Ignatevich, 244

Byliny about Alyosha Popovich and Tugarin Zmeyevich, 357

AP